Case Studies in Contemporary Criticism

EMILY BRONTË

Wuthering Heights

Case Studies in Contemporary Criticism
SERIES EDITOR: Ross C Murfin

Jane Austen, *Emma*
EDITED BY Alistair M. Duckworth, University of Florida

Charlotte Brontë, *Jane Eyre*
EDITED BY Beth Newman, Southern Methodist University

Emily Brontë, *Wuthering Heights,* Second Edition
EDITED BY Linda H. Peterson, Yale University

Geoffrey Chaucer, *The Wife of Bath*
EDITED BY Peter G. Beidler, Lehigh University

Kate Chopin, *The Awakening,* Second Edition
EDITED BY Nancy A. Walker, Vanderbilt University

Samuel Taylor Coleridge, *The Rime of the Ancient Mariner*
EDITED BY Paul H. Fry, Yale University

Joseph Conrad, *Heart of Darkness,* Second Edition
EDITED BY Ross C Murfin, Southern Methodist University

Joseph Conrad, *The Secret Sharer*
EDITED BY Daniel R. Schwarz, Cornell University

Charles Dickens, *Great Expectations*
EDITED BY Janice Carlisle, Tulane University

E. M. Forster, *Howards End*
EDITED BY Alistair M. Duckworth, University of Florida

Thomas Hardy, *Tess of the d'Urbervilles*
EDITED BY John Paul Riquelme, Boston University

Nathaniel Hawthorne, *The Scarlet Letter*
EDITED BY Ross C Murfin, Southern Methodist University

Henry James, *The Turn of the Screw*
EDITED BY Peter G. Beidler, Lehigh University

James Joyce, *The Dead*
EDITED BY Daniel R. Schwarz, Cornell University

James Joyce, *A Portrait of the Artist as a Young Man*
EDITED BY R. B. Kershner, University of Florida

A Companion to James Joyce's Ulysses
EDITED BY Margot Norris, University of California, Irvine

Thomas Mann, *Death in Venice*
EDITED BY Naomi Ritter, University of Missouri

William Shakespeare, *Hamlet*
EDITED BY Susanne L. Wofford, University of Wisconsin — Madison

Mary Shelley, *Frankenstein,* Second Edition
EDITED BY Johanna M. Smith, University of Texas at Arlington

Bram Stoker, *Dracula*
EDITED BY John Paul Riquelme, Boston University

Jonathan Swift, *Gulliver's Travels*
EDITED BY Christopher Fox, University of Notre Dame

Edith Wharton, *The House of Mirth*
EDITED BY Shari Benstock, University of Miami

Case Studies in Contemporary Criticism

SERIES EDITOR: Ross C Murfin, *Southern Methodist University*

EMILY BRONTË
Wuthering Heights

Complete, Authoritative Text with
Biographical, Historical, and Cultural Contexts,
Critical History, and Essays from
Contemporary Critical Perspectives

SECOND EDITION

EDITED BY

Linda H. Peterson

Yale University

Bedford/St. Martin's

BOSTON ♦ NEW YORK

For Bedford/St. Martin's

Executive Editor: Stephen A. Scipione
Editorial Assistant: Anne Noyes
Associate Editor, Publishing Services: Maria Teresa Burwell
Senior Production Supervisor: Dennis J. Conroy
Production Associate: Christie Gross
Marketing Manager: Richard Cadman
Project Management: Stratford Publishing Services, Inc.
Cover Design: Mark McKie
Cover Art: Dawn's New Day by Ashley Jackson. © Ashley Jackson Galleries, West Yorkshire.
Composition: Stratford Publishing Services, Inc.
Printing and Binding: Haddon Craftsmen, an RR Donnelley & Sons Company

President: Joan E. Feinberg
Editorial Director: Denise B. Wydra
Director of Marketing: Karen R. Melton
Director of Editing, Design, and Production: Marcia Cohen
Manager, Publishing Services: Emily Berleth

Library of Congress Control Number: 2002111900

Manufactured in the United States of America.

8 7 6 5
f e d c

For information, write: Bedford/St. Martin's,
75 Arlington Street, Boston, MA 02116 (617-399-4000)

ISBN: 0-312-25686-8

Published and distributed outside North America by:
PALGRAVE
Houndmills, Basingstoke, Hampshire RG21 6XS and London
Companies and representatives throughout the world.
PALGRAVE is the new global academic imprint of St. Martin's Press LLC Scholarly and Reference Division and Palgrave Publishers Ltd. (formerly Macmillan Press Ltd.).
ISBN: 0-333-97349-6
A catalogue record for this book is available from the British Library.

Acknowledgments

Acknowledgments and copyrights are continued at the back of the book on p. 532, which constitutes an extension of the copyright page.

About the Series

Volumes in the *Case Studies in Contemporary Criticism* series introduce college students to the current critical and theoretical ferment in literary studies. Each volume reprints the complete text of a significant literary work, together with critical essays that approach the work from different theoretical perspectives and editorial matter that introduces both the literary work and the critics' theoretical perspectives.

The volume editor of each *Case Study* has selected and prepared an authoritative text of a classic work, written introductions (sometimes supplemented by cultural documents) that place the work in biographical and historical context, and surveyed the critical responses to the work since its original publication. Thus situated biographically, historically, and critically, the work is subsequently examined in several critical essays that have been prepared especially for students. The essays show theory in practice; whether written by established scholars or exceptional young critics, they demonstrate how current theoretical approaches can generate compelling readings of great literature.

As series editor, I have prepared introductions to the critical essays and to the theoretical approaches they entail. The introductions, accompanied by bibliographies, explain and historicize the principal concepts, major figures, and key works of particular theoretical approaches as a prelude to discussing how they pertain to the critical essays that follow. It is my hope that the introductions will reveal to students that effective criticism — including their own — is informed by a set of coherent assumptions that can be not only articulated but also modified and extended through comparison of different theoretical approaches. Finally, I have included a glossary of key terms that recur in these volumes and in the discourse of contemporary theory and criticism. I hope that the *Case Studies in Contemporary Criticism* series will reaffirm the richness of its literary works, even as it presents invigorating new ways to mine their apparently inexhaustible wealth.

I would like to thank Supryia M. Ray, with whom I wrote *The Bedford Glossary of Critical and Literary Terms,* for her invaluable help in revising the introductions to the critical approaches represented in this volume.

Ross C Murfin
Provost, Southern Methodist University
Series Editor

About This Volume

Part One takes as its basis the 1847 edition of *Wuthering Heights,* the only edition published during Emily Brontë's lifetime. Unfortunately, Brontë's publisher, Thomas C. Newby, was lackadaisical in his procedures and produced a text riddled with spelling and punctuation errors. Subsequent editors have found it necessary to correct Newby's errata, many of which Emily had revised in page proofs. Some nineteenth-century editors, including Emily's sister Charlotte, altered more than orthography and punctuation, even to the extent of rewriting the dialect and reorganizing the paragraphs. Although I have annotated some of the dialect, I have tried not to intervene in Emily Brontë's original text. Like most modern editors of *Wuthering Heights,* I have returned to the 1847 edition, letting Emily's written presentation stand but consulting Charlotte Brontë's 1850 and Clement Shorter's 1911 editions for corrections that may have been marked in Emily's personal copy of the novel. The text printed here is thus close to, but not identical with, the original 1847 edition and the scholarly 1976 Clarendon Press edition produced by Hilda Marsden and Ian Jack.

Part Two includes five exemplary critical essays that analyze *Wuthering Heights* from different contemporary theoretical perspectives: psychoanalytic, Marxist, cultural studies, feminist, and a synthetic approach that combines the last three with new historicist and postcolonialist insights. Choosing only five essays, given the large and distinguished body of criticism on the novel, was a difficult task, yet certain choices seemed essential: Terry Eagleton's now classic analysis of Brontë's fiction within the context of nineteenth-century capitalism, Lyn Pykett's consolidation of feminist criticism and social history to explain the novel's engagement with nineteenth-century women's political and personal concerns, and Susan Meyer's reading of Heathcliff's actions within the context of British imperialism. Philip Wion's use of modern developmental psychological theory was a real find, and I am especially pleased to include Nancy Armstrong's original discussion of cultural studies and its relevance to the publication and reception of *Wuthering Heights.* My own work on the biographical and historical background to the novel, as well as its critical history since publication, has reminded me (again) how rewardingly complex a novel Emily Brontë wrote.

Acknowledgments

Many of the ideas for this volume originated in a seminar on "The Teaching of English," where over the years graduate students and I have discussed the implications of teaching a novel from a specific theoretical perspective. The novel to which we applied our ideas was *Wuthering Heights* — in part because I regularly teach that work in an undergraduate course, in part because I knew that the critical debates about the text would produce rich discussion. My thanks to the graduate students in this seminar and the teaching assistants in the Victorian novel lecture course for their many suggestions, some of which influenced this volume, others of which will (I hope) appear in future criticism on *Wuthering Heights.*

Of the people at Bedford/St. Martin's, I owe special thanks to Joan Feinberg, whose conversations about the series hooked me on the idea; to Steve Scipione, who read through mounds of literary criticism and kept the project on track; to Emily Berleth and Linda DeMasi, who saw the book through production with admirable sympathy and efficiency; and to Andrea Nagy, who proofread the text of the novel for this edition.

Finally, I owe thanks to Fred Strebeigh, who helped me obtain slides of the illustrations for the Cultural Contexts and who, over the past two decades, has shared many other intellectual joys and professional tasks. It has been a pleasure to collaborate once again with Ross Murfin, whose friendship predates the contemporary critical debates encapsulated in this volume.

Linda H. Peterson
Yale University

Contents

PART ONE
Wuthering Heights: The Complete Text in Cultural Context

PART TWO
Wuthering Heights:
A Case Study in Contemporary Criticism

PART ONE

Wuthering Heights: The Complete Text in Cultural Context

Introduction: Biographical and Historical Contexts

Emily Brontë published only one novel and, with her sisters, one small volume of poetry. Born in 1818, she died in 1848 — just after *Wuthering Heights* appeared and just before her thirtieth birthday. Yet her novel is one of the most widely read books in the English language, and its literary originality and power have won Brontë lasting fame.

Brontë's life was in some ways the ordinary life of a nineteenth-century woman: as a child she attended a girls' boarding school to obtain the rudiments of an education; at home she learned such domestic skills as sewing, cooking, and baking; and in her early twenties, she tried a stint at governessing in a private school. In many other ways, however, Brontë's life was unusual, even eccentric, and these more unusual aspects of her life contributed to the originality of her novel.

Brontë grew up in the tiny Yorkshire village of Haworth, in a remote region of northern England. Elizabeth Gaskell, a contemporary novelist and family friend, described the village as "situated on the side of a pretty steep hill, with a background of dun and purple moors, rising and sweeping away yet higher than the church which is built at the very summit of the long narrow street." Gaskell found these moors "grand," evoking "ideas of solitude and loneliness which they suggest." But they also could seem "oppressive from the feeling which they give of being pent-up by some monotonous and illimitable barrier" (55).[1] Brontë obviously responded to the grandeur of the moors, for they inspired many of her poems and are loved with passionate intensity by the heroines of *Wuthering Heights,* Catherine Earnshaw and her daughter Catherine Linton.

Growing up on the Yorkshire moors was different from growing up in London, where most of Brontë's readers lived. Life was more rugged, emotion more raw, on the moors. As Emily's sister and fellow novelist Charlotte explained in her preface to the 1850 edition of the novel, city-bred ladies and gentlemen "hardly know what to make of the rough, strong utterance" and "harshly manifested passions" of "unlettered moorland hinds and rugged moorland squires" (p. 21 in this volume). Brontë ran into trouble for depicting the lives of such moorland characters in *Wuthering Heights;* their language and manners were considered too "coarse" for civilized readers to endure, and from the beginning, readers complained of the odiousness of her characters and scenes.

Even more atypical, however, was Brontë's family history, which included the early deaths of her mother and two older sisters. Maria Branwell Brontë died in 1821, leaving three-year-old Emily and her young siblings to the care of their elder sisters, Maria and Elizabeth, and their well-meaning but eccentric father. Four years later, in 1825, the elder sisters died in an outbreak of typhus. The domestic functions of the family were taken over by an unmarried aunt, Elizabeth Branwell, who moved to Haworth to keep house and raise the children. Although her aunt made every effort, Emily never felt much affection for her; "conscientious" but "somewhat narrow" in her views, Miss Branwell was not someone whom children could love easily or freely (Gaskell 96–97). In some respects, the mother's place was taken by a family servant, Tabitha Aykroyd, perhaps a prototype of Nelly Dean.

It was Emily's father, Patrick Brontë, however, who had the most significant influence on her development. Mr. Brontë was a clergyman, appointed as perpetual curate of the Haworth church, but he was not conventional in background or beliefs. Born into a poor Irish family, he had struggled for an education, first tutoring in Ireland to earn money,

[1]Gaskell's biography, which focuses on Charlotte Brontë but discusses the entire family, was originally published in 1857, using interviews and evidence gathered from contemporary sources.

then working his way through Cambridge University and winning a position (respected but low-paying) in the Anglican Church. The family's Irish heritage seems to have had little effect on Emily Brontë's fiction, though some biographers believe that a family legend about Patrick Brontë's father Hugh, a foundling discovered on a Liverpool boat, may be a source for Heathcliff's mysterious origins.[2] Brontë's poverty remained a constant feature of life, but so did more important values: intellectual independence, unconventional thinking, and literary sensitivity.

Mr. Brontë raised his children to be hardy and to scorn conventional notions about food and dress. According to one of Gaskell's informants, one day when the children had been playing on the moors and the rain had set in, their nurse got out some prettily colored boots and put them round the fire to warm. When the children got home, the boots were nowhere to be seen. Mr. Brontë had found them and tossed them into the fire, thinking they were "too gay and luxurious for his children" (89).[3] No record remains of Emily's reaction, but we know from *Wuthering Heights* that young Catherine was always ready for a "scamper on the moors," even on a day "flooding with rain" (pp. 40, 38). Catherine seems also to have scorned conventional dress — at least until her capture and initiation at Thrushcross Grange.

Patrick Brontë fostered in his children an intellectual passion and love of literature. Emily and her sisters had free access to the books in their father's library and in the nearby Keighley Mechanics' Institute Library; no one censored their reading or attempted to direct their interests toward suitable "feminine" literature. And, despite their straitened circumstances, the family subscribed to newspapers and literary periodicals, often reading articles aloud to each other. Mr. Brontë was a poet himself, as well as a storyteller. His children seem to have picked up his intellectual tastes and, quite precociously, developed their own games of storytelling, playacting, and adventure writing.

The most famous of their juvenile storytelling activities began when Mr. Brontë brought home a box of wooden soldiers. Officially, the

[2]The Irish heritage is discussed in Chitham (8–13) and in Constable. Chitham suggests that all the Brontë children had a fascination with Irish folk legends and tales of haunted spirits.

[3]Brontë was also reported to have cut up one of his wife's silk gowns because it offended his sense of appropriate dress. Some modern biographers, such as Juliet Barker, have questioned these stories of Patrick Brontë's eccentric behavior.

soldiers belonged to Branwell, the only son, but he soon divided them up with his sisters, who named them after contemporary heroes like the Duke of Wellington and Napoléon Bonaparte. Emily called her soldier either "Gravey" or "Parry" (after the arctic explorer Captain Edward Parry), and though she was only eight years old, began to invent adventures that involved her soldier in the tales that the Brontë children called "The Islanders." Sometimes the adventures were acted out — much to the dismay of Tabby, the family nurse and servant, who thought their boisterous dramatic activities got out of hand. Sometimes the adventures were written down and made into "books" — at first by Charlotte, who was the eldest, but eventually by all the others: Branwell, Emily, and Anne.

This imaginative life — filled with fair-haired queens and dark heroes, political wars and private love affairs — was sustained for nearly twenty years. The children split into teams, with Charlotte and Branwell producing the "Glasstown Chronicles" and then tales of "Angria"; Anne and Emily writing their own independent saga of "Gondal," a mythical island. Unlike the kingdom of her elder siblings, Emily's Gondal was a feminist and royalist realm. The leading parts went to female characters — variously named Augusta, Rosina, and Geraldine — while the weaker part was invariably given to a young male (a relationship that anticipates the stronger Catherine Earnshaw and weaker Edgar Linton of *Wuthering Heights*). As one Brontë scholar has noted, in her siblings' Angria it is Arthur Wellesley "for love of whom ladies went into romantic decline and commoners gave their lives," whereas in Emily's Gondol it is the queen whose "compelling beauty and charm . . . bring all men to her feet" (Ratchford 22).[4] Men lost their lives — or their minds — for the love of Emily's fair-haired heroines.

Late in adolescence, Brontë began writing poetry to accompany the Gondal narratives. The prose narratives of Gondal have been lost, except for brief summaries and fragments, but much of the poetry has survived — perhaps because Emily valued it more and copied it into a small notebook. In addition to the Gondal poems, she wrote personal and private lyrics, keeping these in a separate notebook utterly secret from her family. Her sister Charlotte "accidentally lighted" upon this

[4]Ratchford argues that Emily consciously established a moral viewpoint antithetical to that of Charlotte and Branwell: "in place of Charlotte and Branwell's pageantry of war, . . . Emily showed wounded and bleeding men, devastated countrysides, and broken homes. To Emily war was real and terrible" (23).

poetry one day in 1845 — much to Emily's anger at the invasion of privacy.[5] But Charlotte, convinced of her sister's literary genius, nagged until Emily agreed to let some of her poems be published, along with selections written by Charlotte and Anne.

In 1846, then, Emily Brontë's first literary work was published under the title *Poems by Currer, Ellis, and Acton Bell.* Pseudonyms were used because the sisters wanted their poetry to be taken seriously: "we had a vague impression," Charlotte later explained, "that authoresses are liable to be looked on with prejudice." But they also worried about dishonesty and so chose names ambiguous as to gender, "being dictated by a sort of conscientious scruple at assuming Christian names positively masculine" (p. 16). During her lifetime Emily Brontë kept the *nom de plume* Ellis Bell. Although her sisters Charlotte and Anne eventually made their real names public, Emily refused, leaving it for Charlotte to explain after Emily's death who "Ellis Bell" really was.

Because Emily's Gondal poems in the 1846 edition are not labeled as such and because so many deal with passionate, often tragic love, biographers have speculated about a secret passion that Emily might have felt for an unknown lover. The Heaton boys of Ponden Hall, thought to be a model for Thrushcross Grange, have been suggested.[6] So, too, biographers have speculated about unknown men at Law Hill, where Emily tried governessing, or in Brussels, where she went to school with Charlotte. No lover has turned up, despite more than 150 years of close, detective-like reading in Emily Brontë's poetry and prose.

Unfortunately, at the time of their publication, the poems received no such close attention, whether for biographical or other purposes. There were brief reviews in *The Critic* and the *Athenaeum,* the latter praising Emily's work for "its music" and "power of wing." Critics recognized Ellis Bell as the most original writer of the three "brothers" (qtd. in Allott 218). But, generally, the volume of poetry went unnoticed and unsold (except for two copies). A year later the sisters sent the

[5]Charlotte Brontë tells the story of her discovery of Emily's poetry in the "Biographical Notice of Ellis and Acton Bell," which she wrote to preface the 1850 edition of *Wuthering Heights* and *Agnes Grey* (pp. 15–21).

[6]In a novel, *White Windows,* Emily Heaton ascribes a love affair to Emily Brontë and Michael Heaton. As Gerin points out, this is highly unlikely, as Michael was only twelve when Emily died. The eldest Heaton son, Robert, was closer to Emily's age, though still four years younger (32).

extras to well-known English poets and critics, explaining their predicament and thanking them for "the pleasure and profit we have often and long derived from your work" (qtd. in Gerin 206). No one seems to have responded to their gift.

No response by Emily Brontë — either to the reviews or to the critical neglect — has been discovered either. She remained utterly silent about the reception of her poetry, as she did about *Wuthering Heights*. We do know, however, that even before their poetry was published, Charlotte had convinced her sisters to try their luck at writing novels. When they began is uncertain, but by July 1846, all three had manuscripts ready to mail to London publishers: *The Professor* by Currer Bell, *Wuthering Heights* by Ellis Bell, and *Agnes Grey* by Acton Bell.

It took a year of rejection letters before *Wuthering Heights* was finally accepted by T. C. Newby of Mortimer Street, Cavendish Square. Newby was a publisher of dubious reputation, and his arrangement with the Brontës was ungenerous. He rejected Charlotte's manuscript of *The Professor* outright and only agreed to publish Emily's *Wuthering Heights* and Anne's *Agnes Grey* if they paid him an advance of £50 (to be refunded after the sale of 250 copies — a detail of the contract he later conveniently ignored). Despite Newby's shoddy publishing practices, Emily and Anne Brontë stuck with him. In December 1847, *Wuthering Heights* and *Agnes Grey* appeared as a three-volume set.

Brontë was never to realize the impact that her novel had on English literature. By January 1848, the entire family had caught a serious form of cold-influenza. This illness — either the cause or a result of tuberculosis — struck down three family members within a year. Branwell, the only son, died on September 24, 1848. Emily attended her brother's funeral, but that was the last day she left the house. She died on December 19, 1848, of "inflammation of the lungs" — a symptom of "consumption," as tuberculosis was called in those days. Her sister Anne followed in less than six months, leaving only Charlotte to carry on and explain Ellis Bell to the world.

Because all three Brontë sisters wrote poetry and fiction, it has been common to amalgamate their achievements and treat them as a single unit. Early readers speculated whether Currer, Ellis, and Acton Bell were just one person and whether *Wuthering Heights* was really written by Currer Bell, author of *Jane Eyre*. Reviewers noted that the Bells's books were closely related "in cast of thought, incident and language" (*Athenaeum* qtd. in Allott 218).[7] In one of his many dubious publishing strategies, T. C. Newby put out advertisements implying that Ellis Bell was the true author of all the novels. Eventually, Charlotte and Anne journeyed to London to set the record straight. (Emily refused to go, as she would have nothing to do with worldly details of fame or infamy.)

This tendency to treat the Brontës as a single author continued into the twentieth century, long after readers knew the biographical facts. (The eminent English critic F. R. Leavis wrote, "It is tempting to retort that there is only one Brontë" [41].)[8] Despite their identical background, the Brontë sisters were quite different — in everything from physical appearance to mental outlook. Charlotte was small and plain — much like the heroine she created for *Jane Eyre*. Emily was much taller (5'6") and, at least as a child, more attractive. One family servant recalled that all the Brontë children "were good little creatures," but that "Emily was the prettiest" (qtd. in Chitham 22). Ellen Nussey, a friend from adolescence, remembered Emily's "beautiful eyes" and "lithesome graceful figure" (qtd. in Gerin 35). So, too, were Emily's and Charlotte's personalities different. Charlotte was known to be excitable and hot-tempered, whereas Emily was stubborn and silent (Gerin 34). This silence developed into extreme taciturnity during adolescence, so much so that Charlotte feared her sister might be seen as socially rude or psychologically withdrawn.

As writers, too, the Brontës differed in their responses to common themes of life and literature: school and education, love and marriage, moral failure and evil. Readers of *Jane Eyre* will recall, for example, that Charlotte found education at once traumatic and exhilarating. Jane Eyre's experiences at Lowood School, including the death of Helen Burns, were based on Charlotte's encounter with cruelty and deprivation at the Cowan Bridge School, where she and Emily were sent as children and where their elder sisters Maria and Elizabeth became fatally ill. Yet Charlotte, like Jane Eyre, considered education a means of female liberation; it allowed her to achieve intellectual and financial independence.

Emily was less enamored of formal education and, apparently, less influenced by her school experiences. She was never particularly good

[7]The confusion over the Brontës' identity is usefully summarized in Gerin (209–13).

[8]Leavis makes this remark in a "Note on the Brontës," intended to justify his omission of their work from his "great tradition."

at bookwork and performed less well than Charlotte, both at Roe Head, which she attended at age seventeen, and in Brussels, where she and Charlotte prepared for careers as private teachers. When Emily tried her hand at teaching, she found it unsuitable employment. Once she told a classroom of unruly students that the only individual she liked in the whole place was the house-dog (Gerin 81). At school, Emily Brontë rebelled against the routine and suffered from homesickness.

Brontë seems ambivalent, moreover, about the effects of education. In *Wuthering Heights* the denial of education to Heathcliff is a demeaning form of social punishment. Yet Hareton's education, later in the novel, has both positive and negative impact: he learns the mental and social skills necessary for marrying Catherine and living a civilized life at Thrushcross Grange, but, as many critics have pointed out, Hareton also loses power — including masculine sexual power — by submitting to conventional forms of nineteenth-century education.

Brontë was even less conventional, more critical, in her attitudes toward love and marriage. Both her sisters suffered from unfulfilled romantic attachments — Anne to a curate who died in his early twenties, Charlotte to a married Belgian teacher, Monsieur Constantin Heger — and they transferred their strong desire for marriage into their novels. In a poem written in 1845, Emily reflects on "Poor slaves, subdued by passion strong,"[9] implying that she has never been so subdued. Yet she certainly understood strong passion, as her depiction of Catherine and Heathcliff's love shows. The institution of marriage, however, she treats with deep ambivalence. Catherine Earnshaw dies from it, first losing freedom and self-confidence, then mental stability, and finally her life.

If Brontë looked critically at sacred Victorian institutions such as school, love, and marriage, she also was less bound by conventional notions of morality. This was no more true than in her treatment of her brother Branwell and his many moral failings. As an only son, Branwell had been the focus of his family's hopes and affection. His talents as a writer and painter were made much of — possibly exaggerated — and he was sent for special art training to London, where he failed miserably. After this failure there were many other disasters, as Branwell became more and more addicted to alcohol and opium, and less able to sustain a career.

[9] "How Beautiful the Earth Is Still," written June 2, 1845, in *Complete Poems* (232).

Charlotte and Anne Brontë viewed their brother's demise with horror and embarrassment. Charlotte refused to speak to him, especially when he returned home in disgrace from a tutorial position and sent the household into chaos with his mad, drunken ravings. Anne, pious by temperament, wrote *The Tenant of Wildfell Hall* as a warning against such moral failings. Emily seems to have had more compassion than her sisters — and more interest in the psychology of cases such as his. It was she who let Branwell back into the parsonage at night after his drunken binges and she, too, who genuinely mourned his early death from alcoholism, drug addiction, and mental collapse. Some biographers even claim that Emily willed her own death after the loss of her brother.

The differences between Charlotte's and Emily's moral perspectives emerge in the heroes they create for their novels. In Charlotte's *Jane Eyre* Edward Rochester may have sinned in his past and may tempt Jane to sin by living with him out of wedlock, but the novel's plot demands that he repent and reform. In *Wuthering Heights* Heathcliff undergoes no such plot of repentance; as Charlotte said of her sister's hero in her "Editor's Preface" to the new 1850 edition, "Heathcliff, indeed, stands unredeemed; never once swerving in his arrow-straight course to perdition" (p. 23). That Emily thought her hero doomed to perdition is unlikely. Critics have pointed out that the novel has little concern with traditional definitions of good and evil, but rather that it represents a vision of cosmic forces transcending human morality.

Questions about Brontë's vision — whether it is social and historical or essentially philosophical, spiritual, and transcendent — have recurred frequently in critical studies of *Wuthering Heights.* Some critics believe that the novel is a timeless romance, best read in terms of the motifs, symbols, and archetypes that express human longing for otherworldly union. Other critics maintain that the novel is vitally historical, responding to pressing social, political, and economic issues of the mid-nineteenth century.

Emily Brontë was less explicitly historical in her writing than her sister Charlotte, whose novels address such contemporary issues as women's education, church politics, and labor movements and strikes. But *Wuthering Heights* is nonetheless rooted in its historical context. Brontë's heroines suffer from the same gender limitations that affected their real-life counterparts. Modern readers may wonder how

Catherine Earnshaw could marry Edgar Linton for the financial security and social status that he offers, but in the nineteenth century young women were similarly pressured into a marriage market that valued marrying "well" over marrying for love. So, too, modern readers may need to have explained the marriage laws that allowed Linton Heathcliff, and then his father, to take control of Cathy Linton's real and personal property. But nineteenth-century readers, living before the passage of the Married Women's Rights and Properties Act (1857), did not need an explanation: they understood, often to their dismay, that husbands became sole possessors of everything that wives "owned" or inherited.

Brontë's readers also understood Heathcliff's story within the context of the social upheavals of the 1830s and 1840s. They knew about unemployed textile workers who burned power looms to protest industrialization; they watched working-class Chartists agitate for the vote in massive urban demonstrations; and they saw thousands of hungry Irish refugees pour into English ports to escape a potato famine that starved more than 700,000 to death in the 1840s. Heathcliff, a foundling from the port of Liverpool, represented to Victorians a common enough social problem: perhaps an orphaned Irish child, perhaps the bastard product of a drunken sailor and a prostitute mother, or perhaps (as Nelly Dean puts it) a "gipsy brat" (p. 51).

Whether historical context should provide the primary basis for interpreting *Wuthering Heights* has been the subject of much critical debate. Three decades ago, in the heyday of formalist criticism, critics tended to emphasize the archetypes, symbols, and motifs that linked the novel to a long, almost timeless tradition of Western literature — for instance, binaries of storm and calm, of exposure and enclosure, or elemental images of fire, wind, and water. (See Part Two, "A Critical History of *Wuthering Heights*.") More recent criticism, however, has tended to treat the novel as participating in, and responding to, its historical moment.

In her feminist reading, for example, Lyn Pykett interprets the dilemma of "the two Catherines" in terms of the traditional marriage plot of the English domestic novel; she sees this literary pattern as reflective of the eighteenth- and nineteenth-century society from which the novel emerges. In his Marxist analysis, Terry Eagleton is even more historically specific, linking the novel to early industrial society in Britain and arguing that all the Brontës' fiction is "rooted in, without being reduced to, specific social conditions"; he finds in Emily Brontë's work "an abnormally stark opposition" between a "'pre-industrial' imaginative creativity" and "the felt pressures of a drably spiritless society to which that imagination must either tortuously adapt or suffer extinction" (Eagleton 3, 12). For him, this is a novel from and about 1847. Similarly, Nancy Armstrong reads *Wuthering Heights* as both a product — and producer — of its culture, but she focuses on the increasing regionalization of Britain in the nineteenth century, an effect of British imperialism and urbanization; Armstrong finds parallels between the novel's regional features and the increasing commodification of regionalism in capitalist England. For Susan Meyer, the historical link lies with British imperialism, particularly with the ways in which the nonwhite races of Britain's colonies were perceived and represented in the language of the colonizer. And, although he draws primarily on modern psychological theory, Philip Wion's approach is partially historical, too, in the connections he draws between Brontë's private history, especially the early loss of her mother, and the themes of "oneness" and "otherness" he finds in *Wuthering Heights.* For Wion, the "absent mother" explains many of the psychological and social disturbances that Brontë depicts. Whether we view the novel historically or from some other perspective, *Wuthering Heights* challenges its readers to come to terms with Brontë's vision.

WORKS CITED

Allott, Miriam, ed. *The Brontës: The Critical Heritage.* London: Routledge, 1974.

Barker, Juliet. *The Brontës.* New York: St. Martin's, 1994.

Brontë, Emily Jane. *Complete Poems.* Ed. C. W. Hatfield. New York: Columbia UP, 1941.

Chitham, Edward. *A Life of Emily Brontë.* Oxford: Basil Blackwell, 1987.

Constable, Kathleen. *A Stranger Within the Gates: Charlotte Brontë and Victorian Irishness.* Lanham, MD: University Press of America, 2000.

Eagleton, Terry. *Myths of Power: A Marxist Study of the Brontës.* London: Macmillan, 1975.

Gaskell, Elizabeth. *The Life of Charlotte Brontë.* 1857; Harmondsworth, UK: Penguin, 1975.

Gerin, Winifred. *Emily Brontë: A Biography.* Oxford: Clarendon, 1971.

Heaton, Emily. *White Windows.* London: Lincoln Williams, 1932.

Leavis, F. R. *The Great Tradition: A Study of the English Novel.* Garden City, NY: Doubleday, 1954.

Ratchford, Fannie. *Gondal's Queen: A Novel in Verse by Emily Jane Brontë.* Austin: U of Texas P, 1955.

Wuthering Heights

BIOGRAPHICAL NOTICE OF ELLIS AND ACTON BELL°

It has been thought that all the works published under the names of Currer, Ellis, and Acton Bell, were, in reality, the production of one person. This mistake I endeavored to rectify by a few words of disclaimer prefixed to the third edition of *Jane Eyre*. These, too, it appears, failed to gain general credence, and now, on the occasion of a reprint of *Wuthering Heights* and *Agnes Grey*, I am advised distinctly to state how the case really stands.

Indeed, I feel myself that it is time the obscurity attending those two names — Ellis and Acton — was done away. The little mystery, which formerly yielded some harmless pleasure, has lost its interest; circumstances are changed. It becomes, then, my duty to explain briefly the origin and authorship of the books written by Currer, Ellis, and Acton Bell.

About five years ago, my two sisters and myself, after a somewhat prolonged period of separation, found ourselves reunited, and at home. Resident in a remote district where education had made little progress, and where, consequently, there was no inducement to seek social intercourse beyond our own domestic circle, we were wholly dependent on

Biographical Notice . . . Acton Bell: Charlotte Brontë wrote this brief biography of her sisters, in part to dispel rumors that Currer, Ellis, and Acton Bell were multiple pseudonyms for the same person.

ourselves and each other, on books and study, for the enjoyments and occupations of life. The highest stimulus, as well as the liveliest pleasure we had known from childhood upwards, lay in attempts at literary composition; formerly we used to show each other what we wrote, but of late years this habit of communication and consultation had been discontinued; hence it ensued, that we were mutually ignorant of the progress we might respectively have made.

One day, in the autumn of 1845, I accidentally lighted on a MS. volume of verse in my sister Emily's handwriting. Of course, I was not surprised, knowing that she could and did write verse: I looked it over, and something more than surprise seized me, — a deep conviction that these were not common affusions, not at all like the poetry women generally write. I thought them condensed and terse, vigorous and genuine. To my ear, they had also a peculiar music — wild, melancholy, and elevating.

My sister Emily was not a person of demonstrative character, nor one, on the recesses of whose mind and feelings, even those nearest and dearest to her could, with impunity, intrude unlicensed; it took hours to reconcile her to the discovery I had made, and days to persuade her that such poems merited publication. I knew, however, that a mind like hers could not be without some latent spark of honourable ambition, and refused to be discouraged in my attempts to fan that spark to flame.

Meantime, my younger sister quietly produced some of her own compositions, intimating that since Emily's had given me pleasure, I might like to look at hers. I could not but be a partial judge, yet I thought that these verses too had a sweet sincere pathos of their own.

We had very early cherished the dream of one day becoming authors. This dream, never relinquished even when distance divided and absorbing tasks occupied us, now suddenly acquired strength and consistency: it took the character of a resolve. We agreed to arrange a small selection of our poems, and, if possible, get them printed. Averse to personal publicity, we veiled our own names under those of Currer, Ellis, and Acton Bell; the ambiguous choice being dictated by a sort of conscientious scruple at assuming Christian names positively masculine, while we did not like to declare ourselves women, because — without at that time suspecting our mode of writing and thinking was not what is called "feminine" — we had a vague impression that authoresses are liable to be looked on with prejudice; we had noticed how critics sometimes use for their chastisement the weapon of personality, and for their reward, a flattery, which is not true praise.

The bringing out of our little book was hard work. As was to be expected, neither we nor our poems were at all wanted; but for this we had been prepared at the outset; though inexperienced ourselves, we had read the experience of others. The great puzzle lay in the difficulty of getting answers of any kind from the publishers to whom we applied. Being greatly harassed by this obstacle, I ventured to apply to the Messrs. Chambers, of Edinburgh, for a word of advice; *they* may have forgotten the circumstance, but *I* have not, for from them I received a brief and business-like, but civil and sensible reply, on which we acted, and at last made a way.

The book was printed: it is scarcely known, and all of it that merits to be known are the poems of Ellis Bell. The fixed conviction I held, and hold, of the worth of these poems has not indeed received the confirmation of much favourable criticism; but I must retain it notwithstanding.

Ill-success failed to crush us; the mere effort to succeed had given a wonderful zest to existence; it must be pursued. We each set to work on a prose tale: Ellis Bell produced *Wuthering Heights*, Acton Bell *Agnes Grey*, and Currer Bell also wrote a narrative in one volume. These MSS. were perseveringly obtruded upon various publishers for the space of a year and a half; usually, their fate was an ignominious and abrupt dismissal.

At last *Wuthering Heights* and *Agnes Grey* were accepted on terms somewhat impoverishing to the two authors; Currer Bell's book found acceptance nowhere, nor any acknowledgment of merit, so that something like the chill of despair began to invade his heart. As a forlorn hope, he tried one publishing house more — Messrs. Smith and Elder. Ere long, in a much shorter space than that on which experience had taught him to calculate — there came a letter, which he opened in the dreary expectation of finding two hard hopeless lines, intimating that Messrs. Smith and Elder "were not disposed to publish the MS.," and, instead, he took out of the envelope a letter of two pages. He read it trembling. It declined, indeed, to publish that tale, for business reasons, but it discussed its merits and demerits so courteously, so considerately, in a spirit so rational, with a discrimination so enlightened, that this very refusal cheered the author better than a vulgarly-expressed acceptance would have done. It was added, that a work in three volumes would meet with careful attention.

I was then just completing *Jane Eyre*, at which I had been working while the one volume tale was plodding its weary round in London: in three weeks I sent if off; friendly and skilful hands took it in. This was in the commencement of September 1847; it came out before the close of

October following, while *Wuthering Heights* and *Agnes Grey*, my sisters' works, which had already been in the press for months, still lingered under a different management.

They appeared at last. Critics failed to do them justice. The immature but very real powers revealed in *Wuthering Heights* were scarcely recognised; its import and nature were misunderstood; the identity of its author was misrepresented; it was said that this was an earlier and ruder attempt of the same pen which had produced *Jane Eyre*. Unjust and grievous error! We laughed at it at first, but I deeply lament it now. Hence, I fear, arose a prejudice against the book. That writer who could attempt to palm off an inferior and immature production under cover of one successful effort, must indeed be unduly eager after the secondary and sordid result of authorship, and pitiably indifferent to its true and honourable meed. If reviewers and the public truly believed this, no wonder that they looked darkly on the cheat.

Yet I must not be understood to make these things subject for reproach or complaint; I dare not do so; respect for my sister's memory forbids me. By her any such querulous manifestation would have been regarded as an unworthy, and offensive weakness.

It is my duty, as well as my pleasure, to acknowledge one exception to the general rule of criticism. One writer,[1] endowed with the keen vision and fine sympathies of genius, has discerned the real nature of *Wuthering Heights*, and has, with equal accuracy, noted its beauties and touched on its faults. Too often do reviewers remind us of the mob of Astrologers, Chaldeans, and Soothsayers gathered before the "writing on the wall," and unable to read the characters or make known the interpretation. We have a right to rejoice when a true seer comes at last, some man in whom is an excellent spirit, to whom have been given light, wisdom, and understanding, who can accurately read the "Mene, Mene, Tekel, Upharsin"[2] of an original mind (however unripe, however inefficiently cultured and partially expanded that mind may be); and who can say with confidence, "this is the interpretation thereof."

Yet even the writer to whom I allude shares the mistake about the authorship, and does me the injustice to suppose that there was equivoque in my former rejection of this honour (as an honour, I regard it). May I assure him that I would scorn in this and in every case to deal in

[1]See the *Palladium* for September 1850. [Charlotte Brontë's note.]

[2]Daniel 5:25. Brontë quotes the next verse, "This is the interpretation of the thing," but suggests that her sister's novel cannot be as easily interpreted as the Hebrew prophet Daniel interpreted the mysterious writing on the wall, "Mene, Tekel, Upharsin," of King Nebuchadnezzar's palace.

equivoque; I believe language to have been given us to make our meaning clear, and not to wrap it in dishonest doubt.

The Tenant of Wildfell Hall, by Acton Bell, had likewise an unfavourable reception. At this I cannot wonder. The choice of subject was an entire mistake. Nothing less congruous with the writer's nature could be conceived. The motives which dictated this choice were pure, but, I think, slightly morbid. She had, in the course of her life, been called on to contemplate, near at hand and for a long time, the terrible effects of talents misused and faculties abused; hers was naturally a sensitive, reserved, and dejected nature; what she saw sank very deeply into her mind; it did her harm. She brooded over it till she believed it to be a duty to reproduce every detail (of course with fictitious characters, incidents, and situations) as a warning to others. She hated her work, but would pursue it. When reasoned with on the subject, she regarded such reasonings as a temptation to self-indulgence. She must be honest; she must not varnish, soften, or conceal. This well-meant resolution brought on her misconstruction and some abuse, which she bore, as it was her custom to bear whatever was unpleasant, with mild, steady patience. She was a very sincere and practical Christian, but the tinge of religious melancholy communicated a sad shade to her brief, blameless life.

Neither Ellis nor Acton allowed herself for one moment to sink under want of encouragement; energy nerved the one, and endurance upheld the other. They were both prepared to try again; I would fain think that hope and the sense of power was yet strong within them. But a great change approached: affliction came in that shape which to anticipate is dread; to look back on, grief. In the very heat and burden of the day, the labourers failed over their work.

My sister Emily first declined. The details of her illness are deep-branded in my memory, but to dwell on them, either in thought or narrative, is not in my power. Never in all her life had she lingered over any task that lay before her, and she did not linger now. She sank rapidly. She made haste to leave us. Yet, while physically she perished, mentally, she grew stronger than we had yet known her. Day by day, when I saw with what a front she met suffering, I looked on her with an anguish of wonder and love. I have seen no other like it; but, indeed, I have never seen her parallel in anything. Stronger than a man, simpler than a child, her nature stood alone. The awful point was, that, while full of ruth for others, on herself she had no pity; the spirit was inexorable to the flesh; from the trembling hand, the unnerved limbs, the faded eyes, the same service was exacted as they had rendered in health. To stand by and witness this, and not dare to remonstrate, was a pain no words can render.

Two cruel months of hope and fear passed painfully by, and the day came at last when the terrors and pains of death were to be undergone by this treasure, which had grown dearer and dearer to our hearts as it wasted before our eyes. Towards the decline of that day, we had nothing left of Emily but her mortal remains as consumption left them. She died December 19, 1848.

We thought this enough; but we were utterly and presumptuously wrong. She was not buried ere Anne fell ill. She had not been committed to the grave a fortnight, before we received distinct intimation that it was necessary to prepare our minds to see the younger sister go after the elder. Accordingly, she followed in the same path with slower step, and with a patience that equalled the other's fortitude. I have said that she was religious, and it was by leaning on those Christian doctrines in which she firmly believed, that she found support through her most painful journey. I witnessed their efficacy in her latest hour and greatest trial, and must bear my testimony to the calm triumph with which they brought her through. She died May 28, 1849.

What more shall I say about them? I cannot and need not say much more. In externals, they were two unobtrusive women; a perfectly secluded life gave them retiring manners and habits. In Emily's nature the extremes of vigour and simplicity seemed to meet. Under an unsophisticated culture, inartificial tastes, and an unpretending outside, lay a secret power and fire that might have informed the brain and kindled the veins of a hero; but she had no worldly wisdom; her powers were unadapted to the practical business of life; she would fail to defend her most manifest rights, to consult her most legitimate advantage. An interpreter ought always to have stood between her and the world. Her will was not very flexible, and it generally opposed her interest. Her temper was magnanimous, but warm and sudden; her spirit altogether unbending.

Anne's character was milder and more subdued; she wanted the power, the fire, the originality of her sister, but was well-endowed with quiet virtues of her own. Long-suffering, self-denying, reflective, and intelligent, a constitutional reserve and taciturnity placed and kept her in the shade, and covered her mind, and especially her feelings, with a sort of nun-like veil, which was rarely lifted. Neither Emily nor Anne was learned; they had no thought of filling their pitchers at the wellspring of other minds; they always wrote from the impulse of nature, the dictates of intuition, and from such stores of observation as their limited experience had enabled them to amass. I may sum up all by saying, that for strangers they were nothing, for superficial observers less than nothing; but for those who had known them all their lives in the intimacy of close relationship, they were genuinely good and truly great.

This notice has been written, because I felt it a sacred duty to wipe the dust off their gravestones, and leave their dear names free from soil.

Currer Bell.

September 19, 1850

EDITOR'S PREFACE TO THE NEW [1850] EDITION OF WUTHERING HEIGHTS°

I have just read over *Wuthering Heights*, and, for the first time, have obtained a clear glimpse of what are termed (and, perhaps, really are) its faults; have gained a definite notion of how it appears to other people — to strangers who knew nothing of the author; who are unacquainted with the locality where the scenes of the story are laid; to whom the inhabitants, the customs, the natural characteristics of the outlying hills and hamlets in the West-Riding of Yorkshire are things alien and unfamiliar.

To all such *Wuthering Heights* must appear a rude and strange production. The wild moors of the north of England can for them have no interest; the language, the manners, the very dwellings and household customs of the scattered inhabitants of those districts, must be to such readers in a great measure unintelligible, and — where intelligible — repulsive. Men and women who, perhaps, naturally very calm, and with feelings moderate in degree, and little marked in kind, have been trained from their cradle to observe the utmost evenness of manner and guardedness of language, will hardly know what to make of the rough, strong utterance, the harshly manifested passions, the unbridled aversions, and headlong partialities of unlettered moorland hinds and rugged moorland squires, who have grown up untaught and unchecked, except by mentors as harsh as themselves. A large class of readers, likewise, will suffer greatly from the introduction into the pages of this work of words printed with all their letters, which it has become the custom to represent by the initial and final letter only — a blank line filling the interval. I may as well say at once that, for this circumstance, it is out of my power to apologize; deeming it, myself, a rational plan to write words at full length. The

Editor's Preface . . . Wuthering Heights: Charlotte Brontë wrote this preface to the second (1850) edition of her sister's novel, *Wuthering Heights*.

practice of hinting by single letters those expletives with which profane and violent people are wont to garnish their discourse, strikes me as a proceeding which, however well meant, is weak and futile. I cannot tell what good it does — what feeling it spares — what horror it conceals.

With regard to the rusticity of *Wuthering Heights,* I admit the charge, for I feel the quality. It is rustic all through. It is moorish, and wild, and knotty as the root of heath. Nor was it natural that it should be otherwise; the author being herself a native and nursling of the moors. Doubtless, had her lot been cast in a town, her writings, if she had written at all, would have possessed another character. Even had chance or taste led her to choose a similar subject, she would have treated it otherwise. Had Ellis Bell been a lady or a gentleman accustomed to what is called "the world," her view of a remote and unclaimed region, as well as the dwellers therein, would have differed greatly from that actually taken by the home-bred country girl. Doubtless it would have been wider — more comprehensive: whether it would have been more original or more truthful is not so certain. As far as the scenery and locality are concerned, it could scarcely have been so sympathetic: Ellis Bell did not describe as one whose eye and taste alone found pleasure in the prospect; her native hills were far more to her than a spectacle; they were what she lived in, and by, as much as the wild birds, their tenants, or as the heather, their produce. Her descriptions, then, of natural scenery, are what they should be, and all they should be.

Where delineation of human character is concerned, the case is different. I am bound to avow that she had scarcely more practical knowledge of the peasantry amongst whom she lived, than a nun has to the country people who sometimes pass her convent gates. My sister's disposition was not naturally gregarious; circumstances favoured and fostered her tendency to seclusion; except to go to church or take a walk on the hills, she rarely crossed the threshold of home. Though her feeling for the people round was benevolent, intercourse with them she never sought; nor, with very few exceptions, ever experienced. And yet she knew them: knew their ways, their language, their family histories; she could hear of them with interest, and talk of them with detail, minute, graphic, and accurate; but *with* them, she rarely exchanged a word. Hence it ensued that what her mind had gathered of the real concerning them, was too exclusively confined to those tragic and terrible traits of which, in listening to the secret annals of every rude vicinage, the memory is sometimes compelled to receive the impress. Her imagination, which was a spirit more sombre than sunny, more powerful than sportive, found in such traits material whence it wrought creations like Heathcliff, like Earnshaw, like Catherine. Having formed these beings, she did not know what she had done. If the auditor of her work when read in manuscript, shuddered under the grinding influence of natures so relentless and implacable, of spirits so lost and fallen; if it was complained that the mere hearing of certain vivid and fearful scenes banished sleep by night, and disturbed mental peace by day, Ellis Bell would wonder what was meant, and suspect the complainant of affectation. Had she but lived, her mind would of itself have grown like a strong tree, loftier, straighter, wider-spreading, and its matured fruits would have attained a mellower ripeness and sunnier bloom; but on that mind time and experience alone could work: to the influence of other intellects, it was not amenable.

Having avowed that over much of *Wuthering Heights* there broods "a horror of great darkness"; that, in its storm-heated and electrical atmosphere, we seem at times to breathe lightning, let me point to those spots where clouded daylight and the eclipsed sun still attest their existence. For a specimen of true benevolence and homely fidelity, look at the character of Nelly Dean; for an example of constancy and tenderness, remark that of Edgar Linton. (Some people will think these qualities do not shine so well incarnate in a man as they would do in a woman, but Ellis Bell could never be brought to comprehend this notion: nothing moved her more than any insinuation that the faithfulness and clemency, the long-suffering and loving-kindness which are esteemed virtues in the daughters of Eve, become foibles in the sons of Adam. She held that mercy and forgiveness are the divinest attributes of the Great Being who made both man and woman, and that what clothes the Godhead in glory, can disgrace no form of feeble humanity.) There is a dry saturnine humour in the delineation of old Joseph, and some glimpses of grace and gaiety animate the younger Catherine. Nor is even the first heroine of the name destitute of a certain strange beauty in her fierceness, or of honesty in the midst of perverted passion and passionate perversity.

Heathcliff, indeed, stands unredeemed; never once swerving in his arrow-straight course to perdition, from the time when "the little black-haired, swarthy thing, as dark as if it came from the Devil," was first unrolled out of the bundle and set on its feet in the farm-house kitchen, to the hour when Nelly Dean found the grim, stalwart corpse laid on its back in the panel-enclosed bed, with wide-gazing eyes that seemed "to sneer at her attempt to close them, and parted lips and sharp white teeth that sneered too."

Heathcliff betrays one solitary human feeling, and that is *not* his love for Catherine; which is a sentiment fierce and inhuman: a passion such as might boil and glow in the bad essence of some evil genius; a fire that might form the tormented centre — the ever-suffering soul of a magnate of the infernal world: and by its quenchless and ceaseless ravage effect the execution of the decree which dooms him to carry Hell with him wherever he wanders. No; the single link that connects Heathcliff with humanity is his rudely confessed regard for Hareton Earnshaw — the young man whom he has ruined; and then his half-implied esteem for Nelly Dean. These solitary traits omitted, we should say he was child neither of Lascar nor gipsy, but a man's shape animated by demon life — a Ghoul — an Afreet.

Whether it is right or advisable to create beings like Heathcliff, I do not know: I scarcely think it is. But this I know; the writer who possesses the creative gift owns something of which he is not always master — something that at times strangely wills and works for itself. He may lay down rules and devise principles, and to rules and principles it will perhaps for years lie in subjection; and then, haply without any warning of revolt, there comes a time when it will no longer consent to "harrow the vallies, or be bound with a band in the furrow" — when it "laughs at the multitude of the city, and regards not the crying of the driver" — when, refusing absolutely to make ropes out of sea-sand any longer, it sets to work on statue-hewing, and you have a Pluto or a Jove, a Tisiphone or a Psyche, a Mermaid or a Madonna, as Fate or Inspiration direct. Be the work grim or glorious, dread or divine, you have little choice left but quiescent adoption. As for you — the nominal artist — your share in it has been to work passively under dictates you neither delivered nor could question — that would not be uttered at your prayer, nor suppressed nor changed at your caprice. If the result be attractive, the World will praise you, who little deserve praise; if it be repulsive, the same World will blame you, who almost as little deserve blame.

Wuthering Heights was hewn in a wild workshop, with simple tools, out of homely materials. The statuary found a granite block on a solitary moor: gazing thereon, he saw how from the crag might be elicited the head, savage, swart, sinister; a form moulded with at least one element of grandeur — power. He wrought with a rude chisel, and from no model but the vision of his meditations. With time and labour, the crag took human shape; and there it stands colossal, dark, and frowning, half statue, half rock: in the former sense, terrible and goblin-like; in the latter, almost beautiful, for its colouring is of mellow grey, and moorland moss clothes it; and heath, with its blooming bells and balmy fragrance, grows faithfully close to the giant's foot.

Currer Bell.
[*Charlotte Brontë*]

CHAPTER 1

1801. — I have just returned from a visit to my landlord — the solitary neighbour that I shall be troubled with. This is certainly a beautiful country! In all England, I do not believe that I could have fixed on a situation so completely removed from the stir of society. A perfect misanthropist's Heaven — and Mr. Heathcliff and I are such a suitable pair to divide the desolation between us. A capital fellow! He little imagined how my heart warmed towards him when I beheld his black eyes withdraw so suspiciously under their brows, as I rode up, and when his fingers sheltered themselves, with a jealous resolution, still further in his waistcoat, as I announced my name.

"Mr. Heathcliff?" I said.

A nod was the answer.

"Mr. Lockwood, your new tenant, sir — I do myself the honour of calling as soon as possible after my arrival, to express the hope that I have not inconvenienced you by my perseverance in soliciting the occupation of Thrushcross Grange: I heard, yesterday, you had had some thoughts — "

"Thrushcross Grange is my own, sir," he interrupted wincing, "I should not allow any one to inconvenience me, if I could hinder it — walk in!"

The "walk in" was uttered with closed teeth and expressed the sentiment, "Go to the Deuce!" Even the gate over which he leant manifested no sympathizing movement to the words; and I think that circumstances determined me to accept the invitation: I felt interested in a man who seemed more exaggeratedly reserved than myself.

When he saw my horse's breast fairly brushing the barrier, he did pull out his hand to unchain it, and then sullenly preceded me up the causeway, calling, as we entered the court:

"Joseph, take Mr. Lockwood's horse; and bring up some wine."

"Here we have the whole establishment of domestics, I suppose," was the reflection, suggested by this compound order, "No wonder the grass grows up between the flags, and cattle are the only hedge-cutters."

Joseph was an elderly man, nay, an old man, very old, perhaps, though hale and sinewy.

"The Lord help us!" he soliloquised in an undertone of peevish displeasure, while relieving me of my horse: looking, meantime, in my face so sourly that I charitably conjectured he must have need of divine aid to digest his dinner, and his pious ejaculation had no reference to my unexpected advent.

Wuthering Heights is the name of Mr. Heathcliff's dwelling. "Wuthering" being a significant provincial adjective, descriptive of the atmospheric tumult to which its station is exposed in stormy weather. Pure, bracing ventilation they must have up there, at all times, indeed: one may guess the power of the north wind, blowing over the edge, by the excessive slant of a few stunted firs at the end of the house; and by a range of gaunt thorns all stretching their limbs one way, as if craving alms of the sun. Happily, the architect had foresight to build it strong: the narrow windows are deeply set in the wall, and the corners defended with large jutting stones.

Before passing the threshold, I paused to admire a quantity of grotesque carving lavished over the front, and especially about the principal door, above which, among a wilderness of crumbling griffins and shameless little boys, I detected the date "1500," and the name "Hareton Earnshaw." I would have made a few comments, and requested a short history of the place from the surly owner, but his attitude at the door appeared to demand my speedy entrance, or complete departure, and I had no desire to aggravate his impatience, previous to inspecting the penetralium.

One step brought us into the family sitting-room, without any introductory lobby or passage: they call it here "the house" pre-eminently. It includes kitchen and parlour, generally, but I believe at Wuthering Heights the kitchen is forced to retreat altogether into another quarter: at least I distinguished a chatter of tongues, and a clatter of culinary utensils, deep within; and I observed no signs of roasting, boiling, or baking, about the huge fire-place; nor any glitter of copper saucepans and tin cullenders on the walls. One end, indeed, reflected splendidly both light and heat, from ranks of immense pewter dishes, interspersed with silver jugs and tankards, towering row after row, in a vast oak dresser, to the very roof. The latter had never been underdrawn, its entire anatomy lay bare to an inquiring eye, except where a frame of wood laden with oatcakes, and clusters of legs of beef, mutton, and ham, concealed it. Above the chimney were sundry villainous old guns, and a couple of horse-pistols, and, by way of ornament, three gaudily painted canisters disposed along its ledge. The floor was of smooth, white stone: the chairs, high-backed, primitive structures, painted green: one or two heavy black ones lurking in the shade. In an arch, under the dresser, reposed a huge, liver-coloured bitch pointer surrounded by a swarm of squealing puppies, and other dogs haunted other recesses.

The apartment and furniture would have been nothing extraordinary as belonging to a homely, northern farmer with a stubborn countenance, and stalwart limbs, set out to advantage in knee-breeches, and gaiters. Such an individual, seated in his armchair, his mug of ale frothing on the round table before him, is to be seen in any circuit of five or six miles among these hills, if you go at the right time, after dinner. But, Mr. Heathcliff forms a singular contrast to his abode and style of living. He is a dark skinned gipsy, in aspect, in dress and manners a gentleman, that is, as much a gentleman as many a country squire: rather slovenly, perhaps, yet not looking amiss with his negligence, because he has an erect and handsome figure — and rather morose — possibly, some people might suspect him of a degree of underbred pride — I have a sympathetic chord within that tells me it is nothing of the sort; I know, by instinct, his reserve springs from an aversion to showy displays of feeling — to manifestations of mutual kindness. He'll love and hate, equally under cover, and esteem it a species of impertinence, to be loved or hated again — No, I'm running on too fast — I bestow my own attributes over-liberally on him. Mr. Heathcliff may have entirely dissimilar reasons for keeping his hand out of the way, when he meets a would-be acquaintance, to those which actuate me. Let me hope my constitution is almost peculiar: my dear mother used to say I should never have a comfortable home, and only last summer, I proved myself perfectly unworthy of one.

While enjoying a month of fine weather at the sea-coast, I was thrown into the company of a most fascinating creature, a real goddess, in my eyes, as long as she took no notice of me. I "never told my love" vocally; still, if looks have language, the merest idiot might have guessed I was over head and ears: she understood me, at last, and looked a return — the sweetest of all imaginable looks — and what did I do? I confess it with shame — shrunk icily into myself, like a snail, at every glance retired colder and farther; till, finally, the poor innocent was led to doubt her own senses, and, overwhelmed with confusion at her supposed mistake, persuaded her mamma to decamp.

By this curious turn of disposition I have gained the reputation of deliberate heartlessness, how undeserved, I alone can appreciate.

I took a seat at the end of the hearthstone opposite that towards which my landlord advanced, and filled up an interval of silence by attempting to caress the canine mother, who had left her nursery, and was sneaking wolfishly to the back of my legs, her lip curled up, and her white teeth watering for a snatch.

My caress provoked a long, guttural snarl.

"You'd better let the dog alone," growled Mr. Heathcliff, in unison, checking fiercer demonstrations with a punch of his foot. "She's not accustomed to be spoiled — not kept for a pet."

Then, striding to a side-door, he shouted again.

"Joseph!"

Joseph mumbled indistinctly in the depths of the cellar, but gave no intimation of ascending; so his master dived down to him, leaving me *vis-à-vis* the ruffianly bitch, and a pair of grim, shaggy sheep dogs, who shared with her a jealous guardianship over all my movements.

Not anxious to come in contact with their fangs, I sat still — but, imagining they would scarcely understand tacit insults, I unfortunately indulged in winking and making faces at the trio, and some turn of my physiognomy so irritated madam, that she suddenly broke into a fury, and leapt on my knees. I flung her back, and hastened to interpose the table between us. This proceeding aroused the whole hive. Half-a-dozen four-footed fiends, of various sizes and ages, issued from hidden dens to the common centre. I felt my heels and coat-laps peculiar subjects of assault; and, parrying off the larger combatants, as effectually as I could, with the poker, I was constrained to demand, aloud, assistance from some of the household, in re-establishing peace.

Mr. Heathcliff and his man climbed the cellar steps with vexatious phlegm. I don't think they moved one second faster than usual, though the hearth was an absolute tempest of worrying and yelping.

Happily, an inhabitant of the kitchen made more dispatch; a lusty dame, with tucked-up gown, bare arms, and fire-flushed cheeks, rushed into the midst of us flourishing a frying-pan; and used that weapon, and her tongue, to such purpose, that the storm subsided magically, and she only remained, heaving like a sea after a high wind, when her master entered on the scene.

"What the devil is the matter?" he asked, eyeing me in a manner I could ill endure after this inhospitable treatment.

"What the devil, indeed!" I muttered. "The herd of possessed swine could have had no worse spirits in them than those animals of yours, sir. You might as well leave a stranger with a brood of tigers!"

"They won't meddle with persons who touch nothing," he remarked, putting the bottle before me, and restoring the displaced table. "The dogs do right to be vigilant. Take a glass of wine?"

"No, thank you."

"Not bitten, are you?"

"If I had been, I would have set my signet on the biter."

Heathcliff's countenance relaxed into a grin.

"Come, come," he said, "you are flurried, Mr. Lockwood. Here, take a little wine. Guests are so exceedingly rare in this house that I and my dogs, I am willing to own, hardly know how to receive them. Your health, sir."

I bowed and returned the pledge; beginning to perceive that it would be foolish to sit sulking for the misbehaviour of a pack of curs: besides, I felt loath to yield the fellow further amusement, at my expense; since his humour took that turn.

He — probably swayed by prudential considerations of the folly of offending a good tenant — relaxed, a little, in the laconic style of chipping off his pronouns and auxiliary verbs, and introduced what he supposed would be a subject of interest to me, a discourse on the advantages and disadvantages of my present place of retirement.

I found him very intelligent on the topics we touched; and, before I went home, I was encouraged so far as to volunteer another visit, tomorrow.

He evidently wished no repetition of my intrusion. I shall go, notwithstanding. It is astonishing how sociable I feel myself compared with him.

CHAPTER 2

Yesterday afternoon set in misty and cold. I had half a mind to spend it by my study fire, instead of wading through heath and mud to Wuthering Heights.

On coming up from dinner, however (N.B. I dine between twelve and one o'clock; the housekeeper, a matronly lady taken as a fixture along with the house, could not, or would not comprehend my request that I might be served at five), — on mounting the stairs with this lazy intention, and stepping into the room, I saw a servant-girl on her knees, surrounded by brushes and coal-scuttles, and raising an infernal dusk as she extinguished the flames with heaps of cinders. This spectacle drove me back immediately; I took my hat, and, after a four miles walk, arrived at Heathcliff's garden gate just in time to escape the first feathery flakes of a snow shower.

On that bleak hilltop the earth was hard with a black frost, and the air made me shiver through every limb. Being unable to remove the chain, I jumped over, and, running up the flagged causeway bordered with straggling gooseberry bushes, knocked vainly for admittance, till my knuckles tingled and the dogs howled.

"Wretched inmates!" I ejaculated, mentally, "you deserve perpetual isolation from your species for your churlish inhospitality. At least, I would not keep my doors barred in the day time — I don't care — I will get in!"

So resolved, I grasped the latch, and shook it vehemently. Vinegar-faced Joseph projected his head from a round window of the barn.

"Whet are ye for?" he shouted. "T' maister's dahn i' t' fowld.° Goa rahned by th' end ut' laith,° if yah went tuh spake tull him."

"Is there nobody inside to open the door?" I hallooed, responsively.

"They's nobbut° t' missis; and shoo'll nut oppen 't an ye mak yer flaysome° dins till neeght."

"Why? cannot you tell her who I am, eh, Joseph?"

"Nor-ne me!° Aw'll hae noa hend° wi't," muttered the head vanishing.

The snow began to drive thickly. I seized the handle to essay another trial; when a young man, without coat, and shouldering a pitchfork, appeared in the yard behind. He hailed me to follow him, and, after marching through a washhouse, and a paved area containing a coal-shed, pump, and pigeon cote, we at length arrived in the large, warm, cheerful apartment, where I was formerly received.

It glowed delightfully in the radiance of an immense fire, compounded of coal, peat, and wood: and near the table, laid for a plentiful evening meal, I was pleased to observe the "missis," an individual whose existence I had never previously suspected.

I bowed and waited, thinking she would bid me take a seat. She looked at me, leaning back in her chair, and remained motionless and mute.

"Rough weather!" I remarked. "I'm afraid, Mrs. Heathcliff, the door must bear the consequence of your servants' leisure attendance: I had hard work to make them hear me!"

She never opened her mouth. I stared — she stared also. At any rate, she kept her eyes on me, in a cool, regardless manner, exceedingly embarrassing and disagreeable.

"Sit down," said the young man, gruffly. "He'll be in soon."

I obeyed; and hemmed, and called the villain Juno, who deigned, at this second interview, to move the extreme tip of her tail, in token of owning my acquaintance.

"A beautiful animal!" I commenced again. "Do you intend parting with the little ones, madam?"

t' fowld: The fold. ***ut' laith:*** Of the barn. ***nobbut:*** Only, merely, none but. ***flaysome:*** Frightening. ***Nor-ne me!:*** Not me! ***hae noa hend:*** Have no hand, take no part.

"They are not mine," said the amiable hostess more repellingly than Heathcliff himself could have replied.

"Ah, your favourites are among these!" I continued, turning to an obscure cushion full of something like cats.

"A strange choice of favourites," she observed scornfully.

Unluckily, it was a heap of dead rabbits — I hemmed once more, and drew closer to the hearth, repeating my comment on the wildness of the evening.

"You should not have come out," she said, rising and reaching from the chimney-piece two of the painted canisters.

Her position before was sheltered from the light: now, I had a distinct view of her whole figure and countenance. She was slender, and apparently scarcely past girlhood: an admirable form, and the most exquisite little face that I have ever had the pleasure of beholding: small features, very fair; flaxen ringlets, or rather golden, hanging loose on her delicate neck; and eyes — had they been agreeable in expression, they would have been irresistible — fortunately for my susceptible heart, the only sentiment they evidenced hovered between scorn and a kind of desperation, singularly unnatural to be detected there.

The canisters were almost out of her reach; I made a motion to aid her; she turned upon me as a miser might turn, if any one attempted to assist him in counting his gold.

"I don't want your help," she snapped, "I can get them for myself."

"I beg your pardon," I hastened to reply.

"Were you asked to tea?" she demanded, tying an apron over her neat black frock, and standing with a spoonful of leaf poised over the pot.

"I shall be glad to have a cup," I answered.

"Were you asked?" she repeated.

"No," I said, half smiling. "You are the proper person to ask me."

She flung the tea back, spoon and all; and resumed her chair in a pet, her forehead corrugated, and her red underlip pushed out, like a child's, ready to cry.

Meanwhile, the young man had slung onto his person a decidedly shabby upper garment, and, erecting himself before the blaze, looked down on me, from the corner of his eyes, for all the world as if there were some mortal feud unavenged between us. I began to doubt whether he were a servant or not; his dress and speech were both rude, entirely devoid of the superiority observable in Mr. and Mrs. Heathcliff; his thick, brown curls were rough and uncultivated, his whiskers encroached bearishly over his cheeks, and his hands were embrowned like those of the common labourour: still his bearing was free, almost haughty; and he showed none of a domestic's assiduity in attending on the lady of the house.

In the absence of clear proofs of his condition, I deemed it best to abstain from noticing his curious conduct, and, five minutes afterwards, the entrance of Heathcliff relieved me, in some measure, from my uncomfortable state.

"You see, sir, I am come according to promise!" I exclaimed, assuming the cheerful; "and I fear I shall be weatherbound for half an hour, if you can afford me shelter during that space."

"Half an hour?" he said, shaking the white flakes from his clothes; "I wonder you should select the thick of a snow-storm to ramble about in. Do you know that you run a risk of being lost in the marshes? People familiar with these moors often miss their road on such evenings, and, I can tell you, there is no chance of a change at present."

"Perhaps I can get a guide among your lads, and he might stay at the Grange till morning — could you spare me one?"

"No, I could not."

"Oh, indeed! Well then, I must trust to my own sagacity."

"Umph!"

"Are you going to make th' tea?" demanded he of the shabby coat, shifting his ferocious gaze from me to the young lady.

"Is *he* to have any?" she asked, appealing to Heathcliff.

"Get it ready, will you?" was the answer, uttered so savagely that I started. The tone in which the words were said revealed a genuine bad nature. I no longer felt inclined to call Heathcliff a capital fellow.

When the preparations were finished, he invited me with —

"Now, sir, bring forward your chair." And we all, including the rustic youth, drew round the table, an austere silence prevailing while we discussed our meal.

I thought, if I had caused the cloud, it was my duty to make an effort to dispel it. They could not every day sit so grim and taciturn, and it was impossible, however ill-tempered they might be, that the universal scowl they wore was their everyday countenance.

"It is strange," I began in the interval of swallowing one cup of tea and receiving another, "it is strange how custom can mould our tastes and ideas; many could not imagine the existence of happiness in a life of such complete exile from the world as you spend, Mr. Heathcliff; yet, I'll venture to say, that, surrounded by your family, and with your amiable lady as the presiding genius over your home and heart — "

"My amiable lady!" he interrupted, with an almost diabolical sneer on his face. "Where is she — my amiable lady?"

"Mrs. Heathcliff, your wife, I mean."

"Well, yes — Oh! you would intimate that her spirit has taken the post of ministering angel, and guards the fortunes of Wuthering Heights, even when her body is gone. It that it?"

Perceiving myself in a blunder, I attempted to correct it. I might have seen that there was too great a disparity in the ages of the parties to make it likely that they were man and wife. One was about forty; a period of mental vigour at which men seldom cherish the delusion of being married for love, by girls: that dream is reserved for the solace of our declining years. The other did not look seventeen.

Then it flashed upon me — "The clown at my elbow, who is drinking his tea out of a basin, and eating his bread with unwashed hands, may be her husband. Heathcliff, junior, of course. Here is the consequence of being buried alive: she has thrown herself away upon that boor, from sheer ignorance that better individuals existed! A sad pity — I must beware how I cause her to regret her choice."

The last reflection may seem conceited; it was not. My neighbour struck me as bordering on repulsive. I knew, through experience, that I was tolerably attractive.

"Mrs. Heathcliff is my daughter-in-law," said Heathcliff, corroborating my surmise. He turned, as he spoke, a peculiar look in her direction, a look of hatred unless he has a most perverse set of facial muscles that will not, like those of other people, interpret the language of his soul.

"Ah, certainly — I see now: you are the favoured possessor of the beneficent fairy," I remarked, turning to my neighbor.

This was worse than before: the youth grew crimson, and clenched his fist with every appearance of a meditated assault. But he seemed to recollect himself, presently; and smothered the storm in a brutal curse, muttered on my behalf, which, however, I took care not to notice.

"Unhappy in your conjectures, sir!" observed my host; "we neither of us have the privilege of owning your good fairy; her mate is dead. I said she was my daughter-in-law, therefore, she must have married my son."

"And this young man is — "

"Not my son, assuredly!"

Heathcliff smiled again, as if it were rather too bold a jest to attribute the paternity of that bear to him.

"My name is Hareton Earnshaw," growled the other; "and I'd counsel you to respect it!"

"I've shown no disrespect," was my reply, laughing internally at the dignity with which he announced himself.

He fixed his eye on me longer than I cared to return the stare, for fear I might be tempted either to box his ears, or render my hilarity audible. I began to feel unmistakably out of place in that pleasant family circle. The dismal spiritual atmosphere overcame, and more than neutralised the glowing physical comforts round me; and I resolved to be cautious how I ventured under those rafters a third time.

The business of eating being concluded, and no one uttering a word of sociable conversation, I approached a window to examine the weather.

A sorrowful sight I saw; dark night coming down prematurely, and sky and hills mingled in one bitter whirl of wind and suffocating show.

"I don't think it possible for me to get home now, without a guide," I could not help exclaiming. "The roads will be buried already; and, if they were bare, I could scarcely distinguish a foot in advance."

"Hareton, drive those dozen sheep into the barn porch. They'll be covered if left in the fold all night; and put a plank before them," said Heathcliff.

"How must I do?" I continued, with rising irritation.

There was no reply to my questions; and on looking around, I saw only Joseph bringing in a pail of porridge for the dogs and Mrs. Heathcliff leaning over the fire, diverting herself with burning a bundle of matches which had fallen from the chimney-piece as she restored the tea-canister to its place.

The former, when he had deposited his burden, took a critical survey of the room; and, in cracked tones, grated out:

"Aw woonder hagh yah can faishion° tuh stand thear i' idleness un war,° when all on 'em's goan aght! bud yah're a nowt,° and it's noa use talking — yah'll niver mend uh yer il ways; bud, goa raight tuh t' divil, like yer mother afore ye!"

I imagined, for a moment, that this piece of eloquence was addressed to me; and, sufficiently enraged, stepped towards the aged rascal with an intention of kicking him out of the door.

Mrs. Heathcliff, however, checked me by her answer.

"You scandalous old hypocrite!" she replied. "Are you not afraid of being carried away bodily, whenever you mention the devil's name? I warn you to refrain from provoking me, or I'll ask your abduction as a special favour. Stop, look here, Joseph," she continued, taking a long, dark book from a shelf. "I'll show you how far I've progressed in the Black Art — I shall soon be competent to make a clear house of it. The

faishion: Manage, contrive. ***un war:*** And worse. ***yah're a nowt:*** You're a nothing.

red cow didn't die by chance; and your rheumatism can hardly be reckoned among providential visitations!"

"Oh, wicked, wicked!" gasped the elder; "may the Lord deliver us from evil!"

"No, reprobate! you are a castaway — be off, or I'll hurt you seriously! I'll have you all modelled in wax and clay; and the first who passes the limits I fix, shall — I'll not say what he shall be done to — but, you'll see! Go, I'm looking at you!"

The little witch put a mock malignity into her beautiful eyes, and Joseph, trembling with sincere horror, hurried out praying and ejaculating "wicked" as he went.

I thought her conduct must be prompted by a species of dreary fun; and, now that we were alone, I endeavoured to interest her in my distress.

"Mrs. Heathcliff," I said, earnestly, "you must excuse me for troubling you — I presume, because, with that face, I'm sure you cannot help being good-hearted. Do point out some landmarks by which I may know my way home — I have no more idea how to get there than you would have how to get to London!"

"Take the road you came," she answered, ensconcing herself in a chair, with a candle, and the long book open before her. "It is brief advice, but as sound as I can give."

"Then, if you hear of me being discovered dead in a bog, or a pit full of snow, your conscience won't whisper that it is partly your fault?"

"How so? I cannot escort you. They couldn't let me go to the end of the garden-wall."

"*You!* I should be very sorry to ask you to cross the threshold, for my convenience, on such a night," I cried. "I want you to *tell* me my way, not to *show* it; or else to persuade Mr. Heathcliff to give me a guide."

"Who? There is himself, Earnshaw, Zillah, Joseph, and I. Which would you have?"

"Are there no boys at the farm?"

"No, those are all."

"Then, it follows that I am compelled to stay."

"That you may settle with your host. I have nothing to do with it."

"I hope it will be a lesson to you, to make no more rash journeys on these hills," cried Heathcliff's stern voice from the kitchen entrance. "As to staying here, I don't keep accommodations for visitors; you must share a bed with Hareton, or Joseph, if you do."

"I can sleep on a chair in this room," I replied.

"No, no. A stranger is a stranger, be he rich or poor — it will not suit me to permit any one the range of the place while I am off guard!" said the unmannerly wretch.

With this insult my patience was at an end. I uttered an expression of disgust, and pushed past him into the yard, running against Earnshaw in my haste. It was so dark that I could not see the means of exit, and, as I wandered round, I heard another specimen of their civil behaviour amongst each other.

At first, the young man appeared about to befriend me.

"I'll go with him as far as the park," he said.

"You'll go with him to hell!" exclaimed his master, or whatever relation he bore. "And who is to look after the horses, eh?"

"A man's life is of more consequence than one evening's neglect of the horses; somebody must go," murmured Mrs. Heathcliff, more kindly than I expected.

"Not at your command!" retorted Hareton. "If you set store on him, you'd better be quiet."

"Then I hope his ghost will haunt you; and I hope Mr. Heathcliff will never get another tenant, till the Grange is a ruin!" she answered sharply.

"Hearken, hearken, shoo's cursing on 'em!" muttered Joseph, towards whom I had been steering.

He sat within earshot, milking the cows by the light of a lantern, which I seized unceremoniously, and, calling out that I would send it back on the morrow, rushed to the nearest postern.

"Maister, maister, he's staling t' lantern!" shouted the ancient, pursuing my retreat. "Hey, Gnasher! Hey, dog! Hey, Wolf, holld him, holld him!"

On opening the little door, two hairy monsters flew at my throat, bearing me down and extinguishing the light, while a mingled guffaw, from Heathcliff and Hareton, put the copestone on my rage and humiliation.

Fortunately, the beasts seemed more bent on stretching their paws, and yawning, and flourishing their tails, then devouring me alive; but, they would suffer no resurrection, and I was forced to lie till their malignant masters pleased to deliver me: then hatless, and trembling with wrath, I ordered the miscreants to let me out — on their peril to keep me one minute longer — with several incoherent threats of retaliation that, in their indefinite depth of virulency, smacked of King Lear.

The vehemence of my agitations brought on a copious bleeding at the nose, and still Heathcliff laughed, and still I scolded. I don't know what would have concluded the scene had there not been one person at hand rather more rational than myself, and more benevolent than my entertainer. This was Zillah, the stout housewife; who at length issued forth to inquire into the nature of the uproar. She thought that some of them had been laying violent hands on me; and, not daring to attack her master, she turned her vocal artillery against the younger scoundrel.

"Well, Mr. Earnshaw," she cried, "I wonder what you'll have agait° next! Are we going to murder folk on our very door-stones? I see this house will never do for me — look at t' poor lad, he's fair choking! Wisht, wisht! you mun'n't go on so — come in, and I'll cure that. There now, hold ye still."

With these words she suddenly splashed a pint of icy water down my neck, and pulled me into the kitchen. Mr. Heathcliff followed, his accidental merriment expiring quickly in his habitual moroseness.

I was sick exceedingly, and dizzy and faint; and thus compelled, perforce, to accept lodgings under his roof. He told Zillah to give me a glass of brandy, and then passed on to the inner room, while she condoled with me on my sorry predicament, and having obeyed his orders, whereby I was somewhat revived, ushered me to bed.

CHAPTER 3

While leading the way up-stairs, she recommended that I should hide the candle, and not make a noise, for her master had an odd notion about the chamber she would put me in; and never let anybody lodge there willingly.

I asked the reason.

She did not know, she answered; she had only lived there a year or two; and they had so many queer goings on, she could not begin to be curious.

Too stupified to be curious myself, I fastened my door and glanced round for the bed. The whole furniture consisted of a chair, a clothes-press, and a large oak case, with squares cut out near the top, resembling coach windows.

Having approached this structure, I looked inside, and perceived it to be a singular sort of old-fashioned couch, very conveniently designed to obviate the necessity for every member of the family having a room to himself. In fact, it formed a little closet, and the ledge of a window, which it enclosed, served as a table.

agait: A-going.

I slid back the panelled sides, got in with my light, pulled them together again, and felt secure against the vigilance of Heathcliff, and everyone else.

The ledge, where I placed my candle, had a few mildewed books piled up in one corner; and it was covered with writing scratched on the paint. This writing, however, was nothing but a name repeated in all kinds of characters, large and small — *Catherine Earnshaw,* here and there varied to *Catherine Heathcliff,* and then again to *Catherine Linton.*

In vapid listlessness I leant my head against the window, and continued spelling over Catherine Earnshaw — Heathcliff — Linton, till my eyes closed; but they had not rested five minutes when a glare of white letters started from the dark, as vivid as spectres — the air swarmed with Catherines; and rousing myself to dispel the obtrusive name, I discovered my candle wick reclining on one of the antique volumes, and perfuming the place with an odour of roasted calf-skin.

I snuffed it off, and, very ill at ease, under the influence of cold and lingering nausea, sat up, and spread open the injured tome on my knee. It was a Testament, in lean type, and smelling dreadfully musty: a fly-leaf bore the inscription — "Catherine Earnshaw, her book," and a date some quarter of a century back.

I shut, and took up another, and another, till I had examined them all. Catherine's library was select; and its state of dilapidation proved it to have been well used, though not altogether for a legitimate purpose; scarcely one chapter had escaped pen and ink commentary — at least, the appearance of one — covering every morsel of blank that the printer had left.

Some were detached sentences; other parts took the form of a regular diary, scrawled in an unformed, childish hand. At the top of an extra page, quite a treasure probably when first lighted on, I was greatly amused to behold an excellent caricature of my friend Joseph, rudely yet powerfully sketched.

An immediate interest kindled within me for the unknown Catherine, and I began, forthwith, to decipher her faded hieroglyphics.

"An awful Sunday!" commenced the paragraph beneath. "I wish my father were back again. Hindley is a detestable substitute — his conduct to Heathcliff is atrocious — H. and I are going to rebel — we took our initiatory step this evening.

"All day had been flooding with rain; we could not go to church, so Joseph must needs get up a congregation in the garret; and, while Hindley and his wife basked down stairs before a comfortable fire; doing anything but reading their Bibles, I'll answer for it — Heathcliff, myself, and the unhappy plough-boy were commanded to take our Prayer-books and mount — we were ranged in a row, on a sack of corn, groaning and shivering, and hoping that Joseph would shiver too, so that he might give us a short homily for his own sake. A vain idea! The service lasted precisely three hours; and yet my brother had the face to exclaim, when he saw us descending,

"'What, done already?'

"On Sunday evenings we used to be permitted to play, if we did not make much noise; now a mere titter is sufficient to send us into corners!

"'You forget you have a master here,' says the tyrant. 'I'll demolish the first who puts me out of temper! I insist on perfect sobriety and silence. Oh, boy! was that you? Frances, darling, pull his hair as you go by; I heard him snap his fingers.'

"Frances pulled his hair heartily; and then went and seated herself on her husband's knee, and there they were, like two babies, kissing and talking nonsense by the hour — foolish palaver that we should be ashamed of.

"We made ourselves as snug as our means allowed in the arch of the dresser. I had just fastened our pinafores together, and hung them up for a curtain, when in comes Joseph, on an errand from the stables. He tears down my handywork, boxes my ears, and croaks:

"'T' maister nobbut° just buried, and Sabbath nut oe'red,° und t' sahnd uh't gospel still i' yer lugs,° and yah darr be laiking!° shame on ye! sit ye dahn, ill childer!° they's good books eneugh if ye'll read 'em; sit ye dahn, and think uh yer sowls!'

"Saying this, he compelled us to square our positions that we might receive, from the far-off fire, a dull ray to show us the text of the lumber he thrust upon us.

"I could not bear the employment. I took my dingy volume by the scroop, and hurled it into the dog-kennel, vowing I hated a good book.

"Heathcliff kicked his to the same place.

"Then there was a hubbub!

"'Maister Hindley!' shouted our chaplain. 'Maister, coom hither! Miss Cathy's riven° th' back off "Th' Helmet uh Salvation," un' Heathcliff's pawsed his fit° intuh t' first part uh "T' Broad Way to Destruction!" It's fair flaysome° ut yah, let 'em goa on this gait.° Ech! th' owd man ud uh laced° 'em properly — bud he's goan!'

nobbut: Only. ***nut oe'red:*** Not gone by. ***t' sahnd uh 't gospel still i' yer lugs:*** The sound of the gospel still in your ears. ***darr be laiking:*** Dare be playing. ***ill childer:*** Bad children. ***riven:*** Split, torn. ***pawsed his fit:*** Kicked his foot. ***fair flaysome:*** Downright frightening. ***gait:*** Course, way. ***laced:*** Lashed, thrashed.

"Hindley hurried up from his paradise on the hearth, and seizing one of us by the collar, and the other by the arm, hurled both in the back-kitchen; where, Joseph asseverated, 'owd Nick'° would fetch us as sure as we were living; and, so comforted, we each sought a separate nook to await his advent.

"I reached this book, and a pot of ink from the shelf, and pushed the house-door ajar to give me light, and I have got the time on with writing for twenty minutes; but my companion is impatient and proposes that we should appropriate the dairy woman's cloak, and have a scamper on the moors, under its shelter. A pleasant suggestion — and then, if the surly old man come in, he may believe his prophecy verified — we cannot be damper, or colder, in the rain than we are here."

I suppose Catherine fulfilled her project, for the next sentence took up another subject: she waxed lachrymose.

"How little did I dream that Hindley would ever make me cry so!" she wrote. "My head aches, till I cannot keep it on the pillow; and still I can't give over. Poor Heathcliff! Hindley calls him a vagabond, and won't let him sit with us, nor eat with us any more; and, he says, he and I must not play together, and threatens to turn him out of the house if we break his orders.

"He has been blaming our father (how dared he?) for treating H. too liberally; and swears he will reduce him to his right place — "

I began to nod drowsily over the dim page; my eye wandered from manuscript to print. I saw a red-ornamented title — "Seventy Times Seven, and the First of the Seventy-First. A Pious Discourse delivered by the Reverend Jabes Branderham, in the Chapel of Gimmerden Sough." And while I was, half consciously, worrying my brain to guess what Jabes Branderham would make of his subject, I sank back in bed, and fell asleep.

Alas, for the effects of bad tea and bad temper! what else could it be that made me pass such a terrible night? I don't remember another that I can at all compare with it since I was capable of suffering.

I began to dream, almost before I ceased to be sensible of my locality. I thought it was morning; and I had set out on my way home, with Joseph for a guide. The snow lay yards deep in our road; and, as we floundered on, my companion wearied me with constant reproaches that I had not brought a pilgrim's staff: telling me that I could never

owd Nick: Old Nick, the devil.

get into the house without one, and boastfully flourishing a heavy-headed cudgel, which I understood to be so denominated.

For a moment I considered it absurd that I should need such a weapon to gain admittance into my own residence. Then, a new idea flashed across me. I was not going there; we were journeying to hear the famous Jabes Branderham preach from the text — "Seventy Times Seven"; and either Joseph, the preacher, or I had committed the "First of the Seventy-First," and were to be publicly exposed and excommunicated.

We came to the chapel — I had passed it really in my walks, twice or thrice: it lies in a hollow, between two hills — an elevated hollow — near a swamp, whose peaty moisture is said to answer all the purposes of embalming on the few corpses deposited there. The roof has been kept whole hitherto, but, as the clergyman's stipend is only twenty pounds per annum, and a house with two rooms, threatening speedily to determine into one, no clergyman will undertake the duties of pastor, especially as it is currently reported that his flock would rather let him starve than increase the living by one penny from their own pockets. However, in my dream, Jabes had a full and attentive congregation: and he preached — good God — what a sermon! divided into *four hundred and ninety* parts — each fully equal to an ordinary address from the pulpit — and each discussing a separate sin! Where he searched for them, I cannot tell; he had his private manner of interpreting the phrase, and it seemed necessary the brother should sin different sins on every occasion.

They were of the most curious character — odd transgressions that I never imagined previously.

Oh, how weary I grew. How I writhed, and yawned, and nodded, and revived! How I pinched and pricked myself, and rubbed my eyes, and stood up, and sat down again, and nudged Joseph to inform me if he would *ever* have done!

I was condemned to hear all out — finally, he reached the "*First of the Seventy-First.*" At that crisis, a sudden inspiration descended on me; I was moved to rise and denounce Jabes Branderham as the sinner of the sin that no Christian need pardon.

"Sir," I exclaimed, "sitting here, within these four walls, at one stretch, I have endured and forgiven the four hundred and ninety heads of your discourse. Seventy times seven times have I plucked up my hat and been about to depart — Seventy times seven times have you preposterously forced me to resume my seat. The four hundred and ninety-first is too much. Fellow-martyrs, have at him! Drag him down, and crush him to atoms, that the place which knows him may know him no more!"

"*Thou art the Man!*" cried Jabes, after a solemn pause, leaning over his cushion. "Seventy times seven didst thou gapingly contort thy visage — seventy times seven did I take counsel with my soul — Lo, this is human weakness; this also may be absolved! The First of the Seventy-First is come. Brethren, execute upon him the judgment written! Such honour have all His saints!"

With that concluding word, the whole assembly, exalting their pilgrim's staves, rushed round me in a body, and I, having no weapon to raise in self-defence, commenced grappling with Joseph, my nearest and most ferocious assailant, for his. In the confluence of the multitude, several clubs crossed; blows, aimed at me, fell on other sconces. Presently the whole chapel resounded with rappings and counter-rappings. Every man's hand was against his neighbor; and Branderham, unwilling to remain idle, poured forth his zeal in a shower of loud taps on the boards of the pulpit which responded so smartly that, at last, to my unspeakable relief, they woke me.

And what was it that had suggested the tremendous tumult, what had played Jabes' part in the row? Merely, the branch of a fir-tree that touched my lattice, as the blast wailed by, and rattled its dry cones against the panes!

I listened doubtingly an instant; detected the disturber, then turned and dozed, and dreamt again; if possible, still more disagreeably than before.

This time, I remembered I was lying in the oak closet, and I heard distinctly the gusty wind, and the driving of the snow; I heard, also, the fir bough repeat its teasing sound, and ascribed it to the right cause; but it annoyed me so much, that I resolved to silence it, if possible; and, I thought, I rose and endeavoured to unhasp the casement. The hook was soldered into the staple, a circumstance observed by me when awake, but forgotten.

"I must stop it, nevertheless!" I muttered, knocking my knuckles through the glass, and stretching an arm out to seize the importunate branch: instead of which, my fingers closed on the fingers of a little, ice-cold hand!

The intense horror of nightmare came over me; I tried to draw back my arm, but the hand clung to it, and a most melancholy voice sobbed,

"Let me in — let me in!"

"Who are you?" I asked, struggling, meanwhile, to disengage myself.

"Catherine Linton," it replied shiveringly (why did I think of *Lin-*

ton? I had read *Earnshaw* twenty times for Linton.) "I'm come home, I'd lost my way on the moor!"

As it spoke, I discerned, obscurely, a child's face looking through the window — Terror made me cruel; and, finding it useless to attempt shaking the creature off, I pulled its wrist on to the broken pane, and rubbed it to and fro till the blood ran down and soaked the bedclothes; still it wailed, "Let me in!" and maintained its tenacious gripe,° almost maddening me with fear.

"How can I?" I said at length. "Let *me* go, if you want me to let you in!"

The fingers relaxed, I snatched mine through the hole, hurriedly piled the books up in a pyramid against it, and stopped my ears to exclude the lamentable prayer.

I seemed to keep them closed above a quarter of an hour, yet, the instant I listened, again, there was the doleful cry moaning on!

"Begone!" I shouted, "I'll never let you in, not if you beg for twenty years!"

"It's twenty years," mourned the voice, "twenty years, I've been a waif for twenty years!"

Thereat began a feeble scratching outside, and the pile of books moved as if thrust forward.

I tried to jump up, but could not stir a limb; and so yelled aloud, in a frenzy of fright.

To my confusion, I discovered the yell was not ideal. Hasty footsteps approached my chamber door: somebody pushed it open, with a vigorous hand, and a light glimmered through the squares at the top of the bed. I sat shuddering yet, and wiping the perspiration from my forehead: the intruder appeared to hesitate, and muttered to himself.

At last, he said in a half-whisper, plainly not expecting an answer,

"Is anyone here?"

I considered it best to confess my presence, for I knew Heathcliff's accents, and feared he might search further, if I kept quiet.

With this intention, I turned and opened the panels — I shall not soon forget the effect my action produced.

Heathcliff stood near the entrance, in his shirt and trousers, with a candle dripping over his fingers, and his face as white as the wall behind him. The first creak of the oak startled him like an electric shock: the light leaped from his hold to a distance of some feet, and his agitation was so extreme, that he could hardly pick it up.

gripe: Grip.

"It is only your guest, sir," I called out, desirous to spare him the humiliation of exposing his cowardice further. "I had the misfortune to scream in my sleep, owing to a frightful nightmare. I'm sorry I disturbed you."

"Oh, God confound you, Mr. Lockwood! I wish you were at the — " commenced my host, setting the candle on a chair, because he found it impossible to hold it steady.

"And who showed you up to this room?" he continued, crushing his nails into his palms, and grinding his teeth to subdue the maxillary convulsions. "Who was it? I've a good mind to turn them out of the house this moment!"

"It was your servant, Zillah," I replied, flinging myself on to the floor, and rapidly resuming my garments. "I should not care if you did, Mr. Heathcliff; she richly deserves it. I suppose that she wanted to get another proof that the place was haunted, at my expense — Well, it is — swarming with ghosts and goblins! You have reason in shutting it up, I assure you. No one will thank you for a doze in such a den!"

"What do you mean?" asked Heathcliff, "and what are you doing? Lie down and finish out the night, since you *are* here; but, for Heaven's sake! don't repeat that horrid noise — Nothing could excuse it, unless you were having your throat cut!"

"If the little fiend had got in at the window, she probably would have strangled me!" I returned. "I'm not going to endure the persecutions of your hospitable ancestors again — Was not the Reverend Jabes Branderham akin to you on the mother's side? And the minx, Catherine Linton, or Earnshaw, or however she was called — she must have been a changeling — wicked little soul! She told me she had been walking the earth these twenty years: a just punishment for her mortal transgressions, I've no doubt!"

Scarcely were these words uttered, when I recollected the association of Heathcliff's with Catherine's name in the book, which had completely slipped from my memory till thus awakened. I blushed at my inconsideration; but, without showing further consciousness of the offence, I hastened to add,

"The truth is, sir, I passed the first part of the night — " Here I stopped afresh — I was about to say "perusing those old volumes," then it would have revealed my knowledge of their written, as well as their printed contents; so, correcting myself, I went on,

"In spelling over the name scratched on the window-ledge. A monotonous occupation, calculated to set me asleep, like counting, or — "

"What *can* you mean by talking in this way to *me!*" thundered Heathcliff with savage vehemence. "How — how *dare* you, under my roof? — God! he's mad to speak so!" And he struck his forehead with rage.

I did not know whether to resent this language, or pursue my explanation; but he seemed so powerfully affected that I took pity and proceeded with my dreams; affirming I had never heard the appellation of "Catherine Linton" before, but reading it often over produced an impression which personified itself when I had no longer my imagination under control.

Heathcliff gradually fell back into the shelter of the bed, as I spoke, finally, sitting down almost concealed behind it. I guessed, however, by his irregular and intercepted breathing, that he struggled to vanquish an access of violent emotion.

Not liking to show him that I heard the conflict, I continued my toilette rather noisily, looked at my watch, and soliloquised on the length of the night:

"Not three o'clock yet! I could have taken oath it had been six — time stagnates here — we must surely have retired to rest at eight!"

"Always at nine in winter, and always rise at four," said my host, suppressing a groan; and, as I fancied, by the motion of his shadow's arm, dashing a tear from his eyes.

"Mr. Lockwood," he added, "you may go into my room; you'll only be in the way, coming down stairs so early: and your childish outcry has sent sleep to the devil for me."

"And for me too," I replied. "I'll walk in the yard till daylight, and then I'll be off; and you need not dread a repetition of my intrusion. I am now quite cured of seeking pleasure in society, be it country or town. A sensible man ought to find sufficient company in himself."

"Delightful company!" muttered Heathcliff. "Take the candle, and go where you please. I shall join you directly. Keep out of the yard, though, the dogs are unchained; and the house — Juno mounts sentinel there — and — nay, you can only ramble about the steps and passages — but, away with you! I'll come in two minutes!"

I obeyed, so far as to quit the chamber; when, ignorant where the narrow lobbies led, I stood still, and was witness, involuntarily, to a piece of superstition on the part of my landlord, which belied, oddly, his apparent sense.

He got onto the bed, and wrenched open the lattice, bursting, as he pulled at it, into an uncontrollable passion of tears.

"Come in! come in!" he sobbed. "Cathy, do come. Oh do — *once* more! Oh! my heart's darling! hear me *this* time — Catherine, at last!"

The spectre showed a spectre's ordinary caprice; it gave no sign of being; but the snow and wind whirled wildly through, even reaching my station, and blowing out the light.

There was such anguish in the gush of grief that accompanied this raving, that my compassion made me overlook its folly, and I drew off, half angry to have listened at all, and vexed at having related my ridiculous nightmare, since it produced that agony; though *why,* was beyond my comprehension.

I descended cautiously to the lower regions and landed in the back-kitchen, where a gleam of fire, raked compactly together, enabled me to rekindle my candle.

Nothing was stirring except a brindled, grey cat, which crept from the ashes, and saluted me with a querulous mew.

Two benches, shaped in sections of a circle, nearly enclosed the hearth; on one of these I stretched myself, and Grimalkin mounted the other. We were both of us nodding, ere any one invaded our retreat; and then it was Joseph shuffling down a wooden ladder that vanished in the roof, through a trap, the ascent to his garret, I suppose.

He cast a sinister look at the little flame which I had enticed to play between the ribs, swept the cat from its elevation, and bestowing himself in the vacancy, commenced the operation of stuffing a three-inch pipe with tobacco; my presence in his sanctum was evidently esteemed a piece of impudence too shameful for remark. He silently applied the tube to his lips, folded his arms, and puffed away.

I let him enjoy the luxury, unannoyed; and after sucking out the last wreath, and heaving a profound sigh, he got up, and departed as solemnly as he came.

A more elastic footstep entered next, and now I opened my mouth for a "good morning," but closed it again, the salutation unachieved; for Hareton Earnshaw was performing his orisons, *sotto voce,* in a series of curses directed against every object he touched, while he rummaged a corner for a spade or shovel to dig through the drifts. He glanced over the back of the bench dilating his nostrils, and thought as little of exchanging civilities with me as with my companion, the cat.

I guessed by his preparations that egress was allowed, and leaving my hard couch, made a movement to follow him. He noticed this, and thrust at an inner door with the end of his spade, intimating by an inarticulate sound, that there was the place I must go, if I changed my locality.

It opened into the house, where the females were already astir, Zillah urging flakes of flame up the chimney with a colossal bellows, and Mrs. Heathcliff, kneeling on the hearth, reading a book by the aid of the blaze.

She held her hand interposed between the furnace-heat and her eyes, and seemed absorbed in her occupation: desisting from it only to chide the servant for covering her with sparks, or to push away a dog, now and then, that snoozled its nose over-forwardly into her face.

I was surprised to see Heathcliff there also. He stood by the fire, his back towards me, just finishing a stormy scene to poor Zillah, who ever and anon interrupted her labour to pluck up the corner of her apron, and heave an indignant groan.

"And you, you worthless — " he broke out as I entered, turning to his daughter-in-law, and employing an epithet as harmless as duck, or sheep, but generally represented by a dash.

"There you are at your idle tricks again! The rest of them do earn their bread — you live on my charity! Put your trash away, and find something to do. You shall pay me for the plague of having you eternally in my sight — do you hear, damnable jade?"

"I'll put my trash away, because you can make me, if I refuse," answered the young lady, closing her book, and throwing it on a chair. "But I'll not do anything, though you should swear your tongue out, except what I please!"

Heathcliff lifted his hand, and the speaker sprang to a safer distance, obviously acquainted with its weight.

Having no desire to be entertained by a cat and dog combat, I stepped forward briskly, as if eager to partake the warmth of the hearth, and innocent of any knowledge of the interrupted dispute. Each had enough decorum to suspend further hostilities; Heathcliff placed his fists, out of temptation, in his pockets: Mrs. Heathcliff curled her lip, and walked to a seat far off, where she kept her word by playing the part of a statue during the remainder of my stay.

That was not long. I declined joining their breakfast, and, at the first gleam of dawn, took an opportunity of escaping into the free air, now clear, and still, and cold as impalpable ice.

My landlord hallooed for me to stop ere I reached the bottom of the garden, and offered to accompany me across the moor. It was well he did, for the whole hill-back was one billowy, white ocean; the swells and falls not indicating corresponding rises and depressions in the ground — many pits, at least, were filled to a level; and entire ranges of mounds, the refuse of the quarries, blotted out from the chart which my yesterday's walk left pictured in my mind.

I had remarked on one side of the road, at intervals of six or seven yards, a line of upright stones, continued through the whole length of the barren: these were erected, and daubed with lime on purpose to serve as guides in the dark, and also, when a fall, like the present, confounded the deep swamps on either hand with the firmer path: but, excepting a dirty dot pointing up, here and there, all traces of their existence had vanished; and my companion found it necessary to warn me frequently to steer to the right, or left, when I imagined I was following, correctly, the windings of the road.

We exchanged little conversation, and he halted at the entrance of Thrushcross park, saying I could make no error there. Our adieux were limited to a hasty bow, and then I pushed forward, trusting to my own resources, for the porter's lodge is untenanted as yet.

The distance from the gate to the Grange is two miles: I believe I managed to make it four, what with losing myself among the trees, and sinking up to the neck in snow, a predicament which only those who have experienced it can appreciate. At any rate, whatever were my wanderings, the clock chimed twelve as I entered the house; and that gave exactly an hour for every mile of the usual way from Wuthering Heights.

My human fixture and her satellites rushed to welcome me; exclaiming, tumultuously, they had completely given me up; everybody conjectured that I perished last night; and they were wondering how they must set about the search for my remains.

I bid them be quiet, now that they saw me returned, and, benumbed to my very heart, I dragged upstairs, whence, after putting on dry clothes, and pacing to and fro, thirty or forty minutes, to restore the animal heat, I am adjourned to my study, feeble as a kitten, almost too much so to enjoy the cheerful fire and smoking coffee which the servant has prepared for my refreshment.

CHAPTER 4

What vain weather-cocks we are! I, who had determined to hold myself independent of all social intercourse, and thanked my stars that, at length, I had lighted on a spot where it was next to impracticable. I, weak wretch, after maintaining till dusk a struggle with low spirits, and solitude, was finally compelled to strike my colours; and, under pretence of gaining information concerning the necessities of my establishment, I desired Mrs. Dean, when she brought in supper, to sit down while I ate it, hoping sincerely she would prove a regular gossip, and either rouse me to animation, or lull me to sleep by her talk.

"You have lived here a considerable time," I commenced; "did you not say sixteen years?"

"Eighteen, sir; I came, when the mistress was married, to wait on her; after she died, the master retained me for his housekeeper."

"Indeed."

There ensued a pause. She was not a gossip, I feared, unless about her own affairs, and those could hardly interest me.

However, having studied for an interval, with a fist on either knee, and a cloud of meditation over her ruddy countenance, she ejaculated —

"Ah, times are greatly changed since then!"

"Yes," I remarked, "you've seen a good many alterations, I suppose?"

"I have: and troubles, too," she said.

"Oh, I'll turn the talk on my landlord's family!" I thought to myself. "A good subject to start — and that pretty girl-widow, I should like to know her history; whether she be a native of the country, or, as is more probable, an exotic that the surly indigenae will not recognise for kin."

With this intention I asked Mrs. Dean why Heathcliff let Thrushcross Grange, and preferred living in a situation and residence so much inferior.

"Is he not rich enough to keep the estate in good order?" I enquired.

"Rich, sir!" she returned. "He has, nobody knows what money, and every year it increases. Yes, yes, he's rich enough to live in a finer house than this; but he's very near — close-handed; and, if he had meant to flit to Thrushcross Grange, as soon as he heard of a good tenant, he could not have borne to miss the change of getting a few hundreds more. It is strange people should be so greedy, when they are alone in the world!"

"He had a son, it seems?"

"Yes, he had one — he is dead."

"And that young lady, Mrs. Heathcliff, is his widow?"

"Yes."

"Where did she come from originally?"

"Why, sir, she is my late master's daughter; Catherine Linton was her maiden name. I nursed her, poor thing! I did wish Mr. Heathcliff would remove here, and then we might have been together again."

"What, Catherine Linton!" I exclaimed, astonished. But a minute's reflection convinced me it was not my ghostly Catherine. "Then," I continued, "my predecessor's name was Linton?"

"It was."

"And who is that Earnshaw, Hareton Earnshaw, who lives with Mr. Heathcliff? are they relations?"

"No; he is the late Mr. Linton's nephew."

"The young lady's cousin, then?"

"Yes; her husband was her cousin also — one, on the mother's — the other, on the father's side — Heathcliff married Mr. Linton's sister."

"I see the house at Wuthering Heights has 'Earnshaw' carved over the front door. Are they an old family?"

"Very old, sir; and Hareton is the last of them, as our Miss Cathy is of us — I mean, of the Lintons. Have you been to Wuthering Heights? I beg pardon for asking; but I should like to hear how she is."

"Mrs. Heathcliff? she looked very well, and very handsome; yet, I think, not very happy."

"Oh dear, I don't wonder! And how did you like the master?"

"A rough fellow, rather, Mrs. Dean. Is not that his character?"

"Rough as a saw-edge, and hard as whinstone! The less you meddle with him the better."

"He must have had some ups and downs in life to make him such a churl. Do you know anything of his history?"

"It's a cuckoo's, sir — I know all about it; except where he was born, and who were his parents, and how he got his money, at first — And Hareton has been cast out like an unfledged dunnock — The unfortunate lad is the only one, in all this parish, that does not guess how he has been cheated!"

"Well, Mrs. Dean, it will be a charitable deed to tell me something of my neighbors — I feel I shall not rest, if I go to bed; so be good enough to sit and chat an hour."

"Oh, certainly, sir! I'll just fetch a little sewing, and then I'll sit as long as you please. But you've caught cold, I saw you shivering, and you must have some gruel to drive it out."

The worthy woman bustled off, and I crouched nearer the fire: my head felt hot, and the rest of me chill: moreover I was excited, almost to a pitch of foolishness through my nerves and brain. This caused me to feel, not uncomfortable, but rather fearful, as I am still, of serious effects from the incidents of to-day and yesterday.

She returned presently, bringing a smoking basin and a basket of work; and, having placed the former on the hob, drew in her seat, evidently pleased to find me so companionable.

Before I came to live here, she commenced, waiting no further invitation to her story; I was almost always at Wuthering Heights; because my mother had nursed Mr. Hindley Earnshaw, that was Hareton's father, and I got used to playing with the children — I ran errands too, and helped to make hay, and hung about the farm ready for anything that anybody would set me to.

One fine summer morning — it was the beginning of harvest, I remember — Mr. Earnshaw, the old master, came down stairs, dressed for a journey; and, after he had told Joseph what was to be done during the day, he turned to Hindley and Cathy, and me — for I sat eating my porridge, with them — and he said, speaking to his son,

"Now, my bonny man, I'm going to Liverpool today . . . What shall I bring you? You may choose what you like; only let it be little, for I shall walk there and back; sixty miles each way, that is a long spell!"

Hindley named a fiddle, and then he asked Miss Cathy; she was hardly six years old, but she could ride any horse in the stable, and she chose a whip.

He did not forget me, for he had a kind heart, though he was rather severe, sometimes. He promised to bring me a pocketful of apples and pears, and then he kissed his children good-bye, and set off.

It seemed a long while to us all — the three days of his absence — and often did little Cathy ask when he would be home. Mrs. Earnshaw expected him by supper-time, on the third evening; and she put off the meal hour after hour; there were no signs of his coming, however, and at last the children got tired of running down to the gate to look — Then it grew dark, she would have had them to bed, but they begged sadly to be allowed to stay up; and just about eleven o'clock, the door-latch was raised quietly and in stept the master. He threw himself into a chair, laughing and groaning, and bid them all stand off, for he was nearly killed — he would not have another such walk for the three kingdoms.

"And at the end of it, to be flighted to death!" he said, opening his great coat, which he held bundled up in his arms. "See here, wife; I was never so beaten with anything in my life; but you must e'en take it as a gift of God; though it's as dark almost as if it came from the devil."

We crowded round, and, over Miss Cathy's head, I had a peep at a dirty, ragged, black-haired child; big enough both to walk and talk — indeed, its face looked older than Catherine's — yet, when it was set on its feet, it only stared round, and repeated over and over again some gibberish that nobody could understand. I was frightened, and Mrs. Earnshaw was ready to fling it out of doors: she did fly up — asking how he could fashion to bring that gipsy brat into the house, when they had their own bairns to feed, and fend for? What he meant to do with it, and whether he were mad?

The master tried to explain the matter; but he was really half dead with fatigue, and all that I could make out, amongst her scolding, was a tale of his seeing it starving, and houseless, and as good as dumb in the streets of Liverpool where he picked it up and inquired for its owner — Not a soul knew to whom it belonged, he said, and his money and time, being both limited, he thought it better to take it home with him, at once, than run into vain expences there; because he was determined he would not leave it as he found it.

Well, the conclusion was that my mistress grumbled herself calm; and Mr. Earnshaw told me to wash it, and give it clean things, and let it sleep with the children.

Hindley and Cathy contented themselves with looking and listening till peace was restored; then, both began searching their father's pockets for the presents he had promised them. The former was a boy of fourteen, but when he drew out what had been a fiddle, crushed to morsels in the great-coat, he blubbered aloud, and Cathy, when she learnt the master had lost her whip in attending on the stranger, showed her humour by grinning and spitting at the stupid little thing, earning for her pains a sound blow from her father to teach her cleaner manners.

They entirely refused to have it in bed with them, or even in their room, and I had no more sense, so, I put it on the landing of the stairs, hoping it might be gone on the morrow. By chance, or else attracted by hearing his voice, it crept to Mr. Earnshaw's door, and there he found it on quitting his chamber. Inquiries were made as to how it got there; I was obliged to confess, and in recompense for my cowardice and inhumanity was sent out of the house.

This was Heathcliff's first introduction to the family: on coming back a few days afterwards, for I did not consider my banishment perpetual, I found they had christened him "Heathcliff": it was the name of a son who died in childhood, and it has served him ever since, both for Christian and surname.

Miss Cathy and he were now very thick; but Hindley hated him, and to say the truth I did the same; and we plagued and went on with him shamefully, for I wasn't reasonable enough to feel my injustice, and the mistress never put in a word on his behalf, when she saw him wronged.

He seemed a sullen, patient child; hardened, perhaps, to ill-treatment: he would stand Hindley's blows without winking or shedding a tear, and my pinches moved him only to draw in a breath, and open his eyes as if he had hurt himself by accident, and nobody was to blame.

This endurance made old Earnshaw furious when he discovered his son persecuting the poor, fatherless child, as he called him. He took to Heathcliff strangely, believing all he said (for that matter, he said precious little, and generally the truth) and petting him up far above Cathy, who was too mischievous and wayward for a favourite.

So, from the very beginning, he bred bad feeling in the house; and at Mrs. Earnshaw's death, which happened in less than two years after, the young master had learnt to regard his father as an oppressor rather than a friend, and Heathcliff as a usurper of his parent's affections and his privileges, and he grew bitter with brooding over these injuries.

I sympathised awhile, but, when the children fell ill of the measles and I had to tend them, and take on me the cares of a woman, at once, I changed my ideas. Heathcliff was dangerously sick, and while he lay at the worst he would have me constantly by his pillow; I suppose he felt I did a good deal for him, and he hadn't wit to guess that I was compelled to do it. However, I will say this, he was the quietest child that ever nurse watched over. The difference between him and the others forced me to be less partial: Cathy and her brother harassed me terribly: *he* was as uncomplaining as a lamb; though hardness, not gentleness, made him give little trouble.

He got through, and the doctor affirmed it was in a great measure owing to me, and praised me for my care. I was vain of his commendations, and softened towards the being by whose means I earned them, and thus Hindley lost his last ally; still I couldn't dote on Heathcliff, and I wondered often what my master saw to admire so much the sullen boy who never, to my recollection, repaid his indulgence by any sign of gratitude. He was not insolent to his benefactor; he was simply insensible, though knowing perfectly the hold he had on his heart, and conscious he had only to speak and all the house would be obliged to bend to his wishes.

As an instance, I remember Mr. Earnshaw once bought a couple of colts at the parish fair, and gave the lads each one. Heathcliff took the handsomest, but it soon fell lame, and when he discovered it, he said to Hindley,

"You must exchange horses with me; I don't like mine, and if you won't I shall tell your father of the three thrashings you've given me this week, and show him my arm, which is black to the shoulder."

Hindley put out his tongue, and cuffed him over the ears.

"You'd better do it at once," he persisted, escaping to the porch (they were in the stable): "you will have to, and if I speak of these blows, you'll get them again with interest."

"Off, dog!" cried Hindley, threatening him with an iron weight, used for weighing potatoes and hay.

"Throw it," he replied, standing still, "and then I'll tell how you boasted that you would turn me out of doors as soon as he died, and see whether he will not turn you out directly."

Hindley threw it, hitting him on the breast, and down he fell, but staggered up immediately, breathless and white, and had not I prevented it he would have gone just so to the master, and got full revenge by letting his condition plead for him, intimating who had caused it.

"Take my colt, gipsy, then!" said young Earnshaw, "And I pray that he may break your neck, take him, and be damned, you beggarly interloper! and wheedle my father out of all he has, only, afterwards, show him what you are, imp of Satan — And take that, I hope he'll kick out your brains!"

Heathcliff had gone to loose the beast, and shift it to his own stall — He was passing behind it, when Hindley finished his speech by knocking him under its feet, and without stopping to examine whether his hopes were fulfilled, ran away as fast as he could.

I was surprised to witness how coolly the child gathered himself up, and went on with his intention, exchanging saddles and all; and then sitting down on a bundle of hay to overcome the qualm which the violent blow occasioned, before he entered the house.

I persuaded him easily to let me lay the blame of his bruises on the horse; he minded little what tale was told since he had what he wanted. He complained so seldom, indeed, of such stirs as these, that I really thought him not vindictive — I was deceived, completely, as you will hear.

CHAPTER 5

In the course of time, Mr. Earnshaw began to fail. He had been active and healthy, yet his strength left him suddenly; and when he was confined to the chimney-corner he grew grievously irritable. A nothing vexed him, and suspected slights of his authority nearly threw him into fits.

This was especially to be remarked if any one attempted to impose upon, or domineer over, his favourite: he was painfully jealous lest a word should be spoken amiss to him, seeming to have got into his head the notion that, because he liked Heathcliff, all hated, and longed to do him an ill-turn.

It was a disadvantage to the lad, for the kinder among us did not wish to fret the master, so we humoured his partiality; and that humouring was rich nourishment to the child's pride and black tempers. Still it became in a manner necessary; twice, or thrice, Hindley's manifestations of scorn, while his father was near, roused the old man to a fury. He seized his stick to strike him, and shook with rage that he could not do it.

At last, our curate (we had a curate then who made the living answer by teaching the little Lintons and Earnshaws, and farming his bit of land himself), he advised that the young man should be sent to college, and Mr. Earnshaw agreed, though with a heavy spirit, for he said —

"Hindley was naught, and would never thrive as where he wandered."

I hoped heartily we should have peace now. It hurt me to think the master should be made uncomfortable by his own good deed. I fancied the discontent of age and disease arose from his family disagreements, as he would have it that it did — really, you know, sir, it was in his sinking frame.

We might have got on tolerably, notwithstanding, but for two people, Miss Cathy, and Joseph, the servant; you saw him, I dare say, up yonder. He was, and is yet, most likely, the wearisomest, self-righteous pharisee that ever ransacked a Bible to take the promises to himself, and fling the curses on his neighbors. By his knack of sermonising and pious discoursing, he contrived to make a great impression on Mr. Earnshaw, and, the more feeble the master became, the more influence he gained.

He was relentless in worrying him about his soul's concerns, and about ruling his children rigidly. He encouraged him to regard Hindley as a reprobate; and, night after night, he regularly grumbled out a long string of tales against Heathcliff and Catherine; always minding to flatter Earnshaw's weakness by heaping the heaviest blame on the last.

Certainly, she had ways with her such as I never saw a child take up before; and she put all of us past our patience fifty times and oftener in a day: from the hour she came down stairs, till the hour she went to bed, we had not a minute's security that she wouldn't be in mischief. Her spirits were always at high-water mark, her tongue always going — singing, laughing, and plaguing everybody who would not do the same. A wild, wick slip she was — but she had the bonniest eye, and sweetest smile, and lightest foot in the parish; and, after all, I believe she meant no harm; for when once she made you cry in good earnest, it seldom happened that she would not keep you company; and oblige you to be quiet that you might comfort her.

She was much too fond of Heathcliff. The greatest punishment we could invent for her was to keep her separate from him: yet she got chided more than any of us on his account.

In play, she liked, exceedingly, to act the little mistress; using her hands freely, and commanding her companions: she did so to me, but I would not bear slapping and ordering; and so I let her know.

Now, Mr. Earnshaw did not understand jokes for his children: he had always been strict and grave with them; and Catherine, on her part, had no idea why her father should be crosser and less patient in his ailing condition, than he was in his prime.

His peevish reproofs wakened in her a naughty delight to provoke him; she was never so happy as when we were all scolding her at once, and she defying us with her bold, saucy look, and her ready words; turning Joseph's religious curses into ridicule, baiting me, and doing just what her father hated most, showing how her pretended insolence, which he thought real, had more power over Heathcliff than his kindness. How the boy would do *her* bidding in anything, and *his* only when it suited his own inclination.

After behaving as badly as possible all day, she sometimes came fondling to make it up at night.

"Nay, Cathy," the old man would say, "I cannot love thee; thou'rt worse than thy brother. Go, say thy prayers, child, and ask God's pardon. I doubt thy mother and I must rue that we ever reared thee!"

That made her cry, at first; and then, being repulsed continually hardened her, and she laughed if I told her to say she was sorry for her faults, and beg to be forgiven.

But the hour came, at last, that ended Mr. Earnshaw's troubles on earth. He died quietly in his chair one October evening, seated by the fire-side.

A high wind blustered round the house, and roared in the chimney: it sounded wild and stormy, yet it was not cold, and we were all together — I, a little removed from the hearth, busy at my knitting, and Joseph reading his Bible near the table, (for the servants generally sat in the house then, after their work was done). Miss Cathy had been sick, and that made her still; she leant against her father's knee, and Heathcliff was lying on the floor with his head in her lap.

I remember the master, before he fell into a doze, stroking her bonny hair — it pleased him rarely to see her gentle — and saying —

"Why canst thou not always be a good lass, Cathy?"

And she turned her face up to his, and laughed, and answered —

"Why cannot you always be a good man, father?"

But as soon as she saw him vexed again, she kissed his hand, and said she would sing him to sleep. She began singing very low, till his fingers dropped from hers, and his head sank on his breast. Then I told her to hush, and not stir, for fear she would wake him. We all kept as mute as mice a full half-hour, and should have done longer, only Joseph, having finished his chapter, got up and said that he must rouse the master for prayers and bed. He stepped forward, and called him by name, and touched his shoulder, but he would not move — so he took the candle and looked at him.

I thought there was something wrong as he set down the light; and seizing the children each by an arm, whispered them to "frame° upstairs, and make little din — they might pray alone that evening — he had summut to do."

"I shall bid father good-night first," said Catherine, putting her arms round his neck, before we could hinder her.

The poor thing discovered her loss directly — she screamed out —

"Oh, he's dead, Heathcliff! he's dead!"

And they both set up a heart-breaking cry.

I joined my wail to theirs, loud and bitter; but Joseph asked what we could be thinking of to roar in that way over a saint in heaven.

He told me to put on my cloak and run to Gimmerton for the doctor and the parson. I could not guess the use that either would be of, then. However, I went, through wind and rain, and brought one, the doctor, back with me; the other said he would come in the morning.

Leaving Joseph to explain matters, I ran to the children's room; their door was ajar, I saw they had never laid down, though it was past midnight; but they were calmer, and did not need me to console them. The little souls were comforting each other with better thoughts than I could have hit on; no parson in the world ever pictured heaven so beautifully as they did, in their innocent talk; and, while I sobbed, and listened, I could not help wishing we were all there safe together.

CHAPTER 6

Mr. Hindley came home to the funeral; and — a thing that amazed us, and set the neighbours gossiping right and left — he brought a wife with him.

frame: Go, get on with it.

What she was, and where she was born, he never informed us; probably, she had neither money nor name to recommend her, or he would scarcely have kept the union from his father.

She was not one that would have disturbed the house much on her own account. Every object she saw, the moment she crossed the threshold, appeared to delight her; and every circumstance that took place about her, except the preparing for the burial, and the presence of the mourners.

I thought she was half silly from her behaviour while that went on; she ran into her chamber, and made me come with her, though I should have been dressing the children; and there she sat shivering and clasping her hands, and asking repeatedly —

"Are they gone yet?"

Then she began describing with hysterical emotion the effect it produced on her to see black; and started, and trembled, and, at last, fell a-weeping — and when I asked what was the matter? answered, she didn't know; but she felt so afraid of dying!

I imagined her as little likely to die as myself. She was rather thin, but young, and fresh complexioned, and her eyes sparkled as bright as diamonds. I did remark, to be sure, that mounting the stairs made her breathe very quick, that the least sudden noise set her all in a quiver, and that she coughed troublesomely sometimes: but, I knew nothing of what these symptoms portended, and had no impulse to sympathise with her. We don't in general take to foreigners here, Mr. Lockwood, unless they take to us first.

Young Earnshaw was altered considerably in the three years of his absence. He had grown sparer, and lost his colour, and spoke and dressed quite differently: and, on the very day of his return, he told Joseph and me we must thenceforth quarter ourselves in the back-kitchen, and leave the house for him. Indeed, he would have carpeted and papered a small spare room for a parlour; but his wife expressed such pleasure at the white floor, and huge glowing fire-place, at the pewter dishes, and delf-case, and dog-kennel, and the wide space there was to move about in, where they usually sat, that he thought it unnecessary to her comfort, and so dropped the intention.

She expressed pleasure, too, at finding a sister among her new acquaintance, and she prattled to Catherine, and kissed her, and ran about with her, and gave her quantities of presents, at the beginning. Her affection tired very soon, however, and when she grew peevish, Hindley became tyrannical. A few words from her, evincing a dislike to Heathcliff, were enough to rouse in him all his old hatred of the boy. He drove him from their company to the servants, deprived him of the instructions of the curate, and insisted that he should labour out of doors instead, compelling him to do so, as hard as any other lad on the farm.

He bore his degradation pretty well at first, because Cathy taught him what she learnt, and worked or played with him in the fields. They both promised fair to grow up as rude as savages, the young master being entirely negligent how they behaved, and what they did, so they kept clear of him. He would not even have seen after their going to church on Sundays, only Joseph and the curate reprimanded his carelessness when they absented themselves, and that reminded him to order Heathcliff a flogging, and Catherine a fast from dinner or supper.

But it was one of their chief amusements to run away to the moors in the morning and remain there all day, and the after punishment grew a mere thing to laugh at. The curate might set as many chapters as he pleased for Catherine to get by heart, and Joseph might thrash Heathcliff till his arm ached; they forgot everything the minute they were together again, at least the minute they had contrived some naughty plan of revenge, and many a time I've cried to myself to watch them growing more reckless daily, and I not daring to speak a syllable for fear of losing the small power I still retained over the unfriended creatures.

One Sunday evening, it chanced that they were banished from the sitting-room, for making a noise, or a light offence of the kind, and when I went to call them to supper, I could discover them nowhere.

We searched the house, above and below, and the yard and stables; they were invisible; and, at last, Hindley in a passion told us to bolt the doors, and swore nobody should let them in that night.

The household went to bed; and I, too anxious to lie down, opened my lattice and put my head out to hearken, though it rained, determined to admit them in spite of the prohibition, should they return.

In a while, I distinguished steps coming up the road, and the light of a lantern glimmered through the gate.

I threw a shawl over my head and ran to prevent them from waking Mr. Earnshaw by knocking. There was Heathcliff, by himself; it gave me a start to see him alone.

"Where is Miss Catherine?" I cried hurriedly. "No accident, I hope?"

"At Thrushcross Grange," he answered, "and I would have been there too, but they had not the manners to ask me to stay."

"Well, you will catch it!" I said, "you'll never be content till you're sent about your business. What in the world led you wandering to Thrushcross Grange?"

"Let me get off my wet clothes, and I'll tell you all about it, Nelly," he replied.

I bid him beware of rousing the master, and while he undressed, and I waited to put out the candle, he continued —

"Cathy and I escaped from the wash-house to have a ramble at liberty, and getting a glimpse of the Grange lights, we thought we would just go and see whether the Lintons passed their Sunday evenings standing shivering in corners, while their father and mother sat eating and drinking, and singing and laughing, and burning their eyes out before the fire. Do you think they do? Or reading sermons, and being catechised by their man-servant, and set to learn a column of Scripture names, if they don't answer properly?"

"Probably not," I responded. "They are good children, no doubt, and don't deserve the treatment you receive, for your bad conduct."

"Don't you cant, Nelly," he said. "Nonsense! We ran from the top of the Heights to the park, without stopping — Catherine completely beaten in the race, because she was barefoot. You'll have to seek for her shoes in the bog to-morrow. We crept through a broken hedge, groped our way up the path, and planted ourselves on a flower-pot under the drawing-room window. The light came from thence; they had not put up the shutters, and the curtains were only half closed. Both of us were able to look in by standing on the basement, and clinging to the ledge, and we saw — ah! it was beautiful — a splendid place carpeted with crimson, and crimson-covered chairs and tables, and a pure white ceiling bordered by gold, a shower of glass-drops hanging in silver chains from the centre, and shimmering with little soft tapers. Old Mr. and Mrs. Linton were not there. Edgar and his sister had it entirely to themselves; shouldn't they have been happy? We should have thought ourselves in heaven! And now, guess what your good children were doing? Isabella — I believe she is eleven, a year younger than Cathy — lay screaming at the farther end of the room, shrieking as if witches were running red hot needles into her. Edgar stood on the hearth weeping silently, and in the middle of the table sat a little dog shaking its paw and yelping, which, from their mutual accusations, we understood they had nearly pulled in two between them. The idiots! That was their pleasure! to quarrel who should hold a heap of warm hair, and each begin to cry because both, after struggling to get it, refused to take it. We laughed outright at the petted things, we did despise them! When would you catch me wishing to have what Catherine wanted? or find us by ourselves, seeking entertainment in yelling, and sobbing, and rolling on the ground, divided by the whole room? I'd not exchange, for a thousand lives, my condition here, for Edgar Linton's at Thrushcross Grange — not if I might have the privilege of flinging Joseph off the highest gable, and painting the house-front with Hindley's blood!"

"Hush, hush!" I interrupted. "Still you have not told me, Heathcliff, how Catherine is left behind?"

"I told you we laughed," he answered. "The Lintons heard us, and with one accord, they shot like arrows to the door; there was silence, and then a cry, 'Oh, mamma, mamma! Oh, papa! Oh, mamma, come here. Oh, papa, oh!' They really did howl out, something in that way. We made frightful noises to terrify them still more, and then we dropped off the ledge, because somebody was drawing the bars, and we felt we had better flee. I had Cathy by the hand, and was urging her on, when all at once she fell down.

" 'Run, Heathcliff, run!' she whispered. 'They have let the bulldog loose, and he holds me!'

"The devil had seized her ankle, Nelly; I heard his abominable snorting. She did not yell out — no! She would have scorned to do it, if she had been spitted on the horns of a mad cow. I did, though, I vociferated curses enough to annihilate any fiend in Christendom, and I got a stone and thrust it between his jaws, and tried with all my might to cram it down his throat. A beast of a servant came up with a lantern at last, shouting —

" 'Keep fast, Skulker, keep fast!'

"He changed his note, however, when he saw Skulker's game. The dog was throttled off, his huge, purple tongue hanging half a foot out of his mouth, and his pendant lips streaming with bloody slaver.

"The man took Cathy up; she was sick; not from fear, I'm certain, but from pain. He carried her in; I followed, grumbling execrations and vengeance.

" 'What prey, Robert?" hallooed Linton from the entrance.

" 'Skulker has caught a little girl, sir,' he replied, 'and there's a lad here,' he added, making a clutch at me, 'who looks an out-and-outer! Very like, the robbers were for putting them through the window, to open the doors to the gang after all were asleep, that they might murder us at their ease. Hold your tongue, you foul-mouthed thief, you! you shall go to the gallows for this. Mr. Linton, sir, don't lay by your gun!'

" 'No, no, Robert!' said the old fool. 'The rascals knew that yesterday was my rent-day; they thought to have me cleverly. Come in; I'll furnish them a reception. There, John, fasten the chain. Give Skulker some water, Jenny. To beard a magistrate in his stronghold, and on the Sabbath, too! where will their insolence stop? Oh, my dear Mary, look here! don't be afraid, it is but a boy — yet, the villain scowls so plainly in his face, would it not be a kindness to the country to hang him at once, before he shows his nature in acts, as well as features?'

"He pulled me under the chandelier, and Mrs. Linton placed her spectacles on her nose and raised her hands in horror. The cowardly children crept nearer also, Isabella lisping —

" 'Frightful thing! Put him in the cellar, papa. He's exactly like the son of the fortune-teller, that stole my tame pheasant. Isn't he, Edgar?'

"While they examined me, Cathy came round; she heard the last speech, and laughed. Edgar Linton, after an inquisitive stare, collected sufficient wit to recognise her. They see us at church, you know, though we seldom meet them elsewhere.

" 'That's Miss Earnshaw!' he whispered to his mother, 'and look how Skulker has bitten her — how her foot bleeds!'

" 'Miss Earnshaw? Nonsense!' cried the dame. 'Miss Earnshaw scouring the country with a gipsy! And yet, my dear, the child is in mourning — surely it is — and she may be lamed for life!'

" 'What culpable carelessness in her brother!' exclaimed Mr. Linton, turning from me to Catherine. 'I've understood from Shielders' " (that was the curate, sir) " 'that he lets her grow up in absolute heathenism. But who is this? Where did she pick up this companion? Oho! I declare he is that strange acquisition my late neighbour made in his journey to Liverpool — a little Lascar, or an American or Spanish castaway.'

" 'A wicked boy, at all events,' remarked the old lady, 'and quite unfit for a decent house! Did you notice his language, Linton? I'm shocked that my children should have heard it.'

"I recommenced cursing — don't be angry, Nelly — and so Robert was ordered to take me off — I refused to go without Cathy — he dragged me into the garden, pushed the lantern into my hand, assured me that Mr. Earnshaw should be informed of my behaviour, and bidding me march, directly, secured the door again.

"The curtains were still looped at one corner; and I resumed my station as spy, because, if Catherine had wished to return, I intended shattering their great glass panes to a million of fragments, unless they let her out.

"She sat on the sofa quietly. Mrs. Linton took off the grey cloak of the dairy maid which we had borrowed for our excursion, shaking her head, and expostulating with her, I suppose; she was a young lady and they made a distinction between her treatment and mine. Then the woman servant brought a basin of warm water, and washed her feet;

and Mr. Linton mixed a tumbler of negus, and Isabella emptied a plate of cakes into her lap, and Edgar stood gaping at a distance. Afterwards, they dried and combed her beautiful hair, and gave her a pair of enormous slippers, and wheeled her to the fire, and I left her, as merry as she could be, dividing her food between the little dog and Skulker, whose nose she pinched as she ate; and kindling a spark of spirit in the vacant blue eyes of the Lintons — a dim reflection from her own enchanting face — I saw they were full of stupid admiration; she is so immeasurably superior to them — to everybody on earth; is she not, Nelly?"

"There will more come of this business than you reckon on," I answered, covering him up and extinguishing the light, "You are incurable Heathcliff, and Mr. Hindley will have to proceed to extremities, see if he won't."

My words came truer than I desired. The luckless adventure made Earnshaw furious — And then, Mr. Linton, to mend matters, paid us a visit himself, on the morrow; and read the young master such a lecture on the road he guided his family, that he was stirred to look about him, in earnest.

Heathcliff received no flogging, but he was told that the first word he spoke to Miss Catherine should ensure a dismissal; and Mrs. Earnshaw undertook to keep her sister-in-law in due restraint, when she returned home; employing art, not force — with force she would have found it impossible.

CHAPTER 7

Cathy stayed at Thrushcross Grange five weeks, till Christmas. By that time her ankle was thoroughly cured, and her manners much improved. The mistress visited her often, in the interval, and commenced her plan of reform by trying to raise her self-respect with fine clothes and flattery, which she took readily: so that, instead of a wild, hatless little savage jumping into the house, and rushing to squeeze us all breathless, there lighted from a handsome black pony a very dignified person, with brown ringlets falling from the cover of a feathered beaver, and a long cloth habit which she was obliged to hold up with both hands that she might sail in.

Hindley lifted her from her horse, exclaiming delightedly,

"Why, Cathy, you are quite a beauty! I should scarcely have known you — you look like a lady now — Isabella Linton is not to be compared with her, is she, Frances?"

"Isabella has not her natural advantages," replied his wife, "but she must mind and not grow wild again here. Ellen, help Miss Catherine off with her things — Stay, dear, you will disarrange your curls — let me untie your hat."

I removed the habit, and there shone forth beneath, a grand plaid silk frock, white trousers, and burnished shoes; and, while her eyes sparkled joyfully when the dogs came bounding up to welcome her, she dare hardly touch them lest they should fawn upon her splendid garments.

She kissed me gently, I was all flour making the Christmas cake, and it would not have done to give me a hug; and, then, she looked round for Heathcliff. Mr. and Mrs. Earnshaw watched anxiously their meeting, thinking it would enable them to judge, in some measure, what grounds they had for hoping to succeed in separating the two friends.

Heathcliff was hard to discover, at first — If he were careless, and uncared for, before Catherine's absence, he had been ten times more so, since.

Nobody but I even did him the kindness to call him a dirty boy, and bid him wash himself, once a week; and children of his age seldom have a natural pleasure in soap and water. Therefore, not to mention his clothes, which had seen three months' service, in mire and dust, and his thick uncombed hair, the surface of his face and hands was dismally beclouded. He might well skulk behind the settle, on beholding such a bright, graceful damsel enter the house, instead of a rough-headed counterpart to himself, as he expected.

"Is Heathcliff not here?" she demanded, pulling off her gloves, and displaying fingers wonderfully whitened with doing nothing, and staying indoors.

"Heathcliff, you may come forward," cried Mr. Hindley, enjoying his discomfiture and gratified to see what a forbidding young blackguard he would be compelled to present himself. "You may come and wish Miss Catherine welcome, like the other servants."

Cathy, catching a glimpse of her friend in his concealment, flew to embrace him, she bestowed seven or eight kisses on his neck within the second, and then stopped, and drawing back, burst into a laugh, exclaiming,

"Why, how very black and cross you look! and how — how funny and grim! but that's because I'm used to Edgar and Isabella Linton. Well, Heathcliff, have you forgotten me?"

She had some reason to put the question, for shame and pride threw double gloom over his countenance, and kept him immovable.

"Shake hands, Heathcliff," said Mr. Earnshaw, condescendingly; "once in a way, that is permitted."

"I shall not!" replied the boy, finding his tongue at last. "I shall not stand to be laughed at, I shall not bear it!"

And he would have broken from the circle, but Miss Cathy seized him again.

"I did not mean to laugh at you," she said, "I could not hinder myself. Heathcliff, shake hands, at least! What are you sulky for? it was only that you looked odd — If you wash your face, and brush your hair, it will be all right. But you are so dirty!"

She gazed concernedly at the dusky fingers she held in her own, and also at her dress, which she feared had gained no embellishment from its contact with his.

"You needn't have touched me!" he answered, following her eye and snatching away his hand. "I shall be as dirty as I please, and I like to be dirty, and I will be dirty."

With that he dashed head foremost out of the room, amid the merriment of the master and mistress, and to the serious disturbance of Catherine, who could not comprehend how her remarks should have produced such an exhibition of bad temper.

After playing lady's maid to the new comer, and putting my cakes in the oven, and making the house and kitchen cheerful with great fires befitting Christmas eve, I prepared to sit down and amuse myself by singing carols, all alone; regardless of Joseph's affirmations that he considered the merry tunes I chose as next door to songs.

He had retired to private prayer in his chamber, and Mr. and Mrs. Earnshaw were engaging Missy's attention by sundry gay trifles bought for her to present to the little Lintons, as an acknowledgment of their kindness.

They had invited them to spend the morrow at Wuthering Heights, and the invitation had been accepted, on one condition: Mrs. Linton begged that her darlings be kept carefully apart from that "naughty, swearing boy."

Under the circumstances I remained solitary. I smelt the rich scent of the heating spices; and admired the shining kitchen utensils, the polished clock, decked in holly, the silver mugs ranged on a tray ready to be filled with mulled ale for supper; and, above all, the speckless purity of my particular care — the scoured and well-swept floor.

I gave due inward applause to every object, and, then, I remembered how old Earnshaw used to come in when all was tidied, and call me a cant lass, and slip a shilling into my hand, as a Christmas box: and from that I went on to think of his fondness for Heathcliff, and his dread lest he should suffer neglect after death had removed him; and that naturally led me to consider the poor lad's situation now, and from singing I changed my mind to crying. It struck me soon, however, there would be more sense in endeavouring to repair some of his wrongs than shedding tears over them — I got up and walked into the court to seek him.

He was not far: I found him smoothing the glossy coat of the new pony in the stable, and feeding the other beasts, according to custom.

"Make haste, Heathcliff!" I said, "the kitchen is so comfortable — and Joseph is up-stairs; make haste, and let me dress you smart before Miss Cathy comes out — and then you can sit together, with the whole hearth to yourselves, and have a long chatter till bedtime."

He proceeded with his task and never turned his head towards me.

"Come — are you coming?" I continued. "There's a little cake for each of you, nearly enough; and you'll need half an hour's donning."

I waited five minutes, but getting no answer left him. . . . Catherine supped with her brother and sister-in-law: Joseph and I joined at an unsociable meal, seasoned with reproofs on one side and sauciness on the other. His cake and cheese remained on the table all night, for the fairies. He managed to continue work till nine o'clock, and, then, marched dumb and dour to his chamber.

Cathy sat up late; having a world of things to order for the reception of her new friends: she came into the kitchen, once, to speak to her old one, but he was gone, and she only stayed to ask what was the matter with him, and then went back.

In the morning, he rose early; and, as it was a holiday, carried his ill-humour onto the moors; not re-appearing till the family were departed for church. Fasting and reflection seemed to have brought him to a better spirit. He hung about me for a while, and having screwed up his courage, exclaimed abruptly,

"Nelly, make me decent, I'm going to be good."

"High time, Heathcliff," I said; "you *have* grieved Catherine; she's sorry she ever came home, I dare say! It looks as if you envied her, because she is more thought of than you."

The notion of *envying* Catherine was incomprehensible to him, but the notion of grieving her he understood clearly enough.

"Did she say she was grieved?" he inquired, looking very serious.

"She cried when I told her you were off again this morning."

"Well, *I* cried last night," he returned, "and I had more reason to cry than she."

"Yes, you had the reason of going to bed with a proud heart and an empty stomach," said I. "Proud people breed sad sorrows for themselves — But, if you be ashamed of your touchiness, you must ask pardon, mind, when she comes in. You must go up, and offer to kiss her, and say — you know best what to say, only, do it heartily, and not as if you thought her converted into a stranger by her grand dress. And now, though I have dinner to get ready, I'll steal time to arrange you so that Edgar Linton shall look quite a doll beside you: and that he does — You are younger, and yet, I'll be bound, you are taller and twice as broad across the shoulders — you could knock him down in a twinkling; don't you feel that you could?"

Heathcliff's face brightened a moment; then it was overcast afresh, and he sighed.

"But, Nelly, if I knocked him down twenty times, that wouldn't make him less handsome, or me more so. I wish I had light hair and a fair skin, and was dressed, and behaved as well, and had a chance of being as rich as he will be!"

"And cried for momma, at every turn — " I added, "and trembled if a country lad heaved his fist against you, and sat at home all day for a shower of rain. — Oh, Heathcliff, you are showing a poor spirit! Come to the glass, and I'll let you see what you should wish. Do you mark those two lines between your eyes, and those thick brows, that instead of rising arched, sink in the middle, and that couple of black fiends, so deeply buried, who never open their windows boldly, but lurk glinting under them, like devil's spies? Wish and learn to smooth away the surly wrinkles, to raise your lids frankly, and change the fiends to confident, innocent angels, suspecting and doubting nothing, and always seeing friends where they are not sure of foes — Don't get the expression of a vicious cur that appears to know the kicks it gets are its desert, and yet hates all the world, as well as the kicker, for what it suffers."

"In other words, I must wish for Edgar Linton's great blue eyes, and even forehead," he replied. "I do — and that won't help me to them."

"A good heart will help you to a bonny face, my lad," I continued, "if you were a regular black; and a bad one will turn the bonniest into something worse than ugly. And now that we've done washing, and combing, and sulking — tell me whether you don't think yourself rather handsome? I'll tell you, I do. You're fit for a prince in disguise. Who knows, but your father was Emperor of China, and your mother an Indian queen, each of them able to buy up, with one week's income, Wuthering Heights and Thrushcross Grange together? And you were kidnapped by wicked sailors, and brought to England. Were I in your place, I would frame high notions of my birth; and the thoughts of what I was should give me courage and dignity to support the oppressions of a little farmer!"

So I chattered on; and Heathcliff gradually lost his frown, and began to look quite pleasant; when all at once our conversation was interrupted by a rumbling sound moving up the road and entering the court. He ran to the window, and I to the door, just in time to behold the two Lintons descend from the family carriage, smothered in cloaks and furs, and the Earnshaws dismount from their horses — they often rode to church in winter. Catherine took a hand of each of the children, and brought them into the house, and set them before the fire, which quickly put colour into their white faces.

I urged my companion to hasten now, and show his amiable humour; and he willingly obeyed: but ill-luck would have it that, as he opened the door leading from the kitchen on one side, Hindley opened it on the other; they met, and the master, irritated at seeing him clean and cheerful, or, perhaps, eager to keep his promise to Mrs. Linton, shoved him back with a sudden thrust, and angrily bade Joseph "keep the fellow out of the room — send him into the garret till dinner is over. He'll be cramming his fingers in the tarts, and stealing the fruit, if left alone with them a minute."

"Nay, sir," I could not avoid answering, "he'll touch nothing, not he — and, I suppose, he must have his share of the dainties as well as we."

"He shall have his share of my hand, if I catch him down stairs again till dark," cried Hindley. "Begone, you vagabond! What, you are attempting the coxcomb, are you? Wait till I get hold of those elegant locks — see if I won't pull them a bit longer!"

"They are long enough already," observed Master Linton, peeping from the doorway; "I wonder they don't make his head ache. It's like a colt's mane over his eyes!"

He ventured this remark without any intention to insult; but Heathcliff's violent nature was not prepared to endure the appearance of impertinence from one whom he seemed to hate, even then, as a rival. He seized a tureen of hot apple-sauce, the first thing that came under his gripe, and dashed it full against the speaker's face and neck — who instantly commenced a lament that brought Isabella and Catherine hurrying to the place.

Mr. Earnshaw snatched up the culprit directly and conveyed him to his chamber, where, doubtless, he administered a rough remedy to cool the fit of passion, for he re-appeared red and breathless. I got the dish-cloth, and, rather spitefully, scrubbed Edgar's nose and mouth, affirming it served him right for meddling. His sister began weeping to go home, and Cathy stood by confounded, blushing for all.

"You should not have spoken to him!" she expostulated with Master Linton. "He was in a bad temper, and now you've spoilt your visit, and he'll be flogged — and I hate him to be flogged! I can't eat my dinner. Why did you speak to him, Edgar!"

"I didn't," sobbed the youth, escaping from my hands, and finishing the remainder of the purification with his cambric pocket-handkerchief. "I promised mamma that I wouldn't say one word to him, and I didn't!"

"Well, don't cry!" replied Catherine, contemptuously. "You're not killed — don't make more mischief — my brother is coming — be quiet! Give over, Isabella! Has anybody hurt *you?*"

"There, there, children — to your seats!" cried Hindley, bustling in. "That brute of a lad has warmed me nicely. Next time, Master Edgar, take the law into your own fists — it will give you an appetite!"

The little party recovered its equanimity at sight of the fragrant feast. They were hungry after their ride, and easily consoled, since no real harm had befallen them.

Mr. Earnshaw carved bountiful platefuls; and the mistress made them merry with lively talk. I waited behind her chair, and was pained to behold Catherine, with dry eyes and an indifferent air, commence cutting up the wing of a goose before her.

"An unfeeling child," I thought to myself, "how lightly she dismisses her old playmate's troubles. I could not have imagined her to be so selfish."

She lifted a mouthful to her lips; then, set it down again: her cheeks flushed, and the tears gushed over them. She slipped her fork to the floor, and hastily dived under the cloth to conceal her emotion. I did not call her unfeeling long, for I perceived she was in purgatory throughout the day, and wearying to find an opportunity of getting by herself, or paying a visit to Heathcliff, who had been locked up by the master, as I discovered, on endeavouring to introduce to him a private mess of victuals.

In the evening we had a dance. Cathy begged that he might be liberated then, as Isabella Linton had no partner; her entreaties were vain, and I was appointed to supply the deficiency.

We got rid of all gloom in the excitement of the exercise, and our pleasure was increased by the arrival of the Gimmerton band, mustering fifteen strong; a trumpet, a trombone, clarionets, bassoons, French horns, and a bass viol, besides singers. They go the rounds of all the respectable houses and receive contributions every Christmas, and we esteemed it a first-rate treat to hear them.

After the usual carols had been sung, we set them to songs and glees. Mrs. Earnshaw loved the music, and, so, they gave us plenty.

Catherine loved it too; but she said it sounded sweetest at the top of the steps, and she went up in the dark: I followed. They shut the house door below, never noting our absence, it was so full of people. She made no stay at the stairs' head, but mounted farther, to the garret where Heathcliff was confined; and called him. He stubbornly declined answering for a while — she persevered, and finally persuaded him to hold communion with her through the boards.

I let the poor things converse unmolested, till I supposed the songs were gong to cease, and the singers to get some refreshment: then, I clambered up to the ladder to warn her.

Instead of finding her outside, I heard her voice within. The little monkey had crept by the skylight of one garret, along the roof, into the skylight of the other, and it was with the utmost difficulty I could coax her out again.

When she did come, Heathcliff came with her; and she insisted that I should take him into the kitchen, as my fellow-servant had gone to a neighbour's to be removed from the sound of our "devil's psalmody," as it pleased him to call it. I told them I intended, by no means, to encourage their tricks; but as the prisoner had never broken his fast since yesterday's dinner, I would wink at his cheating Mr. Hindley that once.

He went down; I set him a stool by the fire, and offered him a quantity of good things; but, he was sick and could eat little: and my attempts to entertain him were thrown away. He leant his two elbows on his knees, and his chin on his hands, and remained wrapt in dumb meditation. On my inquiring the subject of his thoughts, he answered gravely —

"I'm trying to settle how I shall pay Hindley back. I don't care how long I wait, if I can only do it, at last. I hope he will not die before I do!"

"For shame, Heathcliff!" said I. "It is for God to punish wicked people; we should learn to forgive."

"No, God won't have the satisfaction that I shall," he returned. "I only wish I knew the best way! Let me alone, and I'll plan it out: while I'm thinking of that, I don't feel pain."

But, Mr. Lockwood, I forget these tales cannot divert you. I'm annoyed how I should dream of chattering on at such a rate; and your gruel cold, and you nodding for bed! I could have told Heathcliff's history, all that you need hear, in half-a-dozen words.

Thus interrupting herself, the housekeeper rose, and proceeded to lay aside her sewing; but I felt incapable of moving from the hearth, and I was very far from nodding.

"Sit still, Mrs. Dean," I cried, "do sit still, another half hour! You've done just right to tell the story leisurely. That is the method I like; and you must finish in the same style. I am interested in every character you have mentioned, more or less."

"The clock is on the stroke of eleven, sir."

"No matter — I'm not accustomed to go to bed in the long hours. One or two is early enough for a person who lies till ten."

"You shouldn't lie till ten. There's the very prime of the morning gone long before that time. A person who has not done one half his day's work by ten o'clock, runs a chance of leaving the other half undone."

"Nevertheless, Mrs. Dean, resume your chair; because to-morrow I intend lengthening the night till afternoon. I prognosticate for myself an obstinate cold, at least."

"I hope not, sir. Well, you must allow me to leap over some three years; during that space, Mrs. Earnshaw — "

"No, no, I'll allow nothing of the sort! Are you acquainted with the mood of mind in which, if you were seated alone, and the cat licking its kitten on the rug before you, you would watch the operation so intently that puss's neglect of one ear would put you seriously out of temper?"

"A terribly lazy mood, I should say."

"On the contrary, a tiresomely active one. It is mine, at present, and, therefore, continue minutely. I perceive that people in these regions acquire over people in towns the value that a spider in a dungeon does over a spider in a cottage, to their various occupants; and yet the deepened attraction is not entirely owing to the situation of the looker-on. They *do* live more in earnest, more in themselves, and less in surface change, and frivolous external things. I could fancy a love for life here almost possible; and I was a fixed unbeliever in any love of a year's standing — one state resembles setting a hungry man down to a single dish on which he may concentrate his entire appetite, and do it justice — the other, introducing him to a table laid out by French cooks; he can perhaps extract as much enjoyment from the whole; but each part is a mere atom in his regard and remembrance."

"Oh! here we are the same as anywhere else, when you get to know us," observed Mrs. Dean, somewhat puzzled at my speech.

"Excuse me," I responded; "you, my good friend, are a striking evidence against that assertion. Excepting a few provincialisms of slight consequence, you have no marks of the manners which I am habituated to consider as peculiar to your class. I am sure you have thought a great deal more than the generality of servants think. You have been compelled to cultivate your reflective faculties, for want of occasions for frittering your life away in silly trifles."

Mrs. Dean laughed.

"I certainly esteem myself a steady, reasonable kind of body," she said, "not exactly from living among the hills, and seeing one set of faces, and one series of actions, from year's end to year's end: but I have undergone sharp discipline which has taught me wisdom; and then, I have read more than you would fancy, Mr. Lockwood. You could not open a book in this library that I have not looked into, and got something out of also; unless it be that range of Greek and Latin, and that of French — and those I know one from another: it is as much as you can expect of a poor man's daughter.

"However, if I am to follow my story in true gossip's fashion, I had better go on; and instead of leaping three years, I will be content to pass to the next summer — the summer of 1778, that is nearly twenty-three years ago."

CHAPTER 8

On the morning of a fine June day, my first bonny little nursling, and the last of the ancient Earnshaw stock was born.

We were busy with the hay in a far away field, when the girl that usually brought out breakfasts came running, an hour too soon, across the meadow and up the lane, calling me as she ran.

"Oh, such a grand bairn!°" she panted out. "The finest lad that ever breathed! But the doctor says misiss must go; he says she's been in a consumption these many months. I heard him tell Mr. Hindley — and now she has nothing to keep her, and she'll be dead before winter. You must come home directly. You're to nurse it, Nelly — to feed it with sugar and milk, and take care of it, day and night — I wish I were you, because it will be all yours when there is no missis!"

grand bairn: Fine child.

"But is she very ill?" I asked, flinging down my rake, and tying my bonnet.

"I guess she is; yet she looks bravely," replied the girl, "and she talks as if she thought of living to see it grow a man. She's out of her head for joy, it's such a beauty! If I were her I'm certain I should not die. I should get better at the bare sight of it, in spite of Kenneth. I was fairly mad at him. Dame Archer brought the cherub down to master, in the house, and his face just began to light up, then the old croaker steps forward, and, says he: — 'Earnshaw, it's a blessing your wife has been spared to leave you this son. When she came, I felt convinced we shouldn't keep her long; and now, I must tell you, the winter will probably finish her. Don't take on, and fret about it too much, it can't be helped. And besides, you should have known better than to choose such a rush of a lass!' "

"And what did the master answer?" I enquired.

"I think he swore — but, I didn't mind, I was straining to see the bairn," and she began again to describe it rapturously. I, as zealous as herself, hurried eagerly home to admire, on my part, though I was very sad for Hindley's sake; he had room in his heart only for two idols — his wife and himself — he doted on both, and adored one, and I couldn't conceive how he would bear the loss.

When we got to Wuthering Heights, there he stood at the front door; and, as I passed in, I asked how was the baby?

"Nearly ready to run about, Nell!" he replied, putting on a cheerful smile.

"And the mistress?" I ventured to inquire, "the doctor says she's — "

"Damn the doctor!" he interrupted, reddening. "Frances is quite right — she'll be perfectly well by this time next week. Are you going upstairs? will you tell her that I'll come, if she'll promise not to talk. I left her because she would not hold her tongue; and she must — tell her Mr. Kenneth says she must be quiet."

I delivered this message to Mrs. Earnshaw; she seemed in flighty spirits, and replied merrily —

"I hardly spoke a word, Ellen, and there he has gone out twice, crying. Well, say I promise I won't speak; but that does not bind me not to laugh at him!"

Poor soul! Till within a week of her death that gay heart never failed her; and her husband persisted doggedly, nay, furiously, in affirming her health improved every day. When Kenneth warned him that his medicines were useless at that stage of the malady, and he needn't put him to further expense by attending her, he retorted —

"I know you need not — she's well — she does not want any more attendance from you! She never was in a consumption. It was a fever; and it is gone — her pulse is as slow as mine now, and her cheek as cool."

He told his wife the same story, and she seemed to believe him; but one night, while leaning on his shoulder, in the act of saying she thought she should be able to get up to-morrow, a fit of coughing took her — a very slight one — he raised her in his arms; she put her two hands about his neck, her face changed, and she was dead.

As the girl had anticipated, the child, Hareton, fell wholly into my hands. Mr. Earnshaw, provided he saw him healthy, and never heard him cry, was contented, as far as regarded him. For himself, he grew desperate; his sorrow was of that kind that will not lament, he neither wept nor prayed — he cursed and defied — execrated God and man, and gave himself up to reckless dissipation.

The servants could not bear his tyrannical and evil conduct long: Joseph and I were the only two that would stay. I had not the heart to leave my charge; and besides, you know, I had been his foster sister, and excused his behaviour more readily than a stranger would.

Joseph remained to hector over tenants and labourers; and because it was his vocation to be where he had plenty of wickedness to reprove.

The master's bad ways and bad companions formed a pretty example for Catherine and Heathcliff. His treatment of the latter was enough to make a fiend of a saint. And, truly, it appeared as if the lad *were* possessed of something diabolical at that period. He delighted to witness Hindley degrading himself past redemption; and became daily more notable for savage sullenness and ferocity.

I could not half tell what an infernal house we had. The curate dropped calling, and nobody decent came near us, at last; unless Edgar Linton's visits to Miss Cathy might be an exception. At fifteen she was the queen of the country-side; she had no peer: and she did turn out a haughty, headstrong creature! I own I did not like her, after her infancy was past; and I vexed her frequently by trying to bring down her arrogance; she never took an aversion to me, though. She had a wondrous constancy to old attachments; even Heathcliff kept his hold on her affections unalterably, and young Linton, with all his superiority, found it difficult to make an equally deep impression.

He was my late master; that is his portrait over the fireplace. It used to hang on one side, and his wife's on the other; but hers has been removed, or else you might see something of what she was. Can you make that out?

Mrs. Dean raised the candle, and I discerned a soft-featured face, exceedingly resembling the young lady at the Heights, but more pensive and amiable in expression. It formed a sweet picture. The long light hair curled slightly on the temples; the eyes were large and serious; the figure almost too graceful. I did not marvel how Catherine Earnshaw could forget her first friend for such an individual. I marvelled much how he, with a mind to correspond with his person, could fancy my idea of Catherine Earnshaw.

"A very agreeable portrait," I observed to the housekeeper. "Is it like?"

"Yes," she answered; "but he looked better when he was animated; that is his every day countenance; he wanted spirit in general."

Catherine had kept up her acquaintance with the Lintons since her five weeks' residence among them; and as she had no temptation to show her rough side in their company, and had the sense to be ashamed of being rude where she experienced such invariable courtesy, she imposed unwittingly on the old lady and gentleman, by her ingenious cordiality; gained the admiration of Isabella, and the heart and soul of her brother — acquisitions that flattered her from the first, for she was full of ambition — and led her to adopt a double character without exactly intending to deceive any one.

In the place where she had heard Heathcliff termed a "vulgar young ruffian," and "worse than a brute," she took care not to act like him; but at home she had small inclination to practise politeness that would only be laughed at, and restrain an unruly nature when it would bring her neither credit nor praise.

Mr. Edgar seldom mustered courage to visit Wuthering Heights openly. He had a terror of Earnshaw's reputation, and shrunk from encountering him, and yet, he was always received with our best attempts at civility: the master himself avoided offending him — knowing why he came, and if he could not be gracious, kept out of the way. I rather think his appearance there was distasteful to Catherine; she was not artful, never played the coquette, and had evidently an objection to her two friends meeting at all: for when Heathcliff expressed contempt of Linton, in his presence, she could not half coincide, as she did in his absence; and when Linton evinced disgust and antipathy to Heathcliff, she dared not treat his sentiments with indifference, as if depreciation of her playmate were of scarcely any consequence to her.

I've had many a laugh at her perplexities and untold troubles, which she vainly strove to hide from my mockery. That sounds ill-natured — but she was so proud, it became really impossible to pity her distresses, till she should be chastened into more humility.

She did bring herself, finally, to confess, and confide in me. There was not a soul else that she might fashion into an adviser.

Mr. Hindley had gone from home, one afternoon; and Heathcliff presumed to give himself a holiday on the strength of it. He had reached the age of sixteen then, I think, and without having bad features or being deficient in intellect, he contrived to convey an impression of inward and outward repulsiveness that his present aspect retains no traces of.

In the first place, he had, by that time, lost the benefit of his early education: continual hard work, begun soon and concluded late, had extinguished any curiosity he once possessed in pursuit of knowledge, and any love for books or learning. His childhood's sense of superiority, instilled into him by the favours of old Mr. Earnshaw, was faded away. He struggled long to keep up an equality with Catherine in her studies and yielded with poignant though silent regret: but he yielded completely; and there was no prevailing on him to take a step in the way of moving upward, when he found he must, necessarily, sink beneath his former level. Then personal appearance sympathised with mental deterioration; he acquired a slouching gait, and ignoble look; his naturally reserved disposition was exaggerated into an almost idiotic excess of unsociable moroseness; and he took a grim pleasure, apparently, in exciting the aversion rather than the esteem of his few acquaintance.

Catherine and he were constant companions still, at his seasons of respite from labour; but he had ceased to express his fondness for her in words, and recoiled with angry suspicion from her girlish caresses, as if conscious there could be no gratification in lavishing such marks of affection on him. On the before-named occasion he came into the house to announce his intention of doing nothing, while I was assisting Miss Cathy to arrange her dress — she had not reckoned on his taking it into his head to be idle, and imagining she would have the whole place to herself, she managed, by some means, to inform Mr. Edgar of her brother's absence, and was then preparing to receive him.

"Cathy, are you busy this afternoon?" asked Heathcliff. "Are you going anywhere?"

"No, it is raining," she answered.

"Why have you that silly frock on, then?" he said, "Nobody coming here, I hope?"

"Not that I know of," stammered Miss, "but you should be in the field now, Heathcliff. It is an hour past dinner time; I thought you were gone."

"Hindley does not often free us from his accursed presence," observed the boy, "I'll not work any more to-day, I'll stay with you."

"Oh, but Joseph will tell," she suggested; "you'd better go!"

"Joseph is loading lime on the farther side of Pennistow Crag; it will take him till dark, and he'll never know."

So saying, he lounged by the fire, and sat down. Catherine reflected an instant, with knitted brows — she found it needful to smooth the way for an intrusion.

"Isabella and Edgar Linton talked of calling this afternoon," she said at the conclusion of a minute's silence. "As it rains, I hardly expect them; but, they may come, and if they do, you run the risk of being scolded for no good."

"Order Ellen to say you are engaged, Cathy," he persisted. "Don't turn me out for those pitiful, silly friends of yours! I'm on the point, sometimes, of complaining that they — but I'll not — "

"That they what?" cried Catherine, gazing at him with a troubled countenance. "Oh, Nelly!" she added petulantly, jerking her head away from my hands, "you've combed my hair quite out of curl! That's enough, let me alone. What are you on the point of complaining about, Heathcliff?"

"Nothing — only look at the almanack, on that wall." He pointed to a framed sheet hanging near the window, and continued:

"The crosses are for the evenings you have spent with the Lintons, the dots for those spent with me — Do you see, I've marked every day?"

"Yes — very foolish; as if I took notice!" replied Catherine in a peevish tone. "And where is the sense of that?"

"To show that I *do* take notice," said Heathcliff.

"And should I always be sitting with you?" she demanded, growing more irritated. "What good do I get — What do you talk about? You might be dumb or a baby for anything you say to amuse me, or for anything you do, either!"

"You never told me before that I talked too little, or that you disliked my company, Cathy!" exclaimed Heathcliff in much agitation.

"It's no company at all, when people know nothing and say nothing," she muttered.

Her companion rose up, but he hadn't time to express his feelings further, for a horse's feet were heard on the flags, and, having knocked gently, young Linton entered, his face brilliant with delight at the unexpected summons he had received.

Doubtless Catherine marked the difference between her friends as one came in, and the other went out. The contrast resembled what you see in exchanging a bleak, hilly, coal country for a beautiful fertile valley; and his voice and greeting were as opposite as his aspect — He had a sweet, low manner of speaking, and pronounced his words as you do, that's less gruff than we talk here and softer.

"I'm not come too soon, am I?" he said, casting a look at me. I had begun to wipe the plate, and tidy some drawers at the far end in the dresser.

"No," answered Catherine. "What are you doing there, Nelly?"

"My work, Miss," I replied. (Mr. Hindley had given me directions to make a third party in any private visits Linton chose to pay.)

She stepped behind me and whispered crossly, "Take yourself and your dusters off! when company are in the house, servants don't commence scouring and cleaning in the room where they are!"

"It's a good opportunity, now that master is away," I answered aloud; "he hates me to be fidgeting over things in his presence — I'm sure Mr. Edgar will excuse me."

"I hate you to be fidgeting in *my* presence," exclaimed the young lady imperiously, not allowing her guest time to speak — she had failed to recover her equanimity since the little dispute with Heathcliff.

"I'm sorry for it, Miss Catherine!" was my response; and I proceeded assiduously with my occupation.

She, supposing Edgar could not see her, snatched the cloth from my hand, and pinched me, with a prolonged wrench, very spitefully on the arm.

I've said I did not love her, and rather relished mortifying her vanity, now and then; besides, she hurt me extremely, so I started up from my knees, and screamed out.

"Oh, Miss, that's a nasty trick! you have no right to nip me, and I'm not going to bear it!"

"I didn't touch you, you lying creature!" cried she, her fingers tingling to repeat the act, and her ears red with rage. She never had power to conceal her passion, it always set her whole complexion in a blaze.

"What's that, then?" I retorted, showing a decided purple witness to refute her.

She stamped her foot, wavered a moment, and then, irresistibly impelled by the naughty spirit within her, slapped me on the cheek a stinging blow that filled both eyes with water.

"Catherine, love! Catherine!" interposed Linton, greatly shocked at the double assault of falsehood and violence which his idol had committed.

"Leave the room, Ellen!" she repeated, trembling all over.

Little Hareton, who followed me everywhere, and was sitting near me on the floor, at seeing my tears commenced crying himself, and sobbed out complaints against "wicked aunt Cathy," which drew her fury on to his unlucky head: she seized his shoulders, and shook him till the poor child waxed livid, and Edgar thoughtlessly laid hold of her hands to deliver him. In an instant one was wrung free, and the astonished young man felt it applied over his own ear in a way that could not be mistaken for jest.

He drew back in consternation — I lifted Hareton in my arms, and walked off to the kitchen with him, leaving the door of communication open, for I was curious to watch how they would settle their disagreement.

The insulted visitor moved to the spot where he had laid his hat, pale and with a quivering lip.

"That's right," I said to myself, "Take warning and begone! It's a kindness to let you have a glimpse of her genuine disposition."

"Where are you going?" demanded Catherine, advancing to the door.

He swerved aside and attempted to pass.

"You must not go!" she exclaimed energetically.

"I must and shall!" he replied in a subdued voice.

"No," she persisted, grasping the handle; "not yet, Edgar Linton — sit down, you shall not leave me in that temper. I should be miserable all night, and I won't be miserable for you!"

"Can I stay after you have struck me?" asked Linton.

Catherine was mute.

"You've made me afraid, and ashamed of you," he continued; "I'll not come here again!"

Her eyes began to glisten and her lids to twinkle.

"And you told a deliberate untruth!" he said.

"I didn't!" she cried, recovering her speech. "I did nothing deliberately — Well, go, if you please — get away! And now I'll cry — I'll cry myself sick!"

She dropped down on her knees by a chair and set to weeping in serious earnest.

Edgar persevered in his resolution as far as the court; there, he lingered. I resolved to encourage him.

"Miss is dreadfully wayward, sir!" I called out. "As bad as any marred child° — you'd better be riding home, or else she will be sick, only to grieve us."

marred child: Spoiled child.

The soft thing looked askance through the window — he possessed the power to depart, as much as a cat possesses the power to leave a mouse half killed, or a bird half eaten.

Ah, I thought, there will be no saving him — He's doomed, and flies to his fate!

And, so it was; he turned abruptly, hastened into the house again, shut the door behind him; and, when I went in a while after to inform them that Earnshaw had come home rabid drunk, ready to pull the old place about our ears (his ordinary frame of mind in that condition), I saw the quarrel had merely effected a closer intimacy — had broken the outworks of youthful timidity, and enabled them to forsake the disguise of friendship, and confess themselves lovers.

Intelligence of Mr. Hindley's arrival drove Linton speedily to his horse, and Catherine to her chamber. I went to hide little Hareton, and to take the shot out of the master's fowling piece which he was fond of playing with in his insane excitement, to the hazard of the lives of any who provoked, or even attracted his notice too much; and I had hit upon the plan of removing it, that he might do less mischief, if he did go the length of firing the gun.

CHAPTER 9

He entered, vociferating oaths dreadful to hear; and caught me in the act of stowing his son away in the kitchen cupboard. Hareton was impressed with a wholesome terror of encountering either his wild-beast's fondness, or his madman's rage — for in one he ran a chance of being squeezed and kissed to death, and in the other of being flung into the fire, or dashed against the wall — and the poor thing remained perfectly quiet wherever I chose to put him.

"There, I've found it out at last!" cried Hindley, pulling me back by the skin of my neck, like a dog. "By heaven and hell, you've sworn between you to murder that child! I know how it is, now, that he is always out of my way. But with the help of Satan, I shall make you swallow the carving knife, Nelly! You needn't laugh, for, I've just crammed Kenneth, head-downmost, in the Blackhorse marsh; and two is the same as one — and I want to kill some of you, I shall have no rest till I do!"

"But I don't like the carving knife, Mr. Hindley," I answered, "it has been cutting red herrings — I'd rather be shot if you please."

"You'd rather be damned!" he said, "and so you shall — no law in England can hinder a man from keeping his house decent, and mine's abominable! open your mouth."

He held the knife in his hand, and pushed its point between my teeth: but, for my part, I was never much afraid of his vagaries. I spat it out, and affirmed it tasted detestably — I would not take it on any account.

"Oh!" said he, releasing me, "I see that hideous little villain is not Hareton — I beg your pardon, Nell — if it be, he deserves flaying alive for not running to welcome me, and for screaming as if I were a goblin. Unnatural cub, come hither! I'll teach thee to impose on a good-hearted, deluded father — Now, don't you think the lad would be handsomer cropped? It makes a dog fiercer, and I love something fierce — Get me a scissors — something fierce and trim! Besides, it's infernal affectation — devilish conceit it is, to cherish our ears — we're asses enough without them. Hush, child, hush! well, then, it is my darling! wisht,° dry thy eyes — there's a joy; kiss me; what! it won't? kiss me, Hareton! Damn thee, kiss me! By God, as if I would rear such a monster! As sure as I'm living, I'll break the brat's neck."

Poor Hareton was squalling and kicking in his father's arms with all his might, and redoubled his yells when he carried him upstairs and lifted him over the banister. I cried out that he would frighten the child into fits, and ran to rescue him.

As I reached them, Hindley leant forward on the rails to listen to a noise below: almost forgetting what he had in his hands.

"Who is that?" he asked, hearing some one approaching the stair's-foot.

I leant forward, also, for the purpose of signing to Heathcliff, whose step I recognized, not to come further; and, at the instant when my eye quitted Hareton, he gave a sudden spring, delivered himself from the careless grasp that held him, and fell.

There was scarcely time to experience a thrill of horror before we saw that the little wretch was safe. Heathcliff arrived underneath just at the critical moment; by a natural impulse, he arrested his descent, and setting him on his feet, looked up to discover the author of the accident.

A miser who has parted with a lucky lottery ticket for five shillings and finds next day he has lost in the bargain five thousand pounds,

wisht: Hush.

could not show a blanker countenance than he did on beholding the figure of Mr. Earnshaw above — It expressed, plainer than words could do, the intensest anguish at having made himself the instrument of thwarting his own revenge. Had it been dark, I dare say, he would have tried to remedy the mistake by smashing Hareton's skull on the steps; but, we witnessed his salvation; and I was presently below with my precious charge pressed to my heart.

Hindley descended more leisurely, sobered and abashed.

"It is your fault, Ellen," he said, "you should have kept him out of sight; you should have taken him from me! Is he injured anywhere?"

"Injured!" I cried, angrily. "If he's not killed, he'll be an idiot! Oh! I wonder his mother does not rise from her grave to see how you use him. You're worse than a heathen — treating your own flesh and blood in that manner!"

He attempted to touch the child, who, on finding himself with me, sobbed off his terror directly. At the first finger his father laid on him, however, he shrieked again louder than before, and struggled as if he would go into convulsions.

"You shall not meddle with him!" I continued. "He hates you — they all hate you — that's the truth! A happy family you have; and a pretty state you're come to!"

"I shall come to a prettier yet, Nelly!" laughed the misguided man, recovering his hardness. "At present, convey yourself and him away — And, hark you, Heathcliff! clear you too, quite from my reach and hearing . . . I wouldn't murder you tonight, unless, perhaps, I set the house on fire; but that's as my fancy goes — "

While saying this, he took a pint bottle of brandy from the dresser, and poured some into a tumbler.

"Nay, don't!" I entreated, "Mr. Hindley, do take warning. Have mercy on this unfortunate boy, if you care nothing for yourself!"

"Any one will do better for him, than I shall," he answered.

"Have mercy on your own soul!" I said, endeavouring to snatch the glass from his hand.

"Not I! on the contrary, I shall have great pleasure in sending it to perdition, to punish its maker," exclaimed the blasphemer. "Here's to its hearty damnation!"

He drank the spirits, and impatiently bade us go; terminating his command with a sequel of horrid imprecations, too bad to repeat, or remember.

"It's a pity he cannot kill himself with drink," observed Heathcliff, muttering an echo of curses back when the door was shut. "He's doing his very utmost; but his constitution defies him — Mr. Kenneth says he would wager his mare, that he'll outlive any man on this side Gimmerton, and go to the grave a hoary sinner; unless, some happy chance out of the common course befall him."

I went into the kitchen and sat down to lull my little lamb to sleep. Heathcliff, as I thought, walked through to the barn. It turned out, afterwards, that he only got as far as the other side the settle, when he flung himself on a bench by the wall, removed from the fire, and remained silent.

I was rocking Hareton on my knee, and humming a song that began,

"It was far in the night, and the bairnies grat,°
The mither° beneath the mools° heard that."

when Miss Cathy, who had listened to the hubbub from her room, put her head in, and whispered,

"Are you alone, Nelly?"

"Yes, Miss," I replied.

She entered and approached the hearth. I, supposing she was going to say something, looked up. The expression of her face seemed disturbed and anxious. Her lips were half asunder, as if she meant to speak; and she drew a breath, but it escaped in a sigh, instead of a sentence.

I resumed my song, not having forgotten her recent behaviour.

"Where's Heathcliff?" she said, interrupting me.

"About his work in the stable," was my answer.

He did not contradict me; perhaps he had fallen into a doze.

There followed another long pause, during which I perceived a drop or two trickle from Catherine's cheek to the flags.

Is she sorry for her shameful conduct? I asked myself. That will be a novelty, but she may come to the point as she will — I shan't help her!

No, she felt small trouble regarding any subject, save her own concerns.

"Oh, dear!" she cried at last, "I'm very unhappy!"

"A pity," observed I, "you're hard to please — so many friends and so few cares, and can't make yourself content!"

"Nelly, will you keep a secret for me?" she pursued, kneeling down by me, and lifting her winsome eyes to my face with that sort of look when turns off bad temper, even when one has all the right in the world to indulge it.

bairnies grat: Little children cried. ***mither:*** Mother. ***mools:*** Mould, earth.

"Is it worth keeping?" I inquired, less sulkily.

"Yes, and it worries me, and I must let it out! I want to know what I should do — To-day, Edgar Linton has asked me to marry him, and I've given him an answer — Now, before I tell you whether it was a consent, or denial — you tell me which it ought to have been."

"Really, Miss Catherine, how can I know?" I replied. "To be sure, considering the exhibition you performed in his presence, this afternoon, I might say it would be wise to refuse him — since he asked you after that, he must either be hopelessly stupid, or a venturesome fool."

"If you talk so, I won't tell you any more," she returned, peevishly, rising to her feet. "I accepted him, Nelly. Be quick, and say whether I was wrong!"

"You accepted him? then what good is it discussing the matter? You have pledged your word, and cannot retract."

"But, say whether I should have done so — do!" she exclaimed in an irritated tone; chafing her hands together, and frowning.

"There are many things to be considered, before that question can be answered properly," I said sententiously. "First and foremost, do you love Mr. Edgar?"

"Who can help it? Of course I do," she answered.

Then I put her though the following catechism — for a girl of twenty-two it was not injudicious.

"Why do you love him, Miss Cathy?"

"Nonsense, I do — that's sufficient."

"By no means; you must say why?"

"Well, because he is handsome, and pleasant to be with."

"Bad," was my commentary.

"And because he is young and cheerful."

"Bad, still."

"And, because he loves me."

"Indifferent, coming there."

"And he will be rich, and I shall like to be the greatest woman of the neighbourhood, and I shall be proud of having such a husband."

"Worst of all! And, now, say how you love him?"

"As everybody loves — You're silly, Nelly."

"Not at all — Answer."

"I love the ground under his feet, and the air over his head, and everything he touches, and every word he says — I love all his looks, and all his actions, and him entirely, and altogether. There now!"

"And why?"

"Nay — you are making a jest of it; it is exceedingly ill-natured! It's no jest to me!" said the young lady, scowling, and turning her face to the fire.

"I'm very far from jesting, Miss Catherine," I replied, "you love Mr. Edgar, because he is handsome, and young, and cheerful, and rich, and loves you. The last, however goes for nothing — You would love him without that, probably, and with it, you wouldn't, unless he possessed the four former attractions."

"No, to be sure not — I should only pity him — hate him, perhaps, if he were ugly, and a clown."

"But there are several other handsome, rich young men in the world; handsomer, possibly, and richer than he is — What should hinder you from loving them?"

"If there be any, they are out of my way — I've seen none like Edgar."

"You may see some; and he won't always be handsome, and young, and may not always be rich."

"He is now; and I have only to do with the present — I wish you would speak rationally."

"Well, that settles it — If you have only to do with the present, marry Mr. Linton."

"I don't want your permission for that — I *shall* marry him; and yet, you have not told me whether I'm right."

"Perfectly right; if people be right to marry only for the present. And now, let us hear what you are unhappy about. Your brother will be pleased . . . The old lady and gentleman will not object, I think — you will escape from a disorderly, comfortless home into a wealthy, respectable one; and you love Edgar, and Edgar loves you. All seems smooth and easy — where is the obstacle?"

"*Here!* and *here!*" replied Catherine, striking one hand on her forehead, and the other on her breast. "In whichever place the soul lives — in my soul, and in my heart, I'm convinced I'm wrong!"

"That is very strange! I cannot make it out."

"It's my secret; but if you will not mock me, I'll explain it; I can't do it distinctly — but I'll give you a feeling of how I feel."

She seated herself by me again: her countenance grew sadder and graver, and her clasped hands trembled.

"Nelly, do you never dream queer dreams?" she said, suddenly, after some minutes' reflection.

"Yes, now and then," I answered.

"And so do I. I've dreamt in my life dreams that have stayed with me ever after, and changed my ideas; they've gone through and through me, like wine through water, and altered the colour of my mind. And this is one — I'm going to tell it — but take care not to smile at any part of it."

"Oh! don't, Miss Catherine!" I cried. "We're dismal enough without conjuring up ghosts and visions to perplex us. Come, come, be merry, and like yourself! Look at little Hareton — *he's* dreaming nothing dreary. How sweetly he smiles in his sleep!"

"Yes; and how sweetly his father curses in his solitude! You remember him, I dare say, when he was just such another as that chubby thing — nearly as young and innocent. However, Nelly, I shall oblige you to listen — it's not long; and I've no power to be merry to-night."

"I won't hear it, I won't hear it!" I repeated, hastily.

I was superstitious about dreams then, and am still; and Catherine had an unusual gloom in her aspect, that made me dread something from which I might shape a prophecy, and foresee a fearful catastrophe.

She was vexed, but she did not proceed. Apparently taking up another subject, she re-commenced in a short time.

"If I were in heaven, Nelly, I should be extremely miserable."

"Because you are not fit to go there," I answered. "All sinners would be miserable in heaven."

"But it is not for that. I dreamt, once, that I was there."

"I tell you I won't hearken to your dreams, Miss Catherine! I'll go to bed," I interrupted again.

She laughed, and held me down, for I made a motion to leave my chair.

"This is nothing," cried she; "I was only going to say that heaven did not seem to be my home; and I broke my heart with weeping to come back to earth; and the angels were so angry that they flung me out, into the middle of the heath on the top of Wuthering Heights; where I woke sobbing for joy. That will do to explain my secret, as well as the other. I've no more business to marry Edgar Linton than I have to be in heaven; and if the wicked man in there had not brought Heathcliff so low, I shouldn't have thought of it. It would degrade me to marry Heathcliff, now; so he shall never know how I love him; and that, not because he's handsome, Nelly, but because he's more myself than I am. Whatever our souls are made of, his and mine are the same, and Linton's is as different as a moonbeam from lightning, or frost from fire."

Ere this speech ended, I became sensible of Heathcliff's presence. Having noticed a slight movement, I turned my head, and saw him rise from the bench, and steal out, noiselessly. He had listened till he heard Catherine say it would degrade her to marry him, and then he stayed to hear no farther.

My companion, sitting on the ground, was prevented by the back of the settle from remarking his presence or departure; but I started, and bade her hush!

"Why?" she asked, gazing nervously around.

"Joseph is here," I answered, catching, opportunely, the roll of his cartwheels up the road; "and Heathcliff will come in with him. I'm not sure whether he was not at the door this moment."

"Oh, he couldn't overhear me at the door!" said she. "Give me Hareton, while you get the supper, and when it is ready ask me to sup with you. I want to cheat my uncomfortable conscience, and be convinced that Heathcliff has no notion of these things — he has not, has he? He does not know what being in love is?"

"I see no reason that he should not know, as well as you," I returned; "and if *you* are his choice, he'll be the most unfortunate creature that was ever born! As soon as you become Mrs. Linton, he loses friend, and love, and all! Have you considered how you'll bear the separation, and how he'll bear to be quite deserted in the world? Because, Miss Catherine — "

"He quite deserted! we separated!" she exclaimed, with an accent of indignation. "Who is to separate us, pray? They'll meet the fate of Milo! Not as long as I live, Ellen — for no mortal creature. Every Linton on the face of the earth might melt into nothing, before I could consent to forsake Heathcliff. Oh, that's not what I intend — that's not what I mean! I shouldn't be Mrs. Linton were such a price demanded! He'll be as much to me as he has been all his lifetime. Edgar must shake off his antipathy, and tolerate him, at least. He will when he learns my true feelings towards him. Nelly, I see now, you think me a selfish wretch, but did it never strike you that, if Heathcliff and I married, we should be beggars? whereas, if I marry Linton, I can aid Heathcliff to rise, and place him out of my brother's power."

"With your husband's money, Miss Catherine?" I asked. "You'll find him not so pliable as you calculate upon: and, though I'm hardly a judge, I think that's the worst motive you've given yet for being the wife of young Linton."

"It is not," retorted she, "it is the best! The others were the satisfaction of my whims; and for Edgar's sake, too, to satisfy him. This is for the sake of one who comprehends in his person my feelings to Edgar and myself. I cannot express it; but surely you and everybody have a notion that there is, or should be an existence of yours beyond you. What were the use of my creation if I were entirely contained here? My great miseries in this world have been Heathcliff's miseries, and I watched and felt each from the beginning; my great thought in living is himself. If all else perished, and *he* remained, I should still continue to be; and, if all else remained, and he were annihilated, the Universe would turn to a mighty stranger. I should not seem a part of it. My love for Linton is like the foliage in the woods. Time will change it, I'm well aware, as winter changes the trees — my love for Heathcliff resembles the eternal rocks beneath — a source of little visible delight, but necessary. Nelly, I *am* Heathcliff — he's always, always in my mind — not as a pleasure, any more than I am always a pleasure to myself — but, as my own being — so, don't talk of our separation again — it is impracticable; and — "

She paused, and hid her face in the folds of my gown; but I jerked it forcibly away. I was out of patience with her folly!

"If I can make sense of your nonsense, Miss," I said, "it only goes to convince me that you are ignorant of the duties you undertake in marrying; or else, that you are a wicked, unprincipled girl. But trouble me with no more secrets. I'll not promise to keep them."

"You'll keep that?" she asked, eagerly.

"No, I'll not promise," I repeated.

She was about to insist, when the entrance of Joseph finished our conversation; and Catherine removed her seat to a corner, and nursed Hareton, while I made the supper.

After it was cooked, my fellow servant and I began to quarrel who should carry some to Mr. Hindley; and we didn't settle it till all was nearly cold. Then we came to the agreement that we would let him ask, if he wanted any, for we feared particularly to go into his presence when he had been some time alone.

"Und hah isn't that nowt comed in frough th' field,° be this time? What is he abaht? girt eedle seeght!"° demanded the old man, looking round for Heathcliff.

"I'll call him," I replied. "He's in the barn, I've no doubt."

I went and called, but got no answer. On returning, I whispered to Catherine that he had heard a good part of what she said, I was sure; and told how I saw him quit the kitchen just as she complained of her brother's conduct regarding him.

"Und hah isn't that nowt comed in frough th' field: And how is it that nothing [has] come in from the field. ***girt eedle seeght:*** Great idle sight.

She jumped up in a fine fright — flung Hareton onto the settle, and ran to seek for her friend herself, not taking leisure to consider why she was so flurried, or how her talk would have affected him.

She was absent such a while that Joseph proposed we should wait no longer. He cunningly conjectured they were staying away in order to avoid hearing his protracted blessing. They were "ill eneugh for ony fahl manners," he affirmed. And, on their behalf, he added that night a special prayer to the usual quarter of an hour's supplication before meat, and would have tacked another to the end of the grace, had not his young mistress broken in upon him with a hurried command that he must run down the road, and, wherever Heathcliff had rambled, find and make him re-enter directly!

"I want to speak to him, and I *must,* before I go upstairs," she said. "And the gate is open, he is somewhere out of hearing; for he would not reply, though I shouted at the top of the fold as loud as I could."

Joseph objected at first; she was too much in earnest, however, to suffer contradiction; and, at last he placed his hat on his head, and walked grumbling forth.

Meantime, Catherine paced up and down the floor, exclaiming —

"I wonder where he is — I wonder where he *can* be! What did I say, Nelly? I've forgotten. Was he vexed at my bad humour this afternoon? Dear! tell me what I've said to grieve him? I do wish he'd come. I do wish he would!"

"What a noise for nothing!" I cried, though rather uneasy myself. "What a trifle scares you! It's surely no great cause of alarm that Heathcliff should take a moonlight saunter on the moors, or even lie too sulky to speak to us in the hay-loft. I'll engage he's lurking there. See if I don't ferret him out!"

I departed to renew my search; its result was disappointment, and Joseph's quest ended in the same.

"Yon lad gets war un war!"° observed he on re-entering. "He's left th' yate° ut t' full swing, and miss's pony has trodden dahn two rigs° uh corn, un plottered° through, raight o'er intuh t' meadow! Hahsomdiver, t' maister 'ull play t' divil to-morn, and he'll do weel. He's patience itsseln wi' sich careless, offald craters° — patience itsseln he is! Bud he'll nut be soa allus — yah's see, all on ye! Yah mumn't drive him aht uf his heead fur nowt!"

war un war: Worse and worse. ***yate:*** Gate. ***rigs:*** The elevation between each pair of plough-furrows in a field. ***plottered:*** Plodded. ***careless, offald craters:*** Careless, worthless creatures.

"Have you found Heathcliff, you ass?" interrupted Catherine. "Have you been looking for him, as I ordered?"

"Aw sud more likker° look for th' horse," he replied. "It 'ud be tuh more sense. Bud, aw can look for norther horse, nur man uf a neeght loike this° — as black as t' chimbley! und Hathecliff's noan t' chap tuh coom ut *maw* whistle — happen he'll be less hard uh hearing wi' *ye!*"

It *was* a very dark evening for summer: the clouds appeared inclined to thunder, and I said we had better all sit down; the approaching rain would be certain to bring him home without further trouble.

However, Catherine would not be persuaded into tranquillity. She kept wandering to and fro, from the gate to the door, in a state of agitation which permitted no repose; and, at length, took up a permanent position on one side of the wall, near the road; where, heedless of my expostulations, and the growling thunder, and the great drops that began to plash around her, she remained calling, at intervals, and then listening, and then crying outright. She beat Hareton, or any child, at a good, passionate fit of crying.

About midnight, while we still sat up, the storm came rattling over the Heights in full fury. There was a violent wind, as well as thunder, and either one or the other split a tree off at the corner of the building; a huge bough fell across the roof, and knocked down a portion of the east chimney-stack, sending a clatter of stones and soot into the kitchen fire.

We thought a bolt had fallen in the middle of us, and Joseph swung onto his knees, beseeching the Lord to remember the Patriarchs Noah and Lot; and, as in former times, spare the righteous, though he smote the ungodly. I felt some sentiment that it must be a judgment on us also. The Jonah, in my mind, was Mr. Earnshaw, and I shook the handle of his den that I might ascertain if he were yet living. He replied audibly enough, in a fashion which made my companion vociferate more clamorously than before that a wide distinction might be drawn between saints like himself and sinners like his master. But the uproar passed away in twenty minutes, leaving us all unharmed, excepting Cathy, who got thoroughly drenched for her obstinacy in refusing to take shelter, and standing bonnetless and shawlless to catch as much water as she could with her hair and clothes.

She came in, and lay down on the settle, all soaked as she was, turning her face to the back, and putting her hands before it.

Aw sud more likker: I should more likely. ***norther horse, nur man uf a neeght loike this:*** Neither horse nor man on a night like this.

"Well, Miss!" I exclaimed, touching her shoulder. "You are not bent on getting your death, are you? Do you know what o'clock it is? Half-past twelve. Come! come to bed; there's no use waiting longer on that foolish boy — he'll be gone to Gimmerton, and he'll stay there now. He guesses we shouldn't wake° for him till this late hour; at least, he guesses that only Mr. Hindley would be up; and he'd rather avoid having the door opened by the master."

"Nay, nay, he's noan at Gimmerton!" said Joseph. "Aw's niver wonder, bud he's at t' bothom uf a bog-hoile.° This visitation worn't for nowt, and Aw wod hev ye tuh look aht, Miss — yah muh be t' next. Thank Hivin for all! All warks togither for gooid tuh them as is chozzen, and piked aht froo' th' rubbidge!° Yah knaw whet t' Scripture ses — "

And he began quoting several texts; referring us to the chapters and verses, where we might find them.

I, having vainly begged the wilful girl to rise and remove her wet things, left him preaching, and her shivering, and betook myself to bed with little Hareton; who slept as fast as if every one had been sleeping round him.

I heard Joseph read on a while afterwards; then, I distinguished his slow step on the ladder, and then I dropt asleep.

Coming down somewhat later than usual, I saw, by the sunbeams piercing the chinks of the shutters, Miss Catherine still seated near the fire-place. The house door was ajar, too; light entered from its unclosed windows; Hindley had come out, and stood on the kitchen hearth, haggard and drowsy.

"What ails you, Cathy?" he was saying when I entered; "You look as dismal as a drowned whelp — Why are you so damp and pale, child?"

"I've been wet," she answered reluctantly, "and I'm cold, that's all."

"Oh, she is naughty!" I cried, perceiving the master to be tolerably sober; "She got steeped in the shower of yesterday evening, and there she has sat, the night through, and I couldn't prevail on her to stir."

Mr. Earnshaw stared at us in surprise. "The night through," he repeated. "What kept her up, not fear of the thunder, surely? That was over, hours since."

Neither of us wished to mention Heathcliff's absence, as long as we could conceal it; so, I replied, I didn't know how she took it into her head to sit up; and she said nothing.

wake: Wait up, stand watch. ***bothom uf a bog-hoile:*** Bottom of a bog hole. ***piked aht froo' th' rubbidge:*** Picked out from the rubbish.

The morning was fresh and cool; I threw back the lattice, and presently the room filled with sweet scents from the garden: but Catherine called peevishly to me.

"Ellen, shut the window. I'm starving!" And her teeth chattered as she shrunk closer to the almost extinguished embers.

"She's ill — " said Hindley, taking her wrist; "I suppose that's the reason she would not go to bed — Damn it! I don't want to be troubled with more sickness, here — What took you into the rain?"

"Running after t' lads, as usuald!" croaked Joseph, catching an opportunity, from our hesitation, to thrust in his evil tongue. "If Aw wur yah, maister, Aw'd just slam t' boards° i' their faces all on 'em, gentle and simple! Never a day ut yah're off, but yon cat uh Linton comes sneaking hither — and Miss Nelly, shoo's a fine lass! shoo° sits watching for ye i' t' kitchen; and as yah're in at one door, he's aht at t' other — Und, then, wer° grand lady goes a coorting uf hor side! It's bonny behaviour, lurking amang t' fields, after twelve ut night, wi' that fahl, flaysome divil uf a gipsy, Heathcliff! They think *Aw'm* blind; but Aw'm noan, nowt ut t' soart! Aw seed young Linton, boath coming and going, and Aw seed *yah*" (directing his discourse to me). "Yah gooid fur nowt, slattenly witch! nip up and bolt intuh th' hahs,° t' minute yah heard t' maister's horse fit° clatter up t' road."

"Silence, eavesdropper!" cried Catherine, "None of your insolence, before me! Edgar Linton came yesterday, by chance, Hindley: and it was *I* who told him to be off: because I knew you would not like to have met him as you were."

"You lie, Cathy, no doubt," answered her brother, "and you are a confounded simpleton! But never mind Linton at present — Tell me, were you not with Heathcliff last night? Speak the truth, now. You need not be afraid of harming him — though I hate him as much as ever, he did me a good turn, a short time since, that will make my conscience tender of breaking his neck. To prevent it, I shall send him about his business, this very morning; and after he's gone, I'll advise you to look sharp, I shall only have the more humour for you."

"I never saw Heathcliff last night," answered Catherine, beginning to sob bitterly: "and if you do turn him out of doors, I'll go with him. But, perhaps, you'll never have an opportunity — perhaps, he's gone." Here she burst into uncontrollable grief, and the remainder of her words were inarticulate.

t' boards: The doors. ***shoo's . . . shoo:*** She's, she,. ***wer:*** Our. ***hahs:*** House. ***horse fit:*** Horse's feet.

Hindley lavished on her a torrent of scornful abuse, and bid her get to her room immediately, or she shouldn't cry for nothing! I obliged her to obey; and I shall never forget what a scene she acted, when we reached her chamber. It terrified me — I thought she was going mad, and I begged Joseph to run for the doctor.

It proved the commencement of delirium; Mr. Kenneth, as soon as he saw her, pronounced her dangerously ill; she had a fever.

He bled her, and he told me to let her live on whey and water gruel; and take care she did not throw herself down stairs, or out of the window; and then he left, for he had enough to do in the parish where two or three miles was the ordinary distance between cottage and cottage.

Though I cannot say I make a gentle nurse, and Joseph and the master were no better; and though our patient was as wearisome and headstrong as a patient could be, she weathered it through.

Old Mrs. Linton paid us several visits, to be sure, and set things to rights, and scolded, and ordered us all; and when Catherine was convalescent, she insisted on conveying her to Thrushcross Grange; for which deliverance we were very grateful. But the poor dame had reason to repent of her kindness; she, and her husband, both took the fever, and died within a few days of each other.

Our young lady returned to us, saucier, and more passionate, and haughtier than ever. Heathcliff had never been heard of since the evening of the thunder-storm, and, one day, I had the misfortune, when she provoked me exceedingly, to lay the blame of his disappearance on her (where indeed it belonged, as she well knew). From that period for several months, she ceased to hold any communication with me, save in the relation of a mere servant. Joseph fell under a ban also; he *would* speak his mind, and lecture her all the same as if she were a little girl; and she esteemed herself a woman, and our mistress, and thought that her recent illness gave her a claim to be treated with consideration. Then the doctor had said that she would not bear crossing much, she ought to have her own way; and it was nothing less than murder, in her eyes, for any one to presume to stand up and contradict her.

From Mr. Earnshaw and his companions she kept aloof, and tutored by Kenneth, and serious threats of a fit that often attended her rages, her brother allowed her whatever she pleased to demand, and generally avoided aggravating her fiery temper. He was rather *too* indulgent in humouring her caprices; not from affection, but from pride; he wished earnestly to see her bring honor to the family by an alliance with the Lintons, and, as long as she let him alone, she might trample us like slaves for ought he cared!

Edgar Linton, as multitudes have been before and will be after him, was infatuated; and believed himself the happiest man alive on the day he led her to Gimmerton Chapel, three years subsequent to his father's death.

Much against my inclination, I was persuaded to leave Wuthering Heights and accompany her here. Little Hareton was nearly five years old, and I had just begun to teach him his letters. We made a sad parting, but Catherine's tears were more powerful than ours — When I refused to go, and when she found her entreaties did not move me, she went lamenting to her husband and brother. The former offered me munificent wages; the latter ordered me to pack up — he wanted no women in the house, he said, now that there was no mistress; and as to Hareton, the curate should take him in hand, by and by. And so, I had but one choice left, to do as I was ordered — I told the master he got rid of all decent people only to run to ruin a little faster; I kissed Hareton good-bye; and since then, he has been a stranger, and it's very queer to think it, but I've no doubts, he has completely forgotten all about Ellen Dean and that he was ever more than all the world to her, and she to him!

At this point of the housekeeper's story she chanced to glance towards the time-piece over the chimney; and was in amazement, on seeing the minute-hand measure half past one. She would not hear of staying a second longer — In truth, I felt rather disposed to defer the sequel of her narrative, myself: and now, that she is vanished to her rest, and I have meditated for another hour or two, I shall summon courage to go, also, in spite of aching laziness of head and limbs.

CHAPTER 10

A charming introduction to a hermit's life! Four weeks' torture, tossing and sickness! Oh, these bleak winds, and bitter, northern skies, and impassable roads, and dilatory country surgeons! And, oh, this dearth of the human physiognomy, and, worse than all, the terrible intimation of Kenneth that I need not expect to be out of doors till spring!

Mr. Heathcliff has just honoured me with a call. About seven days ago he sent me a brace of grouse — the last of the season. Scoundrel! He is not altogether guiltless in this illness of mine; and that I had a great mind to tell him. But, alas! how could I offend a man who was charitable enough to sit at my bedside a good hour, and talk on some other subjects than pills, and draughts, blisters, and leeches!

This is quite an easy interval. I am too weak to read, yet I feel as if I could enjoy something interesting. Why not have up Mrs. Dean to finish her tale? I can recollect its chief incidents, as far as she had gone. Yes, I remember her hero had run off, and never been heard of for three years: and the heroine was married: I'll ring; she'll be delighted to find me capable of talking cheerfully.

Mrs. Dean came.

"It wants twenty minutes, sir, to taking the medicine," she commenced.

"Away, away with it!" I replied; "I desire to have — "

"The doctor says you must drop the powders."

"With all my heart! Don't interrupt me. Come and take your seat here. Keep your fingers from that bitter phalanx of vials. Draw your knitting out of your pocket — that will do — now continue the history of Mr. Heathcliff, from where you left off, to the present day. Did he finish his education on the Continent, and come back a gentleman? or did he get a sizer's place at college? or escape to America, and earn honours by drawing blood from his foster country? or make a fortune more promptly, on the English highways?"

"He may have done a little in all these vocations, Mr. Lockwood; but I couldn't give my word for any. I stated before that I didn't know how he gained his money; neither am I aware of the means he took to raise his mind from the savage ignorance into which it was sunk; but, with your leave, I'll proceed in my own fashion, if you think it will amuse, and not weary you. Are you feeling better this morning?

"Much."

"That's good news."

I got Miss Catherine and myself to Thrushcross Grange: and to my agreeable disappointment, she behaved infinitely better than I dared to expect. She seemed almost over fond of Mr. Linton; and even to his sister, she showed plenty of affection. They were both very attentive to her comfort, certainly. It was not the thorn bending to the honeysuckles, but the honeysuckles embracing the thorn. There were no mutual concessions; one stood erect, and the others yielded; and who *can* be ill-natured and bad-tempered, when they encounter neither opposition nor indifference?

I observed that Mr. Edgar had a deep-rooted fear of ruffling her humour. He concealed it from her; but if ever he heard me answer sharply, or saw any other servant grow cloudy at some imperious order of hers, he would show his trouble by a frown of displeasure that never darkened on his own account. He, many a time, spoke sternly to me about my pertness; and averred that the stab of a knife could not inflict a worse pang than he suffered at seeing his lady vexed.

Not to grieve a kind master I learned to be less touchy; and, for the space of half a year, the gunpowder lay as harmless as sand, because no fire came near to explode it. Catherine had seasons of gloom and silence, now and then: they were respected with sympathising silence by her husband, who ascribed them to an alteration in her constitution, produced by her perilous illness, as she was never subject to depression of spirits before. The return of sunshine was welcomed by answering sunshine from him. I believe I may assert that they were really in possession of deep and growing happiness.

It ended. Well, we *must* be for ourselves in the long run; the mild and generous are only more justly selfish than the domineering — and it ended when circumstances caused each to feel that the one's interest was not the chief consideration in the other's thoughts.

On a mellow evening in September, I was coming from the garden with a heavy basket of apples which I had been gathering. It had got dusk, and the moon looked over the high wall of the court, causing undefined shadows to lurk in the corners of the numerous projecting portions of the building. I set my burden on the house steps by the kitchen door, and lingered to rest, and drew in a few more breaths of the soft, sweet air; my eyes were on the moon, and my back to the entrance, when I heard a voice behind me say —

"Nelly, is that you?"

It was a deep voice, and foreign in tone; yet, there was something in the manner of pronouncing my name which made it sound familiar. I turned to discover who spoke, fearfully, for the doors were shut, and I had seen nobody on approaching the steps.

Something stirred in the porch; and moving nearer, I distinguished a tall man dressed in dark clothes, with dark face and hair. He leant against the side, and held his fingers on the latch, as if intending to open for himself.

"Who can it be?" I thought. "Mr. Earnshaw? Oh, no! The voice has no resemblance to his."

"I have waited here an hour," he resumed, while I continued staring; "and the whole of that time all round has been as still as death. I dared not enter. You do not know me? Look, I'm not a stranger!"

A ray fell on his features; the cheeks were sallow, and half covered with black whiskers; the brows lowering, the eyes deep set and singular. I remembered the eyes.

"What!" I cried, uncertain whether to regard him as a worldly visitor, and I raised my hands in amazement. "What! you come back? Is it really you? Is it?"

"Yes, Heathcliff," he replied, glancing from me up to the windows which reflected a score of glittering moons, but showed no lights from within. "Are they at home — where is she? Nelly, you are not glad — you needn't be so disturbed. Is she here? Speak! I wait to have one word with her — your mistress. Go, and say some person from Gimmerton desires to see her."

"How will she take it?" I exclaimed, "what will she do? The surprise bewilders me — it will put her out of her head! And you *are* Heathcliff? But altered! Nay, there's no comprehending it. Have you been for a soldier?"

"Go, and carry my message," he interrupted impatiently; "I'm in hell till you do!"

He lifted the latch, and I entered; but when I got to the parlour where Mr. and Mrs. Linton were, I could not persuade myself to proceed.

At length I resolved on making an excuse to ask if they would have the candles lighted, and I opened the door.

They sat together in a window whose lattice lay back against the wall, and displayed, beyond the garden trees and the wild green park, the valley of Gimmerton, with a long line of mist winding nearly to its top (for very soon after you pass the chapel, as you may have noticed, the sough that runs from the marshes joins a beck which follows the bend of the glen). Wuthering Heights rose above this silvery vapour; but our old house was invisible — it rather dips down on the other side.

Both the room, and its occupants, and the scene they gazed on, looked wondrously peaceful. I shrank reluctantly from performing my errand: and was actually going away, leaving it unsaid, after having put my question about the candles, when a sense of my folly compelled me to return, and mutter:

"A person from Gimmerton wishes to see you, ma'am."

"What does he want?" asked Mrs. Linton.

"I did not question him," I answered.

"Well, close the curtains, Nelly," she said; "and bring up tea. I'll be back again directly."

She quitted the apartment; Mr. Edgar inquired carelessly, who it was?

"Some one mistress does not expect," I replied. "That Heathcliff, you recollect him, sir, who used to live at Mr. Earnshaw's."

"What, the gipsy — the plough-boy?" he cried. "Why did you not say so to Catherine?"

"Hush! you must not call him by those names, master," I said. "She'd be sadly grieved to hear you. She was nearly heartbroken when he ran off; I guess his return will make a jubilee to her."

Mr. Linton walked to a window on the other side of the room that overlooked the court. He unfastened it, and leant out. I suppose they were below, for he exclaimed, quickly:

"Don't stand there, love! Bring the person in, if it be any one particular."

Ere long, I heard the click of the latch, and Catherine flew upstairs, breathless and wild, too excited to show gladness; indeed, by her face, you would rather have surmised an awful calamity.

"Oh, Edgar, Edgar!" she panted, flinging her arms round his neck. "Oh, Edgar, darling! Heathcliff's come back — he is!" And she tightened her embrace to a squeeze.

"Well, well," cried her husband, crossly, "don't strangle me for that! He never struck me as such a marvellous creature. There is no need to be frantic!"

"I know you didn't like him," she answered, repressing a little the intensity of her delight. "Yet, for my sake, you must be friends now. Shall I tell him to come up?"

"Here?" he said, "into the parlour?"

"Where else?" she asked.

He looked vexed, and suggested the kitchen as a more suitable place for him.

Mrs. Linton eyed him with a droll expression — half angry, half laughing at his fastidiousness.

"No," she added, after a while: "I cannot sit in the kitchen. Set two tables here, Ellen; one for your master and Miss Isabella, being gentry; the other for Heathcliff and myself, being of the lower orders. Will that please you, dear? Or must I have a fire lighted elsewhere? If so, give directions. I'll run down and secure my guest. I'm afraid the joy is too great to be real!"

She was about to dart off again; but Edgar arrested her.

"*You* bid him step up," he said, addressing me; "and Catherine, try to be glad, without being absurd! The whole household need not witness the sight of your welcoming a runaway servant as a brother."

I descended and found Heathcliff waiting under the porch, evidently anticipating an invitation to enter. He followed my guidance without waste of words, and I ushered him into the presence of the master and mistress, whose flushed cheeks betrayed signs of warm talking. But the lady's glowed with another feeling when her friend appeared at the door; she sprang forward, took both his hands, and led him to Linton; and then she seized Linton's reluctant fingers and crushed them into his.

Now fully revealed by the fire and candlelight, I was amazed, more than ever, to behold the transformation of Heathcliff. He had grown a tall, athletic, well-formed man, beside whom, my master seemed quite slender and youth-like. His upright carriage suggested the idea of his having been in the army. His countenance was much older in expression and decision of feature than Mr. Linton's; it looked intelligent, and retained no marks of former degradation. A half-civilized ferocity lurked yet in the depressed brows, and eyes full of black fire, but it was subdued; and his manner was even dignified, quite divested of roughness though too stern for grace.

My master's surprise equalled or exceeded mine: he remained for a minute at a loss how to address the ploughboy, as he had called him; Heathcliff dropped his slight hand, and stood looking at him coolly till he chose to speak.

"Sit down, sir," he said, at length. "Mrs. Linton, recalling old times, would have me give you a cordial reception, and, of course, I am gratified when anything occurs to please her."

"And I also," answered Heathcliff, "especially if it be anything in which I have a part. I shall stay an hour or two willingly."

He took a seat opposite Catherine, who kept her gaze fixed on him as if she feared he would vanish were she to remove it. He did not raise his to her, often; a quick glance now and then sufficed; but it flashed back, each time more confidently, the undisguised delight he drank from hers.

They were too much absorbed in their mutual joy to suffer embarrassment; not so Mr. Edgar, he grew pale with pure annoyance, a feeling that reached its climax when his lady rose — and stepping across the rug, seized Heathcliff's hands again, and laughed like one beside herself.

"I shall think it a dream to-morrow!" she cried. "I shall not be able to believe that I have seen, and touched, and spoken to you once more — and yet, cruel Heathcliff! you don't deserve this welcome. To be absent and silent for three years, and never to think of me!"

"A little more than you have thought of me!" he murmured. "I heard of your marriage, Cathy, not long since; and, while waiting in the yard below, I meditated this plan — just to have one glimpse of your face — a stare of surprise, perhaps, and pretended pleasure; afterwards settle my score with Hindley; and then prevent the law by doing execution on myself. Your welcome has put these ideas out of my mind; but beware of meeting me with another aspect next time! Nay, you'll not drive me off again — you were really sorry for me, were you? Well, there was cause. I've fought through a bitter life since I last heard your voice, and you must forgive me, for I struggled only for you!"

"Catherine, unless we are to have cold tea, please to come to the table," interrupted Linton, striving to preserve his ordinary tone, and a due measure of politeness. "Mr. Heathcliff will have a long walk, wherever he may lodge to-night; and I'm thirsty."

She took her post before the urn; and Miss Isabella came, summoned by the bell; then, having handed their chairs forward, I left the room.

The meal hardly endured ten minutes — Catherine's cup was never filled, she could neither eat nor drink. Edgar had made a slop in his saucer, and scarcely swallowed a mouthful.

Their guest did not protract his stay, that evening, above an hour longer. I asked, as he departed, if he went to Gimmerton?

"No, to Wuthering Heights," he answered, "Mr. Earnshaw invited me when I called this morning."

Mr. Earnshaw invited *him!* and *he* called on Mr. Earnshaw! I pondered this sentence painfully, after he was gone. Is he turning out a bit of a hypocrite, and coming into the country to work mischief under a cloak? I mused — I had a presentiment, in the bottom of my heart, that he had better have remained away.

About the middle of the night, I was awakened from my first nap by Mrs. Linton gliding into my chamber, taking a seat on my bed-side, and pulling me by the hair to rouse me.

"I cannot rest, Ellen," she said by way of apology. "And I want some living creature to keep me company in my happiness! Edgar is sulky, because I'm glad of a thing that does not interest him — He refuses to open his mouth, except to utter pettish, silly speeches; and he affirmed I was cruel and selfish for wishing to talk when he was so sick and sleepy. He always contrives to be sick at the least cross! I gave a few sentences of commendation to Heathcliff, and he, either for a headache or a pang of envy, began to cry: so I got up and left him.

"What use is it praising Heathcliff to him?" I answered. "As lads they had an aversion to each other, and Heathcliff would hate just as much to hear him praised — it's human nature. Let Mr. Linton alone about him, unless you would like an open quarrel between them."

"But does it not show great weakness?" pursued she. "I'm not envious — I never feel hurt at the brightness of Isabella's yellow hair, and the whiteness of her skin; at her dainty elegance, and the fondness all the family exhibit for her. Even you, Nelly, if we have a dispute sometimes, you back Isabella, at once; and I yield like a foolish mother — I call her a darling, and flatter her into a good temper. It pleases her brother to see us cordial, and that pleases me. But they are very much alike: they are spoiled children, and fancy the world was made for their accommodation; and, though I humour both, I think a smart chastisement might improve them, all the same."

"You're mistaken, Mrs. Linton," said I, "They humour you — I know what there would be to do if they did not! You can well afford to indulge their passing whims, as long as their business is to anticipate all your desires — You may, however, fall out, at last, over something of equal consequence to both sides; and, then those you term weak are very capable of being as obstinate as you!"

"And then we shall fight to the death, shan't we, Nelly?" she returned, laughing, "No, I tell you, I have such faith in Linton's love that I believe I might kill him, and he wouldn't wish to retaliate."

I advised her to value him the more for his affection.

"I do," she answered; "but he needn't resort to whining for trifles. It is childish; and, instead of melting into tears, because I said that Heathcliff was now worthy of any one's regard, and it would honour the first gentleman in the country to be his friend; he ought to have said it for me, and been delighted from sympathy — He must get accustomed to him, and he may as well like him — considering how Heathcliff has reason to object to him, I'm sure he behaved excellently!"

"What do you think of his going to Wuthering Heights?" I inquired. "He is reformed in every respect, apparently — quite a Christian — offering the right hand of fellowship to his enemies all round!"

"He explained it," she replied. "I wondered as much as you — He said he called to gather information concerning me, from you, supposing you resided there still; and Joseph told Hindley, who came out, and fell to questioning him of what he had been doing, and how he had been living: and finally, desired him to walk in — There were some persons sitting at cards — Heathcliff joined them; my brother lost some money to him; and, finding him plentifully supplied, he requested that he would come again in the evening, to which he consented. Hindley is too reckless to select his acquaintance prudently; he doesn't trouble himself to reflect on the causes he might have for mistrusting one whom he has basely injured — But Heathcliff affirms his principal reason for resuming a connection with his ancient persecutor is a wish to install himself in quarters at walking distance from the Grange, and an attachment to the house where we lived together, and likewise a hope that I shall have more opportunities of seeing him there than I could have if he settled in Gimmerton. He means to offer liberal payment for permission to lodge at the Heights; and doubtless my brother's covetousness will prompt him to accept the terms; he was always greedy, though what he grasps with one hand, he flings away with the other."

"It's a nice place for a young man to fix his dwelling in!" said I. "Have you no fear of the consequences, Mrs. Linton?"

"None for my friend," she replied, "his strong head will keep him from danger — a little for Hindley; but he can't be made morally worse than he is; and I stand between him and bodily harm — The event of this evening has reconciled me to God, and humanity! I had risen in angry rebellion against providence — Oh, I've endured very, very bitter misery, Nelly! If that creature knew how bitter, he'd be ashamed to cloud its removal with idle petulance — It was kindness for him which induced me to bear it alone: had I expressed the agony I frequently felt, he would have been taught to long for its alleviation as ardently as I — However, it's over, and I'll take no revenge on his folly — I can afford to suffer anything, hereafter! should the meanest thing alive slap me on the cheek, I'd not only turn the other, but I'd ask pardon for provoking it — and, as a proof, I'll go make my peace with Edgar instantly — Good night — I'm an angel!"

In this self-complacent conviction she departed; and the success of her fulfilled resolution was obvious on the morrow — Mr. Linton had not only abjured his peevishness (though his spirits seemed still subdued by Catherine's exuberance of vivacity) but he ventured no objection to her taking Isabella with her to Wuthering Heights in the afternoon; and she rewarded him with such a summer of sweetness and affection, in return, as made the house a paradise for several days; both master and servants profiting from the perpetual sunshine.

Heathcliff — Mr. Heathcliff I should say in future — used the liberty of visiting Thrushcross Grange cautiously, at first: he seemed estimating how far its owner would bear his intrusion. Catherine, also, deemed it judicious to moderate her expressions of pleasure in receiving him; and he gradually established his right to be expected.

He retained a great deal of the reserve for which his boyhood was remarkable, and that served to repress all startling demonstrations of feeling. My master's uneasiness experienced a lull, and further circumstances diverted it into another channel for a space.

His new source of trouble sprang from the not anticipated misfortune of Isabella Linton evincing a sudden and irresistible attraction towards the tolerated guest — She was at that time a charming young lady of eighteen; infantile in manners, although possessed of keen wit, keen feelings, and a keen temper, too, if irritated. Her brother, who loved her tenderly, was appalled at this fantastic preference. Leaving aside the degradation of an alliance with a nameless man, and the possible fact that his property, in default of heirs male, might pass into such a one's power, he had sense to comprehend Heathcliff's disposition — to know that, though his exterior was altered, his mind was unchangeable, and unchanged. And he dreaded that mind; it revolted him; he shrank forebodingly from the idea of committing Isabella to its keeping.

He would have recoiled still more had he been aware that her attachment rose unsolicited, and was bestowed where it awakened no reciprocation of sentiment; for the minute he discovered its existence, he laid the blame on Heathcliff's deliberate designing.

We had all remarked, during some time, that Miss Linton fretted and pined over something. She grew cross and wearisome, snapping at and teasing Catherine continually, at the imminent risk of exhausting her limited patience. We excused her to a certain extent, on the plea of ill-health — she was dwindling and fading before our eyes — But, one day when she had been particularly wayward, rejecting her breakfast, complaining that the servants did not do what she told them; that the mistress would allow her to be nothing in the house, and Edgar neglected her; that she had caught a cold with the doors being left open, and we let the parlour fire go out on purpose to vex her; with a hundred yet more frivolous accusations; Mrs. Linton peremptorily insisted that she should get to-bed; and, having scolded her heartily, threatened to send for the doctor.

Mention of Kenneth caused her to exclaim, instantly, that her health was perfect, and it was only Catherine's harshness which made her unhappy.

"How can you say I'm harsh, you naughty fondling?" cried the mistress, amazed at the unreasonable assertion. "You are surely losing your reason. When have I been harsh, tell me?"

"Yesterday," sobbed Isabella, "and now!"

"Yesterday!" said her sister-in-law. "On what occasion?"

"In our walk along the moor; you told me to ramble where I pleased, while you sauntered on with Mr. Heathcliff!"

"And that's your notion of harshness?" said Catherine, laughing. "It was no hint that your company was superfluous; we didn't care whether you kept with us or not; I merely thought Heathcliff's talk would have nothing entertaining for your ears."

"Oh no," wept the young lady, "you wished me away, because you knew I liked to be there!"

"Is she sane?" asked Mrs. Linton, appealing to me. "I'll repeat our conversation, word for word, Isabella; and you point out any charm it could have had for you."

"I don't mind the conversation," she answered: "I wanted to be with — "

"Well!" said Catherine, perceiving her hesitate to complete the sentence.

"With him; and I won't be always sent off!" she continued, kindling up. "You are a dog in the manger, Cathy, and desire no one to be loved but yourself!"

"You are an impertinent little monkey!" exclaimed Mrs. Linton, in surprise. "But I'll not believe this idiocy! It is impossible that you can covet the admiration of Heathcliff — that you can consider him an agreeable person! I hope I have misunderstood you, Isabella?"

"No, you have not," said the infatuated girl. "I love him more than ever you loved Edgar; and he might love me, if you would let him!"

"I wouldn't be you for a kingdom, then!" Catherine declared, emphatically — and she seemed to speak sincerely. "Nelly, help me to convince her of her madness. Tell her what Heathcliff is — an unreclaimed creature, without refinement — without cultivation; an arid wilderness of furze and whinstone. I'd as soon put that little canary into the park on a winter's day as recommend you to bestow your heart on him! It is deplorable ignorance of his character, child, and nothing else, which makes that dream enter your head. Pray, don't imagine that he conceals depths of benevolence and affections beneath a stern exterior! He's not a rough diamond — a pearl-containing oyster of a rustic; he's a fierce, pitiless, wolfish man. I never say to him let this or that enemy alone, because it would be ungenerous or cruel to harm them — I say let them alone, because *I* should hate them to be wronged: and he'd crush you, like a sparrow's egg, Isabella, if he found you a troublesome charge. I know he couldn't love a Linton; and yet, he'd be quite capable of marrying your fortune and expectations. Avarice is growing with him a besetting sin. There's my picture; and I'm his friend — so much so, that had he thought seriously to catch you, I should, perhaps, have held my tongue, and let you fall into his trap."

Miss Linton regarded her sister-in-law with indignation.

"For shame! for shame!" she repeated, angrily. "You are worse than twenty foes, you poisonous friend!"

"Ah, you won't believe me, then?" said Catherine. "You think I speak from wicked selfishness?"

"I'm certain you do," retorted Isabella; "and I shudder at you!"

"Good!" cried the other. "Try for yourself, if that be your spirit; I have done, and yield the argument to your saucy insolence."

"And I must suffer for her egotism!" she sobbed, as Mrs. Linton left the room. "All, all is against me; she has blighted my single consolation. But she uttered falsehoods, didn't she? Mr. Heathcliff is not a fiend; he has an honourable soul, and a true one, or how could he remember her?"

"Banish him from your thoughts, Miss," I said. "He's a bird of bad omen; no mate for you. Mrs. Linton spoke strongly, and yet, I can't contradict her. She is better acquainted with his heart than I, or any one besides; and she never would represent him as worse than he is. Honest people don't hide their deeds. How has he been living? how has he got rich? why is he staying at Wuthering Heights, the house of a man whom he abhors? They say Mr. Earnshaw is worse and worse since he came. They sit up all night together continually: and Hindley has been borrowing money on his land; and does nothing but play and drink, I heard only a week ago; it was Joseph who told me — I met him at Gimmerton.

"'Nelly,' he said, 'we's hae a Crahnr's 'quest° each, at ahr folks. One on 'em's a'most getten his finger cut off wi' hauding° t' other froo' sticking hisseln loike a cawlf. That's maister, yah knaw, ut's soa up uh going tuh t' grand 'sizes.° He's noan feard up t' Bench uh judges, norther Paul, nur Peter, nur John, nur Mathew, nur noan on 'em, nut he! He fair likes he langs tuh set his brazened face agean 'em! And yon bonny lad Heathcliff, yah mind, he's a rare un! He can girn° a laugh, as weel's onybody at a raight divil's jest. Does he niver say nowt of his fine living amang us, when he goas tuh t' Grange? This is t' way on 't — up at sun-dahn; dice, brandy, cloised shutters, und can'le lught till next day, at nooin — then, t' fooil gangs banning un raving° tuh his cham'er, makking dacent fowks dig thur fingers i' thur lugs fur varry shaume; un'th' knave, wah, he carn cahnt his brass,° un' ate, un' sleep, un' off tuh his neighbour's tuh gossip wi' t' wife. I' course, he tells

a Crahnr's 'quest: A Coroner's inquest. ***hauding:*** Holding. ***t' grand 'sizes:*** The grand assizes (county court sessions). ***girn:*** Show one's teeth, snarl. ***t' fooil gangs banning un raving:*** The fool goes cursing and raving. ***wah, he carn cahnt his brass:*** Why, he can count his brass (coins, money).

Dame Catherine hah hor fathur's goold runs intuh his pocket, and her father's son gallops dahn t' Broad road, while he flees afore tuh oppen t' pikes?'° Now, Miss Linton, Joseph is an old rascal, but no liar; and, if his account of Heathcliff's conduct be true, you would never think of desiring such a husband, would you?"

"You are leagued with the rest, Ellen!" she replied. "I'll not listen to your slanders. What malevolence you must have to wish to convince me that there is no happiness in the world!"

Whether she would have got over this fancy if left to herself, or persevered in nursing it perpetually, I cannot say; she had little time to reflect. The day after, there was a justice-meeting at the next town; my master was obliged to attend; and Mr. Heathcliff, aware of his absence, called rather earlier than usual.

Catherine and Isabella were sitting in the library, on hostile terms, but silent. The latter alarmed at her recent indiscretion, and the disclosure she had made of her secret feelings in a transient fit of passion; the former, on mature consideration, really offended with her companion; and, if she laughed again at her pertness, inclined to make it no laughing matter to *her*.

She did laugh as she saw Heathcliff pass the window. I was sweeping the hearth, and I noticed a mischievous smile on her lips. Isabella, absorbed in her meditations, or a book, remained till the door opened, and it was too late to attempt an escape, which she would gladly have done had it been practicable.

"Come in, that's right!" exclaimed the mistress, gaily, pulling a chair to the fire. "Here are two people sadly in need of a third to thaw the ice between them; and you are the very one we should both of us choose. Heathcliff, I'm proud to show you, at last, somebody that dotes on you more than myself. I expect you to feel flattered — nay, it's not Nelly; don't look at her! My poor little sister-in-law is breaking her heart by mere contemplation of your physical and moral beauty. It lies in your own power to be Edgar's brother! No, no, Isabella, you sha'n't run off," she continued, arresting, with feigned playfulness, the confounded girl, who had risen indignantly. "We were quarrelling like cats about you, Heathcliff; and I was fairly beaten in protestations of devotion and admiration; and, moreover, I was informed that if I would but have the manners to stand aside, my rival, as she will have herself to be, would shoot a shaft into your soul that would fix you for ever, and send my image into eternal oblivion!"

tuh oppen t' pikes: To open the turnpike gates.

"Catherine!" said Isabella, calling up her dignity, and disdaining to struggle from the tight grasp that held her. "I'd thank you to adhere to the truth and not slander me, even in joke! Mr. Heathcliff, be kind enough to bid this friend of yours release me — she forgets that you and I are not intimate acquaintances, and what amuses her is painful to me beyond expression."

As the guest answered nothing, but took his eat, and looked thoroughly indifferent what sentiments she cherished concerning him, she turned, and whispered an earnest appeal for liberty to her tormentor.

"By no means!" cried Mrs. Linton in answer. "I won't be named a dog in the manger again. You *shall* stay, now then! Heathcliff, why don't you evince satisfaction at my pleasant news? Isabella swears that the love Edgar has for me is nothing to that she entertains for you. I'm sure she made some speech of the kind, did she not, Ellen? And she has fasted ever since the day before yesterday's walk, from sorrow and rage that I despatched her out of your society, under the idea of its being unacceptable."

"I think you belie her," said Heathcliff, twisting his chair to face them. "She wishes to be out of my society now, at any rate!"

And he stared hard at the object of discourse, as one might do at a strange repulsive animal, a centipede from the Indies, for instance, which curiosity leads one to examine in spite of the aversion it raises.

The poor thing couldn't bear that; she grew white and red in rapid succession, and while tears beaded her lashes, bent the strength of her small fingers to loosen the firm clutch of Catherine, and perceiving that, as fast as she raised one finger off her arm, another closed down, and she could not remove the whole together, she began to make use of her nails, and their sharpness presently ornamented the detainer's with crescents of red.

"There's a tigress!" exclaimed Mrs. Linton, setting her free, and shaking her hand with pain. "Begone, for God's sake, and hide your vixen face! How foolish to reveal those talons to *him*. Can't you fancy the conclusions he'll draw? Look, Heathcliff! they are instruments that will do execution — you must beware of your eyes."

"I'd wrench them off her fingers, if they ever menaced me," he answered, brutally, when the door had closed after her. "But what did you mean by teasing the creature in that manner, Cathy? You were not speaking the truth, were you?"

"I assure you I was," she returned. "She has been pining for your sake several weeks; and raving about you this morning, and pouring forth a deluge of abuse, because I represented your failings in a plain light for the purpose of mitigating her adoration. But don't notice it further. I wished to punish her sauciness, that's all — I like her too well, my dear Heathcliff, to let you absolutely seize and devour her up."

"And I like her too ill to attempt it," said he, "except in a very ghoulish fashion. You'd hear of odd things, if I lived alone with that mawkish, waxen face; the most ordinary would be painting on its white the colours of the rainbow, and turning the blue eyes black, every day or two; they detestably resemble Linton's."

"Delectably," observed Catherine. "They are dove's eyes — angel's!"

"She's her brother's heir, is she not?" he asked, after a brief silence.

"I should be sorry to think so," returned his companion. "Half-a-dozen nephews shall erase her title, please Heaven! Abstract your mind from the subject, at present — you are too prone to covet your neighbour's goods: remember, *this* neighbour's goods are mine."

"If they were *mine,* they would be none the less that," said Heathcliff, "but though Isabella Linton may be silly, she is scarcely mad; and — in short, we'll dismiss the matter, if you advise."

From their tongues, they did dismiss it; and Catherine, probably, from her thoughts. The other, I felt certain, recalled it often in the course of the evening; I saw him smile to himself — grin rather — and lapse into ominous musing whenever Mrs. Linton had occasion to be absent from the apartment.

I determined to watch his movements. My heart invariably cleaved to the master's, in preference to Catherine's side; with reason, I imagined, for he was kind, and trustful, and honourable; and she — she could not be called the *opposite,* yet she seemed to allow herself such wide latitude, that I had little faith in her principles, and still less sympathy for her feelings. I wanted something to happen which might have the effect of freeing both Wuthering Heights and the Grange of Mr. Heathcliff, quietly, leaving us as we had been prior to his advent. His visits were a continual nightmare to me; and, I suspected, to my master also. His abode at the Heights was an oppression past explaining. I felt that God had forsaken the stray sheep there to its own wicked wanderings, and an evil beast prowled between it and the fold, waiting his time to spring and destroy.

CHAPTER 11

Sometimes, while meditating on these things in solitude, I've got up in sudden terror, and put on my bonnet to go and see how all was at the farm; I've persuaded my conscience that it was a duty to warn him how people talked regarding his ways; and then I've recollected his confirmed bad habits, and hopeless of benefiting him, have flinched from re-entering the dismal house, doubting if I could bear to be taken at my word.

One time, I passed the old gate, going out of my way, on a journey to Gimmerton. It was about the period that my narrative has reached — a bright frosty afternoon; the ground bare, and the road hard and dry.

I came to a stone where the highway branches off on to the moor at your left hand; a rough sand-pillar, with the letters W.H. cut on its north side, on the east, G., and on the south-west, T.G. It serves as guide-post to the Grange, and Heights, and village.

The sun shone yellow on its grey head, reminding me of summer; and I cannot say why, but all at once, a rush of child's sensations flowed into my heart. Hindley and I held it a favourite spot twenty years before.

I gazed long at the weather-worn block; and, stooping down, perceived a hole near the bottom still full of snail-shells and pebbles which we were very fond of storing there with more perishable things — and, as fresh as reality, it appeared that I beheld my early playmate seated on the withered turf, his dark, square head bent forward, and his little hand scooping out the earth with a piece of slate.

"Poor Hindley!" I exclaimed, involuntarily.

I started — my bodily eye was cheated into a momentary belief that the child lifted its face and stared straight into mine! It vanished in a twinkling; but, immediately, I felt an irresistible yearning to be at the Heights. Superstition urged me to comply with this impulse — supposing he should be dead! I thought — or should die soon! — supposing it were a sign of death!

The nearer I got to the house the more agitated I grew: and on catching sight of it, I trembled every limb. The apparition had outstripped me; it stood looking through the gate. That was my first idea on observing an elf-locked, brown-eyed boy setting his ruddy countenance against the bars. Further reflection suggested this must be Hareton, *my* Hareton, not altered greatly since I left him, ten months since.

"God bless thee, darling!" I cried, forgetting instantaneously my foolish fears. "Hareton, it's Nelly — Nelly, thy nurse."

He retreated out of arm's length, and picked up a large flint.

"I am come to see thy father, Hareton," I added, guessing from the action that Nelly, if she lived in his memory at all, was not recognised as one with me.

He raised his missile to hurl it; I commenced a soothing speech, but could not stay the hand. The stone struck my bonnet, and then ensued, from the stammering lips of the little fellow, a string of curses which, whether he comprehended them or not, were delivered with a practised emphasis, and distorted his baby features into a shocking expression of malignity.

You may be certain this grieved more than angered me. Fit to cry, I took an orange from my pocket, and offered it to propitiate him.

He hesitated, and then snatched it from my hold, as if he fancied I only intended to tempt and disappoint him.

I showed another, keeping it out of his reach.

"Who has taught you those fine words, my barn?"° I inquired. "The curate?"

"Damn the curate, and thee! Gie me that," he replied.

"Tell us where you got your lessons, and you shall have it," said I. "Who's your master?"

"Devil daddy," was his answer.

"And what do you learn from Daddy?" I continued.

He jumped at the fruit; I raised it higher. "What does he teach you?" I asked.

"Naught," said he, "but to keep out of his gait° — Daddy cannot bide me, because I swear at him."

"Ah! and the devil teaches you to swear at Daddy?" I observed.

"Aye — nay," he drawled.

"Who then?"

"Heathcliff."

I asked if he liked Mr. Heathcliff?

"Aye!" he answered again.

Desiring to have his reasons for liking him, I could only gather the sentences "I known't — he pays Dad back what he gies to me — he curses Daddy for cursing me — He says I mun do as I will."

"And the curate does not teach you to read and write, then?" I pursued.

"No, I was told the curate should have his — teeth dashed down his — throat if he stepped over the threshold — Heathcliff had promised that!"

I put the orange in his hand; and bade him tell his father that a woman called Nelly Dean was waiting to speak with him, by the garden gate.

He went up the walk, and entered the house; but, instead of Hindley, Heathcliff appeared on the door stones, and I turned directly and

barn: Bairn, little child. ***gait:*** Way, course.

ran down the road as hard as ever I could race, making no halt till I gained the guide post, and feeling as scared as if I had raised a goblin.

This is not much connected with Miss Isabella's affair; except that it urged me to resolve further on mounting vigilant guard, and doing my utmost to check the spread of such bad influence at the Grange, even though I should wake a domestic storm, by thwarting Mrs. Linton's pleasure.

The next time Heathcliff came, my young lady chanced to be feeding some pigeons in the court. She had never spoken a word to her sister-in-law, for three days; but she had likewise dropped her fretful complaining, and we found it a great comfort.

Heathcliff had not the habit of bestowing a single unnecessary civility on Miss Linton, I knew. Now, as soon as he beheld her, his first precaution was to take a sweeping survey of the housefront. I was standing by the kitchen window, but I drew out of sight. He then stept across the pavement to her, and said something: she seemed embarrassed, and desirous of getting away; to prevent it, he laid his hand on her arm: she averted her face; he apparently put some question which she had no mind to answer. There was another rapid glance at the house, and supposing himself unseen, the scoundrel had the impudence to embrace her.

"Judas! Traitor!" I ejaculated. "You are a hypocrite, too, are you? A deliberate deceiver."

"Who is, Nelly?" said Catherine's voice at my elbow — I had been over-intent on watching the pair outside to mark her entrance.

"Your worthless friend!" I answered, warmly, "the sneaking rascal yonder — Ah, he has caught a glimpse of us — he is coming in! I wonder will he have the art to find a plausible excuse for making love to Miss, when he told you he hated her?"

Mrs. Linton saw Isabella tear herself free, and run into the garden; and a minute after, Heathcliff opened the door.

I couldn't withhold giving some loose to my indignation; but Catherine angrily insisted on silence, and threatened to order me out of the kitchen, if I dared to be so presumptuous as to put in my insolent tongue.

"To hear you, people might think *you* were the mistress!" she cried. "You want setting down in your right place! Heathcliff, what are you about, raising this stir? I said you must let Isabella alone! — I beg you will, unless you are tired of being received here, and wish Linton to draw the bolts against you!"

"God forbid that he should try!" answered the black villain — I detested him just then. "God keep him meek and patient! Every day I grow madder after sending him to heaven!"

"Hush!" said Catherine, shutting the inner door. "Don't vex me. Why have you disregarded my request? Did she come across you on purpose?"

"What is it to you?" he growled, "I have a right to kiss her, if she chooses, and you have no right to object — I'm not *your* husband, *you* needn't be jealous of me!"

"I'm not jealous of you," replied the mistress, "I'm jealous for you. Clear your face, you shan't scowl at me! If you like Isabella, you shall marry her. But, do you like her, tell the truth, Heathcliff? There, you won't answer, I'm certain you don't!"

"And would Mr. Linton approve of his sister marrying that man?" I inquired.

"Mr. Linton should approve," returned my lady decisively.

"He might spare himself the trouble," said Heathcliff, "I could do as well without his approbation — And, as to you, Catherine, I have a mind to speak a few words now, while we are at it — I want you to be aware that I *know* you have treated me infernally — infernally! Do you hear? And, if you flatter yourself that I don't perceive it you are a fool — and if you think I can be consoled by sweet words you are an idiot — and if you fancy I'll suffer unrevenged, I'll convince you of the contrary, in a very little while! Meantime, thank you for telling me your sister-in-law's secret — I swear I'll make the most of it, and stand you aside!"

"What new phase of his character is this?" exclaimed Mrs. Linton, in amazement. "I've treated you infernally — and you'll take revenge! How will you take it, ungrateful brute? How have I treated you infernally?"

"I seek no revenge on you," replied Heathcliff less vehemently. "That's not the plan — The tyrant grinds down his slaves and they don't turn against him, they crush those beneath them — You are welcome to torture me to death for your amusement, only, allow me to amuse myself a little in the same style — And refrain from insult, as much as you are able. Having levelled my palace, don't erect a hovel and complacently admire your own charity in giving me that for a home. If I imagined you really wished me to marry Isabella, I'd cut my throat!"

"Oh, the evil is that I am *not* jealous, is it?" cried Catherine. "Well, I won't repeat my offer of a wife — It is as bad as offering Satan a lost soul — Your bliss lies, like his, in inflicting misery — You prove it —

Edgar is restored from the ill-temper he gave way to at your coming; I begin to be secure and tranquil; and you, restless to know us at peace, appear resolved on exciting a quarrel — quarrel with Edgar if you please, Heathcliff, and deceive his sister; you'll hit on exactly the most efficient method of revenging yourself on me."

The conversation ceased. Mrs. Linton sat down by the fire, flushed and gloomy. The spirit which served her was growing intractable: she could neither lay nor control it. He stood on the hearth, with folded arms, brooding on his evil thoughts; and in this position I left them, to seek the master, who was wondering what kept Catherine below so long.

"Ellen," said he, when I entered, "have you seen your mistress?"

"Yes, she's in the kitchen, sir," I answered. "She's sadly put out by Mr. Heathcliff's behaviour; and, indeed, I do think it's time to arrange his visits on another footing. There's harm in being too soft, and now it's come to this — " And I related the scene in the court, and, as near as I dared, the whole subsequent dispute. I fancied it could not be very prejudicial to Mrs. Linton, unless she made it so, afterwards, by assuming the defensive for her guest.

Edgar Linton had difficulty in hearing me to the close. His first words revealed that he did not clear his wife of blame.

"This is insufferable!" he exclaimed. "It is disgraceful that she should own him for a friend, and force his company on me! Call me two men out of the hall, Ellen — Catherine shall linger no longer to argue with the low ruffian — I have humoured her enough."

He descended, and bidding the servants wait in the passage went, followed by me, to the kitchen. Its occupants had recommenced their angry discussion; Mrs. Linton, at least, was scolding with renewed vigour; Heathcliff had moved to the window, and hung his head, somewhat cowed by her violent rating apparently.

He saw the master first, and made a hasty motion that she should be silent; which she obeyed, abruptly, on discovering the reason of his intimation.

"How is this?" said Linton, addressing her; "what notion of propriety must you have to remain here, after the language which has been held to you by that blackguard? I suppose, because it is his ordinary talk, you think nothing of it — you are habituated to his baseness, and, perhaps, imagine I can get used to it too!"

"Have you been listening at the door, Edgar?" asked the mistress, in a tone particularly calculated to provoke her husband, implying both carelessness and contempt of his irritation.

Heathcliff, who had raised his eyes at the former speech, gave a sneering laugh at the latter, on purpose, it seemed, to draw Mr. Linton's attention to him.

He succeeded; but Edgar did not mean to entertain him with any high flights of passion.

"I have been so far forbearing with you, sir," he said, quietly; "not that I was ignorant of your miserable, degraded character, but I felt you were only partly responsible for that; and Catherine wishing to keep your acquaintance, I acquiesced — foolishly. Your presence is a moral poison that would contaminate the most virtuous — for that cause, and to prevent worse consequences, I shall deny you, hereafter, admission into this house, and give notice, now, that I require your instant departure. Three minutes' delay will render it involuntary and ignominious."

Heathcliff measured the height and breadth of the speaker with an eye full of derision.

"Cathy, this lamb of yours threatens like a bull!" he said. "It is in danger of splitting its skull against my knuckles. By God, Mr. Linton, I'm mortally sorry that you are not worth knocking down!"

My master glanced towards the passage, and signed me to fetch the men — he had no intention of hazarding a personal encounter.

I obeyed the hint; but Mrs. Linton, suspecting something, followed, and when I attempted to call them, she pulled me back, slammed the door to, and locked it.

"Fair means!" she said, in answer to her husband's look of angry surprise. "If you have not the courage to attack him, make an apology, or allow yourself to be beaten. It will correct you of feigning more valour than you possess. No, I'll swallow the key before you shall get it! I'm delightfully rewarded for my kindness to each! After constant thanks, two samples of blind ingratitude, stupid to absurdity! Edgar, I was defending you and yours; and I wish Heathcliff may flog you sick, for daring to think an evil thought of me!"

It did not need the medium of a flogging to produce that effect on the master. He tried to wrest the key from Catherine's grasp; and for safety she flung it into the hottest part of the fire; whereupon Mr. Edgar was taken with a nervous trembling, and his countenance grew deadly pale. For his life he could not avert that access of emotion — mingled anguish and humiliation overcame him completely. He leant on the back of a chair, and covered his face.

"Oh! Heavens! In old days this would win you knighthood!" exclaimed Mrs. Linton. "We are vanquished! we are vanquished! Heathcliff would as soon lift a finger at you as the king would march his army against a colony of mice. Cheer up, you sha'n't be hurt! Your type is not a lamb, it's a sucking leveret."

"I wish you joy of the milk-blooded coward, Cathy!" said her friend. "I compliment you on your taste: and that is the slavering, shivering thing you preferred to me! I would not strike him with my fist, but I'd kick him with my foot, and experience considerable satisfaction. Is he weeping, or is he going to faint for fear?"

The fellow approached and gave the chair on which Linton rested a push. He'd better have kept his distance: my master quickly sprang erect, and struck him full on the throat a blow that would have levelled a slighter man.

It took his breath for a minute; and, while he choked, Mr. Linton walked out by the back door into the yard, and from thence, to the front entrance.

"There! you've done with coming here," cried Catherine. "Get away, now — he'll return with a brace of pistols, and a half a dozen assistants. If he did overhear us, of course, he'd never forgive you. You've played me an ill turn, Heathcliff! But, go — make haste! I'd rather see Edgar at bay than you."

"Do you suppose I'm going with that blow burning in my gullet?" he thundered. "By Hell, no! I'll crush his ribs in like a rotten hazelnut, before I cross the threshold! If I don't floor him now, I shall murder him some time, so, as you value his existence, let me get at him!"

"He is not coming," I interposed, framing a bit of a lie. "There's the coachman, and the two gardeners; you'll surely not wait to be thrust into the road by them! Each has a bludgeon, and master will, very likely, be watching from the parlour windows to see that they fulfil his orders."

The gardeners and coachman *were* there; but Linton was with them. They had already entered the court — Heathcliff, on second thoughts, resolved to avoid a struggle against three underlings; he seized the poker, smashed the lock from the inner door, and made his escape as they tramped in.

Mrs. Linton, who was very much excited, bid me accompany her upstairs. She did not know my share in contributing to the disturbance, and I was anxious to keep her in ignorance.

"I'm nearly distracted, Nelly!" she exclaimed, throwing herself on the sofa. "A thousand smiths' hammers are beating in my head! Tell Isabella to shun me — this uproar is owing to her; and should she or any one else aggravate my anger at present, I shall get wild. And, Nelly, say to Edgar, if you see him again to-night, that I'm in danger of being seriously ill — I wish it may prove true. He has startled and distressed me shockingly! I want to frighten him. Besides, he might come and begin a string of abuse, or complainings; I'm certain I should recriminate, and God knows where we should end! Will you do so, my good Nelly? You are aware that I am no way blameable in this matter. What possessed him to turn listener? Heathcliff's talk was outrageous after you left us; but I could soon have diverted him from Isabella, and the rest meant nothing. Now, all is dashed wrong by the fool's-craving to hear evil of self that haunts some people like a demon! Had Edgar never gathered our conversation, he would never have been the worse for it. Really, when he opened on me in that unreasonable tone of displeasure, after I had scolded Heathcliff till I was hoarse for *him,* I did not care, hardly, what they did to each other, especially as I felt that, however the scene closed, we should all be driven asunder for nobody knows how long! Well, if I cannot keep Heathcliff for my friend — if Edgar will be mean and jealous — I'll try to break their hearts by breaking my own. That will be a prompt way of finishing all, when I am pushed to extremity! But it's a deed to be reserved for a forlorn hope — I'd not take Linton by surprise with it. To this point he has been discreet in dreading to provoke me; you must represent the peril of quitting that policy; and remind him of my passionate temper, verging, when kindled, on frenzy — I wish you could dismiss that apathy out of your countenance, and look rather more anxious about me!"

The stolidity with which I received these instructions was, no doubt, rather exasperating; for they were delivered in perfect sincerity, but I believed a person who could plan the turning of her fits of passion to account, beforehand, might, by exerting her will, manage to control herself tolerably even while under their influence; and I did not wish to "frighten" her husband, as she said, and multiply his annoyances for the purpose of serving her selfishness.

Therefore I said nothing when I met the master coming towards the parlour; but I took the liberty of turning back to listen whether they would resume their quarrel together.

He began to speak first.

"Remain where you are, Catherine," he said, without any anger in his voice, but with much sorrowful despondency. "I shall not stay. I am neither come to wrangle, nor be reconciled; but I wish just to learn whether, after this evening's events, you intend to continue your intimacy with — "

"Oh, for mercy's sake," interrupted the mistress, stamping her foot, "for mercy's sake, let us hear no more of it now! Your cold blood cannot be worked into a fever — your veins are full of ice-water — but mine are boiling, and the sight of such chilliness makes them dance."

"To get rid of me — answer my question," persevered Mr. Linton. "You *must* answer it; and that violence does not alarm me. I have found that you can be as stoical as any one, when you please. Will you give up Heathcliff hereafter, or will you give up me? It is impossible for you to be *my* friend, and *his* at the same time; and I absolutely *require* to know which you choose."

"I require to be let alone!" exclaimed Catherine, furiously. "I demand it! Don't you see I can scarcely stand? Edgar, you — you leave me!"

She rung the bell till it broke with a twang: I entered leisurely. It was enough to try the temper of a saint, such senseless, wicked rages! There she lay dashing her head against the arm of the sofa, and grinding her teeth, so that you might fancy she would crash them to splinters!

Mr. Linton stood looking at her in sudden compunction and fear. He told me to fetch some water. She had no breath for speaking.

I brought a glass full; and, as she would not drink, I sprinkled it on her face. In a few seconds she stretched herself out stiff, and turned up her eyes, while her cheeks, at once blanched and livid, assumed the aspect of death.

Linton looked terrified.

"There is nothing in the world the matter," I whispered. I did not want him to yield, though I could not help being afraid in my heart.

"She has blood on her lips!" he said, shuddering.

"Never mind!" I answered, tartly. And I told him how she had resolved, previous to his coming, on exhibiting a fit of frenzy.

I incautiously gave the account aloud, and she heard me, for she started up — her hair flying over her shoulders, her eyes flashing, the muscles of her neck and arms standing out preternaturally. I made up my mind for broken bones, at least; but she only glared about her, for an instant, and then rushed from the room.

The master directed me to follow; I did, to her chamber door; she hindered me from gong farther by securing it against me.

As she never offered to descend to breakfast next morning, I went to ask whether she would have some carried up.

"No!" she replied, peremptorily.

The same question was repeated at dinner and tea; and again on the morrow after, and received the same answer.

Mr. Linton, on his part, spent his time in the library, and did not inquire concerning his wife's occupations. Isabella and he had had an hour's interview, during which he tried to elicit from her some sentiment of proper horror for Heathcliff's advances; but he could make nothing of her evasive replies, and was obliged to close the examination, unsatisfactorily; adding, however, a solemn warning, that if she were so insane as to encourage that worthless suitor, it would dissolve all bonds of relationship between herself and him.

CHAPTER 12

While Miss Linton moped about the park and garden, always silent, and almost always in tears; and her brother shut himself up among books that he never opened; wearying, I guessed, with a continual vague expectation that Catherine, repenting her conduct, would come of her own accord to ask pardon, and seek a reconciliation; and *she* fasted pertinaciously, under the idea, probably, that at every meal, Edgar was ready to choke for her absence, and pride alone held him from running to cast himself at her feet; I went about my household duties, convinced that the Grange had but one sensible soul in its walls, and that lodged in my body.

I wasted no condolences on miss, nor any expostulation on my mistress, nor did I pay attention to the sighs of my master, who yearned to hear his lady's name, since he might not hear her voice.

I determined they should come about as they pleased for me; and though it was a tiresomely slow process, I began to rejoice at length in a faint dawn of its progress, as I thought at first.

Mrs. Linton, on the third day, unbarred her door; and having finished the water in her pitcher and decanter, desired a renewed supply, and a basin of gruel, for she believed she was dying. That I set down as a speech meant for Edgar's ears; I believed no such thing, so I kept it to myself, and brought her some tea and dry toast.

She ate and drank eagerly; and sank back on her pillow again, clenching her hands and groaning.

"Oh, I will die," she exclaimed, "since no one cares anything about me. I wish I had not taken that."

Then a good while after I heard her murmur,

"No, I'll not die — he'd be glad — he does not love me at all — he would never miss me!"

"Did you want anything, ma'am?" I enquired, still preserving my external composure, in spite of her ghastly countenance and strange exaggerated manner.

"What is that apathetic being doing?" she demanded, pushing the thick entangled locks from her wasted face. "Has he fallen into a lethargy, or is he dead?"

"Neither," replied I; "if you mean Mr. Linton. He's tolerably well, I think, though his studies occupy him rather more than they ought; he is continually among his books, since he has no other society."

I should not have spoken so, if I had known her true condition, but I could not get rid of the notion that she acted a part of her disorder.

"Among his books!" she cried, confounded. "And I dying! I on the brink of the grave! My God! does he know how I'm altered?" continued she, staring at her reflection in the mirror, hanging against the opposite wall. "Is that Catherine Linton? He imagines me in a pet — in play, perhaps. Cannot you inform him that it is frightful earnest? Nelly, if it be not too late, as soon as I learn how he feels, I'll choose between these two — either to starve, at once, that would be no punishment unless he had a heart — or to recover and leave the country. Are you speaking the truth about him now? Take care. Is he actually so utterly indifferent for my life?"

"Why, ma'am," I answered, "the master has no idea of your being deranged; and, of course, he does not fear that you will let yourself die of hunger."

"You think not? Cannot you tell him I will?" she returned; "persuade him — speak of your own mind — say you are certain I will!"

"No, you forget, Mrs. Linton," I suggested, "that you have eaten some food with a relish this evening, and to-morrow you will perceive its good effects."

"If I were only sure it would kill him," she interrupted, "I'd kill myself directly! These three awful nights, I've never closed my lids — and oh, I've been tormented! I've been haunted, Nelly! But I begin to fancy you don't like me. How strange! I thought, though everybody hated and despised each other, they could not avoid loving me — and they have all turned to enemies in a few hours. *They* have, I'm positive, the people *here*. How dreary to meet death, surrounded by their cold faces! Isabella, terrified and repelled, afraid to enter the room, it would be so dreadful to watch Catherine go. And Edgar standing solemnly by to see it over; then offering prayers of thanks to God for restoring peace to his house, and going back to his *books!* What in the name of all that feels, has he to do with *books,* when I am dying?"

She could not bear the notion which I had put into her head of Mr. Linton's philosophical resignation. Tossing about, she increased her feverish bewilderment to madness, and tore the pillow with her teeth, then raising herself up all burning, desired that I would open the window. We were in the middle of winter, the wind blew strong from the northeast, and I objected.

Both the expressions flitting over her face, and the changes of her moods, began to alarm me terribly; and brought to my recollection her former illness, and the doctor's injunction that she should not be crossed.

A minute previously she was violent; now, supported on one arm, and not noticing my refusal to obey her, she seemed to find childish diversion in pulling the feathers from the rents she had just made, and ranging them on the sheet according to their different species: her mind had strayed to other associations.

"That's a turkey's," she murmured to herself; "and this is a wild-duck's; and this is a pigeon's. Ah, they put pigeons' feathers in the pillows — no wonder I couldn't die! Let me take care to throw it on the floor when I lie down. And here's a moor-cock's; and this — I should know it among a thousand — it's a lapwing's. Bonny bird; wheeling over our heads in the middle of the moor. It wanted to get to its nest, for the clouds touched the swells, and it felt rain coming. This feather was picked up from the heath, the bird was not shot — we saw its nest in the winter, full of little skeletons. Heathcliff set a trap over it, and the old ones dare not come. I made him promise he'd never shoot a lapwing, after that, and he didn't. Yes, here are more! Did he shoot my lapwings, Nelly? Are they red, any of them? Let me look."

"Give over with that baby-work!" I interrupted, dragging the pillow away, and turning the holes toward the mattress, for she was removing its contents by handfuls. "Lie down and shut your eyes, you're wandering. There's a mess! The down is flying about like snow!"

I went here and there collecting it.

"I see you, Nelly," she continued, dreamily, "an aged woman — you have grey hair, and bent shoulders. This bed is the fairy cave under Penistone Crag, and you are gathering elf-bolts to hurt our heifers; pretending, while I am near, that they are only locks of wool. That's what you'll come to fifty years hence; I know you are not so now. I'm not wandering, you're mistaken, or else I should believe you really *were* that withered hag, and I should think I *was* under Penistone Crag, and I'm conscious it's night, and there are two candles on the table making the black press° shine like jet."

press: Clothes press, clothes closet.

"The black press? where is that?" I asked. "You are talking in your sleep!"

"It's against the wall, as it always is," she replied. "It *does* appear odd — I see a face in it!"

"There is no press in the room, and never was," said I, resuming my seat, and looping up the curtain that I might watch her.

"Don't *you* see that face?" she enquired, gazing earnestly at the mirror.

And say what I could, I was incapable of making her comprehend it to be her own; so I rose and covered it with a shawl.

"It's behind there still!" she pursued, anxiously. "And it stirred. Who is it? I hope it will not come out when you are gone! Oh! Nelly, the room is haunted! I'm afraid of being alone!"

I took her hand in mine, and bid her to be composed, for a succession of shudders convulsed her frame, and she *would* keep straining her gaze towards the glass.

"There's nobody here!" I insisted. "It was *yourself,* Mrs. Linton; you knew it a while since."

"Myself!" she gasped, "and the clock striking twelve! It's true then; that's dreadful!"

Her fingers clutched the clothes, and gathered them over her eyes. I attempted to steal to the door with an intention of calling her husband; but I was summoned back by a piercing shriek. The shawl had dropped from the frame.

"Why, what *is* the matter?" cried I. "Who is coward now? Wake up! That is the glass — the mirror, Mrs. Linton; and you see yourself in it, and there am I too by your side."

Trembling and bewildered, she held me fast, but the horror gradually passed from her countenance; its paleness gave place to a glow of shame.

"Oh, dear! I thought I was at home," she sighed. "I thought I was lying in my chamber at Wuthering Heights. Because I'm weak, my brain got confused, and I screamed unconsciously. Don't say anything; but stay with me. I dread sleeping, my dreams appal me."

"A sound sleep would do you good, ma'am," I answered; "and I hope this suffering will prevent your trying starving again."

"Oh, if I were but in my own bed in the old house!" she went on bitterly, wringing her hands. "And that wind sounding in the firs by the lattice. Do let me feel it — it comes straight down the moor — do let me have one breath!"

To pacify her, I held the casement ajar, a few seconds. A cold blast rushed through; I closed it, and returned to my post.

She lay still, now; her face bathed in tears — Exhaustion of body had entirely subdued her spirit; our fiery Catherine was no better than a wailing child!

"How long is it since I shut myself in here?" she asked, suddenly reviving.

"It was Monday evening," I replied, "and this is Thursday night, or rather Friday morning, at present."

"What! of the same week?" she claimed. "Only that brief time?"

"Long enough to live on nothing but cold water and ill-temper," observed I.

"Well, it seems a weary number of hours," she muttered doubtfully, "it must be more — I remember being in the parlour, after they had quarrelled; and Edgar being cruelly provoking, and me running into this room desperate — As soon as ever I had barred the door, utter blackness overwhelmed me, and I fell on the floor — I couldn't explain to Edgar how certain I felt of having a fit, or going raging mad, if he persisted in teasing me! I had no command of tongue, or brain, and he did not guess my agony, perhaps; it barely left me sense to try to escape from him and his voice — Before I recovered sufficiently to see and hear, it began to be dawn; and Nelly, I'll tell you what I thought, and what has kept recurring and recurring till I feared for my reason — I thought as I lay there, with my head against that table leg, and my eyes dimly discerning the grey square of the window, that I was enclosed in the oak-panelled bed at home; and my heart ached with some great grief which, just waking, I could not recollect — I pondered, and worried myself to discover what it could be; and most strangely, the whole last seven years of my life grew a blank! I did not recall that they had been at all. I was a child; my father was just buried, and my misery arose from the separation that Hindley had ordered between me and Heathcliff — I was laid alone, for the first time, and rousing from a dismal doze after a night of weeping — I lifted my hand to push the panels aside, it struck the tabletop! I swept it along the carpet, and then, memory burst in — my late anguish was swallowed in a paroxysm of despair — I cannot say why I felt so wildly wretched — it must have been temporary derangement for there is scarcely cause — But, supposing at twelve years old, I had been wrenched from the Heights, and every early association, and my all in all, as Heathcliff was at that time, and been converted, at a stroke, into Mrs. Linton, the lady of Thrushcross Grange, and the wife of a stranger; an exile, and outcast, thenceforth, from what had been my world — You may fancy a glimpse of the abyss where I grovelled! Shake your head as you will, Nelly, *you* have helped to unsettle me! You should have spoken to Edgar, indeed you should, and compelled him to leave me quiet! Oh, I'm burning! I wish I were out of doors — I wish I were a girl again, half savage and hardy, and free . . . and laughing at injuries, not maddening under them! Why am I so changed? why does my blood rush into a hell of tumult at a few words? I'm sure I should be myself were I once among the heather of those hills . . . Open the window again wide, fasten it open! Quick, why don't you move?"

"Because I won't give you your death of cold," I answered.

"You won't give me a chance of life, you mean," she said, sullenly. "However, I'm not helpless yet, I'll open it myself."

And sliding from the bed before I could hinder her, she crossed the room, walking very uncertainly, threw it back, and bent out, careless of the frosty air that cut about her shoulders as keen as a knife.

I entreated, and finally attempted to force her to retire. But I soon found her delirious strength much surpassed mine (she *was* delirious, I became convinced by her subsequent actions and ravings).

There was no moon, and everything beneath lay in misty darkness; not a light gleamed from any house, far or near; all had been extinguished long ago; and those at Wuthering Heights were never visible . . . still she asserted she caught their shining.

"Look!" she cried eagerly, "that's my room, with the candle in it, and the trees swaying before it . . . and the other candle is in Joseph's garret. Joseph sits up late, doesn't he? He's waiting till I come home that he may lock the gate. Well, he'll wait a while yet. It's a rough journey, and a sad heart to travel it; and we must pass by Gimmerton Kirk, to go that journey! We've braved its ghosts often together, and dared each other to stand among the graves and ask them to come . . . But Heathcliff, if I dare you now, will you venture? If you do, I'll keep you. I'll not lie there by myself; they may bury me twelve feet deep, and throw the church down over me; but I won't rest till you are with me. . . . I never will!"

She paused, and resumed with a strange smile, "He's considering . . . he'd rather I'd come to him! Find a way, then! not through that Kirkyard . . . You are slow! be content, you always followed me!"

Perceiving it vain to argue against her insanity, I was planning how I could reach something to wrap about her, without quitting my hold of herself, for I could not trust her alone by the gaping lattice, when, to my consternation, I heard the rattle of the doorhandle, and Mr. Linton entered. He had only then come from the library; and, in passing through the lobby, had noticed our talking and been attracted by curiosity, or fear, to examine what it signified, at that late hour.

"Oh, sir!" I cried, checking the exclamation risen to his lips at the sight which met him, and the bleak atmosphere of the chamber.

"My poor Mistress is ill, and she quite masters me; I cannot manage her at all; pray, come and persuade her to go to bed. Forget your anger, for she's hard to guide any way but her own."

"Catherine ill?" he said, hastening to us. "Shut the window, Ellen! Catherine! why . . . "

He was silent; the haggardness of Mrs. Linton's appearance smote him speechless, and he could only glance from her to me in horrified astonishment.

"She's been fretting here," I continued, "and eating scarcely anything, and never complaining, she would admit none of us till this evening, and so we couldn't inform you of her state, as we were not aware of it ourselves, but it is nothing."

I felt I uttered my explanations awkwardly; the master frowned. "It is nothing, is it, Ellen Dean?" he said sternly. "You shall account more clearly for keeping me ignorant of this!" And he took his wife in his arms, and looked at her with anguish.

At first, she gave him no glance of recognition . . . he was invisible to her abstract gaze. The delirium was not fixed, however; having weaned her eyes from contemplating the outer darkness, by degrees, she centred her attention on him, and discovered who it was that held her.

"Ah! you are come, are you, Edgar Linton?" she said, with angry animation . . . "You are one of those things that are ever found when least wanted, and when you are wanted, never! I suppose we shall have plenty of lamentations, now. . . . I see we shall . . . but they can't keep me from my narrow home out yonder — My resting-place where I'm bound before Spring is over! There it is, not among the Lintons, mind, under the chapel-roof; but in the open air with a head-stone, and you may please yourself, whether you go to them, or come to me!"

"Catherine, what have you done?" commenced the master. "Am I nothing to you, any more? Do you love that wretch, Heath — "

"Hush!" cried Mrs. Linton. "Hush, this moment! You mention that name and I end the matter, instantly, by a spring from the window! What you touch at present, you may have; but my soul will be on that hill-top before you lay hands on me again. I don't want you, Edgar; I'm past wanting you . . . Return to your books . . . I'm glad you possess a consolation, for all you had in me is gone."

"Her mind wanders, sir," I interposed. "She has been talking nonsense the whole evening; but, let her have quiet and proper attendance, and she'll rally . . . Hereafter, we must be cautious how we vex her."

"I desire no further advice from you," answered Mr. Linton. "You knew your mistress's nature, and you encouraged me to harass her. And not to give me one hint of how she has been these three days! It was heartless! months of sickness could not cause such a change!"

I began to defend myself, thinking it too bad to be blamed for another's wicked waywardness!

"I knew Mrs. Linton's nature to be headstrong and domineering," cried I; "but I didn't know that you wished to foster her fierce temper! I didn't know that, to humour her, I should wink at Mr. Heathcliff. I performed the duty of a faithful servant in telling you, and I have got a faithful servant's wages! Well, it will teach me to be careful next time. Next time you may gather intelligence for yourself!"

"The next time you bring a tale to me, you shall quit my service, Ellen Dean," he replied.

"You'd rather hear nothing about it, I suppose, then, Mr. Linton?" said I. "Heathcliff has your permission to come a-courting to Miss and to drop in at every opportunity your absence offers, on purpose to poison the mistress against you?"

Confused as Catherine was, her wits were alert at applying our conversation.

"Ah! Nelly has played traitor," she exclaimed passionately. "Nelly is my hidden enemy — you witch! So you do seek elf-bolts to hurt us! Let me go, and I'll make her rue! I'll make her howl a recantation!"

A maniac's fury kindled under her brows; she struggled desperately to disengage herself from Linton's arms. I felt no inclination to tarry the event; and resolving to seek medical aid on my own responsibility, I quitted the chamber.

In passing the garden to reach the road, at a place where a bridle hook is driven into the wall, I saw something white moved irregularly, evidently by another agent than the wind. Notwithstanding my hurry, I staid to examine it, lest ever after I should have the conviction impressed on my imagination that it was a creature of the other world.

My surprise and perplexity were great to discover, by touch more than vision, Miss Isabella's springer, Fanny, suspended to a handkerchief, and nearly at its last gasp.

I quickly released the animal, and lifted it into the garden. I had seen it follow its mistress upstairs, when she went to bed, and wondered much how it could have got out there, and what mischievous person had treated it so.

While untying the knot round the hook, it seemed to me that I repeatedly caught the beat of horses' feet galloping at some distance;

but there were such a number of things to occupy my reflections that I hardly gave the circumstance a thought, though it was a strange sound, in that place, at two o'clock in the morning.

Mr. Kenneth was fortunately just issuing from his house to see a patient in the village as I came up the street; and my account of Catherine Linton's malady induced him to accompany me back immediately.

He was a plain, rough man; and he made no scruple to speak his doubts of her surviving this second attack; unless she were more submissive to his directions than she had shown herself before.

"Nelly Dean," said he, "I can't help fancying there's an extra cause for this. What has there been to do at the Grange? we've odd reports up here. A stout, hearty lass like Catherine does not fall ill for a trifle; and that sort of people should not either. It's hard work bringing them through fevers, and such things. How did it begin?"

"The master will inform you," I answered; "but you are acquainted with the Earnshaws' violent dispositions, and Mrs. Linton caps them all. I may say this; it commenced in a quarrel. She was struck during a tempest of passion with a kind of fit. That's her account, at least; for she flew off in the height of it, and locked herself up. Afterwards, she refused to eat, and now she alternately raves, and remains in a half-dream, knowing those about her, but having her mind filled with all sorts of strange ideas and illusions."

"Mr. Linton will be sorry?" observed Kenneth, interrogatively.

"Sorry? He'll break his heart should anything happen!" I replied. "Don't alarm him more than necessary."

"Well, I told him to beware," said my companion, "and he must bide the consequences of neglecting my warning! Hasn't he been thick with Mr. Heathcliff lately?"

"Heathcliff frequently visits at the Grange," answered I, "though more on the strength of the mistress having known him when a boy, than because the master likes his company. At present, he's discharged from the trouble of calling; owing to some presumptuous aspirations after Miss Linton which he manifested. I hardly think he'll be taken in again."

"And does Miss Linton turn a cold shoulder on him?" was the doctor's next question.

"I'm not in her confidence," returned I, reluctant to continue the subject.

"No, she's a sly one," he remarked, shaking his head. "She keeps her own counsel! But she's a real little fool. I have it on good authority, that, last night (and a pretty night it was!) she and Heathcliff were walking in the plantation at the back of your house, above two hours; and he pressed her not to go in again, but just mount his horse and away with him! My informant said she could only put him off by pledging her word of honour to be prepared on their first meeting after that: when it was to be, he didn't hear, but you urge Mr. Linton to look sharp!"

This news filled me with fresh fears; I outstripped Kenneth, and ran most of the way back. The little dog was yelping in the garden yet. I spared a minute to open the gate for it, but instead of going to the house door, it crossed up and down snuffing the grass, and would have escaped to the road, had I not seized and conveyed it in with me.

On ascending to Isabella's room, my suspicions were confirmed; it was empty. Had I been a few hours sooner, Mrs. Linton's illness might have arrested her rash step. But what could be done now? There was a bare possibility of overtaking them if pursued instantly. *I* could not pursue them, however; and I dare not rouse the family, and fill the place with confusion; still less unfold the business to my master, absorbed as he was in his present calamity, and having no heart to spare for a second grief!

I saw nothing for it but to hold my tongue, and suffer matters to take their course: and Kenneth being arrived, I went with a badly composed countenance to announce him.

Catherine lay in a troubled sleep; her husband had succeeded in soothing the access of frenzy; he now hung over her pillow, watching every shade, and every change of her painfully expressive features.

The doctor, on examining the case for himself, spoke hopefully to him of its having a favourable termination, if we could only preserve around her perfect and constant tranquility. To me, he signified the threatening danger was, not so much death, as permanent alienation of intellect.

I did not close my eyes that night, nor did Mr. Linton; indeed, we never went to bed: and the servants were all up long before the usual hour, moving through the house with stealthy tread, and exchanging whispers as they encountered each other in their vocations. Every one was active, but Miss Isabella; and they began to remark how sound she slept — her brother too asked if she had risen, and seemed impatient for her presence, and hurt that she showed so little anxiety for her sister-in-law.

I trembled lest he should send me to call her; but I was spared the pain of being the first proclaimant of her flight. One of the maids, a thoughtless girl, who had been on an early errand to Gimmerton, came panting upstairs, open-mouthed, and dashed into the chamber, crying,

"Oh, dear, dear! What mun we have next? Master, master, our young lady — "

"Hold your noise!" cried I hastily, enraged at her clamorous manner.

"Speak lower, Mary — What is the matter?" said Mr. Linton. "What ails your young lady?"

"She's gone, she's gone! Yon' Heathcliff's run off wi' her!" gasped the girl.

"That is not true!" exclaimed Linton, rising in agitation. "It cannot be — how has the idea entered your head? Ellen Dean, go and seek her — it is incredible — it cannot be."

As he spoke he took the servant to the door, and, then, repeated his demand to know her reasons for such an assertion.

"Why I met on the road a lad that fetches milk here," she stammered, "and he asked whether we weren't in trouble at the Grange — I thought he meant for Missis's sickness, so I answered, yes. Then says he, 'they's somebody gone after 'em, I guess?' I stared. He saw I knew naught about it, and he told how a gentleman and lady had stopped to have a horse's shoe fastened at a blacksmith's shop, two miles out of Gimmerton, not very long after midnight! and how the blacksmith's lass had got up to spy who they were: she knew them both directly — And she noticed the man — Heathcliff it was, she felt certain, nob'dy could mistake him, besides — put a sovereign in her father's hand for payment. The lady had a cloak about her face; but having desired a sup of water, while she drank, it fell back, and she saw her very plain — Heathcliff held both bridles as they walked on, and they set their faces from the village, and went as fast as the rough roads would let them. The lass said nothing to her father, but she told it all over Gimmerton this morning."

I ran and peeped, for form's sake, into Isabella's room: confirming, when I returned, the servant's statement. Mr. Linton had resumed his seat by the bed; on my re-entrance, he raised his eyes, read the meaning of my blank aspect, and dropped them without giving an order, or uttering a word.

"Are we to try any measures for overtaking and bringing her back?" I inquired. "How should we do?"

"She went of her own accord," answered the master; "she had a right to go if she pleased — Trouble me no more about her — Hereafter she is only my sister in name; not because I disown her, but because she has disowned me."

And that was all he said on the subject; he did not make a single inquiry further, or mention her in any way, except directing me to send what property she had in the house to her fresh home, wherever it was, when I knew it.

CHAPTER 13

For two months the fugitives remained absent; in those two months, Mrs. Linton encountered and conquered the worst shock of what was denominated a brain fever. No mother could have nursed an only child more devotedly than Edgar tended her. Day and night, he was watching, and patiently enduring all the annoyances that irritable nerves and a shaken reason could inflict: and, though Kenneth remarked that what he saved from the grave would only recompense his care by forming the source of constant future anxiety, in fact, that his health and strength were being sacrificed to preserve a mere ruin of humanity, he knew no limits in gratitude and joy when Catherine's life was declared out of danger; and hour after hour, he would sit beside her, tracing the gradual return to bodily health, and flattering his too sanguine hopes with the illusion that her mind would settle back to its right balance also, and she would soon be entirely her former self.

The first time she left her chamber, was at the commencement of the following March. Mr. Linton had put on her pillow, in the morning, a handful of golden crocuses; her eye, long stranger to any gleam of pleasure, caught them in waking, and shone delighted as she gathered them eagerly together.

"These are the earliest flowers at the Heights!" she exclaimed. "They remind me of soft thaw winds, and warm sunshine, and nearly melted snow — Edgar, is there not a south wind, and is not the snow almost gone?"

"The snow is quite gone down here, darling!" replied her husband, "and I only see two white spots on the whole range of moors — The sky is blue, and the larks are singing, and the becks and brooks are all brim full. Catherine, last spring at this time, I was longing to have you under this roof — now, I wish you were a mile or two up those hills; the air blows so sweetly, I feel that it would cure you."

"I shall never be there, but once more!" said the invalid; "and then you'll leave me, and I shall remain, for ever. Next spring you'll long again to have me under this roof, and you'll look back and think you were happy to-day."

Linton lavished on her the kindest caresses, and tried to cheer her by the fondest words, but vaguely regarding the flowers, she let the tears collect on her lashes, and stream down her cheeks unheeding.

We knew she was really better, and therefore, decided that long confinement to a single place produced much of this despondency, and it might be partially removed by a change of scene.

The master told me to light a fire in the many-weeks-deserted parlour, and to set an easy-chair in the sunshine by the window; and then he brought her down, and she sat a long while enjoying the genial heat, and, as we expected, revived by the objects round her, which, though familiar, were free from the dreary associations investing her hated sick-chamber. By evening, she seemed greatly exhausted; yet no arguments could persuade her to return to that apartment, and I had to arrange the parlour sofa for her bed, till another room could be prepared.

To obviate the fatigue of mounting and descending the stairs, we fitted up this, where you lie at present, on the same floor with the parlour: and she was soon strong enough to move from one to the other, leaning on Edgar's arm.

Ah, I thought myself, she might recover, so waited on as she was. And there was double cause to desire it, for on her existence depended that of another; we cherished the hope that in a little while, Mr. Linton's heart would be gladdened, and his lands secured from a stranger's gripe, by the birth of an heir.

I should mention that Isabella sent to her brother, some six weeks from her departure, a short note, announcing her marriage with Heathcliff. It appeared dry and cold; but at the bottom was dotted in with pencil an obscure apology, and an entreaty for kind remembrance, and reconciliation, if her proceeding had offended him; asserting that she could not help it then, and being done, she had now no power to repeal it.

Linton did not reply to this, I believe; and, in a fortnight more, I got a long letter which I considered odd coming from the pen of a bride just out of the honeymoon. I'll read it, for I keep it yet. Any relic of the dead is precious, if they were valued living.

Dear Ellen, it begins.

I came last night to Wuthering Heights, and heard, for the first time, that Catherine has been, and is yet, very ill. I must not write to her, I suppose, and my brother is either too angry or too distressed to answer what I send him. Still, I must write to somebody, and the only choice left me is you.

Inform Edgar that I'd give the world to see his face again — that my heart returned to Thrushcross Grange in twenty-four hours after I left it, and is there at this moment, full of warm feelings for him and Catherine! *I can't follow it through* — (those words are underlined) —

they need not expect me, and they may draw what conclusions they please; taking care, however, to lay nothing at the door of my weak will, or deficient affection.

The remainder of the letter is for yourself alone. I want to ask you two questions: the first is,

How did you contrive to preserve the common sympathies of human nature when you resided here? I cannot recognise any sentiment which those around share with me.

The second question, I have great interest in; it is this —

Is Mr. Heathcliff a man? If so, is he mad? and if not, is he a devil? I shan't tell my reasons for making this inquiry; but, I beseech you to explain, if you can, what I have married — that is, when you call to see me; and you must call, Ellen, very soon. Don't write, but come, and bring me something from Edgar.

Now, you shall hear how I have been received in my new home, as I am led to imagine the Heights will be. It is to amuse myself that I dwell on such subjects as the lack of external comforts; they never occupy my thoughts, except at the moment when I miss them — I should laugh and dance for joy, if I found their absence was the total of my miseries, and the rest was an unnatural dream!

The sun set behind the Grange, as we turned on to the moors; by that, I judged it to be six o'clock; and my companion halted half-an-hour, to inspect the park, and the gardens, and, probably, the place itself, as well as he could; so it was dark when we dismounted in the paved yard of the farmhouse, and your old fellow-servant, Joseph, issued out to receive us by the light of a dip candle. He did it with a courtesy that redounded to his credit. His first act was to elevate his torch to a level with my face, squint malignantly, project his under lip, and turn away.

Then he took the two horses, and led them into the stables; reappearing for the purpose of locking the outer gate, as if we lived in an ancient castle.

Heathcliff stayed to speak to him, and I entered the kitchen — a dingy, untidy hole; I dare say you would not know it, it is so changed since it was in your charge.

By the fire stood a ruffianly child, strong in limb, and dirty in garb, with a look of Catherine in his eyes and about his mouth.

"This is Edgar's legal nephew," I reflected — "mine in a manner; I must shake hands, and — yes — I must kiss him. It is right to establish a good understanding at the beginning."

I approached, and, attempting to take his chubby fist, said —

"How do you do, my dear?"

He replied in a jargon I did not comprehend.

"Shall you and I be friends, Hareton?" was my next essay at conversation.

An oath, and a threat to set Throttler on me if I did not "frame off"° rewarded my perseverance.

"Hey, Throttler, lad!" whispered the little wretch, rousing a half-bred bull-dog from its lair in a corner. "Now, wilt tuh be ganging?"° he asked authoritatively.

Love for my life urged compliance; I stepped over the threshold to wait till the others should enter. Mr. Heathcliff was nowhere visible; and Joseph, whom I followed to the stables, and requested to accompany me in, after staring and muttering to himself, screwed up his nose and replied —

"Mim! mim! mim! Did iver Christian body hear owt like it? Minching un' munching!° Hah can Aw tell whet ye say?"

"I say, I wish you to come with me into the house!" I cried, thinking him deaf, yet highly disgusted at his rudeness.

"Nor nuh me!° Aw getten summut else to do," he answered, and continued his work, moving his lantern jaws meanwhile, and surveying my dress and countenance (the former a great deal too fine, but the latter, I'm sure, as sad as he could desire) with sovereign contempt.

I walked round the yard, and through a wicket, to another door, at which I took the liberty of knocking, in hopes some more civil servant might shew himself.

After a short suspense, it was opened by a tall, gaunt man, without neckerchief, and otherwise extremely slovenly; his features were lost in masses of shaggy hair that hung on his shoulders; and *his* eyes, too, were like a ghostly Catherine's, with all their beauty annihilated.

"What's your business here?" he demanded grimly. "Who are you?"

"My name *was* Isabella Linton," I replied. "You've seen me before, sir. I'm lately married to Mr. Heathcliff; and he has brought he here — I suppose by your permission."

"Is he come back, then?" asked the hermit, glaring like a hungry wolf.

"Yes — we came just now," I said; "but he left me by the kitchen door; and when I would have gone in, your little boy played sentinel over the place, and frightened me off by the help of a bull-dog."

"It's well the hellish villain has kept his word!" growled my future host, searching the darkness beyond me in expectation of discovering

frame off: Be gone. ***Now, wilt tuh be ganging?:*** Will you be going? ***Minching un' munching:*** Mincing and mouthing. ***Nor nuh me!:*** Not me!

Heathcliff, and then he indulged in a soliloquy of execrations, and threats of what he would have done had the "fiend" deceived him.

I repented having tried this second entrance; and was almost inclined to slip away before he finished cursing, but ere I could execute that intention, he ordered me in, and shut and refastened the door.

There was a great fire, and that was all the light in the huge apartment, whose floor had grown a uniform grey; and the once brilliant pewter dishes which used to attract my gaze when I was a girl partook of a similar obscurity, created by tarnish and dust.

I inquired whether I might call the maid, and be conducted to a bed-room? Mr. Earnshaw vouchsafed no answer. He walked up and down, with his hands in his pockets, apparently quite forgetting my presence; and his abstraction was evidently so deep, and his whole aspect so misanthropical, that I shrank from disturbing him again.

You'll not be surprised, Ellen, at my feeling particularly cheerless, seated in worse than solitude on that inhospitable hearth, and remembering that four miles distant lay my delightful home, containing the only people I loved on earth: and there might as well be the Atlantic to part us, instead of those four miles, I could not overpass them!

I questioned with myself — where must I turn for comfort? and — mind you don't tell Edgar, or Catherine — above every sorrow beside, this rose pre-eminent — despair at finding nobody who could or would be my ally against Heathcliff!

I had sought shelter at Wuthering Heights, almost gladly, because I was secured by that arrangement from living alone with him; but he knew the people we were coming amongst, and he did not fear their intermeddling.

I sat and thought a doleful time; the clock struck eight, and nine, and still my companion paced to and fro, his head bent on his breast, and perfectly silent, unless a groan, or a bitter ejaculation forced itself out at intervals.

I listened to detect a woman's voice in the house, and filled the interim with wild regrets, and dismal anticipations, which, at last, spoke audibly in irrepressible sighing and weeping.

I was not aware how openly I grieved, till Earnshaw halted opposite, in his measured walk, and gave me a stare of newly awakened surprise. Taking advantage of his recovered attention, I exclaimed —

"I'm tired with my journey, and I want to go to bed! Where is the maid-servant? Direct me to her, as she won't come to me!"

"We have none," he answered; "you must wait on yourself!"

"Where must I sleep, then?" I sobbed — I was beyond regarding self-respect, weighed down by fatigue and wretchedness.

"Joseph will show you Heathcliff's chamber," said he; "open that door — he's in there."

I was going to obey, but he suddenly arrested me, and added in the strangest tone —

"Be so good as to turn your lock, and draw your bolt — don't omit it!"

"Well!" I said. "But why, Mr. Earnshaw?" I did not relish the notion of deliberately fastening myself in with Heathcliff.

"Look here!" he replied, pulling from his waistcoat a curiously constructed pistol, having a double-edged spring knife attached to the barrel. "That's a great tempter to a desperate man, is it not? I cannot resist going up with this every night, and trying his door. If once I find it open, he's done for! I do it invariably, even though the minute before I have been recalling a hundred reasons that should make me refrain — it is some devil urges me to thwart my own schemes by killing him — you fight against that devil, for love, as long as you may; when the time comes, not all the angels in heaven shall save him!"

I surveyed the weapon inquisitively; a hideous notion struck me. How powerful I should be possessing such an instrument! I took it from his hand, and touched the blade. He looked astonished at the expression my face assumed during a brief second. It was not horror, it was covetousness. He snatched the pistol back, jealously; shut the knife, and returned it to its concealment.

"I don't care if you tell him," said he. "Put him on his guard, and watch for him. You know the terms we are on, I see; his danger does not shock you."

"What has Heathcliff done to you?" I asked. "In what has he wronged you to warrant this appalling hatred? Wouldn't it be wiser to bid him quit the house?"

"No!" thundered Earnshaw, "should he offer to leave me, he's a dead man, persuade him to attempt it, and you are a murderess! Am I to lose *all*, without a chance of retrieval? Is Hareton to be a beggar? Oh, damnation! I *will* have it back; and I'll have *his* gold too; and then his blood; and hell shall have his soul! It will be ten times blacker with that guest than ever it was before!"

You've acquainted me, Ellen, with your old master's habits. He is clearly on the verge of madness — he was so, last night, at least. I shuddered to be near him, and thought on the servant's ill-bred moroseness as comparatively agreeable.

He now recommenced his moody walk, and I raised the latch, and escaped into the kitchen.

Joseph was bending over the fire, peering into a large pan that swung above it; and a wooden bowl of oatmeal stood on the settle close by. The contents of the pan began to boil, and he turned to plunge his hand into the bowl; I conjectured that this preparation was probably for our supper, and, being hungry, I resolved it should be eatable — so, crying out sharply — "*I'll* make the porridge!" I removed the vessel out of his reach, and proceeded to take off my hat and riding habit. "Mr. Earnshaw," I continued, "directs me to wait on myself — I will — I'm not going to act the lady among you, for fear I should starve."

"Gooid Lord!" he muttered, sitting down, and stroking his ribbed stockings from the knee to the ankle. "If they's tuh be fresh ortherings° — just when Aw getten used tuh two maisters, if Aw mun hev a *mistress* set o'er my heead, it's loike time tuh be flitting. Aw never *did* think tuh say t'day ut Aw mud lave th' owld place — but Aw daht it's nigh at hend!"

This lamentation drew no notice from me; I went briskly to work; sighing to remember a period when it would have been all merry fun; but compelled speedily to drive off the remembrance. It racked me to recall past happiness, and the greater peril there was of conjuring up its apparition, the quicker the thible° ran round, and the faster the handfuls of meal fell into the water.

Joseph beheld my style of cookery with growing indignation.

"Thear!" he ejaculated. "Hareton, thah willn't sup thy porridge tuh neeght; they'll be nowt bud lumps as big as maw nave.° Thear, agean! Aw'd fling in bowl un all, if Aw were yah! Thear, pale t' guilp off,° un' then yah'll hae done wi't. Bang, bang. It's amarcy t' bothom isn't deaved° aht!

It *was* a rather a rough mess, I own, when poured into the basins; four had been provided, and a gallon pitcher of new milk was brought from the dairy, which Hareton seized and commenced drinking and spilling from the expansive lip.

I expostulated, and desired that he should have his in a mug, affirming that I could not taste the liquid treated so dirtily. The old cynic chose to be vastly offended at this nicety; assuring me, repeatedly, that "the barn was every bit as gooid" as I, "and every bit as wollsome," and wondering how I could fashion to be so conceited; meanwhile, the

ortherings: Orders (orderings). ***thible:*** A stick for stirring porridge or broth. ***as big as maw nave:*** As big as my fist. ***pale t' guilp off:*** Scoop a little out of the pot (to make it cool off). ***deaved:*** Stunned, deafened with noise.

infant ruffian continued sucking; and glowered up at me defyingly, as he slavered into the jug.

"I shall have my supper in another room," I said. "Have you a place you call a parlour?"

"*Parlour!*" he said sneeringly, "*parlour!* Nay, we've noa *parlours.* If yah dunnut loike wer company, they's maister's; un' if yah dunnot loike maister, they's us."

"Then I shall go upstairs," I answered; "show me a chamber."

I put my basin on a tray, and went myself to fetch some more milk.

With great grumblings, the fellow rose, and preceded me in my ascent: we mounted to the garrets; he opening a door, now and then, to look into the apartments we passed.

"Here's a rahm," he said, at last, flinging back a cranky board on hinges. "It's weel eneugh tuh ate a few porridge in. They's a pack uh corn i' t' corner, thear, meeterly clane;° if yah're feared uh muckying yer grand silk cloes,° spread yer hankerchir ut t' top on 't."

The "rahm" was a kind of lumber-hole smelling strong of malt and grain; various sacks of which articles were piled around, leaving a wide, bare space in the middle.

"Why man!" I exclaimed, facing him angrily, "this is not a place to sleep in. I wish to see my bed-room."

"*Bed-rume!*" he repeated, in a tone of mockery. "Yah's see all t' *bed-rumes* thear is — yon's mine."

He pointed into the second garret, only differing from the first in being more naked about the walls, and having a large, low, curtainless bed, with an indigo-coloured quilt, at one end.

"What do I want with yours?" I retorted. "I suppose Mr. Heathcliff does not lodge at the top of the house, does he?"

"Oh, it's Maister *Hathecliff's* yah're wenting?" cried he, as if making a new discovery. "Couldn't ye uh said soa, at onst? un then Aw mud uh telled ye, baht all this wark, ut that's just one yah cannut sea — he allas keeps it locked, un' nob'dy iver mells on't° but hisseln."

"You've a nice house, Joseph," I could not refrain from observing, "and pleasant inmates; and I think the concentrated essence of all the madness in the world took up its abode in my brain the day I linked my fate with theirs! However, that is not to the present purpose — there are other rooms. For Heaven's sake, be quick, and let me settle somewhere!"

meeterly clane: Fairly clean. ***muckying yer grand silk cloes:*** Dirtying your grand silk clothes. ***mells on't:*** Meddles with it.

He made no reply to this adjuration; only plodding doggedly down the wooden steps, and halting before an apartment which, from that halt, and the superior quality of the furniture, I conjectured to be the best one.

There was a carpet, a good one; but the pattern was obliterated by dust; a fireplace hung with cut paper dropping to pieces; a handsome oak-bedstead with ample crimson curtains of rather expensive material, and modern make. But they had evidently experienced rough usage: the valances hung in festoons, wrenched from their rings, and the iron rod supporting them was bent in an arc, on one side, causing the drapery to trail upon the floor. The chairs were also damaged, many of them severely; and deep indentations deformed the panels of the walls.

I was endeavouring to gather resolution for entering, and taking possession, when my fool of a guide announced —

"This here is t' maister's."

My supper by this time was cold, my appetite gone, and my patience exhausted. I insisted on being provided instantly with a place of refuge, and means of repose.

"Whear the divil," began the religious elder. "The Lord bless us! The Lord forgie us! Whear the *hell*, wold ye gang? ye marred, wearisome nowt!° Yah seen all bud Hareton's bit uf a cham'er. They's nut another hoile tuh lig dahn in° i' th' hahse!"

I was so vexed, I flung my tray and its contents on the ground; and then seated myself at the stairs-head, hid my face in my hands, and cried.

"Ech! ech!" exclaimed Joseph. "Weel done, Miss Cathy! weel done, Miss Cathy! Hahsiver, t' maister sall just tum'le o'er them brocken pots; un' then we's hear summut; we's hear hah it's tuh be. Gooid-for-nowt madling! yah desarve pining° froo this tuh Churstmas, flingin' t' precious gifts uh God under fooit i' yer flaysome rages! Bud, Aw'm mista'en if yah shew yer sperrit long. Will Hathecliff bide sich bonny ways think ye? Aw nobbut wish he muh cotch ye i' that plisky.° Aw nobbut wish he may."

And so he went scolding to his den beneath, taking the candle with him, and I remained in the dark.

The period of reflection succeeding this silly action, compelled me to admit the necessity of smothering my pride, and choking my wrath, and bestirring myself to remove its effects.

ye marred, wearisome nowt: You spoiled, wearisome nothing. ***hoile tuh lig dahn in:*** Room to lie down in. ***pining:*** Starving. ***Aw nobbut wish he muh cotch ye i' that plisky:*** I only wish he may catch you in that mischievous trick.

An unexpected aid presently appeared in the shape of Throttler, whom I now recognized as a son of our old Skulker; it had spent its whelphood at the Grange, and was given by my father to Mr. Hindley. I fancy it knew me — it pushed its nose against mine by way of salute, and then hastened to devour the porridge, while I groped from step to step, collecting the shattered earthenware, and drying the splatters of milk from the banisters with my pocket-handkerchief.

Our labours were scarcely over when I heard Earnshaw's tread in the passage; my assistant tucked in his tail, and pressed to the wall; I stole into the nearest doorway. The dog's endeavour to avoid him was unsuccessful, as I guessed by a scutter down stairs, and a prolonged, piteous yelping. I had better luck. He passed on, entered his chamber, and shut the door.

Directly after, Joseph came up with Hareton, to put him to bed. I had found shelter in Hareton's room, and the old man, on seeing me, said —

"They's rahm fur boath yah, un' yer pride, nah, Aw sud think i' th' hahse. It's empty; yah muh hev it all tuh yerseln, un Him as allas maks a third, i' sich ill company!"

Gladly did I take advantage of this intimation; and the minute I flung myself into a chair, by the fire, I nodded, and slept.

My slumber was deep, and sweet, though over far too soon. Mr. Heathcliff awoke me; he had just come in, and demanded, in his loving manner, what I was doing there?

I told him the cause of my staying up so late — that he had the key of our room in his pocket.

The adjective *our* gave mortal offence. He swore it was not, nor ever should be mine; and he'd — but I'll not repeat his language, nor describe his habitual conduct; he is ingenious and unresting in seeking to gain my abhorrence! I sometimes wonder at him with an intensity that deadens my fear: yet, I assure you, a tiger or a venomous serpent could not rouse terror in me equal to that which he wakens. He told me of Catherine's illness, and accused my brother of causing it; promising that I should be Edgar's proxy in suffering, till he could get a hold of him.

I do hate him — I am wretched — I have been a fool! Beware of uttering one breath of this to any one at the Grange. I shall expect you every day — don't disappoint me!

Isabella

CHAPTER 14

As soon as I had perused this epistle, I went to the master, and informed him that his sister had arrived at the Heights, and sent me a letter expressing her sorrow for Mrs. Linton's situation, and her ardent desire to see him; with a wish that he would transmit to her, as early as possible, some token of forgiveness by me.

"Forgiveness!" said Linton. "I have nothing to forgive her, Ellen — you may call at Wuthering Heights this afternoon, if you like, and say that I am not *angry*, but I'm *sorry* to have lost her: especially as I can never think she'll be happy. It is out of the question my going to see her, however; we are eternally divided; and should she really wish to oblige me, let her persuade the villain she has married to leave the country."

"And you won't write her a little note, sir?" I asked, imploringly.

"No," he answered. "It is needless. My communication with Heathcliff's family shall be as sparing as his with mine. It shall not exist!"

Mr. Edgar's coldness depressed me exceedingly; and all the way from the Grange, I puzzled my brains how to put more heart into what he said, when I repeated it; and how to soften his refusal of even a few lines to console Isabella.

I dare say she had been on watch for me since morning: I saw her looking through the lattice, as I came up the garden causeway, and I nodded to her; but she drew back, as if afraid of being observed.

I entered without knocking. There never was such a dreary, dismal scene as the formerly cheerful house presented! I must confess that, if I had been in the young lady's place, I would, at least, have swept the hearth, and wiped the tables with a duster. But she already partook of the pervading spirit of neglect which encompassed her. Her pretty face was wan and listless; her hair uncurled: some locks hanging lankly down, and some carelessly twisted round her head. Probably she had not touched her dress since yester evening.

Hindley was not there. Mr. Heathcliff sat at a table, turning over some papers in his pocket-book; but he rose when I appeared, asked me how I did, quite friendly, and offered me a chair.

He was the only thing there that seemed decent, and I thought he never looked better. So much had circumstances altered their positions, that he would certainly have struck a stranger as a born and bred gentleman, and his wife as a thorough little slattern!

She came forward eagerly to greet me; and held out one hand to take the expected letter.

I shook my head. She wouldn't understand the hint, but followed me to a sideboard, where I went to lay my bonnet, and importuned me in a whisper to give her directly what I had brought.

Heathcliff guessed the meaning of her manœuvres, and said —

"If you have got anything for Isabella, as no doubt you have, Nelly, give it to her. You needn't make a secret of it; we have no secrets between us."

"Oh, I have nothing," I replied, thinking it best to speak the truth at once. "My master bid me tell his sister that she must not expect either a letter or a visit from him at present. He sends his love, ma'am, and his wishes for your happiness, and his pardon for the grief you have occasioned; but he thinks that after this time, his household, and the household here, should drop intercommunication, as nothing good could come of keeping it up."

Mrs. Heathcliff's lip quivered slightly, and she returned to her seat in the window. Her husband took his stand on the hearthstone, near me, and began to put questions concerning Catherine.

I told him as much as I thought proper of her illness, and he extorted from me, by cross-examination, most of the facts connected with its origin.

I blamed her, as she deserved, for bringing it all on herself; and ended by hoping that he would follow Mr. Linton's example, and avoid future interference with his family, for good or evil.

"Mrs. Linton is now just recovering," I said, "she'll never be like she was, but her life is spared, and if you really have a regard for her, you'll shun crossing her way again. Nay, you'll move out of this country entirely; and that you may not regret it, I'll inform you Catherine Linton is as different now, from your old friend Catherine Earnshaw, as that young lady is different from me! Her appearance is changed greatly, her character much more so; and the person, who is compelled, of necessity, to be her companion, will only sustain his affection hereafter, by the remembrance of what she once was, by common humanity, and a sense of duty!"

"That is quite possible," remarked Heathcliff, forcing himself to seem calm, "quite possible that your master should have nothing but common humanity and a sense of duty to fall back upon. But do you imagine that I shall leave Catherine to his *duty* and *humanity*? and can you compare my feelings respecting Catherine, to his? Before you leave this house, I must exact a promise from you, that you'll get me an interview with her — consent, or refuse, I *will* see her! What do you say?"

"I say, Mr. Heathcliff," I replied, "you must not — you never shall through my means. Another encounter between you and the master would kill her altogether!"

"With your aid that may be avoided," he continued; "and should there be danger of such an event — should he be the cause of adding a single trouble more to her existence — why, I think, I shall be justified in going to extremes! I wish you had sincerity enough to tell me whether Catherine would suffer greatly from his loss. The fear that she would restrains me: and there you see the distinction between our feelings — Had he been in my place, and I in his, though I hated him with a hatred that turned my life to gall, I never would have raised a hand against him. You may look incredulous, if you please! I never would have banished him from her society, as long as she desired his. The moment her regard ceased, I would have torn his heart out, and drank his blood! But, till then — if you don't believe me, you don't know me — till then, I would have died by inches before I touched a single hair of his head!"

"And yet," I interrupted, "you have no scruples in completely ruining all hopes of her perfect restoration, by thrusting yourself into her remembrance, now, when she has nearly forgotten you, and involving her in a new tumult of discord and distress."

"You suppose she has nearly forgotten me?" he said. "Oh, Nelly! you know she has not! You know as well as I do, that for every thought she spends on Linton, she spends a thousand on me! At a most miserable period of my life, I had a notion of the kind, it haunted me on my return to the neighbourhood, last summer, but only her own assurance could make me admit the horrible idea again. And then, Linton would be nothing, nor Hindley, nor all the dreams that ever I dreamt. Two words would comprehend my future, *death* and *hell* — existence, after losing her, would be hell.

"Yet I was a fool to fancy for a moment that she valued Edgar Linton's attachment more than mine — If he loved with all the powers of his puny being, he couldn't love as much in eighty years, as I could in a day. And Catherine has a heart as deep as I have; the sea could be as readily contained in that horse-trough, as her whole affection be monopolized by him — Tush! He is scarcely a degree dearer to her than her dog, or her horse — it is not in him to be loved like me, how can she love in him what he has not?"

"Catherine and Edgar are as fond of each other as any two people can be!" cried Isabella with sudden vivacity. "No one has a right to talk in that manner, and I won't hear my brother depreciated in silence!"

"Your brother is wondrous fond of you too, isn't he?" observed Heathcliff scornfully. "He turns you adrift on the world with surprising alacrity."

"He is not aware of what I suffer," she replied. "I didn't tell him that."

"You have been telling him something, then — you have written, have you?"

"To say that I was married, I did write — you saw the note."

"And nothing since?"

"No."

"My young lady is looking sadly the worse for her change of condition," I remarked. "Somebody's love comes short in her case, obviously — whose I may guess; but, perhaps, I shouldn't say."

"I should guess it was her own," said Heathcliff. "She degenerates into a mere slut! She is tired of trying to please me, uncommonly early — You'd hardly credit it, but the very morrow of our wedding, she was weeping to go home. However, she'll suit this house so much the better for not being over nice, and I'll take care she does not disgrace me by rambling abroad."

"Well, sir," returned I, "I hope you'll consider that Mrs. Heathcliff is accustomed to be looked after, and waited on; and that she has been brought up like an only daughter whom every one was ready to serve — You must let her have a maid to keep things tidy about her, and you must treat her kindly — Whatever be your notion of Mr. Edgar, you cannot doubt that she has a capacity for strong attachments, or she wouldn't have abandoned the elegancies, and comforts, and friends of her former home, to fix contentedly, in such a wilderness as this, with you."

"She abandoned them under a delusion," he answered; "picturing in me a hero of romance, and expecting unlimited indulgences from my chivalrous devotion. I can hardly regard her in the light of a rational creature, so obstinately has she persisted in forming a fabulous notion of my character, and acting on the false impressions she cherished. But, at last, I think she begins to know me — I don't perceive the silly smiles and grimaces that provoked me, at first; and the senseless incapability of discerning that I was in earnest when I gave her my opinion of her infatuation, and herself — It was a marvellous effort of perspicacity to discover that I did not love her. I believed, at one time, no lessons could teach her that! and yet it is poorly learnt; for this morning she announced, as a piece of appalling intelligence, that I had actually succeeded in making her hate me! A positive labour of Hercules, I assure you! If it be achieved, I have cause to return thanks — Can I trust your assertion, Isabella? are you sure you hate me? If I let you alone for a half a day, won't you come sighing and wheedling to me again? I dare say she would rather I had seemed all tenderness before you; it wounds her vanity to have the truth exposed. But I don't care who knows that the passion was wholly on one side, and I never told her a lie about it. She cannot accuse me of showing a bit of deceitful softness. The first thing she saw me do, on coming out of the Grange, was to hang up her little dog, and when she pleaded for it, the first words I uttered were a wish that I had the hanging of every being belonging to her, except one: possibly, she took that exception for herself— But no brutality disgusted her — I suppose she has an innate admiration of it, if only her precious person were secure from injury! Now, was it not the depth of absurdity — of genuine idiocy, for that pitiful, slavish, mean-minded brach to dream that I could love her? Tell your master, Nelly, that I never, in all my life, met with such an abject thing as she is — She even disgraces the name of Linton; and I've sometimes relented, from pure lack of invention, in my experiments on what she could endure, and still creep shamefully cringing back! But tell him, also, to set his fraternal and magisterial heart at ease, that I keep strictly within the limits of the law — I have avoided, up to this period, giving her the slightest right to claim a separation; and what's more, she'd thank nobody for dividing us — if she desired to go she might — the nuisance of her presence outweighs the gratification to be derived from tormenting her!"

"Mr. Heathcliff," said I, "this is the talk of a madman, and your wife, most likely, is convinced you are mad; and, for that reason, she has borne with you hitherto: but now that you say she may go, she'll doubtless avail herself of the permission — You are not so bewitched, ma'am, are you, as to remain with him of your own accord?"

"Take care, Ellen!" answered Isabella, her eyes sparkling irefully — there was no misdoubting their expression, the full success of her partner's endeavours to make himself detested. "Don't put faith in a single word he speaks. He's a lying fiend, a monster, and not a human being! I've been told I might leave him before; and I've made the attempt, but I dare not repeat it! Only, Ellen, promise you'll not mention a syllable of his infamous conversation to my brother or Catherine — whatever he may pretend, he wishes to provoke Edgar to desperation — he says he has married me on purpose to obtain power over him; and he shan't obtain it — I'll die first! I just hope, I pray that he may forget his diabolical prudence, and kill me! The single pleasure I can imagine is to die, or to see him dead!"

"There — that will do for the present!" said Heathcliff. "If you are called upon in a court of law, you'll remember her language, Nelly! and take a good look at that countenance — she's near the point which would suit me. No, you're not fit to be your own guardian, Isabella, now; and I, being your legal protector, must retain you in my custody, however distasteful the obligation may be — Go upstairs; I have something to say to Ellen Dean, in private. That's not the way — upstairs, I tell you! Why this is the road upstairs, child!"

He seized, and thrust her from the room; and returned muttering,

"I have no pity! I have no pity! The more the worms writhe, the more I yearn to crush out their entrails! It is a moral teething, and I grind with greater energy, in proportion to the increase of pain."

"Do you understand what the word pity means?" I said, hastening to resume my bonnet. "Did you ever feel a touch of it in your life?"

"Put that down!" he interrupted, perceiving my intention to depart. "You are not going yet — Come here now, Nelly — I must either persuade or compel you to aid me in fulfilling my determination to see Catherine, and that without delay — I swear that I meditate no harm; I don't desire to cause any disturbance, or to exasperate or insult Mr. Linton; I only wish to hear from herself how she is, and why she has been ill; and to ask, if anything that I could do would be of use to her. Last night, I was in the Grange garden six hours, and I'll return there to-night; and every night I'll haunt the place, and every day, till I find an opportunity of entering. If Edgar Linton meets me, I shall not hesitate to knock him down, and give him enough to insure his quiescence while I stay — If his servants oppose me, I shall threaten them off with these pistols — But wouldn't it be better to prevent my coming in contact with them, or their master? And you could do it so easily! I'd warn you when I came, and then you might let me in unobserved, as soon as she was alone, and watch till I departed — your conscience quite calm, you would be hindering mischief."

I protested against playing that treacherous part in my employer's house; and besides, I urged the cruelty and selfishness of his destroying Mrs. Linton's tranquillity for his satisfaction.

"The commonest occurrence startles her painfully," I said. "She's all nerves, and she couldn't bear the surprise, I'm positive — Don't persist, sir! or else, I shall be obliged to inform my master of your designs, and he'll take measures to secure his house and its inmates from any such unwarrantable intrusions!"

"In that case, I'll take measures to secure you, woman!" exclaimed Heathcliff, "you shall not leave Wuthering Heights till to-morrow morning. It is a foolish story to assert that Catherine could not bear to see me; and as to surprising her, I don't desire it, you must prepare her — ask her if I may come. You say she never mentions my name, and that I am never mentioned to her. To whom should she mention me if I am a forbidden topic in the house? She thinks you are all spies for her husband — Oh, I've no doubt she's in hell among you! I guess, by her silence, as much as anything, what she feels. You say she is often restless, and anxious-looking — is that a proof of tranquillity? You talk of her mind being unsettled — How the devil could it be otherwise, in her frightful isolation. And that insipid, paltry creature attending her from *duty* and *humanity!* From *pity* and *charity!* He might as well plant an oak in a flower-pot, and expect it to thrive, as imagine he can restore her to vigour in the soil of his shallow cares! Let us settle it at once; will you stay here, and am I to fight my way to Catherine over Linton and his footmen? Or will you be my friend, as you have been hitherto, and do what I request? Decide! because there is no reason for my lingering another minute, if you persist in your stubborn ill-nature!"

Well, Mr. Lockwood, I argued and complained, and flatly refused him fifty times; but in the long run he forced me to an agreement — I engaged to carry a letter from him to my mistress; and, should she consent, I promised to let him have intelligence of Linton's next absence from home, when he might come, and get in as he was able — I wouldn't be there, and my fellow servants should be equally out of the way.

Was it right or wrong? I fear it was wrong, though expedient. I thought I prevented another explosion by my compliance; and I thought, too, it might create a favourable crisis in Catherine's mental illness: and then I remembered Mr. Edgar's stern rebuke of my carrying tales; and I tried to smooth away all disquietude on the subject, by affirming, with frequent iteration, that that betrayal of trust, if it merited so harsh an appellation, should be the last.

Notwithstanding, my journey homeward was sadder than my journey thither; and many misgivings I had, ere I could prevail on myself to put the missive into Mrs. Linton's hand.

But here is Kenneth — I'll go down, and tell him how much better you are. My history is *dree,*° as we say, and will serve to wile away another morning.

Dree, and dreary! I reflected as the good woman descended to receive the doctor; and not exactly of a kind which I should have chosen to amuse me; but never mind! I'll extract wholesome medicines from Mrs. Dean's bitter herbs; and firstly, let me beware of the

dree: Heavy, full of trouble.

fascination that lurks in Catherine Heathcliff's brilliant eyes. I should be in a curious taking if I surrendered my heart to that young person, and the daughter turned out a second edition of the mother!

CHAPTER 15

Another week over — and I am so many days nearer health, and spring! I have now heard all my neighbour's history, at different sittings, as the housekeeper could spare time from more important occupations. I'll continue it in her own words, only a little condensed. She is, on the whole, a very fair narrator and I don't think I could improve her style.

In the evening, she said, the evening of my visit to the Heights, I knew, as well as if I saw him, that Mr. Heathcliff was about the place; and I shunned going out, because I still carried his letter in my pocket, and didn't want to be threatened, or teased any more.

I had made up my mind not to give it till my master went somewhere, as I could not guess how its receipt would affect Catherine. The consequence was, that it did not reach her before the lapse of three days. The fourth was Sunday, and I brought it into her room, after the family were gone to church.

There was a man servant left to keep the house with me, and we generally made a practice of locking the doors during the hours of service; but on that occasion, the weather was so warm and pleasant that I set them wide open; and to fulfil my engagement, as I knew who would be coming, I told my companion that the mistress wished very much for some oranges, and he must run over to the village and get a few, to be paid for on the morrow. He departed, and I went upstairs.

Mrs. Linton sat in a loose, white dress, with a light shawl over her shoulders, in the recess of the open window, as usual. Her thick, long hair had been partly removed at the beginning of her illness, and now, she wore it simply combed in its natural tresses over her temples and neck. Her appearance was altered, as I had told Heathcliff, but when she was calm, there seemed unearthly beauty in the change.

The flash of her eyes had been succeeded by a dreamy and melancholy softness: they no longer gave the impression of looking at the objects around her; they appeared always to gaze beyond, and far beyond — you would have said out of this world — Then, the paleness of her face, its haggard aspect having vanished as she recovered flesh, and the peculiar expression arising from her mental state, though painfully suggestive of their causes, added to the touching interest which she awakened; and invariably to me, I know, and to any person who saw her, I should think, refuted more tangible proofs of convalescence and stamped her as one doomed to decay.

A book lay spread on the sill before her, and the scarcely perceptible wind fluttered its leaves at intervals. I believe Linton had laid it there, for she never endeavoured to divert herself with reading, or occupation of any kind; and he would spend many an hour trying to entice her attention to some subject which had formerly been her amusement.

She was conscious of his aim, and in her better moods, endured his efforts placidly, only showing their uselessness by now and then suppressing a wearied sigh, and checking him at last, with the saddest of smiles and kisses. At other times, she would turn petulantly away, and hide her face in her hands, or even push him off angrily; and then he took care to let her alone, for he was certain of doing no good.

Gimmerton chapel bells were still ringing; and the full, mellow flow of the beck in the valley came soothingly on the ear. It was a sweet substitute for the yet absent murmur of the summer foliage, which drowned that music about the Grange, when the trees were in leaf. At Wuthering Heights it always sounded on quiet days, following a great thaw, or a season of steady rain — and, of Wuthering Heights, Catherine was thinking as she listened; that is, if she thought, or listened, at all; but she had the vague, distant look I mentioned before, which expressed no recognition of material things either by ear or eye.

"There's a letter for you, Mrs. Linton," I said, gently inserting it in one hand that rested on her knee. "You must read it immediately, because it wants an answer. Shall I break the seal?"

"Yes," she answered, without altering the direction of her eyes.

I opened it — it was very short.

"Now," I continued, "read it."

She drew away her hand, and let it fall. I replaced it in her lap, and stood waiting till it should please her to glance down; but that movement was so long delayed that at last I resumed —

"Must I read it, ma'am? It is from Mr. Heathcliff."

There was a start, and a troubled gleam of recollection, and a struggle to arrange her ideas. She lifted the letter, and seemed to peruse it; and when she came to the signature she sighed; yet still I found she had not gathered its import, for upon my desiring to hear her reply, she merely pointed to the name, and gazed at me with mournful and questioning eagerness.

"Well, he wishes to see you," said I, guessing her need of an interpreter. "He's in the garden by this time, and impatient to know what answer I shall bring."

As I spoke, I observed a large dog, lying on the sunny grass beneath, raise its ears, as if about to bark, and then smoothing them back, announce by a wag of the tail that some one approached whom it did not consider a stranger.

Mrs. Linton bent forward, and listened breathlessly. The minute after a step traversed the hall; the open house was too tempting for Heathcliff to resist walking in: most likely he supposed that I was inclined to shirk my promise, and so resolved to trust to his own audacity.

With straining eagerness Catherine gazed towards the entrance of her chamber. He did not hit the right room directly; she motioned me to admit him; but he found it out, ere I could reach the door, and in a stride or two was at her side, and had her grasped in his arms.

He neither spoke, nor loosed his hold for some five minutes, during which period he bestowed more kisses than ever he gave in his life before, I dare say; but then my mistress had kissed him first, and I plainly saw that he could hardly bear, for downright agony, to look into her face! The same conviction had stricken him as me, from the instant he beheld her, that there was no prospect of ultimate recovery there — she was fated, sure to die.

"O, Cathy! Oh, my life! how can I bear it?" was the first sentence he uttered, in a tone that did not seek to disguise his despair.

And now he stared at her so earnestly that I thought the very intensity of his gaze would bring tears into his eyes; but they burned with anguish, they did not melt.

"What now?" said Catherine, leaning back, and returning his look with a suddenly clouded brow — her humour was a mere vane for constantly varying caprices. "You and Edgar have broken my heart, Heathcliff! And you both come to bewail the deed to me, as if you were the people to be pitied! I shall not pity you, not I. You have killed me — and thriven on it, I think. How strong you are! How many years do you mean to live after I am gone?"

Heathcliff had knelt on one knee to embrace her; he attempted to rise, but she seized his hair, and kept him down.

"I wish I could hold you," she continued, bitterly, "till we were both dead! I shouldn't care what you suffered. I care nothing for your sufferings. Why shouldn't you suffer? I do! Will you forget me — will you be happy when I am in the earth? Will you say twenty years hence, 'That's the grave of Catherine Earnshaw. I loved her long ago, and was wretched to lose her; but it is past. I've loved many others since — my children are dearer to me than she was, and, at death, I shall not rejoice that I am going to her, I shall be sorry that I must leave them!' Will you say so, Heathcliff?"

"Don't torture me till I'm as mad as yourself," cried he, wrenching his head free, and grinding his teeth.

The two, to a cool spectator, made a strange and fearful picture. Well might Catherine deem that heaven would be a land of exile to her, unless, with her mortal body, she cast away her mortal character also. Her present countenance had a wild vindictiveness in its white cheek, and a bloodless lip, and scintillating eye; and she retained, in her closed fingers, a portion of the locks she had been grasping. As to her companion, while raising himself with one hand, he had taken her arm with the other; and so inadequate was his stock of gentleness to the requirements of her condition, that on his letting go, I saw four distinct impressions left blue in the colourless skin.

"Are you possessed with a devil," he pursued, savagely, "to talk in that manner to me, when you are dying? Do you reflect that all those words will be branded in my memory, and eating deeper eternally, after you have left me? You know you lie to say I have killed you; and, Catherine, you know that I could as soon forget you, as my existence! Is it not sufficient for your infernal selfishness, that while you are at peace I shall writhe in the torments of hell?"

"I shall not be at peace," moaned Catherine, recalled to a sense of physical weakness by the violent, unequal throbbing of her heart, which beat visibly and audibly under this excess of agitation.

She said nothing further till the paroxysm was over; then she continued, more kindly —

"I'm not wishing you greater torment than I have, Heathcliff. I only wish us never to be parted — and should a word of mine distress you hereafter, think I feel the same distress underground, and for my own sake, forgive me! Come here and kneel down again! You never harmed me in your life. Nay, if you nurse anger, that will be worse to remember than my harsh words! Won't you come here again? Do!"

Heathcliff went to the back of her chair, and leant over, but not so far as to let her see his face, which was livid with emotion. She bent round to look at him; he would not permit it; turning abruptly, he walked to the fire-place, where he stood, silent, with his back towards us.

Mrs. Linton's glance followed him suspiciously: every movement woke a new sentiment in her. After a pause, and a prolonged gaze, she resumed, addressing me in accents of indignant disappointment.

"Oh, you see, Nelly! he would not relent a moment, to keep me out of the grave! *That* is how I am loved! Well, never mind! That is not *my* Heathcliff. I shall love mine yet; and take him with me — he's in my soul. And," added she, musingly, "the thing that irks me most is this shattered prison, after all. I'm tired, tired of being enclosed here. I'm wearying to escape into that glorious world, and to be always there; not seeing it dimly through tears, and yearning for it through the walls of an aching heart; but really with it, and in it. Nelly, you think you are better and more fortunate than I; in full health and strength — you are sorry for me — very soon that will be altered. I shall be sorry for *you*. I shall be incomparably beyond and above you all. I *wonder* he won't be near me!" she went on to herself. "I thought he wished it. Heathcliff, dear! you should not be sullen now. Do come to me, Heathcliff."

In her eagerness she rose, and supported herself on the arm of the chair. At that earnest appeal, he turned to her, looking absolutely desperate. His eyes wide, and wet, at last, flashed fiercely on her; his breast heaved convulsively. An instant they held asunder; and then how they met I hardly saw, but Catherine made a spring, and he caught her, and they were locked in an embrace from which I thought my mistress would never be released alive. In fact, to my eyes, she seemed directly insensible. He flung himself into the nearest seat, and on my approaching hurriedly to ascertain if she had fainted, he gnashed at me, and foamed like a mad dog, and gathered her to him with greedy jealousy. I did not feel as if I were in the company of a creature of my own species; it appeared that he would not understand, though I spoke to him; so, I stood off, and held my tongue, in great perplexity.

A movement of Catherine's relieved me a little presently: she put up her hand to clasp his neck, and bring her cheek to his, as he held her: while he, in return, covering her with frantic caresses, said wildly —

"You teach me now how cruel you've been — cruel and false. *Why* did you despise me? *Why* did you betray your own heart, Cathy! I have not one word of comfort — you deserve this. You have killed yourself. Yes, you may kiss me, and cry; and wring out my kisses and tears. They'll blight you — they'll damn you. You loved me — then what *right* had you to leave me? What right — answer me — for the poor fancy you felt for Linton? Because misery, and degradation, and death, and nothing that God or satan could inflict would have parted us, *you*, of your own will, did it. I have not broken your heart — *you* have broken it — and in breaking it, you have broken mine. So much the worse for me, that I am strong. Do I want to live? What kind of living will it be when you — oh, God! would *you* like to live with your soul in the grave?"

"Let me alone. Let me alone," sobbed Catherine. "If I've done wrong, I'm dying for it. It is enough! You left me too; but I won't upbraid you! I forgive you. Forgive me!"

"It is hard to forgive, and to look at those eyes, and feel those wasted hands," he answered. "Kiss me again; and don't let me see your eyes! I forgive what you have done to me. I love *my* murderer — but *yours!* How can I?"

They were silent — their faces hid against each other, and washed by each other's tears. At least, I suppose the weeping was on both sides; as it seemed Heathcliff *could* weep on a great occasion like this.

I grew very uncomfortable, meanwhile; for the afternoon wore fast away, the man whom I had sent off returned from his errand, and I could distinguish, by the shine of the westering sun up the valley, a concourse thickening outside Gimmerton chapel porch.

"Service is over," I announced. "My master will be here in half-an-hour."

Heathcliff groaned a curse, and strained Catherine closer — she never moved.

Ere long I perceived a group of the servants passing up the road towards the kitchen wing. Mr. Linton was not far behind; he opened the gate himself, and sauntered slowly up, probably enjoying the lovely afternoon that breathed as soft as summer.

"Now he is here," I exclaimed. "For Heaven's sake, hurry down! You'll not meet any one of the front stairs. Do be quick; and stay among the trees till he is fairly in."

"I must go, Cathy," said Heathcliff, seeking to extricate himself from his companion's arms. "But, if I live, I'll see you again before you are asleep. I won't stay five yards from your window."

"You must not go!" she answered, holding him as firmly as her strength allowed. "You shall not, I tell you."

"For one hour," he pleaded, earnestly.

"Not for one minute," she replied.

"I *must* — Linton will be up immediately," persisted the alarmed intruder.

He would have risen, and unfixed her fingers by the act — she clung fast, gasping; there was mad resolution in her face.

"No!" she shrieked. "Oh, don't, don't go. It is the last time! Edgar will not hurt us. Heathcliff, I shall die! I shall die!"

"Damn the fool! There he is," cried Heathcliff, sinking back into his seat. "Hush, my darling! Hush, hush, Catherine! I'll stay. If he shot me so, I'd expire with a blessing on my lips."

And there they were fast again. I heard my master mounting the stairs — the cold sweat ran from my forehead; I was horrified.

"Are you going to listen to her ravings?" I said, passionately. "She does not know what she says. Will you ruin her, because she has not wit to help herself? Get up! You could be free instantly. That is the most diabolical deed that ever you did. We are all done for — master, mistress, and servant."

I wrung my hands, and cried out; and Mr. Linton hastened his step at the noise. In the midst of my agitation, I was sincerely glad to observe that Catherine's arms had fallen relaxed, and her head hung down.

"She's fainted or dead," I thought; "so much the better. Far better that she should be dead, than lingering a burden and a misery-maker to all about her."

Edgar sprang to his unbidden guest, blanched with astonishment and rage. What he meant to do, I cannot tell; however, the other stopped all demonstrations, at once, by placing the lifeless-looking form in his arms.

"Look here!" he said. "Unless you be a fiend, help her first — then you shall speak to me!"

He walked into the parlour, and sat down. Mr. Linton summoned me, and with great difficulty, and after resorting to many means, we managed to restore her to sensation; but she was all bewildered; she sighed, and moaned, and knew nobody. Edgar, in his anxiety for her, forgot her hated friend. I did not. I went, at the earliest opportunity, and besought him to depart, affirming that Catherine was better, and he should hear from me in the morning, how she passed the night.

"I shall not refuse to go out of doors," he answered; "but I shall stay in the garden; and, Nelly, mind you keep your word to-morrow. I shall be under those larch trees, mind! or I pay another visit, whether Linton be in or not."

He sent a rapid glance through the half-open door of the chamber, and, ascertaining that what I stated was apparently true, delivered the house of his luckless presence.

CHAPTER 16

About twelve o'clock, that night, was born the Catherine you saw at Wuthering Heights, a puny, seven months' child; and two hours after the mother died, having never recovered sufficient consciousness to miss Heathcliff, or know Edgar.

The latter's distraction at his bereavement is a subject too painful to be dwelt on; its after effects showed how deep the sorrow sunk.

A great addition, in my eyes, was his being left without an heir. I bemoaned that, as I gazed on the feeble orphan; and I mentally abused old Linton for, what was only natural partiality, the securing his estate to his own daughter, instead of his son's.

An unwelcomed infant it was, poor thing! It might have wailed out of life, and nobody cared a morsel, during those first hours of existence. We redeemed the neglect afterwards; but its beginning was as friendless as its end is likely to be.

Next morning — bright and cheerful out of doors — stole softened in through the blinds of the silent room, and suffused the couch and its occupant with a mellow, tender glow.

Edgar Linton had his head laid on the pillow, and his eyes shut. His young and fair features were almost as deathlike as those of the form beside him, and almost as fixed; but *his* was the hush of exhausted anguish, and *hers* of perfect peace. Her brow smooth, her lids closed, her lips wearing the expression of a smile. No angel in heaven could be more beautiful than she appeared; and I partook of the infinite calm in which she lay. My mind was never in a holier frame than while I gazed on that untroubled image of Divine rest. I instinctively echoed the words she had uttered a few hours before. "Incomparably beyond, and above us all! Whether still on earth or now in heaven, her spirit is at home with God!"

I don't know if it be a peculiarity in me, but I am seldom otherwise than happy while watching in the chamber of death, should no frenzied or despairing mourner share the duty with me. I see a repose that neither earth nor hell can break; and I feel an assurance of the endless and shadowless hereafter — the Eternity they have entered — where life is boundless in its duration, and love in its sympathy, and joy in its fulness. I noticed on that occasion how much selfishness there is even in a love like Mr. Linton's, when he so regretted Catherine's blessed release!

To be sure one might have doubted, after the wayward and impatient existence she had led, whether she merited a haven of peace at last. One might doubt in seasons of cold reflection, but not then, in the presence of her corpse. It asserted its own tranquillity, which seemed a pledge of equal quiet to its former inhabitant.

"Do you believe such people *are* happy in the other world, sir? I'd give a great deal to know."

I declined answering Mrs. Dean's question, which struck me as something heterodox. She proceeded:

"Retracing the course of Catherine Linton, I fear we have no right to think she is: but we'll leave her with her Maker."

The master looked asleep, and I ventured soon after sunrise to quit the room and steal out to the pure, refreshing air. The servants thought me gone to shake off the drowsiness of my protracted watch; in reality my chief motive was seeing Mr. Heathcliff. If he had remained among the larches all night he would have heard nothing of the stir at the Grange, unless, perhaps, he might catch the gallop of the messenger going to Gimmerton. If he had come nearer he would probably be aware, from the lights flitting to and fro, and the opening and shutting of the outer doors, that all was not right within.

I wished yet feared to find him. I felt the terrible news must be told, and I longed to get it over, but *how* to do it I did not know.

He was there — at least a few yards further in the park; leant against an old ash tree, his hat off, and his hair soaked with the dew that had gathered on the budded branches, and fell pattering round him. He had been standing a long time in that position, for I saw a pair of ousels passing and repassing, scarcely three feet from him, busy in building their nest, and regarding his proximity no more than that of a piece of timber. They flew off at my approach, and he raised his eyes and spoke:

"She's dead!" he said: "I've not waited for you to learn that. Put your handkerchief away — don't snivel before me. Damn you all! she wants none of *your* tears!"

I was weeping as much for him as her: we do sometimes pity creatures that have none of the feeling either for themselves or others; and when I first looked into his face I perceived that he had got intelligence of the catastrophe; and a foolish notion struck me that his heart was quelled, and he prayed, because his lips moved, and his gaze was bent on the ground.

"Yes, she's dead!" I answered, checking my sobs, and drying my cheeks. "Gone to heaven, I hope, where we may, everyone, join her, if we take due warning, and leave our evil ways to follow good!"

"Did *she* take due warning, then?" asked Heathcliff, attempting a sneer. "Did she die like a saint? Come, give me a true history of the event. How did — "

He endeavored to pronounce the name, but could not manage it; and compressing his mouth, he held a silent combat with his inward agony, defying, meanwhile, my sympathy with an unflinching, ferocious stare.

"How did she die?" he resumed, at last — fain, notwithstanding his hardihood, to have a support behind him for, after the struggle, he trembled, in spite of himself, to his very finger-ends.

"Poor wretch!" I thought; "you have a heart and nerves the same as your brother men! Why should you be anxious to conceal them? Your pride cannot blind God! You tempt him to wring them, till he forces a cry of humiliation!"

"Quietly as a lamb!" I answered, aloud. "She drew a sigh, and stretched herself, like a child reviving, and sinking again to sleep; and five minutes after I felt one little pulse at her heart, and nothing more!"

"And — did she ever mention me?" he asked, hesitating, as if he dreaded the answer to his question would introduce details that he could not bear to hear.

"Her senses never returned — she recognised nobody from the time you left her," I said. "She lies with a sweet smile on her face; and her latest ideas wandered back to pleasant early days. Her life closed in a gentle dream — may she wake as kindly in the other world!"

"May she wake in torment!" he cried, with frightful vehemence, stamping his foot, and groaning in a sudden paroxysm of ungovernable passion. "Why, she's a liar to the end! Where is she? Not *there* — not in heaven — not perished — where? Oh! you said you cared nothing for my sufferings! And I pray one prayer — I repeat till my tongue stiffens — Catherine Earnshaw, may you not rest, as long as I am living! You said I killed you — haunt me then! The murdered *do* haunt their murderers. I believe — I know that ghosts *have* wandered on earth. Be with me always — take any form — drive me mad! only *do* not leave me in this abyss, where I cannot find you! Oh God! it is unutterable! I *cannot* live without my life! I *cannot* live without my soul!"

He dashed his head against the knotted trunk; and, lifting up his eyes, howled, not like a man, but like a savage beast getting goaded to death with knives and spears.

I observed several splashes of blood about the bark of the tree, and his hands and forehead were both stained; probably the scene I witnessed was a repetition of others acted during the night. It hardly moved my compassion — it appalled me; still I felt reluctant to quit him so. But the moment he recollected himself enough to notice me watching, he thundered a command for me to go, and I obeyed. He was beyond my skill to quiet or console!

Mrs. Linton's funeral was appointed to take place on the Friday following her decease; and till then her coffin remained uncovered, and strewn with flowers and scented leaves, in the great drawing-room. Linton spent his days and nights there, a sleepless guardian; and — a circumstance concealed from all but me — Heathcliff spent his nights, at least, outside, equally a stranger to repose.

I held no communication with him; still I was conscious of his design to enter, if he could; and on the Tuesday, a little after dark, when my master, from sheer fatigue, had been compelled to retire a couple of hours, I went and opened one of the windows, moved by his perseverance to give him a chance of bestowing on the fading image of his idol one final adieu.

He did not omit to avail himself of the opportunity, cautiously and briefly; too cautiously to betray his presence by the slightest noise; indeed, I shouldn't have discovered that he had been there, except for the disarrangement of the drapery about the corpse's face, and for observing on the floor a curl of light hair, fastened with a silver thread, which, on examination, I ascertained to have been taken from a locket hung round Catherine's neck. Heathcliff had opened the trinket and cast out its contents, replacing them by a black lock of his own. I twisted the two, and enclosed them together.

Mr. Earnshaw was, of course, invited to attend the remains of his sister to the grave; and he sent no excuse, but he never came; so that, besides her husband, the mourners were wholly composed of tenants and servants. Isabella was not asked.

The place of Catherine's interment, to the surprise of the villagers, was neither in the chapel, under the carved monument of the Lintons, nor yet by the tombs of her own relations, outside. It was dug on a green slope, in a corner of the kirkyard, where the wall is so low that heath and bilberry plants have climbed over it from the moor; and peat mould almost buries it. Her husband lies in the same spot, now; and they have each a simple headstone above, and a plain grey block at their feet, to mark the graves.

CHAPTER 17

That Friday made the last of our fine days, for a month. In the evening, the weather broke; the wind shifted from south to north-east, and brought rain first, and then sleet, and snow.

On the morrow one could hardly imagine that there had been three weeks of summer: the primroses and crocuses were hidden under wintry drifts: the larks were silent, the young leaves of the early trees smitten and blackened — And dreary, and chill, and dismal that morrow did creep over! My master kept his room — I took possession of the lonely parlour, converting it into a nursery; and there I was sitting, with the moaning doll of a child laid on my knee; rocking it to and fro, and watching, meanwhile, the still driving flakes build up the uncurtained window, when the door opened, and some person entered, out of breath, and laughing!

My anger was greater than my astonishment for a minute; I supposed it one of the maids, and I cried,

"Have done! How dare you show your giddiness, here? What would Mr. Linton say if he heard you?"

"Excuse me!" answered a familiar voice, "but I know Edgar is in bed, and I cannot stop myself."

With that, the speaker came forward to the fire, panting and holding her hand to her side.

"I have run the whole way from Wuthering Heights!" she continued, after a pause. "Except where I've flown — I couldn't count the number of falls I've had — Oh, I'm aching all over! Don't be alarmed — There shall be an explanation as soon as I can give it — only just have the goodness to step out and order the carriage to take me on to Gimmerton, and tell a servant to seek up a few clothes in my wardrobe."

The intruder was Mrs. Heathcliff — She certainly seemed in no laughing predicament: her hair streaming on her shoulders, dripping with snow and water; she was dressed in the girlish dress she commonly wore, befitting her age more than her position; a low frock, with short sleeves, and nothing on either head or neck. The frock was of light silk, and clung to her with wet; and her feet were protected merely by thin slippers; add to this a deep cut under one ear, which only the cold prevented from bleeding profusely, a white face scratched and bruised, and a frame hardly able to support itself through fatigue, and you may fancy my first fright was not much allayed when I had leisure to examine her.

"My dear young lady," I exclaimed, "I'll stir nowhere, and hear nothing, till you have removed every article of your clothes, and put on dry things; and certainly you shall not go to Gimmerton to-night, so it is needless to order the carriage."

"Certainly, I shall," she said; "walking or riding — yet I've no objection to dress myself decently; and — ah, see how it flows down my neck now! The fire does make it smart."

She insisted on my fulfilling her directions, before she would let me touch her; and not till after the coachman had been instructed to get ready, and a maid set to pack up some necessary attire, did I obtain her consent for binding the wound, and helping to change her garments.

"Now, Ellen," she said, when my task was finished, and she was seated in an easy chair on the hearth, with a cup of tea before her, "you sit down opposite me, and put poor Catherine's baby away — I don't like to see it! You mustn't think I care little for Catherine, because I behaved so foolishly on entering — I've cried too, bitterly — yes, more than any one else has reason to cry — we parted unreconciled, you remember, and I shan't forgive myself. But for all that, I was not going to sympathise with him — the brute beast! Oh, give me the poker! This is the last thing of his I have about me." She slipped the gold ring from her third finger, and threw it on the floor. "I'll smash it!" she continued, striking it with childish spite. "And then I'll burn it!" and she took and dropped the misused article among the coals. "There! he shall buy another, if he gets me back again. He'd be capable of coming to seek me, to tease Edgar — I dare not stay, lest that notion should possess his wicked head! And besides, Edgar has not been kind, has he? And I won't come suing for his assistance; nor will I bring him into more trouble — Necessity compelled me to seek shelter here; though if I had not learnt he was out of the way, I'd have halted at the kitchen, washed my face, warmed myself, got you to bring what I wanted, and departed again to anywhere out of the reach of my accursed — of that incarnate goblin! Ah, he was in such a fury — if he had caught me! It's a pity, Earnshaw is not his match in strength — I wouldn't have run, till I'd seen him all but demolished, had Hindley been able to do it!"

"Well, don't talk so fast, Miss!" I interrupted, "you'll disorder the handkerchief I have tied round your face, and make the cut bleed again — Drink your tea, and take breath and give over laughing — Laughter is sadly out of place under this roof, and in your condition!"

"An undeniable truth," she replied, "Listen to that child! It maintains a constant wail — send it out of my hearing, for an hour; I shan't stay any longer."

I rang the bell, and committed it to a servant's care; and then I inquired what had urged her to escape from Wuthering Heights in such an unlikely plight — and where she meant to go, as she refused remaining with us.

"I ought, and I wish to remain," answered she, "to cheer Edgar, and take care of the baby, for two things, and because the Grange is my right home — but I tell you, he wouldn't let me! Do you think he could bear to see me grow fat and merry; and could bear to think that we were tranquil, and not resolve on poisoning our comfort? Now, I have the satisfaction of being sure that he detests me to the point of its annoying him seriously to have me within ear-shot, or eye-sight — I notice, when I enter his presence, the muscles of his countenance are involuntarily distorted into an expression of hatred; partly arising from his knowledge of the good causes I have to feel that sentiment for him, and partly from original aversion — It is strong enough to make me feel pretty certain that he would not chase me over England, supposing I contrived a clear escape; and therefore I must get quite away. I've recovered from my first desire to be killed by him. I'd rather he'd kill himself! He has extinguished my love effectually, and so I'm at my ease. I can recollect yet how I loved him; and can dimly imagine that I could still be loving him, if — No, no! Even if he had doted on me, the devilish nature would have revealed its existence, somehow. Catherine had an awfully perverted taste to esteem him so dearly, knowing him so well — Monster! would that he could be blotted out of creation, and out of my memory!"

"Hush, hush! He's a human being," I said. "Be more charitable; there are worse men then he is yet!"

"He's not a human being," she retorted; "and he has no claim on my charity — I gave him my heart, and he took and pinched it to death; and flung it back to me — people feel with their hearts, Ellen, and since he has destroyed mine, I have not power to feel for him, and I would not, though he groaned from this, to his dying day; and wept tears of blood for Catherine! No, indeed, indeed, I wouldn't!" And here Isabella began to cry; but, immediately dashing the water from her lashes, she recommenced.

"You asked, what has driven me to flight at last? I was compelled to attempt it, because I had succeeded in rousing his rage a pitch above his malignity. Pulling out the nerves with red hot pincers requires more coolness than knocking on the head. He was worked up to forget the fiendish prudence he boasted of, and proceeded to murderous violence: I experienced pleasure in being able to exasperate him: the sense of pleasure woke my instinct of self-preservation; so, I fairly broke free, and if ever I come into his hands again he is welcome to a signal revenge.

"Yesterday, you know, Mr. Earnshaw should have been at the funeral. He kept himself sober, for the purpose — tolerably sober; not going to bed mad at six o'clock and getting up drunk at twelve. Consequently, he rose, in suicidal low spirits, as fit for the church as for a dance; and instead, he sat down by the fire, and swallowed gin or brandy by tumblerfuls.

"Heathcliff — I shudder to name him! has been a stranger in the house from last Sunday till to-day — Whether the angels have fed him, or his kin beneath, I cannot tell; but he has not eaten a meal with us for nearly a week — He has just come home at dawn, and gone upstairs to his chamber; locking himself in — as if anybody dreamt of coveting his company! There he has continued, praying like a methodist; only the deity he implored is senseless dust and ashes; and God, when addressed, was curiously confounded with his own black father! After concluding these precious orisons — and they lasted generally till he grew hoarse, and his voice was strangled in his throat — he would be off again; always straight down to the Grange! I wonder Edgar did not send for a constable, and give him into custody! For me, grieved as I was about Catherine, it was impossible to avoid regarding this season of deliverance from degrading oppression as a holiday.

"I recovered spirits sufficient to hear Joseph's eternal lectures without weeping; and to move up and down the house, less with the foot of a frightened thief than formerly. You wouldn't think that I should cry at anything Joseph could say, but he and Hareton are detestable companions. I'd rather sit with Hindley, and hear his awful talk, than with 't' little maister,' and his staunch supporter, that odious old man!

"When Heathcliff is in, I'm often obliged to seek the kitchen, and their society, or starve among the damp, uninhabited chambers; when he is not, as was the case this week, I establish a table and chair at one corner of the house fire, and never mind how Mr. Earnshaw may occupy himself; and he does not interfere with my arrangements: he is quieter, now, than he used to be, if no one provokes him; more sullen and depressed, and less furious. Joseph affirms he's sure he's an altered man, that the Lord has touched his heart, and he is saved 'so as by fire.' I'm puzzled to detect signs of the favourable change, but it is not my business.

"Yester-evening, I sat in my nook reading some old books, till late on towards twelve. It seemed so dismal to go upstairs, with the wild snow blowing outside, and my thoughts continually reverting to the kirkyard and the new-made grave! I dared hardly lift my eyes from the page before me, that melancholy scene so instantly usurped its place.

"Hindley sat opposite; his head leant on his hand, perhaps meditating on the same subject. He had ceased drinking at a point below irrationality, and had neither stirred nor spoken during two or three hours. There was no sound through the house, but the moaning wind which shook the windows every now and then: the faint crackling of the coals, and the click of my snuffers as I removed at intervals the long wick of the candle. Hareton and Joseph were probably fast asleep in bed. It was very, very sad, and while I read, I sighed, for it seemed as if all joy had vanished from the world, never to be restored.

"The doleful silence was broken, at length, by the sound of the kitchen latch — Heathcliff had returned from his watch earlier than usual, owing, I suppose, to the sudden storm.

"That entrance was fastened; and we heard him coming round to get in by the other. I rose with an irrepressible expression of what I felt on my lips, which induced my companion, who had been staring towards the door, to turn and look at me.

"'I'll keep him out five minutes,' he exclaimed. 'You won't object?'

"'No, you may keep him out the whole night, for me,' I answered. 'Do! put the key in the lock, and draw the bolts.'

"Earnshaw accomplished this ere his guest reached the front; he then came and brought his chair to the other side of my table, leaning over it, and searching in my eyes a sympathy with the burning heat that gleamed from his: as he both looked and felt like an assassin, he couldn't exactly find that; but he discovered enough to encourage him to speak.

"'You and I,' he said, 'have each a great debt to settle with the man out yonder! If we were neither of us cowards, we might combine to discharge it. Are you as soft as your brother? Are you willing to endure to the last, and not once attempt a repayment?'

"'I'm weary of enduring now,' I replied, 'and I'd be glad of a retaliation that wouldn't recoil on myself; but treachery and violence are spears pointed at both ends — they wound those who resort to them, worse than their enemies.'

"'Treachery and violence are a just return for treachery and violence!' cried Hindley. 'Mrs. Heathcliff, I'll ask you to do nothing, but sit still, and be dumb — Tell me now, can you? I'm sure you would have as much pleasure as I, in witnessing the conclusion of the fiend's existence; he'll be *your* death unless you overreach him — and he'll be *my* ruin — Damn the hellish villain! He knocks at the door, as if he were master here already! Promise to hold your tongue, and before that clock strikes — it wants three minutes of one — you're a free woman!'

"He took the implements which I described to you in my letter from his breast, and would have turned down the candle — I snatched it away, however, and seized his arm.

"'I'll not hold my tongue!' I said. 'You mustn't touch him . . . Let the door remain shut and be quiet!'

"'No! I've formed my resolution, and by God, I'll execute it!' cried the desperate being. 'I'll do you a kindness, in spite of yourself, and Hareton justice! And you needn't trouble your head to screen me, Catherine is gone — Nobody alive would regret me, or be ashamed, though I cut my throat this minute — and it's time to make an end!'

"I might as well have struggled with a bear, or reasoned with a lunatic. The only resource left me was to run to a lattice, and warn his intended victim of the fate which awaited him.

"'You'd better seek shelter somewhere else to-night!' I exclaimed in a rather triumphant tone. 'Mr. Earnshaw has a mind to shoot you, if you persist in endeavouring to enter.'

"'You'd better open the door, you — ,' he answered, addressing me by some elegant term that I don't care to repeat.

"'I shall not meddle in the matter,' I retorted again. 'Come in, and get shot, if you please! I've done my duty.'

"With that I shut the window, and returned to my place by the fire; having too small a stock of hypocrisy at my command to pretend any anxiety for the danger that menaced him.

"Earnshaw swore passionately at me, affirming that I loved the villain yet, and calling me all sorts of names for the base spirit I evinced. And I, in my secret heart (and conscience never reproached me), thought what a blessing it would be for *him,* should Heathcliff put him out of misery; and what a blessing for *me,* should he send Heathcliff to his right abode! As I sat nursing these reflections, the casement behind me was banged on to the floor by a blow from the latter individual; and his black countenance looked blightingly through. The stanchions stood too close to suffer his shoulders to follow; and I smiled, exulting in my fancied security. His hair and clothes were whitened with snow, and his sharp cannibal teeth, revealed by cold and wrath, gleamed through the dark.

"'Isabella, let me in, or I'll make you repent!' he 'girned,' as Joseph calls it.

"'I cannot commit murder,' I replied. 'Mr. Hindley stands sentinel with a knife and loaded pistol.'

"'Let me in by the kitchen door!' he said.

"'Hindley will be there before me,' I answered. 'And that's a poor love of yours, that cannot bear a shower of snow! We were left at peace in our beds, as long as the summer moon shone, but the moment a blast of winter returns, you must run for shelter! Heathcliff, if I were you, I'd go stretch myself over her grave, and die like a faithful dog . . . The world is surely not worth living in now, is it? You had distinctly impressed on me, the idea that Catherine was the whole joy of your life — I can't imagine how you think of surviving her loss.'

"'He's there . . . is he?' exclaimed my companion, rushing to the gap. 'If I can get my arm out I can hit him!'

"I'm afraid, Ellen, you'll set me down as really wicked — but you don't know all, so don't judge! I wouldn't have aided or abetted an attempt on even *his* life, for anything — Wish that he were dead, I must; and therefore, I was fearfully disappointed, and unnerved by terror for the consequences of my taunting speech, when he flung himself on Earnshaw's weapon and wrenched it from his grasp.

"The charge exploded, and the knife, in springing back, closed into its owner's wrist. Heathcliff pulled it away by main force, slitting up the flesh as it passed on, and thrust it dripping into his pocket. He then took a stone, struck down the division between the two windows, and sprung in. His adversary had fallen senseless with excessive pain, and the flow of blood that gushed from an artery, or a large vein.

"The ruffian kicked and trampled on him, and dashed his head repeatedly against the flags, holding me with one hand, meantime, to prevent me summoning Joseph.

"He exerted preter-human self-denial in abstaining from finishing him, completely; but getting out of breath, he finally desisted, and dragged the apparently inanimate body onto the settle.

"There he tore off the sleeve of Earnshaw's coat, and bound up the wound with brutal roughness, spitting and cursing during the operation, as energetically as he had kicked before.

"Being at liberty, I lost no time in seeking the old servant; who, having gathered by degrees the purport of my hasty tale, hurried below, gasping, as he descended the steps two at once.

" 'Whet is thur tuh do, nah? whet is thur tuh do, nah?'

" 'There's this to do,' thundered Heathcliff, 'that your master's mad; and should he last another month, I'll have him to an asylum. And how the devil did you come to fasten me out, you toothless hound? Don't stand muttering and mumbling there. Come, I'm not going to nurse him. Wash that stuff away; and mind the sparks of your candle — it is more than half brandy!'

" 'Und, soa, yah been murthering on him?' exclaimed Joseph, lifting his hands and eyes in horror. 'If iver Aw seed a seeght loike this! May the Lord — '

"Heathcliff gave him a push onto his knees, in the middle of the blood, and flung a towel to him; but instead of proceeding to dry it up, he joined his hands, and began a prayer which excited my laughter from its odd phraseology. I was in the condition of mind to be shocked at nothing; in fact, I was as reckless as some malefactors show themselves at the foot of the gallows.

" 'Oh, I forgot you,' said the tyrant. 'You shall do that. Down with you. And you conspire with him against me, do you, viper? There, that is work fit for you!'

"He shook me till my teeth rattled, and pitched me beside Joseph, who steadily concluded his supplications, and then rose, vowing he would set off for the Grange directly. Mr. Linton was a magistrate, and though he had fifty wives dead, he should inquire into this.

"He was so obstinate in his resolution, that Heathcliff deemed it expedient to compel, from my lips, a recapitulation of what had taken place; standing over me, heaving with malevolence, as I reluctantly delivered the account in answer to his questions.

"It required a great deal of labour to satisfy the old man that he was not the aggressor; especially with my hardly wrung replies. However, Mr. Earnshaw soon convinced him that he was alive still; he hastened to administer a dose of spirits, and by their succour his master presently regained motion and consciousness.

"Heathcliff, aware that he was ignorant of the treatment received while insensible, called him deliriously intoxicated; and said he should not notice his atrocious conduct further, but advised him to get to bed. To my joy, he left us after giving this judicious counsel, and Hindley stretched himself on the hearth-stone. I departed to my own room, marvelling that I had escaped so easily.

"This morning, when I came down, about half-an-hour before noon, Mr. Earnshaw was sitting by the fire, deadly sick; his evil genius, almost as gaunt and ghastly, leant against the chimney. Neither appeared inclined to dine; and having waited till all was cold on the table, I commenced alone.

"Nothing hindered me from eating heartily; and I experienced a certain sense of satisfaction and superiority, as, at intervals, I cast a look towards my silent companions, and felt the comfort of a quiet conscience within me.

"After I had done, I ventured on the unusual liberty of drawing near the fire, going round Earnshaw's seat, and kneeling in the corner beside him.

"Heathcliff did not glance my way and I gazed up, and contemplated his features, almost as confidently as if they had been turned to stone. His forehead, that I once thought so manly, and that I now think so diabolical, was shaded with a heavy cloud; his basilisk eyes were nearly quenched by sleeplessness — and weeping, perhaps, for the lashes were wet then; his lips devoid of their ferocious sneer, and sealed in an expression of unspeakable sadness. Had it been another, I would have covered my face, in the presence of such grief. In *his* case, I was gratified, and ignoble as it seems to insult a fallen enemy, I couldn't miss this chance of sticking in a dart; his weakness was the only time when I could taste the delight of paying wrong for wrong."

"Fie, fie, Miss!" I interrupted. "One might suppose you have never opened a Bible in your life. If God afflict your enemies, surely that ought to suffice you. It is both mean and presumptuous to add your torture to his!"

"In general, I'll allow that it would be, Ellen," she continued. "But what misery laid on Heathcliff would content me, unless I have a hand in it? I'd rather he suffered *less*, if I might cause his sufferings, and he might *know* that I was the cause. Oh, I owe him so much. On only one condition can I hope to forgive him. It is, if I may take an eye for an eye, a tooth for a tooth, for every wrench of agony, return a wrench, reduce him to my level. As he was the first to injure, make him the first to implore pardon; and then — why then, Ellen, I might show you some generosity. But it is utterly impossible I can ever be revenged, and therefore I cannot forgive him. Hindley wanted some water, and I handed him a glass, and asked him how he was.

" 'Not as ill as I wish,' he replied. 'But leaving out my arm, every inch of me is as sore as if I had been fighting with a legion of imps!'

" 'Yes, no wonder,' was my next remark. 'Catherine used to boast that she stood between you and bodily harm — she meant that certain persons could not hurt you, for fear of offending her. It's well people don't *really* rise from their grave, or, last night, she might have witnessed a repulsive scene! Are not you bruised, and cut over your chest and shoulders?'

" 'I can't say,' he answered; 'but what do you mean? Did he dare to strike me when I was down?'

" 'He trampled on, and kicked you, and dashed you on the ground,' I whispered. 'And his mouth watered to tear you with his teeth; because he's only half a man — not so much.'

"Mr. Earnshaw looked up, like me, to the countenance of our mutual foe; who, absorbed in his anguish, seemed insensible to anything around him; the longer he stood, the plainer his reflections revealed their blackness through his features.

" 'Oh, if God would but give me the strength to strangle him in my last agony, I'd go to hell with joy,' groaned the impatient man, writhing to rise, and sinking back in despair, convinced of his inadequacy for the struggle.

" 'Nay, it's enough that he has murdered one of you,' I observed aloud. 'At the Grange, every one knows your sister would have been living now, had it not been for Mr. Heathcliff. After all, it is preferable to be hated than loved by him. When I recollect how happy we were — how happy Catherine was before he came — I'm fit to curse the day.'

"Most likely, Heathcliff noticed more the truth of what was said, than the spirit of the person who said it. His attention was roused, I saw, for his eyes rained down tears among the ashes, and he drew his breath in suffocating sighs.

"I stared full at him, and laughed scornfully. The clouded windows of hell flashed a moment towards me; the fiend which usually looked out, however, was so dimmed and drowned that I did not fear to hazard another sound of derision.

" 'Get up, and begone out of my sight,' said the mourner.

"I guessed he uttered those words, at least, though his voice was hardly intelligible.

" 'I beg your pardon,' I replied. 'But I loved Catherine too; and her brother requires attendance which, for her sake, I shall supply. Now that she's dead, I see her in Hindley; Hindley has exactly her eyes, if you had not tried to gouge them out, and made them black and red, and her — '

" 'Get up, wretched idiot, before I stamp you to death!' he cried, making a movement that caused me to make one also.

" 'But then,' I continued, holding myself ready to flee; 'if poor Catherine had trusted you, and assumed the ridiculous, contemptible, degrading title of Mrs. Heathcliff, she would soon have presented a similar picture. *She* wouldn't have borne your abominable behaviour quietly; her detestation and disgust must have found voice.'

"The back of the settle and Earnshaw's person interposed between me and him; so instead of endeavouring to reach me, he snatched a dinner knife from the table, and flung it at my head. It struck beneath my ear, and stopped the sentence I was uttering; but pulling it out, I sprang to the door, and delivered another which I hope went a little deeper than his missile.

"The last glimpse I caught of him was a furious rush on his part, checked by the embrace of his host; and both fell locked together on the hearth.

"In my flight through the kitchen I bid Joseph speed to his master; I knocked over Hareton, who was hanging a litter of puppies from a chair-back in the doorway; and, blest as a soul escaped from purgatory, I bounded, leaped, and flew down the steep road: then, quitting its windings, shot direct across the moor, rolling over banks, and wading through marshes; precipitating myself, in fact, towards the beacon light of the Grange. And far rather would I be condemned to a perpetual dwelling in the infernal regions, than even for one night abide beneath the roof of Wuthering Heights again."

Isabella ceased speaking, and took a drink of tea; then she rose, and bidding me put on her bonnet, and a great shawl I had brought, and turning a deaf ear to my entreaties for her to remain another hour, she stepped onto a chair, kissed Edgar's and Catherine's portraits, bestowed a similar salute on me, and descended to the carriage accompanied by Fanny, who yelped wild with joy at recovering her mistress. She was driven away, never to revisit this neighbourhood; but a regular correspondence was established between her and my master when things were more settled.

I believe her new abode was in the south, near London; there she had a son born, a few months subsequent to her escape. He was christened Linton, and, from the first, she reported him to be an ailing, peevish creature.

Mr. Heathcliff, meeting me one day in the village, inquired where she lived. I refused to tell. He remarked that it was not of any moment, only she must beware of coming to her brother: she should not be with him, if he had to keep her himself.

Though I would give no information, he discovered, through some of the other servants, both her place of residence and the existence of the child. Still he didn't molest her; for which forbearance she might thank his aversion, I suppose.

He often asked about the infant, when he saw me; and on hearing its name, smiled grimly, and observed:

"They wish me to hate it too, do they?"

"I don't think they wish you to know anything about it," I answered.

"But I'll have it," he said, "when I want it. They may reckon on that!"

Fortunately, its mother died before the time arrived, some thirteen years after the decease of Catherine, when Linton was twelve, or a little more.

On the day succeeding Isabella's unexpected visit, I had no opportunity of speaking to my master: he shunned conversation, and was fit for discussing nothing. When I could get him to listen, I saw it pleased him that his sister had left her husband, whom he abhorred with an intensity which the mildness of his nature would scarcely seem to allow. So deep and sensitive was his aversion, that he refrained from going anywhere where he was likely to see or hear of Heathcliff. Grief, and that together, transformed him into a complete hermit: he threw up his office of magistrate, ceased even to attend church, avoided the village on all occasions, and spent a life of entire seclusion within the limits of his park and grounds: only varied by solitary rambles on the moors, and visits to the grave of his wife, mostly at evening, or early morning, before other wanderers were abroad.

But he was too good to be thoroughly unhappy long. *He* didn't pray for Catherine's soul to haunt him: Time brought resignation, and a melancholy sweeter than common joy. He recalled her memory with ardent, tender love, and hopeful aspiring to the better world, where he doubted not she was gone.

And he had earthly consolation and affections, also. For a few days, I said, he seemed regardless of the puny successor to the departed: that coldness melted as fast as snow in April, and ere the tiny thing could stammer a word or totter a step, it wielded a despot's sceptre in his heart.

It was named Catherine, but he never called it the name in full, as he had never called the first Catherine short, probably because Heathcliff had a habit of doing so. The little one was always Cathy, it formed to him a distinction from the mother, and yet, a connection with her; and his attachment sprang from its relation to her, far more than from its being his own.

I used to draw a comparison between him, and Hindley Earnshaw, and perplex myself to explain satisfactorily, why their conduct was so opposite in similar circumstances. They had both been fond husbands, and were both attached to their children; and I could not see how they shouldn't both have taken the same road, for good or evil. But, I thought in my mind, Hindley, with apparently the stronger head, has shown himself sadly the worse and the weaker man. When his ship struck, the captain abandoned his post; and the crew, instead of trying to save her, rushed into riot and confusion, leaving no hope for their luckless vessel. Linton, on the contrary, displayed the true courage of a loyal and faithful soul: he trusted God; and God comforted him. One hoped, and the other despaired; they chose their own lots, and were righteously doomed to endure them.

But you'll not want to hear my moralizing, Mr. Lockwood; you'll judge as well as I can, all these things; at least, you'll think you will, and that's the same.

The end of Earnshaw was what might have been expected: it followed fast on his sister's, there was scarcely six months between them. We, at the Grange, never got a very succinct account of his state preceding it; all that I did learn, was on occasion of going to aid in the preparation for the funeral. Mr. Kenneth came to announce the event to my master.

"Well, Nelly," said he, riding into the yard one morning, too early not to alarm me with an instant presentiment of bad news. "It's yours and my turn to go into mourning at present. Who's given us the slip now, do you think?"

"Who?" I asked in a flurry.

"Why, guess!" he returned, dismounting, and slinging his bridle on a hook by the door. "And nip up the corner of your apron; I'm certain you'll need it."

"Not Mr. Heathcliff, surely?" I exclaimed.

"What! would you have tears for him?" said the doctor. "No, Heathcliff's a tough young fellow; he looks blooming to-day — I've just seen him. He's rapidly regaining flesh since he lost his better half."

"Who is it, then, Mr. Kenneth?" I repeated impatiently.

"Hindley Earnshaw! Your old friend Hindley — " he replied. "And my wicked gossip; though he's been too wild for me this long while. There! I said we should draw water — But cheer up! He died true to his character, drunk as a lord — Poor lad; I'm sorry, too. One can't help missing an old companion; though he had the worst tricks with him that ever man imagined, and has done me many a rascally turn — He's barely twenty-seven, it seems; that's your own age; who would have thought you were born in one year!"

I confess this blow was greater to me than the shock of Mrs. Linton's death: ancient associations lingered round my heart; I sat down in the porch, and wept as for a blood relation, desiring Kenneth to get another servant to introduce him to the master.

I could not hinder myself from pondering on the question — "Had he had fair play?" Whatever I did, that idea would bother me: it was so tiresomely pertinacious that I resolved on requesting leave to go to Wuthering Heights, and assist in the last duties to the dead. Mr. Linton was extremely reluctant to consent, but I pleaded eloquently for the friendless condition in which he lay; and I said my old master and foster brother had a claim on my services as strong as his own. Besides, I reminded him that the child, Hareton, was his wife's nephew; and, in the absence of nearer kin, he ought to act as its guardian; and he ought to and must inquire how the property was left, and look over the concerns of his brother-in-law.

He was unfit for attending to such matters then, but he bid me speak to his lawyer; and at length permitted me to go. His lawyer had been Earnshaw's also: I called at the village, and asked him to accompany me. He shook his head, and advised that Heathcliff should be let alone; affirming, if the truth were known, Hareton would be found little else than a beggar.

"His father died in debt," he said; "the whole property is mortgaged, and the sole chance for the natural heir is to allow him an opportunity of creating some interest in the creditor's heart, that he may be inclined to deal leniently towards him."

When I reached the Heights, I explained that I had come to see everything carried on decently, and Joseph, who appeared in sufficient distress, expressed satisfaction at my presence. Mr. Heathcliff said he did not perceive that I was wanted, but I might stay and order the arrangements for the funeral, if I chose.

"Correctly," he remarked, "that fool's body should be buried at the cross-roads, without ceremony of any kind — I happened to leave him ten minutes, yesterday afternoon; and, in that interval, he fastened the two doors of the house against me, and he has spent the night drinking himself to death deliberately! We broke in this morning, for we heard him snorting like a horse; and there he was, laid over the settle — flaying and scalping would not have wakened him — I sent for Kenneth, and he came; but not till the beast had changed into carrion — he was both dead and cold, and stark; and so you'll allow, it was useless making more stir about him!"

The old servant confirmed his statement, but muttered,

"Aw'd rayther he'd goan hisseln fur t' doctor! Aw sud uh taen tent uh t' maister better nur him° — un he warn't deead when Aw left, nowt uh t' soart!"°

I insisted on the funeral being respectable — Mr. Heathcliff said I might have my own way there too; only, he desired me to remember that the money for the whole affair came out of his pocket.

He maintained a hard, careless deportment, indicative of neither joy nor sorrow; if anything, it expressed a flinty gratification at a piece of difficult work successfully executed. I observed once, indeed, something like exultation in his aspect. It was just when the people were bearing the coffin from the house; he had the hypocrisy to represent a mourner; and previous to following with Hareton, he lifted the unfortunate child on to the table, and muttered, with peculiar gusto,

"Now, my bonny lad, you are *mine!* And we'll see if one tree won't grow as crooked as another, with the same wind to twist it!"

The unsuspecting thing was pleased at this speech; he played with Heathcliff's whiskers, and stroked his cheek, but I divined its meaning, and observed tartly,

Aw sud uh taen tent uh t' maister better nur him: I should have taken care of the master better than him. ***nowt uh t' soart:*** Nothing of the sort.

"That boy must go back with me to Thrushcross Grange, sir. There is nothing in the world less yours than he is!"

"Does Linton say so?" he demanded.

"Of course — he has ordered me to take him," I replied.

"Well," said the scoundrel, "we'll not argue the subject now; but I have a fancy to try my hand at rearing a young one, so intimate to your master, that I must supply the place of this with my own, if he attempt to remove it. I don't engage to let Hareton go, undisputed; but I'll be pretty sure to make the other come! Remember to tell him."

This hint was enough to bind our hands. I repeated its substance on my return, and Edgar Linton, little interested at the commencement, spoke no more of interfering. I'm not aware that he could have done it to any purpose, had he been ever so willing.

The guest was now the master of Wuthering Heights: he held firm possession, and proved it to the attorney, who, in his turn, proved it to Mr. Linton, that Earnshaw had mortgaged every yard of land he owned for cash to supply his mania for gaming; and he, Heathcliff, was the mortgagee.

In that manner, Hareton, who should now be the first gentleman in the neighbourhood, was reduced to a state of complete dependence on his father's inveterate enemy; and lives in his own house as a servant deprived of the advantage of wages, and quite unable to right himself, because of his friendlessness, and his ignorance that he has been wronged.

CHAPTER 18

The twelve years, continued Mrs. Dean, following that dismal period, were the happiest of my life: my greatest troubles, in their passage, rose from our little lady's trifling illnesses, which she had to experience in common with all children, rich or poor.

For the rest, after the first six months, she grew like a larch; and could walk and talk too, in her own way, before the heath bloomed a second time over Mrs. Linton's dust.

She was the most winning thing that ever brought sunshine into a desolate house — a real beauty in face — with the Earnshaws' handsome dark eyes, but the Lintons' fair skin, and small features, and yellow curling hair. Her spirit was high, though not rough, and qualified by a heart, sensitive and lively to excess in its affections. That capacity for intense attachments reminded me of her mother; still she did not resemble her; for she could be soft and mild as a dove, and she had a gentle voice, and pensive expression: her anger was never furious; her love never fierce; it was deep and tender.

However, it must be acknowledged, she had faults to foil her gifts. A propensity to be saucy was one; and a perverse will that indulged children invariably acquire, whether they be good tempered or cross. If a servant chanced to vex her, it was always, "I shall tell papa!" and if he reproved her, even by a look, you would have thought it a heart-breaking business: I don't believe he ever did speak a harsh word to her.

He took her education entirely on himself, and made it an amusement: fortunately, curiosity and a quick intellect urged her into an apt scholar; she learnt rapidly and eagerly, and did honour to his teaching.

Till she reached the age of thirteen, she had not once been beyond the range of the park by herself. Mr. Linton would take her with him, a mile or so outside, on rare occasions; but he trusted her to no one else. Gimmerton was an unsubstantial name in her ears; the chapel, the only building she had approached or entered, except her own home. Wuthering Heights and Mr. Heathcliff did not exist for her; she was a perfect recluse; and, apparently, perfectly contented. Sometimes, indeed, while surveying the country from her nursery window, she would observe —

"Ellen, how long will it be before I can walk to the top of those hills? I wonder what lies on the other side — is it the sea?'

"No, Miss Cathy," I would answer, "it is hills again just like these."

"And what are those golden rocks like, when you stand under them?" she once asked.

The abrupt descent of Penistone Crags particularly attracted her notice, especially when the setting sun shone on it, and the topmost heights, and the whole extent of landscape besides lay in shadow.

I explained that they were bare masses of stone, with hardly enough earth in their clefts to nourish a stunted tree.

"And why are they bright so long after it is evening here?" she pursued.

"Because they are a great deal higher up than we are," replied I; "you could not climb them, they are too high and steep. In winter the frost is always there before it comes to us; and deep into summer, I have found snow under that black hollow on the north-east side!"

"Oh, you have been on them!" she cried, gleefully. "Then I can go, too, when I am a woman. Has papa been, Ellen?"

"Papa would tell you, Miss," I answered hastily, "that they are not worth the trouble of visiting. The moors, where you ramble with him, are much nicer; and Thrushcross park is the finest place in the world."

"But I know the park, and I don't know those," she murmured to herself. "And I should delight to look round me, from the brow of that tallest point — my little pony, Minny, shall take me sometime."

One of the maids mentioning the Fairy cave, quite turned her head with a desire to fulfil this project; she teased Mr. Linton about it; and he promised she should have the journey when she got older; but Miss Catherine measured her age by months, and —

"Now, am I old enough to go to Penistone Crags?" was the constant question in her mouth.

The road thither wound close to Wuthering Heights. Edgar had not the heart to pass it; so she received as constantly the answer,

"Not yet, love, not yet."

I said Mrs. Heathcliff lived about a dozen years after quitting her husband. Her family were of a delicate constitution: she and Edgar both lacked the ruddy health that you will generally meet in these parts. What her last illness was, I am not certain; I conjecture, they died of the same thing, a kind of fever, slow at its commencement, but incurable, and rapidly consuming life towards the close.

She wrote to inform her brother of the probable conclusion of a four months' indisposition, under which she had suffered; and entreated him to come to her, if possible, for she had much to settle, and she wished to bid him adieu, and deliver Linton safely into his hands. Her hope was, that Linton might be left with him, as he had been with her; his father, she would fain convince herself, had no desire to assume the burden of his maintenance or education.

My master hesitated not a moment in complying with her request; reluctant as he was to leave home at ordinary calls, he flew to answer this; commending Catherine to my peculiar vigilance, in his absence, with reiterated orders that she must not wander out of the park, even under my escort; he did not calculate on her going unaccompanied.

He was away three weeks: the first day or two, my charge sat in a corner of the library, too sad for either reading or playing: in that quiet state she caused me little trouble; but it was succeeded by an interval of impatient, fretful weariness; and being too busy, and too old then, to run up and down amusing her, I hit on a method by which she might entertain herself.

I used to send her on travels round the grounds — now on foot, and now on a pony; indulging her with a patient audience of all her real and imaginary adventures, when she returned.

The summer shone in full prime; and she took such a taste for this solitary rambling that she often contrived to remain out from breakfast till tea; and then the evenings were spent in recounting her fanciful tales. I did not fear her breaking bounds, because the gates were generally locked, and I thought she would scarcely venture forth alone, if they had stood wide open.

Unluckily, my confidence proved misplaced. Catherine came to me, one morning, at eight o'clock, and said she was that day an Arabian merchant, going to cross the Desert with his caravan; and I must give her plenty of provision for herself and beasts: a horse and three camels, personated by a large hound and a couple of pointers.

I got together good store of dainties, and slung them in a basket on one side of the saddle; and she sprang up as gay as a fairy, sheltered by her wide-brimmed hat and gauze veil from the July sun, and trotted off with a merry laugh, mocking my cautious counsel to avoid galloping, and come back early.

The naughty thing never made her appearance at tea. One traveller, the hound, being an old dog, and fond of its ease, returned; but neither Cathy, nor the pony, nor the two pointers were visible in any direction; and I despatched emissaries down this path, and that path, and, at last, went wandering in search of her myself.

There was a labourer working at a fence round a plantation, on the borders of the grounds. I enquired of him if he had seen our young lady?

"I saw her at morn," he replied; "she would have me to cut her a hazel switch; and then she leapt her galloway over the hedge yonder, where it is lowest, and galloped out of sight."

You may guess how I felt at hearing this news. It struck me directly she must have started for Penistone Crags.

"What will become of her?" I ejaculated, pushing through a gap which the man was repairing, and making straight to the high road.

I walked as if for a wager, mile after mile, till a turn brought me in view of the Heights, but no Catherine could I detect, far or near.

The Crags lie about a mile and a half beyond Mr. Heathcliff's place, and that is four from the Grange, so I began to fear night would fall ere I could reach them.

"And what if she should have slipped in clambering among them," I reflected, "and been killed, or broken some of her bones?"

My suspense was truly painful; and, at first, it gave me delightful relief to observe, in hurrying by the farmhouse, Charlie, the fiercest of the pointers, lying under a window, with swelled head and bleeding ear. I opened the wicket, and ran to the door, knocking vehemently for admittance. A woman whom I knew, and who formerly lived at

Gimmerton, answered — she had been servant there since the death of Mr. Earnshaw.

"Ah," said she, "you are come a-seeking your little mistress! don't be frightened. She's here safe — but I'm glad it isn't the master."

"He is not at home then, is he?" I panted, quite breathless with quick walking and alarm.

"No, no," she replied, "both he and Joseph are off, and I think they won't return this hour or more. Step in and rest you a bit."

I entered, and beheld my stray lamb, seated on the hearth, rocking herself in a little chair that had been her mother's, when a child. Her hat was hung against the wall, and she seemed perfectly at home, laughing and chattering, in the best spirits imaginable, to Hareton, now a great, strong lad of eighteen, who stared at her with considerable curiosity and astonishment; comprehending precious little of the fluent succession of remarks and questions which her tongue never ceased pouring forth.

"Very well, Miss," I exclaimed, concealing my joy under an angry countenance. "This is your last ride, till papa comes back. I'll not trust you over the threshold again, you naughty, naughty girl!"

"Aha, Ellen!" she cried, gaily, jumping up, and running to my side. "I shall have a pretty story to tell to-night — and so you've found me out. Have you ever been here in your life before?"

"Put that hat on, and home at once," said I. "I'm dreadfully grieved at you, Miss Cathy, you've done extremely wrong! It's no use pouting and crying; that won't repay the trouble I've had, scouring the country after you. To think how Mr. Linton charged me to keep you in; and you stealing off so; it shows you are a cunning little fox, and nobody will put faith in you any more."

"What have I done?" sobbed she, instantly checked. "Papa charged me nothing — he'll not scold me, Ellen — he's never cross, like you!"

"Come, come!" I repeated. "I'll tie the riband. Now, let us have no petulance. Oh, for shame. You thirteen years old, and such a baby!"

This exclamation was caused by her pushing the hat from her head, and retreating to the chimney out of my reach.

"Nay," said the servant, "don't be hard on the bonny lass, Mrs. Dean. We made her stop — she'd fain have ridden forwards, afeard you should be uneasy. But Hareton offered to go with her, and I thought he should. It's a wild road over the hills."

Hareton, during the discussion, stood with his hands in his pockets, too awkward to speak, though he looked as if he did not relish my intrusion.

"How long am I to wait?" I continued, disregarding the woman's interference. "It will be dark in ten minutes. Where is the pony, Miss Cathy? And where is Phenix? I shall leave you, unless you be quick, so please yourself."

"The pony is in the yard," she replied, "and Phenix is shut in there. He's bitten — and so is Charlie. I was going to tell you all about it; but you are in a bad temper, and don't deserve to hear."

I picked up her hat, and approached to reinstate it; but perceiving that the people of the house took her part, she commenced capering round the room; and, on my giving chase, ran like a mouse, over and under, and behind the furniture, rendering it ridiculous for me to pursue.

Hareton and the woman laughed; and she joined them, and waxed more impertinent still; till I cried, in great irritation,

"Well, Miss Cathy, if you were aware whose house this is, you'd be glad enough to get out."

"It's *your* father's, isn't it?" said she, turning to Hareton.

"Nay," he replied, looking down, and blushing bashfully.

He could not stand a steady gaze from her eyes, though they were just his own.

"Whose then — your master's?" she asked.

He coloured deeper, with a different feeling, muttered an oath, and turned away.

"Who is his master?" continued the tiresome girl, appealing to me. "He talked about 'our house,' and 'our folk.' I thought he had been the owner's son. And he never said, Miss; he should have done, shouldn't he, if he's a servant?"

Hareton grew black as a thunder-cloud, at this childish speech. I silently shook my questioner, and, at last, succeeded in equipping her for departure.

"Now, get my horse," she said, addressing her unknown kinsman as she would one of the stable-boys at the Grange. "And you may come with me. I want to see where the goblin hunter rises in the marsh, and to hear about the *fairishes,*° as you call them — but make haste! What's the matter? Get my horse, I say."

"I'll see thee damned, before I be *thy* servant!" growled the lad.

"You'll see me *what?*" asked Catherine in surprise.

"Damned — thou saucy witch!" he replied.

"There, Miss Cathy! you see you have got into pretty company," I interposed. "Nice words to be used to a young lady! Pray don't begin

fairishes: Fairies.

to dispute with him — Come, let us seek for Minny ourselves, and begone."

"But Ellen," cried she, staring, fixed in astonishment. "How dare he speak so to me? Mustn't he be made to do as I ask him? You wicked creature, I shall tell papa what you said — Now then!"

Hareton did not appear to feel this threat; so the tears sprung into her eyes with indignation. "You bring the pony," she exclaimed, turning to the woman, "and let my dog free this moment!"

"Softly, Miss," answered the addressed. "You'll lose nothing by being civil. Though Mr. Hareton, there, be not the master's son, he's your cousin; and I was never hired to serve you."

"*He* my cousin!" cried Cathy with a scornful laugh.

"Yes, indeed," responded her reprover.

"Oh, Ellen! don't let them say such things," she pursued in great trouble. "Papa is gone to fetch my cousin from London — my cousin is a gentleman's son — That my — " she stopped, and wept outright; upset at the bare notion of relationship with such a clown.

"Hush, hush!' I whispered, "people can have many cousins and of all sorts, Miss Cathy, without being any the worse for it; only they needn't keep their company, if they be disagreeable and bad."

"He's not, he's not my cousin, Ellen!" she went on, gathering fresh grief from reflection, and flinging herself into my arms for refuge from the idea.

I was much vexed at her and the servant for their mutual revelations; having no doubt of Linton's approaching arrival, communicated by the former, being reported to Mr. Heathcliff; and feeling as confident that Catherine's first thought on her father's return, would be to seek an explanation of the latter's assertion concerning her rude-bred kindred.

Hareton, recovering from his disgust at being taken for a servant, seemed moved by her distress; and, having fetched the pony round to the door, he took, to propitiate her, a fine crooked-legged terrier whelp from the kennel; and putting it into her hand, bid her wisht;° for he meant naught.

Pausing in her lamentations, she surveyed him with a glance of awe and horror, then burst forth anew.

I could scarcely refrain from smiling at this antipathy to the poor fellow; who was a well-made, athletic youth, good looking in features, and stout and healthy, and attired in garments befitting his daily occupations of working on the farm, and lounging among the moors after rabbits and

wisht: Hush.

game. Still, I thought I could detect in his physiognomy a mind owning better qualities than his father ever possessed. Good things lost amid a wilderness of weeds, to be sure, whose rankness far over-topped their neglected growth; yet notwithstanding, evidence of a wealthy soil that might yield luxuriant crops under other and favourable circumstances. Mr. Heathcliff, I believe, had not treated him physically ill; thanks to his fearless nature, which offered no temptation to that course of oppression; it had none of the timid susceptibility that would have given zest to ill-treatment, in Heathcliff's judgment. He appeared to have bent his malevolence on making him a brute; he was never taught to read or write; never rebuked for any bad habit which did not annoy his keeper; never led a single step towards virtue, or guarded by a single precept against vice. And from what I heard, Joseph contributed much to his deterioration by a narrow-minded partiality which prompted him to flatter and pet him, as a boy, because he was the head of the old family. And as he had been in the habit of accusing Catherine Earnshaw and Heathcliff, when children, of putting the master past his patience, and compelling him to seek solace in drink, by what he termed their "offald° ways," so at present he laid the whole burden of Hareton's faults on the shoulders of the usurper of his property.

If the lad swore he wouldn't correct him; nor however culpably he behaved. It gave Joseph satisfaction, apparently, to watch him go the worst lengths. He allowed that he was ruined; that his soul was abandoned to perdition; but then, he reflected that Heathcliff must answer for it. Hareton's blood would be required at his hands; and there lay immense consolation in that thought.

Joseph had instilled into him a pride of name, and of his lineage; he would, had he dared, have fostered hate between him and the present owner of the Heights, but his dread of that owner amounted to superstition; and he confined his feelings, regarding him, to muttered innuendoes and private communications.

I don't pretend to be intimately acquainted with the mode of living customary in those days at Wuthering Heights. I only speak from hearsay; for I saw little. The villagers affirmed Mr. Heathcliff was *near,*° and a cruel hard landlord to his tenants; but the house, inside, had regained its ancient aspect of comfort under female management; and the scenes of riot common in Hindley's time were not now enacted within its walls. The master was too gloomy to seek companionship with any people, good or bad, and he is yet —

offald: Worthless or trashy. ***near:*** Stingy.

This, however, is not making progress with my story. Miss Cathy rejected the peace-offering of the terrier, and demanded her own dogs, Charlie and Phenix. They came limping, and hanging their heads; and we set out for home, sadly out of sorts, every one of us.

I could not wring from my little lady how she had spent the day; except that, as I supposed, the goal of her pilgrimage was Penistone Crags; and she arrived without adventure to the gate of the farmhouse, when Hareton happened to issue forth, attended by some canine followers who attacked her train.

They had a smart battle, before their owners could separate them: that formed an introduction. Catherine told Hareton who she was, and where she was going; and asked him to show her the way, finally, beguiling him to accompany her.

He opened the mysteries of the Fairy cave, and twenty other queer places; but being in disgrace, I was not favoured with a description of the interesting objects she saw.

I could gather, however, that her guide had been a favourite till she hurt his feelings by addressing him as a servant, and Heathcliff's housekeeper hurt hers by calling him her cousin.

Then the language he had held to her rankled in her heart; she who was always "love," and "darling," and "queen," and "angel," with everybody at the Grange, to be insulted so shockingly by a stranger! She did not comprehend it; and hard work I had, to obtain a promise that she would not lay the grievance before her father.

I explained how he objected to the whole household at the Heights, and how sorry he would be to find she had been there; but I insisted most on the fact, that if she revealed my negligence of his orders, he would perhaps be so angry that I should have to leave; and Cathy couldn't bear that prospect; she pledged her word, and kept it, for my sake — after all, she was a sweet little girl.

CHAPTER 19

A letter, edged with black, announced the day of my master's return. Isabella was dead; and he wrote to bid me to get mourning for his daughter, and arrange a room, and other accommodations, for his youthful nephew.

Catherine ran wild with joy at the idea of welcoming her father back: and indulged most sanguine anticipations of the innumerable excellences of her "real" cousin.

The evening of their expected arrival came. Since early morning, she had been busy, ordering her own small affairs; and now, attired in her new black frock — poor thing! her aunt's death impressed her with no definite sorrow — she obliged me, by constant worrying, to walk with her, down through the grounds, to meet them.

"Linton is just six months younger than I am," she chattered as we strolled leisurely over the swells and hollows of mossy turf, under shadow of the trees. "How delightful it will be to have him for a playfellow! Aunt Isabella sent papa a beautiful lock of his hair; it was lighter than mine — more flaxen, and quite as fine. I have it carefully preserved in a little glass box; and I've often thought what pleasure it would be to see its owner — Oh! I am happy — and papa, dear, dear papa! Come, Ellen, let us run! come run!"

She ran, and returned and ran again, many times before my sober footsteps reached the gate, and then she seated herself on the grassy bank beside the path, and tried to wait patiently; but that was impossible; she couldn't be still a minute.

"How long they are!" she exclaimed. "Ah, I see some dust on the road — they are coming! No! When will they be here? May we not go a little way — half a mile, Ellen, only just half a mile? Do say yes, to that clump of birches at the turn!"

I refused staunchily: and, at length, her suspense was ended: the travelling carriage rolled in sight.

Miss Cathy shrieked, and stretched out her arms, as soon as she caught her father's face, looking from the window. He descended, nearly as eager as herself; and a considerable interval elapsed, ere they had a thought to spare for any but themselves.

While they exchanged caresses, I took a peep in to see after Linton. He was asleep, in a corner, wrapped in a warm, fur-lined cloak, as if it had been winter. A pale, delicate, effeminate boy, who might have been taken for my master's younger brother, so strong was the resemblance, but there was a sickly peevishness in his aspect, that Edgar Linton never had.

The latter saw me looking; and having shaken hands, advised me to close the door, and leave him undisturbed; for the journey had fatigued him.

Cathy would fain have taken one glance; but her father told her to come on, and they walked together up the park, while I hastened before to prepare the servants.

"Now, darling," said Mr. Linton, addressing his daughter, as they halted at the bottom of the front steps. "Your cousin is not so strong or so merry as you are, and he has lost his mother, remember, a very short time since; therefore, don't expect him to play and run about with you directly. And don't harass him much by talking — let him be quiet this evening, at least, will you?"

"Yes, yes, papa," answered Catherine; "but I do want to see him; and he hasn't once looked out."

The carriage stopped; and the sleeper, being roused, was lifted to the ground by his uncle.

"This is your cousin Cathy, Linton," he said, putting their little hands together. "She's fond of you already; and mind you don't grieve her by crying to-night. Try to be cheerful now; the travelling is at an end, and you have nothing to do but rest and amuse yourself as you please."

"Let me go to bed then," answered the boy, shrinking from Catherine's salute; and he put his fingers to his eyes to remove incipient tears.

"Come, come, there's a good child," I whispered, leading him in. "You'll make her weep, too — see how sorry she is for you!"

I do not know whether it were sorrow for him, but his cousin put on as sad a countenance as himself, and returned to her father. All three entered, and mounted to the library, where tea was laid ready.

I proceeded to remove Linton's cap and mantle, and placed him on a chair by the table; but he was no sooner seated than he began to cry afresh. My master inquired what was the matter.

"I can't sit on a chair," sobbed the boy.

"Go to the sofa then, and Ellen shall bring you some tea," answered his uncle, patiently.

He had been greatly tried during the journey, I felt convinced, by his fretful, ailing charge.

Linton slowly trailed himself off, and lay down. Cathy carried a foot-stool and her cup to his side.

At first she sat silent; but that could not last; she had resolved to make a pet of her little cousin, as she would have him to be; and she commenced stroking his curls, and kissing his cheek, and offering him tea in her saucer, like a baby. This pleased him, for he was not much better; he dried his eyes, and lightened into a faint smile.

"Oh, he'll do very well," said the master to me, after watching them a minute. "Very well, if we can keep him, Ellen. The company of a child of his own age will instil new spirit into him soon: and by wishing for strength he'll gain it."

"Aye, if we can keep him!" I mused to myself; and sore misgivings came over me that there was slight hope of that. And then, I thought, however will that weakling live at Wuthering Heights, between his father and Hareton? What playmates and instructors they'll be.

Our doubts were presently decided; even earlier than I expected. I had just taken the children upstairs, after tea was finished, and had seen Linton asleep — he would not suffer me to leave him, till that was the case — I had come down, and was standing by the table in the hall, lighting a bed-room candle for Mr. Edgar, when a maid stepped out of the kitchen, and informed me that Mr. Heathcliff's servant, Joseph, was at the door, and wished to speak with the master.

"I shall ask him what he wants first," I said, in considerable trepidation. "A very unlikely hour to be troubling people, and the instant they have returned from a long journey. I don't think the master can see him."

Joseph had advanced through the kitchen, as I uttered these words, and now presented himself in the hall. He was donned in his Sunday garments, with his most sanctimonious and sourest face; and holding his hat in one hand, and his stick in the other, he proceeded to clean his shoes on the mat.

"Good evening, Joseph," I said, coldly. "What business brings you here to-night?"

"It's Maister Linton Aw mun spake tull," he answered, waving me disdainfully aside.

"Mr. Linton is going to bed; unless you have something particular to say, I'm sure he won't hear it now," I continued. "You had better sit down in there, and entrust your message to me."

"Which is his rahm?" pursued the fellow, surveying the range of closed doors.

I perceived he was bent on refusing my mediation; so very reluctantly I went up to the library, and announced the unseasonable visitor, advising that he should be dismissed till next day.

Mr. Linton had not time to empower me to do so, for he mounted close at my heels, and pushing into the apartment, planted himself at the far side of the table, with his two fists clapped on the head of his stick, and began in an elevated tone, as if anticipating opposition.

"Heathcliff has sent me for his lad, un Aw munn't goa back 'baht him."°

Edgar Linton was silent for a minute; an expression of exceeding sorrow overcast his features; he would have pitied the child on his own account; but, recalling Isabella's hopes and fears, and anxious wishes for her son, and her commendations of him to his care, he grieved bitterly

Aw munn't goa back 'baht him: I must not go back without him.

at the prospect of yielding him up, and searched in his heart how it might be avoided. No plan offered itself: the very exhibition of any desire to keep him would have rendered the claimant more peremptory: there was nothing left but to resign him. However, he was not going to rouse him from his sleep.

"Tell Mr. Heathcliff," he answered, calmly, "that his son shall come to Wuthering Heights to-morrow. He is in bed, and too tired to go any distance now. You may also tell him that the mother of Linton desired him to remain under my guardianship; and, at present, his health is very precarious."

"Noa!" said Joseph, giving a thud with his prop on the floor, and assuming an authoritative air. "Noa! that manes nowt° — Hathecliff maks noa 'cahnt° uh t' mother, nor yah norther° — bud he'll hev his lad; und Aw mun tak him — soa nah yah knaw!"

"You shall not to-night!" answered Linton, decisively. "Walk down stairs at once, and repeat to your master what I have said. Ellen, show him down. Go — "

And, aiding the indignant elder with a lift by the arm, he rid the room of him, and closed the door.

"Varrah weel!" shouted Joseph, as he slowly drew off. "Tuh morn, he's come hisseln, un' thrust *him* aht, if yah darr!"

CHAPTER 20

To obviate the danger of his threat being fulfilled, Mr. Linton commissioned me to take the boy home early, on Catherine's pony, and said he —

"As we shall now have no influence over his destiny, good or bad, you must say nothing of where he is gone to my daughter; she cannot associate with him hereafter; and it is better for her to remain in ignorance of his proximity lest she should be restless and anxious to visit the Heights — merely tell her, his father sent for him suddenly, and he has been obliged to leave us."

Linton was very reluctant to be roused from his bed, at five o'clock, and astonished to be informed that he must prepare for further travelling: but I softened off the matter by stating that he was gong to spend some time with his father, Mr. Heathcliff, who wished to see him so much, he did not like to defer the pleasure till he should recover from his late journey.

manes nowt: Means nothing. ***maks noa 'cahnt:*** Takes no account. ***nor yah norther:*** Nor you neither.

"My father?" he cried, in strange perplexity. "Mamma never told me I had a father. Where does he live? I'd rather stay with uncle."

"He lives a little distance from the Grange," I replied, "just beyond those hills — not so far, but you may walk over here, when you get hearty. And you should be glad to go home, and to see him. You must try to love him, as you did your mother, and then he will love you."

"But why have I not heard of him before?" asked Linton; "why didn't mamma and he live together, as other people do?"

"He had business to keep him in the north," I answered; "and your mother's health required her to reside in the south."

"And why didn't mamma speak to me about him?" persevered the child. "She often talked of uncle, and I learnt to love him long ago. How am I to love papa? I don't know him."

"Oh, all children love their parents," I said. "Your mother, perhaps, thought you would want to be with him, if she mentioned him often to you. Let us make haste. An early ride on such a beautiful morning is much preferable to an hour's more sleep."

"Is *she* to go with us," he demanded. "The little girl I saw yesterday?"

"Not now," replied I.

"Is uncle?" he continued.

"No, I shall be your companion there," I said.

Linton sank back on his pillow, and fell into a brown study.

"I won't go without uncle," he cried at length; "I can't tell where you mean to take me."

I attempted to persuade him of the naughtiness of showing reluctance to meet his father: still he obstinately resisted any progress towards dressing, and I had to call for my master's assistance, in coaxing him out of bed.

The poor thing was finally got off with several delusive assurances that his absence should be short; that Mr. Edgar and Cathy would visit him; and other promises, equally ill-founded, which I invented and reiterated, at intervals, throughout the way.

The pure heather-scented air, and the bright sunshine, and the gentle canter of Minny relieved his despondency, after a while. He began to put questions concerning his new home, and its inhabitants, with greater interest and liveliness.

"Is Wuthering Heights as pleasant a place as Thrushcross Grange?" he inquired, turning to take a last glance into the valley, whence a light mist mounted, and formed fleecy cloud, on the skirts of the blue.

"It is not so buried in trees," I replied, "and it is not quite so large, but you can see the country beautifully, all round; and the air is healthier for you — fresher, and dryer. You will, perhaps, think the building old and dark, at first — though it is a respectable house, the next best in the neighbourhood. And you will have such nice rambles on the moors! Hareton Earnshaw — that is Miss Cathy's other cousin, and so yours in a manner — will show you all the sweetest spots; and you can bring a book in fine weather, and make a green hollow your study; and, now and then, your uncle may join you in a walk; he does, frequently, walk out on the hills."

"And what is my father like?" he asked. "Is he as young and handsome as uncle?"

"He's as young," said I "but he has black hair and eyes; and looks sterner, and he is taller and bigger altogether. He'll not seem to you so gentle and kind at first, perhaps, because, it is not his way — still, mind you be frank and cordial with him; and naturally, he'll be fonder of you than any uncle, for you are his own."

"Black hair and eyes!" mused Linton. "I can't fancy him. Then I am not like him, am I?"

"Not much," I answered . . . Not a morsel, I thought, surveying with regret the white complexion and slim frame of my companion, and his large languid eyes . . . his mother's eyes save that, unless a morbid touchiness kindled them a moment, they had not a vestige of her sparkling spirit.

"How strange that he should never come to see momma and me!" he murmured. "Has he ever seen me? If he have, I must have been a baby — I remember not a single thing about him!"

"Why, Master Linton," said I, "three hundred miles is a great distance: and ten years seem very different in length to a grown-up person, compared with what they do to you. It is probable Mr. Heathcliff proposed going, from summer to summer, but never found a convenient opportunity: and now it is too late — Don't trouble him with questions on the subject: it will disturb him for no good."

The boy was fully occupied with his own cogitations for the remainder of the ride, till we halted before the farm-house garden gate. I watched to catch his impressions in his countenance. He surveyed the carved front and low-bowed lattices, the straggling gooseberry bushes and crooked firs, with solemn intentness, and then shook his head: his private feelings entirely disapproved of the exterior of his new abode; but he had sense to postpone complaining — there might be compensation within.

Before he dismounted, I went and opened the door. It was half-past six; the family had just finished breakfast; the servant was clearing and wiping down the table; Joseph stood by his master's chair telling some tale concerning a lame horse; and Hareton was preparing for the hay-field.

"Hallo, Nelly!" cried Mr. Heathcliff when he saw me. "I feared I should have to come down and fetch my property myself — You've brought it, have you? Let's see what we can make of it."

He got up and strode to the door: Hareton and Joseph followed in gaping curiosity. Poor Linton ran a frightened eye over the faces of the three.

"Sure-ly," said Joseph after a grave inspection, "he's swopped wi' ye, maister, an' yon's his lass!"

Heathcliff, having stared his son into an ague of confusion, uttered a scornful laugh.

"God! what a beauty! what a lovely, charming thing!" he exclaimed. "Haven't they reared it on snails and sour milk, Nelly? Oh, damn my soul! but that's worse than I expected — and the devil knows I was not sanguine!"

I bid the trembling and bewildered child get down, and enter. He did not thoroughly comprehend the meaning of his father's speech, or whether it were intended for him: indeed, he was not yet certain that the grim, sneering stranger was his father; but he clung to me with growing trepidation; and on Mr. Heathcliff's taking a seat, and bidding him "come hither," he hid his face on my shoulder, and wept.

"Tut, tut!" said Heathcliff, stretching out a hand and dragging him roughly between his knees, and then holding up his head by the chin. "None of that nonsense! We're not going to hurt thee, Linton — isn't that thy name? Thou art thy mother's child, entirely! Where is *my* share in thee, puling chicken?"

He took off the boy's cap and pushed back his thick flaxen curls, felt his slender arms, and his small fingers; during which examination, Linton ceased crying, and lifted his great blue eyes to inspect the inspector.

"Do you know me?" asked Heathcliff, having satisfied himself that the limbs were all equally frail and feeble.

"No!" said Linton, with a gaze of vacant fear.

"You've heard of me, I dare say?"

"No," he replied again.

"No? What a shame of your mother, never to waken your filial regard for me! You are my son, then, I'll tell you; and your mother was a wicked slut to leave you in ignorance of the sort of father you possessed — Now don't wince, and colour up! Though it *is* something to see you have not white blood — Be a good lad; and I'll do for you —

Nelly, if you be tired you may sit down; if not, get home again — I guess you'll report what you hear, and see, to the cipher at the Grange; and this thing won't be settled while you linger about it."

"Well," replied I, "I hope you'll be kind to the boy, Mr. Heathcliff, or you'll not keep him long, and he's all you have akin in the wide world that you will ever know — remember."

"I'll be *very* kind to him, you needn't fear," he said, laughing. "Only nobody else must be kind to him — I'm jealous of monopolising his affection — And, to begin my kindness, Joseph! bring the lad some breakfast — Hareton, you infernal calf, begone to your work. Yes, Nell," he added when they had departed, "my son is prospective owner of your place, and I should not wish him to die till I was certain of being his successor. Besides, he's *mine,* and I want the triumph of seeing *my* descendent fairly lord of their estates; my child hiring their children, to till their fathers' land for wages — That is the sole consideration which can make me endure the whelp — I despise him for himself, and hate him for the memories he revives! But, that consideration is sufficient; he's as safe with me, and shall be tended as carefully, as your master tends his own — I have a room upstairs, furnished for him in handsome style — I've engaged a tutor, also, to come three times a week, from twenty miles distance, to teach him what he pleases to learn. I've ordered Hareton to obey him: and in fact, I've arranged every thing with a view to preserve the superior and the gentleman in him, above his associates — I do regret, however, that he so little deserves the trouble — if I wished any blessing in the world, it was to find him a worthy object of pride, and I'm bitterly disappointed with the whey-faced whining wretch!"

While he was speaking, Joseph returned, bearing a basin of milk-porridge, and placed it before Linton. He stirred round the homely mess with a look of aversion, and affirmed he could not eat it.

I saw the old man-servant shared largely in his master's scorn of the child, though he was compelled to retain the sentiment in his heart, because Heathcliff plainly meant his underlings to hold him in honour.

"Cannot ate it?" repeated he, peering in Linton's face, and subduing his voice to a whisper, for fear of being overheard. "But Maister Hareton nivir ate nowt else, when he were a little un: und what wer gooid eneugh fur him's gooid eneugh fur yah, Aw's rayther think!"

"I *shan't* eat it!" answered Linton snappishly. "Take it away."

Joseph snatched up the food indignantly, and brought it to us.

"Is there owt ails th' victuals?" he asked, thrusting the tray under Heathcliff's nose.

"What should ail them?" he said.

"Wah!" answered Joseph, "yon dainty chap says he cannut ate 'em. Bud aw guess it's raight! His mother wer just soa — we wer a'most too mucky° tuh sow t' corn fur makking her breead."

"Don't mention his mother to me," said the master, angrily. "Get him something that he can eat, that's all. What is his usual food, Nelly?"

I suggested boiled milk or tea; and the housekeeper received instructions to prepare some.

Come, I reflected, his father's selfishness may contribute to his comfort. He perceives his delicate constitution, and the necessity of treating him tolerably. I'll console Mr. Edgar by acquainting him with the turn Heathcliff's humour has taken.

Having no excuse for lingering longer, I slipped out, while Linton was engaged in timidly rebuffing the advances of a friendly sheep-dog. But he was too much on the alert to be cheated — as I closed the door, I heard a cry, and a frantic repetition of the words —

"Don't leave me! I'll not stay here! I'll not stay here!"

Then the latch was raised and fell — they did not suffer him to come forth. I mounted Minny, and urged her to a trot; and so my brief guardianship ended.

CHAPTER 21

We had sad work with little Cathy that day: she rose in high glee, eager to join her cousin; and such passionate tears and lamentations followed the news of his departure, that Edgar himself was obliged to soothe her, by affirming he should come back soon; he added, however, "if I can get him"; and there were no hopes of that.

This promise poorly pacified her; but time was more potent; and though still, at intervals, she inquired of her father, when Linton would return, before she did see him again, his features had waxed so dim in her memory that she did not recognise him.

When I chanced to encounter the housekeeper of Wuthering Heights, in paying business-visits to Gimmerton, I used to ask how the young master got on; for he lived almost as secluded as Catherine herself, and was never to be seen. I could gather from her that he continued in weak health, and was a tiresome inmate. She said Mr. Heathcliff seemed to dislike him ever longer and worse, though he took some trouble to conceal it. He had an antipathy to the sound of his voice, and

mucky: Dirty, filthy.

could not do at all with his sitting in the same room with him many minutes together.

There seldom passed much talk between them; Linton learnt his lessons, and spent his evenings in a small apartment they called the parlour; or else lay in bed all day; for he was constantly getting coughs, and colds, and aches, and pains of some sort.

"And I never knew such a faint-hearted creature," added the woman; "nor one so careful of hisseln. He *will* go on, if I leave the window open, a bit late in the evening. Oh! it's killing, a breath of night air! And he must have a fire in the middle of summer; and Joseph's 'bacca pipe is poison; and he must always have sweets and dainties, and always milk, milk for ever — heeding naught how the rest of us are pinched in winter — and there he'll sit, wrapped in his furred cloak in his chair by the fire, and some toast and water, or other slop on the hob to sip at; and if Hareton, for pity, comes to amuse him — Hareton is not bad-natured, though he's rough — they're sure to part, one swearing, and the other crying. I believe the master would relish Earnshaw's thrashing him to a mummy, if he were not his son: and, I'm certain, he would be fit to turn him out of doors, if he knew half the nursing he gives hisseln. But then, he won't go into danger of temptation; he never enters the parlour, and should Linton show those ways in the house where he is, he sends him upstairs directly."

I divined, from this account, that utter lack of sympathy had rendered young Heathcliff selfish and disagreeable, if he were not so originally; and my interest in him, consequently, decayed; though still I was moved with a sense of grief at his lot, and a wish that he had been left with us.

Mr. Edgar encouraged me to gain information; he thought a great deal about him, I fancy, and would have run some risk to see him; and he told me once to ask the housekeeper whether he ever came into the village?

She said he had only been twice, on horseback, accompanying his father: and both times he pretended to be quite knocked up for three or four days afterwards.

That housekeeper left, if I recollect rightly, two years after he came; and another, whom I did not know, was her successor; she lives there still.

Time wore on at the Grange in its former pleasant way, till Miss Cathy reached sixteen. On the anniversary of her birth we never manifested any signs of rejoicing, because it was, also, the anniversary of my late mistress's death. Her father invariably spent that day alone in the library; and walked, at dusk, as far as Gimmerton kirkyard, where he would frequently prolong his stay beyond midnight. Therefore Catherine was thrown on her own resources for amusement.

This twentieth of March was a beautiful spring day, and when her father had retired, my young lady came down dressed for going out, and said she had asked to have a ramble on the edge of the moors with me; and Mr. Linton had given her leave, if we went only a short distance, and were back within the hour.

"So make haste, Ellen!" she cried. "I know where I wish to go; where a colony of moor-game are settled; I want to see whether they have made their nests yet."

"That must be a good distance up," I answered; "they don't breed on the edge of the moor."

"No, it's not," she said. "I've gone very near with papa."

I put on my bonnet and sallied out, thinking nothing more of the matter. She bounded before me, and returned to my side, and was off again like a young greyhound; and, at first, I found plenty of entertainment in listening to the larks singing far and near; and enjoying the sweet, warm sunshine; and watching her, my pet, and my delight, with her golden ringlets flying loose behind, and her bright cheek, as soft and pure in its bloom as a wild rose, and her eyes radiant with cloudless pleasure. She was a happy creature, and an angel, in those days. It's a pity she could not be content.

"Well," said I, "where are your moor-game, Miss Cathy? We should be at them — the Grange park-fence is a great way off now."

"Oh, a little further — only a little further, Ellen," was her answer, continually. "Climb to that hillock, pass that bank, and by the time you reach the other side, I shall have raised the birds."

But there were so many hillocks and banks to climb and pass, that, at length, I began to be weary, and told her we must halt, and retrace our steps.

I shouted to her, as she had outstripped me, a long way; she either did not hear, or did not regard, for she still sprang on, and I was compelled to follow. Finally, she dived into a hollow; and before I came in sight of her again, she was two miles nearer Wuthering Heights than her own home; and I beheld a couple of persons arrest her, one of whom I felt convinced was Mr. Heathcliff himself.

Cathy had been caught in the act of plundering, or, at least, hunting out the nests of the grouse.

The Heights were Heathcliff's land, and he was reproving the poacher.

"I've neither taken any nor found any," she said, as I toiled to them, expanding her hands in corroboration of the statement. "I didn't mean to take them; but papa told me there were quantities up here, and I wished to see the eggs."

Heathcliff glanced at me with an ill-meaning smile, expressing his acquaintance with the party, and, consequently, his malevolence towards it, and demanded who "papa" was.

"Mr. Linton of Thrushcross Grange," she replied. "I thought you did not know me, or you wouldn't have spoken in that way."

"You suppose papa is highly esteemed and respected, then?" he said, sarcastically.

"And what are you?" inquired Catherine, gazing curiously on the speaker. "That man I've seen before. Is he your son?"

She pointed to Hareton, the other individual, who had gained nothing but increased bulk and strength by the addition of two years to his age: he seemed as awkward and rough as ever.

"Miss Cathy," I interrupted, "it will be three hours instead of one that we are out, presently. We really must go back."

"No, that man is not my son," answered Heathcliff, pushing me aside. "But I have one, and you have seen him before too; and, though your nurse is in a hurry, I think both you and she would be the better for a little rest. Will you just turn this nab° of heath, and walk into my house? You'll get home earlier for the ease; and you shall receive a kind welcome."

I whispered Catherine that she mustn't, on any account, accede to the proposal; it was entirely out of the question.

"Why?" she asked, aloud. "I'm tired of running, and the ground is dewy — I can't sit here. Let us go, Ellen! Besides, he says I have seen his son. He's mistaken, I think; but I guess where he lives — at the farm-house I visited in coming from Penistone Crags. Don't you?"

"I do. Come, Nelly, hold your tongue — it will be a treat for her to look in on us. Hareton, get forwards with the lass. You shall walk with me, Nelly."

"No, she's not going to any such place," I cried, struggling to release my arm, which he had seized; but she was almost at the door-stones already, scampering round the brow at full speed. Her appointed companion did not pretend to escort her; he shied off by the road-side, and vanished.

nab: A projecting or jutting out part of a hill.

"Mr. Heathcliff, it's very wrong," I continued; "you know you mean no good; and there she'll see Linton, and all will be told, as soon as ever we return; and I shall have the blame."

"I want her to see Linton," he answered; "he's looking better these few days; it's not often he's fit to be seen. And we'll soon persuade her to keep the visit secret — where is the harm of it?"

"The harm of it is, that her father would hate me, if he found I suffered her to enter your house; and I am convinced you have a bad design in encouraging her to do so," I replied.

"My design is as honest as possible. I'll inform you of its whole scope," he said. "That the two cousins may fall in love, and get married. I'm acting generously to your master; his young chit has no expectations, and should she second my wishes, she'll be provided for, at once, as joint successor with Linton."

"If Linton died," I answered, "and his life is quite uncertain, Catherine would be the heir."

"No, she would not," he said. "There is no clause in the will to secure it so; his property would go to me; but, to prevent disputes, I desire their union, and am resolved to bring it about."

"And I'm resolved she shall never approach your house with me again," I returned, as we reached the gate, where Miss Cathy waited our coming.

Heathcliff bid me to be quiet; and preceding us up the path, hastened to open the door. My young lady gave him several looks, as if she could not exactly make up her mind what to think of him; but now he smiled when he met her eye, and softened his voice in addressing her, and I was foolish enough to imagine the memory of her mother might disarm him from desiring her injury.

Linton stood on the hearth. He had been out walking in the fields; for his cap was on, and he was calling to Joseph to bring him dry shoes.

He had grown tall of his age, still wanting some months of sixteen. His features were pretty yet, and his eye and complexion brighter than I remembered them, though with merely temporary lustre borrowed from the salubrious air and genial sun.

"Now, who is that?" asked Mr. Heathcliff, turning to Cathy. "Can you tell?"

"Your son?" she said, having doubtfully surveyed, first one, and then the other.

"Yes, yes," answered he; "but is this the only time you have beheld him? Think! Ah! you have a short memory. Linton, don't you recall your cousin, that you used to tease us so with wishing to see?"

"What, Linton!" cried Cathy, kindling into joyful surprise at the name. "Is that little Linton? He's taller than I am! Are you, Linton?"

The youth stepped forward, and acknowledged himself: she kissed him fervently, and they gazed with wonder at the change time had wrought in the appearance of each.

Catherine had reached her full height; her figure was both plump and slender, elastic as steel, and her whole aspect sparkling with health and spirits. Linton's looks and movements were very languid, and his form extremely slight; but there was a grace in his manner that mitigated these defects, and rendered him not unpleasing.

After exchanging numerous marks of fondness with him, his cousin went to Mr. Heathcliff, who lingered by the door, dividing his attention between the objects inside, and those that lay without, pretending, that is, to observe the latter, and really noting the former alone.

"And you are my uncle, then!" she cried, reaching up to salute him. "I thought I liked you, though you were cross, at first. Why don't you visit the Grange with Linton? To live all these years such close neighbours, and never see us, is odd; what have you done so for?"

"I visited it once or twice too often before you were born," he answered. "There — damn it! If you have any kisses to spare, give them to Linton — they are thrown away on me."

"Naughty Ellen!" exclaimed Catherine, flying to attack me next with her lavish caresses. "Wicked Ellen! to try to hinder me from entering. But I'll take this walk every morning in future — may I, uncle — and sometimes bring papa? Won't you be glad to see us?"

"Of course!" replied the uncle, with a hardly suppressed grimace, resulting from his deep aversion to both the proposed visitors. "But stay," he continued, turning towards the young lady. "Now I think of it, I'd better tell you. Mr. Linton has a prejudice against me; we quarrelled at one time of our lives, with unchristian ferocity; and, if you mention coming here to him, he'll put a veto on your visits altogether. Therefore, you must not mention it, unless you be careless of seeing your cousin hereafter — you may come, if you will, but you must not mention it."

"Why did you quarrel?" asked Catherine, considerably crestfallen.

"He thought me too poor to wed his sister," answered Heathcliff, "and was grieved that I got her — his pride was hurt, and he'll never forgive it."

"That's wrong!" said the young lady: "some time, I'll tell him so; but Linton and I have no share in your quarrel. I'll not come here, then, he shall come to the Grange."

"It will be too far for me," murmured her cousin, "to walk four miles would kill me. No, come here, Miss Catherine, now and then, not every morning, but once or twice a week."

The father launched towards his son a glance of bitter contempt.

"I am afraid, Nelly, I shall lose my labour," he muttered to me. "Miss Catherine, as the ninny calls her, will discover his value, and send him to the devil. Now, if it had been Hareton — do you know that, twenty times a day, I covet Hareton, with all his degradation? I'd have loved the lad had he been some one else. But I think he's safe from *her* love. I'll pit him against that paltry creature, unless it bestir itself briskly. We calculate it will scarcely last till it is eighteen. Oh, confound the vapid thing! He's absorbed in drying his feet, and never looks at her — Linton!"

"Yes, father," answered the boy.

"Have you nothing to show your cousin, anywhere about; not even a rabbit, or a weasel's nest? Take her into the garden, before you change your shoes; and into the stable to see your horse."

"Wouldn't you rather sit here?" asked Linton, addressing Cathy in a tone which expressed reluctance to move again.

"I don't know," she replied, casting a longing look to the door, and evidently eager to be active.

He kept his seat, and shrank closer to the fire.

Heathcliff rose, and went into the kitchen, and then from thence to the yard, calling out for Hareton.

Hareton responded, and presently the two re-entered. The young man had been washing himself, as was visible by the glow on his cheeks, and his wetted hair.

"Oh, I'll ask *you,* uncle," cried Miss Cathy, recollecting the housekeeper's assertion. "That is not my cousin, is he?"

"Yes," he replied, "your mother's nephew. Don't you like him?"

Catherine looked queer.

"Is he not a handsome lad?" he continued.

The uncivil little thing stood on tiptoe, and whispered a sentence in Heathcliff's ear.

He laughed; Hareton darkened; I perceived he was very sensitive to suspected slights, and had obviously a dim notion of his inferiority. But his master or guardian chased the frown by exclaiming —

"You'll be the favourite among us, Hareton! She says you are a — what was it? Well, something very flattering — Here! you go with her round the farm. And behave like a gentleman, mind! Don't use any bad words; and don't stare, when the young lady is not looking at you, and be ready to hide your face when she is; and, when you speak, say your words slowly, and keep your hands out of your pockets. Be off, and entertain her as nicely as you can."

He watched the couple walking past the window. Earnshaw had his countenance completely averted from his companion. He seemed studying the familiar landscape with a stranger's and an artist's interest.

Catherine took a sly look at him, expressing small admiration. She then turned her attention to seeking out objects of amusement for herself, and tripped merrily on, lilting a tune to supply the lack of conversation.

"I've tied his tongue," observed Heathcliff. "He'll not venture a single syllable, all the time! Nelly, you recollect me at his age — nay, some years younger — Did I ever look so stupid, so 'gaumless,'° as Joseph calls it?"

"Worse," I replied, "because more sullen with it."

"I've a pleasure in him!" he continued reflecting aloud. "He has satisfied my expectations — If he were a born fool I should not enjoy it half so much — But he's no fool; and I can sympathise with all his feelings, having felt them myself — I know what he suffers now, for instance, exactly — it is merely a beginning of what he shall suffer, though. And he'll never be able to emerge from his bathos of coarseness and ignorance. I've got him faster than his scoundrel of a father secured me, and lower; for he takes a pride in his brutishness. I've taught him to scorn everything extra-animal as silly and weak — Don't you think Hindley would be proud of his son, if he could see him? almost as proud as I am of mine — But there's this difference, one is gold put to the use of paving-stones; and the other is tin polished to ape a service of silver — *Mine* has nothing valuable about it; yet I shall have the merit of making it go as far as such poor stuff can go. *His* had first-rate qualities, and they are lost — rendered worse than unavailing — I have nothing to regret; he would have more than any, but I, are aware of — And the best of it is, Hareton is damnably fond of me! You'll own that I've outmatched Hindley there — If the dead villain could rise from his grave to abuse me for his offspring's wrongs, I should have the fun of seeing the said offspring fight him back again, indignant that he should dare to rail at the one friend he has in the world!"

Heathcliff chuckled a fiendish laugh at the idea; I made no reply, because I saw he expected none.

Meantime, our young companion, who sat too removed from us to hear what was said, began to evince symptoms of uneasiness: probably

gaumless: Witless, lacking intelligence.

repenting that he had denied himself the treat of Catherine's society, for fear of a little fatigue.

His father remarked the restless glances wandering to the window, and the hand irresolutely extended towards his cap.

"Get up, you idle boy!" he exclaimed with assumed heartiness. "Away after them . . . they are just at the corner, by the stand of hives."

Linton gathered his energies and left the hearth. The lattice was open, and, as he stepped out, I heard Cathy inquiring of her unsociable attendant, what was that inscription over the door?

Hareton stared up, and scratched his head like a true clown.

"It's some damnable writing," he answered. "I cannot read it."

"Can't read it?" cried Catherine. "I can read it . . . It's English . . . but I want to know, why it is there."

Linton giggled — the first appearance of mirth he had exhibited.

"He does not know his letters," he said to his cousin. "Could you believe in the existence of such a colossal dunce?"

"Is he all as he should be?" asked Miss Cathy seriously, "or is he simple . . . not right? I've questioned him twice now, and each time he looked so stupid, I think he does not understand me; I can hardly understand *him*, I'm sure!"

Linton repeated his laugh, and glanced at Hareton tauntingly, who certainly did not seem quite clear of comprehension at that moment.

"There's nothing the matter, but laziness, is there, Earnshaw?" he said. "My cousin fancies you are an idiot . . . There you experience the consequence of scorning 'book-larning,' as you would say . . . Have you noticed, Catherine, his frightful Yorkshire pronunciation?"

"Why, where the devil is the use on 't?" growled Hareton, more ready in answering his daily companion. He was about to enlarge further, but the two youngsters broke into a noisy fit of merriment; my giddy Miss being delighted to discover that she might turn his strange talk to matter of amusement.

"Where is the use of the devil in that sentence?" tittered Linton. "Papa told you not to say any bad words, and you can't open your mouth without one . . . Do try to behave like a gentleman, now do!"

"If thou weren't more a lass than a lad, I'd fell thee this minute, I would; pitiful lath of a crater!" retorted the angry boor, retreating, while his face burnt with mingled rage and mortification; for he was conscious of being insulted, and embarrassed how to resent it.

Mr. Heathcliff having overheard the conversation, as well as I, smiled when he saw him go, but immediately afterwards, cast a look of singular aversion on the flippant pair, who remained chattering in the door-way.

The boy finding animation enough while discussing Hareton's faults and deficiencies, and relating anecdotes of his goings on; and the girl relishing his pert and spiteful sayings, without considering the ill-nature they evinced: but I began to dislike, more than to compassionate, Linton, and to excuse his father, in some measure, for holding him cheap.

We staid till afternoon: I could not tear Miss Cathy away, before: but happily my master had not quitted his apartment, and remained ignorant of our prolonged absence.

As we walked home, I would fain have enlightened my charge on the characters of the people we had quitted; but she got it into her head that I was prejudiced against them.

"Aha!" she cried, "you take papa's side, Ellen — you are partial . . . I know, or else you wouldn't have cheated me so many years, into the notion that Linton lived a long way from here. I'm really extremely angry, only, I'm so pleased, I can't show it! But you must hold your tongue about my uncle . . . he's *my* uncle, remember, and I'll scold papa for quarrelling with him."

And so she ran on, till I dropped endeavouring to convince her of her mistake.

She did not mention the visit that night, because she did not see Mr. Linton. Next day it all came out, sadly to my chagrin; and still I was not altogether sorry: I thought the burden of directing and warning would be more efficiently borne by him than me, but he was too timid in giving satisfactory reasons for his wish that she would shun connection with the household of the Heights, and Catherine liked good reasons for every restraint that harassed her petted will.

"Papa!" she exclaimed, after the morning's salutations, "guess whom I saw yesterday, in my walk on the moors . . . Ah, papa, you started! you've not done right, have you, now? I saw — But listen, and you shall hear how I found you out, and Ellen, who is in league with you, and yet pretended to pity me so, when I kept hoping, and was always disappointed about Linton's coming back!"

She gave a faithful account of her excursion and its consequences; and my master, though he cast more than one reproachful look at me, said nothing, till she had concluded. Then he drew her to him, and asked if she knew why he had concealed Linton's near neighbourhood from her? Could she think it was to deny her a pleasure that she might harmlessly enjoy?

"It was because you disliked Mr. Heathcliff," she answered.

"Then you believe I care more for my own feelings than yours, Cathy?" he said. "No, it was not because I disliked Mr. Heathcliff; but because Mr. Heathcliff dislikes me; and is a most diabolical man, delighting to wrong and ruin those he hates, if they give him the slightest opportunity. I knew that you could not keep up an acquaintance with your cousin, without being brought into contact with him; and I knew he would detest you, on my account; so, for your own good, and nothing else, I took precautions that you should not see Linton again — I meant to explain this some time as you grew older, and I'm sorry I delayed it!"

"But Mr. Heathcliff was quite cordial, papa," observed Catherine, not at all convinced; "and *he* didn't object to our seeing each other: he said I might come to his house, when I pleased, only I must not tell you, because you had quarrelled with him, and would not forgive him for marrying Aunt Isabella. And you won't — *you* are the one to be blamed — he is willing to let *us* be friends, at least; Linton and I — and you are not."

My master, perceiving that she would not take his word for her uncle-in-law's evil disposition, gave a hasty sketch of his conduct to Isabella, and the manner in which Wuthering Heights became his property. He could not bear to discourse long upon the topic, for though he spoke little of it, he still felt the same horror and detestation of his ancient enemy that had occupied his heart ever since Mrs. Linton's death. "She might have been living yet, if it had not been for him!" was his constant bitter reflection; and, in his eyes, Heathcliff seemed a murderer.

Miss Cathy, conversant with no bad deeds except her own slight acts of disobedience, injustice, and passion, rising from hot temper and thoughtlessness, and repented of on the day they were committed, was amazed at the blackness of spirit that could brood on and cover revenge for years, and deliberately prosecute its plans, without a visitation of remorse. She appeared so deeply impressed and shocked at this new view of human nature — excluded from all her studies and all her ideas till now — that Mr. Edgar deemed it unnecessary to pursue the subject. He merely added,

"You will know hereafter, darling, why I wish you to avoid his house and family — now, return to your old employments and amusements, and think no more about them!"

Catherine kissed her father, and sat down quietly to her lessons for a couple of hours, according to custom: then she accompanied him into the grounds, and the whole day passed as usual: but in the evening, when she had retired to her room, and I went to help her undress, I found her crying, on her knees by the bedside.

"Oh, fie, silly child!" I exclaimed. "If you had any real griefs, you'd be ashamed to waste a tear on this little contrariety. You never had one shadow of substantial sorrow, Miss Catherine. Suppose, for a minute, that master and I were dead, and you were by yourself in the world — how would you feel, then? Compare the present occasion with such an affliction as that, and be thankful for the friends you have, instead of coveting more."

"I'm not crying for myself, Ellen," she answered, "it's for him — He expected to see me again, to-morrow, and there, he'll be so disappointed — and he'll wait for me, and I shan't come!"

"Nonsense!" said I: "do you imagine he has thought as much of you, as you have of him? Hasn't he Hareton for a companion? Not one in a hundred would weep at losing a relation they had just seen twice, for two afternoons — Linton will conjecture how it is, and trouble himself no further about you."

"But may I not write a note to tell him why I cannot come?" she asked, rising to her feet. "And just send those books, I promised to lend him — his books are not as nice as mine, and he wanted to have them extremely, when I told him how interesting they were — May I not, Ellen?"

"No, indeed, no, indeed!" replied I with decision. "Then he would write to you, and there'd never be an end of it — No, Miss Catherine, the acquaintance must be dropped entirely — so papa expects, and I shall see that it is done."

"But how can one little note — " she recommenced, putting on an imploring countenance.

"Silence!" I interrupted. "We will not begin with your little notes — Get into bed."

She threw me a very naughty look, so naughty that I would not kiss her good-night at first: I covered her up, and shut her door, in great displeasure — but, repenting half-way, I returned softly, and, lo! there was Miss, standing at the table with a bit of blank paper before her, and a pencil in her hand, which she guiltily slipped out of sight, on my re-entrance.

"You'll get nobody to take that, Catherine," I said, "if you write it; and at present I shall put out your candle."

I set the extinguisher on the flame, receiving as I did so, a slap on my hand, and a petulant "cross thing!" I then quitted her again, and she drew the bolt in one of her worst, most peevish humours.

The letter was finished and forwarded to its destination by a milk-fetcher who came from the village, but that I didn't learn till some time afterwards. Weeks passed on, and Cathy recovered her temper, though she grew wondrous fond of stealing off to corners by herself, and often, if I came near her suddenly while reading, she would start, and bend over the book, evidently desirous to hide it; and I detected edges of loose paper sticking out beyond the leaves.

She also got a trick of coming down early in the morning, and lingering about the kitchen, as if she were expecting the arrival of something; and she had a small drawer in a cabinet in the library, which she would trifle over for hours, and whose key she took special care to remove when she left it.

One day, as she inspected this drawer, I observed that the playthings and trinkets, which recently formed its contents, were transmuted into bits of folded paper.

My curiosity and suspicions were roused; I determined to take a peep at her mysterious treasures; so, at night, as soon as she and my master were safe upstairs, I searched and readily found among my house keys, one that would fit the lock. Having opened, I emptied the whole contents into my apron, and took them with me to examine at leisure in my own chamber.

Though I could not but suspect, I was still surprised to discover that they were a mass of correspondence, daily, almost, it must have been, from Linton Heathcliff, answers to documents forwarded by her. The earlier dated were embarrassed and short; gradually, however, they expanded into copious love letters, foolish as the age of the writer rendered natural, yet with touches, here and there, which, I thought, were borrowed from a more experienced source.

Some of them struck me as singularly odd compounds of ardour and flatness; commencing in strong feeling, and concluding in the affected, wordy way that a schoolboy might use to a fancied, incorporeal sweet-heart.

Whether they satisfied Cathy, I don't know, but they appeared very worthless trash to me.

After turning over as many as I thought proper, I tied them in a handkerchief and set them aside, re-locking the vacant drawer.

Following her habit, my young lady descended early, and visited the kitchen: I watched her go to the door, on the arrival of a certain little boy; and, while the diary maid filled his can, she tucked something into his jacket pocket, and plucked something out.

I went round by the garden, and laid wait for the messenger; who fought valorously to defend his trust, and we spilt the milk between us;

but I succeeded in abstracting the epistle; and, threatening serious consequences if he did not look sharp home, I remained under the wall, and perused Miss Cathy's affectionate composition. It was more simple and more eloquent than her cousin's, very pretty and very silly. I shook my head, and went meditating into the house.

The day being wet, she could not divert herself with rambling about the park; so, at the conclusion of her morning studies, she resorted to the solace of the drawer. Her father sat reading at the table; and I, on purpose, had sought a bit of work in some unripped fringes of the window curtain, keeping my eye steadily fixed on her proceedings.

Never did any bird flying back to a plundered nest which it had left brim-full of chirping young ones, express more complete despair in its anguished cries and flutterings, than she by her single "Oh!" and the change that transfigured her late happy countenance. Mr. Linton looked up.

"What is the matter, love? Have you hurt yourself?" he said.

His tone and look assured her *he* had not been the discoverer of the hoard.

"No, papa — " she gasped, "Ellen! Ellen! come upstairs — I'm sick!"

I obeyed her summons, and accompanied her out.

"Oh, Ellen! you have got them," she commenced immediately, dropping on her knees, when we were enclosed alone. "Oh, give them to me, and I'll never never do so again! Don't tell papa — You have not told papa, Ellen, say you have not! I've been exceedingly naughty, but I won't do it any more!"

With a grave severity in my manner, I bid her stand up.

"So," I exclaimed, "Miss Catherine, you are tolerably far on, it seems — you may well be ashamed of them! A fine bundle of trash you study in your leisure hours, to be sure — Why, it's good enough to be printed! And what do you suppose the master will think, when I display it before him? I haven't shown it yet, but you needn't imagine I shall keep your ridiculous secrets — For shame! And you must have led the way in writing such absurdities, he would not have thought of beginning, I'm certain."

"I didn't! I didn't!" sobbed Cathy, fit to break her heart. "I didn't once think of loving him till — "

"*Loving!*" cried I, as scornfully as I could utter the word. "*Loving!* Did anybody ever hear the like! I might just as well talk of loving the miller who comes once a year to buy our corn. Pretty loving, indeed, and both times together you have seen Linton hardly four hours, in your life! Now here is the babyish trash. I'm going with it to the library; and we'll see what your father says to such *loving*."

She sprang at her precious epistles, but I held them above my head; and then she poured out further frantic entreaties that I would burn them — do anything rather than show them. And being really fully as inclined to laugh as scold, for I esteemed it all girlish vanity, I at length relented in a measure, and asked,

"If I consent to burn them, will you promise faithfully, neither to send nor receive a letter again, nor a book, for I perceive you have sent him books, nor locks of hair, nor rings, nor playthings?"

"We don't send playthings!" cried Catherine, her pride overcoming her shame.

"Nor anything at all, then, my lady!" I said. "Unless you will, here I go."

"I promise, Ellen!" she cried, catching my dress. "Oh, put them in the fire, do, do!"

But when I proceeded to open a place with the poker, the sacrifice was too painful to be borne — She earnestly supplicated that I would spare her one or two.

"One or two, Ellen, to keep for Linton's sake!"

I unknotted the handkerchief, and commenced dropping them in from an angle, and the flame curled up the chimney.

"I will have one, you cruel wretch!" she screamed, darting her hand into the fire, and drawing forth some half consumed fragments, at the expense of her fingers.

"Very well — and I will have some to exhibit to papa!" I answered, shaking back the rest into the bundle, and turning anew to the door.

She emptied her blackened pieces into the flames, and motioned me to finish the immolation. It was done; I stirred up the ashes, and interred them under a shovel full of coals; and she mutely, and with a sense of intense injury, retired to her private apartment. I descended to tell my master that the young lady's qualm of sickness was almost gone, but I judged it best for her to lie down a while.

She wouldn't dine; but she re-appeared at tea, pale and red about the eyes, and marvelously subdued in outward aspect.

Next morning, I answered the letter by a slip of paper, inscribed, "Master Heathcliff is requested to send no more notes to Miss Linton, as she will not receive them." And, thenceforth, the little boy came with vacant pockets.

CHAPTER 22

Summer drew to an end, and early Autumn — it was past Michaelmas, but the harvest was late that year, and a few of our fields were still uncleared.

Mr. Linton and his daughter would frequently walk out among the reapers: at the carrying of the last sheaves, they stayed till dusk, and the evening happening to be chill and damp, my master caught a bad cold, that settling obstinately on his lungs, confined him indoors throughout the whole of the winter, nearly without intermission.

Poor Cathy, frightened from her little romance, had been considerably sadder and duller since its abandonment: and her father insisted on her reading less, and taking more exercise. She had his companionship no longer; I esteemed it a duty to supply its lack, as much as possible, with mine; an inefficient substitute, for I could only spare two or three hours, from my numerous diurnal occupations, to follow her footsteps, and then, my society was obviously less desirable than his.

On an afternoon in October, or the beginning of November, a fresh watery afternoon, when the turf and path were rustling with moist, withered leaves, and the cold, blue sky was half hidden by clouds, dark grey streamers, rapidly mounting from the west, and boding abundant rain; I requested my young lady to forego her ramble because I was certain of showers. She refused; and I unwillingly donned a cloak, and took my umbrella to accompany her on a stroll to the bottom of the park; a formal walk which she generally affected if low-spirited — and that she invariably was when Mr. Edgar had been worse than ordinary; a thing never known from his confession, but guessed both by her and me from his increased silence, and the melancholy of his countenance.

She went sadly on; there was no running or bounding now, though the chill wind might well have tempted her to a race. And often, from the side of my eye, I could detect her raising a hand, and brushing something off her cheek.

I gazed round for a means of diverting her thoughts. On one side of the road rose a high, rough bank, where hazels and stunted oaks, with their roots half exposed, held uncertain tenure: the soil was too loose for the latter; and strong winds had blown some nearly horizontal. In summer, Miss Catherine delighted to climb among these trunks, and sit in the branches, swinging twenty feet above the ground; and I, pleased with her agility and her light, childish heart, still considered it proper to scold every time I caught her at such an elevation; but so that she knew there was no necessity for descending. From dinner to tea she would lie in her breeze-rocked cradle, doing nothing except singing old songs — my nursery lore — to herself, or watching the birds, joint tenants, feed and entice their young ones to fly, or nestling with closed lids, half thinking, half dreaming, happier than words can express.

"Look, Miss!" I exclaimed, pointing to a nook under the roots of one twisted tree. "Winter is not here yet. There's a little flower, up yonder, the last bud from the multitude of blue-bells that clouded those turf steps in July with a lilac mist. Will you clamber up, and pluck it to show to papa?"

Cathy stared a long time at the lonely blossom trembling in is earthly shelter, and replied, at length —

"No, I'll not touch it — but it looks melancholy, does it not, Ellen?"

"Yes," I observed, "about as starved and sackless° as you — your cheeks are bloodless; let us take hold of hands and run. You're so low, I dare say I shall keep up with you."

"No," she repeated, and continued sauntering on, pausing, at intervals, to muse over a bit of moss, or a tuft of blanched grass, or a fungus spreading its bright orange among the heaps of brown foliage; and, ever and anon, her hand was lifted to her averted face.

"Catherine, why are you crying, love?" I asked, approaching and putting my arm over her shoulder. "You mustn't cry because papa has a cold; be thankful it is nothing worse."

She now put no further restraint on her tears; her breath was stifled by sobs.

"Oh, it *will* be something worse," she said. "And what shall I do when papa and you leave me, and I am by myself? I can't forget your words, Ellen, they are always in my ear. How life will be changed, how dreary the world will be, when papa and you are dead."

"None can tell, whether you won't die before us," I replied. "It's wrong to anticipate evil — we'll hope there are years and years to come before any of us go — master is young, and I am strong, and hardly forty-five. My mother lived till eighty, a canty° dame to the last. And suppose Mr. Linton were spared till he saw sixty, that would be more years than you have counted, Miss. And would it not be foolish to mourn a calamity above twenty years beforehand?"

"But Aunt Isabella was younger than papa," she remarked, gazing up with timid hope to seek further consolation.

sackless: Harmless, lacking energy. ***canty:*** Lively, active.

"Aunt Isabella had not you and me to nurse her," I replied. "She wasn't as happy as master; she hadn't as much to live for. All you need do, is to wait well on your father, and cheer him by letting him see you cheerful; and avoid giving him anxiety on any subject — mind that, Cathy! I'll not disguise, but you might kill him, if you were wild and reckless, and cherished a foolish, fanciful affection for the son of a person who would be glad to have him in his grave — and allowed him to discover that you fretted over the separation he has judged it expedient to make."

"I fret about nothing on earth except papa's illness," answered my companion. "I care for nothing in comparison with papa. And I'll never — never — oh, never while I have my senses, do an act or say a word to vex him. I love him better than myself, Ellen; and I know it by this — I pray every night that I may live after him; because I would rather be miserable than that he should be — that proves I love him better than myself."

"Good words," I replied. "But deeds must prove it also; and after he is well, remember you don't forget resolutions formed in the hour of fear."

As we talked, we neared a door that opened on the road: and my young lady, lightening into sunshine again, climbed up, and seated herself on the top of the wall, reaching over to gather some hips that bloomed scarlet on the summit branches of the wild rose trees, shadowing the highway side: the lower fruit had disappeared, but only birds could touch the upper, except from Cathy's present station.

In stretching to pull them, her hat fell off; and as the door was locked, she proposed scrambling down to recover it. I bid her be cautious lest she got a fall, and she nimbly disappeared.

But the return was no such easy matter; the stones were smooth and neatly cemented, and the rosebushes and the blackberry stragglers could yield no assistance in re-ascending. I, like a fool, didn't recollect that till I heard her laughing, and exclaiming —

"Ellen, you'll have to fetch the key, or else I must run round to the porter's lodge. I can't scale the ramparts on this side!"

"Stay where you are," I answered, "I have my bundle of keys in my pocket; perhaps I may manage to open it; if not, I'll go."

Catherine amused herself with dancing to and fro before the door, while I tried all the large keys in succession. I had applied the last, and found that none would do; so, repeating my desire that she would remain there, I was about to hurry home as fast I could, when an approaching sound arrested me. It was the trot of a horse; Cathy's dance stopped; and in a minute the horse stopped also.

"Who is that?" I whispered.

"Ellen, I wish you could open the door," whispered back my companion, anxiously.

"Ho, Miss Linton!" cried a deep voice (the rider's). "I'm glad to meet you. Don't be in haste to enter, for I have an explanation to ask and obtain."

"I shan't speak to you, Mr. Heathcliff!" answered Catherine. "Papa says you are a wicked man, and you hate both him and me; and Ellen says the same."

"That is nothing to the purpose," said Heathcliff. (He it was.) "I don't hate my son, I suppose, and it is concerning him that I demand your attention. Yes! you have cause to blush. Two or three months since, were you not in the habit of writing to Linton? making love in play, eh? You deserved, both of you, flogging for that! You especially, the elder, and less sensitive, as it turns out. I've got your letters, and if you give me any pertness, I'll send them to your father. I presume you grew weary of the amusement, and dropped it, didn't you? Well, you dropped Linton with it, into a Slough of Despond. He was in earnest — in love — really. As true as I live, he's dying for you — breaking his heart at your fickleness, not figuratively, but actually. Though Hareton has made him a standing jest for six weeks, and I have used more serious measures, and attempted to frighten him out of his idiocy, he gets worse daily, and he'll be under the sod before summer, unless you restore him!"

"How can you lie so glaringly to the poor child!" I called from the inside. "Pray ride on! How can you deliberately get up such paltry falsehoods? Miss Cathy, I'll knock the lock off with a stone. You won't believe that vile nonsense. You can feel in yourself, it is impossible that a person should die for the love of a stranger."

"I was not aware there were eaves-droppers," muttered the detected villain. "Worthy Mrs. Dean, I like you, but I don't like your double dealing," he added, aloud. "How could *you* lie so glaringly, as to affirm I hated the 'poor child'? And invent bugbear stories to terrify her from my door-stones? Catherine Linton (the very name warms me), my bonny lass, I shall be from home all this week; go and see if I have not spoken truth; do, there's a darling! Just imagine your father in my place, and Linton in yours; then think how you would value your careless lover, if he refused to stir a step to comfort you, when your father, himself, entreated him; and don't, from pure stupidity, fall into the same error. I swear, on my salvation, he's going to his grave, and none but you can save him!"

The lock gave way, and I issued out.

"I swear Linton is dying," repeated Heathcliff, looking hard at me. "And grief and disappointment are hastening his death. Nelly, if you won't let her go, you can walk over yourself. But I shall not return till this time next week; and I think your master himself would scarcely object to her visiting her cousin!"

"Come in," said I, taking Cathy by the arm and half forcing her to re-enter, for she lingered, viewing, with troubled eyes, the features of the speaker, too stern to express his inward deceit.

He pushed his horse close, and bending down, observed —

"Miss Catherine, I'll own to you that I have little patience with Linton — and Hareton and Joseph have less. I'll own that he's with a harsh set. He pines for kindness, as well as love; and a kind word from you would be his best medicine. Don't mind Mrs. Dean's cruel cautions, but be generous, and contrive to see him. He dreams of you day and night, and cannot be persuaded that you don't hate him, since you neither write nor call."

I closed the door, and rolled a stone to assist the loosened lock in holding it; and spreading my umbrella, I drew my charge underneath, for the rain began to drive through the moaning branches of the trees, and warned us to avoid delay.

Our hurry prevented any comment on the encounter with Heathcliff, as we stretched towards home; but I divined instinctively that Catherine's heart was clouded now in double darkness. Her features were so sad, they did not seem hers; she evidently regarded what she had heard as every syllable true.

The master had retired to rest before we came in. Cathy stole to his room to inquire how he was; he had fallen asleep. She returned, and asked me to sit with her in the library. We took our tea together; and afterwards she lay down on the rug, and told me not to talk for she was weary.

I got a book, and pretended to read. As soon as she supposed me absorbed in my occupation, she recommenced her silent weeping: it appeared, at present, her favourite diversion. I suffered her to enjoy it a while; then, I expostulated; deriding and ridiculing all Mr. Heathcliff's assertions about his son, as if I were certain she would coincide. Alas! I hadn't skill to counteract the effect his account had produced; it was just what he intended.

"You may be right, Ellen," she answered; "but I shall never feel at ease till I know — and I must tell Linton it is not my fault that I don't write; and convince him that I shall not change."

What use were anger and protestations against her silly credulity? We parted that night hostile — but next day beheld me on the road to Wuthering Heights, by the side of my wilful young mistress's pony. I couldn't bear to witness her sorrow, to see her pale, dejected countenance, and heavy eyes; and I yielded in the faint hope that Linton himself might prove, by his reception of us, how little of the tale was founded on fact.

CHAPTER 23

The rainy night had ushered in a misty morning — half frost, half drizzle — and temporary brooks crossed our path, gurgling from the uplands. My feet were thoroughly wetted; I was cross and low, exactly the humour for making the most of these disagreeable things.

We entered the farm-house by the kitchen way to ascertain whether Mr. Heathcliff were really absent; because I put slight faith in his own affirmation.

Joseph seemed sitting in a sort of elysium alone, beside a roaring fire; a quart of ale on the table near him, bristling with large pieces of toasted oat cake; and his black, short pipe in his mouth.

Catherine ran to the hearth to warm herself. I asked if the master were in?

My questions remained so long unanswered, that I thought the old man had grown deaf, and repeated it louder.

"Na — ay!" he snarled, or rather screamed through his nose. "Na — ay! yah muh goa back whear yah coom frough."

"Joseph!" cried a peevish voice, simultaneously with me, from the inner room. "How often am I to call you? There are only a few red ashes now. Joseph! come at this moment."

Vigorous puffs, and a resolute stare into the grate, declared he had ear for this appeal. The housekeeper and Hareton were invisible; one on an errand, and the other at his work, probably. We knew Linnes and entered.

hope you'll die in a garret! starved to death," said the boy, r approach for that of his negligent attendant.

, on observing his error; his cousin flew to him.

"Is that you, Miss Linton?" he said, raising his head from the arm of the great chair, in which he reclined. "No — don't kiss me. It takes my breath — dear me! Papa said you would call," continued he, after recovering a little from Catherine's embrace; while she stood by looking very contrite. "Will you shut the door, if you please? you left it open; and those — those *detestable* creatures won't bring coals to the fire. It's so cold!"

I stirred up the cinders, and fetched a scuttle full myself. The invalid complained of being covered with ashes; but he had a tiresome cough, and looked feverish and ill, so I did not rebuke his temper.

"Well, Linton," murmured Catherine, when his corrugated brow relaxed. "Are you glad to see me? Can I do you any good?"

"Why didn't you come before?" he said. "You should have come, instead of writing. It tired me dreadfully, writing those long letters. I'd far rather have talked to you. Now, I can neither bear to talk, nor anything else. I wonder where Zillah is! Will you (looking at me) step into the kitchen and see?"

I had received no thanks for my other service; and being unwilling to run to and fro at his behest, I replied —

"Nobody is out there but Joseph."

"I want to drink," he exclaimed, fretfully, turning away. "Zillah is constantly gadding off to Gimmerton since papa went. It's miserable! And I'm obliged to come down here — they resolved never to hear me upstairs."

"Is your father attentive to you, Master Heathcliff?" I asked, perceiving Catherine to be checked in her friendly advances.

"Attentive? He makes *them* a little more attentive, at least," he cried. "The wretches! Do you know, Miss Linton, that brute Hareton laughs at me — I hate him — indeed, I hate them all — they are odious beings."

Cathy began searching for some water; she lighted on a pitcher in the dresser, filled a tumbler, and brought it. He bid her add a spoonful of wine from a bottle on the table; and having swallowed a small portion, appeared more tranquil, and said she was very kind.

"And are you glad to see me?" asked she, reiterating her former question, and pleased to detect the faint dawn of a smile.

"Yes, I am — It's something new to hear a voice like yours!" he replied. "But I *have* been vexed, because you wouldn't come — And papa swore it was owing to me; he called me a pitiful, shuffling, worthless thing; and said you despised me; and if he had been in my place, he would be more the master of the Grange than your father, by this time. But you don't despise me, do you, Miss — "

"I wish you would say Catherine, or Cathy!" interrupted my young lady. "Despise you? No! Next to papa, and Ellen, I love you better than anybody living. I don't love Mr. Heathcliff, though; and I dare not come when he returns; will he stay away many days?"

"Not many," answered Linton, "but he goes onto the moors frequently, since the shooting season commenced, and you might spend an hour or two with me, in his absence — Do! say you will! I think I should not be peevish with you; you'd not provoke me, and you'd be always ready to help me, wouldn't you?"

"Yes," said Catherine, stroking his long soft hair, "if I could only get papa's consent, I'd spend half my time with you — Pretty Linton! I wish you were my brother."

"And then you would like me as well as your father?" observed he more cheerfully. "But papa says you would love me better than him, and all the world, if you were my wife — so I'd rather you were that!"

"No! I should never love anybody better than papa," she returned gravely. "And people hate their wives, sometimes; but not their sisters and brothers, and if you were the latter, you would live with us, and papa would be as fond of you, as he is of me."

Linton denied that people ever hated their wives; but Cathy affirmed they did, and in her wisdom, instanced his own father's aversion to her aunt.

I endeavoured to stop her thoughtless tongue — and I couldn't succeed, till everything she knew was out. Master Heathcliff, much irritated, asserted her relation was false.

"Papa told me; and papa does not tell falsehoods!" she answered pertly.

"*My* papa scorns yours!" cried Linton. "He calls him a sneaking fool!"

"Yours is a wicked man," retorted Catherine, "and you are very naughty to dare to repeat what he says — He must be wicked, to have made Aunt Isabella leave him as she did!"

"She didn't leave him," said the boy; "you shan't contradict me!"

"She did!" cried my young lady.

"Well, I'll tell *you* something!" said Linton. "Your mother hated your father, now then."

"Oh!" exclaimed Catherine, too enraged to continue.

"And she loved mine!" added he.

"You little liar! I hate you now," she panted, and her face grew red with passion.

"She did! she did!" sang Linton, sinking into the recess of his chair, and leaning back his head to enjoy the agitation of the other disputant, who stood behind.

"Hush, Master Heathcliff!" I said, "that's your father's tale too, I suppose."

"It isn't — you hold your tongue!" he answered. "She did, she did, Catherine, she did, she did!"

Cathy, beside herself, gave the chair a violent push, and caused him to fall against one arm. He was immediately seized by a suffocating cough that soon ended his triumph.

It lasted so long, that it frightened even me. As to his cousin, she wept with all her might, aghast at the mischief she had done, though she said nothing.

I held him, till the fit exhausted itself. Then he thrust me away; and leant his head down, silently — Catherine quelled her lamentations also, took a seat opposite, and looked solemnly into the fire.

"How do you feel now, Master Heathcliff?" I inquired after waiting ten minutes.

"I wish *she* felt as I do," he replied, "spiteful, cruel thing! Hareton never touches me, he never struck me in his life — And I was better to-day — and there — " his voice died in a whimper.

"*I* didn't strike you!" muttered Cathy, chewing her lip to prevent another burst of emotion.

He signed and moaned like one under great suffering; and kept it up for a quarter of an hour, on purpose to distress his cousin, apparently, for whenever he caught a stifled sob from her, he put renewed pain and pathos into the inflexions of his voice.

"I'm sorry I hurt you, Linton!" she said at length, racked beyond endurance. "But *I* couldn't have been hurt by that little push; and I had no idea that you could, either — you're not much, are you, Linton? Don't let me go home thinking I've done you harm! Answer, speak to me."

"I can't speak to you," he murmured, "you've hurt me so, that I shall lie awake all night, choking with this cough! If you had it you'd know what it was — but *you'll* be comfortably asleep, while I'm in agony — and nobody near me! I wonder how you would like to pass those fearful nights!" And he began to wail aloud for very pity of himself.

"Since you are in the habit of passing dreadful nights," I said, "it won't be Miss who spoils your ease; you'd be the same, had she never come — However, she shall not disturb you, again — and perhaps, you'll get quieter when we leave you."

"Must I go?" asked Catherine dolefully, bending over him. "Do you want me to go, Linton?"

"You can't alter what you've done," he replied pettishly, shrinking from her, "unless you alter it for the worse, by teasing me into a fever!"

"Well, then I must go?" she repeated.

"Let me alone, at least," said he; "I can't bear your talking!"

She lingered, and resisted my persuasions to departure, a tiresome while, but as he neither looked up nor spoke, she finally made a movement to the door, and I followed.

We were recalled by a scream — Linton had slid from his seat on to the hearthstone, and lay writhing in the mere perverseness of an indulged plague of a child, determined to be as grievous and harassing as it can.

I thoroughly gauged his disposition from his behaviour, and saw at once it would be folly to attempt humouring him. Not so my companion: she ran back in terror, knelt down, and cried, and soothed, and entreated, till he grew quiet from lack of breath, by no means from compunction at distressing her.

"I shall lift him on the settle," I said, "and he may roll about as he pleases; we can't stop to watch him — I hope you are satisfied, Miss Cathy, that *you* are not the person to benefit him, and that his condition of health is not occasioned by attachment to you. Now then, there it is! Come away; as soon as he knows there is nobody by to care for his nonsense, he'll be glad to lie still!"

She placed a cushion under his head, and offered him some water; he rejected the latter, and tossed uneasily on the former, as if it were a stone, or a block of wood.

She tried to put it more comfortably.

"I can't do with that," he said, "it's not high enough!"

Catherine brought another to lay above it.

"That's *too* high!" murmured the provoking thing.

"How must I arrange it, then?" she asked despairingly.

He twined himself up to her, as she half knelt by the settle, and converted her shoulder into a support.

"No, that won't do!" I said. "You'll be content with the cushion, Master Heathcliff! Miss has wasted too much time on you, already; we cannot remain five minutes longer."

"Yes, yes, we can!" replied Cathy. "He's good and patient, now — He's beginning to think I shall have far greater misery than he will, to-night, if I believe he is the worse for my visit; and then, I dare not come again — Tell the truth about it, Linton — for I mustn't come, if I have hurt you."

"You must come, to cure me," he answered. "You ought to come because you have hurt me — You know you have, extremely! I was not as ill, when you entered, as I am at present — was I?"

"But you've made yourself ill by crying, and being in a passion. I didn't do it all," said his cousin. "However, we'll be friends now. And you want me — you would wish to see me sometimes, really?"

"I told you, I did!" he replied impatiently. "Sit on the settle and let me lean on your knee — That's as mamma used to do, whole afternoons together — Sit quite still, and don't talk, but you may sing a song if you can sing, or you may say a nice, long interesting ballad — one of those you promised to teach me, or a story — I'd rather have a ballad, though: begin."

Catherine repeated the longest she could remember. The employment pleased both mightily. Linton would have another, and after that another, notwithstanding my strenuous objections; and so they went on, until the clock struck twelve, and we heard Hareton in the court, returning for his dinner.

"And to-morrow, Catherine, will you be here to-morrow?" asked young Heathcliff, holding her frock, as she rose reluctantly.

"No!' I answered, "nor the next day either." She, however, gave a different response, evidently, for his forehead cleared as she stooped and whispered in his ear.

"You won't go to-morrow, recollect, Miss!" I commenced, when we were out of the house. "You are not dreaming of it, are you?"

She smiled.

"Oh, I'll take good care!" I continued. "I'll have that lock mended, and you can escape by no way else."

"I can get over the wall," she said, laughing. "The Grange is not a prison, Ellen, and you are not my jailer. And besides, I'm almost seventeen. I'm a woman — and I'm certain Linton would recover quickly if he had me to look after him — I'm older than he is, you know, and wiser, less childish, am I not? And he'll soon do as I direct him with some slight coaxing — He's a pretty little darling when he's good. I'd make such a pet of him, if he were mine — We should never quarrel, should we, after we were used to each other? Don't you like him, Ellen?"

"Like him?" I exclaimed. "The worst-tempered bit of a sickly slip that ever struggled into his teens! Happily, as Mr. Heathcliff conjectured, he'll not win twenty! I doubt whether he'll see spring, indeed — and small loss to his family, whenever he drops off; and lucky it is for us that his father took him — The kinder he was treated, the more tedious and selfish he'd be! I'm glad you have no chance of having him for a husband, Miss Catherine!"

My companion waxed serious at hearing this speech — To speak of his death so regardlessly wounded her feelings.

"He's younger than I," she answered, after a protracted pause of meditation, "and he ought to live the longest, he will — he must live as long as I do. He's as strong now as when he first came into the North, I'm positive of that! It's only a cold that ails him, the same as papa has — You say papa will get better, and why shouldn't he?"

"Well, well," I cried, "after all, we needn't trouble ourselves; for listen, Miss — and mind, I'll keep my word — If you attempt going to Wuthering Heights again, with or without me, I shall inform Mr. Linton, and, unless he allow it, the intimacy with your cousin must not be revived."

"It has been revived!" muttered Cathy sulkily.

"Must not be continued, then!" I said.

"We'll see!" was her reply, and she set off at a gallop, leaving me to toil in the rear.

We both reached home before our dinner-time: my master supposed we had been wandering through the park, and therefore, he demanded no explanation of our absence. As soon as I entered, I hastened to change my soaked shoes and stockings; but sitting such a while at the Heights, had done the mischief. On the succeeding morning, I was laid up; and during three weeks I remained incapacitated for attending to my duties — a calamity never experienced prior to that period, and never, I am thankful to say, since.

My little mistress behaved like an angel in coming to wait on me, and cheer my solitude: the confinement brought me exceedingly low — It is wearisome, to a stirring active body — but few have slighter reasons for complaint than I had. The moment Catherine left Mr. Linton's room, she appeared at my bed-side. Her day was divided between us; no amusement usurped a minute: she neglected her meals, her studies, and her play; and she was the fondest nurse that ever watched: she must have had a warm heart, when she loved her father so, to give so much to me!

I said her days were divided between us; but the master retired early, and I generally needed nothing after six o'clock, thus the evening was her own.

Poor thing, I never considered what she did with herself after tea. And though frequently, when she looked in to bid me goodnight, I remarked a fresh colour in her cheeks, and a pinkness over her slender fingers; instead of fancying the hue borrowed from a cold ride across the moors, I laid it to the charge of a hot fire in the library.

CHAPTER 24

At the close of three weeks, I was able to quit my chamber, and move about the house. And on the first occasion of my sitting up in the evening, I asked Catherine to read to me, because my eyes were weak. We were in the library, the master having gone to bed: she consented, rather unwillingly, I fancied; and imagining my sort of books did not suit her, I bid her please herself in the choice of what she perused.

She selected one of her own favourites, and got forward steadily about an hour; then came frequent questions.

"Ellen, are not you tired? Hadn't you better lie down now? You'll be sick, keeping up so long, Ellen."

"No, no, dear, I'm not tired," I returned, continually.

Perceiving me immovable, she essayed another method of showing her dis-relish for her occupation. It changed to yawning, and stretching, and —

"Ellen, I'm tired."

"Give over then and talk," I answered.

That was worse; she fretted and sighed, and looked at her watch till eight; and finally went to her room, completely overdone with sleep, judging by her peevish, heavy look, and the constant rubbing she inflicted on her eyes.

The following night she seemed more impatient still; and on the third from recovering her company, she complained of a head-ache, and left me.

I thought her conduct odd; and having remained alone a long while, I resolved on going, and inquiring whether she were better, and asking her to come and lie on the sofa, instead of upstairs, in the dark.

No Catherine could I discover upstairs, and none below. The servants affirmed they had not seen her. I listened at Mr. Edgar's door — all was silence. I returned to her apartment, extinguished my candle, and seated myself in the window.

The moon shone bright; a sprinkling of snow covered the ground, and I reflected that she might, possibly, have taken it into her head to walk about the garden, for refreshment. I did detect a figure creeping along the inner fence of the park; but it was not my young mistress; on its emerging into the light, I recognised one of the grooms.

He stood a considerable period, viewing the carriage-road through the grounds; then started off at a brisk pace, as if he had detected something, and reappeared presently, leading Miss's pony; and there she was, just dismounted, and walking by its side.

The man took his charge stealthily across the grass towards the stable. Cathy entered by the casement-window of the drawing-room, and glided noiselessly up to where I awaited her.

She put the door gently to, slipped off her snowy shoes, untied her hat, and was proceeding, unconscious of my espionage, to lay aside her mantle, when I suddenly rose and revealed myself. The surprise petrified her an instant: she uttered an inarticulate exclamation, and stood fixed.

"My dear Miss Catherine," I began, too vividly impressed by her recent kindness to break into a scold, "where have you been riding out at this hour? And why should you try to deceive me, by telling a tale? Where have you been? Speak!"

"To the bottom of the park," she stammered. "I didn't tell a tale."

"And nowhere else?" I demanded.

"No," was the muttered reply.

"Oh, Catherine," I cried, sorrowfully. "You know you have been doing wrong, or you wouldn't be driven to uttering an untruth to me. That does grieve me. I'd rather be three months ill, than hear you frame a deliberate lie."

She sprang forward, and bursting into tears, threw her arms round my neck.

"Well, Ellen, I'm so afraid of you being angry," she said. "Promise not to be angry, and you shall know the very truth. I hate to hide it."

We sat down in the window-seat; I assured her I would not scold, whatever her secret might be, and I guessed it, of course; so she commenced —

"I've been to Wuthering Heights, Ellen, and I've never missed going a day since you fell ill; except thrice before, and twice after you left your room. I gave Michael books and pictures to prepare Minny every evening, and to put her back in the stable; you mustn't scold *him* either, mind. I was at the Heights by half-past six, and generally stayed till half-past eight, and then galloped home. It was not to amuse myself that I went; I was often wretched all the time. Now and then, I was happy, once in a week perhaps. At first, I expected there would be sad work persuading you to let me keep my word to Linton, for I had engaged to call again next day, when we quitted him; but, as you stayed upstairs on the morrow, I escaped that trouble; and while Michael was refastening the lock of the park door in the afternoon, I got possession of the key, and told him how my cousin wished me to visit him, because he was sick, and couldn't come to the Grange: and how papa would object to my going. And then I negotiated with him about the pony. He is fond of reading, and he thinks of leaving soon to get married, so he offered, if I would lend him books out of the library, to do what I wished; but I preferred giving him my own, and that satisfied him better.

"On my second visit, Linton seemed in lively spirits; and Zillah (that is their housekeeper) made us a clean room and a good fire, and told us that, as Joseph was out at a prayer-meeting, and Hareton Earnshaw was off with his dogs, robbing our woods of pheasants, as I heard afterwards, we might do what we liked.

"She brought me some warm wine and gingerbread, and appeared exceedingly good-natured; and Linton sat in the armchair, and I in the little rocking chair on the hearthstone, and we laughed and talked so merrily, and found so much to say; we planned where we would go, and what we would do in summer. I needn't repeat that, because you would call it silly.

"One time, however, we were near quarrelling. He said the pleasantest manner of spending a hot July day was lying from morning till evening on a bank of heath in the middle of the moors, with the bees humming dreamily about among the bloom, and the larks singing high up over head, and the blue sky and bright sun shining steadily and cloudlessly. That was his most perfect idea of heaven's happiness — mine was rocking in a rustling green tree, with a west wind blowing, and bright, white clouds flitting rapidly above; and not only larks, but throstles, and blackbirds, and linnets, and cuckoos pouring out music on every side, and the moors seen at a distance, broken into cool dusky dells; but close by great swells of long grass undulating in waves to the breeze; and woods and sounding water, and the whole world awake and wild with joy. He wanted all to lie in an ecstacy of peace; I wanted all to sparkle, and dance in a glorious jubilee.

"I said his heaven would be only half alive, and he said mine would be drunk; I said I should fall asleep in his, and he said he could not breathe in mine, and began to grow very snappish. At last, we agreed to try both as soon as the right weather came; and then we kissed each other and were friends. After sitting still an hour, I looked at the great room with its smooth, uncarpeted floor; and thought how nice it would be to play in, if we removed the table; and I asked Linton to call Zillah in to help us — and we'd have a game at blind-man's buff — she should try to catch us — you used to, you know, Ellen. He wouldn't, there was no pleasure in it, he said; and he consented to play at ball with me. We found two, in a cupboard, among a heap of old toys; tops, and hoops, and battledoors, and shuttlecocks. One was marked C., and the other H.; I wished to have the C., because that stood for Catherine, and the H. might be for Heathcliff, his name; but the bran came out of H., and Linton didn't like it.

"I beat him constantly; and he got cross again, and coughed, and returned to his chair: that night, though, he easily recovered his good humour; he was charmed with two or three pretty songs — *your* songs, Ellen; and when I was obliged to go, he begged and entreated me to come the following evening, and I promised.

"Minny and I went flying home as light as air: and I dreamt of Wuthering Heights, and my sweet, darling cousin, till morning.

"On the morrow, I was sad; partly because you were poorly, and partly that I wished my father knew, and approved of my excursion: but it was beautiful moonlight after tea; and, as I rode on, the gloom cleared.

"I shall have another happy evening, I thought to myself; and what delights me more, my pretty Linton will.

"I trotted up their garden, and was turning round to the back, when that fellow Earnshaw met me, took my bridle, and bid me go in by the front entrance. He patted Minny's neck, and said she was a bonny beast, and appeared as if he wanted me to speak to him. I only told him to leave my horse alone, or else it would kick him.

"He answered in his vulgar accent,

" 'It wouldn't do mitch hurt if it did;' and surveyed its legs with a smile.

"I was half inclined to make a try; however, he moved off to open the door, and, as he raised the latch, he looked up to the inscription above, and said, with a stupid mixture of awkwardness and elation —

" 'Miss Catherine! I can read yon, nah.'

" 'Wonderful,' I exclaimed. 'Pray let us hear you — you *are* grown clever!'

"He spelt, and drawled over by syllables, the name — 'Hareton Earnshaw.'

" 'And the figures?' I cried, encouragingly, perceiving that he came to a dead halt.

" 'I cannot tell them yet,' he answered.

" 'Oh, you dunce!' I said, laughing heartily at his failure.

"The fool stared, with a grin hovering about his lips, and a scowl gathering over his eyes, as if uncertain whether he might not join in my mirth; whether it were not pleasant familiarity, or what it really was, contempt.

"I settled his doubts by suddenly retrieving my gravity, and desiring him to walk away, for I came to see Linton not him.

"He reddened — I saw that by the moonlight — dropped his hand from the latch, and skulked off, a picture of mortified vanity. He imagined himself to be as accomplished as Linton, I suppose, because he could spell his own name; and was marvellously discomfited that I didn't think the same."

"Stop, Miss Catherine, dear!" I interrupted. "I shall not scold, but I don't like your conduct there. If you had remembered that Hareton was your cousin, as much as Master Heathcliff, you would have felt how improper it was to behave in that way. At least, it was praiseworthy ambition for him to desire to be as accomplished as Linton: and probably he did not learn merely to show off; you had made him ashamed of his ignorance, before: I have no doubt; and he wished to remedy it and please you. To sneer at his imperfect attempt was very bad breeding — had *you* been brought up in his circumstances, would you be less rude? He was as quick and as intelligent a child as ever you were, and I'm hurt that he should be despised now, because that base Heathcliff has treated him so unjustly."

"Well, Ellen, you won't cry about it, will you?" she exclaimed, surprised at my earnestness. "But wait, and you shall hear if he conned his A B C to please me; and if it were worth while being civil to the brute. I entered; Linton was lying on the settle, and half got up to welcome me.

"'I'm ill to-night, Catherine, love,' he said, 'and you must have all the talk, and let me listen. Come, and sit by me — I was sure you wouldn't break your word, and I'll make you promise again, before you go.'

"I knew now that I mustn't tease him, as he was ill; and I spoke softly and put no questions, and avoided irritating him in any way. I had brought some of my nicest books for him; he asked me to read a little of one, and I was about to comply, when Earnshaw burst the door open, having gathered venom with reflection. He advanced direct to us; seized Linton by the arm, and swung him off the seat.

"'Get to thy own room!' he said, in a voice almost inarticulate with passion, and his face looked swelled and furious. 'Take her there if she comes to see thee — thou shalln't keep me out of this. Begone, wi' ye both!'

"He swore at us, and left Linton no time to answer, nearly throwing him into the kitchen; and he clenched his fist, as I followed, seemingly longing to knock me down. I was afraid, for a moment, and I let one volume fall; he kicked it after me, and shut us out.

"I heard a malignant, crackly laugh by the fire, and turning beheld that odious Joseph, standing rubbing his bony hands, and quivering.

"'Aw wer sure he'd sarve ye eht!° He's a grand lad! He's getten t' raight sperrit in him! *He* knaws — Aye, he knaws, as weel as Aw do, who sud be t' maister yonder — Ech, ech, ech! He mad ye skift properly!° Ech, ech, ech!'

"'Where must we go?' I said to my cousin, disregarding the old wretch's mockery.

"Linton was white and trembling. He was not pretty then, Ellen! Oh, no! he looked frightful! for his thin face and large eyes were wrought into an expression of frantic, powerless fury. He grasped the handle of the door, and shook it — it was fastened inside.

"'If you don't let me in I'll kill you! If you don't let me in I'll kill you!' he rather shrieked than said. 'Devil! devil! I'll kill you, I'll kill you!'

"Joseph uttered his croaking laugh again.

"'Thear, that's t' father!' he cried. 'That's father! We've allas summut uh orther side in us° — Niver heed Hareton, lad — dunnut be 'feard — he cannot get at thee!'

"I took hold of Linton's hands, and tried to pull him away; but he shrieked so shockingly that I dared not proceed. At last, his cries were choked by a dreadful fit of coughing; blood gushed from his mouth, and he fell on the ground.

"I ran into the yard, sick with terror; and called for Zillah, as loud as I could. She soon heard me; she was milking the cows in a shed behind the barn, and hurrying from her work, she inquired what there was to do?

"I hadn't breath to explain; dragging her in, I looked about for Linton. Earnshaw had come out to examine the mischief he had caused, and he was then conveying the poor thing upstairs. Zillah and I ascended after him; but he stopped me, at the top of the steps, and said I shouldn't go in, I must go home.

"I exclaimed that he had killed Linton, and I *would* enter.

"Joseph locked the door, and declared I should do 'no sich stuff,' and asked me whether I were 'bahn° to be as mad as him.'

"I stood crying, till the housekeeper re-appeared; she affirmed that he would be better in a bit; but he couldn't do with that shrieking and din; and she took me, and nearly carried me into the house.

sarve ye eht: Serve you properly, give you what's coming. ***mad ye skift properly:*** Made you move suitably, quickly. ***summut uh orther side in us:*** Something of the other side in us (inherited from Heathcliff's genes). ***bahn:*** Born.

"Ellen, I was ready to tear my hair off my head! I sobbed and wept so that my eyes were almost blind: and the ruffian you have such sympathy with stood opposite, presuming every now and then to bid me 'wisht,' and denying that it was his fault; and finally, frightened by my assertions that I would tell papa, and that he should be put in prison, and hanged, he commenced blubbering himself, and hurried out to hide his cowardly agitation.

"Still, I was not rid of him: when at length they compelled me to depart, and I had got some hundred yards off the premises, he suddenly issued from the shadow of the road-side, and checked Minny and took hold of me.

"'Miss Catherine, I'm ill grieved,' he began, 'but it's raything too bad — '

"I gave him a cut with my whip, thinking, perhaps he would murder me — He let go, thundering one of his horrid curses, and I galloped home more than half out of my senses.

"I didn't bid you good-night, that evening; and I didn't go to Wuthering Heights, the next — I wished to, exceedingly; but I was strangely excited, and dreaded to hear that Linton was dead, sometimes; and sometimes shuddered at the thought of encountering Hareton.

"On the third day I took courage; at least, I couldn't bear longer suspense and stole off, once more. I went at five o'clock, and walked, fancying I might manage to creep into the house, and up to Linton's room, unobserved. However, the dogs gave notice of my approach: Zillah received me, and saying 'the lad was mending nicely,' showed me into a small, tidy, carpeted apartment, where, to my inexpressible joy, I beheld Linton laid on a little sofa, reading one of my books. But he would neither speak to me nor look at me, through a whole hour, Ellen — He has such an unhappy temper — and what quite confounded me, when he did open his mouth it was to utter a falsehood, that I had occasioned the uproar, and Hareton was not to blame!

"Unable to reply, except passionately, I got up, and walked from the room. He sent after me a faint 'Catherine!' He did not reckon on being answered so — but I wouldn't turn back; and the morrow was the second day on which I stayed home, nearly determined to visit him no more.

"But it was so miserable going to bed, and getting up, and never hearing anything about him, that my resolution melted into air, before it was properly formed. It *had* appeared wrong to take the journey once; now it seemed wrong to refrain. Michael came to ask if he must saddle Minny; I said 'Yes,' and considered myself doing a duty as she bore me over the hills.

"I was forced to pass the front windows to get to the court; it was no use trying to conceal my presence.

" 'Young master is in the house,' said Zillah, as she saw me making for the parlour.

"I went in, Earnshaw was there also, but he quitted the room directly. Linton sat in the great arm chair half asleep; walking up to the fire, I began in a serious tone, partly meaning it to be true.

" 'As you don't like me, Linton, and as you think I come on purpose to hurt you, and pretend that I do so every time, this is our last meeting — let us say good-bye; and tell Mr. Heathcliff that you have no wish to see me, and that he mustn't invent any more falsehoods on the subject.'

" 'Sit down and take your hat off, Catherine,' he answered. 'You are so much happier than I am, you ought to be better. Papa talks enough of my defects, and shows enough scorn of me, to make it natural I should doubt myself — I doubt whether I am not altogether as worthless as he calls me, frequently; and then I feel so cross and bitter, I hate everybody! I *am* worthless, and bad in temper, and bad in spirit, almost always — and if you choose, you *may* say good-bye — you'll get rid of an annoyance — Only, Catherine, do me this justice; believe that if I might be as sweet, and as kind, and as good as you are, I would be, as willingly, and more so, than as happy and as healthy. And, believe that your kindness has made me love you deeper than if I deserved your love, and though I couldn't, and cannot help showing my nature to you, I regret it and repent it, and shall regret and repent it, till I die!'

"I felt he spoke the truth; and I felt I must forgive him; and though he should quarrel the next moment, I must forgive him again. We were reconciled, but we cried, both of us, the whole time I stayed. Not entirely for sorrow, yet I *was* sorry Linton had that distorted nature. He'll never let his friends be at ease, and he'll never be at ease himself!

"I have always gone to his little parlour, since that night; because his father returned the day after. About three times, I think, we have been merry, and hopeful, as we were the first evening; the rest of my visits were dreary and troubled — now, with his selfishness and spite, and now with his sufferings: but I've learnt to endure the former with nearly as little resentment as the latter.

"Mr. Heathcliff purposely avoids me. I have hardly seen him at all. Last Sunday, indeed, coming earlier than usual, I heard him abusing poor Linton, cruelly, for his conduct of the night before. I can't tell how he knew of it, unless he listened. Linton had certainly behaved provokingly; however, it was the business of nobody but me; and I interrupted Mr. Heathcliff's lecture, by entering and telling him so. He burst into a laugh, and went away, saying he was glad I took that view of the matter. Since then, I've told Linton he must whisper his bitter things.

"Now, Ellen, you have heard all; and I can't be prevented from going to Wuthering Heights, except by inflicting misery on two people — whereas, if you'll only not tell papa, my going need disturb the tranquillity of none. You'll not tell, will you? It will be very heartless if you do."

"I'll make up my mind on that point by to-morrow, Miss Catherine," I replied, "It requires some study; and so I'll leave you to your rest, and go think it over."

I thought it over aloud, in my master's presence; walking straight from her room to his, and relating the whole story, with the exception of her conversations with her cousin, and any mention of Hareton.

Mr. Linton was alarmed and distressed more than he would acknowledge to me. In the morning, Catherine learnt my betrayal of her confidence, and she learnt that her secret visits were to end.

In vain she wept and writhed against the interdict, and implored her father to have pity on Linton: all she got to comfort her was a promise that he would write, and give him leave to come to the Grange when he pleased; but explaining that he must no longer expect to see Catherine at Wuthering Heights. Perhaps, had he been aware of his nephew's disposition and state of health, he would have seen fit to withhold even that slight consolation.

CHAPTER 25

"These things happened last winter, sir," said Mrs. Dean; "hardly more than a year ago. Last winter, I did not think, at another twelve months' end, I should be amusing a stranger to the family with relating them! Yet, who knows how long you'll be a stranger? You're too young to rest always contented, living by yourself; and I some way fancy, no one could see Catherine Linton, and not love her. You smile; but why do you look so lively and interested, when I talk about her — and why have you asked me to hang her picture over your fireplace? and why — "

"Stop, my good friend!" I cried. "It may be very possible that *I* should love her; but would she love me? I doubt it too much to venture my tranquillity, by running into temptation; and then my home is not here. I'm of the busy world, and to its arms I must return. Go on. Was Catherine obedient to her father's commands?"

"She was," continued the housekeeper, "Her affection for him was still the chief sentiment in her heart; and he spoke without anger; he spoke in the deep tenderness of one about to leave his treasure amid perils and foes, where his remembered words would be the only aid that he could bequeath to guide her.

"He said to me, a few days afterwards,

"'I wish my nephew would write, Ellen, or call. Tell me, sincerely, what you think of him — is he changed for the better, or is there a prospect of improvement, as he grows a man?'

"'He's very delicate, sir,' I replied; 'and scarcely likely to reach manhood; but this I can say, he does not resemble his father; and if Miss Catherine had the misfortune to marry him, he would not be beyond her control, unless she were extremely and foolishly indulgent. However, master, you'll have plenty of time to get acquainted with him, and see whether he would suit her — it wants four years and more to his being of age.'

Edgar sighed; and, walking to the window, looked out towards Gimmerton Kirk. It was a misty afternoon, but the February sun shone dimly, and we could just distinguish the two fir trees in the yard, and the sparely scattered gravestones.

"I've prayed often," he half soliloquized, "for the approach of what is coming; and now I begin to shrink, to fear it. I thought the memory of the hour I came down that glen a bridegroom, would be less sweet than the anticipation that I was soon, in a few months, or, possibly, weeks, to be carried up, and laid in its lonely hollow! Ellen, I've been very happy with my little Cathy. Through winter nights and summer days she was a living hope at my side — but I've been as happy musing by myself among those stones, under that old church — lying, through the long June evenings, on the green mound of her mother's grave, and wishing, yearning for the time when I might lie beneath it. What can I do for Cathy? How must I quit her? I'd not care one moment for Linton being Heathcliff's son; nor for his taking her from me, if he could console her for my loss. I'd not care that Heathcliff gained his ends, and triumphed in robbing me of my last blessing! But should Linton be unworthy — only a feeble tool to his father — I cannot abandon her to him! And, hard though it be to crush her buoyant spirit, I must persevere in making her sad while I live, and leaving her solitary when I die. Darling! I'd rather resign her to God, and lay her in the earth before me."

"Resign her to God, as it is, sir," I answered, "and if we should lose you — which may He forbid — under His providence, I'll stand her friend and counsellor to the last. Miss Catherine is a good girl; I don't fear that she will go wilfully wrong; and people who do their duty are always finally rewarded."

Spring advanced; yet my master gathered no real strength, though he resumed his walks in the grounds with his daughter. To her inexperienced notions, this itself was a sign of convalescence; and then his cheek was often flushed, and his eyes were bright, she felt sure of his recovering.

On her seventeenth birthday, he did not visit the churchyard; it was raining, and I observed —

"You'll surely not go out to-night, sir?"

He answered —

"No, I'll defer it, this year, a little longer."

He wrote again to Linton, expressing his great desire to see him; and, had the invalid been presentable, I've no doubt his father would have permitted him to come. As it was, being instructed, he returned an answer, intimating that Mr. Heathcliff objected to his calling at the Grange; but his uncle's kind remembrance delighted him, and he hoped to meet him, sometimes, in his rambles, and personally to petition that his cousin and he might not remain long so utterly divided.

That part of his letter was simple, and probably his own. Heathcliff knew he could plead eloquently enough for Catherine's company, then—

"I do not ask" he said, "that she may visit here; but, am I never to see her, because my father forbids me to go to her home, and you forbid her to come to mine? Do, now and then, ride with her towards the Heights; and let us exchange a few words, in your presence! We have done nothing to deserve this separation; and you are not angry with me — you have no reason to dislike me — you allow yourself. Dear uncle! send me a kind note to-morrow; and leave to join you anywhere you please, except at Thrushcross Grange. I believe an interview would convince you that my father's character is not mine; he affirms I am more your nephew than his son; and though I have faults which render me unworthy of Catherine, she has excused them, and for her sake, you should also. You inquire about my health — it is better; but while I remain cut off from all hope, and doomed to solitude, or the society of those who never did, and never will like me, how can I be cheerful and well?"

Edgar, though he felt for the boy, could not consent to grant his request; because he could not accompany Catherine.

He said, in summer, perhaps, they might meet: meantime, he wished him to continue writing at intervals, and engaged to give him what advice and comfort he was able by letter; being well aware of his hard position in his family.

Linton complied; and had he been unrestrained, would probably have spoiled all by filling his epistles with complaints and lamentations; but his father kept a sharp watch over him; and, of course, insisted on every line that my master sent being shown; so, instead of penning his peculiar personal sufferings and distresses, the themes constantly uppermost in this thoughts, he harped on the cruel obligation of being held asunder from his friend and love; and gently intimated that Mr. Linton must allow an interview soon, or he should fear he was purposely deceiving him with empty promises.

Cathy was a powerful ally at home; and, between them, they, at length, persuaded my master to acquiesce in their having a ride or a walk together, about once a week, under my guardianship, and on the moors nearest the Grange; for June found him still declining; and though he had set aside, yearly, a portion of his income for my young lady's fortune, he had a natural desire that she might retain, or, at least, return, in a short time, to the house of her ancestors; and he considered her only prospect of doing that was by a union with his heir: he had no idea that the latter was failing almost as fast as himself; nor had any one, I believe; no doctor visited the Heights, and no one saw Master Heathcliff to make report of his condition, among us.

I, for my part, began to fancy my forebodings were false, and that he must be actually rallying, when he mentioned riding and walking on the moors, and seemed so earnest in pursuing his object.

I could not picture a father treating a dying child as tyrannically and wickedly as I afterwards learnt Heathcliff had treated him, to compel this apparent eagerness; his efforts redoubling the more imminently his avaricious and unfeeling plans were threatened with defeat by death.

CHAPTER 26

Summer was already past its prime, when Edgar reluctantly yielded his assent to their entreaties, and Catherine and I set out on our first ride to join her cousin.

It was a close, sultry day; devoid of sunshine, but with a sky too dappled and hazy to threaten rain; and our place of meeting had been fixed at the guide-stone, by the cross-roads. On arriving there, however, a little herd-boy, despatched as a messenger, told us that —

"Maister Linton wer just ut this side th' Heights: and he'd be mitch obleeged to us to gang on a bit further."

"Then Master Linton has forgot the first injunction of his uncle," I observed: "he bid us keep on the Grange land, and here we are, off at once."

"Well, we'll turn our horses' heads round, when we reach him," answered my companion, "our excursion shall lie towards home."

But when we reached him, and that was scarcely a quarter of a mile from his own door, we found he had no horse, and we were forced to dismount, and leave ours to graze.

He lay on the heath, awaiting our approach, and did not rise till we came within a few yards. Then, he walked so feebly, and looked so pale, that I immediately exclaimed —

"Why, Master Heathcliff, you are not fit for enjoying a ramble, this morning. How ill you do look!"

Catherine surveyed him with grief and astonishment; and changed the ejaculation of joy on her lips, to one of alarm; and the congratulation of their long postponed meeting, to an anxious inquiry, whether he were worse than usual?

"No — better — better!" he panted, trembling, and retaining her hand as if he needed its support, while his large blue eyes wandered timidly over her; the hollowness round them, transforming to haggard wildness, the languid expression they once possessed.

"But you have been worse," persisted his cousin, "worse than when I saw you last — you are thinner, and — "

"I'm tired," he interrupted, hurriedly. "It is too hot for walking, let us rest here. And, in the morning, I often feel sick — papa says I grow so fast."

Badly satisfied, Cathy sat down, and he reclined beside her.

"This is something like your paradise," said she, making an effort at cheerfulness. "You recollect the two days we agreed to spend in the place and way each thought pleasantest? This is nearly yours, only there are clouds; but then, they are so soft and mellow, it is nicer than sunshine. Next week, if you can, we'll ride down to the Grange Park, and try mine."

Linton did not appear to remember what she talked of; and he had evidently a great difficulty in sustaining any kind of conversation. His lack of interest in the subjects she started, and his equal incapacity to contribute to her entertainment were so obvious, that she could not conceal her disappointment. An indefinite alteration had come over his whole person and manner. The pettishness that might be caressed into fondness, had yielded to a listless apathy; there was less of the peevish temper of a child which frets and teases on purpose to be soothed, and more of the self-absorbed moroseness of a confirmed invalid, repelling consolation, and ready to regard the good-humoured mirth of others, as an insult.

Catherine perceived, as well as I did, that he held it rather a punishment, than a gratification, to endure our company; and she made no scruple of proposing, presently, to depart.

That proposal, unexpectedly, roused Linton from his lethargy and threw him into a strange state of agitation. He glanced fearfully towards the Heights, begging she would remain another half-hour, at least.

"But, I think," said Cathy, "you'd be more comfortable at home than sitting here; and I cannot amuse you to-day, I see, by my tales, and songs, and chatter; you have grown wiser than I, in these six months; you have little taste for my diversions now; or else, if I could amuse you, I'd willingly stay."

"Stay to rest yourself," he replied. "And, Catherine, don't think, or say that I'm *very* unwell — it is the heavy weather and heat that make me dull; and I walked about, before you came, a great deal, for me. Tell uncle, I'm in tolerable health, will you?"

"I'll tell him that *you* say so, Linton. I couldn't affirm that you are," observed my young lady, wondering at his pertinacious assertion of what was evidently an untruth.

"And be here again next Thursday," continued he, shunning her puzzled gaze. "And give him my thanks for permitting you to come — my best thanks, Catherine. And — and, if you *did* meet my father, and he asked you about me, don't lead him to suppose that I've been extremely silent and stupid — don't look sad and downcast, as you *are* doing — he'll be angry."

"I care nothing for his anger," exclaimed Cathy, imagining she would be its object.

"But I do," said her cousin, shuddering. "*Don't* provoke him against me, Catherine, for he is very hard."

"Is he severe to you, Master Heathcliff?" I inquired. "Has he grown weary of indulgence, and passed from passive to active hatred?"

Linton looked at me, but did not answer; and, after keeping her seat by his side, another ten minutes, during which his head fell drowsily on his breast, and he uttered nothing except suppressed moans of exhaustion or pain, Cathy began to seek solace in looking for bilberries, and sharing the produce of her researches with me: she did not offer them to him, for she saw further notice would only weary and annoy.

"Is it half an hour now, Ellen!" she whispered in my ear, at last. "I can't tell why we should stay. He's asleep, and papa will be wanting us back."

"Well, we must not leave him asleep," I answered; "wait till he wakes and be patient. You were mighty eager to set off, but your longing to see poor Linton has soon evaporated!"

"Why did *he* wish to see me?" returned Catherine. "In his crossest humours, formerly, I liked him better than I do in his present curious mood. It's just as if it were a task he was compelled to perform — this interview — for fear his father should scold him. But I'm hardly going to come to give Mr. Heathcliff pleasure; whatever reason he may have for ordering Linton to undergo this penance. And, though I'm glad he's better in health, I'm sorry he's so much less pleasant, and so much less affectionate to me."

"You think *he is* better in health, then?" I said.

"Yes," she answered; "because he always made such a great deal of his sufferings, you know. He is not tolerably well, as he told me to tell papa, but he's better, very likely."

"There you differ with me, Miss Cathy," I remarked; "I should conjecture him to be far worse."

Linton here started from his slumber in bewildered terror, and asked if any one had called his name.

"No," said Catherine; "unless in dreams. I cannot conceive how you manage to doze, out of doors, in the morning."

"I thought I heard my father," he gasped, glancing up to the frowning nab above us. "You are sure nobody spoke?"

"Quite sure," replied his cousin. "Only Ellen and I were disputing concerning your health. Are you truly stronger, Linton, than when we separated in winter? If you be, I'm certain one thing is not stronger — your regard for me — speak, are you?"

The tears gushed from Linton's eyes as he answered —

"Yes, yes, I am!"

And, still under the spell of the imaginary voice, his gaze wandered up and down to detect its owner.

Cathy rose.

"For to-day we must part," she said. "And I won't conceal that I have been sadly disappointed with our meeting, though I'll mention it to nobody but you — not that I stand in awe of Mr. Heathcliff!"

"Hush," murmured Linton; "for God's sake, hush! He's coming." And he clung to Catherine's arm, striving to detain her; but, at that announcement, she hastily disengaged herself, and whistled to Minny, who obeyed like a dog.

"I'll be here next Thursday," she cried, springing to the saddle. "Good-bye. Quick, Ellen!"

And so we left him, scarcely conscious of our departure, so absorbed was he in anticipating his father's approach.

Before we reached home, Catherine's displeasure softened into a perplexed sensation of pity and regret, largely blended with vague, uneasy doubts about Linton's actual circumstances, physical and social; in which I partook, though I counselled her not to say much, for a second journey would make us better judges.

My master requested an account of our on goings: his nephew's offering of thanks was duly delivered, Miss Cathy gently touching on the rest: I also threw little light on his inquiries, for I hardly knew what to hide, and what to reveal.

CHAPTER 27

Seven days glided away, every one marking its course by the henceforth rapid alteration of Edgar Linton's state. The havoc that months had previously wrought, was now emulated by the inroads of hours.

Catherine, we would fain have deluded yet, but her own quick spirit refused to delude her. It divined, in secret, and brooded on the dreadful probability, gradually ripening into certainty.

She had not the heart to mention her ride, when Thursday came round; I mentioned it for her, and obtained permission to order her out of doors; for the library, where her father stopped a short time daily — the brief period he could bear to sit up — and his chamber had become her whole world. She grudged each moment that did not find her bending over his pillow, or seated by his side. Her countenance grew wan with watching and sorrow, and my master gladly dismissed her to what he flattered himself would be a happy change of scene and society, drawing comfort from the hope that she would not now be left entirely alone after his death.

He had a fixed idea, I guessed by several observations he let fall, that as his nephew resembled him in person, he would resemble him in mind; for Linton's letters bore few or no indications of his defective character. And I through pardonable weakness refrained from correcting the error; asking myself what good there would be in disturbing his last moments with information that he had neither power nor opportunity to turn to account.

We deferred our excursion till the afternoon; a golden afternoon of August — every breath from the hills so full of life, that it seemed whoever respired it, though dying, might revive.

Catherine's face was just like the landscape — shadows and sunshine flitting over it, in rapid succession; but the shadows rested longer and the sunshine was more transient, and her poor little heart reproached itself for even that passing forgetfulness of its cares.

We discerned Linton watching at the same spot he had selected before. My young mistress alighted, and told me that as she was resolved to stay a very little while, I had better hold the pony and remain on horseback; but I dissented, I wouldn't risk losing sight of the charge committed to me a minute; so we climbed the slope of heath, together.

Master Heathcliff received us with greater animation on this occasion; not the animation of high spirits though, nor yet of joy; it looked more like fear.

"It is late!" he said, speaking short, and with difficulty. "Is not your father very ill? I thought you wouldn't come."

"*Why* won't you be candid?" cried Catherine, swallowing her greeting. "Why cannot you say at once, you don't want me? It is strange, Linton, that for the second time, you have brought me here on purpose, apparently to distress us both, and for no reason besides!"

Linton shivered, and glanced at her, half supplicating, half ashamed, but his cousin's patience was not sufficient to endure this enigmatical behaviour.

"My father *is* very ill," she said, "and why am I called from his bedside — why didn't you send to absolve me from my promise, when you wished I wouldn't keep it? Come! I desire an explanation — playing and trifling are completely banished out of my mind: and I can't dance attendance on your affectations, now!"

"My affectations!" he murmured, "what are they? For Heaven's sake, Catherine, don't look so angry! Despise me as much as you please; I am a worthless, cowardly wretch — I can't be scorned enough! but I'm too mean for your anger — hate my father, and spare me, for contempt!"

"Nonsense!" cried Catherine in a passion. "Foolish, silly boy! And there! he trembles, as if I were really going to touch him! You needn't bespeak contempt, Linton; anybody will have it spontaneously, at your service. Get off! I shall return home — it is folly dragging you from the hearthstone, and pretending — what do we pretend? Let go my frock — if I pitied you for crying, and looking so very frightened, you should spurn such pity! Ellen, tell him how disgraceful this conduct is. Rise, and don't degrade yourself into an abject reptile — *don't*."

With streaming face and an expression of agony, Linton had thrown his nerveless frame along the ground; he seemed convulsed with exquisite terror.

"Oh!" he sobbed, "I cannot bear it! Catherine, Catherine, I'm a traitor, too, and I dare not tell you! But leave me and I shall be killed! *Dear* Catherine, my life is in your hands; and you have said you loved me — and if you did, it wouldn't harm you. You'll not go, then? kind, sweet, good Catherine! And perhaps you *will* consent — and he'll let me die with you!"

My young lady, on witnessing his intense anguish, stooped to raise him. The old feeling of indulgent tenderness overcame her vexation, and she grew thoroughly moved and alarmed.

"Consent to what?" she asked. "To stay? Tell me the meaning of this strange talk, and I will. You contradict your own words, and distract me! Be calm and frank, and confess at once, all that weighs on your heart. You wouldn't injure me, Linton, would you? You wouldn't let any enemy hurt me, if you could prevent it? I'll believe you are a coward, for yourself, but not a cowardly betrayer of your best friend."

"But my father threatened me," gasped the boy, clasping his attenuated fingers, "and I dread him — I dread him! I *dare* not tell!"

"Oh well!" said Catherine, with scornful compassion, "keep your secret, *I'm* no coward — save yourself, I'm not afraid!"

Her magnanimity provoked his tears; he wept wildly, kissing her supporting hands, and yet could not summon courage to speak out.

I was cogitating what the mystery might be, and determined Catherine should never suffer to benefit him or any one else, by my good will. When hearing a rustle among the ling, I looked up, and saw Mr. Heathcliff almost close upon us, descending the Heights. He didn't cast a glance towards my companions, though they were sufficiently near for Linton's sobs to be audible; but hailing me in the almost hearty tone he assumed to none besides, and the sincerity of which, I couldn't avoid doubting, he said —

"It is something to see you so near my house, Nelly! How are you at the Grange? Let us hear! The rumour goes," he added in a lower tone, "that Edgar Linton is on his deathbed — perhaps they exaggerate his illness?"

"No; my master is dying," I replied, "it is true enough. A sad thing it will be for us all, but a blessing for him!"

"How long will he last, do you think?" he asked.

"I don't know," I said.

"Because," he continued, looking at the two young people, who were fixed under his eye — Linton appeared as if he could not venture to stir, or raise his head, and Catherine could not move, on his account — "Because that lad yonder, seems determined to beat me — and I'd thank his uncle to be quick, and go before him — Hallo! Has the whelp been playing that game long? I *did* give him some lessons about sniveling. Is he pretty lively with Miss Linton generally?"

"Lively? no — he has shown the greatest distress," I answered. "To see him, I should say, that instead of rambling with his sweetheart on the hills, he ought to be in bed, under the hands of a doctor."

"He shall be, in a day or two," muttered Heathcliff. "But first — get up, Linton! Get up!" he shouted. "Don't grovel on the ground there — up this moment!"

Linton had sunk prostrate again in another paroxysm of helpless fear, caused by his father's glance towards him, I suppose: there was nothing else to produce such humiliation. He made several efforts to obey, but his little strength was annihilated, for the time, and he fell back again with a moan.

Mr. Heathcliff advanced, and lifted him to lean against a ridge of turf.

"Now," said he, with curbed ferocity, "I'm getting angry — and if you don't command that paltry spirit of yours — *Damn* you! Get up, directly!"

"I will father!" he panted. "Only, let me alone, or I shall faint! I've done as you wished — I'm sure. Catherine will tell you that I — that I — have been cheerful. Ah! keep by me, Catherine; give me your hand."

"Take mine," said his father, "stand on your feet! There now — she'll lend you her arm . . . that's right, look at *her*. You would imagine I was the devil himself, Miss Linton, to excite such horror. Be so kind as to walk home with him, will you? He shudders, if I touch him."

"Linton, dear!" whispered Catherine, "I can't go to Wuthering Heights . . . papa has forbidden me . . . He'll not harm you, why are you so afraid?"

"I can never re-enter that house," he answered. "I am *not* to re-enter it without you!"

"Stop . . . " cried his father. "We'll respect Catherine's filial scruples. Nelly, take him in, and I'll follow your advice concerning the doctor, without delay."

"You'll do well," replied I, "but I must remain with my mistress. To mind your son is not my business."

"You are very stiff!" said Heathcliff. "I know that — but you'll force me to pinch the baby, and make it scream, before it moves your charity. Come then, my hero. Are you willing to return, escorted by me?"

He approached once more, and made as if he would seize the fragile being; but shrinking back, Linton clung to his cousin, and implored her to accompany him, with a frantic importunity that admitted no denial.

However I disapproved, I couldn't hinder her; indeed, how could she have refused him herself? What was filling him with dread, we had no means of discerning, but there he was, powerless under its gripe, and any addition seemed capable of shocking him into idiocy.

We reached the threshold; Catherine walked in; and I stood waiting till she had conducted the invalid to a chair, expecting her out immediately; when Mr. Heathcliff, pushing me forward, exclaimed —

"My house is not stricken with the plague, Nelly; and I have a mind to be hospitable to-day, sit down, and allow me to shut the door."

He shut and locked it also. I started.

"You shall have tea, before you go home," he added. "I am by myself. Hareton is gone with some cattle to the Lees — and Zillah and Joseph are off on a journey of pleasure. And, though I'm used to being alone, I'd rather have some interesting company, if I can get it. Miss Linton, take your seat by *him*. I give you what I have; the present is hardly worth accepting; but, I have nothing else to offer. It is Linton, I mean. How she does stare! It's odd what a savage feeling I have to anything that seems afraid of me! Had I been born where laws are less strict, and tastes less dainty, I should treat myself to a slow vivisection of those two, as an evening's amusement."

He drew in his breath, struck the table, and swore to himself.

"By hell! I hate them."

"I'm not afraid of you!" exclaimed Catherine, who could not hear the latter part of his speech.

She stepped close up; her black eyes flashing with passion and resolution.

"Give me that key — I will have it!" she said. "I wouldn't eat or drink here, if I were starving."

Heathcliff had the key in his hand that remained on the table. He looked up, seized with a sort of surprise at her boldness, or, possibly, reminded by her voice and glance, of the person from whom she inherited it.

She snatched at the instrument, and half succeeded in getting it out of his loosened fingers; but her action recalled him to the present; he recovered it speedily.

"Now, Catherine Linton," he said, "stand off, or I shall knock you down; and that will make Mrs. Dean mad."

Regardless of his warning, she captured his closed hand and its contents again.

"We *will* go!" she repeated, exerting her utmost efforts to cause the iron muscles to relax; and finding that her nails made no impression, she applied her teeth pretty sharply.

Heathcliff glanced at me a glance that kept me from interfering a moment. Catherine was too intent on his fingers to notice his face. He opened them, suddenly, and resigned the object of dispute; but, ere she had well secured it, he seized her with the liberated hand, and, pulling her on his knee, administered with the other, a shower of terrific slaps on both sides of the head, each sufficient to have fulfilled his threat, had she been able to fall.

At this diabolical violence, I rushed on him furiously.

"You villain!" I began to cry, "you villain!"

A touch on the chest silenced me; I am stout, and soon put out of breath; and what with that and the rage, I staggered dizzily back, and felt ready to suffocate, or to burst a blood-vessel.

The scene was over in two minutes; Catherine, released, put her two hands to her temples, and looked just as if she were not sure whether her ears were off or on. She trembled like a reed, poor thing, and leant against the table perfectly bewildered.

"I know how to chastise children, you see," said the scoundrel, grimly, as he stooped to repossess himself of the key, which had dropped to the floor. "Go to Linton now, as I told you; and cry at your ease! I shall be your father to-morrow — all the father you'll have in a few days — and you shall have plenty of that — you can bear plenty — you're no weakling — you shall have a daily taste, if I catch such a devil of a temper in your eyes again!"

Cathy ran to me instead of Linton, and knelt down and put her burning cheek on my lap, weeping aloud. Her cousin had shrunk into a corner of the settle, as quiet as a mouse, congratulating himself, I dare say, that the correction had lighted on another than him.

Mr. Heathcliff, perceiving us all confounded, rose, and expeditiously made the tea himself. The cups and saucers were laid ready. He poured it out, and handed me a cup.

"Wash away your spleen," he said. "And help your own naughty pet and mine. It is not poisoned, though I prepared it. I'm going out to seek your horses."

Our first thought, on his departure, was to force an exit somewhere. We tried the kitchen door, but that was fastened outside; we looked at the windows — they were too narrow for even Cathy's little figure.

"Master Linton," I cried, seeing we were regularly imprisoned, "you know what your diabolical father is after, and you shall tell us, or I'll box your ears, as he has done your cousin's."

"Yes, Linton; you must tell," said Catherine. "It was for your sake I came; and it will be wickedly ungrateful if you refuse."

"Give me some tea, I'm thirsty, and then I'll tell you," he answered. "Mrs. Dean, go away. I don't like you standing over me. Now, Catherine, you are letting your tears fall into my cup! I won't drink that. Give me another."

Catherine pushed another to him, and wiped her face. I felt disgusted at the little wretch's composure, since he was no longer in terror for himself. The anguish he had exhibited on the moor subsided as soon as ever he entered Wuthering Heights; so I guessed he had been menaced with the awful visitation of wrath, if he failed in decoying us there; and, that accomplished, he had no further immediate fears.

"Papa wants us to be married," he continued, after sipping some of the liquid. "And he knows your papa wouldn't let us marry now; and he's afraid of my dying, if we wait; so we are to be married in the morning, and you are to stay here all night; and, if you do as he wishes, you shall return home next day, and take me with you."

"Take you with her, pitiful changeling?" I exclaimed. "*You* marry? Why, the man is mad, or he thinks us fools, every one. And do you imagine that beautiful young lady, that healthy, hearty girl, will tie herself to a little perishing monkey like you? Are you cherishing the notion that *anybody*, let alone Miss Catherine Linton, would have you for a husband? You want whipping for bringing us in here at all, with your dastardly, puling tricks; and — don't look so silly now! I've a very good mind to shake you severely, for your contemptible treachery, and your imbecile conceit."

I did give him a slight shaking, but it brought on the cough, and he took to his ordinary resource of moaning and weeping, and Catherine rebuked me.

"Stay all night? No!" she said, looking slowly round. "Ellen, I'll burn that door down, but I'll get out."

And she would have commenced the execution of her threat directly, but Linton was up in alarm, for his dear self, again. He clasped her in his two feeble arms, sobbing —

"Won't you have me, and save me — not let me come to the Grange? Oh! darling Catherine! you mustn't go, and leave me, after all. You *must* obey my father, you *must!*"

"I must obey my own," she replied, "and relieve him from this cruel suspense. The whole night! What would he think? he'll be distressed already. I'll either break or burn a way out of the house. Be quiet! You're in no danger — but, if you hinder me — Linton, I love papa better than you!"

The mortal terror he felt of Mr. Heathcliff's anger, restored to the boy his coward's eloquence. Catherine was near distraught — still, she persisted that she must go home, and tried entreaty, in her turn, persuading him to subdue his selfish agony.

While they were thus occupied, our jailer re-entered.

"Your beasts have trotted off," he said, "and — now, Linton! snivelling again? What has she been doing to you? Come, come — have done, and get to bed. In a month or two, my lad, you'll be able to pay her back her present tyrannies, with a vigorous hand — you're pining for pure love, are you not? nothing else in the world — and she shall have you! There, to bed! Zillah won't be here to-night; you must undress yourself. Hush! hold your noise! Once in your own room, I'll not come near you, you needn't fear. By chance, you've managed tolerably. I'll look to the rest."

He spoke these words, holding the door open for his son to pass; and the latter achieved his exit exactly as a spaniel might, which suspected the person who attended on it of designing a spiteful squeeze.

The lock was re-secured. Heathcliff approached the fire, where my mistress and I stood silent. Catherine looked up, and instinctively raised her hand to her cheek — his neighbourhood revived a painful sensation. Anybody else would have been incapable of regarding the childish act with sternness, but he scowled on her and muttered —

"Oh, you are not afraid of me? Your courage is well disguised — you *seem* damnably afraid!"

"I *am* afraid now," she replied; "because if I stay, papa will be miserable; and how can I endure making him miserable — when he — when he — Mr. Heathcliff, *let* me go home! I promise to marry Linton — papa would like me to, and I love him — and why should you wish to force me to do what I'll willingly do of myself?"

"Let him dare to force you!" I cried. "There's law in the land, thank God, there is! though we *be* in an out-of-the-way place. I'd inform, if he were my own son, and it's felony without benefit of clergy!"

"Silence!" said the ruffian. "To the devil with your clamour! I don't want *you* to speak. Miss Linton, I shall enjoy myself remarkably in thinking your father will be miserable; I shall not sleep for satisfaction. You could have hit on no surer way of fixing your residence under my roof, for the next twenty-four hours, than informing me that such an event would follow. As to your promise to marry Linton, I'll take care you shall keep it, for you shall not quit this place till it is fulfilled."

"Send Ellen then, to let papa know I'm safe!" exclaimed Catherine, weeping bitterly. "Or marry me now. Poor papa! Ellen, he'll think we're lost. What shall we do?"

"Not he! He'll think you are tired of waiting on him, and run off, for a little amusement," answered Heathcliff. "You cannot deny that you entered my house of your own accord, in contempt of his injunctions to the contrary. And it is quite natural that you should desire amusement at your age; and that you should weary of nursing a sick man, and that man, *only* your father. Catherine, his happiest days were over when your days began. He cursed you, I dare say, for coming into the world (I did, at least). And it would just do if he cursed you as *he* went out of it. I'd join him. I don't love you! How should I? Weep away. As far as I can see, it will be your chief diversion hereafter: unless Linton makes amends for other losses; and your provident parent appears to fancy he may. His letters of advice and consolation entertained me vastly. In his last, he recommended my jewel to be careful of his; and kind to her when he got her. Careful and kind — that's paternal! But Linton requires his whole stock of care and kindness for himself. Linton can play the little tyrant well. He'll undertake to torture any number of cats if their teeth be drawn, and their claws pared. You'll be able to tell his uncle fine tales of his *kindness*, when you get home again, I assure you."

"You're right there!" I said, "explain your son's character. Show his resemblance to yourself; and then, I hope, Miss Cathy will think twice, before she takes the cockatrice!"

"I don't much mind speaking of his amiable qualities now," he answered, "because she must either accept him, or remain a prisoner, and you along with her, till your master dies. I can detain you both, quite concealed, here. If you doubt, encourage her to retract her word, and you'll have an opportunity of judging!"

"I'll not retract my word," said Catherine. "I'll marry him, within this hour, if I may go to Thrushcross Grange afterwards. Mr. Heathcliff, you're a cruel man, but you're not a fiend; and you won't, from *mere* malice, destroy, irrevocably, all my happiness. If papa thought I had left him, on purpose, and if he died before I returned, could I bear to live? I've given over crying; but I'm going to kneel here, at your knee; and I'll not get up, and I'll not take my eyes off your face, till you look back at me! No, don't turn away! *do* look! You'll see nothing to provoke you. I don't hate you. I'm not angry that you struck me. Have you never loved *anybody,* in all your life, uncle? *never?* Ah! you must look once — I'm so wretched — you can't help being sorry and pitying me."

"Keep your eft's° fingers off; and move, or I'll kick you!" cried Heathcliff, brutally repulsing her. "I'd rather be hugged by a snake. How the devil can you dream of fawning on me? I *detest* you!"

He shrugged his shoulders — shook himself, indeed, as if his flesh crept with aversion; and thrust back his chair, while I got up, and opened my mouth, to commence a downright torrent of abuse; but I was rendered dumb in the middle of the first sentence, by a threat that I should be shown into a room by myself, the very next syllable I uttered.

It was growing dark — we heard a sound of voices at the garden gate. Our host hurried out, instantly; *he* had his wits about him; *we* had not. There was a talk of two or three minutes, and he returned alone.

"I thought it had been your cousin, Hareton," I observed to Catherine. "I wish he would arrive! Who knows but he might take our part?"

"It was three servants sent to seek you from the Grange," said Heathcliff, overhearing me. "You should have opened a lattice and called out; but I could swear that chit is glad you didn't. She's glad to be obliged to stay, I'm certain."

At learning the chance we had missed, we both gave vent to our grief without control; and he allowed us to wail on till nine o'clock; then he bid us go upstairs, through the kitchen, to Zillah's chamber; and I whispered my companion to obey; perhaps, we might contrive to get through the window there, or into a garret, and out by its skylight.

The window, however, was narrow, like those below, and the garret trap was safe from our attempts; for we were fastened in as before.

We neither of us lay down: Catherine took her station by the lattice, and watched anxiously for morning — a deep sigh being the only answer I could obtain to my frequent entreaties that she would try to rest.

I seated myself in a chair, and rocked, to and fro, passing harsh judgment on my many derelictions of duty; from which, it struck me

eft's: Newt's (from Middle English *efeta,* lizard).

then, all the misfortunes of all my employers sprang. It was not the case, in reality, I am aware; but it was, in my imagination, that dismal night, and I thought Heathcliff himself less guilty than I.

At seven o'clock he came, and inquired if Miss Linton had risen.

She ran to the door immediately, and answered —

"Yes."

"Here, then," he said, opening it, and pulling her out.

I rose to follow, but he turned the lock again. I demanded my release.

"Be patient," he replied; "I'll send up your breakfast in a while."

I thumped on the panels, and rattled the latch angrily; and Catherine asked why I was still shut up? He answered, I must try to endure it another hour, and they went away.

I endured it two or three hours; at length, I heard a footstep, not Heathcliff's.

"I've brought you something to eat," said a voice; "oppen t' door!"

Complying eagerly, I beheld Hareton, laden with food enough to last me all day.

"Tak' it," he added, thrusting the tray into my hand.

"Stay one minute," I began.

"Nay!" cried he, and retired, regardless of any prayers I could pour forth to detain him.

And there I remained enclosed, the whole day, and the whole of the next night; and another, and another. Five nights and four days I remained, altogether, seeing nobody but Hareton, once every morning, and he was a model of a jailer — surly, and dumb, and deaf to every attempt at moving his sense of justice or compassion.

CHAPTER 28

On the fifth morning, or rather afternoon, a different step approached — lighter and shorter — and, this time, the person entered the room. It was Zillah; donned in her scarlet shawl, with a black silk bonnet on her head, and a willow basket swung to her arm.

"Eh, dear! Mrs. Dean," she exclaimed. "Well! there is a talk about you at Gimmerton. I never thought, but you were sunk in the Blackhorse marsh, and Missy with you, till master told me you'd been found, and he'd lodged you here! What, and you must have got on an island, sure? And how long were you in the hole? Did master save you, Mrs. Dean? But you're not so thin — you've not been so poorly have you?"

"Your master is a true scoundrel!" I replied. "But he shall answer for it. He needn't have raised that tale — it shall all be laid bare!"

"What do you mean?" asked Zillah. "It's not his tale — they tell that in the village — about your being lost in the marsh; and I calls to Earnshaw, when I come in —

" 'Eh, they's queer things, Mr. Hareton, happened since I went off. It's a sad pity of that likely young lass, and cant Nelly Dean.'

"He stared. I thought he had not heard aught, so I told him the rumour.

"The master listened, and he just smiled to himself, and said —

" 'If they have been in the marsh, they are out now, Zillah. Nelly Dean is lodged, at this minute, in your room. You can tell her to flit, when you go up; here is the key. The bog-water got into her head, and she would have run home, quite flighty, but I fixed her, till she came round to her senses. You can bid her go to the Grange, at once, if she be able, and carry a message from me, that her young lady will follow in time to attend the squire's funeral.' "

"Mr. Edgar is not dead?" I gasped. "Oh! Zillah, Zillah!"

"No, no — sit you down, my good mistress," she replied; "you're right sickly yet. He's not dead: Doctor Kenneth thinks he may last another day — I met him on the road and asked."

Instead of sitting down, I snatched my outdoor things, and hastened below, for the way was free.

On entering the house, I looked about for some one to give information of Catherine.

The place was filled with sunshine, and the door stood wide open, but nobody seemed at hand.

As I hesitated whether to go off at once, or return and seek my mistress, a slight cough drew my attention to the hearth.

Linton lay on the settle, sole tenant, sucking a stick of sugar-candy, and pursuing my movements with apathetic eyes.

"Where is Miss Catherine?" I demanded, sternly, supposing I could frighten him into giving intelligence, by catching him thus, alone.

He sucked on like an innocent.

"Is she gone?" I said.

"No," he replied; "she's upstairs — she's not to go; we won't let her."

"You won't let her, little idiot!" I exclaimed. "Direct me to her room immediately, or I'll make you sing out sharply."

"Papa would make you sing out, if you attempted to get there," he answered. "He says I'm not to be soft with Catherine — she's my wife, and it's shameful that she should wish to leave me! He says, she hates me, and wants me to die, that she may have my money, but she shan't have it; and she shan't go home! She never shall! she may cry, and be sick as much as she pleases!"

He resumed his former occupation, closing his lids, as if he meant to drop asleep.

"Master Heathcliff," I resumed, "have you forgotten all Catherine's kindness to you, last winter, when you affirmed you loved her, and when she brought you books, and sung you songs, and came many a time through wind and snow to see you? She wept to miss one evening, because you would be disappointed; and you felt then, that she was a hundred times too good to you; and now you believe the lies your father tells, though you know he detests you both! And you join him against her. That's fine gratitude, is it not?"

The corner of Linton's mouth fell, and he took the sugar-candy from his lips.

"Did she come to Wuthering Heights, because she hated you?" I continued. "Think for yourself! As to your money, she does not even know that you will have any. And you say she's sick; and yet, you leave her alone, up there in a strange house! *You,* who have felt what it is to be so neglected! You could pity your own sufferings, and she pitied them, too, but you won't pity hers! I shed tears, Master Heathcliff, you see — an elderly woman — a servant merely — and you, after pretending such affection, and having reason to worship her, almost, store every tear you have for yourself, and lie there quite at ease. Ah! you're a heartless, selfish boy!"

"I can't stay with her," he answered crossly. "I'll not stay, by myself. She cries so I can't bear it. And she won't give over, though I say I'll call my father — I did call him once; and he threatened to strangle her, if she was not quiet, but she began again, the instant he left the room; moaning and grieving, all night long, though I screamed for vexation that I couldn't sleep."

"Is Mr. Heathcliff out?" I inquired, perceiving that the wretched creature had no power to sympathise with his cousin's mental tortures.

"He's in the court," he replied, "talking to Doctor Kenneth who says uncle is dying, at last — I'm glad, for I shall be master of the Grange after him — and Catherine always spoke of it as *her* house. It isn't hers! It's mine — papa says everything she has is mine, all her nice books are mine — she offered to give me them, and her pretty birds, and her pony Minny, if I would get the key of our room, and let her out: but I told her she had nothing to give, they were all, all mine. And then she cried, and took a little picture from her neck, and said I should have that — two pictures in a gold case — on one side her mother, and on the other, uncle, when they were young. That was yesterday — I said *they* were mine, too; and tried to get them from her. The spiteful thing wouldn't let me; she pushed me off, and hurt me. I shrieked out — that frightens her — she heard papa coming, and she broke the hinges, and divided the case and gave me her mother's portrait; the other she attempted to hide; but papa asked what was the matter and I explained it. He took the one I had away; and ordered her to resign hers to me; she refused, and he — he struck her down, and wrenched it off the chain, and crushed it with his foot."

"And were you pleased to see her struck?" I asked: having my designs in encouraging his talk.

"I winked," he answered. "I wink to see my father strike a dog, or a horse, he does it so hard — yet I was glad at first — she deserved punishing for pushing me: but when papa was gone, she made me come to the window and showed me her cheek cut on the inside, against her teeth, and her mouth filling with blood; and then she gathered up the bits of the picture, and went and sat down with her face to the wall, and she has never spoken to me since; and I sometimes think she can't speak for pain. I don't like to think so! but she's a naughty thing for crying continually; and she looks so pale and wild, I'm afraid of her!"

"And you can get the key if you choose?" I said.

"Yes, when I am upstairs," he answered; "but I can't walk upstairs now."

"In what apartment is it?" I asked.

"Oh," he cried, "I shan't tell *you* where it is! It is our secret. Nobody, neither Hareton, nor Zillah are to know. There! you've tired me — go away, go away!" And he turned his face onto his arm, and shut his eyes, again.

I considered it best to depart without seeing Mr. Heathcliff; and bring a rescue for my young lady, from the Grange.

On reaching it, the astonishment of my fellow servants to see me, and their joy also, was intense; and when they heard that their little mistress was safe, two or three were about to hurry up, and shout the news at Mr. Edgar's door: but I bespoke the announcement of it, myself.

How changed I found him, even in those few days! He lay an image of sadness, and resignation, waiting his death. Very young he looked: though his actual age was thirty-nine, one would have called him ten years younger, at least. He thought of Catherine for he murmured her name. I touched his hand, and spoke.

"Catherine is coming, dear master!" I whispered; "she is alive, and well; and will be here, I hope, to-night."

I trembled at the first effects of this intelligence: he half rose up, looked eagerly round the apartment, and then sunk back in a swoon.

As soon as he recovered, I related our compulsory visit, and detention at the Heights: I said Heathcliff forced me to go in, which was not quite true; I uttered as little as possible against Linton; nor did I describe all his father's brutal conduct — my intentions being to add no bitterness, if I could help it, to his already overflowing cup.

He divined that one of his enemy's purposes was to secure the personal property, as well as the estate, to his son, or rather himself; yet why he did not wait till his decease, was a puzzle to my master, because ignorant how nearly he and his nephew would quit the world together.

However, he felt that his will had better be altered — instead of leaving Catherine's fortune at her own disposal, he determined to put it in the hands of trustees, for her use during life; and for her children, if she had any, after her. By that means, it could not fall to Mr. Heathcliff should Linton die.

Having received his orders, I despatched a man to fetch the attorney, and four more, provided with serviceable weapons, to demand my young lady of her jailer. Both parties were delayed very late. The single servant returned first.

He said Mr. Green, the lawyer, was out when he arrived at his house, and he had to wait two hours for his re-entrance: and then Mr. Green told him he had a little business in the village that must be done, and he would be at Thrushcross Grange before morning.

The four men came back unaccompanied, also. They brought word that Catherine was ill, too ill to quit her room, and Heathcliff would not suffer them to see her.

I scolded the stupid fellow well, for listening to that tale, which I would not carry to my master; resolving to take a whole bevy up to the Heights, at daylight, and storm it, literally, unless the prisoner were quietly surrendered to me.

Her father *shall* see her, I vowed, and vowed again, if that devil be killed on his own door-stones in trying to prevent it!

Happily, I was spared the journey, and the trouble.

I had gone downstairs at three o'clock to fetch a jug of water; and was passing through the hall, with it in my hand, when a sharp knock, at the front door, made me jump.

"Oh! it is Green" — I said, recollecting myself — "only Green," and I went on, intending to send somebody else to open it; but the knock was repeated, not loud, and still importunately.

I put the jug on the banister, and hastened to admit him, myself.

The harvest moon shone clear outside. It was not the attorney. My own sweet little mistress sprung on my neck, sobbing,

"Ellen! Ellen! is papa alive?"

"Yes!" I cried, "yes, my angel, he is! God be thanked, you are safe with us again!"

She wanted to run, breathless as she was, upstairs to Mr. Linton's room; but I compelled her to sit down on a chair, and made her drink, and washed her pale face, chafing it into a faint colour with my apron. Then I said I must go first, and tell of her arrival; imploring her to say, she should be happy with young Heathcliff. She stared, but soon comprehending why I counselled her to utter the falsehood, she assured me she would not complain.

I couldn't abide to be present at their meeting. I stood outside the chamber-door a quarter of an hour, and hardly ventured near the bed, then.

All was composed, however; Catherine's despair was as silent as her father's joy. She supported him calmly, in appearance; and he fixed on her features his raised eyes that seemed dilating with ecstacy.

He died blissfully, Mr. Lockwood; he died so. Kissing her cheek, he murmured,

"I am going to her, and you, darling child, shall come to us;" and never stirred or spoke again, but continued that rapt, radiant gaze, till his pulse imperceptibly stopped, and his soul departed. None could have noticed the exact minute of his death, it was so entirely without a struggle.

Whether Catherine had spent her tears, or whether the grief were too weighty to let them flow, she sat there dry-eyed till the sun rose — she sat till noon, and would have remained, brooding over that death-bed, but I insisted on her coming away, and taking some repose.

It was well I succeeded in removing her, for at dinner-time appeared the lawyer, having called at Wuthering Heights to get his instructions how to behave. He had sold himself to Mr. Heathcliff, and that was the cause of his delay in obeying my master's summons. Fortunately, no thought of worldly affairs crossed the latter's mind, to disturb him, after his daughter's arrival.

Mr. Green took upon himself to order everything and everybody about the place. He gave all the servants but me, notice to quit. He would have carried his delegated authority to the point of insisting that Edgar Linton should not be buried beside his wife, but in the chapel, with his family. There was the will, however, to hinder that, and my loud protestations against any infringement of its directions.

The funeral was hurried over; Catherine, Mrs. Linton Heathcliff now, was suffered to stay at the Grange, till her father's corpse had quitted it.

She told me that her anguish had at last spurred Linton to incur the risk of liberating her. She heard the men I sent, disputing at the door, and she gathered the sense of Heathcliff's answer. It drove her desperate — Linton, who had been conveyed up to the little parlour soon after I left, was terrified into fetching the key before his father re-ascended.

He had the cunning to unlock, and re-lock the door, without shutting it; and when he should have gone to bed, he begged to sleep with Hareton, and his petition was granted, for once.

Catherine stole out before break of day. She dare not try the doors, lest the dogs should raise an alarm; she visited the empty chambers, and examined their windows; and, luckily, lighting on her mother's, she got easily out of its lattice, and onto the ground, by means of the fir tree, close by. Her accomplice suffered for his share in the escape, notwithstanding his timid contrivances.

CHAPTER 29

The evening after the funeral, my young lady and I were seated in the library; now musing mournfully, one of us despairingly, on our loss; now venturing conjectures as to the gloomy future.

We had just agreed the best destiny which could await Catherine, would be a permission to continue resident at the Grange, at least, during Linton's life: he being allowed to join her there, and I to remain as housekeeper. That seemed rather too favourable an arrangement to be hoped for, and yet I did hope, and began to cheer up under the prospect of retaining my home, and my employment, and, above all, my beloved young mistress, when a servant — one of the discarded ones, not yet departed — rushed hastily in, and said, "that devil Heathcliff" was coming through the court, should he fasten the door in his face?

If we had been mad enough to order that proceeding, we had not time. He made no ceremony of knocking, or announcing his name; he was master, and availed himself of the master's privilege to walk straight in, without saying a word.

The sound of our informant's voice directed him to the library: he entered; and motioning him out, shut the door.

It was the same room into which he had been ushered, as a guest, eighteen years before: the same moon shone through the window; and the same autumn landscape lay outside. We had not yet lighted a candle, but all the apartment was visible, even to the portraits on the wall — the splendid head of Mrs. Linton and the graceful one of her husband.

Heathcliff advanced to the hearth. Time had little altered his person either. There was the same man; his dark face rather sallower, and more composed, his frame a stone or two heavier, perhaps, with no other difference.

Catherine had risen with an impulse to dash out, when she saw him.

"Stop!" he said, arresting her by the arm. "No more runnings away! Where would you go? I'm come to fetch you home; and I hope you'll be a dutiful daughter, and not encourage my son to further disobedience. I was embarrassed how to punish him, when I discovered his part in the business — he's such a cobweb, a pinch would annihilate him — but, you'll see by his look that he has received his due! I brought him down one evening, the day before yesterday, and set him in a chair, and never touched him afterwards. I sent Hareton out, and we had the room to ourselves. In two hours, I called Joseph to carry him up again; and, since then, my presence is as potent on his nerves, as a ghost; and I fancy he sees me often, though I am not near. Hareton says he wakes and shrieks in the night by the hour together; and calls you to protect him from me; and, whether you like your precious mate or not, you must come — he's your concern now; I yield all my interest in him to you."

"Why not let Catherine continue here?" I pleaded, "and send Master Linton to her. As you hate them both, you'd not miss them — they *can* only be a daily plague to your unnatural heart."

"I'm seeking a tenant for the Grange," he answered; "and I want my children about me, to be sure — besides, that lass owes me her services for her bread; I'm not going to nurture her in luxury and idleness after Linton is gone. Make haste and get ready now. And don't oblige me to compel you."

"I shall," said Catherine. "Linton is all I have to love in the world, and, though you have done what you could to make him hateful to me, and me to him, you *cannot* make us hate each other! and I defy you to hurt him when I am by, and I defy you to frighten me."

"You are a boastful champion!" replied Heathcliff; "but I don't like you well enough to hurt him — you shall get the full benefit of the torment, as long as it lasts. It is not I who will make him hateful to you— it is his own sweet spirit. He's as bitter as gall at your desertion, and its consequences — don't expect thanks for this noble devotion. I heard him draw a pleasant picture to Zillah of what he would do, if he were as strong as I — the inclination is there, and his very weakness will sharpen his wits to find a substitute for strength."

"I know he has a bad nature," said Catherine; "he's your son. But I'm glad I've a better, to forgive it; and I know he loves me and for that reason I love him. Mr. Heathcliff, *you* have *nobody* to love you; and, however miserable you make us, we shall still have the revenge of thinking that your cruelty arises from your greater misery! You *are* miserable, are you not? Lonely, like the devil, and envious like him? *Nobody* loves you — *nobody* will cry for you, when you die! I wouldn't be you!"

Catherine spoke with a kind of dreary triumph: she seemed to have made up her mind to enter into the spirit of her future family, and draw pleasure from the griefs of her enemies.

"You shall be sorry to be yourself presently," said her father-in-law, "if you stand there another minute. Begone, witch, and get your things."

She scornfully withdrew.

In her absence, I began to beg for Zillah's place at the Heights, offering to resign her mine; but he would suffer it on no account. He bid me be silent, and then, for the first time, allowed himself a glance round the room, and a look at the pictures. Having studied Mrs. Linton, he said —

"I shall have that home. Not because I need it, but — "

He turned abruptly to the fire, and continued, with what, for lack of a better word, I must call a smile —

"I'll tell you what I did yesterday! I got the sexton, who was digging Linton's grave, to remove the earth off her coffin lid, and I opened it. I thought, once, I would have stayed there, when I saw her face again — it is hers yet — he had hard work to stir me; but he said it would change, if the air blew on it, and so I struck one side of the coffin loose — and covered it up — not Linton's side, damn him! I wish he'd been soldered in lead — and I bribed the sexton to pull it away, when I'm laid there, and slide mine out too; I'll have it made so, and then, by the time Linton gets to us, he'll not know which is which!"

"You were very wicked, Mr. Heathcliff!" I exclaimed; "were you not ashamed to disturb the dead?"

"I disturbed nobody, Nelly," he replied; "and I gave some ease to myself. I shall be a great deal more comfortable now; and you'll have a better chance of keeping me underground, when I get there. Disturbed her? No! she has disturbed me, night and day, through eighteen years — incessantly — remorselessly — till yesternight — and yesternight, I was tranquil. I dreamt I was sleeping the last sleep, by that sleeper, with my heart stopped, and my cheek frozen against hers."

"And if she had been dissolved into earth, or worse, what would you have dreamt of then?" I said.

"Of dissolving with her, and being more happy still!" he answered. "Do you suppose I dread any change of that sort? I expected such a transformation on raising the lid, but I'm better pleased that it should not commence till I share it. Besides, unless I had received a distinct impression of her passionless features, that strange feeling would hardly have been removed. It began oddly. You know, I was wild after she died, and eternally, from dawn to dawn, praying her to return to me — her spirit — I have a strong faith in ghosts; I have a conviction that they can, and do exist, among us!

"The day she was buried there came a fall of snow. In the evening I went to the churchyard. It blew bleak as winter — all round was solitary: I didn't fear that her fool of a husband would wander up the den so late — and no one else had business to bring them there.

"Being alone, and conscious two yards of loose earth was the sole barrier between us, I said to myself —

"'I'll have her in my arms again! If she be cold, I'll think it is this north wind that chills *me;* and if she be motionless, it is sleep.'

"I got a spade from the toolhouse, and began to delve with all my might — it scraped the coffin; I fell to work with my hands; the wood commenced cracking about the screws, I was on the point of attaining my object, when it seemed that I heard a sigh from some one above, close at the edge of the grave, bending down. 'If I can only get this off,' I muttered, 'I wish they may shovel in the earth over us both!' and I wrenched more desperately still. There was another sigh, close at my ear. I appeared to feel the warm breath of it displacing the sleet-laden wind. I knew no living thing in flesh and blood was by — but as certainly as you perceive the approach to some substantial body in the dark, though it cannot be discerned, so certainly I felt that Cathy was there, not under me, but on the earth.

"A sudden sense of relief flowed, from my heart, through every limb. I relinquished my labour of agony, and turned consoled at once, unspeakably consoled. Her presence was with me; it remained while I re-filled the grave, and led me home. You may laugh, if you will, but I was sure I should see her there. I was sure she was with me, and I could not help talking to her.

"Having reached the Heights, I rushed eagerly to the door. It was fastened; and, I remember, that accursed Earnshaw and my wife opposed my entrance. I remember stopping to kick the breath out of him, and then hurrying upstairs, to my room, and hers — I looked round impatiently — I felt her by me — I could *almost* see her, and yet I *could not!* I ought to have sweat blood then, from the anguish of my yearning, from the fervour of my supplications to have but one glimpse! I had not one. She showed herself, as she often was in life, a devil to me! And, since then, sometimes more, and sometimes less, I've been the sport of that intolerable torture! Infernal — keeping my nerves at such a stretch, that, if they had not resembled catgut, they would, long ago, have relaxed to the feebleness of Linton's.

"When I sat in the house with Hareton, it seemed that on going out, I should meet her; when I walked on the moors I should meet her coming in. When I went from home, I hastened to return, she *must* be somewhere at the Heights, I was certain! And when I slept in her chamber — I was beaten out of that — I couldn't lie there; for the moment I closed my eyes, she was either outside the window, or sliding back the panels, or entering the room, or even resting her darling head on the same pillow as she did when a child. And I must open my lids to see. And so I opened and closed them a hundred times a night — to be always disappointed! It racked me! I've often groaned aloud, till that old rascal Joseph, no doubt, believed that my conscience was playing the fiend inside of me.

"Now since I've seen her, I'm pacified — a little. It was a strange way of killing, not by inches, but by fractions of hair-breadths, to beguile me with the spectre of a hope, through eighteen years!"

Mr. Heathcliff paused and wiped his forehead — his hair clung to it, wet with perspiration; his eyes were fixed on the red embers of the fire; the brows not contracted, but raised next the temples, diminishing the grim aspect of his countenance, but imparting a peculiar look of trouble, and a painful appearance of mental tension towards one absorbing subject. He only half addressed me, and I maintained silence — I didn't like to hear him talk!

After a short period, he resumed his meditation on the picture, took it down, and leant it against the sofa to contemplate it at better advantage; and while so occupied Catherine entered, announcing that she was ready, when her pony should be saddled.

"Send that over to-morrow," said Heathcliff to me, then turning to her he added, "You may do without your pony — it is a fine evening, and you'll need no ponies at Wuthering Heights, for what journeys you take, your own feet will serve you — Come along."

"Good-bye, Ellen!" whispered my dear little mistress. As she kissed me, her lips felt like ice. "Come and see me, Ellen, don't forget."

"Take care you do no such thing, Mrs. Dean!" said her new father. "When I wish to speak to you I'll come here. I want none of your prying at my house!"

He signed her to precede him; and casting back a look that cut my heart, she obeyed.

I watched them from the window, walk down the garden, Heathcliff fixed Catherine's arm under his, though she disputed the act, at first, evidently, and with rapid strides, he hurried her into the alley, whose trees concealed them.

CHAPTER 30

I have paid a visit to the Heights, but I have not seen her since she left; Joseph held the door in his hand, when I called to ask after her, and wouldn't let me pass. He said Mrs. Linton was "thrang,"° and the master was not in. Zillah has told me something of the way they go on, otherwise I should hardly know who was dead, and who living.

She thinks Catherine haughty, and does not like her, I can guess by her talk. My young lady asked some aid of her, when she first came, but Mr. Heathcliff told her to follow her own business, and let his daughter-in-law look after herself, and Zillah willingly acquiesced, being a narrow-minded selfish woman. Catherine evinced a child's annoyance at this neglect; repaid it with contempt, and thus enlisted my informant among her enemies, as securely as if she had done her some great wrong.

I had a long talk with Zillah, about six weeks ago, a little before you came, one day, when we foregathered on the moor; and this is what she told me.

"The first thing Mrs. Linton did," she said, "on her arrival at the Heights, was to run upstairs without even wishing good-evening to me and Joseph; she shut herself into Linton's room, and remained till morning — then, while the master and Earnshaw were at breakfast, she entered the house and asked all in a quiver if the doctor might be sent for? her cousin was very ill.

" 'We know that!' answered Heathcliff, 'but his life is not worth a farthing, and I won't spend a farthing on him.'

thrang: Hard-pressed, busy.

"'But I cannot tell how to do,' she said, 'and if nobody will help me, he'll die!'

"'Walk out of the room!' cried the master, 'and let me never hear a word more about him! None here care what becomes of him; if you do, act the nurse; if you do not, lock him up and leave him.'

"Then she began to bother me, and I said I'd had enough plague with the tiresome thing; we each had our tasks, and hers was to wait on Linton, Mr. Heathcliff bid me leave that labour to her.

"How they managed together, I can't tell. I fancy he fretted a great deal, and moaned hisseln, night and day; and she had precious little rest, one could guess by her white face, and heavy eyes — she sometimes came into the kitchen all wildered like, and looked as if she would fain beg assistance; but I was not going to disobey the master — I never dare disobey him, Mrs. Dean, and though I thought it wrong that Kenneth should not be sent for, it was no concern of mine, either to advise or complain; and I always refused to meddle.

"Once or twice, after we had gone to bed, I've happened to open my door again, and seen her sitting crying, on the stairs' top; and then I've shut myself in, quick, for fear of being moved to interfere. I did pity her then, I'm sure; still I didn't want to lose my place, you know!

"At last, one night she came boldly into my chamber, and frightened me out of my wits by saying —

"'Tell Mr. Heathcliff that his son is dying — I'm sure he is, this time. Get up, instantly, and tell him!'

"Having uttered this speech, she vanished again. I lay a quarter of an hour listening and trembling — Nothing stirred — the house was quiet.

"'She's mistaken,' I said to myself. 'He's got over it. I needn't disturb them.' And I began to doze. But my sleep was marred a second time, by a sharp ringing of the bell — the only bell we have, put up on purpose for Linton; and the master called to me, to see what was the matter, and inform them that he wouldn't have that noise repeated.

"I delivered Catherine's message. He cursed to himself, and in a few minutes, came out with a lighted candle, and proceeded to their room. I followed — Mrs. Heathcliff was seated by the bedside, with her hands folded on her knees. Her father-in-law went up, held the light to Linton's face, looked at him, and touched him, afterwards he turned to her.

"'Now — Catherine,' he said, 'how do you feel?'

"She was dumb.

"'How do you feel, Catherine?' he repeated.

" 'He's safe, and I'm free,' she answered, 'I should feel well — but,' she continued with a bitterness she couldn't conceal, 'you have left me so long to struggle against death, alone, that I feel and see only death! I feel like death!'

"And she looked like it, too! I gave her a little wine. Hareton and Joseph, who had been wakened by the ringing, and the sound of feet, and heard our talk from outside, now entered. Joseph was fain, I believe, of the lad's removal: Hareton seemed a thought bothered, though he was more taken up with staring at Catherine than thinking of Linton. But the master bid him get off to bed again — we didn't want his help. He afterwards made Joseph remove the body to his chamber, and told me to return to mine, and Mrs. Heathcliff remained by herself.

"In the morning, he sent me to tell her she must come down to breakfast — she had undressed, and appeared going to sleep; and said she was ill; at which I hardly wondered. I informed Mr. Heathcliff, and he replied —

" 'Well, let her be till after the funeral; and go up now and then go get her what is needful; and as soon as she seems better, tell me.' "

Cathy stayed upstairs a fortnight, according to Zillah, who visited her twice a-day, and would have been rather more friendly, but her attempts at increasing kindness were proudly and promptly repelled.

Heathcliff went up at once, to show her Linton's will. He had bequeathed the whole of his, and what had been her moveable property to his father. The poor creature was threatened, or coaxed, into that act during her week's absence, when his uncle died. The lands, being a minor, he could not meddle with. However, Mr. Heathcliff has claimed and kept them in his wife's right, and his also — I suppose legally: at any rate, Catherine, destitute of cash and friends, cannot disturb his possession.

"Nobody," said Zillah, "ever approached her door, except that once, but I . . . and nobody asked anything about her. The first occasion of her coming down into the house, was on a Sunday afternoon.

"She had cried out, when I carried up her dinner, that she couldn't bear any longer being in the cold; and I told her the master was going to Thrushcross Grange; and Earnshaw and I needn't hinder her from descending; so, as soon as she heard Heathcliff's horse trot off, she made her appearance, donned in black, and her yellow curls combed back behind her ears, as plain as a quaker: she couldn't comb them out.

"Joseph and I generally go to chapel on Sundays," (the Kirk, you know, has no minister, now, explained Mrs. Dean, and they call the

Methodists' or Baptists' place, I can't say which it is, at Gimmerton, a chapel). "Joseph had gone," she continued, "but I thought proper to bide at home. Young folks are always the better for an elder's overlooking, and Hareton, with all his bashfulness, isn't a model of nice behaviour. I let him know his cousin would very likely sit with us, and she had been always used to see the Sabbath respected, so he had as good leave his guns, and bits of indoor work alone, while she stayed.

"He coloured up at the news; and cast his eyes over his hands and clothes. The train-oil and gunpowder were shoved out of sight in a minute. I saw he meant to give her his company; and I guessed, by his way, he wanted to be presentable; so, laughing, as I durst not laugh when the master is by, I offered to help him, if he would, and joked at his confusion. He grew sullen, and began to swear.

"Now, Mrs. Dean," she went on, seeing me not pleased by her manner, "you happen think your young lady too fine for Mr. Hareton, and happen you're right — but, I own, I should love well to bring her pride a peg lower. And what will all her learning and her daintiness do for her, now? She's as poor as you, or I — poorer — I'll be bound, you're saving — and I'm doing my little all, that road."°

Hareton allowed Zillah to give him her aid; and she flattered him into a good humour; so, when Catherine came, half forgetting her former insults, he tried to make himself agreeable, by the house-keeper's account.

"Missis walked in," she said, "as chill as an icicle, and as high as a princess. I got up and offered her my seat in the armchair. No, she turned up her nose at my civility. Earnshaw rose too, and bid her come to the settle, and sit close by the fire; he was sure she was starved.

"'I've been starved a month and more,' she answered, resting on the word, as scornful as she could.

"And she got a chair for herself, and placed it at a distance from both of us.

"Having sat till she was warm, she began to look round, and discovered a number of books on the dresser; she was instantly upon her feet again, stretching to reach them, but they were too high up.

"Her cousin, after watching her endeavours a while, at last summoned courage to help her; she held her frock, and he filled it with the first that came to hand.

"That was a great advance for the lad — she didn't thank him; still, he felt gratified that she had accepted his assistance, and ventured to stand behind as she examined them, and even to stoop and point out

that road: That way.

what struck his fancy in certain old pictures which they contained — nor was he daunted by the saucy style in which she jerked the page from his finger; he contented himself with going a bit farther back, and looking at her, instead of the book.

"She continued reading, or seeking for something to read. His attention became, by degrees, quite centred in the study of her thick, silky curls — her face he couldn't see, and she couldn't see him. And, perhaps, not quite awake to what he did, but attracted like a child to a candle, at last, he proceeded from staring to touching; he put out his hand and stroked one curl, as gently as if it were a bird. He might have stuck a knife into her neck, she started round in such a taking.

"'Get away, this moment! How dare you touch me? Why are you stopping there?' she cried, in a tone of disgust. 'I can't endure you! I'll go upstairs again, if you come near me.'

"Mr. Hareton recoiled, looking as foolish as he could do; he sat down in the settle, very quiet, and she continued turning over her volumes, another half hour — finally, Earnshaw crossed over, and whispered to me.

"'Will you ask her to read to us, Zillah? I'm stalled of doing naught — and I do like — I could like to hear her! Dunnot say I wanted it, but ask of yourseln.'

"'Mr. Hareton wishes you would read to us, ma'am,' I said, immediately. 'He'd take it very kind — he'd be much obliged.'

"She frowned; and, looking up, answered —

"'Mr. Hareton, and the whole set of you, will be good enough to understand that I reject any pretence at kindness you have the hypocrisy to offer! I despise you, and will have nothing to say to any of you! When I would have given my life for one kind word, even to see one of your faces, you all kept off. But I won't complain to you! I'm driven down here by the cold, not either to amuse you, or enjoy your society.'

"'What could I ha' done?' began Earnshaw. 'How was I to blame?'

"'Oh! you are an exception,' answered Mrs. Heathcliff. 'I never missed such a concern as you.'

"'But, I offered more than once, and asked,' he said, kindling up at her pertness, 'I asked Mr. Heathcliff to let me wake° for you — '

"'Be silent! I'll go out of doors, or anywhere, rather than have your disagreeable voice in my ear!' said my lady.

"Hareton muttered, she might go to hell, for him! and unslinging his gun, restrained himself from his Sunday occupations no longer.

wake: Watch, stand guard.

"He talked now, freely enough; and she presently saw fit to retreat to her solitude: but the frost had set in, and, in spite of her pride, she was forced to condescend to our company, more and more. However, I took care there should be no further scorning of my good nature — ever since, I've been as stiff as herself — and she has no lover or liker among us — and she does not deserve one — for, let them say the least word to her, and she'll curl back without respect of any one! She'll snap at the master himself, and as good as dares him to thrash her; and the more hurt she gets, the more venomous she grows."

At first, on hearing this account from Zillah, I determined to leave my situation, take a cottage, and get Catherine to come and live with me; but Mr. Heathcliff would as soon permit that, as he would set up Hareton in an independent house; and I can see no remedy, at present, unless she could marry again; and that scheme, it does not come within my province to arrange.

Thus ended Mrs. Dean's story. Notwithstanding the doctor's prophecy, I am rapidly recovering strength, and, though it be only the second week in January, I propose getting out on horseback, in a day or two, and riding over to Wuthering Heights, to inform my landlord that I shall spend the next six months in London; and, if he likes, he may look out for another tenant to take the place, after October — I would not pass another winter here, for much.

CHAPTER 31

Yesterday was bright, calm, and frosty. I went to the Heights as I proposed; my housekeeper entreated me to bear a little note from her to her young lady, and I did not refuse, for the worthy woman was not conscious of anything odd in her request.

The front door stood open, but the jealous gate was fastened, as at my last visit; I knocked and invoked Earnshaw from among the garden beds; he unchained it, and I entered. The fellow is as handsome a rustic as need be seen. I took particular notice of him this time; but then, he does his best, apparently, to make the least of his advantages.

I asked if Mr. Heathcliff were at home? He answered, no; but he would be in at dinner-time. It was eleven o'clock, and I announced my intention of going in, and waiting for him, at which he immediately flung down his tools and accompanied me, in the office of watchdog, not as a substitute for the host.

We entered together; Catherine was there, making herself useful in preparing some vegetables for the approaching meal; she looked more sulky, and less spirited than when I had seen her first. She hardly raised her eyes to notice me, and continued her employment with the same disregard to common forms of politeness, as before; never returning my bow and good-morning by the slightest acknowledgment.

"She does not seem so amiable," I thought, "as Mrs. Dean would persuade me to believe. She's a beauty, it is true; but not an angel."

Earnshaw surlily bid her remove her things to the kitchen.

"Remove them yourself," she said, pushing them from her, as soon as she had done; and retiring to a stool by the window, where she began to carve figures of birds and beasts, out of the turnip parings in her lap.

I approached her, pretending to desire a view of the garden; and, as I fancied, adroitly dropped Mrs. Dean's note onto her knee, unnoticed by Hareton — but she asked aloud —

"What is that?" And chucked it off.

"A letter from your old acquaintance, the housekeeper at the Grange," I answered, annoyed at her exposing my kind deed, and fearful lest it should be imagined a missive of my own.

She would gladly have gathered it up, at this information, but Hareton beat her; he seized, and put it in his waistcoat, saying Mr. Heathcliff should look at it first.

Thereat, Catherine silently turned her face from us, and, very stealthily, drew out her pocket-handkerchief and applied it to her eyes; and her cousin, after struggling a while to keep down his softer feelings, pulled out the letter and flung it on the floor beside her as ungraciously as he could.

Catherine caught and perused it eagerly; then she put a few questions to me concerning the inmates, rational and irrational, of her former home; and gazing towards the hills, murmured in soliloquy.

"I should like to be riding Minny down there! I should like to be climbing up there — Oh! I'm tired — I'm *stalled,* Hareton!"

And she leant her pretty head back against the sill, with half a yawn and half a sigh, and lapsed into an aspect of abstracted sadness, neither caring nor knowing whether we remarked her.

"Mrs. Heathcliff," I said, after sitting some time mute, "you are now aware that I am an acquaintance of yours? so intimate, that I think it strange you won't come and speak to me. My housekeeper never wearies of talking about and praising you; and she'll be greatly disappointed if I return with no news of, or from you, except that you received her letter and said nothing!"

She appeared to wonder at this speech and asked,

"Does Ellen like you?"

"Yes, very well," I replied unhesitatingly.

"You must tell her," she continued, "that I would answer her letter, but I have no materials for writing, not even a book from which I might tear a leaf."

"No books!" I exclaimed. "How do you contrive to live here without them — if I may take the liberty to inquire? Though provided with a large library, I'm frequently very dull at the Grange — take my books away, and I should be desperate!"

"I was always reading, when I had them," said Catherine, "and Mr. Heathcliff never reads; so he took it into his head to destroy my books. I have not had a glimpse of one, for weeks. Only once, I searched through Joseph's store of theology, to his great irritation; and once, Hareton, I came upon a secret stock in your room . . . some Latin and Greek, and some tales and poetry; all old friends — I brought the last here — and you gathered them, as a magpie gathers silver spoons, for the mere love of stealing! They are of no use to you — or else you concealed them in the bad spirit, that as you cannot enjoy them, nobody else shall. Perhaps *your* envy counselled Mr. Heathcliff to rob me of my treasures? But I've most of them written on my brain and printed in my heart, and you cannot deprive me of those!"

Earnshaw blushed crimson, when his cousin made this revelation of his private literary accumulations, and stammered an indignant denial of her accusations.

"Mr. Hareton is desirous of increasing his amount of knowledge," I said, coming to his rescue. "He is not *envious* but *emulous* of your attainments — He'll be a clever scholar in a few years!"

"And he wants *me* to sink into a dunce, meantime," answered Catherine. "Yes, I hear him trying to spell and read to himself, and pretty blunders he makes! I wish you would repeat Chevy Chase, as you did yesterday — it was extremely funny! I heard you . . . and I heard you turning over the dictionary, to seek out the hard words, and then cursing, because you couldn't read their explanations!"

The young man evidently thought it too bad that he should be laughed at for his ignorance, and then laughed at for trying to remove it. I had a similar notion, and, remembering Mrs. Dean's anecdotes of his first attempt at enlightening the darkness in which he had been reared, I observed,

"But, Mrs. Heathcliff, we have each had a commencement, and each stumbled and tottered on the threshold, and had our teachers scorned, instead of aiding us, we should stumble and totter yet."

"Oh!" she replied, "I don't wish to limit his acquirements . . . still, he has no right to appropriate what is mine, and make it ridiculous to me with his vile mistakes and mispronunciations! Those books, both prose and verse, were consecrated to me by other associations, and I hate to have them debased and profaned in his mouth! Besides, of all, he has selected my favourite pieces that I love the most to repeat, as if out of deliberate malice!"

Hareton's chest heaved in silence a minute; he laboured under a severe sense of mortification and wrath, which it was no easy task to suppress.

I rose, and from a gentlemanly idea of relieving his embarrassment, took up my station in the doorway, surveying the external prospect, as I stood.

He followed my example, and left the room, but presently reappeared, bearing half a dozen volumes in his hands, which he threw into Catherine's lap, exclaiming —

"Take them! I never want to hear, or read, or think of them again!"

"I won't have them, now," she answered. "I shall connect them with you, and hate them."

She opened one that had obviously been often turned over, and read a portion in the drawling tone of a beginner; then laughed, and threw if from her.

"And listen," she continued provokingly, commencing a verse of an old ballad in the same fashion.

But his self-love would endure no further torment — I heard, and not altogether disapprovingly, a manual check given to her saucy tongue — The little wretch had done her utmost to hurt her cousin's sensitive though uncultivated feelings, and a physical argument was the only mode he had of balancing the account and repaying its effects on the inflicter.

He afterwards gathered the books and hurled them on the fire. I read in his countenance what anguish it was to offer that sacrifice to spleen — I fancied that as they consumed, he recalled the pleasure they had already imparted; and the triumph and ever-increasing pleasure he had anticipated from them — and I fancied, I guessed the incitement to his secret studies, also. He had been content with daily labour and rough animal enjoyments, till Catherine crossed his path — Shame at her scorn, and hope of her approval were his first prompters to higher pursuits; and instead of guarding him from one, and winning him the other, his endeavours to raise himself had produced just the contrary result.

"Yes, that's all the good that such a brute as you can get from them!" cried Catherine, sucking her damaged lip, and watching the conflagration with indignant eyes.

"You'd *better* hold your tongue, now!" he answered fiercely.

And his agitation precluding further speech, he advanced hastily to the entrance, where I made way for him to pass. But, ere he had crossed the door-stones, Mr. Heathcliff, coming up the causeway, encountered him, and laying hold of his shoulder asked —

"What's to do now, my lad?"

"Naught, naught!" he said, and broke away, to enjoy his grief and anger in solitude.

Heathcliff gazed after him, and sighed.

"It will be odd, if I thwart myself!" he muttered, unconscious that I was behind him. "But, when I look for his father in his face, I find *her* every day more! How the devil is he so like? I can hardly bear to see him."

He bent his eyes to the ground, and walked moodily in. There was a restless, anxious expression in his countenance I had never remarked there before, and he looked sparer in person.

His daughter-in-law, on perceiving him through the window, immediately escaped to the kitchen, so that I remained alone.

"I'm glad to see you out of doors again, Mr. Lockwood," he said in reply to my greeting, "from selfish motives partly; I don't think I could readily supply your loss in this desolation. I've wondered, more than once, what brought you here."

"An idle whim, I fear, sir," was my answer, "or else an idle whim is going to spirit me away — I shall set out for London, next week, and I must give you warning, that I feel no disposition to retain Thrushcross Grange, beyond the twelve months I agreed to rent it. I believe I shall not live there any more."

"Oh, indeed! you're tired of being banished from the world, are you?" he said. "But, if you be coming to plead off paying for a place you won't occupy, your journey is useless — I never relent in exacting my due, from any one."

"I'm coming to plead off nothing about it!" I exclaimed, considerably irritated. "Should you wish it, I'll settle with you now," and I drew my note-book from my pocket.

"No, no," he replied coolly, "you'll leave sufficient behind, to cover your debts, if you fail to return . . . I'm not in such a hurry — sit down and take your dinner with us — a guest that is safe from repeating his visit, can generally be made welcome — Catherine! bring the things in — where are you?"

Catherine re-appeared, bearing a tray of knives and forks.

"You may get your dinner with Joseph," muttered Heathcliff aside, "and remain in the kitchen till he is gone."

She obeyed his directions very punctually — perhaps she had no temptation to transgress. Living among clowns and misanthropists, she probably cannot appreciate a better class of people, when she meets them.

With Mr. Heathcliff, grim and saturnine, on one hand, and Hareton, absolutely dumb, on the other, I made a somewhat cheerless meal, and bid adieu early. I would have departed by the back way, to get a last glimpse of Catherine, and annoy old Joseph; but Hareton received orders to lead up my horse, and my host himself escorted me to the door, so I could not fulfil my wish.

"How dreary life gets over in that house!" I reflected, while riding down the road. "What a realization of something more romantic than a fairy tale it would have been for Mrs. Linton Heathcliff, had she and I struck up an attachment, as her good nurse desired, and migrated together, into the stirring atmosphere of the town!"

CHAPTER 32

1802. — This September, I was invited to devastate the moors of a friend, in the North; and, on my journey to his abode, I unexpectedly came within fifteen miles of Gimmerton. The hostler, at a roadside public-house, was holding a pail of water to refresh my horses, when a cart of very green oats, newly reaped, passed by, and he remarked —

"Yon's frough Gimmerton, nah! They're allas three wick' after other folk wi' ther harvest."

"Gimmerton?" I repeated — my residence in that locality had already grown dim and dreamy. "Ah! I know! How far is it from this?"

"Happen fourteen mile' o'er th' hills, and a rough road," he answered.

A sudden impulse seized me to visit Thrushcross Grange. It was scarcely noon, and I conceived that I might as well pass the night under my own roof, as in an inn. Besides, I could spare a day easily, to arrange matters with my landlord, and thus save myself the trouble of invading the neighbourhood again.

Having rested a while, I directed my servant to inquire the way to the village; and, with great fatigue to our beasts, we managed the distance in some three hours.

I left him there, and proceeded down the valley alone. The grey church looked greyer, and the lonely churchyard lonelier. I distinguished a moor sheep cropping the short turf on the graves. It was sweet, warm weather — too warm for travelling; but the heat did not hinder me from enjoying the delightful scenery above and below; had I seen it nearer August, I'm sure it would have tempted me to waste a month among its solitudes. In winter, nothing more dreary, in summer, nothing more divine, than those glens shut in by hills, and those bluff, bold swells of heath.

I reached the Grange before sunset, and knocked for admittance; but the family had retreated into the back premises, I judged by one thin, blue wreath curling from the kitchen chimney, and they did not hear.

I rode into the court. Under the porch, a girl of nine or ten sat knitting, and an old woman reclined on the horse-steps, smoking a meditative pipe.

"Is Mrs. Dean within?" I demanded of the dame.

"Mistress Dean? Nay!" she answered, "shoo doesn't bide here; shoo's up at th' Heights."

"Are you the housekeeper, then?" I continued.

"Eea, Aw keep th' hause," she replied.

"Well, I'm Mr. Lockwood, the master — Are there any rooms to lodge me in, I wonder? I wish to stay here all night."

"T' maister!" she cried in astonishment. "Whet, whoiver knew yah wur coming? Yah sud ha' send word! They's nowt norther dry nor mensful abaht t' place° — nowt there isn't!"

She threw down her pipe and bustled in, the girl followed, and I entered too; soon perceiving that her report was true, and, moreover, that I had almost upset her wits by my unwelcome apparition.

I bid her to be composed — I would go out for a walk; and, meantime, she must try to prepare a corner of a sitting-room for me to sup in, and a bed-room to sleep in — No sweeping and dusting, only good fires and dry sheets were necessary.

She seemed willing to do her best; though she thrust the hearth-brush into the grates in mistake for the poker; and malappropriated several other articles of her craft; but I retired, confiding in her energy for a resting-place against my return.

Wuthering Heights was the goal of my proposed excursion. An after-thought brought me back, when I had quitted the court.

They's nowt norther dry nor mensful abaht t' place: There's nothing neither dry nor tidy about the place.

"All well at the Heights?" I inquired of the woman.

"Eea, f'r owt Ee knaw!" she answered, skurrying away with a pan of hot cinders.

I would have asked why Mrs. Dean had deserted the Grange; but it was impossible to delay her at such a crisis, so I turned away and made my exit, rambling leisurely along with the glow of a sinking sun behind, and the mild glory of a rising moon in front; one fading, and the other brightening, as I quitted the park, and climbed the stony by-road branching off to Mr. Heathcliff's dwelling.

Before I arrived in the sight of it, all that remained of day was a beamless, amber light along the west, but I could see every pebble on the path, and every blade of grass, by that splendid moon.

I had neither to climb the gate, nor to knock — it yielded to my hand.

That is an improvement! I thought. And I noticed another, by the aid of my nostrils; a fragrance of stocks and wall flowers, wafted on the air, from amongst the homely fruit trees.

Both doors and lattices were open; and, yet, as is usually the case in a coal district, a fine, red fire illumined the chimney; the comfort which the eye derives from it, renders the extra heat endurable. But the house of Wuthering Heights is so large, that the inmates have plenty of space for withdrawing out of its influence; and, accordingly, what inmates there were had stationed themselves not far from one of the windows. I could both see them and hear them talk before I entered, and looked and listened in consequence, being moved thereto by a mingled sense of curiosity and envy that grew as I lingered.

"Con-*trary!*" said a voice, as sweet as a silver bell — "That for the third time, you dunce! I'm not going to tell you again — Recollect, or I pull your hair!"

"Contrary, then," answered another, in deep, but softened tones. "And now, kiss me, for minding so well."

"No, read it over first correctly, without a single mistake."

The male speaker began to read — he was a young man, respectably dressed, and seated at a table, having a book before him. His handsome features glowed with pleasure, and his eyes kept impatiently wandering from the page to a small white hand over his shoulder, which recalled him by a smart slap on the cheek, whenever its owner detected such signs of inattention.

Its owner stood behind; her light shining ringlets blending, at intervals, with his brown locks, as she bent to superintend his studies; and her face — it was lucky he could not see her face, or he would never have been so steady — I could, and I bit my lip, in spite, at having thrown away the chance I might have had, of doing something besides staring at its smiting beauty.

The task was done, not free from further blunders, but the pupil claimed a reward and received at least five kisses, which, however, he generously returned. Then, they came to the door, and from their conversation, I judged they were about to issue out and have a walk on the moors. I supposed I should be condemned in Hareton Earnshaw's heart, if not by his mouth, to the lowest pit in the infernal regions if I showed my unfortunate person in his neighbourhood then, and feeling very mean and malignant, I skulked round to seek refuge in the kitchen.

There was unobstructed admittance on that side also; and, at the door, sat my old friend, Nelly Dean, sewing and singing a song, which was often interrupted from within, by harsh words of scorn and intolerance, uttered in far from musical accents.

"Aw'd rayther, by th' haulf, hev 'em swearing i' my lugs° frough morn tuh neeght, nur hearken yah, hahsiver!" said the tenant of the kitchen, in answer to an unheard speech of Nelly's. "It's a blazing shaime, ut Aw cannut oppen t' Blessed Book, bud yah set up them glories tuh sattan,° un' all t' flaysome° wickednesses ut iver wer born intuh t'warld! Oh! yah're a raight nowt; un' shoo's another; un' that poor lad 'ull be lost, atween ye. Poor lad!" he added, with a groan; "he's witched, Aw'm sartin on't! O, Lord, judge 'em, fur they's norther law nur justice amang wer rullers!"°

"No! or we should be sitting in flaming fagots, I suppose," retorted the singer. "But wisht, old man, and read your Bible like a Christian, and never mind me. This is 'Fairy Annie's Wedding' — a bonny tune — it goes to a dance."

Mrs. Dean was about to recommence, when I advanced, and recognising me directly, she jumped to her feet, crying —

"Why, bless you, Mr. Lockwood! How could you think of returning in this way? All's shut up at Thrushcross Grange. You should have given us notice!"

"I've arranged to be accommodated there, for as long as I shall stay," I answered. "I depart again to-morrow. And how are you transplanted here, Mrs. Dean? tell me that."

lugs: Ears. ***sattan:*** Satan. ***flaysome:*** Terrible. ***amang wer rullers:*** Among our rulers.

"Zillah left, and Mr. Heathcliff wished me to come, soon after you went to London, and stay till you returned. But, step in, pray! Have you walked from Gimmerton this evening?"

"From the Grange," I replied; "and, while they make me lodging room there, I want to finish my business with your master, because I don't think of having another opportunity in a hurry."

"What business, sir?" said Nelly, conducting me into the house. "He's gone out, at present, and won't return soon."

"About the rent," I answered.

"Oh! then it is with Mrs. Heathcliff you must settle," she observed, "or rather with me. She has not learnt to manage her affairs yet, and I act for her; there's nobody else."

I looked surprised.

"Ah! you have not heard of Heathcliff's death, I see!" she continued.

"Heathcliff dead?" I exclaimed, astonished. "How long ago?"

"Three months since — but, sit down, and let me take your hat, and I'll tell you all about it. Stop, you have had nothing to eat, have you?"

"I want nothing. I have ordered supper at home. You sit down too. I never dreamt of his dying! Let me hear how it came to pass. You say you don't expect them back for some time — the young people?"

"No — I have to scold them every evening, for their late rambles — but they don't care for me. At least, have a drink of our old ale — it will do you good — you seem weary."

She hastened to fetch it, before I could refuse, and I heard Joseph asking, whether "it warn't a crying scandal that she should have fellies° at her time of life? And then, to get them jocks° out uh t' Maister's cellar! He fair shaamed to 'bide still and see it."

She did not stay to retaliate, but re-entered, in a minute, bearing a reaming, silver pint, whose contents I lauded with becoming earnestness. And afterwards she furnished me with the sequel of Heathcliff's history. He had a "queer" end, as she expressed it.

I was summoned to Wuthering Heights, within a fortnight of your leaving us, she said; and I obeyed joyfully, for Catherine's sake.

My first interview with her grieved and shocked me! she had altered so much since our separation. Mr. Heathcliff did not explain his reasons for taking a new mind about my coming here; he only told me he wanted me, and he was tired of seeing Catherine: I must make the little

fellies: Fellows. *jocks:* Jugs.

parlour my sitting room, and keep her with me. It was enough if he were obliged to see her once or twice a day.

She seemed pleased at this arrangement; and, by degrees, I smuggled over a great number of books, and other articles, that had formed her amusement at the Grange; and flattered myself we should get on in tolerable comfort.

The delusion did not last long. Catherine, contented at first, in a brief space grew irritable and restless. For one thing, she was forbidden to move out of the garden, and it fretted her sadly to be confined to its narrow bounds, as Spring drew on — for another, in following the house, I was forced to quit her frequently, and she complained of loneliness; she preferred quarrelling with Joseph in the kitchen, to sitting at peace in her solitude.

I did not mind their skirmishes; but Hareton was often obliged to seek the kitchen also, when the master wanted to have the house to himself; and, though, in the beginning, she either left it at his approach, or quietly joined in my occupations, and shunned remarking or addressing him — and though he was always as sullen and silent as possible — after a while, she changed her behaviour, and became incapable of letting him alone. Talking at him; commenting on his stupidity and idleness; expressing her wonder how he could endure the life he lived — how he could sit a whole evening staring into the fire, and dozing.

"He's just like a dog, is he not, Ellen?" she once observed, "or a cart-horse? He does his work, eats his food, and sleeps, eternally! What a blank, dreary mind he must have! Do you ever dream, Hareton? And, if you do, what is it about? But you can't speak to me!"

Then she looked at him; but he would neither open his mouth, nor look again.

"He's perhaps, dreaming now," she continued. "He twitched his shoulder as Juno twitches hers. Ask him, Ellen."

"Mr. Hareton will ask the master to send you upstairs, if you don't behave!" I said. He had not only twitched his shoulder, but clenched his fist, as if tempted to use it.

"I know why Hareton never speaks, when I am in the kitchen," she exclaimed, on another occasion. "He is afraid I shall laugh at him. Ellen, what do you think? He began to teach himself to read once; and, because I laughed, he burned his books, and dropped it — was he not a fool?"

"Were not you naughty?" I said; "answer me that."

"Perhaps I was," she went on, "but I did not expect him to be so silly. Hareton, if I gave you a book, would you take it now? I'll try!"

She placed one she had been perusing on his hand; he flung it off, and muttered, if she did not give over, he would break her neck.

"Well, I shall put it here," she said, "in the table drawer, and I'm going to bed."

Then she whispered to me to watch whether he touched it, and departed. But he would not come near it, and so I informed her in the morning, to her great disappointment. I saw she was sorry for his persevering sulkiness and indolence — her conscience reproved her for frightening him off improving himself — she had done it effectually.

But her ingenuity was at work to remedy the injury; while I ironed, or pursued other stationary employments I could not well do in the parlour — she would bring some pleasant volume, and read it aloud to me. When Hareton was there, she generally paused in an interesting part, and left the book lying about — that she did repeatedly; but he was as obstinate as a mule, and, instead of snatching at her bait, in wet weather he took to smoking with Joseph, and they sat like automatons, one on each side of the fire, the elder happily too deaf to understand her wicked nonsense, as he would have called it, the younger doing his best to seem to disregard it. On fine evenings the latter followed his shooting expeditions, and Catherine yawned and sighed, and teased me to talk to her, and ran off into the court or garden, the moment I began; and, as a last resource, cried, and said, she was tired of living, her life was useless.

Mr. Heathcliff, who grew more and more disinclined to society, had almost banished Earnshaw out of his apartment. Owing to an accident, at the commencement of March, he became for some days a fixture in the kitchen. His gun burst, while out on the hills, by himself; a splinter cut his arm, and he lost a good deal of blood before he could reach home. The consequence was, that, perforce, he was condemned to the fire-side and tranquillity, till he made it up again.

It suited Catherine to have him there: at any rate, it made her hate her room upstairs more than ever; and she would compel me to find out business below, that she might accompany me.

On Easter Monday, Joseph went to Gimmerton fair with some cattle; and, in the afternoon, I was busy getting up linen in the kitchen — Earnshaw sat, morose as usual, at the chimney corner, and my little mistress was beguiling an idle hour with drawing pictures on the window panes, varying her amusement by smothered bursts of songs, and whispered ejaculations, and quick glances of annoyance and impatience in the direction of her cousin, who steadfastly smoked, and looked into the grate.

At a notice that I could do with her no longer intercepting my light, she removed to the hearthstone. I bestowed little attention on her proceedings, but, presently, I heard her begin —

"I've found out, Hareton, that I want — that I'm glad — that I should like you to be my cousin, now, if you had not grown so cross to me, and so rough."

Hareton returned no answer.

"Hareton, Hareton, Hareton! do you hear?" she continued.

"Get off wi' ye!" he growled, with uncompromising gruffness.

"Let me take that pipe," she said, cautiously advancing her hand, and abstracting it from his mouth.

Before he could attempt to recover it, it was broken, and behind the fire. He swore at her and seized another.

"Stop," she cried, "you must listen to me first; and I can't speak while those clouds are floating in my face."

"Will you go to the devil!" he exclaimed, ferociously, "and let me be!"

"No," she persisted, "I won't — I can't tell what to do to make you talk to me, and you are determined not to understand. When I call you stupid, I don't mean anything — I don't mean that I despise you. Come, you shall take notice of me, Hareton — You are my cousin, and you shall own me."

"I shall have naught to do wi' you, and your mucky pride, and your damned, mocking tricks!" he answered. "I'll go to hell, body and soul, before I look sideways after you again! Side out of t' gait,° now; this minute!"

Catherine frowned, and retreated to the window-seat, chewing her lip, and endeavouring, by humming an eccentric tune, to conceal a growing tendency to sob.

"You should be friends with your cousin, Mr. Hareton," I interrupted, "since she repents of her sauciness! it would do you a great deal of good — it would make you another man, to have her for a companion."

"A companion?" he cried; "when she hates me, and does not think me fit to wipe her shoon! Nay, if it made me a king, I'd not be scorned for seeking her good will any more."

"It is not I who hate you, it is you who hate me!" wept Cathy, no longer disguising her trouble. "You hate me as much as Mr. Heathcliff does, and more."

"You're a damned liar," began Earnshaw; "why have I made him angry, by taking your part then, a hundred times? and that, when you

Side out of t' gait: Get out of the way.

sneered at, and despised me, and — Go on plaguing me, and I'll step in yonder, and say you worried me out of the kitchen!"

"I didn't know you took my part," she answered, drying her eyes; "and I was miserable and bitter at every body; but, now I thank you, and beg you to forgive me, what can I do besides?"

She returned to the hearth, and frankly extended her hand.

He blackened, and scowled like a thunder cloud, and kept his fists resolutely clenched, and his gaze fixed on the ground.

Catherine, by instinct, must have divined it was obdurate perversity, and not dislike, that prompted this dogged conduct; for, after remaining an instant, undecided, she stooped, and impressed on his cheek a gentle kiss.

The little rogue thought I had not seen her, and, drawing back, she took her former station by the window, quite demurely.

I shook my head reprovingly; and then she blushed, and whispered —

"Well, what should I have done, Ellen? He wouldn't shake hands, and he wouldn't look — I must show him someway that I like him, that I want to be friends."

Whether the kiss convinced Hareton, I cannot tell; he was very careful, for some minutes, that his face should not be seen; and when he did raise it, he was sadly puzzled where to turn his eyes.

Catherine employed herself in wrapping a handsome book neatly in white paper; and having tied it with a bit of ribband, and addressed it to "Mr. Hareton Earnshaw," she desired me to be her ambassadress, and convey the present to its destined recipient.

"And tell him, if he'll take it, I'll come and teach him to read it right," she said, "and, if he refuse it, I'll go upstairs, and never tease him again."

I carried it, and repeated the message, anxiously watched by my employer. Hareton would not open his fingers, so I laid it on his knee. He did not strike it off either. I returned to my work: Catherine leaned her head and arms on the table, till she heard the slight rustle of the covering being removed; then she stole away, and quietly seated herself beside her cousin. He trembled, and his face glowed — all his rudeness, and all his surly harshness had deserted him — he could not summon courage, at first, to utter a syllable, in reply to her questioning look, and her murmured petition.

"Say you forgive me, Hareton, do! You can make me so happy, by speaking that little word."

He muttered something inaudible.

"And you'll be my friend?" added Catherine, interrogatively.

"Nay! you'll be ashamed of me every day of your life," he answered. "And the more, the more you know me, and I cannot bide it."

"So, you won't be my friend?" she said, smiling sweet as honey, and creeping close up.

I overheard no further distinguishable talk; but on looking round again, I perceived two such radiant countenances bent over the page of the accepted book, that I did not doubt the treaty had been ratified, on both sides, and the enemies were, thenceforth, sworn allies.

The work they studied was full of costly pictures; and those, and their position, had charm enough to keep them unmoved, till Joseph came home. He, poor man, was perfectly aghast at the spectacle of Catherine seated on the same bench with Hareton Earnshaw, leaning her hand on his shoulder; and confounded at his favourite's endurance of her proximity. It affected him too deeply to allow an observation on the subject that night. His emotion was only revealed by the immense sighs he drew, as he solemnly spread his large Bible on the table, and overlaid it with dirty blank-notes from his pocket-book, the produce of the day's transactions. At length, he summoned Hareton from his seat.

"Tak' these in tuh t' maister, lad," he said, "un' bide theare; Aw's gang up tuh my awn rahm. This hoile's norther mensful, nor seemly fur us — we mun side aht, and seearch another!"

"Come, Catherine," I said, "we must 'side out,' too — I've done my ironing, are you ready to go?"

"It is not eight o'clock!" she answered, rising unwillingly. "Hareton, I'll leave this book upon the chimney-piece, and I'll bring some more to-morrow."

"Ony books ut yah leave, Aw suall tak' intuh th' hahse," said Joseph, "un' it 'ull be mitch if ya find 'em agean; soa, yah muh plase yourseln!"

Cathy threatened that his library should pay for hers; and, smiling as she passed Hareton, went singing upstairs, lighter of heart, I venture to say, then ever she had been under that roof before; except, perhaps, during her earliest visits to Linton.

The intimacy, thus commenced, grew rapidly; though it encountered temporary interruptions. Earnshaw was not to be civilized with a wish; and my young lady was no philosopher, and no paragon of patience; but both their minds tending to the same point — one loving and desiring to esteem; and the other loving and desiring to be esteemed — they contrived in the end, to reach it.

You see, Mr. Lockwood, it was easy enough to win Mrs. Heathcliff's heart; but now, I'm glad you did not try — the crown of all my wishes will be the union of those two; I shall envy no one on their wedding-day — there won't be a happier woman than myself in England!

CHAPTER 33

On the morrow of that Monday, Earnshaw being still unable to follow his ordinary employments, and, therefore, remaining about the house, I speedily found it would be impracticable to retain my charge beside me, as heretofore.

She got downstairs before me, and out into the garden, where she had seen her cousin performing some easy work; and when I went to bid them come to breakfast, I saw she had persuaded him to clear a large space of ground from currant and gooseberry bushes, and they were busy planning together an importation of plants from the Grange.

I was terrified at the devastation which had been accomplished in a brief half hour; the black currant trees were the apple of Joseph's eye, and she had just fixed her choice of a flower bed in the midst of them!

"There! That will be all shewn to the master," I exclaimed, "the minute it is discovered. And what excuse have you to offer for taking such liberties with the garden? We shall have a fine explosion on the head of it: see if we don't! Mr. Hareton, I wonder you should have no more wit, than to do and make that mess at her bidding!"

"I'd forgotten they were Joseph's," answered Earnshaw, rather puzzled, "but I'll tell him I did it."

We always ate our meals with Mr. Heathcliff. I held the mistress's post in making tea and carving; so I was indispensable at table. Catherine usually sat by me; but to-day, she stole nearer to Hareton, and I presently saw she would have no more discretion in her friendship, than she had in her hostility.

"Now, mind you don't talk with and notice your cousin too much," were my whispered instructions as we entered the room. "It will certainly annoy Mr. Heathcliff, and he'll be mad at you both."

"I'm not going to," she answered.

The minute after, she had sidled to him, and was sticking primroses in his plate of porridge.

He dared not speak to her, there; he dared hardly look; and yet she went on teasing, till he was twice on the point of being provoked to laugh; and I frowned, and then she glanced towards the master, whose mind was occupied on other subjects than his company, as his countenance evinced, and she grew serious for an instant, scrutinising him with deep gravity. Afterwards she turned, and re-commenced her nonsense; at last, Hareton uttered a smothered laugh.

Mr. Heathcliff started; his eyes rapidly surveyed our faces. Catherine met it with her accustomed look of nervousness, and yet defiance, which he abhorred.

"It is well you are out of my reach," he exclaimed. "What fiend possesses you to stare back at me, continually, with those infernal eyes? Down with them! and don't remind me of your existence again. I thought I had cured you of laughing!"

"It was me," muttered Hareton.

"What do you say?" demanded the master.

Hareton looked at his place, and did not repeat the confession.

Mr. Heathcliff looked at him a bit, and then silently resumed his breakfast, and his interrupted musing.

We had nearly finished, and the two young people prudently shifted wider asunder, so I anticipated no further disturbance during that sitting; when Joseph appeared at the door, revealing by his quivering lip, and furious eyes, that the outrage committed on his precious shrubs was detected.

He must have seen Cathy and her cousin about the spot, before he examined it, for while his jaws worked like those of a cow chewing its cud, and rendered his speech difficult to understand, he began:

"Aw mun hev my wage, and Aw mun goa! Aw *hed* aimed tuh dee,° wheare Aw'd sarved fur sixty years; un' Aw thowt Aw'd lug my books up intuh t' garret, un' all my bits uh stuff, un' they sud hev t' kitchen tuh theirseln; fur t' sake uh quietness. It wur hard tuh gie up my awn hearthstun, bud Aw thowt Aw *could* do that! Bud, nah, shoo's taan my garden frough me,° un' by th' heart! Maister, Aw cannot stand it! Yah mun bend tuh th' yoak, an ye will — *Aw* noan used to 't and an ow'd man doesn't sooin get used tuh new barthens — Aw'd rayther arn my bite, an' my sup, wi' a hammer in th' road!"

"Now, now, idiot!" interrupted Heathcliff, "cut it short! What's your grievance? I'll interfere in no quarrels between you and Nelly — She may thrust you into the coal-hole for anything I care."

"It's noan Nelly!" answered Joseph. "Aw sudn't shift fur Nelly° — Nasty, ill nowt as shoo is, Thank God! *shoo* cannot stale t' sowl uh nob'dy! Shoo wer niver soa handsome, bud whet a body mud look at her baht winking. It's yon flaysome, graceless quean,° ut's witched ahr

dee: Die. ***shoo's taan my garden frough me:*** She's taken my garden from me. ***Aw sudn't shift fur Nelly:*** I shouldn't leave on account of Nelly. ***flaysome, graceless quean:*** Terrible, wicked (i.e., not in a state of grace) hussy.

lad, wi' her bold een, un' her forrard ways — till — Nay! it fair brusts° my heart! He's forgetten all E done for him, un' made on him, un' goan un' riven up° a whole row ut t' grandest currant trees, i' t' garden!" And here he lamented outright, unmanned by a sense of his bitter injuries, and Earnshaw's ingratitude and dangerous condition.

"Is the fool drunk?" asked Mr. Heathcliff. "Hareton, is it you he's finding fault with?"

"I've pulled up two or three bushes," replied the young man, "but I'm going to set 'em again."

"And why have you pulled them up?" said the master.

Catherine wisely put in her tongue.

"We want to plant some flowers there," she cried. "I'm the only person to blame, for I wished him to do it."

"And who the devil gave *you* leave to touch a stick about the place?" demanded her father-in-law, much surprised. "And who ordered *you* to obey her?" he added, turning to Hareton.

The latter was speechless; his cousin replied —

"You shouldn't grudge a few yards of earth, for me to ornament, when you have taken all my land!"

"Your land, insolent slut? You never had any!" said Heathcliff.

"And my money," she continued, returning his angry glare, and meantime, biting a piece of crust, the remnant of her breakfast.

"Silence!" he exclaimed. "Get done, and begone!"

"And Hareton's land, and his money," pursued the reckless thing. "Hareton and I are friends now; and I shall tell him all about you!"

The master seemed confounded a moment; he grew pale, and rose up, eyeing her all the while, with an expression of mortal hate.

"If you strike me, Hareton will strike you!" she said; "so you may as well sit down."

"If Hareton does not turn you out of the room, I'll strike him to Hell," thundered Heathcliff. "Damnable witch! dare you pretend to rouse him against me? Off with her! Do you hear? Fling her into the kitchen! I'll kill her, Ellen Dean, if you let her come into my sight again!"

Hareton tried under his breath to persuade her to go.

"Drag her away!" he cried savagely. "Are you staying to talk?" And he approached to execute his own command.

"He'll not obey you, wicked man, any more!" said Catherine; "and he'll soon detest you, as much as I do!"

brusts: Breaks. ***riven up:*** Torn up.

"Wisht! wisht!" muttered the young man reproachfully. "I will not hear you speak so to him — Have done!"

"But you won't let him strike me?" she cried.

"Come then!" he whispered earnestly.

It was too late — Heathcliff had caught hold of her.

"Now *you* go!" he said to Earnshaw. "Accursed witch! this time she has provoked me, when I could not bear it; and I'll make her repent it for ever!"

He had his hand in her hair; Hareton attempted to release the locks, entreating him not to hurt her that once. His black eyes flashed, he seemed ready to tear Catherine to pieces, and I was just worked up to risk coming to the rescue, when of a sudden, his fingers relaxed, he shifted his grasp from her head, to her arm, and gazed intently in her face — Then, he drew his hand over his eyes, stood a moment to collect himself apparently, and turning anew to Catherine, said with assumed calmness,

"You must learn to avoid putting me in a passion, or I shall really murder you, some time! Go with Mrs. Dean, and keep with her, and confine your insolence to her ears. As to Hareton Earnshaw, if I see him listen to you, I'll send him seeking his bread where he can get it! Your love will make him an outcast, and a beggar — Nelly, take her, and leave me, all of you! Leave me!"

I led my young lady out; she was too glad to escape, to resist; the other followed, and Mr. Heathcliff had the room to himself, till dinner.

I had counselled Catherine to get hers upstairs; but, as soon as he perceived her vacant seat, he sent me to call her. He spoke to none of us, ate very little, and went out directly afterwards, intimating that he should not return before evening.

The two friends established themselves in the house, during his absence, where I heard Hareton sternly check his cousin, on her offering a revelation of her father-in-law's conduct to his father.

He said he wouldn't suffer a word to be uttered to him, in his disparagement; if he were the devil, it didn't signify; he would stand by him; and he'd rather she would abuse himself, as she used to, than begin on Mr. Heathcliff.

Catherine was waxing cross at this; but he found means to make her hold her tongue, by asking, how she would like *him* to speak ill of her father? and then she comprehended that Earnshaw took the master's reputation home to himself: and was attached by ties stronger than reason could break — chains, forged by habit, which it would be cruel to attempt to loosen.

She showed a good heart, thenceforth, in avoiding both complaints and expressions of antipathy concerning Heathcliff; and confessed to me her sorrow that she had endeavoured to raise a bad spirit between him and Hareton — indeed, I don't believe she has ever breathed a syllable, in the latter's hearing, against her oppressor, since.

When this slight disagreement was over, they were thick again, and as busy as possible, in their several occupations, of pupil and teacher. I came in to sit with them, after I had done my work, and I felt so soothed and comforted to watch them, that I did not notice how time got on. You know, they both appeared, in a measure, my children: I had long been proud of one; and now, I was sure, the other would be a source of equal satisfaction. His honest, warm, and intelligent nature shook off rapidly the clouds of ignorance and degradation in which it had been bred; and Catherine's sincere commendations acted as a spur to his industry. His brightening mind brightened his features, and added spirit and nobility to their aspect — I could hardly fancy it the same individual I had beheld on the day I discovered my little lady at Wuthering Heights, after her expedition to the Crags.

While I admired, and they laboured, dusk grew on, and with it returned the master. He came upon us quite unexpectedly, entering by the front way, and had a full view of the whole three, ere we could raise our heads to glance at him.

Well, I reflected, there was never a pleasanter, or more harmless sight; and it will be a burning shame to scold them. The red fire-light glowed on their two bonny heads, and revealed their faces, animated with the eager interest of children; for, though he was twenty-three, and she eighteen, each had so much of novelty to feel and learn, that neither experienced nor evinced the sentiments of sober disenchanted maturity.

They lifted their eyes together, to encounter Mr. Heathcliff — perhaps, you have never remarked that their eyes are precisely similar, and they are those of Catherine Earnshaw. The present Catherine has no other likeness to her, except a breadth of forehead, and a certain arch of the nostril that makes her appear rather haughty, whether she will, or not. With Hareton the resemblance is carried farther; it is singular, at all times — then it was particularly striking: because his senses were alert, and his mental faculties wakened to unwonted activity.

I suppose this resemblance disarmed Mr. Heathcliff: he walked to the hearth in evident agitation, but it quickly subsided, as he looked at the young man; or, I should say, altered its character, for it was there yet.

He took the book from his hand, and glanced at the open page, then returned it without any observation; merely signing Catherine away — her companion lingered very little behind her, and I was about to depart also, but he bid me sit still.

"It is a poor conclusion, is it not," he observed, having brooded a while on the scene he had just witnessed. "An absurd termination to my violent exertions? I get levers and mattocks to demolish the two houses, and train myself to be capable of working like Hercules, and when everything is ready, and in my power, I find the will to lift a slate off either roof has vanished! My old enemies have not beaten me — now would be the precise time to revenge myself on their representatives — I could do it; and none could hinder me — But where is the use? I don't care for striking, I can't take the trouble to raise my hand! That sounds as if I had been labouring the whole time, only to exhibit a fine trait of magnanimity. It is far from being the case — I have lost the faculty of enjoying their destruction, and I am too idle to destroy for nothing.

"Nelly, there is a strange change approaching — I'm in its shadow at present — I take so little interest in my daily life, that I hardly remember to eat, and drink — Those two who have left the room are the only objects which retain a distinct material appearance to me; and, that appearance causes me pain, amounting to agony. About *her* I won't speak; and I don't desire to think; but I earnestly wish she were invisible — her presence invokes only maddening sensations. *He* moves me differently; and yet if I could do it without seeming insane, I'd never see him again! You'll perhaps think me rather inclined to become so," he added, making an effort to smile, "if I try to describe the thousand forms of past associations, and ideas he awakens, or embodies — But you'll not talk of what I tell you, and my mind is so eternally secluded in itself, it is tempting, at last, to turn it out to another.

"Five minutes ago, Hareton seemed a personification of my youth, not a human being — I felt to him in such a variety of ways, that it would have been impossible to have accosted him rationally.

"In the first place, his startling likeness to Catherine connected him fearfully with her — That however which you may suppose the most potent to arrest my imagination, is actually the least — for what is not connected with her to me? and what does not recall her? I cannot look down to this floor, but her features are shaped on the flags! In every cloud, in every tree — filling the air at night, and caught by glimpses in every object by day, I am surrounded with her image! — The most ordinary faces of men and women — my own features — mock me with a resemblance. The entire world is a dreadful collection of memoranda that she did exist, and that I have lost her!

"Well, Hareton's aspect was the ghost of my immortal love, of my wild endeavours to hold my right, my degradation, my pride, my happiness, and my anguish —

"But it is frenzy to repeat these thoughts to you; only it will let you know, why, with a reluctance to be always alone, his society is no benefit, rather an aggravation of the constant torment I suffer — and it partly contributes to render me regardless how he and his cousin go on together. I can give them no attention, any more."

"But what do you mean by a *change*, Mr. Heathcliff?" I said, alarmed at his manner, though he was neither in danger of losing his senses, nor dying; according to my judgment he was quite strong and healthy; and, as to his reason, from childhood, he had a delight in dwelling on dark things, and entertaining odd fancies — he might have had a monomania on the subject of his departed idol; but on every other point his wits were as sound as mine.

"I shall not know that, till it comes," he said, "I'm only half conscious of it now."

"You have no feelings of illness, have you?" I asked.

"No, Nelly, I have not," he answered.

"Then, you are not afraid of death?" I pursued.

"Afraid? No!" he replied. "I have neither a fear, nor a presentiment, nor a hope of death — Why should I? With my hard constitution, and temperate mode of living, and unperilous occupations, I ought to, and probably *shall* remain above ground, till there is scarcely a black hair on my head — And yet I cannot continue in this condition! — I have to remind myself to breathe — almost to remind my heart to beat! And it is like bending back a stiff spring . . . it is by compulsion, that I do the slightest act, not prompted by one thought, and by compulsion, that I notice anything alive or dead, which is not associated with one universal idea. . . . I have a single wish, and my whole being and faculties are yearning to attain it. They have yearned towards it so long, and so unwaveringly, that I'm convinced it *will* be reached — and *soon* — because it has devoured my existence — I am swallowed in the anticipation of its fulfilment.

"My confessions have not relieved me — but, they may account for some otherwise unaccountable phases of humour which I show. O, God! It is a long fight, I wish it were over!"

He began to pace the room, muttering terrible things to himself; till I was inclined to believe, as he said Joseph did, that conscience had turned his heart to an earthly hell — I wondered greatly how it would end.

Though he seldom before had revealed this state of mind, even by looks, it was his habitual mood, I had no doubt: he asserted it himself — but not a soul, from his general bearing, would have conjectured the fact. You did not, when you saw him, Mr. Lockwood — and at the period of which I speak, he was just the same as then, only fonder of continued solitude, and perhaps still more laconic in company.

CHAPTER 34

For some days after that evening, Mr. Heathcliff shunned meeting us at meals; yet he would not consent, formally, to exclude Hareton and Cathy. He had an aversion to yielding so completely to his feelings, choosing, rather, to absent himself — And eating once in twenty-four hours seemed sufficient sustenance for him.

One night, after the family were in bed, I heard him go downstairs, and out at the front door: I did not hear him re-enter and, in the morning, I found him still away.

We were in April then, the weather was sweet and warm, the grass as green as showers and sun could make it, and the two dwarf apple trees, near the southern wall, in full bloom.

After breakfast, Catherine insisted on my bringing a chair, and sitting, with my work, under the fir trees, at the end of the house; and she beguiled Hareton, who had perfectly recovered from his accident, to dig and arrange her little garden, which was shifted to that corner by the influence of Joseph's complaints.

I was comfortably revelling in the spring fragrance around, and the beautiful soft blue overhead, when my young lady, who had run down near the gate to procure some primrose roots for a border, returned only half laden, and informed us that Mr. Heathcliff was coming in.

"And he spoke to me," she added, with a perplexed countenance.

"What did he say?" asked Hareton.

"He told me to begone as fast as I could," she answered. "But he looked so different from his usual look that I stopped a moment to stare at him."

"How?" he inquired.

"Why, almost bright and cheerful — No, almost nothing — *very much* excited, and wild and glad!" she replied.

"Night-walking amuses him, then," I remarked, affecting a careless manner. In reality, as surprised as she was; and, anxious to ascertain the truth of her statement, for to see the master looking glad would not be an everyday spectacle, I framed an excuse to go in.

Heathcliff stood at the open door; he was pale, and he trembled; yet, certainly, he had a strange joyful glitter in his eyes, that altered the aspect of his whole face.

"Will you have some breakfast?" I said. "You must be hungry, rambling about all night!"

I wanted to discover where he had been; but I did not like to ask directly.

"No, I'm not hungry," he answered, averting his head, and speaking rather contemptuously, as if he guessed I was trying to divine the occasion of his good humour.

I felt perplexed — I didn't know whether it were not a proper opportunity to offer a bit of admonition.

"I don't think it right to wander out of doors," I observed, "instead of being in bed: it is not wise, at any rate, this moist season. I dare say you'll catch a bad cold, or a fever — you have something the matter with you now!"

"Nothing but what I can bear," he replied, "and with the greatest pleasure, provided you'll leave me alone — get in, and don't annoy me."

I obeyed; and, in passing, I noticed he breathed as fast as a cat.

"Yes!" I reflected to myself, "we shall have a fit of illness. I cannot conceive what he has been doing!"

That noon, he sat down to dinner with us, and received a heaped-up plate from my hands, as if he intended to make amends for previous fasting.

"I've neither cold nor fever, Nelly," he remarked, in allusion to my morning's speech. "And I'm ready to do justice to the food you give me."

He took his knife and fork, and was going to commence eating, when the inclination appeared to become suddenly extinct. He laid them on the table, looked eagerly towards the window, then rose and went out.

We saw him walking, to and fro, in the garden, while we concluded our meal; and Earnshaw said he'd go and ask why he would not dine; he thought we had grieved him some way.

"Well, is he coming?" cried Catherine, when her cousin returned.

"Nay," he answered; "but he's not angry: he seemed rare and pleased indeed; only, I made him impatient by speaking to him twice; and then he bid me be off to you; he wondered how I could want the company of any body else."

I set his plate, to keep warm, on the fender: and after an hour or two, he re-entered, when the room was clear, in no degree calmer — the same unnatural — it was unnatural — appearance of joy under his black brows; the same bloodless hue; and his teeth visible, now and then, in a kind of smile; his frame shivering, not as one shivers with chill or weakness, but as a tight-stretched cord vibrates — a strong thrilling, rather than trembling.

"Have you heard any good news, Mr. Heathcliff? You look uncommonly animated."

"Where should good news come from, to me?" he said. "I'm animated with hunger; and, seemingly, I must not eat."

"Your dinner is here," I returned; "why won't you get it?"

"I don't want it now," he muttered, hastily. "I'll wait till supper. And, Nelly, once for all, let me beg you to warn Hareton and the other away from me. I wish to be troubled by nobody — I wish to have this place to myself."

"Is there some new reason for this banishment?" I inquired. "Tell me why you are so queer, Mr. Heathcliff? Where were you last night? I'm not putting the question through idle curiosity, but —

"You are putting the question through very idle curiosity," he interrupted, with a laugh. "Yet, I'll answer it. Last night, I was on the threshold of hell. To-day, I am within sight of my heaven — I have my eyes on it — hardly three feet to sever me! And now you'd better go — You'll neither see nor hear anything to frighten you, if you refrain from prying."

Having swept the hearth, and wiped the table, I departed more perplexed than ever.

He did not quit the house again that afternoon, and no one intruded on his solitude, till, at eight o'clock, I deemed it proper, though unsummoned, to carry a candle and his supper to him.

He was leaning against the ledge of an open lattice, but not looking out; his face was turned to the interior gloom. The fire had smouldered to ashes; the room was filled with the damp, mild air of the cloudy evening, and so still, that not only the murmur of the beck down Gimmerton was distinguishable, but its ripples and its gurgling over the pebbles, or through the large stones which it could not cover.

I uttered an ejaculation of discontent at seeing the dismal grate, and commenced shutting the casements, one after another, till I came to his.

"Must I close this?" I asked, in order to rouse him, for he would not stir.

The light flashed on his features, as I spoke. Oh, Mr. Lockwood, I cannot express what a terrible start I got, by the momentary view! Those deep black eyes! That smile, and ghastly paleness! It appeared to me, not Mr. Heathcliff, but a goblin; and, in my terror, I let the candle bend towards the wall, and it left me in darkness.

"Yes, close it," he replied, in his familiar voice. "There, that is pure awkwardness! Why did you hold the candle horizontally? Be quick, and bring another."

I hurried out in a foolish state of dread, and said to Joseph —

"The master wishes you to take him a light, and re-kindle the fire." For I dared not go in myself again just then.

Joseph rattled some fire into the shovel, and went; but he brought it back, immediately, with the supper-tray in his other hand, explaining that Mr. Heathcliff was going to bed, and he wanted nothing to eat till morning.

We heard him mount the stairs directly; he did not proceed to his ordinary chamber, but turned into that with the panelled bed — its window, as I mentioned before, is wide enough for anybody to get through, and it struck me, that he plotted another midnight excursion, which he had rather we had no suspicion of.

"Is he a ghoul, or a vampire?" I mused. I had read of such hideous, incarnate demons. And then, I set myself to reflect, how I had tended him in infancy; and watched him grow to youth; and followed him almost through his whole course; and what absurd nonsense it was to yield to that sense of horror.

"But, where did he come from, the little dark thing, harboured by a good man to his bane?" muttered superstition, as I dozed into unconsciousness. And I began, half dreaming, to weary myself with imaging some fit parentage for him; and repeating my waking meditations, I tracked his existence over again, with grim variations; at last, picturing his death and funeral; of which, all I can remember is, being exceedingly vexed at having the task of dictating the inscription for his monument, and consulting the sexton about it; and, as he had no surname, and we could not tell his age, we were obliged to content ourselves with the single word, "Heathcliff." That came true; we were. If you enter the kirkyard, you'll read on his headstone, only that, and the date of his death.

Dawn restored me to common sense. I rose, and went into the garden, as soon as I could see, to ascertain if there were any footmarks under his window. There were none.

"He stayed at home," I thought, "and he'll be all right, to-day!"

I prepared breakfast for the household, as was my usual custom, but told Hareton and Catherine to get theirs, ere the master came down, for he lay late. They preferred taking it out of doors, under the trees, and I set a little table to accommodate them.

On my re-entrance, I found Mr. Heathcliff below. He and Joseph were conversing about some farming business; he gave clear, minute directions concerning the matter discussed, but he spoke rapidly, and turned his head continually aside, and had the same excited expression, even more exaggerated.

When Joseph quitted the room, he took his seat in the place he generally chose, and I put a basin of coffee before him. He drew it nearer, and then rested his arms on the table, and looked at the opposite wall, as I supposed, surveying one particular portion, up and down, with glittering, restless eyes, and with such eager interest, that he stopped breathing, during half a minute together.

"Come now," I exclaimed, pushing some bread against his hand. "Eat and drink that, while it is hot. It has been waiting near an hour."

He didn't notice me, and yet he smiled. I'd rather have seen him gnash his teeth than smile so.

"Mr. Heathcliff! master!" I cried. "Don't, for God's sake, stare as if you saw an unearthly vision."

"Don't, for God's sake, shout so loud," he replied. "Turn round, and tell me, are we by ourselves?"

"Of course," was my answer, "of course we are!"

Still, I involuntarily obeyed him, as if I were not quite sure.

With a sweep of his hand, he cleared a vacant space in front among the breakfast things, and leant forward to gaze more at his ease.

Now, I perceived he was not looking at the wall, for when I regarded him alone, it seemed, exactly, that he gazed at something within two yards distance. And, whatever it was, it communicated, apparently, both pleasure and pain, in exquisite extremes, at least, the anguished, yet raptured expression of his countenance suggested that idea.

The fancied object was not fixed, either; his eyes pursued it with unwearied vigilance; and, even in speaking to me, were never weaned away.

I vainly reminded him of his protracted abstinence from food; if he stirred to touch anything in compliance with my entreaties, if he stretched his hand out to get a piece of bread, his fingers clenched, before they reached it, and remained on the table, forgetful of their aim.

I sat a model of patience, trying to attract his absorbed attention from its engrossing speculation; till he grew irritable, and got up, asking, why I would not allow him to have his own time in taking his meals? and saying that, on the next occasion, I needn't wait, I might set the things down, and go.

Having uttered these words, he left the house, slowly sauntered down the garden path, and disappeared through the gate.

The hours crept anxiously by: another evening came. I did not retire to rest till late, and when I did, I could not sleep. He returned after midnight, and, instead of going to bed, shut himself into the room beneath. I listened, and tossed about; and, finally, dressed, and descended. It was too irksome to lie up there harassing my brain with a hundred idle misgivings.

I distinguished Mr. Heathcliff's step, restlessly measuring the floor; and he frequently broke the silence, by a deep inspiration, resembling a groan. He muttered detached words, also; the only one I could catch was the name of Catherine, coupled with some wild term of endearment, or suffering; and spoken as one would speak to a person present — low and earnest, and wrung from the depth of his soul.

I had not courage to walk straight into the apartment; but I desired to divert him from his reverie, and, therefore, fell foul of the kitchen fire; stirred it, and began to scrape the cinders. It drew him forth sooner than I expected. He opened the door immediately, and said —

"Nelly, come here — is it morning? Come in with your light."

"It is striking four," I answered; "you want a candle to take upstairs — you might have lit one at this fire."

"No, I don't wish to go upstairs," he said. "Come in, and kindle *me* a fire, and do anything there is to do about the room."

"I must blow the coals red first, before I can carry any," I replied, getting a chair and the bellows.

He roamed to and fro, meantime, in a state approaching distraction: his heavy sighs succeeding each other so thick as to leave no space for common breathing between.

"When day breaks I'll send for Green," he said; "I wish to make some legal inquiries of him while I can bestow a thought on those matters, and while I can act calmly. I have not written my will yet, and how to leave my property, I cannot determine! I wish I could annihilate it from the face of the earth."

"I would not talk so, Mr. Heathcliff," I interposed. "Let your will be, a while — you'll be spared to repent of your many injustices, yet! I never expected that your nerves would be disordered — they are, at present, marvellously so, however; and, almost entirely, through your own fault. The way you've passed these last three days might knock up a

Titan. Do take some food, and some repose. You need only look at yourself, in a glass, to see how you require both. Your cheeks are hollow, and your eyes blood-shot, like a person starving with hunger, and going blind with loss of sleep."

"It is not my fault, that I cannot eat or rest," he replied. "I assure you it is through no settled designs. I'll do both, as soon as I possibly can. But you might as well bid a man struggling in the water, rest within arm's length of the shore! I must reach it first, and then I'll rest. Well, never mind Mr. Green; as to repenting of my injustices, I've done no injustice, and I repent of nothing — I'm too happy, and yet I'm not happy enough. My soul's bliss kills my body, but does not satisfy itself."

"Happy, master?" I cried, "Strange happiness! If you would hear me without being angry, I might offer some advice that would make you happier."

"What is that?" he asked. "Give it."

"You are aware, Mr. Heathcliff," I said, "that from the time you were thirteen years old, you have lived a selfish, unchristian life; and probably hardly had a Bible in your hands, during all that period. You must have forgotten the contents of the book, and you may not have space to search it now. Could it be hurtful to send for some one — some minister of any denomination, it does not matter which, to explain it, and show you how very far you have erred from its precepts, and how unfit you will be for its heaven, unless a change takes place before you die?"

"I'm rather obliged than angry, Nelly," he said, "for you remind me of the manner that I desire to be buried in — It is to be carried to the churchyard, in the evening. You and Hareton may, if you please, accompany me — and mind, particularly, to notice that the sexton obeys my directions concerning the two coffins! No minister need come; nor need anything be said over me — I tell you, I have nearly attained *my* heaven; and that of others is altogether unvalued and uncoveted by me!"

"And supposing you persevered in your obstinate fast, and died by that means, and they refused to bury you in the precincts of the Kirk?" I said, shocked at his godless indifference. "How would you like it?"

"They won't do that," he replied; "if they did, you must have me removed secretly; and if you neglect it, you shall prove, practically, that the dead are not annihilated!"

As soon as he heard the other members of the family stirring he retired to his den, and I breathed freer — But in the afternoon, while Joseph and Hareton were at their work, he came into the kitchen again, and with a wild look, bid me come, and sit in the house — he wanted somebody with him.

I declined, telling him plainly that his strange talk and manner frightened me, and I had neither the nerve nor the will to be his companion, alone.

"I believe you think me a fiend!" he said, with his dismal laugh, "something too horrible to live under a decent roof!"

Then turning to Catherine, who was there, and who drew behind me at his approach, he added, half sneeringly —

"Will *you* come, chuck? I'll not hurt you. No! to you, I've made myself worse than the devil. Well, there is *one* who won't shrink from my company! By God! she's relentless. Oh, damn it! It's unutterably too much for flesh and blood to bear, even mine."

He solicited the society of no one more. At dusk, he went into his chamber — through the whole night, and far into the morning, we heard him groaning, and murmuring to himself. Hareton was anxious to enter, but I bid him fetch Mr. Kenneth, and he should go in, and see him.

When he came, and I requested admittance and tried to open the door, I found it locked; and Heathcliff bid us be damned. He was better, and would be left alone; so the doctor went away.

The following evening was very wet; indeed it poured down, till day-dawn; and, as I took my morning walk round the house, I observed the master's window swinging open, and the rain driving straight in.

"He cannot be in bed," I thought, "those showers would drench him through! He must be either up, or out. But I'll make no more ado, I'll go boldly, and look!"

Having succeeded in obtaining entrance with another key, I ran to unclose the panels, for the chamber was vacant — quickly pushing them aside, I peeped in. Mr. Heathcliff was there — laid on his back. His eyes met mine so keen, and fierce, I started; and then, he seemed to smile.

I could not think him dead — but his face and throat were washed with rain; the bed-clothes dripped, and he was perfectly still. The lattice, flapping to and fro, had grazed one hand that rested on the sill — no blood trickled from the broken skin, and when I put my fingers to it, I could doubt no more — he was dead and stark!

I hasped the window; I combed his black long hair from his forehead; I tried to close his eyes — to extinguish, if possible, that frightful, life-like gaze of exultation, before any one else beheld it. They would not shut — they seemed to sneer at my attempts, and his parted lips and sharp, white teeth sneered too! Taken with another fit of cowardice, I cried for Joseph. Joseph shuffled up, and made a noise, but resolutely refused to meddle with him.

"Th' divil's harried° off his soul," he cried, "and he muh hev his carcass intuh t' bargain, for ow't Aw care! Ech! what a wicked un he looks girnning° at death!" and the old sinner grinned in mockery.

I thought he intended to cut a caper round the bed; but suddenly composing himself, he fell on his knees, and raised his hands, and returned thanks that the lawful master and the ancient stock were restored to their rights.

I felt stunned by the awful event; and my memory unavoidably recurred to former times with a sort of oppressive sadness. But poor Hareton, the most wronged, was the only one that really suffered much. He sat by the corpse all night, weeping in bitter earnest. He pressed its hand, and kissed the sarcastic, savage face that every one else shrank from contemplating; and bemoaned him with that strong grief which springs naturally from a generous heart, though it be tough as tempered steel.

Kenneth was perplexed to pronounce of what disorder the master died. I concealed the fact of his having swallowed nothing for four days, fearing it might lead to trouble, and then, I am persuaded he did not abstain on purpose; it was the consequence of his strange illness, not the cause.

We buried him, to the scandal of the whole neighbourhood, as he had wished. Earnshaw, and I, the sexton, and six men to carry the coffin, comprehended the whole attendance.

The six men departed when they had let it down into the grave: we stayed to see it covered. Hareton, with a streaming face, dug green sods, and laid them over the brown mould himself, at present it is as smooth and verdant as its companion mounds — and I hope its tenant sleeps as soundly. But the country folks, if you asked them, would swear on their Bible that he *walks*. There are those who speak to having met him near the church, and on the moor, and even within this house — Idle tales, you'll say, and so say I. Yet that old man by the kitchen fire affirms he has seen two on 'em looking out of his chamber window, on every rainy night since his death — and an odd thing happened to me about a month ago.

I was going to the Grange one evening — a dark evening threatening thunder — and, just at the turn of the Heights, I encountered a

harried: Laid waste to, stolen. ***girnning:*** Grinning, snarling.

little boy with a sheep and two lambs before him; he was crying terribly, and I supposed the lambs were skittish, and would not be guided.

"What is the matter, my little man?" I asked.

"They's Heathcliff, and a woman, yonder, under t' Nab,"° he blubbered, "un' Aw darnut pass 'em."

I saw nothing; but neither the sheep nor he would go on, so I bid him take the road lower down.

He probably raised the phantoms from thinking, as he traversed the moors alone, on the nonsense he had heard his parents and companions repeat — yet still, I don't like being out in the dark, now — and I don't like being left by myself in this grim house — I cannot help it, I shall be glad when they leave it, and shift to the Grange!

"They are going to the Grange then?" I said.

"Yes," answered Mrs. Dean, "as soon as they are married; and that will be on New Year's day."

"And who will live here then?"

"Why, Joseph will take care of the house, and, perhaps, a lad to keep him company. They will live in the kitchen, and the rest will be shut up."

"For the use of such ghosts as choose to inhabit it," I observed.

"No, Mr. Lockwood," said Nelly, shaking her head. "I believe the dead are at peace, but it is not right to speak of them with levity."

At that moment the garden gate swung to; the ramblers were returning.

"*They* are afraid of nothing," I grumbled, watching their approach through the window. "Together they would brave satan and all his legions."

As they stepped onto the door-stones, and halted to take a last look at the moon, or, more correctly, at each other, by her light, I felt irresistibly impelled to escape them again; and, pressing a remembrance into the hand of Mrs. Dean, and disregarding her expostulations at my rudeness, I vanished through the kitchen, as they opened the house-door, and so should have confirmed Joseph in his opinion of his fellow-servant's gay indiscretions, had he not, fortunately, recognised me for a respectable character, by the sweet ring of a sovereign at his feet.

My walk home was lengthened by a diversion in the direction of the kirk. When beneath its walls, I perceived decay had made progress, even in seven months — many a window showed black gaps deprived of glass; and slates jutted off, here and there, beyond the right line of the roof, to be gradually worked off in coming autumn storms.

Nab: A projecting or jutting out part of a hill.

I sought, and soon discovered, the three head-stones on the slope next the moor — the middle one grey, and half buried in heath — Edgar Linton's only harmonised by the turf, and moss creeping up its foot — Heathcliff's still bare.

I lingered round them, under that benign sky; watched the moths fluttering among the heath, and hare-bells; listened to the soft wind breathing through the grass, and wondered how anyone could ever imagine unquiet slumbers for the sleepers in that quiet earth.

Cultural Documents and Illustrations

Wuthering Heights emerged from — and responds to — a variety of cultural contexts, some regional, others national, still others international and imperial. As Nancy Armstrong's essay, "Imperialist Nostalgia and *Wuthering Heights*," suggests (see pp. 430–50 in this volume), from 1850 onward the novel was marketed as regional literature, as the representation of a remote, alien, and almost extinct group of people living on the northern Yorkshire moors. Readers became fascinated with the Brontë family itself, especially with the tragic deaths of the three sister-novelists and their burial in Haworth church; with the landscape of the moors, the terrain on which so much of the novel occurs; and with the possible real-life sources of the tale in local buildings and ruins, such as Top Withens and Law Hill. Nineteenth-century illustrations or photographs of these regional sites appear in The Regional Context.

At the national level, *Wuthering Heights* responds to two crises of the 1840s: the movement for married women's legal rights and the Irish potato famine. In 1847, when Brontë's novel was published, married women were not allowed to hold property in their own names; once married, both personal and real property (land) came into the possession of their husbands. This legal situation created much misery for women who were abandoned by, or wished to separate from, their husbands — as the case of Lady Caroline Norton revealed. In 1827 Caroline married George Chapple Norton, a young barrister of limited income and a violent temper. Her husband first exploited his wife's friendship with Lord Melbourne to obtain a minor governmental appointment, then accused Lord Melbourne of adultery with his wife and brought a lawsuit against him. Although acquitted, Caroline Norton's reputation was tarnished, and she lived apart from her husband, who nonetheless continued to claim his legal right to her earnings as an author. Norton wrote actively in defense of women's issues during the 1840s and 1850s; her *Letter to the Queen on Lord Chancellor Cranworth's Marriage and Divorce Bill* (1855), which advocates the rights of married women to retain their incomes and the custody of their children, is included in The Political Context. Also included is the petition for increased women's rights, signed by many prominent literary women and presented to Parliament in 1857. This petition eventually led to the passage of the Matrimonial Causes Act of 1857 and the Married Women's Property Act of 1870.

The second national crisis — the Irish famine — is more tangentially treated in Brontë's novel but is nonetheless relevant to Heathcliff's mysterious origins. *Wuthering Heights* never directly mentions Ireland or the potato famine, yet, as Terry Eagleton has argued, its male protagonist is found abandoned in Liverpool and depicted in terms of the starving, emaciated beings who fled Ireland to this port city "with a few rags on them and an animal growth of hair almost obscuring their features."[1] Eagleton notes that the Brontë family, Irish in origin, was well apprised of the condition of the Irish peasantry in the 1840s. The potato blight began in 1845, and continuing crop failures, along with severe winters, caused disease, death, and mass emigration from Ireland from 1845 onward. Branwell Brontë's trip to Liverpool in August 1845 would have made him and his sisters, Charlotte, Emily, and Anne, aware of the condition of thousands starving from the failure of the Irish potato crop. Depictions of conditions in Ireland, taken from *The Illustrated London News* of 1843 and 1847, the years during which the novel was written and published, are reproduced in The Historical Context.

If Heathcliff is visually associated with the Irish poor, he is verbally associated with other figures of empire: with gypsies, lascars (Indian seamen), castaways, Chinese emperors, and Indian royalty. Most of these comparisons, as Susan Meyer argues in "'Your Father Was Emperor of China, and Your Mother an Indian Queen': Reverse Imperialism in *Wuthering Heights*" (pp. 480–502), reflect negative English attitudes

[1]Terry Eagleton, *Heathcliff and the Great Hunger: Studies in Irish Culture* (London: Verso, 1995), pp. 1–5.

toward the racial "others" of the British empire. Yet, as the depictions in Imperial and Racial Contexts reveal, not all depictions were negative. If Hindley Earnshaw calls Heathcliff a "gipsy" and an "imp of Satan" (p. 54), or if Mr. Linton's associations of him with "gypsies," "lascars," and "castaways" (p. 62) make him into "a wicked boy . . . unfit for a decent house," then Nelly's version of his origins in Chinese or Indian royalty also suggests the possibility of high birth, breeding, and power.

How Heathcliff gains power — and legal claim — to Wuthering Heights and Thrushcross Grange is a question raised by several characters in the second half of the novel. One tactic involves the manipulation of English inheritance law. The Legal Context includes a chapter from William Blackstone's *Commentaries on the Laws of England*, which explains the laws of inheritance that controlled the passing down of land (called "real property") to heirs. It pertains to Heathcliff's marriage to Isabella Linton and his later plot to marry their son to Catherine Linton, thereby consolidating all the properties of the Linton and Earnshaw families.

The Regional Context: Haworth, Yorkshire, and the Moors

Emily Brontë, as painted by her brother Branwell (1834). National Portrait Gallery, London.

By courtesy of the National Portrait Gallery, London.

Haworth Church and Vicarage, as drawn by Elizabeth Gaskell for *The Life of Charlotte Brontë* (1857).
Courtesy of Yale University Library.

Wuthering Heights by Edmund Morrison Wimperis, included in the first illustrated edition of the novel (London: Smith, Elder, 1873).
Courtesy of Yale University Library.

Top Withens, often considered the site of Wuthering Heights, from Ellis H. Chadwick's *In the Footsteps of the Brontës* (1914).
Courtesy of Yale University Library.

Law Hill, the school where Emily Brontë taught briefly and whose legend of an adopted son's usurpation of property may have inspired the plot of *Wuthering Heights*, from Ellis H. Chadwick's *In the Footsteps of the Brontës* (1914).
Courtesy of Yale University Library.

The Political Context: The Women's Movement

LADY CAROLINE NORTON

From Letter to the Queen on Lord Chancellor Cranworth's Marriage and Divorce Bill (1855)

A married woman in England has *no legal existence:* her being is absorbed in that of her husband. Years of separation or desertion cannot alter this position. Unless divorced by special enactment in the House of Lords, the legal fiction holds her to be *"one"* with her husband, even though she may never see or hear of him.

She has no possessions, unless by special settlement; her property is *his* property. Lord Ellenborough mentions a case in which a sailor bequeathed "all he was worth" to a woman he cohabited with; and afterwards married, in the West Indies, a woman of considerable fortune. At this man's death it was held, — notwithstanding the hardship of the case, — that the will swept away from his widow, in favour of his mistress, every shilling of the property. It is now provided that a will shall be revoked by marriage: but the claim of *the husband* to all that is his wife's exists in full force. An English wife has no legal right even to her clothes or ornaments; her husband may take them and sell them if he pleases, even though they be the gifts of relatives or friends, or bought before marriage.

An English wife cannot make a will. She may have children or kindred whom she may earnestly desire to benefit; — she may be separated from her husband, who may be living with a mistress; no matter: the law gives what she has to him, and no will she could make would be valid.

An English wife cannot legally claim her own earnings. Whether wages for manual labour, or payment for intellectual exertion, whether she weed potatoes, or keep a school, her salary is *the husband's;* and he could compel a second payment, and treat the first as void, if paid to the wife without his sanction.

An English wife may not leave her husband's house. Not only can he sue her for "restitution of conjugal rights," but he has a right to enter the house of any friend or relation with whom she may take refuge, and who may "harbour her," — as it is termed, — and carry her away by force, with or without the aid of the police.

From *Lady Caroline Norton's Letter to the Queen on Lord Chancellor Cranworth's Marriage and Divorce Bill* (London: Longman, Brown, Green and Longmans, 1855).

If the wife sue for separation for cruelty, it must be "cruelty that endangers life or limb," and if she has once forgiven, or, in legal phrase, *"condoned"* his offences, she cannot plead them; though her past forgiveness only proves that she endured as long as endurance was possible.

If her husband take proceedings for a divorce, she is not, in the first instance, allowed to defend herself. She has no means of proving the falsehood of his allegations. She is not represented by attorney, nor permitted to be considered a party to the suit between him and her supposed lover, for "damages." Lord Brougham affirmed in the House of Lords: *"in that action the character of the woman was at immediate issue, although she was not prosecuted. The consequence not unfrequently was, that the character of a woman was sworn away; instances were known in which, by collusion between the husband and a pretended paramour, the character of the wife has been destroyed. All this could take place, and yet the wife had no defence; she was excluded from Westminster-hall, and behind her back, by the principles of our jurisprudence, her character was tried between her husband and the man called her paramour."*

If an English wife be guilty of infidelity, her husband can divorce *her* so as to marry again; but she cannot divorce the husband *a vinculo*, however profligate he may be. No law court can divorce in England. A special Act of Parliament annulling the marriage, is passed for each case. The House of Lords grants this almost as a matter of course to the husband, but not to the wife. In only four instances (two of which were cases of incest), has the wife obtained a divorce to marry again.

She cannot prosecute for a libel. Her husband must prosecute; and in cases of enmity and separation, of course she is without a remedy.

She cannot sign a lease, or transact responsible business.

She cannot claim support, as a matter of personal right, from her husband. The general belief and nominal rule is, that her husband is "bound to maintain her." That is not the law. He is not bound to *her*. He is bound to his country; bound to see that she does not cumber the parish in which she resides. If it be proved that means sufficient are at her disposal, from relatives or friends, her husband is quit of his obligation, and need not contribute a farthing: even if he have deserted her; or be in receipt of money which is hers by inheritance.

She cannot bind her husband by any agreement, except through a third party. A contract formally drawn out by a lawyer, — witnessed, and signed by her husband, — is *void in law;* and he can evade payment of an income so assured, by the legal quibble that "a man cannot contract with his own wife."

Separation from her husband by consent, or for his ill usage, does not alter their mutual relation. He retains the right to divorce her *after* separation, — as before, — though he himself be unfaithful.

Her being, on the other hand, of spotless character, and without reproach, gives her no advantage in law. She may have withdrawn from his roof knowing that he lives with "his faithful housekeeper": having suffered personal violence at his hands; having "condoned" much, and being able to prove it by unimpeachable testimony: or he may have shut the doors of her house against her: all this is quite immaterial: the law takes no cognisance of which is to blame. As *her husband*, he has a right to all that is hers: as *his wife*, she has no right to anything that is his. As her husband, he may divorce her (if truth or false swearing can do it): as his wife, the utmost "divorce" she could obtain, is permission to reside alone, — married to his name. The marriage ceremony is a civil bond for him, — and an indissoluble sacrament for her; and the rights of mutual property which that ceremony is ignorantly supposed to confer, are made absolute for him, and null for her.

Of course an opposite picture may be drawn. There are bad, wanton, irreclaimable women, as there are vicious, profligate, tyrannical men: but the difference is *this:* that to punish and restrain bad wives, there are laws, and very severe laws (to say nothing of social condemnation); while to punish or restrain bad husbands, there is, in England, no adequate law whatever. Indeed, the English law holds out a sort of premium on infidelity; for there is no doubt that the woman who is divorced for a lover and marries him, suffers less (except in conscience) than the woman who *does not deserve to suffer at all* — the wife of a bad husband, who can inflict what he pleases, whether she remain in her home, or attempt to leave it.

Such, however, is "the law": and if anything could add to the ridicule, confusion, and injustice of its provisions, it would be the fact, that though it is law for the rich, it is not law for the poor; and though it is the law in England, it is not the law in Scotland!

It is not law for the poor.

Since the days of King Henry VIII., for whose passions it was contrived, our method of divorce has remained an indulgence sacred to the aristocracy of England. The poorer classes have no form of divorce amongst them. The rich man makes a new marriage, having divorced his wife in the House of Lords: his new marriage is legal; his children are legitimate; his bride occupies, in all respects, the same social position as if he had never previously been wedded. The poor man makes a new marriage, *not* having divorced his wife in the House of Lords; his new marriage is null; his children are bastards; and he himself is liable to be put on his trial for bigamy: the allotted punishment for which crime, at one time was hanging, and is now imprisonment. Not always offending knowingly, — for nothing can exceed the ignorance of the poor on this subject; they believe a Magistrate can divorce them; that an absence of seven years constitutes a nullity of the marriage tie; or that they can give each other reciprocal permission to divorce: and among some of our rural populations, the grosser belief prevails, that a man may legally *sell* his wife, and so break the bond of union! They believe anything, — rather than what is the fact, — viz., that *they* cannot do legally, that which they know is done legally in the classes above them; that the comfort of the rich man's home, or the indulgence of the rich man's passions, receives a consideration in England which the poor need not expect to obtain.

It is not the law of Scotland. In your Majesty's kingdom, nothing but

"The rapid running of the silver Tweed"

divides that portion of the realm where women are protected by law, — from that portion where they are *un*protected, though living under the same Sovereign and the same government!

When, in Queen Anne's reign, the legislative union of Scotland was completed, the laws relating to trade, customs, and excise, were assimilated to those of England; but other laws remained untouched; and in nothing is there a larger difference than in all matters relating to marriage, divorce, and legitimation of children.

In Scotland, the wife accused of infidelity defends herself as a matter of course, and as a first process, — instead of suffering by the infamous English action for "damages," where she is not allowed to interfere, though the result may be to ruin her.

In Scotland, the property of the wife is protected; rules are made for her "aliment" or support; and her clothes and "paraphernalia" cannot be seized by her husband.

In Scotland, above all, the law *has* power to divorce *a vinculo,* so as to enable *either* party to marry again; and the right of the wife to apply for such divorce is equal with the right of the husband; that license for inconstancy, taken out under the English law by the English husband, — as one of the masculine gender, — being utterly unknown to the Scottish courts.

This condition of the English law; its anomalies, its injustice, its actions for damages and crim. con., and its perpetual contradictions, have long marked it out for reform.

ELIZABETH BARRETT BROWNING, ELIZABETH GASKELL, JANE CARLYLE, HARRIET MARTINEAU, BARBARA LEIGH SMITH, ET AL.

Petition to Parliament (1857)

"TO THE HONOURABLE THE HOUSE OF PEERS (AND COMMONS) IN PARLIAMENT ASSEMBLED. THE PETITION OF THE UNDERSIGNED WOMEN OF GREAT BRITAIN, MARRIED AND SINGLE
Humbly sheweth: —

That the manifold evils occasioned by the present law, by which the property and earnings of the wife are thrown into the absolute power of the husband, become daily more apparent. That the sufferings thereupon ensuing, extend over all classes of society. That it might once have been deemed for the middle and upper ranks, a comparatively theoretical question, but it is so no longer, since married women of education are entering on every side the fields of literature and art, in order to increase the family income by such exertions.

"That it is usual when a daughter marries in these ranks, to make, if possible, some distinct pecuniary provision for her and her children, and to secure the money thus set aside by a cumbrous machinery of trusteeship, proving that few parents are willing entirely to entrust the welfare of their offspring to the irresponsible power of the husband, to the chances of his character, his wisdom, and his success in a profession.

"That another device for the protection of women who can afford to appeal, exists in the action of the Courts of Equity, which attempt, within certain limits, to redress the deficiencies of the law; but that trustees may prove dishonest or unwise in the management of the funds entrusted to their care, and Courts of Equity may fail in adjusting differences which concern the most intimate and delicate relation of life; that legal devices patched upon a law which is radically unjust, can only work clumsily, and that here, as in many other departments of justice, a clearance of the ground is the chief thing necessary. That since this is a

Petition to Parliament Signed by Elizabeth Barrett Browning, Elizabeth Gaskell, Jane Carlyle, Harriet Martineau, Barbara Leigh Smith, and Other Prominent Englishwomen, Presented in the House of Commons, 1857.

truth which has gradually come to be recognised in regard to protective restrictions upon trade, to titles of property in hand, and to legal machinery for conveying such property from one owner to another, etc., we would hope before long it will also come to be recognised in matrimonial legislation.

"That it is proved by well-known cases of hardship suffered by women of station, and also by professional women earning large incomes by pursuit of the arts, how real is the injury inflicted.

"That if these laws often bear heavily upon women protected by the forethought of their relations, the social training of their husbands, and the refined customs of the rank to which they belong, how much more unequivocal is the injury sustained by women in the lower classes, for whom no such provisions can be made by their parents, who possess no means of appeal to expensive legal protection, and in regard to whom the education of the husband and the habits of his associates offer no moral guarantee for tender consideration of his wife.

"That whereas it is customary in manufacturing districts to employ women largely in the processes of trade, and as women are also engaged as sempstresses, laundresses, charwomen, and in other multifarious occupations which cannot here be enumerated, the question must be recognised by all as of practical importance.

"That newspapers constantly detail instances of marital oppression, 'wife-beating' being a new compound noun lately introduced into the English language, and a crime against which English gentlemen have lately enacted stringent regulations.

"But that for the robbery by a man of his wife's hard earnings there is no redress; against the selfishness of a drunken father, who wrings from a mother her children's daily bread, there is no appeal. She may work from morning till night to see the produce of her labour wrested from her, and wasted in a gin palace; and such cases are within the knowledge of every one.

"That the law in depriving the mother of all pecuniary resources, deprives her of the power of giving schooling to her children, and in other ways providing for their moral and physical welfare; it obliges her in short to leave them to the temptations of the street, so fruitful in juvenile crime.

"That there are certain portions of the law of husband and wife which bear unjustly on the husband, as for instance that of making him responsible for his wife's debts, contracted before marriage, even although he may have no fortune with her. Her power also, after marriage, of contracting debts in the name of her husband, for which he is responsible, is too unlimited, and often produces injustice.

"That in rendering the husband responsible for the entire maintenance of his family, the law expresses the necessity of an age, when the man was the only money-getting agent, but that since the custom of the country has greatly changed in this respect the position of the female sex, the law of maintenance no longer meets the whole case. That since modern civilisation, in indefinitely extending the sphere of occupation for women, has in some measure broken down their pecuniary dependence upon men, it is time that legal protection be thrown over the produce of their labour, and that in entering the state of marriage, they no longer pass from freedom into the condition of a slave, all whose earnings belong to his master and not to himself.

"That the laws of various foreign countries are in this respect much more just than our own, and afford precedent for a more liberal precedent than prevails in England; and your Petitioners therefore humbly pray, that your Honourable House will take the foregoing allegations into consideration, and apply such remedy as to its wisdom shall seem fit.

"And your Petitioners will ever pray."

THE HISTORICAL CONTEXT: THE IRISH POTATO FAMINE

From Ireland and the Irish (1843)

Mother and Children, *The Illustrated London News* (August 12, 1843).

Courtesy of Yale University Library.

Connaught Man, *The Illustrated London News* (August 12, 1843). Courtesy of Yale University Library.

Leinster Cottage, *The Illustrated London News* (August 12, 1843). Courtesy of Yale University Library.

Idiot and Mother, *The Illustrated London News* (August 12, 1843).
Courtesy of Yale University Library.

JAMES MAHONY

Sketches in the West of Ireland (February 13, 1847)

Uncoffin'd, unshrouded, his bleak corpse they bore,
From the spot where he died on the Cabin's wet floor,
To a hole which they dug in the garden close by;
Thus a brother hath died — thus a Christian must lie!

Twas a horrible end and a harrowing tale,
To chill the strong heart — to strike revelry pale.
No disease o'er this Victim could mastery claim,
'Twas Famine alone mark'd his skeleton frame!

The bones of his Grandsire and Father too, rest
In the old Abbey-yard, by the holy rites blest;
Their last hours were sooth'd by affections fond cares,
Their last sighs were breath'd midst their Friends tearful prayers!

Unshriven, untended, this man pass'd away,
Ere Time streak'd one hair of his dark locks with gray,
His requiem the wild wind, and Ilen's hoarse roar,
As its swollen waves dash on the rock-girded shore.

C.C.T —.

The accounts from the Irish provincial papers continue to detail the unmitigated sufferings of the starving peasantry. Indeed, they are stated to be on the increase, notwithstanding the very great exertion of public bodies and individuals to assuage their pressure.

With the object of ascertaining the accuracy of the frightful statements received from the West, and of placing them in unexaggerated fidelity before our readers, a few days since, we commissioned our Artist, Mr. James Mahony, of Cork, to visit a seat of extreme suffering, viz., Skibbereen and its vicinity; and we now submit to our readers the graphic results of his journey, accompanied by such descriptive notes as he was enabled to collect whilst sketching the fearful incidents and desolate localities; premising merely, that our Artist must already have been somewhat familiar with such scenes of suffering in his own locality, (Cork), so that he cannot be supposed to have taken an *extreme* view of the greater misery at Skibbereen.

From *The Illustrated London News* (February 13, 1847).

"I started from Cork, by the mail (says our informant), for Skibbereen and saw little until we came to Clonakilty, where the coach stopped for breakfast; and here, for the first time, the horrors of the poverty became visible, in the vast number of famished poor, who flocked around the coach to beg alms: amongst them was a woman carrying in her arms the corpse of a fine child, and making the most distressing appeal to the passengers for aid to enable her to purchase a coffin and bury her dear little baby. This horrible spectacle induced me to make some inquiry about her, when I learned from the people of the hotel that each day brings dozens of such applicants into the town. (*See the Sketch* [below].)

Woman Begging at Clonakilty, *The Illustrated London News* (February 13, 1847).
Courtesy of Yale University Library.

"After leaving Clonakilty, each step that we took westward brought fresh evidence of the truth of the reports of the misery, as we either met a funeral or a coffin at every hundred yards, until we approached the picturesque country of the Shepperton Lakes. (*See the Sketch* [below].) Here, the distress became more striking, from the decrease of numbers at the funerals, none having more than eight or ten attendants, and many only two or three.

"We next reached Skibbereen, a general view of which I send you from Clover Hill House, the residence of J. Macarthy Downing, Esq.; and, it being then late I rested until Monday, when, with the valuable aid of Dr. D. Donovan, and his assistant, Mr. Crowley, I witnessed such scenes of misery and privation as I trust it may never be again my lot to look upon. Up to this morning, I, like a large portion, I fear, of the community, looked on the diaries of Dr. Donovan, as published in *The Cork Southern Reporter,* to be highly-coloured pictures, doubtless, intended for a good and humane purpose; but I can now, with perfect confidence, say that neither pen nor pencil ever could portray the misery and horror, at this moment, to be witnessed in Skibbereen. We first proceeded to Bridgetown, a portion of which is shown in the right hand distance of the sketch; and there I saw the dying, the living, and the dead, lying indiscriminately upon the same floor, without anything between them and the cold earth, save a few miserable rags upon them. To point to any particular house as a proof of this would be a waste of

Funeral at Shepperton Lakes, *The Illustrated London News* (February 13, 1847).
Courtesy of Yale University Library.

time, as all were in the same state; and, not a single house out of 500 could boast of being free from death and fever, though several could be pointed out with the dead lying close to the living for the space of three or four, even six days, without any effort being made to remove the bodies to a last resting place.

"After leaving this abode of death, we proceeded to High-street, or Old Chapel-lane (*See the Sketch* [below]), and there found one house, without door or window, filled with destitute people lying on the bare floor; and one, fine, tall, stout country lad, who had entered some hours previously to find shelter from the piercing cold, lay here dead amongst others likely soon to follow him. The appeals to the feelings and professional skill of my kind attendants here became truly heart-rending; and so distressed Dr. Donovan, that he begged me not to go into the house, and to avoid coming into contact with the people surrounding the doorway.

"We next proceeded to the Chapel-yard, to see the hut, of which Dr. Donovan gives the following graphic account in his diary: —

'On my return home, I remembered that I had yet a visit to pay; having in the morning received a ticket to see six members of one

Old Chapel-Lane, Skibbereen, *The Illustrated London News* (February 13, 1847).
Courtesy of Yale University Library.

family, named Barrett, who had been turned out of the cabin in which they lodged, in the neighbourhood of Old Chapelyard; and who had struggled to this burying-ground, and literally entombed themselves in a small watch-house that was built for the shelter of those who were engaged in guarding against exhumation by the doctors, when more respect was paid to the dead than is at present the case. This shed is exactly seven feet long, by about six in breadth. By the side of the western wall is a long, newly-made grave; by either gable are two of shorter dimensions, which have been recently tenanted; and near the hole that serves as a doorway is the last resting-place of two or three children; in fact, this hut is surrounded by a rampart of human bones, which have accumulated to such a height that the threshold, which was originally on a level with the ground, is now two feet beneath it. In this horrible den, in the midst of a mass of human putrefaction, six individuals, males and females, labouring under most malignant fever, were huddled together, as closely as were the dead in the graves around.

'At the time (eleven o'clock at night) that I went to visit the poor sufferers, it was blowing a perfect hurricane, and such groans of roaring wind and rain I never remember to have heard.

'I was accompanied by my assistant, Crowley, and we took with us some bread, tea and sugar; on reaching this vault, I thrust my head through the hole of entrance, and had immediately to draw back, so intolerable was the effluvium; and, though rendered callous by a companionship for many years with disease and death, yet I was completely unnerved at the humble scene of suffering and misery that was presented to my view; six fellow creatures were almost buried alive in this filthy sepulchre. When they heard my voice, one called out, "Is that the Priest?" another, "Is that the Doctor?" The mother of the family begged in the most earnest manner that I would have them removed, or else that they would 'rot together;' and they all implored that we would give them drink. Mr. Crowley produced the tea and sugar, but they said it was of no use to them, as they had no fire or place to light it in, and that what they wanted was *water;* that they had put a jug under the droppings from the roof, but would not have drink enough for the night. The next day I got the consent of the Poor Law Guardians to have my patients removed from this abode of the dead to the fever hospital, and they are since improving.'

"To complete my melancholy visit to this scene of horror, and to visit every corner of Skibbereen, next morning, accompanied by a Mr. Everett, whose knowledge of the country I found most useful, I started for Ballidichob, and learned upon the road that we should come to a hut or cabin in the parish of Aghadoe, on the property of Mr. Long, where four people had lain dead for six days; and, upon arriving at the hut, the abode of Tim Harrington, we found this to be true; for there lay the four bodies, and a fifth was passing to the same bourne. On hearing our voices, the sinking man made an effort to reach the door, and ask for drink or fire; he fell in the doorway; there, in all probability to lie; as the living cannot be prevailed to assist in the interments, for fear of taking the fever.

"We next got to Skull, where, by the attention of Dr. Traill, vicar of the parish (and whose humanity at the present moment is beyond all praise), we witnessed almost indescribable in-door horrors. In the street, however, we had the best opportunity of judging of the condition of the people; for here, from three to five hundred women, with money in their hands, were seeking to buy food; whilst a few of the Government officers doled out Indian meal to them in their turn. One of the women told me she had been standing there since daybreak, seeking to get food for her family at home.

"This food, it appeared, was being doled out in miserable quantities, at 'famine prices,' to the neighbouring poor, from a stock lately arrived in a sloop, with a Government steamship to protect its cargo of 50 tons; whilst the population amounts to 27,000; so that you may calculate what were the feelings of the disappointed mass.

"In my way out of the town, I made the accompanying Sketch [p. 311]; and, here, again, I had an opportunity of witnessing the efforts of the Vicar's family to relieve the affliction around them; and we met his daughters returning from their work of charity in the poorest portion of the town.

"Having returned to Skibbereen, my next object was to seek out the truth of the following extract from Dr. Donovan's Diary, as published in the *Cork Southern Reporter*, of Jan. 26: —

" 'A man of the name of Leahey died in the parish of Dromdaleague about a fortnight ago; his wife and two children remained in the house until the putrescent exhalations from the body drove them from their companionship with the dead; in a day or two after, some persons in passing the man's cabin, had their attention attracted by a loud snarling, and on entering, found the gnawed and mangled skeleton of Leahey contended for by hungry dogs.'

"This, I need not tell you, I looked upon as designed for an effect; and so I started for Dromdaleague, to reach which we had to pass through the miserable parish of Cahera, where, unless something be done for the poor, and that quickly and effectively, the result will be awful."

The Hut or Watch-House in the Old Chapel Yard, *The Illustrated London News* (February 13, 1847).
Courtesy of Yale University Library.

Here the report must terminate for the present. Next week we shall complete our painfully interesting series of Illustrations.

JAMES MAHONY

Sketches in the West of Ireland (February 20, 1847)

We resume from our Journal of last week our Artist's Sketches of Scenes and Incidents from the distressed district of Skibbereen, and its neighbourhood; premising that our main object in the publication of this Series of Illustrations is to direct public sympathy to the suffering poor of these localities, a result that must, inevitably, follow the right appreciation of their extent and severity.

We left our Artist, last week, on the road to Dromdaleague, to inquire into the horrible circumstances of Leahey's death.

From *The Illustrated London News* (February 20, 1847).

Boy and Girl at Cahera, *The Illustrated London News* (February 20, 1847). Courtesy of Yale University Library.

The first Sketch [above] is taken on the road, at Cahera, of a famished boy and girl turning up the ground to seek for a potato to appease their hunger. "Not far from the spot where I made this sketch," says Mr. M., "and less than fifty perches from the high road, is another of the many sepulchres above ground, where six dead bodies had lain for twelve days, without the least chance of interment, owing to their being so far from the town. After leaving this fearful spot, we soon reached Dromdaleague, where I called upon the Rev. J. Creedon, and inquired of him as to the fate of Leahey. 'Not only do I know the statement to be true,' replied the reverend gentleman, 'but also prepared the man for death, and am ready to accompany you to the spot.' We, accordingly, started; and, within half an hour's drive, reached the village of Meinies, where the house of Leahey is situated, and of which I send you a sketch [p. 313]. Whilst making this, I learned from Mr. Creedon, and one of the villagers, that not only was the account of Leahey's house in the Diary true, but the case was even more disgusting than there stated; and, horrifying as it was, the

The Village of Mienies, *The Illustrated London News* (February 20, 1847). Courtesy of Yale University Library.

man's mother, who found the dogs about him, after having first lain him across the few remaining sparks of fire upon the floor, went out to beg as much as would purchase a coffin to bury him in."

"Having heard much of the wants of Dunmanway, I proceeded thither, and am delighted to say that this large and thriving town (of which I send you a sketch, taken from the bridge on the Cork road) seems to be the barrier to the dreadful want further west. Not, at the same time, but that much want does exist here, though nothing beyond what may be expected upon land where nature is not bountiful. The worst feature presenting itself, at this moment, all through the West, is the entire abandonment of agricultural occupation; and, during my entire excursion from Clonakilty round to Dunmanway, not more than ten or a dozen fields seemed to have been prepared for the spring; and the answer of all those to whom I addressed myself on the subject was, that if they put down, they did not know who would reap; and that in case the crops were sown, the poor famished wretches would be there to eat them up long before they had time to grow.

"Again, all sympathy between the living and the dead seems completely out of the question; and the revolting practice will, doubtless, go on until it works its own remedy. I certainly saw from 150 to 180 funerals of victims to the want of food, the whole number attended by not more than 50 persons; and so hardened are the men regularly employed in the removal of the dead from the workhouses, that I saw one of them, with four coffins in a car, driving to the chuchyard, sitting upon one of the said coffins, and smoking with much apparent enjoyment. The people also say that whoever escapes the fever is sure of falling sick on the road (the Public Works), as they are, in many instances, compelled to walk from three to six miles, and sometimes a greater distance, to work, and back again in the evening, without partaking of a morsel of food. Added to this, they are, in a great number of instances, standing in bogs and wet places, which so affects them, that many of the poor fellows have been known to drop down at their work."

We must here revert to Ballydehob, on the Skibbereen road. Here he was told by the Rev. Mr. Triphook that the destitution was of so frightful a nature that such persons as could command five pounds were leaving the town, to avoid the contagion of fever, as well as the afflicting scene of persons dropping around them daily; and the informant added that the town was more than five times fuller of people from the surrounding country than it had accommodation for.

A specimen of the in-door horrors of Scull may be seen in the annexed sketch [below] of the hut of a poor man named Mullins, who lay dying in a corner upon a heap of straw, supplied by the Relief Com-

Mullins's Hut, at Scull, *The Illustrated London News* (February 20, 1847). Courtesy of Yale University Library.

mittee, whilst his three wretched children crouched over a few embers of turf, as if to raise the last remaining spark of life. This poor man, it appears, had buried his wife some five days previously, and was, in all probability, on the eve of joining her, when he was found out by the untiring efforts of the Vicar, who, for a few short days, saved him from that which no kindness could ultimately avert. Our Artist us assures that the dimensions of the hut do not exceed ten feet square; adding that, to make the sketch, he was compelled to stand up to his ancles in the dirt and filth upon the floor.

"I have thus," observes Mr. M., "been lengthy in my details in order that you may be as well informed upon the subjects as I can enable you to be; and, bearing in mind the horrifying scenes that I have just witnessed, I entreat you to do the best you can for so much suffering humanity; as this visit to the West will, I trust, assist in making this affliction known to the charitable public."

A Typical Gypsy Encampment Sited in the Wooded Areas around London in Mid-Century, *The Illustrated London News* (September 20, 1856).

Courtesy of Yale University Library.

Pig Fleeing Tent: A farmer's pig that does not like a gypsy tent. *The Illustrated London News* (January 3, 1880).

Courtesy of Yale University Library.

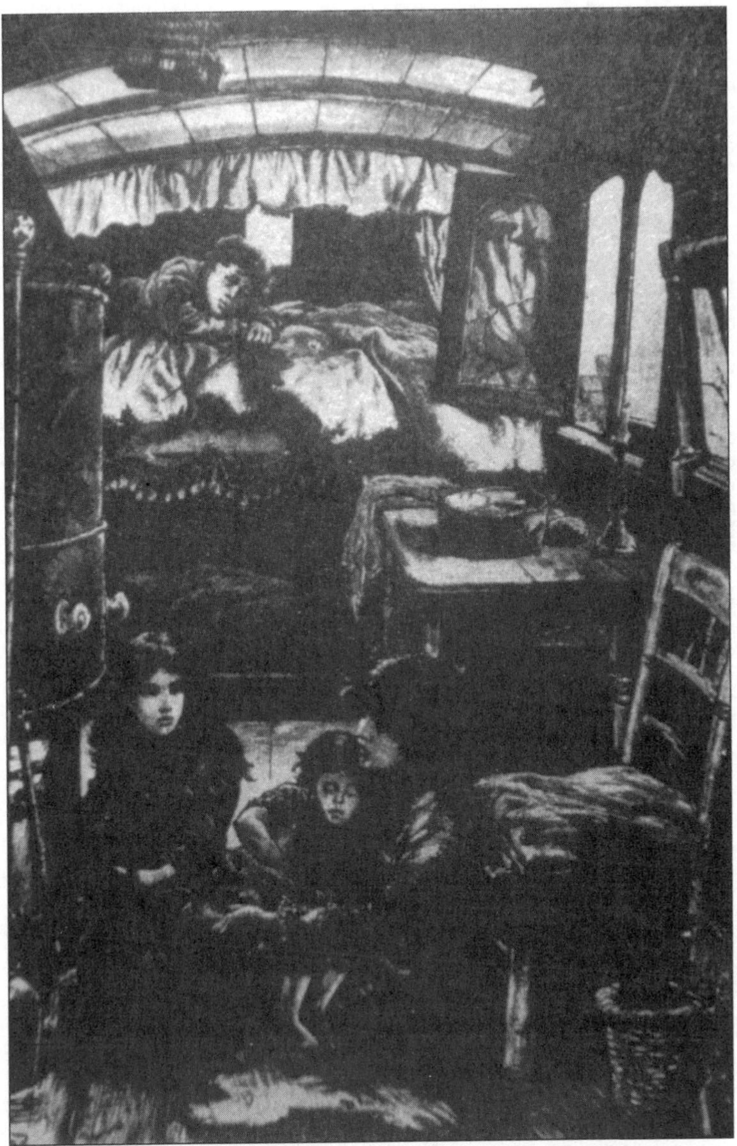

Sketches of Gypsy Life: Interior of a Gypsy Van near Lattimer Road, Notting-Hill, *The Illustrated London News* (December 6, 1879).
Courtesy of Yale University Library.

Lascars in London, from a painting by H. H. Flère. From Rozina Visram, *Ayahs, Lascars and Princes: Indians in Britain 1700–1947* (London: Pluto, 1986).

The East in the West: Oriental Sailors in the London Docks. From Rozina Visram, *Ayahs, Lascars and Princes: Indians in Britain 1700–1947* (London: Pluto, 1986).

Chinese Youths, *The Illustrated London News* (April 15, 1848).
Courtesy of Yale University Library.

Shere Sing and Ajeet Sing, *The Illustrated London News* (November 11, 1843).
Courtesy of Yale University Library.

The Captive, *The Illustrated London News* (April 22, 1848).
Courtesy of Yale University Library.

Mahmoud Shah, The Present King of Persia, illustration for "Our English Triumphs in the East," *The Illustrated London News* (November 26, 1842).
Courtesy of Yale University Library.

Indian Prince: The Maharajah of Kuch Behar, *The Illustrated London News* (October 15, 1887).
Courtesy of Yale University Library.

Indian Princess: The Maharanee of Kuch Behar, *The Illustrated London News* (October 15, 1887).

Courtesy of Yale University Library.

The Legal Context: English Inheritance Laws

WILLIAM BLACKSTONE

From William Blackstone's Commentaries on the Laws of England (1855)

CHAPTER XIV. OF TITLE BY DESCENT

The several *gradations* and *stages*, requisite to form a *complete title* to lands, tenements, and hereditaments, having been briefly stated in the preceding chapter, we are next to consider the several *manners*, in which this complete title (and therein principally the right of *property*) may be reciprocally lost and acquired: whereby the dominion of things real is either continued or transferred from one man to another. And here we must first of all observe, that (as gain and loss are terms of relation, and of a reciprocal nature) by whatever method one man gains an estate, by that same method or its correlative some other man has lost it. As where the heir acquires by descent, the ancestor has first lost or abandoned his estate by his death: where the lord gains land by escheat, the estate of the tenant is first of all lost by the natural or legal extinction of all his hereditary blood: where a man gains an interest by occupancy, the former owner has previously relinquished his right of possession: where one man claims by prescription or immemorial usage, another man has either parted with his right by an ancient and now forgotten grant, or has forfeited it by the supineness or neglect of himself and his ancestors for ages: and so, in case of forfeiture, the tenant by his own misbehaviour or neglect has renounced his interest in the estate; whereupon it devolves to that person who by law may take advantage of such default: and, in alienation by common assurances, the two considerations of loss and acquisition are so interwoven, and so constantly contemplated together, that we never hear of a conveyance, without at once receiving the ideas as well of the grantor as the grantee.

The methods therefore of acquiring on the one hand, and of losing on the other, a title to estates in things real, are reduced by our law to two: *descent*, where the title is vested in a man by the single operation of

From "Of Title by Descent" and "Of Title by Purchase and by Escheat," *Blackstone's Commentaries on the Laws of England,* Chapters XIV, XV (1855).

law; and *purchase,* where the title is vested in him by his own act or agreement.[1]

Descent, or hereditary succession, is the title whereby a man on the death of his ancestor acquires his estate by right of representation, as his heir at law. An heir therefore is he upon whom the law casts the estate immediately on the death of the ancestor[2]: and an estate, so descending to the heir, is in law called the inheritance.

The doctrine of descents, or law of inheritances in fee-simple, is a point of the highest importance; and is indeed the principal object of the laws of real property in England. All the rules relating to purchases, whereby the legal course of descents is broken and altered, perpetually refer to this settled law of inheritance, as a *datum* or first principle universally known, and upon which their subsequent limitations are to work. Thus a gift in tail, or to a man and the heirs of his body, is a limitation that cannot be perfectly understood without a previous knowledge

[1]Purchase in law is used in contradistinction to descent, and is any other mode of acquiring real property, viz. by a man's own art and agreement, by devise, and by every species of gift, or grant; and as the land taken by purchase has very different inheritable qualities from land taken by descent, the distinction is important.

The principal distinctions between these modes of acquiring estates are these; 1. that by purchase, the estate acquires a *new* inheritable quality, and is rendered descendible to the blood *in general* of the person, to whom it is limited, as a feud of indefinite antiquity. 2. That an estate acquired by purchase will not, like a title by descent, render the owner answerable for the acts of his ancestors.

It is a rule, that where the heir takes any thing which *might* have vested in the ancestor, the heir shall be in by descent, but where a person takes an estate which never vested or attached, or might have vested or attached, in the ancestor, he shall take by purchase: as if a son buys an estate and takes a conveyance to him and his heirs; or if a remainder be limited by a stranger to the right heirs of A. who has no estate in the premises, for the remainder might otherwise have been attracted to the particular estate of A. under the rule in Shelley's case, this will be an estate by purchase. The instances of persons taking by *descent* may be classed under the following heads: 1. Where an estate devolves in a regular course of descent from father to son, or from any other ancestor to his heir at law. 2. Where the ancestor, by any gift or conveyance takes an estate of freehold, and in the same conveyance, an estate is limited, either mediately or immediately to his heirs in fee or in tail (the estates becoming both united in the ancestor under the rule in Shelley's case). 3. Where an ancestor devises his estate to his heir at law (the heir then taking by his preferable title, viz. by descent). 4. Where an ancestor by deed, or his will, limits a particular estate to a stranger, and either limits over the remainder (or more properly speaking the reversion) to his right heirs, or leaves the same undisposed of.

[2] Yet though the lands are cast on the heir by the law itself, the heir has not *plenum dominium,* or full and complete ownership, till he has made an actual corporal entry into the lands: for if he dies before *entry* made, *his* heir shall not be entitled to take the possession, but the heir of the person who was last actually seised. It is not therefore only a mere right to enter, but the actual entry that makes a man complete owner; so as to transmit the inheritance to his own heirs: *non jus, sed seisina facit stipitem;* what a sufficient entry and seisin and what not.

of the law of descents in fee-simple. One may well perceive that this is an estate confined in its descent to such heirs only of the donee, as have sprung or shall spring from his body; but who those heirs are, whether all his children both male and female, or the male only, and (among the males) whether the eldest, youngest, or other son alone, or all the sons together, shall be his heirs; this is a point that we must result back to the standing law of descents in fee-simple to be informed of. . . .

I. The first rule is, that inheritances shall lineally descend to the issue of the person who last died actually seised *in infinitum;* but shall never lineally ascend.

To explain the more clearly both this and the subsequent rules, it must first be observed, that by law no inheritance can vest, nor can any person be the actual complete heir of another, till the ancestor is previously dead. *Nemo est haeres viventis.* Before that time the person who is next in the line of succession is called an *heir apparent,* or heir *presumptive.* Heirs *apparent* are such, whose right of inheritance is indefeasible, provided they outlive the ancestor; as the eldest son or his issue, who must by the course of the common law be heir to the father whenever he happens to die. Heirs *presumptive* are such who, if the ancestor should die immediately, would in the present circumstances of things be his heirs; but whose right of inheritance may be defeated by the contingency of some nearer heir being born; as a brother, or nephew, whose presumptive succession may be destroyed by the birth of a child; or a daughter, whose present hopes may be hereafter cut off by the birth of a son. Nay, even if the estate hath descended, by the death of the owner, to such brother, or nephew, or daughter, in the former cases, the estate shall be devested and taken away by the birth of a posthumous child; and, in the latter, it shall also be totally devested by the birth of a posthumous son. . . .

II. A second general rule or canon is, that the male issue shall be admitted before the female.

Thus sons shall be admitted before daughters; or, as our male lawgivers have somewhat uncomplaisantly expressed it, the worthiest of blood shall be preferred. As if John Stiles hath two sons, Matthew and Gilbert, and two daughters, Margaret and Charlotte, and dies; first Matthew, and (in case of his death without issue) then Gilbert shall be admitted to the succession in preference to both the daughters.

This preference of males to females is entirely agreeable to the law of succession among the Jews, and also among the states of Greece, or at least among the Athenians; but was totally unknown to the laws of Rome (such of them I mean as are at present extant), wherein brethren and sisters were allowed to succeed to equal portions of the inheritance. I shall not here enter into the comparative merit of the Roman and the other constitutions in this particular, nor examine into the greater dignity of blood in the male or female sex: but shall only observe, that our present preference of males to females seems to have arisen entirely from the feodal law. For though our British ancestors, the Welsh, appear to have given a preference to males, yet our Danish predecessors (who succeeded them) seem to have made no distinction of sexes, but to have admitted all the children at once to the inheritance. But the feodal law of the Saxons on the continent (which was probably brought over hither, and first altered by the law of king Canute) gives an evident preference of the male to the female sex. . . .

III. A third rule or canon of descent is this: that where there are two or more males, in equal degree, the eldest only shall inherit; but the females all together.[3]

As if a man hath two sons, Matthew and Gilbert, and two daughters, Margaret and Charlotte, and dies; Matthew his eldest son shall alone succeed to his estate, in exclusion of Gilbert the second son and both the daughters; but, if both the sons die without issue before the father, the daughters Margaret and Charlotte shall both inherit the estate as coparceners.

This right of primogeniture in males seems anciently to have only obtained among the Jews, in whose constitution the eldest son had a double portion of the inheritance; in the same manner as with us, by the laws of king Henry the First, the eldest son had the capital fee or principal feud of his father's possessions, and no other pre-eminence; and as the eldest daughter had afterwards the principal mansion, when the estate descended in coparcenary. The Greeks, the Romans, the Britons, the Saxons, and even originally the feudists, divided the lands equally; some among all the children at large, some among the males only. This is certainly the most obvious and natural way; and has the appearance, at least in the opinion of younger brothers, of the greatest impartiality and

[3]Daughters by different venters may inherit together as one heir to their common parent, though half blood is an impediment to the succession by descent from one to the other. Thus lord Hale says, "all the daughters, whether by the same or divers venters, do inherit together to the father." Therefore, if A. marries B. who dies leaving issue a daughter, and A. afterwards has issue one or more daughters by C. his second wife, and dies; all these daughters shall take his estate in equal shares among them in coparcenary, being equally his children. So Robinson says, all the daughters by different wives succeed to the inheritance of which their father was either seised in his own right, or to which their father would have been heir had he survived the person last seised. And the daughters by several husbands succeed, in the same manner, to the inheritance of their mother.

justice. But when the emperors began to create honorary feuds, or titles of nobility, it was found necessary (in order to preserve their dignity) to make them impartible, or (as they styled them) *feuda individua,* and in consequence descendible to the eldest son alone. . . .

IV. A fourth rule, or canon of descents, is this; that the lineal descendants, *in infinitum,* of any person deceased, shall represent their ancestor; that is, shall stand in the same place as the person himself would have done, had he been living.

Thus the child, grandchild, or great-grandchild (either male or female) of the eldest son succeeds before the younger son, and so *in infinitum.* And these representatives shall take neither more nor less, but just so much as their principals would have done. As if there be two sisters, Margaret and Charlotte; and Margaret dies, leaving six daughters; and then John Stiles, the father of the two sisters, dies without other issue: these six daughters shall take among them exactly the same as their mother Margaret would have done, had she been living. . . .

V. A fifth rule is, that on failure of lineal descendants, or issue, of the person last seised, the inheritance shall descend to his collateral relations, being of the blood of the first purchasor; subject to the three preceding rules.[4]

Thus if Geoffrey Stiles purchases land, and it descends to John Stiles his son, and John dies seised thereof without issue; whoever succeeds to this inheritance must be of the blood of Geoffrey, the first purchasor of this family.[5] The first purchasor, *perquisitor,* is he who first acquired the

[4]It should here be noticed, that though it is necessary that a person who would succeed must shew himself to be of the blood of the first purchasor; yet, where the persons who inherit, succeed or derive title to the inheritance, by virtue of remote and intermediate descents from the purchasor, it will be sufficient if they are related by half blood only to the purchasor, or to such other remote and intermediate ancestors who were formerly and intermediately seised of the inheritance in the regular course of descent from the purchasor, provided, according to the rule which follows, they are the worthiest legal relatives of the whole blood to the person last seised.

[5]To be of the blood of Geoffrey, is either to be immediately descended from *him,* or to be descended from the *same couple* of common ancestors. Two persons are *consanguinei,* or are of the blood (that is, whole blood) of each other, who are descended from the same two ancestors.

The heir and ancestor must not only have two common ancestors with the original purchasor of the estate, but must have two common ancestors with each other; and therefore if the son purchases lands and dies without issue, and it descends to any heir on the part of the father, if the line of the father should afterwards become extinct, it cannot pass to the line of the mother. And for the same reason, if it should descend to the line of any female, it can never afterwards, upon failure of that line, be transmitted to the line of any other female, for according to the next rule, viz. the sixth, the heir of the person last seised must be a collateral kinsman of the whole blood.

estate to his family, whether the same was transferred to him by sale or by gift, or by any other method, except only that of descent.

This is a rule almost peculiar to our own laws, and those of a similar original. For it was entirely unknown among the Jews, Greeks, and Romans: none of whose laws looked any farther than the person himself who died seised of the estate; but assigned him an heir, without considering by what title he gained it, or from what ancestor he derived it. . . .

VI. A sixth rule or canon therefore is, that the collateral heir of the person last seised must be his next collateral kinsman, of the *whole blood*.

First, he must be his next collateral kinsman, either personally or *jure representationis;* which proximity is reckoned according to the canonical degrees of consanguinity before mentioned. Therefore, the brother being in the first degree, he and his descendants shall exclude the uncle and his issue, who is only in the second. And herein consists the true reason of the different methods of computing the degrees of consanguinity, in the civil law on the one hand, and in the canon and common laws on the other. The civil law regards consanguinity, principally with respect to successions, and therein very naturally considers only the person deceased, to whom the relation is claimed: it therefore counts the degrees of kindred according to the number of persons through whom the claim must be derived from him; and makes not only his great-nephew but also his first-cousin to be both related to him in the fourth degree; because there are three persons between him and each of them. . . .

CHAPTER XV. OF TITLE BY PURCHASE AND BY ESCHEAT

Purchase, *perquisitio,* taken in its largest and most extensive sense, is thus defined by Littleton; the possession of lands and tenements, which a man hath by his own act or agreement, and not by descent from any of his ancestors or kindred. In this sense it is contradistinguished from acquisition by right of blood, and includes every other method of coming to an estate, but merely that by inheritance: wherein the title is vested in a person, not by his own act or agreement, but by the single operation of law.

Purchase, indeed, in its vulgar and confined acceptation, is applied only to such acquisitions of land, as are obtained by way of bargain and sale for money, or some other valuable consideration. But this falls far short of the legal idea of purchase: for, if I *give* land freely to another, he is in the eye of the law a purchasor, and falls within Littleton's definition, for he comes to the estate by his own agreement; that is, he consents to the gift. A man who has his father's estate settled upon him in tail, before he was born, is also a purchasor; for he takes quite another estate than the law of descents would have given him. Nay, even if the ancestor devises his estate to his heir at law by will, *with* other limitations, *or* in any other shape than the course of descents would direct, such heir shall take by purchase. . . .

The difference, in effect, between the acquisition of an estate by descent and by purchase, consists principally in these two points: 1. That by purchase the estate acquires a new inheritable quality, and is descendible to the owner's blood in general, and not the blood only of some particular ancestor. For, when a man takes an estate by purchase, he takes it not *ut feudum paternum* or *maternum,* which would descend only to the heirs by the father's or the mother's side: but he takes it *ut feudum antiquum,* as a feud of indefinite antiquity, whereby it becomes inheritable to his heirs general, first of the paternal, and then of the maternal line. 2. An estate taken by purchase will not make the heir answerable for the acts of the ancestor, as an estate by descent will. For if the ancestor, by any deed, obligation, covenant, or the like, bindeth himself and his heirs, and dieth; this deed, obligation, or covenant, shall be binding upon the heir, so far forth only as he (or any other in trust for him) had any estate of inheritance vested in him by descent from, (or any estate *per auter vie* coming to him by special occupancy, as heir to) that ancestor, sufficient to answer the charge; whether he remains in possession, or hath alienated it before action brought; which sufficient estate is in the law called *assets:* from the French word, *assez,* enough. Therefore if a man covenants, for himself and his heirs, to keep my house in repair, I can then (and then only) compel his heir to perform this covenant, when he has an estate sufficient for this purpose, at *assets,* by descent from the covenantor: for though the covenant descends to the heir, whether he inherits any estate or no, it lies dormant, and is not compulsory, until he has assets by descent.

PART TWO

Wuthering Heights: A Case Study in Contemporary Criticism

A Critical History of *Wuthering Heights*

Wuthering Heights — Emily Brontë's only novel — was published in mid-December 1847, along with her sister Anne's shorter fiction, *Agnes Grey.* Many stories surround the publication and early reception of *Wuthering Heights,* some true, others apocryphal. One (true) story explains how the three Brontë sisters each wrote a novel and sent their manuscripts to London publishers, hoping their work might appear together in the three-volume, "triple-decker" form popular in the mid-nineteenth century. Charlotte Brontë's novel, *The Professor,* was never accepted, however, and only after several rejections were the novels by Emily and Anne Brontë finally published together under the pseudonyms Ellis and Acton Bell.

A second story, probably apocryphal, goes on to explain how *Wuthering Heights* came to have two parts, the first about the elder Catherine and Heathcliff, the second about the younger Catherine, Linton Heathcliff, and Hareton Earnshaw. Because the publisher had rejected Charlotte's novel, he needed another manuscript to fill out his "triple-decker." Emily Brontë — so the story goes — quickly wrote the second half of *Wuthering Heights* to replace her sister's rejected manuscript and fill out the third volume. Critics who dislike the ending of the novel, or think the second half inferior to the first, sometimes propose this story in support of their views — despite the lack of substantiating facts.

A final story about *Wuthering Heights* is the most persistent, though again not factually accurate. This is the myth of Emily Brontë as a misunderstood genius and her novel as an unrecognized masterpiece. After the deaths of Emily and Anne, their sister Charlotte brought out a new edition of *Wuthering Heights* and *Agnes Grey* (1850). In a "Biographical Notice" attached to this second edition (pp. 15–21 in this volume), Charlotte accused literary critics of failing to do Emily's novel justice. "The immature but very real powers revealed in *Wuthering Heights* were scarcely recognized," Charlotte wrote; "its import and nature were misunderstood; the identity of its author was misrepresented" (p. 18). No doubt, Charlotte was deeply grieved by her sisters' deaths and by her conviction that they had not received sufficient praise for their literary work. But Charlotte either misremembered or misstated the facts. *Wuthering Heights* did not go unrecognized by its early readers. Literary critics repeatedly acknowledged its originality, genius, and imaginative power — if they also complained about its moral ambiguity.

A reviewer for the *Spectator* (December 18, 1847), a nineteenth-century literary magazine, praised Emily Brontë's execution as "good," her delineation of incidents as "forceful and truthful." The *Athenaeum* (December 25, 1847) noted the novel's "power and cleverness," a phrase echoed by the *Examiner* (January 1848) in its estimate of the work as one of "considerable power." Words like "powerful" and "original" and "strange" appear frequently in early reviews of *Wuthering Heights* — as if critics recognized the novel as an exceptional, compelling book, but could not quite figure out what to say about it or how to interpret it. Indeed, the reviewer for the *Literary World* (April 1848) admitted that, despite his hesitation about the book's merits, it was a real page-turner. "We are spellbound," he said, "we cannot choose but read."[1]

If reviewers praised *Wuthering Heights* for its literary merits, they also identified certain problems, particularly its "coarseness" and its "confusion." By "coarseness," they meant the vulgar and profane language that Brontë included in the dialogue. Today it seems strange that expressions like "Go to the Deuce!" or allusions to Catherine as a "bitch" should provoke a fury of moral outrage. But many nineteenth-century readers, especially Americans, objected to "the disgusting coarseness" of the dialogue and accused Ellis Bell of "an ill-mannered contempt for the decencies of language." One American critic even accused Brontë of trying to "corrupt the virtues of the sturdy descendants of the Puritans" (Allott 247–8). Sometimes, too, critics found "coarseness" in the plot and char-

[1]Unsigned reviews collected in Allott, *The Critical Heritage,* pp. 217, 218, 220, 232.

acters. They sensed a "moral taint" about the novel, an obsession with evil, diabolical behavior. In their reviews they argued that novels should depict positive, not just degraded, features of humanity. As the critic for the *Literary World* put it, "In the whole story not a single trait of character is elicited which can command our admiration, not one of the fine feelings of our nature seems to have formed a part in the composition of its principal actors" (Allott 234).

Whether or not we share these judgments, we can see how they led to the further criticisms of the novel: criticisms of its "confusion" or "wildness." By "confusion," critics did not mean that the plot of *Wuthering Heights* was difficult to follow (though one claimed it was hard to "disentangle the incidents and set them forth in chronological order," perhaps because he was too lazy to make the effort [Allott 221]). Rather, critics meant that the novel was morally confused, that it failed to make its "message" clear. "There seems to be great power in this book but a purposeless power" (Allott 228), one reviewer wrote. "The villainy [does] not lead to results sufficient to justify the elaborate pains taken in depicting it," said a second (Allott 225). Such critics were troubled by their inability to discover the meaning of Brontë's text, especially a "meaning" that coincided with their sense of social morality or poetic justice. Already in 1850, they were formulating versions of questions we still ask today: What is *Wuthering Heights* about? What does it mean? How should we interpret it? Is it a subversive novel?

Since its publication, readers have attempted to answer these questions, using a variety of critical strategies. Emily Brontë's sister, Charlotte, was among the first to propose some solutions in her "Editor's Preface to the New [1850] Edition of Wuthering Heights" (pp. 21–24). To complaints of the novel's coarseness, Charlotte Brontë pointed out that her sister was not a town dweller, but "a native of the moors," and that she accurately reproduced "the rough strong utterance, the harshly manifested passions, the unbridled aversions, and headlong partialities" of the "unlettered moorland hinds and rugged moorland squires" among whom she grew up. To suggestions that Emily had written a book with a "moral taint," Charlotte responded by saying that Emily never intended it: "she did not know what she had done."

Charlotte's phrase — "she did not know what she had done" — has had multiple reverberations in subsequent criticism. Charlotte meant that the creative artist works by inspiration, that she (or he) "is not always master" of what she creates. The inspired artist, Charlotte believed, must "work passively under dictates you neither delivered nor could question": "Be the work grim or glorious, dread or divine, you have little choice but quiescent adoption." Thus the artist is never fully aware of, nor fully responsible for, the work of art she produces. This Romantic explanation of Emily Brontë as an inspired artist has led many critics to search for the unconscious meanings of *Wuthering Heights;* it has influenced psychoanalytic criticism and certain kinds of formalist and feminist work in the twentieth century. But, in her 1850 preface to *Wuthering Heights,* Charlotte Brontë also pointed to more immediate sources of her sister's inspiration: to the "tragic and terrible" tales told by local villagers, to "their ways, their language, their family histories." From the search for these sources have come various biographical, historical, and cultural approaches to the novel.

Following Charlotte Brontë's lead, the best nineteenth-century analyses of *Wuthering Heights* emphasized the psychological truth revealed in the novel's plot and characters. Critic and poet Sydney Dobell, for instance, praised Emily Brontë for the "instinctive art" that enabled her to capture the "deep, unconscious" truth of Catherine Earnshaw's personality. He pointed to the psychological conflict within Catherine's "two natures" and the uncanny accuracy with which Brontë prepares for and then depicts Catherine's delirium. According to Dobell, Brontë understood that certain "crimes and sorrows are not so much the result of intrinsic evil as of a false position in the scheme of things" (Allott 281) — a view that anticipates feminist discussions of Catherine's dilemma as psychosocial in origin.

Another nineteenth-century critic, Peter Bayne, similarly approached the novel as "a psychological study" but focused on Heathcliff rather than on Catherine. Whereas many early readers dismissed Heathcliff simply as "evil incarnate," Bayne believed that Brontë meant to depict the psychological forces underlying his actions: "we watch that boyish heart, until, in the furnace of hopeless and agonizing passion, it becomes as insensible to any tender emotion, to any emotion save one, as a mass of glowing iron to trickly dew" (Allott 323).[2] Bayne's descriptions of the novel as "a dream at which we gaze" and a "dream we can never forget" (Allott 323) stress the hallucinatory elements of Brontë's work and anticipate twentieth-century psychoanalytic criticism which, following Freud, treats the literary text as dream material to be interpreted by the literary critic. Bayne's attention to Heathcliff also anticipates later divisions

[2]See also the unsigned review in the *Galaxy,* February 1873, for a view of the novel as "a profound psychological study and complete history of human life and love" (Allott 392–96), and T. W. Reid, who compares Emily Brontë's "wonderful portraits" with the work of "some psychologist, learned in the secrets of morbid human nature" (Allott 400).

among critics over whether primary attention should be paid to the male hero, Heathcliff, or to the two female heroines, both named Catherine.

Most nineteenth-century critics, however, were less interested in psychology than in searching for the biographical, historical, or literary sources of the novel. Today critics tend to prefer other forms of textual analysis, but the sleuthwork of these early biographer-critics unearthed much of what we know about Emily Brontë's life and the imaginative world in which she was immersed.

Brontë's first biographer-critic, A. Mary F. Robinson, traced aspects of Heathcliff's behavior to the experiences of Branwell Brontë, Emily's older brother. While tutoring for a private family, Branwell had fallen in love with the mother of his pupils. The father discovered the affair and, in an insulting letter, dismissed Branwell from his job. Returning home in disgrace, Branwell took to drinking and smoking opium (a common nineteenth-century form of drug addiction). According to Robinson, Branwell's ravings while under the influence resemble Heathcliff's (and later Hindley's) mad, drunken behavior. Robinson even noted parallels between Branwell's letters and Heathcliff's passionate outbursts of love for Catherine:

> BRANWELL: "My own life without her will be hell. What can the so-called love of her wretched sickly husband be to her compared with mine?"
>
> HEATHCLIFF: "Two words would comprehend my future — death and hell; existence after losing her would be hell. Yet I was a fool to fancy for a moment that she valued Edgar Linton's attachment more than mine. If he loved with all the powers of his puny being, he couldn't love in eighty years as much as I could in a day." (Robinson 217)

Typical of early critics, Robinson used a "real" person — in this case Branwell — to explain how an innocent, inexperienced female writer like Brontë could have created a wicked, diabolical male character like Heathcliff.

Other biographer-critics sought the source of Heathcliff's story in local legends and history. One legend involved Jack Sharp, a Heathcliff-like usurper who built Law Hill, the country house which later became the school where Emily briefly taught. Sharp was the orphaned nephew of a man named John Walker, whose estate, Walterclough Hall, stood about a mile from Law Hill. Walker adopted young Jack Sharp and trained him in the wool trade, sending his own sons away to college, just as old Mr. Earnshaw sends Hindley away. While the sons were gone, Jack Sharp supplanted them in Walker's affection and finances — to the extent that the eldest son was virtually unable to reclaim Walterclough Hall when his father died. Eventually, the son did recover the estate, but only after Jack Sharp had stripped it of furniture and fixtures and transported them to his rival establishment, Law Hill. When Emily Brontë taught at Law Hill in 1838, Jack Sharp had long been bankrupt and dead. But the granddaughter of John Walker was still living in the region. Whether or not Emily met Miss Walker, she may have heard the local legend and adapted it as the basis for *Wuthering Heights.*[3]

Biographer-critics of the nineteenth century approached *Wuthering Heights* as if the key to interpreting the novel lay in real people and real events. They assumed that literary criticism ought to explore the relation between fiction and our experiences in the world, between "literature" and "reality." If this assumption led some to complain that the novel was unrealistic or overly obsessed with evil, perhaps it was because their views of "reality" differed from Emily Brontë's. Those who shared views closer to hers continued to exonerate *Wuthering Heights* from charges of coarseness and moral confusion by showing parallels between its plot and their experiences in the world.

Not all nineteenth-century critics believed that moral questions should dominate discussions of *Wuthering Heights* or that the novel could be explained by tracing its connections to real people and events. Another important mode of criticism focused on literary sources for the novel, sometimes turning to French or German "Gothic" tales,[4] at other times turning to English poets such as Byron, whose outcast figures — Cain, Manfred, Lara — resemble Heathcliff in their passionate intensity and lawlessness.[5] Byron's Lara, for example, has origins as mysterious as Heathcliff's:

> He stood a stranger in this breathing world,
> An erring spirit from another hurl'd . . .

[3]The first research on Emily Brontë's experiences at Law Hill was done by Ellis A. Chadwick in *In the Footsteps of the Brontës;* more recently, this research was expanded by Edward Chitham in *A Life of Emily Brontë* (pp. 100–21).

[4]Possible German sources for *Wuthering Heights* were mentioned as early as 1848 in the *Britannia* but were first systematically discussed by Mary Ward in her preface to the Haworth edition of the novel (1898).

[5]Allusions to Byronic heroes were noticed as early as 1848 in the *Examiner,* where the reviewer linked Heathcliff to the Corsair as "melodramatic heroes" who are "Linked to one virtue and a thousand crimes" (Allott 220). The Byronic influences have more recently been discussed by Winifred Gérin in *Emily Brontë: A Biography* (44–46) and by Andrew Elfenbein, *Byron and the Victorians.*

What had he been? What was he, thus unknown?
Who walked their world, his lineage all unknown?

Byron's Manfred suffers from a fatal love; Cain, from an unforgivable crime. All were offered as possible models for Heathcliff.

Besides Byron, it was to Emily Brontë herself and to her early poetry that critics turned for the sources of *Wuthering Heights.* In the Gondal poems, Emily had created a fair-haired heroine, intense but fickle in love, and several dark-haired heroes, all fatally attracted to the heroine. Fannie E. Ratchford, a Brontë scholar of the 1950s, assembled Emily's poems into a narrative titled *Gondal's Queen,* arguing that these poetic figures from Gondal are the precursors of Catherine and Heathcliff. In the Gondal poems, Ratchford believed, we "glimpse *Wuthering Heights* in the making" (37).

By turning to literary sources for *Wuthering Heights,* such critics suggest — contrary to their more biographically oriented counterparts — that literature originates not so much in "real life" as in other literature. Or, to put it another way, that the literature we read is as much a part of real life as anything else that happens to us. The literary texts we create respond to the literary texts we have read: they imitate, they revise, they modify, they reject their predecessors. Thus, in creating a hero like Heathcliff, Emily Brontë was acknowledging Byron's influence and, in a sense, imitating him; but, in creating Catherine, she was also revising Byron and showing a fundamentally masculine myth as it might look from a feminine (or feminist) perspective. More sophisticated versions of this approach continue in contemporary twentieth-century criticism — in, for example, Harold Bloom's reading of *Wuthering Heights* as a critique of Byron's *Manfred,* or in *The Madwoman in the Attic,* where Sandra Gilbert and Susan Gubar argue that Brontë revises the Miltonic myth of the fall, or in *Tradition, Countertradition,* where Joseph Boone shows Brontë playing a traditional novelistic plot of courtship and marriage against a more radical (and modern) plot of wedlock as deadlock.

Modern criticism of *Wuthering Heights* begins earlier, however, with readers who took Brontë's artistry seriously and focused on her literary achievements. As the nineteenth-century criticism reveals, Brontë's artistry was not completely neglected in her own century. Matthew Arnold paid tribute to his fellow poet

whose soul
Knew no fellow for might,

> Passion, vehemence, grief,
> Daring, since Byron died.

Another Victorian poet, Algernon Charles Swinburne, wrote extensively about "the passionate great genius of Emily Brontë," and the late Victorian novelist Mary Ward extensively analyzed the literary sources that shaped Brontë's art. Just after the turn of the century, Virginia Woolf praised Brontë as one who "looked out upon a world cleft into gigantic disorder and felt within her the power to unite it in a book" (159). These writer-critics tended to praise Brontë in general terms rather than look specifically at her literary craft.

Close attention to Brontë's artistry begins with C. P. Sanger's *The Structure of* Wuthering Heights (1926) and Lord David Cecil's *Early Victorian Novelists* (1935), both of which sought to reclaim *Wuthering Heights* from the long-standing charge of confusion and incoherence. Sanger was an English barrister who pointed out Brontë's impressive knowledge of property and inheritance laws and who showed, through detailed charts, how carefully Brontë had worked out the chronology of the novel.[6] Cecil's book was a broader attempt to "illuminate those aesthetic qualities" of Victorian novels "which can still make them a living delight to readers," but he believed that, of all Victorian novels, *Wuthering Heights* was "the one perfect work of art amid the vast varied canvasses of Victorian fiction" (22, 192).

Cecil argued that the novel was constructed on the cosmic principles of "storm" and "calm." He showed how the two major locales of Brontë's setting — Wuthering Heights and Thrushcross Grange — embody these principles and how various characters emerge as either children of storm (Heathcliff, Catherine) or children of calm (Edgar and Isabella Linton). According to this pattern, characters find fulfillment when they unite with a partner for whom they have a natural affinity — as in Catherine's love for Heathcliff "because he's more myself than I am." Things go wrong when characters of storm link themselves wrongly to characters of calm — as in Catherine's marriage to Edgar or Heathcliff's to Isabella. Cecil argued that the novel ends perfectly with the marriage of the younger Catherine and Hareton, both of whom are mixtures of storm and calm and combine the best traits of both realms.

Although Sanger and Cecil were responding to long-standing criticisms, they also helped to establish a basis for subsequent interpreta-

[6]See also the selection from *Blackstone's Commentaries on the Laws of England*, pp. 324–30.

tions of *Wuthering Heights.* In effect, they argued that interpretation should proceed from an analysis of the *formal* elements of the novel, not from preconceived *moral* or *social* standards imposed on the text. Thus Cecil argued against those critics who (mis)read the conflict in *Wuthering Heights* as one "between right and wrong"; rather, it is "between like and unlike," between "conditioning forces of life" that provide the cosmic scheme and artistic principle of the novel (154–55). Cecil was not a "formalist" per se, but like the New Critics who came to dominate Anglo-American criticism in the mid-twentieth century, he paid close attention to the "formal" elements of *Wuthering Heights*: to the narrative strategies, the setting, the symbols, the recurring metaphors, motifs, and imagery that help us discern the aesthetic unity and inherent meaning of a literary work.

The New Criticism, dominant from the 1940s through the 1960s, produced a plethora of critical studies that analyzed such elements in Brontë's novel. One frequent focus of critical attention was on Brontë's use of dual narrators, a technique virtually unprecedented in English fiction. For some critics, such as Sanger and later Bonamy Dobrée, using a commonsensical narrator like Nelly Dean gives credibility to an otherwise difficult tale; Nelly makes the reader "believe it, wholly and utterly accept it," and Lockwood "clinches Nelly's statements; he confirms for us the ghastly truth of what she tells" (Dobrée 112–13, 115). For more skeptical New Critics, however, the dual narrators introduce the problem of ambiguity. As John K. Mathison pointed out in "Nelly Dean and the Power of *Wuthering Heights*" (1956), Nelly's common sense represents a liability as well as an asset in that she can understand and sympathize with conventional actions and emotions, but cannot comprehend the greater passions and social issues that Catherine and Heathcliff raise. Thus "the reader continually decreases in sympathy with a type that he would usually admire," for Nelly reveals "the futility of a tolerant, common-sense attitude which is the result of a desire merely to avoid trouble, to deny serious problems, and to grasp genuinely the emotions of others" (129).

Besides analyzing narrative techniques, New Critics focused on patterns of imagery or recurring symbolism in the novel (a critical choice influenced by the New Criticism's initial concern with the study of poetry and perhaps by the critical tradition that treated *Wuthering Heights* as a "poetic" novel). In "Fiction and the Matrix of Analogy" (1949), a seminal New Critical analysis of *Wuthering Heights,* Mark Schorer noted two dominant imagistic patterns: (1) animal imagery, which Brontë uses to characterize, satirize, or villify her characters, and

(2) imagery of fire, wind, and water, which Brontë associates with elemental human emotions. For Schorer, such imagery reveals a tension between a novelist's conscious and unconscious intentions. In the grand passion of Heathcliff and Catherine, Brontë intended to dramatize "the sense of a stupendous self and an insignificant world"; but what the novel teaches through its imagery is quite different: "the impermanence of the self and the permanence of something larger," death and the survival of nature (Schorer 545).

Other New Critics focused on structural patterns and recurring motifs in *Wuthering Heights.* In "The Circumambient Universe" (1964) J. Frank Goodridge used the two houses — the Heights and the Grange — to explore the metaphors of "exposure" and "enclosure" and to suggest that Brontë depicts "incompatible ways of life"; the novel, in Goodridge's reading, "leads us to question whether there is any one natural and social order, the same for all men and women" (77). In *The English Novel: Form and Function* (1953) Dorothy Van Ghent similarly used paired motifs — the "window" and the "two children" figures — but to reach a different conclusion about the novel's meaning. Van Ghent argued that the various windows (which appear in Lockwood's dream, in Catherine and Heathcliff's first vision of Thrushcross Grange, in Catherine's scenes of delirium, in Heathcliff's death) serve to separate the "inside" from the "outside," the "human" from the alien and terrible "other" (159–64). Windows embody the tension in the novel between two kinds of reality: "the raw, inhuman reality of anonymous natural energies, and the restrictive reality of civilized habits, manners, and codes" (157). Pairs of characters attempt to break through the windows that separate them, hoping to unite the two kinds of reality and the qualities of both sides. Most attempts are unsuccessful, but, in Van Ghent's view, *Wuthering Heights* ends with a successful union in the "domestic romance" of the younger Catherine and Hareton. Unlike David Cecil, who found the novel's ending "perfect," Van Ghent admits that "this successful metamorphosis and mating" suppresses the "daemonic quality" of the "other": "The great magic, the wild power, of the original two has been lost" (169–70).

How could three critics, all analyzing formal elements, reach such different conclusions about the ending of *Wuthering Heights*? The fact that critics frequently reach conflicting interpretations may seem illogical — certainly perplexing — and such differences become even more evident if we add a fourth famous (or perhaps infamous) formalist analysis of the novel. In "What Is the Matter with Emily Jane?: Conflicting Impulses in *Wuthering Heights*" (1962), Thomas Moser treats the same motifs of the window and door that Van Ghent does, but, adding Freudian theory to New Critical analysis, Moser suggests that these are "female" symbols, just as the key and the poker are "male," "phallic" symbols. Moser sees sexual symbolism throughout the novel and argues that "the primary traits which Freud ascribed to the *id* apply perfectly to Heathcliff: the source of psychic energy; the seat of the instincts (particularly sex and death); the essence of dreams; the archaic foundation of personality — selfish, asocial, impulsive" (4). In focusing on Heathcliff, Moser does not share Cecil's or Van Ghent's opinion that Brontë brings *Wuthering Heights* to a successful conclusion. For him, when Heathcliff goes, the energy and interest of the novel go, too. Hareton, in his romance with the younger Catherine, is by comparison a weak, emasculated hero, and the ending of the novel, pallid compared with the first half.

Such differences among critics led to questions about the validity of formalist approaches. To New Critics, "the fact that such differences are possible" is "a tribute to the novel's richness and fascination" (Daiches 15). In a sense, this is true. But not everyone held this opinion of formalist criticism. As J. Hillis Miller observes in "*Wuthering Heights*: Repetition and the 'Uncanny'" (1982), "each [critic] takes some one element in the novel and extrapolates it toward a total explanation. . . . All literary criticism tends to be the presentation of what claims to be the definitive rational explanation of the text in question" (50). For Miller, this critical technique — extrapolating meaning from one element of the novel — cannot suffice. The problem is particularly acute for formalists, who seek the "aesthetic unity" of literary texts. To a deconstructionist like Miller, aesthetic unity is an illusion; *the text itself* tends to deconstruct its own meanings, to contain conflicting and contradictory sets of possibilities for the reader to negotiate. The critic must acknowledge these conflicting possibilities. Indeed, in *Fiction and Repetition* (1982) Miller repudiates his own earlier analysis of Emily Brontë, published in *The Disappearance of God* (1963), in which he had used a phenomenological approach (a version of formalism that seeks to understand the controlling metaphors of an author's entire life's work or oeuvre) to argue that *Wuthering Heights* fictionalizes Brontë's religious vision as expressed in her poems and essays.

Not all critics who question formalism are deconstructionists. There has been a long tradition of historically based criticism of *Wuthering Heights* that grounds interpretation in the social, political, and economic context of the mid-nineteenth century. In *An Introduction to the English Novel* (1951), for example, Arnold Kettle boldly stated, "*Wuthering*

Heights is about England in 1847 and the years before" — not about Byron or Gondal or some other fictional realm (130). For Kettle the values embodied by Thrushcross Grange are "not simply the values of *any* tyranny but specifically those of Victorian society," and the rebellion of Heathcliff is "a particular rebellion, that of the worker physically and spiritually degraded by the conditions and relationships of this same society." The novel thus expresses, in the imaginative terms of art, "the stresses and tensions and conflicts, personal and spiritual, of nineteenth-century capitalist society" (144). Brontë's artistry consists, in Kettle's view, of making the reader sympathize with Heathcliff, a representative of the working classes, even when his actions are extreme and "dreadful." Heathcliff functions as a "moral force" who shows the limited humanity of bourgeois characters like Edgar Linton or Hindley Earnshaw (an argument, we might note, that implicitly answers nineteenth-century charges of "moral confusion").

In analyzing *Wuthering Heights,* Kettle draws on Marxist theory to explain the conflicts in the novel, as his references to the proletariat, bourgeoisie, and capitalist England suggest. Another eminent English critic, Raymond Williams, also used Marxism in *The English Novel from Dickens to Lawrence* (1970), though he did not translate Marxist terms and theories so directly into his reading of *Wuthering Heights.* For Williams, Brontë's novel registers "the unprecedented disturbance of those English years" (50) surrounding 1847, but the disturbance is displaced onto the personal, emotional crises the novel represents. According to Williams, when transformative historical events occur, we need not look in art only "for direct or public historical event and response"; "it can appear as radically and as authentically in what is apparently, what is actually, personal or family experience" (54).

How to use Marxist criticism — whether to demonstrate direct correspondences between the novel's plot and the social, economic, and political forces that produced it or whether to expect some sort of "displacement" from historical to fictional context — is a question that Terry Eagleton takes up in his discussion of *Wuthering Heights* included in his *Myths of Power: A Marxist Study of the Brontës* (see pp. 394–410 in this volume). It is too easy, Eagleton believes, to say that all novels are political novels, all drama historical drama, or all poems social poems. Such statements do "little to broach the question of how literature and society are actually related" (p. 3). According to Eagleton, the challenging question for the Marxist critic is: What relationship holds between the imaginative fiction of the Brontës and the society of their time?

It is appropriate that one modern tradition of interpreting *Wuthering Heights* should derive from Marxist theory, for both Brontë's novel and Marx's theoretical work originate in mid-nineteenth-century Europe. Both writers experienced and responded to the historical forces of industrial capitalism, Brontë in her native region of Yorkshire, where the working-class movement was powerful, and Marx in Germany and later England, where he wrote *Das Kapital* (in the British Museum). Although Brontë did not — indeed, could not — have known Marx or his work, her novel registers, as Eagleton explains, the tensions between the values of the older landed gentry and the newer industrial bourgeoisie.

It is equally appropriate, however, that two other strong nineteenth-century intellectual traditions — psychoanalysis and feminism — should contribute to modern criticism of *Wuthering Heights.* Psychoanalysis began, of course, later in the nineteenth century with the pioneering theoretical work of Freud and his fellow "alienists." But as we saw from the early reviews of *Wuthering Heights,* an interest in psychological motivation dates from the mid-nineteenth century and pervades discussions of Brontë's characters, especially Heathcliff. Modern psychoanalytic critics have applied multiple theories to Brontë's novel, finding everything from Freudian "phallic" symbols to Jungian archetypes to traits of vampirism and lycanthropy (werewolfism). Philip K. Wion's analysis, "The Absent Mother in *Wuthering Heights,*" takes a less extreme (and more convincing) approach by combining details from Brontë's life and literary work with modern psychology's understanding of childhood development, particularly the separation-individuation process that children undergo in relation to their mothers.

So, too, a long tradition of feminism contributes to modern interpretations of *Wuthering Heights.* Emily Brontë was less explicit than her sister Charlotte on issues that nineteenth-century women's rights advocates took up, such as the right to hold property after marriage or the right to a university education or a profession. Nevertheless, Brontë's novel is especially keen in its understanding of the psychosocial tensions women felt in courtship and marriage, and it addresses specific injustices that Victorian feminists fought against, including the inability of women to hold property in their own names, which the Married Women's Rights and Property Act eventually corrected in 1870. Modern feminist interpretations of *Wuthering Heights* do not derive directly from Victorian feminism (although some, including Lyn Pykett's "Changing the Names: The Two Catherines," pp. 468–77, focus on the

Victorian social context). Rather, feminist criticism today tends to have its roots either in the empirically based feminism of Anglo-Americans or in the more theoretically oriented work of French feminists. Lyn Pykett's essay originates in the former tradition and addresses the social and political issues that the English *Bildungsroman* (the novel of development) raises about a young woman's maturation process at mid-nineteenth century.

Finally, within the last decade, we have witnessed a flourishing of cultural studies, as in Nancy Armstrong's "Imperialist Nostalgia and *Wuthering Heights*," and a blending of approaches, as literary critics have combined the insights of feminism, Marxism, new historicism, and cultural studies. Susan Meyer's synthetic essay, "'Your Father Was Emperor of China, and Your Mother an Indian Queen': Reverse Imperialism in *Wuthering Heights*," applies the methods of feminism and Marxism to understand power relations within the novel, even as it draws upon new interests in postcolonial and imperial studies to analyze the frequent allusions in *Wuthering Heights* that affiliate Heathcliff with the dark racial "other" who both constituted and threatened Britain's vast empire in the nineteenth century.

WORKS CITED

Allott, Miriam, ed. *The Brontës: The Critical Heritage*. London: Routledge & Kegan Paul, 1974.

Bloom, Harold, ed. Introduction. *Emily Brontë's Wuthering Heights*. New York: Chelsea, 1987.

Boone, Joseph Allen. *Tradition Counter Tradition: Love and the Forum of Fiction*. Chicago: U of Chicago P, 1987.

Cecil, Lord David. *Early Victorian Novelists*. London: Constable, 1935.

Chadwick, Ellis A. *In the Footsteps of the Brontës*. London: Sir Isaac Pitman, 1914.

Chitham, Edward. *A Life of Emily Brontë*. Oxford: Basil Blackwell, 1987.

Daiches, David. Introduction. *Wuthering Heights*. By Emily Brontë. Harmondsworth: Penguin, 1965.

Dobrée, Bonamy. "The Narrator in 'Wuthering Heights.'" 1953. Rpt. in *Wuthering Heights: An Anthology of Criticism*. Ed. Alastair Everitt. London: Frank Cass, 1967.

Eagleton, Terry. *Myths of Power: A Marxist Study of the Brontës.* London: Macmillan, 1975.

Elfenbein, Andrew. *Byron and the Victorians.* Cambridge: Cambridge UP, 1995.

Gérin, Winifred. *Emily Brontë: A Biography.* Oxford: Clarendon, 1971.

Gilbert, Sandra, and Susan Gubar. *The Madwoman in the Attic: The Woman Writer and the Nineteenth Century Literary Imagination.* New Haven: Yale UP, 1979.

Goodridge, J. Frank. "The Circumambient Universe." *Emily Brontë: Wuthering Heights.* London: Edward Arnold, 1964.

Kettle, Arnold. *An Introduction to the English Novel: Defoe to the Present.* Rev. ed. New York: Harper, 1968.

Mathison, John K. "Nelly Dean and the Power of *Wuthering Heights.*" *Nineteenth-Century Fiction* 11 (1956): 106–29.

Miller, J. Hillis. *The Disappearance of God: Five Nineteenth-Century Writers.* Cambridge, MA: Belknap, 1963.

———. "*Wuthering Heights:* Repetition and the 'Uncanny.'" *Fiction and Repetition: Seven English Novels.* Cambridge: Harvard UP, 1982.

Moser, Thomas. "What Is the Matter with Emily Jane?: Conflicting Impulses in *Wuthering Heights.*" *Nineteenth-Century Fiction* 17 (1962): 1–19.

Ratchford, Fannie E. *Gondal's Queen: A Novel in Verse.* Austin: U of Texas P, 1955.

Robinson, A. Mary F. *Emily Brontë.* Boston: Roberts Brothers, 1883.

Sanger, C. P. *The Structure of* Wuthering Heights. London: Hogarth, 1926.

Schorer, Mark. "Fiction and the Matrix of Analogy." *Kenyon Review* 11 (1949): 539–60.

Van Ghent, Dorothy. *The English Novel: Form and Function.* New York: Holt, 1953.

Williams, Raymond. *The English Novel from Dickens to Lawrence.* 1970. Frogmore: Paladin, 1974.

Woolf, Virginia. "'Jane Eyre' and 'Wuthering Heights.'" *The Common Reader.* First series, 1925. London: Hogarth, 1984.

Psychoanalytic Criticism and *Wuthering Heights*

WHAT IS PSYCHOANALYTIC CRITICISM?

It seems natural to think about novels in terms of dreams. Like dreams, literary works are fictions, inventions of the mind that, although based on reality, are by definition not literally true. Like a literary work, a dream may have some truth to tell, but, like a literary work, it may need to be interpreted before that truth can be grasped. We can live vicariously through romantic fictions, much as we can through daydreams. Terrifying novels and nightmares affect us in much the same way, plunging us into an atmosphere that continues to cling, even after the last chapter has been read — or the alarm clock has sounded.

The notion that dreams allow such psychic explorations, of course, like the analogy between literary works and dreams, owes a great deal to the thinking of Sigmund Freud, the famous Austrian psychoanalyst who in 1900 published a seminal essay, *The Interpretation of Dreams*. But is the reader who feels that Emily Brontë's *Wuthering Heights* is dreamlike — who feels that Mary Shelley's *Frankenstein* is nightmarish — necessarily a Freudian literary critic? To some extent the answer has to be yes. We are all Freudians, really, whether or not we have read a single work by Freud. At one time or another, most of us have referred to ego, libido, complexes, unconscious desires, and sexual repression. The premises of Freud's thought have changed the way the Western world thinks about itself. Psychoanalytic criticism has influenced the teachers our teachers studied with, the works of scholarship and criticism they read, and the critical and creative writers *we* read as well.

What Freud did was develop a language that described, a model that explained, a theory that encompassed human psychology. Many of the elements of psychology he sought to describe and explain are present in the literary works of various ages and cultures, from Sophocles' *Oedipus Rex* to Shakespeare's *Hamlet* to works being written in our own day. When the great novel of the twenty-first century is written, many of these same elements of psychology will probably inform its discourse as well. If, by understanding human psychology according to Freud, we can appreciate literature on a new level, then we should acquaint ourselves with his insights.

Freud's theories are either directly or indirectly concerned with the nature of the unconscious mind. Freud didn't invent the notion of the unconscious; others before him had suggested that even the supposedly "sane" human mind was conscious and rational only at times, and even then at possibly only one level. But Freud went further, suggesting that the powers motivating men and women are *mainly* and *normally* unconscious.

Freud, then, powerfully developed an old idea: that the human mind is essentially dual in nature. He called the predominantly passional, irrational, unknown, and unconscious part of the psyche the *id*, or "it." The *ego*, or "I," was his term for the predominantly rational, logical, orderly, conscious part. Another aspect of the psyche, which he called the *superego*, is really a projection of the ego. The superego almost seems to be outside of the self, making moral judgments, telling us to make sacrifices for good causes even though self-sacrifice may not be quite logical or rational. And, in a sense, the superego *is* "outside," since much of what it tells us to do or think we have learned from our parents, our schools, or our religious institutions.

What the ego and superego tell us *not* to do or think is repressed, forced into the unconscious mind. One of Freud's most important contributions to the study of the psyche, the theory of repression, goes something like this: much of what lies in the unconscious mind has been put there by consciousness, which acts as a censor, driving underground unconscious or conscious thoughts or instincts that it deems unacceptable. Censored materials often involve infantile sexual desires, Freud postulated.

Repressed to an unconscious state, they emerge only in disguised forms: in dreams, in language (so-called Freudian slips), in creative activity that may produce art (including literature), and in neurotic behavior.

According to Freud, all of us have repressed wishes and fears; we all have dreams in which repressed feelings and memories emerge disguised, and thus we are all potential candidates for dream analysis. One of the unconscious desires most commonly repressed is the childhood wish to displace the parent of our own sex and take his or her place in the affections of the parent of the opposite sex. This desire really involves a number of different but related wishes and fears. (A boy — and it should be remarked in passing that Freud here concerns himself mainly with the male — may fear that his father will castrate him, and he may wish that his mother would return to nursing him.) Freud referred to the whole complex of feelings by the word *oedipal,* naming the complex after the Greek tragic hero Oedipus, who unwittingly killed his father and married his mother.

Why are oedipal wishes and fears repressed by the conscious side of the mind? And what happens to them after they have been censored? As Roy P. Basler puts it in *Sex, Symbolism, and Psychology in Literature* (1975), "from the beginning of recorded history such wishes have been restrained by the most powerful religious and social taboos, and as a result have come to be regarded as 'unnatural,'" even though "Freud found that such wishes are more or less characteristic of normal human development":

> In dreams, particularly, Freud found ample evidence that such wishes persisted. . . . Hence he conceived that natural urges, when identified as "wrong," may be repressed but not obliterated. . . . In the unconscious, these urges take on symbolic garb, regarded as nonsense by the waking mind that does not recognize their significance. (14)

Freud's belief in the significance of dreams, of course, was no more original than his belief that there is an unconscious side to the psyche. Again, it was the extent to which he developed a theory of how dreams work — and the extent to which that theory helped him, by analogy, to understand far more than just dreams — that made him unusual, important, and influential beyond the perimeters of medical schools and psychiatrists' offices.

The psychoanalytic approach to literature not only rests on the theories of Freud; it may even be said to have *begun* with Freud, who was interested in writers, especially those who relied heavily on symbols. Such writers regularly cloak or mystify ideas in figures that make sense only when interpreted, much as the unconscious mind of a neurotic disguises secret thoughts in dream stories or bizarre actions that need to be interpreted by an analyst. Freud's interest in literary artists led him to make some unfortunate generalizations about creativity; for example, in the twenty-third lecture in *Introductory Lectures on Psycho-Analysis* (1922), he defined the artist as "one urged on by instinctive needs that are too clamorous" (314). But it also led him to write creative literary criticism of his own, including an influential essay on "The Relation of a Poet to Daydreaming" (1908) and "The Uncanny" (1919), a provocative psychoanalytic reading of E. T. A. Hoffman's supernatural tale "The Sandman."

Freud's application of psychoanalytic theory to literature quickly caught on. In 1909, only a year after Freud had published "The Relation of a Poet to Daydreaming," the psychoanalyst Otto Rank published *The Myth of the Birth of the Hero.* In that work, Rank subscribes to the notion that the artist turns a powerful, secret wish into a literary fantasy, and he uses Freud's notion about the "oedipal" complex to explain why the popular stories of so many heroes in literature are so similar. A year after Rank had published his psychoanalytic account of heroic texts, Ernest Jones, Freud's student and eventual biographer, turned his attention to a tragic text: Shakespeare's *Hamlet.* In an essay first published in the *American Journal of Psychology,* Jones, like Rank, makes use of the oedipal concept: he suggests that Hamlet is a victim of strong feelings toward his mother, the queen.

Between 1909 and 1949, numerous other critics decided that psychological and psychoanalytic theory could assist in the understanding of literature. I. A. Richards, Kenneth Burke, and Edmund Wilson were among the most influential to become interested in the new approach. Not all of the early critics were committed to the approach; neither were all of them Freudians. Some followed Alfred Adler, who believed that writers wrote out of inferiority complexes, and others applied the ideas of Carl Gustav Jung, who had broken with Freud over Freud's emphasis on sex and who had developed a theory of the *collective* unconscious. According to Jungian theory, a great work of literature is not a disguised expression of its author's personal, repressed wishes; rather, it is a manifestation of desires once held by the whole human race but now repressed because of the advent of civilization.

It is important to point out that among those who relied on Freud's models were a number of critics who were poets and novelists as well. Conrad Aiken wrote a Freudian study of American literature, and poets such as Robert Graves and W. H. Auden applied Freudian insights when writing critical prose. William Faulkner, Henry James, James Joyce, D. H. Lawrence, Marcel Proust, and Toni Morrison are only a few of the novelists who have either written criticism influenced by Freud or who have written novels that conceive of character, conflict, and creative writing itself in Freudian terms. The poet H. D. (Hilda Doolittle) was actually a patient of Freud's and provided an account of her analysis in her book *Tribute to Freud*. By giving Freudian theory credibility among students of literature that only they could bestow, such writers helped to endow earlier psychoanalytic criticism with a largely Freudian orientation that has begun to be challenged only in the last two decades.

The willingness, even eagerness, of writers to use Freudian models in producing literature and criticism of their own consummated a relationship that, to Freud and other pioneering psychoanalytic theorists, had seemed fated from the beginning; after all, therapy involves the close analysis of language. René Wellek and Austin Warren included "psychological" criticism as one of the five "extrinsic" approaches to literature described in their influential book *Theory of Literature* (1942). Psychological criticism, they suggest, typically attempts to do at least one of the following: provide a psychological study of an individual writer; explore the nature of the creative process; generalize about "types and laws present within works of literature"; or theorize about the psychological "effects of literature upon its readers" (81). Entire books on psychoanalytic criticism began to appear, such as Frederick J. Hoffman's *Freudianism and the Literary Mind* (1945).

Probably because of Freud's characterization of the creative mind as "clamorous" if not ill, psychoanalytic criticism written before 1950 tended to psychoanalyze the individual author. Poems were read as fantasies that allowed authors to indulge repressed wishes, to protect themselves from deep-seated anxieties, or both. A perfect example of author analysis would be Marie Bonaparte's 1933 study of Edgar Allan Poe. Bonaparte found Poe to be so fixated on his mother that his repressed longing emerges in his stories in images such as the white spot on a black cat's breast, said to represent mother's milk.

A later generation of psychoanalytic critics often paused to analyze the characters in novels and plays before proceeding to their authors. But not for long, since characters, both evil and good, tended to be seen by these critics as the author's potential selves, or projections of various repressed aspects of his or her psyche. For instance, in *A Psychoanalytic Study of the Double in Literature* (1970), Robert Rogers begins with the view that human beings are double or multiple in nature.

Using this assumption, along with the psychoanalytic concept of "dissociation" (best known by its result, the dual or multiple personality), Rogers concludes that writers reveal instinctual or repressed selves in their books, often without realizing that they have done so.

In the view of critics attempting to arrive at more psychological insights into an author than biographical materials can provide, a work of literature is a fantasy or a dream — or at least so analogous to daydream or dream that Freudian analysis can help explain the nature of the mind that produced it. The author's purpose in writing is to gratify secretly some forbidden wish, in particular an infantile wish or desire that has been repressed into the unconscious mind. To discover what the wish is, the psychoanalytic critic employs many of the terms and procedures developed by Freud to analyze dreams.

The literal surface of a work is sometimes spoken of as its "manifest content" and treated as a "manifest dream" or "dream story" would be treated by a Freudian analyst. Just as the analyst tries to figure out the "dream thought" behind the dream story — that is, the latent or hidden content of the manifest dream — so the psychoanalytic literary critic tries to expose the latent, underlying content of a work. Freud used the words *condensation* and *displacement* to explain two of the mental processes whereby the mind disguises its wishes and fears in dream stories. In condensation, several thoughts or persons may be condensed into a single manifestation or image in a dream story; in displacement, an anxiety, a wish, or a person may be displaced onto the image of another, with which or whom it is loosely connected through a string of associations that only an analyst can untangle. Psychoanalytic critics treat metaphors as if they were dream condensations; they treat metonyms — figures of speech based on extremely loose, arbitrary associations — as if they were dream displacements. Thus figurative literary language in general is treated as something that evolves as the writer's conscious mind resists what the unconscious tells it to picture or describe. A symbol is, in Daniel Weiss's words, "a meaningful concealment of truth as the truth promises to emerge as some frightening or forbidden idea" (20).

In a 1970 article entitled "The 'Unconscious' of Literature," Norman Holland, a literary critic trained in psychoanalysis, succinctly sums up the attitudes held by critics who would psychoanalyze authors, but without quite saying that it is the *author* that is being analyzed by the psychoanalytic critic. "When one looks at a poem psychoanalytically," he writes, "one considers it as though it were a dream or as though some ideal patient [were speaking] from the couch in iambic pentameter." One "looks for the general level or levels of fantasy associated with the language. By level I mean the familiar stages of childhood development — oral [when desires for nourishment and infantile sexual desires overlap], anal [when infants receive their primary pleasure from defecation], urethral [when urinary functions are the locus of sexual pleasure], phallic [when the penis or, in girls, some penis substitute is of primary interest], oedipal." Holland continues by analyzing not Robert Frost but Frost's poem "Mending Wall" as a specifically oral fantasy that is not unique to its author. "Mending Wall" is "about breaking down the wall which marks the separated or individuated self so as to return to a state of closeness to some Other"— including and perhaps essentially the nursing mother ("'Unconscious'" 136, 139).

While not denying the idea that the unconscious plays a role in creativity, psychoanalytic critics such as Holland began to focus more on the ways in which authors create works that appeal to *our* repressed wishes and fantasies. Consequently, they shifted their focus away from the psyche of the author and toward the psychology of the reader and the text. Holland's theories, which have concerned themselves more with the reader than with the text, have helped to establish another school of critical theory: reader-response criticism. Elizabeth Wright explains Holland's brand of modern psychoanalytic criticism in this way: "What draws us as readers to a text is the secret expression of what we desire to hear, much as we protest we do not. The disguise must be good enough to fool the censor into thinking that the text is respectable, but bad enough to allow the unconscious to glimpse the unrespectable" (117).

Holland is one of dozens of critics who have revised Freud significantly in the process of revitalizing psychoanalytic criticism. Another such critic is R. D. Laing, whose controversial and often poetical writings about personality, repression, masks, and the double or "schizoid" self have (re)blurred the boundary between creative writing and psychoanalytic discourse. Yet another is D. W. Winnicott, an "object relations" theorist who has had a significant impact on literary criticism. Critics influenced by Winnicott and his school have questioned the tendency to see reader/text as an either/or construct; instead, they have seen reader and text (or audience and play) in terms of a *relationship* taking place in what Winnicott calls a "transitional" or "potential" space — space in which binary terms such as *real* and *illusory, objective* and *subjective,* have little or no meaning.

Psychoanalytic theorists influenced by Winnicott see the transitional or potential reader/text (or audience/play) space as being *like* the space entered into by psychoanalyst and patient. More important, they also see it as being similar to the space between mother and infant: a space characterized by trust in which categorizing terms such as *knowing* and *feeling* mix and merge and have little meaning apart from one another.

Whereas Freud saw the mother-son relationship in terms of the son and his repressed oedipal complex (and saw the analyst-patient relationship in terms of the patient and the repressed "truth" that the analyst could scientifically extract), object-relations analysts see both relationships as *dyadic* — that is, as being dynamic in both directions. Consequently, they don't depersonalize analysis or their analyses. It is hardly surprising, therefore, that contemporary literary critics who apply object-relations theory to the texts they discuss don't depersonalize critics or categorize their interpretations as "truthful," at least not in any objective or scientific sense. In the view of such critics, interpretations are made of language — itself a transitional object — and are themselves the mediating terms or transitional objects of a relationship.

Like critics of the Winnicottian school, the French structuralist theorist Jacques Lacan focused on language and language-related issues. He treated the unconscious *as* a language and, consequently, viewed the dream not as Freud did (that is, as a form and symptom of repression) but rather as a form of discourse. Thus we may study dreams psychoanalytically to learn about literature, even as we may study literature to learn more about the unconscious. In Lacan's seminar on Poe's "The Purloined Letter," a pattern of repetition like that used by psychoanalysts in their analyses is used to arrive at a reading of the story. According to Wright, "the new psychoanalytic structural approach to literature" employs "analogies from psychoanalysis . . . to explain the workings of the text as distinct from the workings of a particular author's, character's, or even reader's mind" (125).

Lacan, however, did far more than extend Freud's theory of dreams, literature, and the interpretation of both. More significantly, he took Freud's whole theory of psyche and gender and added to it a crucial third term — that of language. In the process, he both used and significantly developed Freud's ideas about the oedipal stage and complex.

Lacan pointed out that the pre-oedipal stage, in which the child at first does not even recognize its independence from its mother, is also a pre*verbal* stage, one in which the child communicates without the medium of language, or — if we insist on calling the child's communications a language — in a language that can only be called *literal.* ("Coos," certainly, cannot be said to be figurative or symbolic.) Then, while still in the pre-oedipal stage, the child enters the *mirror* stage.

During the mirror period, the child comes to view itself and its mother, later other people as well, *as* independent selves. This is the stage in which the child is first able to fear the aggressions of another, to desire what is recognizably beyond the self (initially the mother), and, finally, to want to compete with another for the same desired object. This is also the stage at which the child first becomes able to feel sympathy with another being who is being hurt by a third, to cry when another cries. All of these developments, of course, involve projecting beyond the self and, by extension, constructing one's own self (or "ego" or "I") as others view one — that is, as *another.* Such constructions, according to Lacan, are just that: constructs, products, artifacts — fictions of coherence that in fact hide what Lacan called the "absence" or "lack" of being.

The mirror stage, which Lacan also referred to as the *imaginary* stage, is fairly quickly succeeded by the oedipal stage. As in Freud, this stage begins when the child, having come to view itself as self and the father and mother as separate selves, perceives gender and gender differences between its parents and between itself and one of its parents. For boys, gender awareness involves another, more powerful recognition, for the recognition of the father's phallus as the mark of his difference from the mother involves, at the same time, the recognition that his older and more powerful father is also his rival. That, in turn, leads to the understanding that what once seemed wholly his and even indistinguishable from himself is in fact someone else's: something properly desired only at a distance and in the form of socially acceptable *substitutes.*

The fact that the oedipal stage roughly coincides with the entry of the child into language is extremely important for Lacan. For the linguistic order is essentially a figurative or "Symbolic" order; words are not the things they stand for but are, rather, stand-ins or substitutes for those things. Hence boys, who in the most critical period of their development have had to submit to what Lacan called the "Law of the Father"— a law that prohibits direct desire for and communicative intimacy with what has been the boy's whole world — enter more easily into the realm of language and the Symbolic order than do girls, who have never really had to renounce that which once seemed continuous with the self: the mother. The gap that has been opened up for boys, which includes the gap between signs and what they substitute — the gap marked by the phallus and encoded with the boy's sense of his maleness — has not opened up for girls, or has not opened up in the same way, to the same degree.

For Lacan, the father need not be present to trigger the oedipal stage; nor does his phallus have to be seen to catalyze the boy's (easier) transition into the Symbolic order. Rather, Lacan argued, a child's recognition of its gender is intricately tied up with a growing recognition of the system of names and naming, part of the larger system of substitutions we call language. A child has little doubt about who its mother is, but who is its father, and how would one know? The father's claim rests on the mother's *word* that he is in fact the father; the father's relationship to the child is thus established through language and a system of marriage and kinship — names — that in turn is basic to rules of everything from property to law. The name of the father (*nom du père,* which in French sounds like *non du père*) involves, in a sense, nothing of the father — nothing, that is, except his word or name.

Lacan's development of Freud has had several important results. First, his sexist-seeming association of maleness with the Symbolic order, together with his claim that women cannot therefore enter easily into the order, has prompted feminists not to reject his theory out of hand but, rather, to look more closely at the relation between language and gender, language and women's inequality. Some feminists have gone so far as to suggest that the social and political relationships between male and female will not be fundamentally altered until language itself has been radically changed. (That change might begin dialectically, with the development of some kind of "feminine language" grounded in the presymbolic, literal-to-imaginary communication between mother and child.)

Second, Lacan's theory has proved of interest to deconstructors and other poststructuralists, in part because it holds that the ego (which in Freud's view is as necessary as it is natural) is a product or construct. The ego-artifact, produced during the mirror stage, *seems* at once unified, consistent, and organized around a determinate center. But the unified self, or ego, is a fiction, according to Lacan. The yoking together of fragments and destructively dissimilar elements takes its psychic toll, and it is the job of the Lacanian psychoanalyst to "deconstruct," as it were, the ego, to show its continuities to be contradictions as well.

In the essay that follows, Philip K. Wion takes the best-known scene in *Wuthering Heights* — the one in which Catherine says, "I *am* Heathcliff" — and places it in the context not of high, Romantic literature but rather of contemporary psychoanalytic theory. Wion begins by summarizing the work of Margaret Mahler and her associates, post-Freudians (like Lacan) who have divided the first three years of a child's life into three major phases, calling the third phase a "second birth" since it leaves the child for the first time psychologically independent from the mother and able to see the world as being something separate from the self.

This second birth stage, according to Mahler and associates, is not always wholly successful, and an incomplete emergence from it can cause serious, lifelong problems. Wion suggests that for Emily Brontë the process was disturbed by the death of the mother in the child's third year, and that the interruption of Brontë's individuation process caused her to have fantasies of oneness for the rest of her life. Those can be found in *Wuthering Heights,* including in the scene in which Cathy protests to Nelly Dean (a mother figure) that she and Heathcliff are one.

Within the world of the novel, Heathcliff, Wion points out, "usurps" (Brontë's word) the role of the mother — Mrs. Earnshaw — coming into the Earnshaw household as he does against the mother's wishes and almost seeming to cause her death. But Heathcliff is hardly the only mother figure to be found in *Wuthering Heights;* nor is Mrs. Earnshaw the only mother who dies. The latter category includes Hindley's wife Frances, Mrs. Linton, Catherine herself, and Isabella. (In all cases but one, the father outlives the dying mother — just as Emily Brontë's father outlived his wife.) The former category — that of mother figures — would include Nelly, who plays not only a mother's role but also that of the stepmother (Brontë was, of course, raised by one), the "all-bad" mother, and even the "anti-mother" or "witch."

The novel, in Wion's view, is so deeply about a mother's absence and a daughter's uncertain movement into independent being that it even dramatizes what psychoanalysts like Lacan have called the mirror phase: the point at which children first see themselves in the mirrors, recognize themselves *as* themselves, and therefore know of their separateness from mother and world — of their individuality and therefore of their identity. At one point, Catherine looks into a mirror and asks Nelly, "Is that Catherine Linton?" (p. 119 in this volume). At a later point, she does not even recognize her own image *as* her own.

In the end, Wion argues, "Brontë allows Catherine fulfillment — in death — of her wish to escape from separateness and to merge totally with the other" (p. 372). That this fantasized end (that is like life's beginning) can be achieved by this young woman only in death is telling. Like her mother, like Heathcliff, and like her projected self

(Catherine), Brontë was herself quite young when she returned to that "quiet earth" that would seem to suggest, if coldly, the symbiotic oneness between mother and child.

Ross C Murfin

PSYCHOANALYTIC CRITICISM: A SELECTED BIBLIOGRAPHY

Some Short Introductions to Psychological and Psychoanalytic Theory

Holland, Norman. "The 'Unconscious' of Literature: The Psychoanalytic Approach." *Contemporary Criticism.* Ed. Malcolm Bradbury and David Palmer. Stratford-Upon-Avon Studies 12. New York: St. Martin's, 1971. 131–53.

Natoli, Joseph, and Frederik L. Rusch, comps. *Psychocriticism: An Annotated Bibliography.* Westport: Greenwood, 1984.

Scott, Wilbur. *Five Approaches to Literary Criticism.* London: Collier-Macmillan, 1962. See the essays by Burke and Gorer as well as Scott's introduction to the section "The Psychological Approach: Literature in the Light of Psychological Theory."

Wellek, Rene, and Austin Warren. *Theory of Literature.* New York: Harcourt, 1942. See the chapter "Literature and Psychology" in pt. 3, "The Extrinsic Approach to the Study of Literature."

Wright, Elizabeth. "Modern Psychoanalytic Criticism." *Modern Literary Theory: A Comparative Introduction.* Ed. Ann Jefferson and David Robey. Totowa: Barnes, 1982. 113–33.

Freud, Lacan, and Their Influence

Althusser, Louis. *Writings on Psychoanalysis: Freud and Lacan.* Ed. Olivier Corpet and Francois Matheron. Trans. Jeffrey Mehlman. New York: Columbia UP, 1996.

Basler, Roy P. *Sex, Symbolism, and Psychology in Literature.* New York: Octagon, 1975. See especially 13–19.

Clement, Catherine. *The Lives and Legends of Jacques Lacan.* Trans. Arthur Goldhammer. New York: Columbia UP, 1983.

Copjec, Joan. *Read My Desire: Lacan Against the Historicists.* Cambridge: MIT P, 1994.

Feldstein, Richard, Bruce Fink, and Maire Jaanus, eds. *Reading Seminar XI: Lacan's Four Fundamental Concepts of Psychoanalysis.* Albany: State U of New York P, 1995.

Fink, Bruce. *The Lacanian Subject: Between Language and Jouissance.* Princeton: Princeton UP, 1995.

Freud, Sigmund. *Introductory Lectures on Psycho-Analysis.* Trans. Joan Riviere. London: Allen, 1922.

Hill, Philip. *Lacan for Beginners.* New York: Writers and Readers, 1997.

Lacan, Jacques. *Ecrits: A Selection.* Trans. Alan Sheridan. New York: Norton, 1977.

———. *The Ego in Freud's Theory and in the Technique of Psychoanalysis 1954–1955.* Ed. Jacques-Alain Miller. Trans. Sylvana Tomaselli. The Seminar of Jacques Lacan Book II. New York: Norton, 1988.

———. *The Ethics of Psychoanalysis: 1959–1960.* Ed. Jacques-Alain Miller. Trans. Dennis Porter. The Seminar of Jacques Lacan Book VII. New York: Norton, 1992.

———. *Feminine Sexuality: Lacan and the ecole freudienne.* Ed. Juliet Mitchell and Jacqueline Rose. Trans. Rose. New York: Norton, 1982.

———. *The Four Fundamental Concepts of Psychoanalysis.* Trans. Alan Sheridan. London: Penguin, 1980.

———. *Freud's Papers on Technique 1953–1954.* Ed. Jacques-Alain Miller. Trans. John Forrester. The Seminar of Jacques Lacan Book I. New York: Norton, 1988.

———. *On Feminine Sexuality: The Limits of Love and Knowledge.* Ed. Jacques-Alain Miller. Trans. Bruce Fink. The Seminar of Jacques Lacan Book XX: Encore 1972–1973. New York: Norton, 1998.

Lee, Jonathan Scott. *Jacques Lacan.* Boston: Twayne, 1990.

Ragland-Sullivan, Ellie. *Essays on the Pleasures of Death: From Freud to Lacan.* New York: Routledge, 1995.

Roudinesco, Elisabeth. *Jacques Lacan.* Trans. Barbara Bray. New York: Columbia UP, 1997.

Schneiderman, Stuart. *Jacques Lacan: The Death of an Intellectual Hero.* Cambridge: Harvard UP, 1983.

Zizek, Slavoj. *Enjoy Your Symptom: Jacques Lacan in Hollywood and Out.* New York: Routledge, 1992.

———. *The Metastases of Enjoyment: Six Essays on Woman and Causality.* New York: Verso, 1994.

———. *The Sublime Object of Ideology.* New York: Verso, 1989.

Psychoanalysis, Feminism, and Literature

Barr, Marleen S., and Richard Feldstein. *Discontented Discourses: Feminism/Textual Intervention/Psychoanalysis.* Urbana: U of Illinois P, 1989.

Benjamin, Jessica. *The Bonds of Love: Psychoanalysis, Feminism and the Problem of Domination.* New York: Pantheon, 1988.

Bernheimer, Charles, and Claire Kahane, eds. *In Dora's Case: Freud-Hysteria-Feminism.* New York: Columbia UP, 1985.

de Lauretis, Teresa. *The Practice of Love: Lesbian Sexuality and Perverse Desire.* Bloomington: Indiana UP, 1994.

Elliott, Patricia. *From Mastery to Analysis: Theories of Gender in Psychoanalytic Criticism.* Ithaca: Cornell UP, 1991.

Felman, Shoshana. *What Does a Woman Want? Reading and Sexual Difference.* Baltimore: Johns Hopkins UP, 1993.

Gallop, Jane. *The Daughter's Seduction: Feminism and Psychoanalysis.* Ithaca: Cornell UP, 1982.

———. *Thinking Through the Body.* New York: Columbia UP, 1988.

Garner, Shirley Nelson, Claire Kahane, and Madelon Sprengnether. *The (M)other Tongue: Essays in Feminist Psychoanalytic Interpretation.* Ithaca: Cornell UP, 1985.

Grosz, Elizabeth. *Jacques Lacan: A Feminist Introduction.* New York: Routledge, 1990.

Irigaray, Luce. *This Sex Which Is Not One.* Trans. Catherine Porter. Ithaca: Cornell UP, 1985.

———. *Speculum of the Other Woman.* Trans. Gillian C. Gill. Ithaca: Cornell UP, 1985.

Jacobus, Mary. "Is There a Woman in This Text?" *New Literary History* 14 (1982): 117–41.

Kristeva, Julia. *The Kristeva Reader.* Ed. Toril Moi. New York: Columbia UP, 1986. See especially the selection from *Revolution in Poetic Language* 89–136.

MacCannell, Juliet Flower. *The Regime of the Brother: After the Patriarchy.* New York: Routledge, 1991.

Mitchell, Juliet. *Psychoanalysis and Feminism.* New York: Random, 1974.

Mitchell, Juliet, and Jacqueline Rose. Introduction I and Introduction II. Lacan, *Feminine Sexuality: Jacques Lacan and the ecole freudienne* 1–26, 27–57.

Rose, Jacqueline. *Sexuality in the Field of Vision.* New York: Verso, 1986.

Sprengnether, Madelon. *The Spectral Mother: Freud, Feminism, and Psychoanalysis.* Ithaca: Cornell UP, 1990.

Psychological and Psychoanalytic Studies of Literature, Culture, and the Arts

Apollon, Willy, and Richard Feldstein, eds. *Lacan. Politics, Aesthetics.* Albany: State U of New York P, 1996.

Bersani, Leo. *Baudelaire and Freud.* Berkeley: U of California P, 1977.

———. *The Freudian Body: Psychoanalysis and Art.* New York: Columbia UP, 1986.

Bettelheim, Bruno. *The Uses of Enchantment: The Meaning and Importance of Fairy Tales.* New York: Knopf, 1976.

Bracher, Mark. *Lacan, Discourse, and Social Change: A Psychoanalytic Cultural Criticism.* Ithaca: Cornell UP, 1993.

Grosz, Elizabeth. *Space, Time, and Perversion: Essays on the Politics of Bodies.* New York: Routledge, 1995.

Hartman, Geoffrey, ed. *Psychoanalysis and the Question of the Text.* Baltimore: Johns Hopkins UP, 1978.

Hertz, Neil. *The End of the Line: Essays on Psychoanalysis and the Sublime.* New York: Columbia UP, 1985.

Hirsch, Marianne. *The Mother/Daughter Plot: Narrative, Psychoanalysis, Feminism.* Bloomington: Indiana UP, 1989.

Jacobus, Mary. *First Things: The Maternal Imaginary in Literature, Art, and Psychoanalysis.* New York: Routledge, 1995.

Krauss, Rosalind. *The Optical Unconscious.* Cambridge: MIT P, 1994.

Poizat, Michel. *The Angel's Cry: Beyond the Pleasure Principle in Opera.* Trans. Arthur Denner. Ithaca: Cornell UP, 1992.

Salecl, Renata, and Slavoj Zizek, eds. *Gaze and Voice as Love Objects.* Durham: Duke UP, 1996.

Silverman, Kaja. *The Threshold of the Visible World.* New York: Routledge, 1996.

Lacanian Psychoanalytic Studies of Literature

Booker, M. Keith. "Notes Toward a Lacanian Reading of Wallace Stevens." *Journal of Modern Literature* 16 (1990): 493–509.

Davis, Robert Con, ed. *The Fictional Father: Lacanian Readings of the Text.* Amherst: U of Massachusetts P, 1981.

———. *Lacan and Narration: The Psychoanalytic Difference in Narrative Theory.* Baltimore: Johns Hopkins UP, 1984.

Devlin, Kim. "Castration and Its Discontents: A Lacanian Approach to *Ulysses.*" *James Joyce Quarterly* 29 (1991): 117–44.

Felman, Shoshana, ed. *Literature and Psychoanalysis: The Question of Reading: Otherwise.* Baltimore: Johns Hopkins UP, 1982. Includes Lacan's seminar on Shakespeare's *Hamlet.*

Homans, Margaret. *Bearing the Word: Language and Female Experience in Nineteenth-Century Women's Writing.* Chicago: U of Chicago P, 1986.

Lacan, Jacques. "The Essence of Tragedy: A Commentary on Sophocles's *Antigone.*" Lacan, *The Ethics of Psychoanalysis* 243–87.

Mellard, James M. *Using Lacan, Reading Fiction.* Urbana: U of Illinois P, 1991.

Miller, David Lee. "Writing the Specular Son: Jonson, Freud, Lacan, and the (K)not of Masculinity." *Desire in the Renaissance: Psychoanalysis and Literature.* Ed. Valeria Finucci and Regina Schwartz. Princeton: Princeton UP, 1994. 233–60.

Muller, John P., and William J. Richardson, eds. *The Purloined Poe: Lacan, Derrida, and Psychoanalytic Reading.* Baltimore: Johns Hopkins UP, 1988. Includes Lacan's seminar on Poe's "The Purloined Letter."

Netto, Jeffrey A. "Dickens with Kant and Sade." *Style* 29 (1995): 441–58.

Rapaport, Herman. *Between the Sign & the Gaze.* Ithaca: Cornell UP, 1994.

Schad, John. "'No One Dreams': Hopkins, Lacan, and the Unconscious." *Victorian Poetry* 32 (1994): 141–56.

Psychoanalytic Readings of *Wuthering Heights*

Berman, Jeffrey. "Attachment and Loss in *Wuthering Heights.*" In *Narcissism and the Novel.* New York: New York UP, 1990. 78–112.

Gordon, Marci M. "Kristeva's Abject and Sublime in Brontë's *Wuthering Heights.*" *Literature and Psychology* 34 (1988): 44–58.

Homans, Margaret. "Repression and Sublimation of Nature in *Wuthering Heights,*" *PMLA* 93 (1978): 9–19.

Massé, Michelle A. "'He's More Myself than I Am': Narcissism and Gender in *Wuthering Heights.*" In *Psychoanalyses/Feminisms.* Ed. Peter L. Rudnytsky and Andrew M. Gordon. Albany and Buffalo: State U of New York P, 2000. 135–53.

McGuire, Kathryn B. "The Incest Taboo in *Wuthering Heights:* A Modern Appraisal." *American Imago* 45 (1988): 217–24.

Moser, Thomas. "What Is the Matter with Emily Jane?: Conflicting Impulses in *Wuthering Heights.*" *Nineteenth-Century Fiction* 17 (1962): 1–19.

Shapiro, Barbara Ann. "The Rebirth of Catherine Earnshaw: Splitting and Reintegration of Self in *Wuthering Heights.*" In *Literature and the Relational Self.* New York: New York UP, 1994. 46–61.

A PSYCHOANALYTIC PERSPECTIVE

PHILIP K. WION

The Absent Mother in *Wuthering Heights*

"Nelly, I *am* Heathcliff." Readers of *Wuthering Heights* almost always remember these words of Catherine Earnshaw and the scene in which they occur. But the meaning of Catherine's striking declaration is problematic. Catherine's declaration of identity with Heathcliff and the "impracticability" of separating from him comes, ironically, just at the point when she has determined to marry Edgar and when Heathcliff is leaving her. In her confusion, Catherine looks to Nelly Dean for understanding and comfort such as a mother might give, even trying to hide her face in the folds of Nelly's gown; but she only meets with rejection. This scene provides some of the novel's richest statements of its primary relationships and underlying fantasies. The issues which are central to it and to the novel as a whole are, I believe, deep conflicts about oneness and separation which spring from the primary relation between child and mother.

These issues arise from the difficult, painful, but necessary "psychological birth of the human infant" — a process described by the psychologist Margaret Mahler and her associates.[1] The birth of a child is a *physical* process of separation from the mother's body. As Mahler explains, the infant's *psychological* separation from its mother is an equally momentous, but much more complex and gradual, process. Mahler divides the process into three major phases: (1) the "normal

[1]Margaret S. Mahler, Fred Pine, and Anni Bergman, *The Psychological Birth of the Human Infant: Symbiosis and Individuation* (New York: Basic, 1975); see also Louise J. Kaplan, *Oneness and Separateness: From Infant to Individual* (New York: Simon, 1978).

autistic" phase, in which the infant continues to live as if it were still within the mother's womb (41); (2) the "normal symbiotic" phase, in which the infant "behaves and functions as though he and the mother were an omnipotent system" (44); and (3) the phase of "separation-individuation," in which there is "a steady increase in awareness of the separateness of the self and the 'other'" (48). In the "normal autistic" and "normal symbiotic" phases, the child experiences a primal "one-ness" without awareness of boundaries; these phases are followed by a "second birth," the "separation-individuation" process.

Mahler distinguishes four subphases of this second-birth process: "differentiation," "practicing," "rapprochement," and "consolidation of individuality and emotional object constancy." All phases overlap to some extent, as Mahler points out; but the third and fourth subphases are of greatest importance for understanding *Wuthering Heights*. In the third, the child goes through a crisis

> during which the realization of separateness is acute. The toddler's belief in his omnipotence is severely threatened and the environment is coerced as he tries to restore the *status quo*, which is impossible. Ambitendency, which develops into ambivalence, is often intense; the toddler wants to be united with, and at the same time separate from, mother. Temper tantrums, whining, sad moods, and intense separation reactions are at their height.[2]

During the fourth subphase, the "consolidation of individuality," "a degree of object constancy is achieved, and the separation of self and object representations is sufficiently established. Mother is clearly perceived as a separate person in the outside world, and at the same time has an existence in the internal representational world of the child."[3]

Psychoanalysts have become increasingly aware in recent years of the dangers and difficulties attendant upon this process of separation from "oneness" and establishment of individuality. When the relationship between child and mother (or mothering person) is "good enough," the child emerges from the process with a sufficient degree of constancy "to allow him to feel safe in the world even though he now recognizes that his self is separate from the self of his mother. . . . He may occasionally long for her presence, but he does not turn separateness from mother into a fantasy that she is a bad, frustrating mother who has ceased to care about him or love him."[4] But the difficult "second birth" is not always

[2]Mahler 292.
[3]Mahler 289.
[4]Kaplan 30.

accomplished so successfully, and a particularly troubled traversal of this period can lead to serious problems later in life.

Little enough is known directly of Emily Brontë's earliest years; but one crucial fact stands out: her mother died, after a long and painful illness, shortly after Emily's third birthday.[5] I believe that much of what is known of her later life can best be understood in terms of the psychological strategies she developed to deal with the loss of her mother at this crucial point in her development. Likewise, much of what has puzzled readers of *Wuthering Heights* can be understood in terms of struggles, fantasies, and fears associated with the separation-individuation process.

It may seem odd to think of the relationship between Catherine and Heathcliff, which occupies a central position in the novel, as a displaced version of the symbiotic relationship between mother and child. But there is much in the novel to support this view. Emotionally, Heathcliff *is* the world to Catherine, just as the mother *is* the world to the symbiotic child: "'If all else perished, and *he* remained, I should still continue to be; and, if all else remained, and he were annihilated, the Universe would turn to a mighty stranger.'" When Catherine discovers that Heathcliff has left, she seeks him as a mother seeks a lost child — or as a lost child seeks its mother: "calling at intervals, and then listening, and then crying outright. She beat Hareton, or any child, at a good passionate fit of crying" (pp. 88, 90 in this volume).

The boundary between Catherine and her world is ambiguous and problematic, just as it is for the child undergoing the separation-individuation process. The "inner" emotional turmoil into which she is thrown by Heathcliff's disappearance coincides with the "outer" natural turmoil of a thunderstorm, which not only drenches her but damages part of the house. When Nelly finds Catherine near the fireplace in the morning, the door is ajar and the windows are open — the boundaries between inside and outside are not closed. But Catherine tells Nelly peevishly to "'shut the window'" (p. 92). Shortly afterwards, she breaks down into "uncontrollable grief" and behavior so frightening to Nelly that she "thought she was going mad." It takes Catherine several months to recover from her "fever."

[5]Brontë's mother is generally said to have died of cancer, as in Winifred Gérin's authoritative biography, *Emily Brontë* (Oxford: Oxford UP, 1971) 4. But a professor of obstetrics and gynecology, Dr. Philip Rhodes, has suggested that it is more likely she died of "some chronic disorder consequent upon" her "rapid childbearing," probably "chronic pelvic sepsis together with increasing anemia." "A Medical Appraisal of the Brontës," *Brontë Society Transactions* 16 (1972): 101–09.

That Brontë may have been at least partially aware of the extent to which the love of Catherine and Heathcliff is modeled on the primal bond between child and mother is suggested by several references in the same chapter to the relationship between the infant Hareton and Nelly Dean. Hareton's mother is dead, and Nelly has taken her place, serving as Hareton's substitute mother. When Hindley almost kills Hareton by drunkenly dropping him over the banister, Nelly thinks of the child's dead mother and wonders that she "'does not rise from her grave to see how you use him'" (p. 82). Rocking Hareton to sleep shortly afterwards, Nelly hums a song expressing the fantasy of a mother's continuing care for her children after death: "'It was far in the night, and the bairnies grat [little ones wept], / The mither beneath the mools [earth of a grave] heard that'" (p. 83). At the very end of the chapter, Nelly is forced to leave Hareton behind at the Heights when she accompanies Catherine to Thrushcross Grange: "I kissed Hareton good-bye; and, since then, he has been a stranger, and it's very queer to think it, but I've no doubt, he has completely forgotten all about Ellen Dean and that he was ever *more than all the world to her, and she to him!*" (my emphasis; p. 94).

Furthermore, the narrative juxtapositions in this chapter suggest that the mother-child relationship was on Brontë's mind. Of course, by this point in the novel, Mrs. Earnshaw, Catherine's mother, has long since died. But one of the more curious things about the narrative is the casualness with which her death is revealed. All we are told about Mrs. Earnshaw while she is still living is that she reacted with furious resentment to her husband's bringing "that gipsy brat into the house, when they had their own bairns to feed, and fend for," and that she "never put in a word on [Heathcliff's] behalf, when she saw him wronged" (p. 51). Her death is referred to only in passing, in a mere adverbial phrase embedded in a long sentence which focusses attention on another matter — Heathcliff's role as "usurper": "So, from the very beginning, he bred bad feeling in the house; and at Mrs. Earnshaw's death, which happened in less than two years after, the young master [Hindley] had learnt to regard his father as an oppressor rather than a friend, and Heathcliff as a usurper of his parent's affections and his privileges . . ." (p. 53). It is as if the arrival of Heathcliff has somehow caused the death of Mrs. Earnshaw, as if his presence really does displace hers. Something similar happens later in the novel: when Catherine is taken to Thrushcross Grange to convalesce from her "fever," Mr. and Mrs. Linton both promptly die as a result (p. 93).

Quite a few mothers, in fact, die in the course of the novel: Mrs. Earnshaw, Hindley's wife Frances (Hareton's mother), Mrs. Linton,

Catherine herself, and Isabella (Linton's mother). In every case but one (that of Mrs. Linton), the father outlives the mother. But a substitute mother is usually found — and she is usually Nelly Dean. Nelly makes her role as surrogate mother explicit in the cases of Hareton and the younger Catherine: "You know, they both appeared, in a measure, my children" (p. 275). Her role as surrogate mother to Catherine and to Heathcliff (who had evidently been abandoned by his parents) is only slightly less directly suggested, and she constantly watches over their lives, for better and for worse. The one child in the novel she doesn't get a chance to "nurse" for any length of time is Linton; the relative indifference of Zillah, who has taken Nelly's place at the Heights, serves to underline the importance of Nelly's role as surrogate mother. (Linton's sickliness is presented as largely a matter of heredity; but his peevish tendency to nurse himself may also be taken to reflect inadequate mothering from Isabella and the others who care for him.)

When Heathcliff returns after his mysterious three-year absence, his reunion with Catherine is described in terms which derive psychologically from the symbiotic phase of the mother-child relationship. This phase coincides with the oral stage of libidinal development and the imagery Brontë chooses uncannily suggests such orality: Catherine "kept her gaze fixed on him as if she feared he would vanish were she to remove it. He did not raise his to her, often . . . but it flashed back, each time more confidently, the undisguised delight he *drank* from hers. They were too much *absorbed* in their mutual joy to suffer embarrassment" (my emphasis; p. 99). Edgar expresses his envy by urging that they sit down to tea: "'I'm thirsty.'" For Catherine, her joy at being reunited with Heathcliff supersedes her interest in actual food: "she could neither eat nor drink" (p. 100).

The novel is full of such oral imagery. Nearly every social encounter involves food or drink, from Lockwood's uncomfortable first visit to the Heights — he notes the oatcakes and "clusters of legs of beef, mutton, and ham" (p. 26) in a frame under the roof, speculates that Joseph's poor digestion may account for his "sour" looks, and ends up accepting a glass of wine from Heathcliff — to his last visit nearly a year later, when he takes in Nelly's account of Heathcliff's death along with a "drink of our old ale'" (p. 265). More often than not, it is Nelly who provides the food and drink, which is appropriate not only to her socioeconomic role as domestic servant, but also to her psychological role as surrogate mother.

Even characters and relationships of secondary importance tend to be imagined in oral terms. Hindley's drinking himself to death begins as a grief-stricken response to the death of his wife. When Catherine discovers Isabella's infatuation with Heathcliff, she tells him Isabella has been "'fasting'" and "'pining'" for him, but "'I like her too well . . . to let you absolutely seize and *devour* her up'" (my emphasis; p. 108). Heathcliff responds by saying he likes her "'too ill to attempt it . . . except in a very ghoulish fashion'" — one of many references identifying Heathcliff's tendencies toward greed and sadism as primarily oral in orientation. He himself talks (rather melodramatically) of drinking Edgar's blood (p. 141), and he calls his pitiless tormenting of Isabella and the others he despises "'a moral teething'" (p. 144). One of his strongest expressions of contempt for Edgar is to call him "'not a lamb [but] a *sucking* leveret [young hare]'" (my emphasis; p. 115). Isabella refers to "'his sharp cannibal teeth'" (p. 162) and tells Hindley that "'his mouth watered to tear you with his teeth; because he's only half a man — not so much'" (p. 165). Even Nelly, puzzled by Heathcliff's behavior shortly before his death, wonders if he is "'a ghoul, or a vampire'" (p. 281).

Catherine's crisis in the novel may be understood as one that involves a breakdown in the psychological process of "separation-individuation." Catherine's first breakdown is precipitated by the disappearance of Heathcliff. Her second occurs when the conflict between Heathcliff and Edgar has intensified to the point where Edgar insists that she give up one or the other. It begins as an attempt to control Edgar: "'I felt that . . . we should all be driven asunder for nobody knows how long! Well, if I cannot keep Heathcliff for my friend — if Edgar will be mean and jealous — I'll try to break their hearts by breaking my own'" (p. 116). Despite the apparent deliberation of Catherine's project (which Nelly finds so provoking), it reveals the sort of confusion of inside and outside characteristic of an identity insecure at the deepest level. For Catherine, the "driving asunder" of the three of them would be tantamount to a splitting apart of her very self. Moreover, if the identities of Edgar and Heathcliff are (as she assumes) as dependent on attachment to her as hers is on attachment to them, it follows that her suffering will cause them pain and her death will be their destruction. Catherine expresses rage at Edgar's ultimatum and Nelly's apparent indifference by locking herself in her room and refusing to eat — that is, by insisting on her separateness and independence.

The scene that follows in chapter 12 is crucial, I think, to the dynamics of the novel. In it, Catherine expresses more directly than at any other time an intense feeling that Nelly, as surrogate mother, has betrayed her. When Catherine discovers that Nelly has kept Edgar unaware of the seriousness of her "derangement," she tells her that "'I begin to fancy you don't like me. How strange! I thought, though everybody hated and despised each other, they could not avoid loving me — and they have all turned to enemies in a few hours'" (p. 119). Later, she says that she sees Nelly as a witch, "'an aged woman . . . gathering elf-bolts to hurt our heifers'" (p. 120). The scene ends with Catherine in fury at Nelly for having "'played traitor'": "'Nelly is my hidden enemy — you witch! So you do seek elf-bolts to hurt us!'" (p. 125). For the next two months of "brain fever," Edgar takes Nelly's place with Catherine: "No mother could have nursed an only child more devotedly than Edgar tended her" (p. 129).

Nelly as witch is Nelly as all-bad mother or anti-mother, a bad, frustrating mother who has ceased to care about Catherine or love her. This fantasy ties in with other fantasies Catherine expresses in this scene. In her bewildered rage at Edgar's apparent indifference to her suffering, Catherine begins tearing the pillow with her teeth. The feathers evoke a confused but significant memory — or fantasy — of a lapwing seen on the moors: "'It wanted to get to its nest . . . the bird was not shot — we saw its nest in the winter, full of little skeletons. Heathcliff set a trap over it, and the old ones dare not come. I made him promise he'd never shoot a lapwing, after that, and he didn't. . . . Did he shoot my lapwings, Nelly?'" (p. 120). Catherine seems to identify both with the "old" lapwing, which wants to get home but can't, *and* with the starved and abandoned little ones. Heathcliff is here the cause of the separation of parent and child. This fits with Nelly's image of him as a "cuckoo" (p. 50) whose advent leads to the displacement of the birds which belong in the nest — "And Hareton has been cast out like an unfledged dunnock!" (p. 50) — and with her implicit linking of his role as "usurper" to Mrs. Earnshaw's death (p. 53).

Catherine's desire to be at home takes the form of a temporary delusion that she is in her room at Wuthering Heights. Her longing to be there is also associated with her desire to feel the wind from the Heights, and she gets Nelly to open the window for a moment. Afterwards, "our fiery Catherine was no better than a wailing child!" (p. 122). (Nelly's remark is clearly related to Lockwood's account of the "waif" who tried to enter through the window of Catherine's room in his dream.) Separation from her home is linked with separation from Heathcliff in Catherine's account of her confusion when she locked herself in her room:

> "I thought . . . that I was enclosed in the oak-panelled bed at home; and my heart ached with some great grief which, just wak-

> ing, I could not recollect . . . the whole last seven years of my life grew a blank! . . . I was a child; my father was just buried, and my misery arose from the separation that Hindley had ordered between me and Heathcliff — I was laid alone, for the first time . . . supposing, at twelve years old, I had been wrenched from the Heights, and every early association, and my all in all, as Heathcliff was at that time, and been converted, at a stroke, into Mrs. Linton, the lady of Thrushcross Grange, and the wife of a stranger; an exile, and outcast, thenceforth, from what had been my world — You may fancy a glimpse of the abyss where I grovelled! . . . I wish I were a girl again, half savage and hardy, and free . . . I'm sure I should be myself were I once among the heather on those hills . . . Open the window again wide, fasten it open!" (pp. 122–23).

When Nelly refuses, Catherine opens the window herself, and looking out, believes she can see a candle in her room, although in actuality the house at the Heights is not visible from where she is. When she finally ends her stand at the window, she is described as "having *weaned* her eyes from contemplating the outer darkness" (my emphasis; p. 124). The metaphor of "weaning" the eyes, for turning the attention to perception of reality, is thus not only striking but deeply appropriate psychologically, since it links vision to the oral mode of relating to the world which is dominant in the symbiotic phase of development.

Hallucinations and dreams ("'I dread sleeping, my dreams appal me'" [p. 121]) are forms of seeing in which the boundaries between self and world are radically broken down. Catherine's confusion about her reflection in the mirror is also connected with the themes of a blurring of inner and outer and a loss of identity. At the beginning of this scene, Catherine stares at the mirror and asks, "'Is that Catherine Linton?'" (p. 119). She knows at this point that what she sees is her reflection; she is primarily trying to get sympathy for the changes in her appearance caused by her fasting and suffering. Later, however, she really does not recognize the face as her own, and insists that it exists independently and is still there when Nelly has covered the mirror with a shawl: "'Who is it? I hope it will not come out when you are gone'" (p. 121). When Nelly insists, "'It was *yourself,* Mrs. Linton,'" Catherine replies cryptically, "'Myself! . . . and the clock is striking twelve! It's true, then, that's dreadful!'" She covers her eyes; but moments later the shawl slips, and she shrieks in terror.

This episode, like Catherine's account of her momentary amnesia of the past seven years, suggests a deep disturbance in her sense of identity, such as would be traceable to difficulties in the separation-individuation process. Lacan, Winnicott, and other analysts have placed considerable emphasis on the role of mirroring, both literal and figurative, in the child's construction of its sense of self.[6] What seems to be happening to Catherine in this episode is a disintegration of an identity composed precariously of partially incompatible identifications. The names Lockwood found scratched on the windowledge in Catherine's room — Catherine Earnshaw, Catherine Heathcliff, Catherine Linton — are one index, relatively public and social, of the conflicting elements of Catherine's identity.[7] But the depth and intensity of her confusion suggests that her dilemma of choosing between Edgar and Heathcliff (which precipitated this breakdown) screens a deeper problem, that of accepting the fact that she is indeed a separate, individual person, unable to find again the primal oneness with the symbiotic other she has lost. Constancy and continuity of the self depend, ultimately, upon a deep assurance of the constancy of the primary other, and, therefore, of the world. The rebelliousness of Heathcliff, the demands of Edgar, and the coolness of Nelly Dean have created a crisis for Catherine by eliciting her deepest anxieties and insecurities about the constancy of the primary other.

In the end, Brontë allows Catherine fulfillment — in death — of her wish to escape from separateness and to merge totally with the other. Reunited with Heathcliff, she faints in his arms, and dies "having never recovered sufficient consciousness to miss Heathcliff, or know Edgar" (p. 152).

Heathcliff shares Catherine's final scene, of course. Brontë stresses the anger he feels at Catherine for abandoning him, which derives from his boundless need for her. For much of the novel, Heathcliff is presented as an archetypal "other" — outsider, alien, mysterious, danger-

[6]Jacques Lacan, "The mirror stage as formative of the function of the I as revealed in psychoanalytic experience," in *Ecrits,* trans. Alan Sheridan (New York: Norton, 1977) 1–7; D. W. Winnicott, "Mirror-role of Mother and Family in Child Development," in *Playing and Reality* (New York: Basic, 1971) 111–18; Paula Elkisch, "The Psychological Significance of the Mirror," *Journal of the American Psychoanalytic Association* 5 (1965): 235–44.

[7]Two important recent analyses of the novel focus on its dramatization of resistance against the (patriarchal) cultural forces which would direct and limit the self in its struggle to construct a coherent and viable identity: Leo Bersani, *A Future for Astyanax* (Boston: Little, 1976) 198–223; and Sandra M. Gilbert and Susan Gubar, *The Madwoman in the Attic: The Woman Writer and the Nineteenth-Century Literary Imagination* (New Haven: Yale UP, 1979) 248–308. The reading I am offering here is compatible with their analyses, but places greater stress on fantasies from the earliest stages of psychological development.

ous, demonic, subhuman, a force of "external" rather than "human" nature. More than any of the other persons in the book, he seems to be a figure of myth — "demon lover" in the first half and "paternal ogre" in the second, according to Dorothy Van Ghent[8] — or of quasi-Byronic melodrama. The novel would be less powerful than it is, however, if Heathcliff were only "other" for the reader. Much in the novel encourages us to identify strongly with him. Initially he elicits considerable sympathy as abandoned child and as victim of the censures of Joseph, the tyranny of Hindley, and the social condescension of the Lintons and even of Catherine herself. And the most powerful scenes in the second half of the novel are those which focus on his prolonged mourning for Catherine.

Heathcliff's most obvious defense against his pain is his sadistic aggression against others — Hindley, Edgar, Isabella, Linton and the younger Catherine, and even Hareton, though his aggression toward Hareton is increasingly qualified by his identification with the boy. Heathcliff has already linked his need for revenge on the others directly to his anger at Catherine for her "infernal" treatment of him: " 'I seek no revenge on you [Catherine] . . . The tyrant grinds down his slaves and they don't turn against him, they crush those beneath them' " (p. 112). Important as they are, Heathcliff's efforts to gain and maintain power over those around him are clearly revealed in the end to have been secondary and derivative: " 'I get levers and mattocks to demolish the two houses . . . and when everything is ready, and in my power, I find the will to lift a slate off either roof has vanished!' " (p. 276).

Like Catherine before him, Heathcliff undergoes a "strange change" toward the end of his life, marked most strikingly by his loss of interest in eating and drinking. His gaze is increasingly absorbed by a hallucinatory vision: "his eyes pursued it with unwearied vigilance; and . . . were never *weaned* away" (my emphasis; p. 282). His death is presented as the fulfillment of his wish for total union with Catherine, which has " '*devoured* [his] existence' " and *" 'swallowed' "* him (my emphasis, p. 277). The details surrounding it emphasize the dissolution of boundaries, most significantly in the manner of his burial; the reader will remember his insistence that the walls of his coffin and Catherine's be removed, so that their bodies might decompose together. In death, we are encouraged to imagine, Heathcliff and Catherine are completely united, both physically and spiritually, at last.

[8]Dorothy Van Ghent, *The English Novel: Form and Function* (New York: Harper & Row, 1961 [1953]) 156.

The novel does recognize, however, that in life the return to a lost symbiotic oneness, no matter how intensely desired, is not a realistic possibility. Moreover, the wish for complete fusion of identities and overcoming of separateness can also be a source of intense fear and anxiety. One of the main functions of Lockwood in the novel is to dramatize this contrasting reaction to a deep longing for union with the mother.

We learn little about Lockwood's history, but what he does tell us is highly significant. When he reflects that he may have been over-hasty in concluding that his reserve and Heathcliff's spring from similar motives, he recalls that "my dear mother used to say I should never have a comfortable home" (p. 27). He then recounts an episode from the previous summer in which he signaled his interest in a young woman through his glances, but "shrunk icily into myself, like a snail" (p. 27) when she began to return his looks. He next tells of his difficulties in relating to the dogs during his first visit to the Heights: after attempting "to caress the *canine mother*" (my emphasis) when she comes up to him in what he takes to be a threatening manner, "her white teeth watering for a snatch" of his leg (p. 27), he makes faces at the dogs, and is attacked in response. Most commentators rightly point to the emotional inhibition and lack of insight into himself Lockwood reveals in these encounters. I would stress the hints Brontë provides that these qualities may be related to intensely ambivalent feelings toward that mother who predicted he would never find a comfortable home.

Lockwood's dreams reveal the intensity of the emotions he generally denies or represses, as some critics have noted;[9] but the specific nature of those emotions is also important. His first dream begins with the wish to get *home,* thus introducing a theme which, as we have seen, is significant throughout the novel. Joseph warns him that he "could never get into the house" without a pilgrim's staff, such as the cudgel Joseph is carrying. Considering it "absurd that I should need such a weapon to gain admittance into my own residence," the dreamer suddenly realizes he is going somewhere else, to the chapel to hear the Reverend Jabes Branderham preach, and that "either Joseph, the preacher, or I had committed the 'First [sin] of the Seventy-First,' and were to be publicly exposed and excommunicated" (p. 41). It seems to me that this dream can be interpreted persuasively in familiar oedipal

[9]See, for example, Edgar F. Shannon Jr., "Lockwood's Dreams and the Exegesis of *Wuthering Heights*," *Nineteenth-Century Fiction* 14 (1959): 95–109.

terms. If "home" represents the mother (ultimately, the womb), using a phallic "staff" to enter it would indeed be "absurd" — because forbidden by the incest taboo, and therefore a source of intense anxiety. Hence the sudden shift to the theme of sin and guilt. The mutual accusations and struggles for possession of the pilgrims' staves toward which the dream turns suggest unresolved conflicts with father and superego figures. (Throughout the novel Joseph clearly functions as a superego figure, though a systematically discredited one.)

Lockwood's second dream is even more frightening to him than the first. Critics usually emphasize the cruelty of the dreamer, who rubs the hand of the child on the broken glass of the window until blood runs down and soaks the bed-clothes. But we might ask *why* the dreamer is so terrified by the child sobbing, " 'Let me in — let me in!' " A link with the earlier dream is the theme of coming home. The breaking of the window can be interpreted as the breaking of the barrier between self and other. I suggest that by the common dream device of reversal the child, so much younger than the dreamer, may actually represent (among other things) the *older* female other most important to Lockwood, his mother. If Lockwood both longs for his mother and fears being engulfed by her, it makes sense that when he tries to explain his terror to Heathcliff he says that " 'the little fiend . . . probably would have strangled me' " (p. 44). An unconscious association of the child with the mother also helps to account for Lockwood's puzzling question, " 'Was not the Reverend Jabes Branderham akin to you on the mother's side?' " (p. 44).

Brontë is of course using this dream for multiple purposes. But it seems to me that it does express a deep fear of the loss of individual identity which a return to symbiotic union with the mother would entail. Such a return is ultimately equivalent with death, and this equation is present in Lockwood's account as well. When he mentions the chapel in recounting his dream, Lockwood digresses to describe it. What he says serves to give some information about the actual chapel, of course; but it functions more importantly as a set of significant associations to the content of the dream. Like other buildings, the chapel can unconsciously symbolize the female body; here, it is especially connected with fears of the female body as locus of death and dissolution, the womb as tomb. Lockwood's associations refer not only to corpses but to collapsing boundaries and to starvation: the chapel

> lies in a hollow, between two hills — an elevated hollow — near a swamp, whose peaty moisture is said to answer all the purposes of

> embalming on the few corpses deposited there. The roof has been kept whole hitherto, but, as the clergyman's stipend is only twenty pounds per annum, and a house with two rooms, threatening speedily to determine into one, no clergyman will undertake the duties of pastor, especially as it is currently reported that his flock would rather let him starve than increase the living. (p. 41)

Lockwood's fear of death is the other side of his fear of life, and both are linked to a fear of women rooted in his ambivalence toward his mother. His repressed sexuality finds some expression later in the novel, but only in muted, indirect ways. He plays with the idea of loving young Catherine (Nelly even encourages the thought for a while), but nothing comes of it. Near the end of the novel there is even a hint that Lockwood might be sexually interested in the motherly Nelly Dean: Joseph, ever censorious, mutters that it's " 'a crying scandal that she should have fellies at her time of life' " (p. 264). Lockwood counters the suggestion by asserting another, more comfortable relationship, that of social superior: he presses a coin into Nelly's hand and throws one at Joseph's feet as he escapes from the Heights for the last time (p. 287).

Brontë clearly expects us to find Lockwood's defensive solution to the dilemmas of oneness and separation unsympathetic and unsatisfactory (though her own shyness and reserve, and her fierce independence, may in fact have resulted in part from similar dynamics). Total commitment to oneness and denial of separateness, such as that of Catherine and Heathcliff, is presented much more sympathetically; but it is also shown as incompatible with the conditions of actual adult life.

A middle ground is represented by the tamer but more viable love of Hareton and the younger Catherine, which develops under the approving eye of their foster mother, Nelly Dean. Many critics have noted that in the second half of the novel the characters of the second generation recapitulate — with significant differences — the pattern of relationships of the older generation in the first half. The younger Catherine's marriage to Linton Heathcliff parallels Catherine's to Edgar; but this time, it is the husband who dies first, leaving the wife free to marry again. In marrying Hareton, the younger Catherine will be marrying a member of her own family[10] (they are first cousins; but so were she and Linton) and completing the exclusion of Heathcliff, the

[10]It has often been suggested that fantasies of brother-sister incest underlie the relationship between Catherine and Heathcliff, most elaborately by Giles Mitchell, in "Incest, Demonism, and Death in *Wuthering Heights*," *Literature and Psychology* 23 (1973): 27–36. The reading I am presenting does not preclude such a possibility, but regards pregenital fantasies and identifications as more fundamental.

"usurper." But because Hareton is so strongly identified with Heathcliff — "'Hareton's aspect was the ghost of my immortal love, of my wild endeavors to hold my right, my degradation, my pride, my happiness, and my anguish'" (p. 277) — this marriage also represents a less extreme, more conventional, more "mature" version of the union of Catherine and Heathcliff, which for them could take place only in fantasy or in death, not in an actual, day-to-day relationship.

We are led to see the love of young Catherine and Hareton from a different perspective than that from which we see the love of their predecessors. Nelly Dean's puzzled, skeptical, frightened reactions to the intense passions and unconventional behavior of Catherine and Heathcliff are obviously inadequate, however well-intentioned. With them, she is out of her depth. With Hareton and the younger Catherine, however, she can play the role of mother much more appropriately, comfortably, and successfully; and we are encouraged to share her parental perspective on their developing mutual understanding and affection (much as we share Prospero's perspective on the love of Ferdinand and Miranda in Shakespeare's *The Tempest*).

With all her limitations, Nelly Dean plays a very important psychological role in the novel. Nelly's compromises among the conflicting demands of Catherine, Heathcliff, Edgar, Lockwood, and the rest have earned her the disrespect and even hostility of some readers.[11] When she is cornered and temporarily imprisoned by Heathcliff, Nelly herself momentarily passes "harsh judgment on my many derelictions of duty; from which, it struck me then, all the misfortunes of all my employers sprang" (pp. 239–40). However, she soon regains her reasonable perspective: "It was not the case, in reality, I am aware; but it was, in my imagination, that dismal night, and I thought Heathcliff himself less guilty than I." Nelly's main functions in the novel are essentially those attributed to the ego in classic psychoanalytic theory — "reality testing" and mediation among the competing claims of the id, the superego, and the outside world.

But Nelly is not just the novel's principal representative of the values and functions associated with the ego. She is also its most important mother figure. As such, she may represent, in part, an attempt by Emily Brontë to come to terms with the loss of her own mother, by becoming, in fantasy, a kind of mother of herself. Brontë understood the psychological process of introjection, in which a representation of an

[11]Probably the most extreme attack on Nelly Dean is by James Hafley, in "The Villain in *Wuthering Heights*," *Nineteenth-Century Fiction* 13 (1958): 199–215.

important other is located "within" the self: "'That is not *my* Heathcliff. I shall love mine yet; and take him with me — he's in my soul'" (p. 150). It seems to me that among the many conscious and unconscious motives leading to the creation of Nelly Dean and the elaboration of her complex role as narrator and as participant in the events of the novel, not the least in importance for Brontë may have been such a desire (probably unconscious) to re-create and to be, in fantasy, the mother she had lost.

For the younger Catherine, Nelly is a "good enough mother," and her emotional development is presented as quite "normal" and well-balanced. But the positive resolution of the novel's conflicts represented by the love of the younger Catherine and Hareton (so satisfying to Nelly and so disconcerting to Lockwood) is only part of the very complex experience the novel leaves with the reader.

Heathcliff and the elder Catherine (for whom Nelly was *not* a "good enough mother") are dead and buried. But "the country folks" would swear that Heathcliff "walks"; Joseph claims to have seen them every rainy night; a boy and his sheep have been frightened by "Heathcliff, and a woman, yonder, under t' Nab"; and Nelly herself is afraid of being out in the dark now and doesn't like to be left alone in "this grim house" (p. 287). Intense longing for the lost primal oneness remains powerful in the novel, even when it is buried, in the earth or in the unconscious. And if Lockwood wonders "how any one could ever imagine unquiet slumbers for the sleepers in that quiet earth" (p. 288), the limitation is in *his* imagination, not in Emily Brontë's.

Marxist Criticism and *Wuthering Heights*

WHAT IS MARXIST CRITICISM?

To the question "What is Marxist criticism?" it may be tempting to respond with another question: "What does it matter?" In light of the rapid and largely unanticipated demise of Soviet-style communism in the former USSR and throughout Eastern Europe, it is understandable to suppose that Marxist literary analysis would disappear too, quickly becoming an anachronism in a world enamored with full-market capitalism.

In fact, however, there is no reason why Marxist criticism should weaken, let alone disappear. It is, after all, a phenomenon distinct from Soviet and Eastern European communism, having had its beginnings nearly eighty years before the Bolshevik revolution and having thrived since the 1940s, mainly in the West — not as a form of communist propaganda but rather as a form of critique, a discourse for interrogating *all* societies and their texts in terms of certain specific issues. Those issues — including race, class, and the attitudes shared within a given culture — are as much with us as ever, not only in contemporary Russia but also in the United States.

The argument could even be made that Marxist criticism has been strengthened by the collapse of Soviet-style communism. There was a time, after all, when few self-respecting Anglo-American journals would use Marxist terms or models, however illuminating, to analyze Western issues or problems. It smacked of sleeping with the enemy. With the collapse of the Kremlin, however, old taboos began to give way. Even the staid *Wall Street Journal* now seems comfortable using phrases like "worker alienation" to discuss the problems plaguing the American business world.

The assumption that Marxist criticism will die on the vine of a moribund political system rests in part on another mistaken assumption, namely, that Marxist literary analysis is practiced only by people who would like to see society transformed into a Marxist-communist state, one created through land reform, the redistribution of wealth, a tightly and centrally managed economy, the abolition of institutionalized religion, and so on. In fact, it has never been necessary to be a communist political revolutionary to be classified as a Marxist literary critic. (Many of the critics discussed in this introduction actually *fled* communist societies to live in the West.) Nor is it necessary to like only those literary works with a radical social vision or to dislike books that represent or even reinforce a middle-class, capitalist worldview. It is necessary, however, to adopt what most students of literature would consider a radical definition of the purpose and function of literary criticism.

More traditional forms of criticism, according to the Marxist critic Pierre Macherey, "set . . . out to deliver the text from its own silences by coaxing it into giving up its true, latent, or hidden meaning." Inevitably, however, non-Marxist criticism "intrude[s] its own discourse between the reader and the text" (qtd. in Bennett 107). Marxist critics, by contrast, do not attempt to discover hidden meanings in texts. Or if they do, they do so only after seeing the text, first and foremost, as a material product to be understood in broadly historical terms. That is to say, a literary work is first viewed as a product *of* work (and hence of the realm of production and consumption we call economics). Second, it may be looked upon as a work that *does* identifiable work of its own. At one level, that work is usually to enforce and reinforce the prevailing ideology, that is, the network of conventions, values, and opinions to which the majority of people uncritically subscribe.

This does not mean that Marxist critics merely describe the obvious. Quite the contrary: the relationship that the Marxist critic Terry Eagleton outlines in *Criticism and Ideology* (1978) among the soaring cost of books in the nineteenth century, the growth of lending libraries, the practice of publishing "three-decker" novels (so that three borrowers could be reading the same book at the same time), and the changing *content* of those novels is highly complex in its own way. But the complexity Eagleton finds is not that of the deeply buried meaning of the text. Rather, it is that of the complex web of social and economic relationships that were prerequisite to the work's production. Marxist criticism does not seek to be, in Eagleton's words, "a passage from text to reader." Indeed, "its task is to show the text as it cannot know itself, to manifest those conditions of its making (inscribed in its very letter) about which it is necessarily silent" (43).

As everyone knows, Marxism began with Karl Marx, the nineteenth-century German philosopher best known for writing *Das Kapital,* the seminal work of the communist movement. What everyone doesn't know is that Marx was also the first Marxist literary critic (much as Sigmund Freud, who psychoanalyzed E. T. A. Hoffmann's supernatural tale "The Sandman," was the first Freudian literary critic). During the 1830s Marx wrote critical essays on writers such as Goethe and Shakespeare (whose tragic vision of Elizabethan disintegration he praised).

The fact that Marxist literary criticism began with Marx himself is hardly surprising, given Marx's education and early interests. Trained in the classics at the University of Bonn, Marx wrote literary imitations, his own poetry, a failed novel, and a fragment of a tragic drama *(Oulanem)* before turning to contemplative and political philosophy. Even after he met Friedrich Engels in 1843 and began collaborating on works such as *The German Ideology* and *The Communist Manifesto,* Marx maintained a keen interest in literary writers and their works. He and Engels argued about the poetry of Heinrich Heine, admired Hermann Freiligrath (a poet critical of the German aristocracy), and faulted the playwright Ferdinand Lassalle for writing about a reactionary knight in the Peasants' War rather than about more progressive aspects of German history.

As these examples suggest, Marx and Engels would not — indeed, could not — think of aesthetic matters as being distinct and independent from such things as politics, economics, and history. Not surprisingly, they viewed the alienation of the worker in industrialized, capitalist societies as having grave consequences for the arts. How can people mechanically stamping out things that bear no mark of their producer's individuality (people thereby "reified," turned into things themselves) be expected to recognize, produce, or even consume things of beauty? And if there is no one to consume something, there will soon be no one to produce it, especially in an age in which production (even of something like literature) has come to mean *mass* (and therefore profitable) production.

In *The German Ideology* (1846), Marx and Engels expressed their sense of the relationship between the arts, politics, and basic economic reality in terms of a general social theory. Economics, they argued, provides the "base" or "infrastructure" of society, but from that base emerges a "superstructure" consisting of law, politics, philosophy, religion, and art.

Marx later admitted that the relationship between base and superstructure may be indirect and fluid: every change in economics may not be reflected by an immediate change in ethics or literature. In *The Eighteenth Brumaire of Louis Bonaparte* (1852), he came up with the word *homology* to describe the sometimes unbalanced, often delayed, and almost always loose correspondence between base and superstructure. And later in that same decade, while working on an introduction to his *Political Economy,* Marx further relaxed the base–superstructure relationship. Writing on the excellence of ancient Greek art (versus the primitive nature of ancient Greek economics), he conceded that a gap sometimes opens up between base and superstructure — between economic forms and those produced by the creative mind.

Nonetheless, *at* base the old formula was maintained. Economics remained basic and the connection between economics and superstructural elements of society was reaffirmed. Central to Marxism and Marxist literary criticism was and is the following "materialist" insight: consciousness, without which such things as art cannot be produced, is not the source of social forms and economic conditions. It is, rather, their most important product.

Marx and Engels, drawing upon the philosopher G. W. F. Hegel's theories about the dialectical synthesis of ideas out of theses and antitheses, believed that a revolutionary class war (pitting the capitalist class against a proletarian, antithetical class) would lead eventually to the synthesis of a new social and economic order. Placing their faith not in the idealist Hegelian dialectic but, rather, in what they called "dialectical materialism," they looked for a secular and material salvation of humanity — one in, not beyond, history — via revolution and not via divine intervention. And they believed that the communist society eventually established would be one capable of producing new forms of consciousness and belief and therefore, ultimately, great art.

The revolution anticipated by Marx and Engels did not occur in their century, let alone lifetime. When it finally did take place, it didn't happen in places where Marx and Engels had thought it might be successful: the United States, Great Britain, and Germany. It happened, rather, in 1917 Russia, a country long ruled by despotic czars but also enlightened by the works of powerful novelists and playwrights, including Chekhov, Pushkin, Tolstoy, and Dostoyevsky.

Perhaps because of its significant literary tradition, Russia produced revolutionaries like V. I. Lenin, who shared not only Marx's interest in literature but also his belief in literature's ultimate importance. But it was not without some hesitation that Lenin endorsed the significance of texts written during the reign of the czars. Well before 1917 he had questioned what the relationship should be between a society undergoing a revolution and the great old literature of its bourgeois past.

Lenin attempted to answer that question in a series of essays on Tolstoy that he wrote between 1908 and 1911. Tolstoy — the author of *War and Peace* and *Anna Karenina* — was an important nineteenth-century Russian writer whose views did not accord with all of those of young Marxist revolutionaries. Continuing interest in a writer like Tolstoy may be justified, Lenin reasoned, given the primitive and unenlightened economic order of the society that produced him. Since superstructure usually lags behind base (and is therefore usually *more* primitive), the attitudes of a Tolstoy were relatively progressive when viewed in light of the monarchical and precapitalist society out of which they arose.

Moreover, Lenin also reasoned, the writings of the great Russian realists would *have* to suffice, at least in the short run. Lenin looked forward, in essays like "Party Organization and Party Literature," to the day in which new artistic forms would be produced by progressive writers with revolutionary political views and agendas. But he also knew that a great proletarian literature was unlikely to evolve until a thoroughly literate proletariat had been produced by the educational system.

Lenin was hardly the only revolutionary leader involved in setting up the new Soviet state who took a strong interest in literary matters. In 1924 Leon Trotsky published a book called *Literature and Revolution*, which is still acknowledged as a classic of Marxist literary criticism.

Trotsky worried about the direction in which Marxist aesthetic theory seemed to be going. He responded skeptically to groups like Proletkult, which opposed tolerance toward pre- and nonrevolutionary writers, and which called for the establishment of a new, proletarian culture. Trotsky warned of the danger of cultural sterility and risked unpopularity by pointing out that there is no necessary connection between the quality of a literary work and the quality of its author's politics.

In 1927 Trotsky lost a power struggle with Josef Stalin, a man w believed, among other things, that writers should be "engine "human souls." After Trotsky's expulsion from the Soviet Union, views held by groups like Proletkult and the Left Front of Art (LEF), and by theorists such as Nikolai Bukharin and A. A. Zhdanov, became more prevalent. Speaking at the First Congress of the Union of Soviet Writers in 1934, the Soviet author Maxim Gorky called for writing that would "make labor the principal hero of our books." It was at the same writers' congress that "socialist realism," an art form glorifying workers and the revolutionary State, was made Communist party policy and the official literary form of the USSR.

Of the writers active in the USSR after the expulsion of Trotsky and the unfortunate triumph of Stalin, two critics stand out. One, Mikhail Bakhtin, was a Russian, later a Soviet, critic who spent much of his life in a kind of internal exile. Many of his essays were written in the 1930s and not published in the West or translated until the late 1960s. His work comes out of an engagement with the Marxist intellectual tradition as well as out of an indirect, even hidden, resistance to the Soviet government. It has been important to Marxist critics writing in the West because his theories provide a means to decode submerged social critique, especially in early modern texts. He viewed language — especially literary texts — in terms of discourses and dialogues. Within a novel written in a society in flux, for instance, the narrative may include an official, legitimate discourse, plus another infiltrated by challenging comments and even retorts. In a 1929 book on Dostoyevsky and a 1940 study titled *Rabelais and His World,* Bakhtin examined what he calls "polyphonic" novels, each characterized by a multiplicity of voices or discourses. In Dostoyevsky the independent status of a given character is marked by the difference of his or her language from that of the narrator. (The narrator's voice, too, can in fact be a dialogue.) In works by Rabelais, Bakhtin finds that the (profane) language of the carnival and of other popular festivals plays against and parodies the more official discourses, that is, of the king, church, or even socially powerful intellectuals. Bakhtin influenced modern cultural criticism by showing, in a sense, that the conflict between "high" and "low" culture takes place not only between classic and popular texts but also between the "dialogic" voices that exist within many books — whether "high" or "low."

The other subtle Marxist critic who managed to survive Stalin's dictatorship and his repressive policies was Georg Lukács. A Hungarian who had begun his career as an "idealist" critic, Lukács had converted to Marxism in 1919; renounced his earlier, Hegelian work shortly thereafter; visited Moscow in 1930–31; and finally emigrated to the

USSR in 1933, just one year before the First Congress of the Union of Soviet Writers met. Lukács was far less narrow in his views than the most strident Stalinist Soviet critics of the 1930s and 1940s. He disliked much socialist realism and appreciated prerevolutionary, realistic novels that broadly reflected cultural "totalities"— and were populated with characters representing human "types" of the author's place and time. (Lukács was particularly fond of the historical canvasses painted by the early nineteenth-century novelist Sir Walter Scott.) But like his more rigid and censorious contemporaries, he drew the line at accepting nonrevolutionary, modernist works like James Joyce's *Ulysses.* He condemned movements like expressionism and symbolism, preferring works with "content" over more decadent, experimental works characterized mainly by "form."

With Lukács its most liberal and tolerant critic from the early 1930s until well into the 1960s, the Soviet literary scene degenerated to the point that the works of great writers like Franz Kafka were no longer read, either because they were viewed as decadent, formal experiments or because they "engineered souls" in "nonprogressive" directions. Officially sanctioned works were generally ones in which artistry lagged far behind the politics (no matter how bad the politics were).

Fortunately for the Marxist critical movement, politically radical critics *outside* the Soviet Union were free of its narrow, constricting policies and, consequently, able fruitfully to develop the thinking of Marx, Engels, and Trotsky. It was these non-Soviet Marxists who kept Marxist critical theory alive and useful in discussing all *kinds* of literature, written across the entire historical spectrum.

Perhaps because Lukács was the best of the Soviet communists writing Marxist criticism in the 1930s and 1940s, non-Soviet Marxists tended to develop their ideas by publicly opposing those of Lukács. German dramatist and critic Bertolt Brecht countered Lukács by arguing that art ought to be viewed as a field of production, not as a container of "content." Brecht also criticized Lukács for his attempt to enshrine realism at the expense not only of other "isms" but also of poetry and drama, both of which had been largely ignored by Lukács.

Even more outspoken was Brecht's critical champion Walter Benjamin, a German Marxist who, in the 1930s, attacked those conventional and traditional literary forms conveying a stultifying "aura" of culture. Benjamin praised dadaism and, more important, new forms of art ushered in by the age of mechanical reproduction. Those forms — including radio and film — offered hope, he felt, for liberation f capitalist culture, for they were too new to be part of its stultifyingly ritualistic traditions.

But of all the anti-Lukácsians outside the USSR who made a contribution to the development of Marxist literary criticism, the most important was probably Théodor Adorno. Leader since the early 1950s of the Frankfurt school of Marxist criticism, Adorno attacked Lukács for his dogmatic rejection of nonrealist modern literature and for his belief in the primacy of content over form. Art does not equal science, Adorno insisted. He went on to argue for art's autonomy from empirical forms of knowledge and to suggest that the interior monologues of modernist works (by Beckett and Proust) reflect the fact of modern alienation in a way that Marxist criticism ought to find compelling.

In addition to turning against Lukács and his overly constrictive canon, Marxists outside the Soviet Union were able to take advantage of insights generated by non-Marxist critical theories being developed in post–World War II Europe. One of the movements that came to be of interest to non-Soviet Marxists was structuralism, a scientific approach to the study of humankind whose proponents believed that all elements of culture, including literature, could be understood as parts of a system of signs. Using modern linguistics as a model, structuralists like Claude Lévi-Strauss broke down the myths of various cultures into "mythemes" in an attempt to show that there are structural correspondences, or homologies, between the mythical elements produced by various human communities across time.

Of the European structuralist Marxists, one of the most influential was Lucien Goldmann, a Rumanian critic living in Paris. Goldmann combined structuralist principles with Marx's base–superstructure model in order to show how economics determines the mental structures of social groups, which are reflected in literary texts. Goldmann rejected the idea of individual human genius, choosing to see works, instead, as the "collective" products of "trans-individual" mental structures. In early studies, such as *The Hidden God* (1955), he related seventeenth-century French texts (such as Racine's *Phèdre*) to the ideology of Jansenism. In later works, he applied Marx's base–superstructure model even more strictly, describing a relationship between economic conditions and texts unmediated by an intervening, collective consciousness.

In spite of his rigidity and perhaps because of his affinities with structuralism, Goldmann came to be seen in the 1960s as the proponent of a kind of watered-down, "humanist" Marxism. He was certainly viewed that way by the French Marxist Louis Althusser, a disciple not of Lévi-Strauss and structuralism but rather of the psychoanalytic theorist Jacques Lacan and of the Italian communist Antonio Gramsci, famous for his writings about ideology and "hegemony." (Gramsci used the latter word to refer to the pervasive, weblike system of assumptions and values that shapes the way things look, what they mean, and therefore what reality *is* for the majority of people within a culture.)

Like Gramsci, Althusser viewed literary works primarily in terms of their relationship to ideology, the function of which, he argued, is to (re)produce the existing relations of production in a given society. Dave Laing, in *The Marxist Theory of Art* (1978), has attempted to explain this particular insight of Althusser by saying that ideologies, through the "ensemble of habits, moralities, and opinions" that can be found in any literary text, "ensure that the work-force (and those responsible for re-producing them in the family, school, etc.) are maintained in their position of subordination to the dominant class" (91). This is not to say that Althusser thought of the masses as a brainless multitude following only the dictates of the prevailing ideology: Althusser followed Gramsci in suggesting that even working-class people have some freedom to struggle against ideology and to change history. Nor is it to say that Althusser saw ideology as being a coherent, consistent force. In fact, he saw it as being riven with contradictions that works of literature sometimes expose and even widen. Thus Althusser followed Marx and Gramsci in believing that although literature must be seen in *relation* to ideology, it — like all social forms — has some degree of autonomy.

Althusser's followers included Pierre Macherey, who in *A Theory of Literary Production* (1978) developed Althusser's concept of the relationship between literature and ideology. A realistic novelist, he argued, attempts to produce a unified, coherent text, but instead ends up producing a work containing lapses, omissions, gaps. This happens because within ideology there are subjects that cannot be covered, things that cannot be said, contradictory views that aren't recognized as contradictory. (The critic's challenge, in this case, is to supply what the text cannot say, thereby making sense of gaps and contradictions.)

But there is another reason why gaps open up and contradictions become evident in texts. Works don't just reflect ideology (which Goldmann had referred to as "myth" and which Macherey refers to as a system of "illusory social beliefs"); they are also "fictions," works of art, *products* of ideology that have what Goldmann would call a "worldview" to offer. What kind of product, Macherey implicitly asks, is identical to the thing that produced it? It is hardly surprising, then, that Balzac's fiction shows French peasants in two different lights, only one of which is critical and judgmental, only one of which is baldly ideological.

Writing approvingly on Macherey and Macherey's mentor Althusser in *Marxism and Literary Criticism* (1976), Terry Eagleton says: "It is by giving ideology a determinate form, fixing it within certain fictional limits, that art is able to distance itself from [ideology], thus revealing . . . [its] limits" (19).

A follower of Althusser, Macherey is sometimes referred to as a "post-Althusserian Marxist." Eagleton, too, is often described that way, as is his American contemporary Fredric Jameson. Jameson and Eagleton, as well as being post-Althusserians, are also among the few Anglo-American critics who have closely followed and significantly developed Marxist thought.

Before them, Marxist interpretation in English was limited to the work of a handful of critics: Christopher Caudwell, Christopher Hill, Arnold Kettle, E. P. Thompson, and Raymond Williams. Of these, Williams was perhaps least Marxist in orientation: he felt that Marxist critics, ironically, tended too much to isolate economics from culture; that they overlooked the individualism of people, opting instead to see them as "masses"; and that even more ironically, they had become an elitist group. But if the least Marxist of the British Marxists, Williams was also by far the most influential. Preferring to talk about "culture" instead of ideology, Williams argued in works such as *Culture and Society 1780–1950* (1958) that culture is "lived experience" and, as such, an interconnected set of social properties, each and all grounded in and influencing history.

Terry Eagleton's *Criticism and Ideology* is in many ways a response to the work of Williams. Responding to Williams's statement in *Culture and Society* that "there are in fact no masses; there are only ways of seeing people as masses" (289), Eagleton writes:

> That men and women really are now unique individuals was Williams's (unexceptionable) insistence; but it was a proposition bought at the expense of perceiving the fact that they must mass and fight to achieve their full individual humanity. One has only to adapt Williams's statement to "There are in fact no classes; there are only ways of seeing people as classes" to expose its theoretical paucity. (*Criticism* 29)

Eagleton goes on, in *Criticism and Ideology,* to propose an elaborate theory about how history — in the form of "general," "authorial," and "aesthetic" ideology — enters texts, which in turn may revivify, open up, or critique those same ideologies, thereby setting in motion a process that may alter history. He shows how texts by Jane Austen, Matthew Arnold, Charles Dickens, George Eliot, Joseph Conrad, and T. S. Eliot deal with and transmute conflicts at the heart of the general and authorial ideologies behind them: conflicts between morality and individualism, and between individualism and social organicism and utilitarianism.

As all this emphasis on ideology and conflict suggests, a modern British Marxist like Eagleton, even while acknowledging the work of a British Marxist predecessor like Williams, is more nearly developing the ideas of Continental Marxists like Althusser and Macherey. That holds, as well, for modern American Marxists like Fredric Jameson. For although he makes occasional, sympathetic references to the works of Williams, Thompson, and Hill, Jameson makes far more *use* of Lukács, Adorno, and Althusser as well as non-Marxist structuralist, psychoanalytic, and poststructuralist critics.

In the first of several influential works, *Marxism and Form* (1971), Jameson takes up the question of form and content, arguing that the former is "but the working out" of the latter "in the realm of superstructure" (329). (In making such a statement Jameson opposes not only the tenets of Russian formalists, for whom content had merely been the fleshing out of form, but also those of so-called vulgar Marxists, who tended to define form as mere ornamentation or window dressing.) In his later work *The Political Unconscious* (1981), Jameson uses what in *Marxism and Form* he had called "dialectical criticism" to synthesize out of structuralism and poststructuralism, Freud and Lacan, Althusser and Adorno, a set of complex arguments that can only be summarized reductively.

The fractured state of societies and the isolated condition of individuals, he argues, may be seen as indications that there originally existed an unfallen state of something that may be called "primitive communism." History — which records the subsequent divisions and alienations — limits awareness of its own contradictions and of that lost, Better State, via ideologies and their manifestation in texts whose strategies essentially contain and repress desire, especially revolutionary desire, into the collective unconscious. (In Conrad's *Lord Jim,* Jameson shows, the knowledge that governing classes don't *deserve* their power is contained and repressed by an ending that metaphysically blames Nature for the tragedy and that melodramatically blames wicked Gentleman Brown.)

As demonstrated by Jameson in analyses like the one mentioned above, textual strategies of containment and concealment may be discovered by the critic, but only by the critic practicing dialectical criticism, that is to say, a criticism aware, among other things, of its *own* status as ideology. All thought, Jameson concludes, is ideological; only through ideological thought that knows itself as such can ideologies be seen through and eventually transcended.

In the essay that follows, Terry Eagleton upholds the general tenets of Marxist criticism by seeing *Wuthering Heights* not in terms of its intricate, concentric circles of narrative but, rather, in terms of its reference to class, economics, history. Eagleton is, furthermore, interested in the novel's relationship to its culture's ideology — as well as in the different relationships that different novels have to that ideology with which they are inscribed.

Although declaring "suspect" Lucien Goldmann's distinction between ideology and "world-view," Eagleton goes on to use just that distinction to discuss differences between Charlotte Brontë's novel *Jane Eyre* and Emily Brontë's *Wuthering Heights. Jane Eyre,* Eagleton suggests, comes close to merely expressing the ideology of its culture. It is therefore, in a "precise sense," what Goldmann would call a "myth": that is, it achieves "an illusory resolution of real contradictions" (p. 394 in this volume) in such a way as to validate ideology and the societal *status quo.* Although it is coherent in the way that all fairy tales are coherent, it is riven by the strains attendant upon achieving its proper ideological closure.

Wuthering Heights, on the other hand, is a myth of a different, darker color, offering more like what Goldmann calls a "world-view." It is coherent insofar as it offers a coherent perception of the terrible contradictions, the awful choices available, within the culture. Whereas *Jane Eyre* shows a governess ending up rich without compromising either her desire for Lord Rochester or her fidelity to middle-class morality, *Wuthering Heights,* Eagleton shows, depicts characters forced to choose between desire and physical comfort, integrity and social convention, passionate being and economic *well*-being, *living* and surviving.

In a classed, sexist society, Catherine Earnshaw — the younger sister of a middle-class young man who, by the laws of patrimony, will inherit Wuthering Heights — is forced to choose between the man she loves and a man whose class will ensure her well-being, for herself and her children. And, given the fact that Heathcliff has disappeared just before that choice is forced upon her (he has disappeared in an attempt, unbeknownst to Catherine, to acquire enough "cultural capital" to compete with Edgar), Catherine really has little choice to make. Finally, when Heathcliff returns a rich man, he is not only too late to marry Catherine but also a *changed* man. It is simply impossible, Eagleton maintains, to acquire cultural capital and, at the same time, maintain full, personal integrity in the world defined by *Wuthering Heights.* "Authentic" being is always in conflict, and the resolution of such conflicts is never accomplished without someone or something sustaining a terrible loss.

"*Wuthering Heights* remains unriven by the conflicts it releases," Eagleton argues, "and it contrasts as such with those Charlotte works which are formally flawed by the strains and frictions of their 'content'" (pp. 395–96). Although Eagleton does not allude to the work of Pierre Macherey, his analysis of Charlotte Brontë's works — and, especially, *Jane Eyre* — has clearly been influenced by Macherey's thought. For he suggests that *Jane Eyre* can bear its ideological message (that romance is realistic, that a poor girl can become a "lady," that one can be authentic while still remaining quite properly within social convention) only under stress; its author has had to resort to resolutions so flimsy (and therefore so "strained") that they can be seen through, thereby providing gaps through which what cannot be said *within* the ideology can, with the help of Marxist analysis, at least be read from outside it.

However, whereas Eagleton's reading of *Jane Eyre* would seem to owe a great deal to Macherey and his thought, his reading of *Wuthering Heights* as a "form . . . *un*riven" (emphasis added) that reveals *outward* contradictions implicitly reveals the limitations of a method like that of Macherey. Some works, Eagleton suggests — perhaps those Goldmann would see as offering a "world-view" and not just another mythical version of the ideology — resist simple formulations — even Marxist ones.

Ross C Murfin

MARXIST CRITICISM: A SELECTED BIBLIOGRAPHY

Marx, Engels, Lenin, and Trotsky

Engels, Friedrich. *The Condition of the Working Class in England.* Ed. and trans. W. O. Henderson and W. H. Chaloner. Stanford: Stanford UP, 1968.

Lenin, V. I. *On Literature and Art.* Moscow: Progress, 1967.

Marx, Karl. *Selected Writings.* Ed. David McLellan. Oxford: Oxford UP, 1977.

Trotsky, Leon. *Literature and Revolution.* 1924. New York: Russell, 1967.

General Introductions to and Reflections on Marxist Criticism

Bennett, Tony. *Formalism and Marxism.* London: Methuen, 1979.

Demetz, Peter. *Marx, Engels, and the Poets.* Chicago: U of Chicago P, 1967.

Eagleton, Terry. *Literary Theory: An Introduction.* Minneapolis: U of Minnesota P, 1983.

———. *Marxism and Literary Criticism.* Berkeley: U of California P, 1976.

Elster, Jon. *An Introduction to Karl Marx.* Cambridge: Cambridge UP, 1985.

———. *Nuts and Bolts for the Social Sciences.* Cambridge: Cambridge UP, 1989.

Fokkema, D. W., and Elrud Kunne-Ibsch. *Theories of Literature in the Twentieth Century: Structuralism, Marxism, Aesthetics of Reception, Semiotics.* New York: St. Martin's, 1977. See ch. 4, "Marxist Theories of Literature."

Frow, John. *Marxism and Literary History.* Cambridge: Harvard UP, 1986.

Jefferson, Ann, and David Robey. *Modern Literary Theory: A Critical Introduction.* Totowa, NJ: Barnes, 1982. See the essay "Marxist Literary Theories," by David Forgacs.

Laing, Dave. *The Marxist Theory of Art.* Brighton: Harvester, 1978.

Selden, Raman, Peter Widdowson, and Peter Brooker. *A Readers' Guide to Contemporary Literary Theory.* 4th ed. Lexington: U of Kentucky P, 1997. See ch. 5, "Marxist Theories."

Slaughter, Cliff. *Marxism, Ideology, and Literature.* Atlantic Highlands: Humanities, 1980.

Some Classic Marxist Studies and Statements

Adorno, Théodor. *Prisms: Cultural Criticism and Society.* Trans. Samuel Weber and Sherry Weber. Cambridge: MIT P, 1982.

Althusser, Louis. *For Marx.* Trans. Ben Brewster. New York: Pantheon, 1969.

Althusser, Louis, and Étienne Balibar. *Reading Capital.* Trans. Ben Brewster. New York: Pantheon, 1971.

Bakhtin, Mikhail. *The Dialogic Imagination: Four Essays.* Ed. Michael Holquist. Trans. Caryl Emerson. Austin: U of Texas P, 1981.

———. *Rabelais and His World.* Trans. Hélène Iswolsky. Cambridge: MIT P, 1968.

Benjamin, Walter. *Illuminations.* Ed. with introd. by Hannah Arendt. Trans. H. Zohn. New York: Harcourt, 1968.

Brecht, Bertolt. *Brecht on Theatre: The Development of an Aesthetic.* Ed. and trans. John Willett. New York: Hill, 1964.

———. *William Morris: Romantic to Revolutionary.* New York: Pantheon, 1977.

Caudwell, Christopher. *Illusion and Reality.* 1935. New York: Russell, 1955.

———. *Studies in a Dying Culture.* London: Lawrence, 1938.

Goldmann, Lucien. *The Hidden God.* New York: Humanities, 1964.

———. *Towards a Sociology of the Novel.* London: Tavistock, 1975.

Gramsci, Antonio. *Selections from the Prison Notebooks.* Ed. Quintin Hoare and Geoffrey Nowell Smith. New York: International UP, 1971.

Kettle, Arnold. *An Introduction to the English Novel.* New York: Harper, 1960.

Lukács, Georg. *The Historical Novel.* Trans. H. Mitchell and S. Mitchell. Boston: Beacon, 1963.

———. *Studies in European Realism.* New York: Grosset, 1964.

———. *The Theory of the Novel.* Cambridge: MIT P, 1971.

Marcuse, Herbert. *One-Dimensional Man.* Boston: Beacon, 1964.

Thompson, E. P. *The Making of the English Working Class.* New York: Pantheon, 1964.

Williams, Raymond. *Culture and Society 1780–1950.* New York: Harper, 1958.

———. *The Long Revolution.* New York: Columbia UP, 1961.

———. *Marxism and Literature.* Oxford: Oxford UP, 1977.

Wilson, Edmund. *To the Finland Station.* Garden City: Doubleday, 1953.

Studies by and of Post-Althusserian Marxists

Dowling, William C. *Jameson, Althusser, Marx: An Introduction to "The Political Unconscious."* Ithaca: Cornell UP, 1984.

Eagleton, Terry. *Criticism and Ideology: A Study in Marxist Literary Theory.* London: Verso, 1978.

———. *Exiles and Émigrés.* New York: Schocken, 1970.

Goux, Jean-Joseph. *Symbolic Economies after Marx and Freud.* Trans. Jennifer Gage. Ithaca: Cornell UP, 1990.

Jameson, Fredric. *Marxism and Form: Twentieth-Century Dialectical Theories of Literature.* Princeton: Princeton UP, 1971.

———. *The Political Unconscious: Narrative as a Socially Symbolic Act.* Ithaca: Cornell UP, 1981.

Macherey, Pierre. *A Theory of Literary Production.* Trans. G. Wall. London: Routledge, 1978.

Marxist Criticism Relating to *Wuthering Heights*

Eagleton, Terry. "Heathcliff and the Great Hunger." *Heathcliff and the Great Hunger.* London: Verso, 1995. 1–26.

———. *Myths of Power: A Marxist Study of the Brontës.* London: Macmillan, 1975.

Kettle, Arnold. "Emily Brontë: *Wuthering Heights.*" *An Introduction to the English Novel.* New York: Harper, 1968. 130–45.

Lenta, Margaret. "Capitalism or Patriarchy and Immoral Love: A Study of *Wuthering Heights.*" *Theoria: A Journal of Studies in the Arts, Humanities and Social Sciences* 62 (1984): 63–76.

Williams, Raymond. "Charlotte and Emily Brontë." *The English Novel from Dickens to Lawrence.* London: Chatto, 1970. 50–61.

Wilson, David. "Emily Brontë: First of the Moderns." *Modern Quarterly Miscellany* 1 (1947): 94–115.

A MARXIST PERSPECTIVE

TERRY EAGLETON

Myths of Power: A Marxist Study on *Wuthering Heights*

If it is a function of ideology to achieve an illusory resolution of real contradictions, then Charlotte Brontë's novels are ideological in a precise sense — myths. In the fabulous, fairy-tale ambience of a work like *Jane Eyre,* with its dramatic archetypes and magical devices, certain facets of the complex mythology which constitutes Victorian bourgeois consciousness find their aesthetically appropriate form. Yet "myth" is, of course, a term more commonly used of *Wuthering Heights;* and we need therefore to discriminate between different meanings of the word.

For Lucien Goldmann, "ideology" in literature is to be sharply distinguished from what he terms "world-view." Ideology signifies a false, distortive, partial consciousness; "world-view" designates a true, total, and coherent understanding of social relations. This seems to me a highly suspect formulation, but even so, Goldmann's questionable distinction can be used to illuminate a crucial difference between the work of Charlotte and Emily Brontë. Charlotte's fiction is "mythical" in an exact ideological sense: it welds together antagonistic forces, forging from them a pragmatic, precarious coherence of interests. *Wuthering Heights* is mythical in a more traditional sense of the term: an apparently timeless, highly integrated, mysteriously autonomous symbolic universe. Such a notion of myth is itself, of course, ideologically based, and much of this essay will be an attempt to de-mystify it. The world of *Wuthering Heights* is neither external nor self-enclosed; nor is it in the least unriven by internal contradictions. But in the case of this work it does seem necessary to speak of a "world-view," a unified vision of brilliant clarity and consistency. *Wuthering Heights* achieves its coherence of vision from an exhausting confrontation of contending forces, whereas Charlotte's kind of totality depends upon a pragmatic integration of them. Both forms of consciousness are ideological; but insofar as Emily's represents a more penetrative, radical, and honest enterprise, it provides the basis for a finer artistic achievement. *Wuthering Heights* remains formally unfissured by the conflicts it dramatizes; it forges its unity of vision from the very imaginative heat those conflicts generate. The book's genealogical structure is relevant here: familial relations at once provide the substance of antagonism and mold that substance into intricate shape, precipitating a tightly integrated form from the very stuff of struggle and disintegration. The genealogical structure, moreover, allows for a sharply dialectical relation between the "personal" and "impersonal": the family, at once social institution and domain of intensely interpersonal relationships, highlights the complex interplay between an evolving system of given unalterable relations and the creation of individual value. One is tempted, then, to credit Goldmann's dubious dichotomy between ideology and world-view to this extent: that if "ideology" is a coherence of antagonisms, "world-view" is a coherent perception of them.

I have said that *Wuthering Heights* remains unriven by the conflicts it releases, and it contrasts as such with those Charlotte works which are formally flawed by the strains and frictions of their "content." Charlotte's fiction sets out to reconcile thematically what might be crudely termed "Romance" and "realism" but sometimes displays severe structural disjunctions between the two; *Wuthering Heights* fastens thematically on a near-absolute antagonism between these modes but achieves, structurally and stylistically, an astonishing unity between them. Single incidents are inseparably high drama and domestic farce, figures like Catherine Earnshaw contradictory amalgams of the passionate and the pettish. There seems to me an ideological basis to this paradoxical contrast between the two sisters' works. Charlotte's novels, as I have suggested, are ideological in that they exploit fiction and fable to smooth the jagged edges of real conflict, and the evasions which that entails emerge as aesthetic unevennesses — as slanting, overemphasis, idealization, structural dissonance. *Wuthering Heights,* on the other hand, confronts the tragic truth that the passion and society it presents are not fundamentally reconcilable — that there remains at the deepest level an ineradicable contradiction between them which refuses to be unlocked, which obtrudes itself as the very stuff and secret of experience. It is, then, precisely the imagination capable of confronting this tragic duality which has the power to produce the aesthetically superior work — which can synchronize in its internal structures the most shattering passion with the most rigorous realist control. The more authentic social and moral recognitions of the book, in other words, generate a finer artistic control; the unflinchingness with which the novel penetrates into fundamental contradictions is realized in a range of rich imaginative perceptions.

The primary contradiction I have in mind is the choice posed for Catherine between Heathcliff and Edgar Linton. That choice seems to me the pivotal event of the novel, the decisive catalyst of the tragedy; and if this is so, then the crux of *Wuthering Heights* must be conceded by even the most remorselessly mythological and mystical of critics to be a social one. In a crucial act of self-betrayal and bad faith, Catherine rejects Heathcliff as a suitor because he is socially inferior to Linton; and it is from this that the train of destruction follows. Heathcliff's own view of the option is not, of course, to be wholly credited: he is clearly wrong to think that Edgar " 'is scarcely a degree dearer to [Catherine] than her dog, or her horse' " (p. 141). Linton lacks spirit, but he is, as Nelly says, kind, honorable, and trustful, a loving husband to Catherine and utterly distraught at her loss. Even so, the perverse act of *mauvaise foi* by which Catherine trades her authentic selfhood for social privilege is rightly denounced by Heathcliff as spiritual suicide and murder:

> "*Why* did you betray your own heart, Cathy? I have not one word of comfort — you deserve this. You have killed yourself. Yes, you may kiss me, and cry; and wring out my kisses and tears. They'll blight you — they'll damn you. You loved me — then what *right* had you to leave me? What right — answer me — for the poor fancy you felt for Linton? Because misery, and degradation, and death, and nothing that God or satan could inflict would have parted us, *you*, of your own will, did it. I have not broken your heart — *you* have broken it — and in breaking it, you have broken mine." (p. 150)

Catherine tries to lead two lives: she hopes to square authenticity with social convention, running in harness an ontological commitment to Heathcliff with a phenomenal relationship to Linton. "'I *am* Heathcliff!'" (p. 88) is dramatically arresting, but it is also a way of keeping the outcast at arm's length, evading the challenge he offers. Catherine's attempt to compromise unleashes the contradictions which will drive both her and Heathcliff to their deaths. One such contradiction lies in the relation between Heathcliff and the Earnshaw family. As a waif and orphan, Heathcliff is inserted into the close-knit family structure as an alien; he emerges from that ambivalent domain of darkness which is the "outside" of the tightly defined domestic system. That darkness is ambivalent because it is at once fearful and fertilizing, as Heathcliff himself is both gift and threat. Earnshaw's first words about him make this clear: "'See here, wife; I was never so beaten with anything in my life; but you must e'en take it as a gift of God; though it's as dark almost as if it came from the devil'" (p. 51). Stripped as he is of determinate social relations, of a given function within the family, Heathcliff's presence is radically gratuitous; the arbitrary, unmotivated event of his arrival at the Heights offers its inhabitants a chance to transcend the constrictions of their self-enclosed social structure and gather him in. Because Heathcliff's circumstances are so obscure, he is available to be accepted or rejected simply for himself, laying claim to no status other than a human one. He is, of course, proletarian in appearance, but the obscurity of his origins also frees him of any exact social role; as Nelly Dean muses later, he might equally be a prince. He is ushered into the Heights for no good reason other than to be arbitrarily loved; and in this sense he is a touchstone of others' responses, a liberating force for Cathy and a stumbling-block for others. Nelly hates him at first, unable to transcend her bigotry against the new and non-related; she puts him on the landing like a dog, hoping he will be gone by morning.

Earnshaw pets and favors him, and in doing so creates fresh inequalities in the family hierarchy which become the source of Hindley's hatred. As heir to the Heights, Hindley understandably feels his social role subverted by this irrational, unpredictable intrusion.

Catherine, who does not expect to inherit, responds spontaneously to Heathcliff's presence; and because this antagonizes Hindley she becomes after Earnshaw's death a spiritual orphan as Heathcliff is a literal one. Both are allowed to run wild; both become the "outside" of the domestic structure. Because his birth is unknown, Heathcliff is a purely atomized individual, free of generational ties in a novel where genealogical relations are of crucial thematic and structural importance; and it is because he is an internal *émigré* within the Heights that he can lay claim to a relationship of direct personal equality with Catherine who, as the daughter of the family, is the least economically integral member. Heathcliff offers Catherine a friendship which opens fresh possibilities of freedom within the internal system of the Heights; in a situation where social determinants are insistent, freedom can mean only a relative independence of given blood-ties, of the settled, evolving, predictable structures of kinship. Whereas in Charlotte's fiction the severing or lapsing of such relations frees you for progress up the class-system, the freedom which Cathy achieves with Heathcliff takes her down that system, into consorting with a "gypsy." Yet "down" is also "outside," just as gypsy signifies "lower class" but also a social vagrant, classless natural life-form. As the eternal rocks beneath the woods, Heathcliff is both lowly and natural, enjoying the partial freedom from social pressures appropriate to those at the bottom of the class-structure. In loving Heathcliff, Catherine is taken outside the family and society into an opposing realm which can be adequately imaged only as "Nature."

The loving equality between Catherine and Heathcliff stands, then, as a paradigm of human possibilities which reach beyond, and might ideally unlock, the tightly dominative system of the Heights. Yet at the same time Heathcliff's mere presence fiercely intensifies that system's harshness, twisting all the Earnshaw relationships into bitter antagonism. He unwittingly sharpens a violence endemic to the Heights — a violence which springs both from the hard exigencies imposed by its struggle with the land, and from its social exclusiveness as a self-consciously ancient, respectable family. The violence which Heathcliff unwittingly triggers is turned against him: he is cast out by Hindley, culturally deprived, reduced to the status of farm-laborer. What Hindley does, in fact, is to invert the potential freedom symbolized by Heathcliff into a parody of itself, into the non-freedom of neglect. Heathcliff is robbed of liberty in two antithetical ways: exploited as a servant on the one hand, allowed to run wild on the other; and this contradiction is appropriate to childhood, which is a time of relative freedom from convention and yet, paradoxically, a phase of authoritarian repression. In this sense there is freedom for Heathcliff neither within society nor outside it; his two conditions are inverted mirror-images of one another. It is a contradiction which encapsulates a crucial truth about bourgeois society. If there is no genuine liberty on its "inside" — Heathcliff is oppressed by work and the familial structure — neither is there more than a caricature of liberty on the "outside," since the release of running wild is merely a function of cultural impoverishment. The friendship of Heathcliff and Cathy crystallizes under the pressures of economic and cultural violence so that the freedom it seems to signify (" 'half savage and hardy, and free' " [p. 123]) is always the other face of oppression, always exists in its shadow. With Heathcliff and Catherine, bitter social reality breeds Romantic escapism. Romantic intensity is locked in combat with society, but cannot wholly transcend it; your freedom is bred and deformed in the shadow of your oppression, just as, in the adult Heathcliff, oppression is the logical consequence of the exploiter's "freedom."

Just as Hindley withdraws culture from Heathcliff as a mode of domination, so Heathcliff acquires culture as a weapon. He amasses a certain amount of cultural capital in his two years' absence in order to shackle others more effectively, buying up the expensive commodity of gentility in order punitively to re-enter the society from which he was punitively expelled. This is liberty of a kind, in contrast with his previous condition; but the novel is insistent on its ultimately illusory nature. In oppressing others the exploiter imprisons himself; the adult Heathcliff's systematic tormenting is fed by his victims' pain but also drains him of blood, impels and possesses him as an external force. His alienation from Catherine estranges him from himself to the point where his brutalities become tediously perfunctory gestures, the mechanical motions of a man who is already withdrawing himself from his own body. Heathcliff moves from being Hindley's victim to becoming, like Catherine, his own executioner.

Throughout *Wuthering Heights,* labor and culture, bondage and freedom, Nature and artifice appear at once as each other's dialectical negations and as subtly matched, mutually reflective. Culture — gentility — is the opposite of labor for young Heathcliff and Hareton; but it is also a crucial economic weapon, as well as a product of work itself. The delicate spiritless Lintons in their crimson-carpeted drawing-room are radically severed from the labor which sustains them; gentility grows from the production of others, detaches itself from that work (as the Grange is separate from the Heights), and then comes to dominate the labor on which it is parasitic. In doing so, it becomes a form of self-bondage; if work is servitude, so in a subtler sense is civilization. To some extent, these polarities are held together in the yeoman-farming structure of the Heights. Here labor and culture, freedom and necessity, Nature and society are roughly complementary. The Earnshaws are gentlemen yet they work the land; they enjoy the freedom of being their own masters, but that freedom moves within the tough discipline of labor; and because the social unit of the Heights — the family — is both "natural" (biological) and an economic system, it acts to some degree as a mediation between Nature and artifice, naturalizing property relations and socializing blood-ties. Even so, the Heights does pin together contradictions which the entry of Heathcliff will break open. Heathcliff disturbs the Heights because he is simply superfluous: he has no defined place within its biological and economic system. (He may well be Catherine's illegitimate half-brother, just as he may well have passed his two-year absence in Tunbridge Wells.) The superfluity he embodies is that of a sheerly human demand for recognition; but since there is no space for such surplus within the terse economy of the Heights, it proves destructive rather than creative in effect, straining and overloading already taut relationships. Heathcliff catalyzes an aggression intrinsic to Heights society; that sound blow Hindley hands out to Catherine on the evening of Heathcliff's first appearance is slight but significant evidence against the case that conflict starts only with Heathcliff's arrival.

The effect of Heathcliff is to explode those conflicts into antagonisms which finally rip the place apart. In particular, he marks the beginnings of that process whereby passion and personal intensity separate out from the social domain and offer an alternative commitment to it. For farming families like the Earnshaws, work and human relations are roughly coterminous: work is socialized, personal relations mediated through a context of labor. Heathcliff, however, is set to work meaninglessly, as a servant rather than a member of the family; and his fervent emotional life with Catherine is thus forced outside the working environment into the wild Nature of the heath, rather than Nature reclaimed and worked up into significant value in the social activity of labor. Heathcliff is stripped of culture in the sense of gentility, but the result is a paradoxical intensifying of his fertile imaginative liaison with Catherine. It is fitting, then, that their free, neglected wanderings lead them to their adventure at Thrushcross Grange. For if the Romantic childhood culture of Catherine and Heathcliff exists in a social limbo divorced from the minatory world of working relations, the same can be said in a different sense of the genteel culture of the Lintons, surviving as it does on the basis of material conditions it simultaneously conceals. As the children spy on the Linton family, that concealed brutality is unleashed in the shape of bulldogs brought to the defense of civility. The natural energy in which the Lintons' culture is rooted bursts literally through to savage the "savages" who appear to threaten property. The underlying truth of violence, continuously visible at the Heights, is momentarily exposed; old Linton thinks the intruders are after his rents. Culture draws a veil over such brute force but also sharpens it: the more property you have, the more ruthlessly you need to defend it. Indeed, Heathcliff himself seems dimly aware of how cultivation exacerbates "natural" conflict, as we see in his scornful account of the Linton children's petulant squabbling; cultivation, by pampering and swaddling "natural" drives, at once represses serious physical violence and breeds a neurasthenic sensitivity which allows selfish impulse freed rein. "Natural" aggression is nurtured both by an excess and an absence of culture — a paradox demonstrated by Catherine Earnshaw, who is at once wild and pettish, savage and spoilt. Nature and culture, then, are locked in a complex relation of antagonism and affinity.

Nature, in any case, is no true "outside" to society, since its conflicts are transposed into the social arena. In one sense the novel sharply contrasts Nature and society; in another sense it grasps civilized life as a higher distillation of ferocious natural appetite. Nature, then, is a thoroughly ambiguous category, inside and outside society simultaneously. At one level it represents the unsalvaged region beyond the pale of culture; at another level it signifies the all-pervasive reality of which culture itself is a particular outcropping. It is, indeed, this ambiguity which supplies the vital link between the childhood and adult phases of Heathcliff's career. Heathcliff the child is "natural" both because he is allowed to run wild and because he is reduced as Hindley's laborer to a mere physical instrument; Heathcliff the adult is "natural" man in a Hobbesian sense: an appetitive exploiter to whom no tie or tradition is sacred, a callous predator violently sundering the bonds of custom and piety. If the first of "naturalness" is anti-social in its estrangement from the norms of "civilized" life, the second involves the unsociality of one set at the center of a world whose social relations are inhuman. Heathcliff moves from being natural in the sense of an anarchic outsider to adopting the behavior natural to an insider in a viciously competitive society. Of course, to be natural in both senses is at a different level to be unnatural. From the viewpoint of culture, it is unnatural that a child should be degraded to a savage, and unnatural too that a man should behave in the obscene way Heathcliff does. But culture in his novel is as problematical as Nature. The dialectical vision of *Wuthering Heights* puts culture into question in the very act of exploring the "naturalness" which is its negation. Just as being natural involves being either completely outside or inside society, as roaming waif or manipulative landlord, so culture signifies either free-wheeling Romantic fantasy or that well-appointed Linton drawing-room. The adult Heathcliff is the focus of these contradictions: as he worms his way into the social structure he becomes progressively detached in spirit from all it holds dear. But *contradiction* is the essential emphasis. Heathcliff's schizophrenia is symptomatic of a world in which there can be no true dialectic between culture and Nature — a world in which culture is merely refuge from or reflex of material conditions, and so either too estranged from or entwined with those conditions to offer a viable alternative.

I take it that Heathcliff, up to the point at which Cathy rejects him, is in general an admirable character. His account of the Grange adventure, candid, satirical, and self-aware as it is, might itself be enough to enforce this point; and we have in any case on the other side only the self-confessedly biased testimony of Nelly Dean. Even according to Nelly's grudging commentary, Heathcliff as a child is impressively patient and uncomplaining (although Nelly adds "sullen" out of spite), and the heart-rending cry he raises when old Earnshaw dies is difficult to square with her implication that he felt no gratitude to his benefactor. He bears Hindley's vindictive treatment well, and tries pathetically to keep culturally abreast of Catherine despite it. The novel says quite explicitly that Hindley's systematic degradation of Heathcliff "was enough to make a fiend of a saint" (p. 74); and we should not therefore be surprised that what it does, more precisely, is to produce a pitiless capitalist landlord out of an oppressed child. Heathcliff the adult is in one sense an inversion, in another sense an organic outgrowth, of Heathcliff the child. Heathcliff the child was an isolated figure whose freedom from given genealogical ties offered, as I have argued, fresh possibilities of relationship; Heathcliff the adult is the atomic capitalist to whom relational bonds are nothing, whose individualism is now enslaving rather than liberating. The child knew the purely negative freedom of running wild; the adult, as a man vehemently pursuing ends progressively alien to him, knows only the delusory freedom of exploiting others. The point is that such freedom seems the only kind available in this society, once the relationship with Catherine has collapsed; the only mode of self-affirmation left to Heathcliff is that of oppression which, since it involves self-oppression, is no affirmation at all. Heathcliff is a self-tormentor, a man who is in hell because he can avenge himself on the system which has robbed him of his soul only by battling with it on its own hated terms. If as a child he was outside and inside that system simultaneously, wandering on the moors and working on the farm, he lives out of a similar self-division as an adult, trapped in the grinding contradiction between a false social self and the true identity which lies with Catherine. The social self is false, not because Heathcliff is only apparently brutal — that he certainly is — but because it is contradictorily related to the authentic selfhood which is his passion for Catherine. He installs himself at the center of conventional society, but with wholly negative and inimical intent; his social role is a calculated self-contradiction, created first to further, and then fiercely displace, his asocial passion for Catherine.

Heathcliff's social relation to both Heights and Grange is one of the most complex issues in the novel. Lockwood remarks that he looks too genteel for the Heights; and indeed, insofar as he represents the victory of capitalist property-dealing over the traditional yeoman economy of the Earnshaws, he is inevitably aligned with the world of the Grange. Heathcliff is a dynamic force which seeks to destroy the old yeoman settlement by dispossessing Hareton; yet he does this partly to revenge himself on the very Linton world whose weapons (property deals, arranged marriages) he deploys so efficiently. He does this, moreover, with a crude intensity which is a quality of the Heights world; his roughness and resilience link him culturally to Wuthering Heights, and he exploits those qualities to destroy both it and the Grange. He is, then, a force which springs out of the Heights yet subverts it, breaking beyond its constrictions into a new, voracious acquisitiveness. His capitalist brutality is an extension as well as a negation of the Heights world he knew as a child; and to that extent there is continuity between his childhood and adult protests against Grange values, if not against Grange weapons. Heathcliff is subjectively a Heights figure opposing the Grange, and objectively a Grange figure undermining the Heights; he focuses acutely the contradictions between the two worlds. His rise to power symbolizes at once the triumph of the oppressed over capitalism and the triumph of capitalism over the oppressed.

He is, indeed, contradiction incarnate — both progressive and outdated, at once caricature of and traditionalist protest against the agrarian capitalist forces of Thrushcross Grange. He harnesses those forces to worst the Grange, to beat it at its own game; but in doing so he parodies that property-system, operates against the Lintons with an unLinton-like explicitness and extremism. He behaves in this way because his "soul" belongs not to that world but to Catherine; and in that sense his true commitment is an "outdated" one, to a past, increasingly mythical realm of absolute personal value which capitalist social relations cancel. He embodies a passionate human protest against the marriage-market values of both Grange and Heights at the same time as he callously images those values in caricatured form. Heathcliff exacts vengeance from that society precisely by extravagantly enacting its twisted priorities, becoming a darkly satirical commentary on conventional mores. If he is in one sense a progressive historical force, he belongs in another sense to the superseded world of the Heights, so that his death and the closing-up of the house seem logically related. In the end Heathcliff is defeated and the Heights restored to its rightful owner; yet at the same time the trends he epitomizes triumph in the form of the Grange, to which Hareton and young Catherine move away. Hareton wins and loses the Heights simultaneously; dispossessed by Heathcliff, he repossesses the place only to be in that act assimilated by Thrushcross Grange. And if Hareton both wins and loses, then Heathcliff himself is both ousted and victorious.

Quite who has in fact won in the end is a matter of critical contention. Q. D. Leavis and Tom Winnifrith both see the old world as having yielded to the new, in contrast to T. K. Meier, who reads the conclusion as "the victory of tradition over innovation."[1] The critical contention reflects a real ambiguity in the novel. In one sense, the old values have triumphed over the disruptive usurper: Hareton has wrested back his birthright, and the qualities he symbolizes, while preserving their authentic vigor, will be fertilized by the civilizing grace which the Grange, in the form of young Catherine, can bring. Heathcliff's career appears from his perspective as a shattering but short-lived interlude, after which true balance may be slowly recovered. In a more obvious sense, however, the Grange has won: the Heights is shut up and Hareton will become the new squire. Heathcliff, then, has been the blunt instrument by which the remnants of the Earnshaw world have been transformed into a fully-fledged capitalist class — the historical medium whereby that world is at once annihilated and elevated to the Grange. Thrushcross values have entered into productive dialogue with

[1]F. R. and Q. D. Leavis, *Lectures in America* (London: Chatto, 1969) 99; T. K. Meier, *Brontë Society Transactions* 15.3, pt. 78 (1968): 233–36.

rough material reality and, by virtue of this spiritual transfusion, ensured their continuing survival; the Grange comes to the Heights and gathers back to itself what the Heights can yield it. This is why it will not do to read the novel's conclusion as some neatly reciprocal symbolic alliance between the two universes, a symmetrical symbiosis of bourgeois realism and upper-class cultivation. Whatever unity the book finally establishes, it is certainly not symmetrical: in a victory for the progressive forces of agrarian capitalism, Hareton, last survivor of the traditional order, is smoothly incorporated into the Grange.

There is another significant reason why the "defeat" of Heathcliff cannot be read as the resilient recovery of a traditional world from the injuries it has suffered at his hands. As an extreme parody of capitalist activity, Heathcliff is also an untypical deviation from its norms; as a remorseless, crudely transparent revelation of the real historical character of the Grange, he stands askew to that reality in the very act of becoming its paradigm. It is true that Heathcliff, far from signifying some merely ephemeral intervention, is a type of the historically ascendant world of capital; but because he typifies it so "unnaturally" the novel can move beyond him, into the gracefully gradualistic settlement symbolized by the union of Hareton and young Catherine. Heathcliff is finally fought off, while the social values he incarnates can be pried loose from the self-parodic mold in which he cast them and slowly accommodated. His undisguised violence, like the absolutism of his love, come to seem features of a past more brutal but also more heroic than the present; if the decorous, muted milieu of the Grange will not easily accommodate such passionate intensities, neither will it so readily reveal the more unpleasant face of its social and economic power. The "defeat" of Heathcliff, then, is at once the transcending of such naked power and the collapse of that passionate protest against it which was the inner secret of Heathcliff's outrageous dealings.

We can now ask what these contradictions in the figure of Heathcliff actually amount to. It seems to be possible to decipher in the struggle between Heathcliff and the Grange an imaginatively transposed version of that contemporary conflict between bourgeoisie and landed gentry. The relationship holds in no precise detail, since Heathcliff is not literally an industrial entrepreneur; but the double-edgedness of his relation with the Lintons, with its blend of antagonism and emulation, reproduces the complex structure of class-forces we found in Charlotte's fiction. Having mysteriously amassed capital outside agrarian society, Heathcliff forces his way into that society to expropriate the expropriators; and in this sense his machinations reflect the behavior of a contemporary bourgeois class increasingly successful in its penetration of landed property. He belongs fully to neither Heights nor Grange, opposing them both; he embodies a force which at once destroys the traditional Earnshaw settlement and effectively confronts the power of the squirearchy. In his contradictory amalgam of "Heights" and "Grange," then, Heathcliff's career fleshes out a contemporary ideological dilemma which Charlotte also explores: the contradiction that the fortunes of the industrial bourgeoisie belong *economically* to an increasing extent with the landed gentry but that there can still exist between them, socially, culturally, and personally, a profound hostility. If they are increasingly bound up objectively in a single power-bloc, there is still sharp subjective conflict between them. I take it that *Wuthering Heights,* like Charlotte's fiction, needs mythically to resolve this historical contradiction. If the exploitative adult Heathcliff belongs economically with the capitalist power of the Grange, he is culturally closer to the traditional world of the Heights; his contemptuous response to the Grange as a child, and later to Edgar, is of a piece with Joseph's scorn for the finicky Linton Heathcliff and the haughty young Catherine. If Heathcliff exploits Hareton culturally and economically, he nevertheless feels a certain rough-and-ready *rapport* with him. The contradiction Heathcliff embodies, then, is brought home in the fact that he combines Heights violence with Grange methods to gain power over both properties; and this means that while he is economically progressive he is culturally outdated. He represents a turbulent form of capitalist aggression which must historically be civilized — blended with spiritual values, as it will be in the case of his surrogate Hareton. The terms into which the novel casts this imperative are those of the need to refine, in the person of Hareton, the old yeoman class; but since Hareton's achievement of the Grange is an ironic consequence of Heathcliff's own activity, there is a sense in which it is the capitalist drive symbolized by Heathcliff which must submit to spiritual cultivation. It is worth recalling at this point the cultural affinities between the old yeoman and the new industrial classes touched on by David Wilson;[2] and F. M. L. Thompson comments that by the early 1830s a depleted yeomanry were often forced to sell their land either to a large landowner, or to a local tradesman who would put a tenant in.[3] On the

[2]David Wilson, "Emily Brontë: First of the Moderns," *Modern Quarterly Miscellany* 1 (1947): 94–115.

[3]F. M. L. Thompson, *English Landed Society in the Nineteenth Century* (London: Routledge, 1963) 23.

other hand, as Mrs. Gaskell notes, some landed yeomen turned to manufacture. Heathcliff the heartless capitalist and Hareton the lumpish yeoman thus have a real as well as an alliterative relation. Insofar as Heathcliff symbolizes the dispossessing bourgeoisie, he links hands with the large capitalist landowner Linton in common historical opposition to yeoman society; insofar as he himself has sprung from that society and turned to amassing capital outside it, still sharing its dour life-style, he joins spiritual forces with the uncouth Hareton against the pampered squirearchy.

In pitting himself against both yeomanry and large-scale agrarian capitalism, then, Heathcliff is an indirect symbol of the aggressive industrial bourgeoisie of Emily Brontë's own time, a social trend extrinsic to both classes but implicated in their fortunes. The contradiction of the *novel*, however, is that Heathcliff cannot represent at once an absolute metaphysical refusal of an inhuman society and a class which is intrinsically part of it. Heathcliff is both metaphysical hero, spiritually marooned from all material concern in his obsessional love for Catherine, and a skillful exploiter who cannily expropriates the wealth of others. It is a limit of the novel's "possible consciousness" that its absolute metaphysical protest can be socially articulated only in such terms — that its "outside" is in this sense an "inside." The industrial bourgeoisie is outside the farming world of both Earnshaws and Lintons; but it is no longer a *revolutionary* class, and so provides no sufficient social correlative for what Heathcliff "metaphysically" represents. He can thus be presented only as a conflictive unity of spiritual rejection and social integration; and this, indeed, is his personal tragedy.

The novel's final settlement might seem to qualify what I have said earlier about its confronting of irreconcilable contradictions. *Wuthering Heights* does, after all, end on a note of tentative convergence between labor and culture, sinew and gentility. The culture which Catherine imparts to Hareton in teaching him to read promises equality rather than oppression, an unemasculating refinement of physical energy. But this is a consequence rather than a resolution of the novel's tragic action; it does nothing to dissolve the deadlock of Heathcliff's relationship with Catherine, as the language used to describe that culture transfusion unconsciously suggests:

> "Con-*trary!*" said a voice, as sweet as a silver bell — "That for the third time, you dunce! I'm not going to tell you, again — Recollect, or I'll pull your hair!"
>
> "Contrary, then," answered another, in deep but softened tones. "And now, kiss me, for minding so well."

> "No, read it over first correctly, without a single mistake."
>
> The male speaker began to read — he was a young man, respectably dressed, and seated at a table, having a book before him. His handsome features glowed with pleasure, and his eyes kept impatiently wandering from the page to a small white hand over his shoulder, which recalled him by a smart slap on the cheek, whenever its owner detected such signs of inattention.
>
> Its owner stood behind; her light shining ringlets blending, at intervals, with his brown locks, as she bent to superintend his studies; and her face — it was lucky he could not see her face, or he would never have been so steady — I could, and I bit my lip, in spite, at having thrown away the chance I might have had, of doing something besides staring at its smiting beauty. (p. 263)

The aesthetic false moves of this are transparently dictated by ideological comprise. "Sweet as a silver bell," "glowed with pleasure," "shining ringlets," "smiting beauty": there is a coy, beaming, sentimental self-indulgence about the whole passage which belongs more to Lockwood than to Emily Brontë, although her voice has clearly been confiscated by his. It is Jane and Rochester in a different key: yet the difference is as marked as the parallel. The conclusion, while in a sense symbolically resolving the tragic disjunctions which precede it, moves at a level sufficiently distanced from those disjunctions to preserve their significance intact. It is true that *Wuthering Heights* finally reveals the limits of its "possible consciousness" by having recourse to a gradualist model of social change: the antinomies of passion and civility will be harmonized by the genetic fusion of both strains in the offspring of Catherine and Hareton, effecting an equable interchange of Nature and culture, biology and education. But those possibilities of growth are exploratory and underdeveloped, darkened by the shadow of the tragic action. If it is not exactly true to say that Hareton and Catherine play Fortinbras to Heathcliff's Hamlet, since what they symbolize emerges from, rather than merely imposes itself upon, the narrative, there is nonetheless a kernel of truth in that proposition. Hareton and Catherine are the products of their history, but they cannot negate it; the quarrel between their sedate future at Thrushcross Grange and the spectre of Heathcliff and Catherine on the hills lives on, in a way alien to Charlotte's reconciliatory imagination.

There is another reason why the ending of *Wuthering Heights* differs from the ideological integration which concludes Charlotte's novels. I have argued that those novels aim for a balance or fusion of "genteel" and bourgeois traits, enacting a growing convergence of interests between two powerful segments of a ruling social bloc. The union of Hareton and Catherine parallels this complex unity in obvious ways: the brash vigor of the petty-bourgeois yeoman is smoothed and sensitized by the cultivating grace of the squirearchy. But the crucial difference lies in the fact that the yeomanry of *Wuthering Heights* is no longer a significant class but a historically superannuated force. The transfusion of class-qualities in Charlotte's case rests on a real historical symbiosis; in *Wuthering Heights* that symbolic interchange has no such solid historical foundation. The world of the Heights is over, lingering on only in the figure of Hareton Earnshaw; and in that sense Hareton's marriage to Catherine signifies more at the level of symbolism than historical fact, as a salutary grafting of the values of a dying class on to a thriving, progressive one. If Hareton is thought of as a surrogate, symbolic Heathcliff, then the novel's ending suggests a rapprochement between gentry and capitalist akin to Charlotte's mythical resolutions; if he is taken literally, as a survivor of yeoman stock, then there can be no such historical balance of power. Literally, indeed, this is what finally happens: Hareton's social class is effectively swallowed up into the hegemony of the Grange. Symbolically, however, Hareton represents a Heathcliff-like robustness with which the Grange must come to terms. It is this tension between literal and symbolic meanings which makes the ending of *Wuthering Heights* considerably more complex than the conclusion of any Charlotte Brontë novel. Read symbolically, the ending of *Wuthering Heights* seems to echo the fusion of qualities found in Charlotte; but since the basis of that fusion is the absorption and effective disappearance of a class on which the novel places considerable value, Emily's conclusion is a good deal more subtly shaded than anything apparent in her sister's work.

Wuthering Heights has been alternately read as a social and a metaphysical novel — as a work rooted in a particular time and place, or as a novel preoccupied with the eternal grounds rather than the shifting conditions of human relationship. That critical conflict mirrors a crucial thematic dislocation in the novel itself. The social and metaphysical are indeed ripped rudely apart in the book: existences only feebly incarnate essences, the discourse of ethics makes little creative contact with that of ontology. So much is apparent in Heathcliff's scathing dismissal of Edgar Linton's compassion and moral concern: "and that insipid, paltry creature attending her from *duty* and *humanity!* From *pity* and *charity!* He might as well plant an oak in a flower-pot, and expect it to thrive, as imagine he can restore her to vigour in the soil of his shallow cares!" (p. 145). The novel's dialectical vision proves Heathcliff both right and wrong. There is something insipid about Linton, but his concern for Catherine is not in the least shallow; if his pity and charity are less fertile than Heathcliff's passion, they are also less destructive. But if ethical and ontological idioms fail to mesh, if social existence negates rather than realizes spiritual essence, this is itself a profoundly social fact. The novel projects a condition in which the available social languages are too warped and constrictive to be the bearers of love, freedom, and equality; and it follows that in such a condition those values can be sustained only in the realms of myth and metaphysics. It is a function of the metaphysical to preserve those possibilities which a society cancels, to act as its reservoir of unrealized value. This is the history of Heathcliff and Catherine — the history of a wedge driven between the actual and the possible which, by estranging the ideal from concrete existence, twists that existence into violence and despair. The actual is denatured to a mere husk of the ideal, the empty shell of some tormentingly inaccessible truth. It is an index of the dialectical vision of *Wuthering Heights* that it shows at once the terror and the necessity of that denaturing, as it shows both the splendor and the impotence of the ideal.

Cultural Criticism and *Wuthering Heights*

WHAT IS CULTURAL CRITICISM?

What do you think of when you think of culture? The opera or ballet? A performance of a Mozart symphony at Lincoln Center or a Rembrandt show at the De Young Museum in San Francisco? Does the phrase "cultural event" conjure up images of young people in jeans and T-shirts — or of people in their sixties dressed formally? Most people hear "culture" and think "high culture." Consequently, when they first hear of cultural criticism, most people assume it is more formal than, well, say, formalism. They suspect it is "highbrow," in both subject and style.

Nothing could be further from the truth. Cultural critics oppose the view that culture refers exclusively to high culture, Culture with a capital *C*. Cultural critics want to make the term refer to popular, folk, urban, and mass (mass-produced, -disseminated, -mediated, and -consumed) culture, as well as to that culture we associate with the so-called classics. Raymond Williams, an early British cultural critic whose ideas will later be described at greater length, suggested that "art and culture are ordinary"; he did so not to "pull art down" but rather to point out that there is "creativity in all our living. . . . We create our human world as we have thought of art being created" (*Revolution* 37).

Cultural critics have consequently placed a great deal of emphasis on what Michel de Certeau has called "the practice of everyday life."

Rather than approaching literature in the elitist way that academic literary critics have traditionally approached it, cultural critics view it more as an anthropologist would. They ask how it emerges from and competes with other forms of discourse within a given culture (science, for instance, or television). They seek to understand the social contexts in which a given text was written, and under what conditions it was — and is — produced, disseminated, read, and used.

Contemporary cultural critics are as willing to write about *Star Trek* as they are to analyze James Joyce's *Ulysses,* a modern literary classic full of allusions to Homer's *Odyssey.* And when they write about *Ulysses,* they are likely to view it as a collage reflecting and representing cultural forms common to Joyce's Dublin, such as advertising, journalism, film, and pub life. Cultural critics typically show how the boundary we tend to envision between high and low forms of culture — forms thought of as important on one hand and relatively trivial on the other — is transgressed in all sorts of exciting ways within works on both sides of the putative cultural divide.

A cultural critic writing about a revered classic might contrast it with a movie, or even a comic-strip version produced during a later period. Alternatively, the literary classic might be seen in a variety of other ways: in light of some more common form of reading material (a novel by Jane Austen might be viewed in light of Gothic romances or ladies' conduct manuals); as the reflection of some common cultural myths or concerns (*Adventures of Huckleberry Finn* might be shown to reflect and shape American myths about race and concerns about juvenile delinquency); or as an example of how texts move back and forth across the alleged boundary between "low" and "high" culture. For instance, one group of cultural critics has pointed out that although Shakespeare's history plays probably started off as popular works enjoyed by working people, they were later considered "highbrow" plays that only the privileged and educated could appreciate. That view of them changed, however, due to film productions geared toward a national audience. A film version of *Henry V* produced during World War II, for example, made a powerful, popular, patriotic statement about England's greatness during wartime (Humm, Stigant, and Widdowson 6–7). More recently, cultural critics have analyzed the "cultural work" accomplished cooperatively by Shakespeare and Kenneth Branagh in the latter's 1992 film production of *Henry V.*

In combating old definitions of what constitutes culture, of course, cultural critics sometimes end up contesting old definitions of what constitutes the literary canon, that is, the once-agreed-upon honor roll of Great Books. They tend to do so, however, neither by adding books (and movies and television sitcoms) *to* the old list of texts that every "culturally literate" person should supposedly know nor by substituting some kind of counterculture canon. Instead, they tend to critique the very *idea* of canon.

Cultural critics want to get us away from thinking about certain works as the "best" ones produced by a given culture. They seek to be more descriptive and less evaluative, more interested in relating than in rating cultural products and events. They also aim to discover the (often political) reasons *why* a certain kind of aesthetic or cultural product is more valued than others. This is particularly true when the product in question is one produced since 1945, for most cultural critics follow Jean Baudrillard (*Simulations,* 1981) and Andreas Huyssen (*The Great Divide,* 1986) in thinking that any distinctions that may once have existed between high, popular, and mass culture collapsed after the end of World War II. Their discoveries have led them beyond the literary canon, prompting them to interrogate many other value hierarchies. For instance, Pierre Bourdieu in *Distinction: A Social Critique of the Judgment of Taste* (1984) and Dick Hebdige in *Hiding the Light: On Images and Things* (1988) have argued that definitions of "good taste"— which are instrumental in fostering and reinforcing cultural discrimination — tell us at least as much about prevailing social, economic, and political conditions as they do about artistic quality and value.

In an article entitled "The Need for Cultural Studies," four groundbreaking cultural critics have written that "Cultural Studies should . . . abandon the goal of giving students access to that which represents a culture." A literary work, they go on to suggest, should be seen in relation to other works, to economic conditions, or to broad social discourses (about childbirth, women's education, rural decay, and so on) within whose contexts it makes sense. Perhaps most important, critics practicing cultural studies should counter the prevalent notion of culture as some preformed whole. Rather than being static or monolithic, culture is really a set of interactive *cultures,* alive and changing, and cultural critics should be present- and even future-oriented. They should be "resisting intellectuals," and cultural studies should be "an emancipatory project" (Giroux et al. 478–80).

The paragraphs above are peppered with words like *oppose, counter, deny, resist, combat, abandon,* and *emancipatory.* What such words quite accurately suggest is that a number of cultural critics view themselves in political, even oppositional, terms. Not only are they likely to take on the literary canon, they are also likely to oppose the institution of the university, for that is where the old definitions of culture as high culture (and as something formed, finished, and canonized) have been most vigorously preserved, defended, and reinforced.

Cultural critics have been especially critical of the departmental structure of universities, which, perhaps more than anything else, has kept the study of the "arts" relatively distinct from the study of history, not to mention from the study of such things as television, film, advertising, journalism, popular photography, folklore, current affairs, shoptalk, and gossip. By maintaining artificial boundaries, universities have tended to reassert the high/low culture distinction, implying that all the latter subjects are best left to historians, sociologists, anthropologists, and communication theorists. Cultural critics have taken issue with this implication, arguing that the way of thinking reinforced by the departmentalized structure of universities keeps us from seeing the aesthetics of an advertisement as well as the propagandistic elements of a work of literature. Cultural critics have consequently mixed and matched the analytical procedures developed in a variety of disciplines. They have formed — and encouraged other scholars to form — networks and centers, often outside of those enforced departmentally.

Some initially loose interdisciplinary networks have, over time, solidified to become cultural studies programs and majors. As this has happened, a significant if subtle danger has arisen. Richard Johnson, who along with Hebdige, Stuart Hall, and Richard Hoggart was instrumental in developing the Center for Contemporary Cultural Studies at Birmingham University in England, has warned that cultural studies must not be allowed to turn into yet another traditional academic discipline — one in which students encounter a canon replete with soap operas and cartoons, one in which belief in the importance of such popular forms has become an "orthodoxy" (39). The only principles that critics doing cultural studies can doctrinally espouse, Johnson suggests, are the two that have thus far been introduced: the principle that "culture" has been an "inegalitarian" concept, a "tool" of "condescension," and the belief that a new, "interdisciplinary (and even anti-disciplinary)" approach to *true* culture (that is, to the forms in which culture currently lives) is required now that history, art, and the communications media are so complex and interrelated (42).

The object of cultural study should not be a body of works assumed to comprise or reflect a given culture. Rather, it should be human consciousness, and the goal of that critical analysis should be to understand

and show how that consciousness is itself forged and formed, to a great extent, by cultural forces. "Subjectivities," as Johnson has put it, are "produced, not given, and are . . . objects of inquiry" inevitably related to "social practices," whether those involve factory rules, supermarket behavior patterns, reading habits, advertisements, myths, or languages and other signs to which people are exposed (44–45).

Although the United States has probably contributed more than any other nation to the *media* through which culture is currently expressed, and although many if not most contemporary practitioners of cultural criticism are North American, the evolution of cultural criticism and, more broadly, cultural studies has to a great extent been influenced by theories developed in Great Britain and on the European continent.

Among the Continental thinkers whose work allowed for the development of cultural studies are those whose writings we associate with structuralism and poststructuralism. Using the linguistic theory of Ferdinand de Saussure, structuralists suggested that the structures of language lie behind all human organization. They attempted to create a *semiology* — a science of signs — that would give humankind at once a scientific and holistic way of studying the world and its human inhabitants. Roland Barthes, a structuralist who later shifted toward poststructuralism, attempted to recover literary language from the isolation in which it had been studied and to show that the laws that govern it govern all signs, from road signs to articles of clothing. Claude Lévi-Strauss, an anthropologist who studied the structures of everything from cuisine to villages to myths, looked for and found recurring, common elements that transcended the differences within and between cultures.

Of the structuralist and poststructuralist thinkers who have had an impact on the evolution of cultural studies, Jacques Lacan is one of three whose work has been particularly influential. A structuralist psychoanalytic theorist, Lacan posited that the human unconscious is structured like a language and treated dreams not as revealing symptoms of repression but, rather, as forms of discourse. Lacan also argued that the ego, subject, or self that we think of as being natural (our individual human nature) is in fact a product of the social order and its symbolic systems (especially, but not exclusively, language). Lacan's thought has served as the theoretical underpinning for cultural critics seeking to show the way in which subjectivities are produced by social discourses and practices.

Jacques Derrida, a French philosopher whose name has become synonymous with poststructuralism, has had an influence on cultural criticism at least as great as that of Lacan. The linguistic focus of structuralist thought has by no means been abandoned by poststructuralists, despite their opposition to structuralism's tendency to find universal patterns instead of textual and cultural contradictions. Indeed, Derrida has provocatively asserted that *"there is nothing outside the text"* (158), by which he means something like the following: we come to know the world through language, and even our most worldly actions and practices (the Gulf War, the wearing of condoms) are dependent upon discourses (even if they deliberately contravene those discourses). Derrida's "deconstruction" of the world/text distinction, like his deconstruction of so many of the hierarchical oppositions we habitually use to interpret and evaluate reality, has allowed cultural critics to erase the boundaries between high and low culture, classic and popular literary texts, and literature and other cultural discourses that, following Derrida, may be seen as manifestations of the same textuality.

Michel Foucault is the third Continental thinker associated with structuralism and/or poststructuralism who has had a particularly powerful impact on the evolution of cultural studies — and perhaps *the* strongest influence on American cultural criticism and the so-called new historicism, an interdisciplinary form of cultural criticism whose evolution has often paralleled that of cultural criticism. Although Foucault broke with Marxism after the French student uprisings of 1968, he was influenced enough by Marxist thought to study cultures in terms of power relationships. Unlike Marxists, however, Foucault refused to see power as something exercised by a dominant class over a subservient class. Indeed, he emphasized that power is not just repressive power, that is, a tool of conspiracy by one individual or institution against another. Power, rather, is a whole complex of forces; it is that which produces what happens.

Thus even a tyrannical aristocrat does not simply wield power but is empowered by "discourses"— accepted ways of thinking, writing, and speaking — and practices that embody, exercise, and amount to power. Foucault tried to view all things, from punishment to sexuality, in terms of the widest possible variety of discourses. As a result, he traced what he called the "genealogy" of topics he studied through texts that more traditional historians and literary critics would have overlooked, examining (in Lynn Hunt's words) "memoirs of deviants, diaries, political treatises, architectural blueprints, court records, doctors' reports — appl[ying] consistent principles of analysis in search of moments of reversal in discourse, in search of events as loci of the conflict where social practices were transformed" (39). Foucault tended not only to build interdisciplinary bridges but also, in the process, to bring into the study of culture the "histories of women, homosexuals, and minorities"— groups seldom studied by those interested in Culture with a capital *C* (Hunt 45).

Of the British influences on cultural studies and criticism, two stand out prominently. One, the Marxist historian E. P. Thompson, revolutionized the study of the industrial revolution by writing about its impact on human attitudes, even consciousness. He showed how a shared cultural view, specifically that of what constitutes a fair or just price, influenced crowd behavior and caused such things as the "food riots" of the eighteenth and nineteenth centuries (during which the women of Nottingham repriced breads in the shops of local bakers, paid for the goods they needed, and carried them away). The other, even more important early British influence on contemporary cultural criticism and cultural studies was Raymond Williams, who coined the phrase "culture is ordinary." In works like *Culture and Society, 1780–1950* (1958) and *The Long Revolution* (1961) Williams demonstrated that culture is not fixed and finished but, rather, living and evolving. One of the changes he called for was the development of a common socialist culture.

Although Williams dissociated himself from Marxism during the period 1945–58, he always followed the Marxist practice of viewing culture in relation to ideologies, which he defined as the "residual," "dominant," or "emerging" ways of viewing the world held by classes or individuals holding power in a given social group. He avoided dwelling on class conflict and class oppression, however, tending instead to focus on people as people, on how they experience the conditions in which they find themselves and creatively respond to those conditions through their social practices. A believer in the resiliency of the individual, Williams produced a body of criticism notable for what Stuart Hall has called its "humanism" (63).

As is clearly suggested in several of the preceding paragraphs, Marxism is the background to the background of cultural criticism. What isn't as clear is that some contemporary cultural critics consider themselves Marxist critics as well. It is important, therefore, to have some familiarity with certain Marxist concepts — those that would have been familiar to Foucault, Thompson, and Williams, plus those espoused by contemporary cultural critics who self-identify with Marxism. That familiarity can be gained from an introduction to the works of four important Marxist thinkers: Mikhail Bakhtin, Walter Benjamin, Antonio Gramsci, and Louis Althusser.

Bakhtin was a Russian, later a Soviet, critic so original in his thinking and wide-ranging in his influence that some would say he was never a Marxist at all. He viewed literary works in terms of discourses and dialogues *between* discourses. The narrative of a novel written in a society in flux, for instance, may include an official, legitimate discourse, plus others that challenge its viewpoint and even its authority. In a 1929 book on Dostoyevsky and the 1940 study *Rabelais and His World,* Bakhtin examined what he calls "polyphonic" novels, each characterized by a multiplicity of voices or discourses. In Dostoyevsky the independent status of a given character is marked by the difference of his or her language from that of the narrator. (The narrator's language may itself involve a dialogue between opposed points of view.) In works by Rabelais, Bakhtin finds that the (profane) languages of Carnival and of other popular festivities play against and parody the more official discourses of the magistrates and the church. Bakhtin's relevance to cultural criticism lies in his suggestion that the dialogue involving high and low culture takes place not only between classic and popular texts but also between the "dialogic" voices that exist within all great books.

Walter Benjamin was a German Marxist who, during roughly the same period, attacked fascism and questioned the superior value placed on certain traditional literary forms that he felt conveyed a stultifying "aura" of culture. He took this position in part because so many previous Marxist critics (and, in his own day, Georg Lukács) had seemed to prefer nineteenth-century realistic novels to the modernist works of their own time. Benjamin not only praised modernist movements, such as dadaism, but also saw as promising the development of new art forms utilizing mechanical production and reproduction. These forms, including photography, radio, and film, promised that the arts would become a more democratic, less exclusive, domain. Anticipating by decades the work of those cultural critics interested in mass-produced, mass-mediated, and mass-consumed culture, Benjamin analyzed the meanings and (defensive) motivations behind words like *unique* and *authentic* when used in conjunction with mechanically reproduced art.

Antonio Gramsci, an Italian Marxist best known for his *Prison Notebooks* (first published in 1947), critiqued the very concept of literature and, beyond that, of culture in the old sense, stressing the importance of culture more broadly defined and the need for nurturing and developing proletarian, or working-class, culture. He argued that all intellectual or cultural work is fundamentally political and expressed the need for what he called "radical organic" intellectuals. Today's cultural critics urging colleagues to "legitimate the notion of writing reviews and books for the general public," to "become involved in the political reading of popular culture," and more generally to "repoliticize" scholarship have viewed Gramsci as an early precursor (Giroux et al. 482).

Gramsci related literature to the ideologies — the prevailing ideas, beliefs, values, and prejudices — of the culture in which it was produced. He developed the concept of "hegemony," which refers at once to the process of consensus formation and to the authority of the ideologies so formed, that is to say, their power to shape the way things look, what they would seem to mean, and, therefore, what reality *is* for the majority of people. But Gramsci did not see people, even poor people, as the helpless victims of hegemony, as ideology's pathetic robots. Rather, he believed that people have the freedom and power to struggle against and shape ideology, to alter hegemony, to break out of the weblike system of prevailing assumptions and to form a new consensus. As Patrick Brantlinger has suggested in *Crusoe's Footprints: Cultural Studies in Britain and America* (1990), Gramsci rejected the "intellectual arrogance that views the vast majority of people as deluded zombies, the victims or creatures of ideology" (100).

Of those Marxists who, after Gramsci, explored the complex relationship between literature and ideology, the French Marxist Louis Althusser had a significant impact on cultural criticism. Unlike Gramsci, Althusser tended to portray ideology as being in control of people, and not vice versa. He argued that the main function of ideology is to reproduce the society's existing relations of production, and that that function is even carried out in literary texts. In many ways, though, Althusser is as good an example of how Marxism and cultural criticism part company as he is of how cultural criticism is indebted to Marxists and their ideas. For although Althusser did argue that literature is relatively autonomous — more independent of ideology than, say, church, press, or state — he meant literature in the high cultural sense, certainly not the variety of works that present-day cultural critics routinely examine alongside those of Tolstoy and Joyce, Eliot and Brecht. Popular fictions, Althusser assumed, were mere packhorses designed (however unconsciously) to carry the baggage of a culture's ideology, or mere brood mares destined to reproduce it.

Thus, while a number of cultural critics would agree both with Althusser's notion that works of literature reflect certain ideological formations and with his notion that, at the same time, literary works may be relatively distant from or even resistant to ideology, they have rejected the narrow limits within which Althusser and some other Marxists (such as Georg Lukács) have defined literature. In "Marxism and Popular Fiction" (1986), Tony Bennett uses *Monty Python's Flying Circus* and another British television show, *Not the 9 O'clock News,* to argue that the Althusserian notion that all forms of culture belong "among [all those] many material forms which ideology takes . . . under capitalism" is "simply not true." The "entire field" of "popular fiction"— which Bennett takes to include films and television shows as well as books — is said to be "replete with instances" of works that do what Bennett calls the "work" of "distancing." That is, they have the effect of separating the audience from, not rebinding the audience to, prevailing ideologies (249).

Although Marxist cultural critics exist (Bennett himself is one, carrying on through his writings what may be described as a lovers' quarrel with Marxism), most cultural critics are not Marxists in any strict sense. Anne Beezer, in writing about such things as advertisements and women's magazines, contests the "Althusserian view of ideology as the construction of the subject" (qtd. in Punter 103). That is, she gives both the media she is concerned with and their audiences more credit than Althusserian Marxists presumably would. Whereas they might argue that such media make people what they are, she points out that the same magazines that, admittedly, tell women how to please their men may, at the same time, offer liberating advice to women about how to preserve their independence by not getting too serious romantically. And, she suggests, many advertisements advertise their status as ads, just as many people who view or read them see advertising as advertising and interpret it accordingly.

The complex sort of analysis that Beezer has brought to bear on women's magazines and advertisements has been focused on paperback romance novels by Tania Modleski and Janice A. Radway in *Loving with a Vengeance* (1982) and *Reading the Romance* (1984), respectively. Radway, a feminist cultural critic who uses but ultimately goes beyond Marxism, points out that many women who read romances do so in order to carve out a time and space that is wholly their own, not to be intruded upon by husbands or children. Although many such novels end in marriage, the marriage is usually between a feisty and independent heroine and a powerful man she has "tamed," that is, made sensitive and caring. And why do so many of these stories involve such heroines and end as they do? Because, as Radway demonstrates through painstaking research into publishing houses, bookstores, and reading communities, their consumers *want* them to. They don't buy — or, if they buy they don't recommend — romances in which, for example, a heroine is raped: thus, in time, fewer and fewer such plots find their way onto the racks by the supermarket checkout.

Radway's reading is typical of feminist cultural criticism in that it is *political,* but not exclusively about oppression. The subjectivities of women may be "produced" by romances — the thinking of romance readers may be governed by what is read — but the same women also govern, to a great extent, what gets written or produced, thus performing "cultural work" of their own. Rather than seeing all forms of popular culture as manifestations of ideology, soon to be remanifested in the minds of victimized audiences, cultural critics tend to see a sometimes disheartening but always dynamic synergy between cultural forms and the culture's consumers. Their observations have increasingly led to an analysis of consumerism, from a feminist but also from a more general point of view. This analysis owes a great deal to the work of de Certeau, Hall, and, especially, Hebdige, whose 1979 book *Subculture: The Meaning of Style* paved the way for critics like John Fiske (*Television Culture,* 1987), Greil Marcus (*Dead Elvis,* 1991), and Rachel Bowlby (*Shopping with Freud,* 1993). These latter critics have analyzed everything from the resistance tactics employed by television audiences to the influence of consumers on rock music styles to the psychology of consumer choice.

The overlap between feminist and cultural criticism is hardly surprising, especially given the recent evolution of feminism into various femin*isms,* some of which remain focused on "majority" women of European descent, others of which have focused instead on the lives and writings of minority women in Western culture and of women living in Third World (now preferably called postcolonial) societies. The culturalist analysis of value hierarchies within and between cultures has inevitably focused on categories that include class, race, national origin, gender, and sexualities; the terms of its critique have proved useful to contemporary feminists, many of whom differ from their predecessors insofar as they see *woman* not as a universal category but, rather, as one of several that play a role in identity- or subject-formation. The influence of cultural criticism (and, in some cases, Marxist class analysis) can be seen in the work of contemporary feminist critics such as Gayatri Spivak, Trinh T. Minh-ha, and Gloria Anzaldúa, each of whom has stressed that while all women are female, they are something else as well (such as working-class, lesbian, Native American, Muslim, Pakistani) and that that something else must be taken into account when their writings are read and studied.

The expansion of feminism and feminist literary criticism to include multicultural analysis, of course, parallels a transformation of education in general. On college campuses across North America, the field of African-American studies has grown and flourished. African-American critics have been influenced by and have contributed to the cultural approach by pointing out that the white cultural elite of North America has tended to view the oral-musical traditions of African Americans (traditions that include jazz, the blues, sermons, and folktales) as entertaining, but nonetheless inferior. Black writers, in order not to be similarly marginalized, have produced texts that, as Henry Louis Gates has pointed out, fuse the language and traditions of the white Western canon with a black vernacular and traditions derived from African and Caribbean cultures. The resulting "hybridity" (to use Homi K. Bhabha's word), although deplored by a handful of black separatist critics, has proved both rich and complex — fertile ground for many cultural critics practicing African-American criticism.

Interest in race and ethnicity at home has gone hand in hand with a new, interdisciplinary focus on colonial and postcolonial societies abroad, in which issues of race, class, and ethnicity also loom large. Edward Said's book *Orientalism* (1978) is generally said to have inaugurated postcolonial studies, which in Bhabha's words "bears witness to the unequal and uneven forces of cultural representation involved in the contest for political and social authority within the modern world order" ("Postcolonial Criticism" 437). *Orientalism* showed how Eastern and Middle Eastern peoples have for centuries been systematically stereotyped by the West, and how that stereotyping facilitated the colonization of vast areas of the East and Middle East by Westerners. Said's more recent books, along with postcolonial studies by Bhabha and Patrick Brantlinger, are among the most widely read and discussed works of literary scholarship. Brantlinger focuses on British literature of the Victorian period, examining representations of the colonies in works written during an era of imperialist expansion. Bhabha complements Brantlinger by suggesting that modern Western culture is best understood from the postcolonial perspective.

Thanks to the work of scholars like Brantlinger, Bhabha, Said, Gates, Anzaldúa, and Spivak, education in general and literary study in particular are becoming more democratic, decentered (less patriarchal and Eurocentric), and multicultural. The future of literary criticism will owe a great deal indeed to those early cultural critics who demonstrated that the boundaries between high and low culture are at once repressive and permeable, that culture is common and therefore includes all forms of popular culture, that cultural definitions are inevitably political, and that the world we see is seen through society's ideology. In a very real sense, the future of education *is* cultural studies.

In the essay that follows, cultural critic Nancy Armstrong begins by citing formalist predecessors who have suggested that *Wuthering Heights,* more than most works, sprang from a "mind uncontaminated by political concerns." Since, as a cultural critic, Armstrong cannot believe that *any* text can be independent of cultural contexts, including politics, she sets out to show that the novel in fact represents or re-presents a number of things that were going on in mid-Victorian culture. She thereby suggests, implicitly, that no work — no matter how rural its setting or "romantic" its themes — can be divorced from the society whose power structure it was shaped by and shaped.

Even *Wuthering Heights,* Armstrong goes on to show, is doing "cultural work," a fact we can come to realize only once we become aware of "the materials of the 1830s and 1840s out of which Emily Brontë made that novel and with which it therefore carried on a relationship" (p. 431 in this volume). Whereas critics have traditionally pointed out the self-enclosed nature of the novel's Chinese-box narrative structure (thereby justifying the view that the novel is somehow apart from history), Armstrong reminds us that "everyone in the novel crosses at least one threshold with violence and ravishes sacred ground" (p. 431). She implicitly calls into question the view of a novel and novelist generally thought of as somehow separate from "social history" by showing *Wuthering Heights* to be about the impossibility of inviolate apartness — about the ultimate vulnerability of all self-enclosed places, physical and otherwise.

Wuthering Heights, like its characters, is, according to Armstrong, a kind of interloper. For one thing, it bridges boundaries set (by Culture with a capital *C*) between Literature (with a capital *L*) and folklore, the study of which began in the mid-1840s — just before *Wuthering Heights* was written. Looked at in this way, the novel is the account of a folklorist, Lockwood, of what he found in a remote area of Yorkshire, much as the *Foxfire* books written in the second half of the twentieth century offer verbal accounts of the largely verbal history that a folklorist learned in rural Appalachia.

Looked at in another way, though, Lockwood is a version of yet another new type of individual first appearing in the mid-nineteenth century. He is a great deal like a photographer, particularly the photographer who "offered the viewer a countryside that was remote, exotic, and utterly passive to view." (It was "during Emily Brontë's relatively brief lifetime," Armstrong explains, the very years "when folklore became enormously popular," that "an increasing number of amateur photographers went out into the remote areas of Great Britain to document the landscape, customs, and people, in much the same way and presumably for much the same reasons that folklorists had" [pp. 439, 442]). Lockwood, after all, gives us what he calls "pictures" of a remote area but also steps outside the frame of his photographs to comment on them, just as did such mid-nineteenth-century photographers as William Henry Fox Talbot.

Armstrong follows the lead of many a cultural critic in seeing *Wuthering Heights* as but one of many manifestations or expressions (some of them "nonliterary," some would say "low" or "uncultured") of cultural work. However, she is most interesting and original in showing *Wuthering Heights* to be part of a culture cycle of responses; responding *to* photographs (including of Yorkshire laborers), it is also shown to have *influenced* photographs — not necessarily historically accurate ones, but who would expect it to? *Wuthering Heights* is, after all, a novel, and are folklore and photographs not to some extent fictions, too, produced by a culture? And is the culture itself not the product of ideology — *a* way (not *the* way) of seeing the world?

Armstrong's essay continually asks — sometimes explicitly, but just as often implicitly — questions such as these. And, like so many other works of cultural criticism, it asks more questions than it answers. It does so in part because it knows that the answers we must come up with are no more *the* answers than Brontë's ideology was *the* way of seeing the world. Our answers, rather, will be those of our cultural moment. And they will do our culture's work.

Ross C Murfin

CULTURAL CRITICISM: A SELECTED BIBLIOGRAPHY

General Introductions to Cultural Criticism, Cultural Studies

Bathrick, David. "Cultural Studies." *Introduction to Scholarship in Modern Languages and Literatures.* Ed. Joseph Gibaldi. New York: MLA, 1992. 320–40.

Brantlinger, Patrick. *Crusoe's Footprints: Cultural Studies in Britain and America*. New York: Routledge, 1990.

———. "Cultural Studies vs. the New Historicism." *English Studies/Cultural Studies: Institutionalizing Dissent*. Ed. Isaiah Smithson and Nancy Ruff. Urbana: U of Illinois P, 1994. 43–58.

Brantlinger, Patrick, and James Naremore, eds. *Modernity and Mass Culture*. Bloomington: Indiana UP, 1991.

Brummett, Barry. *Rhetoric in Popular Culture*. New York: St. Martin's, 1994.

Desan, Philippe, Priscilla Parkhurst Ferguson, and Wendy Griswold. "Editors' Introduction: Mirrors, Frames, and Demons: Reflections on the Sociology of Literature." *Literature and Social Practice*. Ed. Desan, Ferguson, and Griswold. Chicago: U of Chicago P, 1989. 1–10.

During, Simon, ed. *The Cultural Studies Reader*. New York: Routledge, 1993.

Eagleton, Terry. "Two Approaches in the Sociology of Literature." *Critical Inquiry* 14 (1988): 469–76.

Easthope, Antony. *Literary into Cultural Studies*. New York: Routledge, 1991.

Fisher, Philip. "American Literary and Cultural Studies since the Civil War." *Redrawing the Boundaries: The Transformation of English and American Literary Studies*. Ed. Stephen Greenblatt and Giles Gunn. New York: MLA, 1992. 232–50.

Giroux, Henry, David Shumway, Paul Smith, and James Sosnoski. "The Need for Cultural Studies: Resisting Intellectuals and Oppositional Public Spheres." *Dalhousie Review* 64.2 (1984): 472–86.

Graff, Gerald, and Bruce Robbins. "Cultural Criticism." *Redrawing the Boundaries: The Transformation of English and American Literary Studies*. Ed. Stephen Greenblatt and Giles Gunn. New York: MLA, 1992. 419–36.

Grossberg, Lawrence, Cary Nelson, and Paula A. Treichler, eds. *Cultural Studies*. New York: Routledge, 1992.

Gunn, Giles. *The Culture of Criticism and the Criticism of Culture*. New York: Oxford UP, 1987.

Hall, Stuart. "Cultural Studies: Two Paradigms." *Media, Culture and Society* 2 (1980): 57–72.

Humm, Peter, Paul Stigant, and Peter Widdowson, eds. *Popular Fictions: Essays in Literature and History*. New York: Methuen, 1986.

Hunt, Lynn, ed. *The New Cultural History: Essays*. Berkeley: U of California P, 1989.

Johnson, Richard. "What Is Cultural Studies Anyway?" *Social Text* 16 (1986–87): 38–80.

Pfister, Joel. "The Americanization of Cultural Studies." *Yale Journal of Criticism* 4 (1991): 199–229.

Punter, David, ed. *Introduction to Contemporary Critical Studies.* New York: Longman, 1986. See especially Punter's "Introduction: Culture and Change" 1–18, Tony Dunn's "The Evolution of Cultural Studies" 71–91, and the essay "Methods for Cultural Studies Students" by Anne Beezer, Jean Grimshaw, and Martin Barker 95–118.

Storey, John. *An Introductory Guide to Cultural Theory and Popular Culture.* Athens: U of Georgia P, 1993.

Turner, Graeme. *British Cultural Studies: An Introduction.* Boston: Unwin Hyman, 1990.

Cultural Studies: Some Early British Examples

Hoggart, Richard. *Speaking to Each Other.* 2 vols. London: Chatto, 1970.

———. *The Uses of Literacy: Changing Patterns in English Mass Culture.* Boston: Beacon, 1961.

Thompson, E. P. *The Making of the English Working Class.* New York: Harper, 1958.

———. *William Morris: Romantic to Revolutionary.* New York: Pantheon, 1977.

Williams, Raymond. *Culture and Society, 1780–1950.* New York: Harper, 1966.

———. *The Long Revolution.* New York: Columbia UP, 1961.

Cultural Studies: Continental and Marxist Influences

Althusser, Louis. *For Marx.* Trans. Ben Brewster. New York: Pantheon, 1969.

———. "Ideology and Ideological State Apparatuses." *Lenin and Philosophy.* Trans. Ben Brewster. New York: Monthly Review P, 1971. 127–86.

Althusser, Louis, and Étienne Balibar. *Reading Capital.* Trans. Ben Brewster. New York: Pantheon, 1971.

Bakhtin, Mikhail. *The Dialogic Imagination: Four Essays.* Ed. Michael Holquist. Trans. Caryl Emerson. Austin: U of Texas P, 1981.

———. *Rabelais and His World*. Trans. Hélène Iswolsky. Cambridge: MIT P, 1968.

Baudrillard, Jean. *Simulations*. Trans. Paul Foss, Paul Patton, and Philip Beitchnan. 1981. New York: Semiotext(e), 1983.

Benjamin, Walter. *Illuminations*. Ed. with intro. by Hannah Arendt. Trans. H. Zohn. New York: Harcourt, 1968.

Bennett, Tony. "Marxism and Popular Fiction." Humm, Stigant, and Widdowson 237–65.

Bourdieu, Pierre. *Distinction: A Social Critique of the Judgment of Taste*. Trans. Richard Nice. Cambridge: Harvard UP, 1984.

de Certeau, Michel. *The Practice of Everyday Life*. Trans. Steven F. Rendall. Berkeley: U of California P, 1984.

Derrida, Jacques. *Of Grammatology*. 1969. Trans. Gayatri C. Spivak. Baltimore: Johns Hopkins UP, 1976.

Foucault, Michel. *Discipline and Punish: The Birth of the Prison*. Trans. Alan Sheridan. New York: Pantheon, 1978.

———. *The History of Sexuality*. Trans. Robert Hurley. Vol. 1. New York: Pantheon, 1978.

Gramsci, Antonio. *Selections from the Prison Notebooks*. Ed. Quintin Hoare and Geoffrey Nowell Smith. New York: International, 1971.

Modern Cultural Studies: Selected British and American Examples

Bagdikian, Ben H. *The Media Monopoly*. Boston: Beacon, 1983.

Bowlby, Rachel. *Shopping with Freud*. New York: Routledge, 1993.

Chambers, Iain. *Popular Culture: The Metropolitan Experience*. New York: Methuen, 1986.

Colls, Robert, and Philip Dodd, eds. *Englishness: Politics and Culture, 1880–1920*. London: Croom Helm, 1986.

Denning, Michael. *Mechanic Accents: Dime Novels and Working-Class Culture in America*. New York: Verso, 1987.

Fiske, John. "British Cultural Studies and Television." *Channels of Discourse: Television and Contemporary Criticism*. Ed. Robert C. Allen. Chapel Hill: U of North Carolina P, 1987.

———. *Television Culture*. New York: Methuen, 1987.

Hebdige, Dick. *Hiding the Light: On Images and Things*. New York: Routledge, 1988.

———. *Subculture: The Meaning of Style*. London: Methuen, 1979.

Huyssen, Andreas. *After the Great Divide: Modernism, Mass Culture, Postmodernism*. Bloomington: Indiana UP, 1986.

Marcus, Greil. *Dead Elvis: A Chronicle of a Cultural Obsession.* New York: Doubleday, 1991.

———. *Lipstick Traces: A Secret History of the Twentieth Century.* Cambridge: Harvard UP, 1989.

Modleski, Tania. *Loving with a Vengeance: Mass-Produced Fantasies for Women.* Hamden: Archon, 1982.

Poovey, Mary. *Uneven Developments: The Ideological Work of Gender in Mid-Victorian England.* Chicago: U of Chicago P, 1988.

Radway, Janice A. *Reading the Romance: Women, Patriarchy, and Popular Literature.* Chapel Hill: U of North Carolina P, 1984.

Reed, T. V. *Fifteen Jugglers, Five Believers: Literary Politics and the Poetics of American Social Movements.* Berkeley: U of California P, 1992.

Ethnic and Minority Criticism: Postcolonial Studies

Anzaldúa, Gloria. *Borderlands: La Frontera = The New Mestiza.* San Francisco: Spinsters/Aunt Lute, 1987.

Baker, Houston. *Blues, Ideology, and Afro-American Literature: A Vernacular Theory.* Chicago: U of Chicago P, 1984.

———. *The Journey Back: Issues in Black Literature and Criticism.* Chicago: U of Chicago P, 1980.

Bhabha, Homi K. *The Location of Culture.* New York: Routledge, 1994.

———, ed. *Nation and Narration.* New York: Routledge, 1990.

———. "Postcolonial Criticism." *Redrawing the Boundaries: The Transformation of English and American Literary Studies.* Ed. Stephen Greenblatt and Giles Gunn. New York: MLA, 1992. 437–65.

Brantlinger, Patrick. *Rule of Darkness: British Literature and Imperialism, 1830–1914.* Ithaca: Cornell UP, 1988.

Gates, Henry Louis, Jr. *Black Literature and Literary Theory.* New York: Methuen, 1984.

———, ed. *"Race," Writing, and Difference.* Chicago: U of Chicago P, 1986.

Gayle, Addison. *The Black Aesthetic.* Garden City: Doubleday, 1971.

———. *The Way of the New World: The Black Novel in America.* Garden City: Doubleday, 1975.

JanMohamed, Abdul. *Manichean Aesthetics: The Politics of Literature in Colonial Africa.* Amherst: U of Massachusetts P, 1983.

JanMohamed, Abdul, and David Lloyd, eds. *The Nature and Context of Minority Discourse.* New York: Oxford UP, 1991.

Kaplan, Amy, and Donald E. Pease, eds. *Cultures of United States Imperialism.* Durham: Duke UP, 1983.

Neocolonialism. Spec. issue of *Oxford Literary Review* 13 (1991).

Said, Edward. *After the Last Sky: Palestinian Lives.* New York: Pantheon, 1986.

———. *Culture and Imperialism.* New York: Knopf, 1993.

———. *Orientalism.* New York: Pantheon, 1978.

———. *The World, the Text, and the Critic.* Cambridge: Harvard UP, 1983.

Spivak, Gayatri Chakravorty. *In Other Worlds: Essays in Cultural Politics.* New York: Methuen, 1987.

Stepto, Robert B. *From Behind the Veil: A Study of Afro-American Narrative.* Urbana: U of Illinois P, 1979.

Young, Robert. *White Mythologies: Writing, History, and the West.* London: Routledge, 1990.

Cultural Criticism Relating to *Wuthering Heights*

Armstrong, Nancy. "Emily Brontë In and Out of Her Time." *Genre* 15 (1982): 243–64.

Eagleton, Terry. "Heathcliff and the Great Hunger." *Heathcliff and the Great Hunger.* London: Verso, 1995. 1–26.

Levy, Anita. *Other Women: The Writing of Class, Race, and Gender, 1832–1898.* Princeton: Princeton UP, 1991.

Meyer, Susan. "'Your Father Was Emperor of China, and Your Mother an Indian Queen': Reverse Imperialism in *Wuthering Heights.*" *Imperialism at Home: Race and Victorian Women's Fiction.* Ithaca: Cornell UP, 1996. 96–125.

Michie, Elsie B. "'The Yahoo, Not the Demon': Heathcliff, Rochester, and the Simianization of the Irish." *Outside the Pale: Cultural Exclusion, Gender Difference, and the Victorian Woman Writers.* Ithaca: Cornell UP, 1993. 46–78.

Sneidern, Maja-Lisa. "*Wuthering Heights* and the Liverpool Slave Trade." *ELH* 62 (1995): 171–96.

A CULTURAL CRITICAL PERSPECTIVE

NANCY ARMSTRONG

Imperialist Nostalgia and *Wuthering Heights*

> *Wuthering Heights* was hewn in a wild workshop, with simple tools, out of homely materials.
>
> — CHARLOTTE BRONTË, 1850 Preface to *Wuthering Heights*

> Nostalgia is a particularly appropriate emotion to invoke in establishing one's innocence and at the same time talk about what one has destroyed. Don't most people feel nostalgic about childhood memories? Aren't these memories genuinely innocent? Indeed, much of imperialist nostalgia's force resides in its association with (indeed, its disguise as) more genuinely innocent tender recollections of what is at once an earlier epoch and a previous phase of life.
>
> — RENATO ROSALDO, "Imperialist Nostalgia"

Emily Brontë presents a particularly interesting challenge to cultural criticism. In the words of her sister Charlotte, Emily was "stronger than a man, simpler than a child, her nature stood alone" (19). Child, virgin, man, by nature reclusive and physically on the verge of dying, Emily wrote with "a secret power and fire" that, her sister tells us, came strictly from within. Most scholars and critics have accepted this view. More so than any Romantic poem, they have assumed, *Wuthering Heights* comes to us as the product of a mind detached from history and uncontaminated by political concerns. They as much as ask, "What is there to historicize in a novel so removed from the business of the world? What can such an eccentric document tell us about the culture with which it evidently had so little intercourse?" "Nothing," the literary critic tends to answer, never questioning the fact that *Wuthering Heights* tells us only about its own internal operations and those of the mind from which it sprang. But for the cultural historian, this is just the sort of text that exemplifies the symbolic practices most essential to the social group that produced and/or received it.

To show that such a text is doing a certain kind of cultural work requires special strategies of proof whose success depends on two factors. First, one has to have a feel for those details within a text that can come only from its material surroundings. Such details have the power to dissolve the frame distinguishing what is "inside" a novel like *Wuthering Heights* from the materials of the 1830s and 1840s out of which Emily Brontë made that novel and with which it therefore carried on a relationship. Second, one has to decide exactly how to link these materials together as a field of information, a discourse, or a cultural text (as I am using these terms, they mean much the same thing). This decision hinges on locating the principles of overdetermination. Taken from French philosopher Louis Althusser, overdetermination resembles the logic that in psychoanalytic theory links the disparate materials of a dream into a single coherent message, or wish.[1] The logic I have in mind traces the kind of wish that we express through dreams back to the cultural materials through which we conduct social relationships. If these messages seem to come from the very center of our selves, I believe, it is because the messages in question constitute truth — divine or natural — that one has to accept in order to belong to a particular culture at a specific moment in time.

I have already called attention to the self-enclosure of *Wuthering Heights*. Many literary critics have attributed the Chinese-box structure of this novel to the neurosis of a female author who withdrew from adult sexuality into the sanctuary of her family, fantasy life, and, finally, death. But a second detail must be coupled with its self-enclosure if we are to place the novel squarely within cultural history. All these enclosures — or, more accurately, frames — are violated. No frame remains intact, neither Heights, nor Grange, nor bedroom, nor body, nor book, nor dream, nor even the grave. Everyone in the novel crosses at least one threshold with violence and ravishes some sacred ground. Think of the moment when Lockwood first approaches the portals of Wuthering Heights and is knocked over backwards by one of the housedogs. Or when Catherine and Heathcliff peer in the window of Thrushcross Grange only to be chased away and Catherine seized by another pack of dogs. Or when Linton separates Catherine from Heathcliff and then speeds her decline and death by childbirth. Or when her daughter scales the wall between the Heights and Grange to keep company with her sickly cousin. Or when Heathcliff takes over the Heights, elopes with and dismisses Isabel Linton, takes custody of their son, and forcibly marries him off to the young Catherine. Each intrusion is enacted strictly according to law, and yet each is described in terms of rape, pedophilia, necrophilia, or some combination of these.

[1]Louis Althusser, "Contradiction and Overdetermination: Notes for an Investigation," *For Marx,* trans. Ben Brewster (New York: Vintage, 1970) 101.

The supreme act of violence that seems to sum up all these events occurs in a dream where one cannot distinguish aggressor from victim.

The scene I have in mind is Lockwood's dream. Overwhelmed with the shock suffered from the dog attack, Lockwood retires to a chamber where Heathcliff "never let anyone lodge willingly." Inside the chamber is a bed that provides a second chamber, "a singular sort of old-fashioned couch . . . [that] formed a little closet" (p. 37 in this volume). Once there, he penetrates yet another enclosure: "It was a Testament, in lean type, and smelling dreadfully musty: a fly-leaf bore the inscription — 'Catherine Earnshaw, her book,' and a date some quarter of a century back" (p. 38). As Lockwood drops off to sleep, however, the novel makes it increasingly difficult to tell just where private fantasy ends and social history begins: "I began to dream," Lockwood recalls, "almost before I ceased to be sensible to my locality. I thought it was morning; and I had set out on my way home, with Joseph for a guide" (p. 40). This phase of the dream takes him to a religious meeting that concludes as he enters into mortal combat with Joseph. "And what was it that had suggested the tremendous tumult," Lockwood asks himself, apparently waking:

> Merely, the branch of a fir-tree that touched my lattice, as the blast wailed by, and rattled its dry cones against the panes!
>
> I listened doubtingly an instant; detected the disturber, then turned and dozed, and dreamt again; if possible, still more disagreeably than before.
>
> This time, I remembered I was lying in the oak closet, and I heard distinctly the gusty wind, and the driving of the snow; I heard, also, the fir-bough repeat its teasing sound, and ascribed it to the right cause; but it annoyed me so much, that I resolved to silence it, if possible; and, I thought, I rose and endeavoured to unhasp the casement. The hook was soldered into the staple, a circumstance observed by me when awake, but forgotten.
>
> "I must stop it nevertheless!" I muttered, knocking my knuckles through the glass, and stretching an arm out to seize the importunate branch: instead of which, my fingers closed on the fingers of a little, ice-cold hand! . . .
>
> "Catherine Linton," it replied, shiveringly (why did I think of *Linton*? I had read *Earnshaw* twenty times for Linton), "I'm come home, I'd lost my way on the moor!"
>
> As it spoke, I discerned, obscurely, a child's face looking through the window — Terror made me cruel; and, finding it useless to attempt shaking the creature off, I pulled its wrist on to the broken pane, and rubbed it to and fro till the blood ran

> down and soaked the bedclothes: still it wailed, "Let me in" and maintained its tenacious gripe, almost maddening me with fear. (pp. 42–43).

I have written about this scene on several occasions, and yet I feel it still eludes me, much as Catherine eluded Lockwood. One cannot say if this account of a dream takes the reader outward from a dream into social history or inward from the moors, house, bed, and book to the recesses of a modern person's fantasy life. The dream, in other words, offers us the moment before precisely this difference has been textually produced.

Lockwood would all but slip by without notice were it not for these occasions when he breaks the frame defined by Nelly Dean's narrative. His intrusions always shatter the pastoral beauty of the scene he observes, disclosing a way of life hostile to the expectations of such a tourist. Readers in turn find a very different meaning attached to images once we discover what binds them together within a frame that resists the urbane interpretive reflexes Lockwood brings with him into Yorkshire. Indeed, he requires an entire history of that framework, the land, house, room, and book, before he can begin to understand the human relationships into which he literally stumbles in crossing the threshold. In providing this history of Wuthering Heights, I will argue, the novel itself entered into a massive historical process. The pages to follow will simply outline the cultural project in which I think *Wuthering Heights* played an instrumental role.

1. Folklore

For all practical purposes, folklore took off sometime during the 1820s, and by the 1840s a substantial number of people were collecting stories, superstitions, cures, and arcane practices from every out-of-the-way place in the nation.[2] They began writing them down for weekly and monthly publications. One man who became very influential in folklore, William Thorns, can be credited with coining the term when in 1846 he described "Folk-Lore" as "a vast body of 'traditionary lore' floating among our peasantry."[3] But folklore did not simply familiarize educated readers with life in these regions; it reclassified ordinary life in much of the nation as exotic and backward. For example, John Roby,

[2]For an account of the history of British folklore as it went from the antiquarian interests of a handful of scholars in the late eighteenth and early nineteenth centuries to the mid-nineteenth-century vogue for collecting and publishing British folklore, see Richard M. Dorson, *The British Folklorists, A History* (London: Routledge, 1968).

[3]William John Thoms, "Folk-Lore," *Athenaeum*, 982 (22 Aug. 1846): 862–63.

the author of the extremely popular *Traditions of Lancashire* (1829), is said to have "regarded folk products as disfigured and imperfect specimens in the mouths of peasants."[4] In short, the degree to which a local community depended on custom and oral transmission indicated how ignorant it was.

Proceeding on this assumption, collectors turned the distinction between their class and the rest of England into a matter of cultural rather than economic capital. "Those who mix much amongst the lower orders," wrote the nineteenth-century collector William Henderson, "and have opportunities of enquiring closely into their beliefs, customs, and usages, will find in these remote places, — nay, even in our towns and villages, — a vast mass of superstition holding its ground most tenaciously."[5] "Superstition" indicated a lack of knowledge in two important respects, both of which figure prominently in *Wuthering Heights*. One has to do with the care of the body. The then-budding profession of medicine had to expend considerable energy to invalidate folk ways of caring for the body.[6] But the effort to reclassify popular knowledge as the absence of knowledge extended well beyond any single profession. This effort generated many new kinds of writing, both scientific and literary, across Western Europe. It linked one kind of professional writing to another in an unwitting conspiracy that established a distinctively modern system of belief: knowledge will give us control over nature, the purpose of which is to extend human life.[7]

[4]Qtd in Dorson 100.

[5]William Henderson, *Notes on the Folk Lore of the Northern Counties of England and the Borders* (London: Longmans, Green 1866), qtd in David Vincent, *Literacy and Popular Culture, England 1750–1914* (Cambridge, Eng.: Cambridge UP, 1989) 156.

[6]On this point, see Georges Canguilhem, *The Normal and the Pathological,* trans. Carolyn R. Fawcett and Robert S. Cohen (New York: Zone, 1989); Frank Mort, *Dangerous Sexualities: Medico-Moral Politics in England since 1830* (London: Routledge, 1987); Ivan Waddington, *The Medical Profession in the Industrial Revolution* (Dublin: Gill and Macmillan, 1984); Jacques Donzelot, *The Policing of Families,* trans. Robert Hurley (New York: Pantheon, 1979); Jean Donnison, *Midwives and Medical Men: A History of Inter-Professional Rivalries and Women's Rights* (London: Heinemann, 1977); J. Woodward and D. Richards, eds., *Health Care and Popular Medicine in Nineteenth-Century England* (London: Croom Helm, 1977); Jeanne Brand, *Doctors and the State: The British Medical Profession and Government Acion in Public Health, 1870–1912* (Baltimore: Johns Hopkins UP, 1965).

[7]For an explanation of how nineteenth-century European intellectuals reclassified human nature, disseminated that classification system, and thus established the power of knowledge as the instrument of and justification for domination, see Michel Foucault's *History of Sexuality I: An Introduction,* trans. Robert Hurley (New York: Pantheon, 1978), and *Discipline and Punish: The Birth of the Prison,* trans. Alan Sheridan (New York: Vintage, 1979).

There is a second way in which "superstition" denoted an absence rather than an alternative form of knowledge. To the modern observer, superstition scrambled time in ways that seemed to overturn natural law. Catherine's body, for example, does not decompose in the grave but lingers there, just as her childish voice and image linger outside the bedroom where Lockwood sleeps. Indeed, the novel's plot loops backward in time to establish an essential continuity of Heathcliff present with Heathcliff past where Lockwood can see only change and transformation.[8] In doing so, *Wuthering Heights* encourages us to regard the present as a recycling of past essences. Historians believe that this kind of time organized life in preindustrial England; it was based on the time it took to perform the tasks required by the agricultural year and the demands of cottage industry.[9]

Curiously enough, it was over the issue of time and how to "keep" it that the various objections to "superstition" seem to converge and form a coherent logic. As a result, what we encounter today in the logic motivating and organizing folklore is the very conflict organizing British culture as it was undergoing industrialization. Methods that promoted literacy, particularly the establishment of charity schools, proved to be the best way of inculcating a sense of time that met the requirements of mechanized labor among rural as well as urban populations.[10] But there was far more to the means and effects of such acculturation than we can explain with the economic logic of capitalism. The new sense of time produced a rupture in ordinary life between one setting, where the body belonged to "society," and another, where it belonged to oneself — an irreparable rupture, that is, between social and subjective life.

Such fissures are everywhere apparent in *Wuthering Heights:* in Hindley's concern with facts and figures when he returns to the

[8]In an unpublished but widely circulated essay comparing the first and second editions of *Wuthering Heights,* Masao Miyoshi offers a precise description of the coordinates where the mythic space-time of the Heathcliff-Catherine narrative confronts the clock-time organizing Lockwood's narration. His examination of the first edition of the novel demonstrates that what may appear to be punctuation errors and other evidence of syntactic confusion in fact call attention to the gap between the two different space-time continuums. I thank Professor Miyoshi for allowing me to read his manuscript.

[9]For a historical account of the two conflicting concepts of time, I am drawing on E. P. Thompson, "Time, Work-Discipline, and Industrial Capitalism," *Past and Present* 38 (1967): 56–97.

[10]Thomas Walter Laqueur, *Religion and Respectability: Sunday Schools and Working Class Culture, 1780–1850* (New Haven: Yale UP, 1976) 219–40.

Heights as a married man; in Catherine's concern with propriety after she has been taken in by the Lintons; and in the curses that Heathcliff hurls at her daughter for reading in his presence. But we can use Lockwood's dream to identify the strong sense of violence that infuses them all. The dream translates that violence into metaphysical terms — the violence of enclosing consciousness and confining it to the body, on the one hand, and the violence of violating such self-enclosure, on the other. Lockwood commits violence in the first sense when he insists on a kind of self-enclosure that severs the bond of common humanity linking him to the place and to its history, as represented by the phantom child. But the child causes violence of another kind. Her consciousness permeates such things as the place, the book, and the name. Unconfined to the body of the woman it once inhabited, the essential Catherine enjoys a sinister afterlife in those things. What is more, the voice and image that once were hers tend to enter other people's minds. From Heathcliff's point of view, Lockwood committed an act of violence by cutting off and shutting out the child. Such people are shallow, heartless, and unreal — "dolls," he calls them. From Lockwood's point of view, however, the only violence done was Catherine's violation of the boundary surrounding the self and confining it to the body, and that he dismisses as a phantom of his own imagination.

Lockwood's journey into the wastelands, farms, and villages is a journey back in time. As the story regresses through preceding generations of the Earnshaw family, it appears to be taking us back to the primitive beginnings of the culture. At the same time, this is an utterly civilized excursion made of a series of well-composed shots of the ancient house and its interior, the closeted bed with a bookshelf and window frame in turn nested within it. In *Wuthering Heights,* as in Charlotte Brontë's novel *Jane Eyre,* the pictorial in general and landscapes in particular are at once deliberately framed to announce their artificiality and yet used to represent naked emotions that would otherwise elude verbal expression. Thus alongside the world of work and clock-time, we can observe the twin worlds of leisure and dreams in the process of being carved from the materials of another culture.

Lockwood encounters the rural landscape as a tourist, converting that landscape and its occupants into a private aesthetic experience. He takes secret satisfaction in prying into out-of-the-way places with his eyes. In this respect, we might say he also resembles the folklorist, except for the fact there is a special thrill in tourism, an erotic thrill of sorts. Whereas eighteenth-century gentlemen could find this form of erotic gratification in the privacy of their gardens, Lockwood has to travel to a region in the north of England.[11] Here he encounters a very different nature from the one that yielded to the taste of the eighteenth-century gentleman gardener. Lockwood is not the owner but an intruder and, as such, can not take the same satisfaction in strolling across its contours and exploring its passageways. In offering readers the following explanation for his seclusion at Thrushcross Grange, Lockwood reveals the fact that people, and especially women, exist for him only as texts to contemplate and, in this way, to appropriate for his private fantasy life:

> While enjoying a month of fine weather at the sea-coast, I was thrown into the company of a most fascinating creature, a real goddess in my eyes, as long as she took no notice of me . . . She understood me, at last, and looked a return — the sweetest of all imaginable looks — and what did I do? I confess it with shame — shrunk icily into myself, like a snail . . . finally, the poor innocent was led to doubt her own senses, and, overwhelmed with confusion at her supposed mistake, persuaded her mamma to decamp. (p. 27)

He gives us this single bit of background just as he is about to repeat the same scene several times over, first with Catherine Heathcliff and then with the ghost of her mother cast as the "fascinating creature."

What becomes clear through such repetition is that, like an eighteenth-century gentleman, Lockwood wants nothing so much as the pornographic thrill of *just* looking. When the girl catches him in the act of looking, then, the thrill is gone. He is no longer the gentlemanly connoisseur of nature whom readers encountered both in pastoral poetry and in picturesque accounts of the English countryside.[12] Nor does the nature he observes in Yorkshire submit passively to his gaze. It is much closer to the sexually motivated nature that Robert Malthus described in his influential *Essay on the Principle of Population* (1798) as

[11]Simon Pugh, "Loitering with Intent: From Arcadia to the Arcades," *Reading Landscape: Country-City-Capital,* ed. Simon Pugh (Manchester, Eng.: Manchester UP, 1990) 145–60. Pugh's analysis of what a tour around the eighteenth-century garden did to one's view of nature suggests that it was an erotic experience: "The journey round the garden is the equivalent of the pornographer's journey round the female figure, dimensions, angles, postures, views, zones, absurd unnatural contortions of the landscape . . . to secure the best shots, odd styles of dress thrown together for effect to emphasise or to conceal a feature" (152).

[12]One might recall Wordsworth's "solitary reaper" and "old leech gatherer" as well as the Lucy of the Lucy poems, all of which remain quiescent beneath the poet's gaze and are thus easily translated into figures of imagination. In contrast with the phantom Catherine, they do not call attention to the rupture between modern subject and folkloric object.

well as the dog-eat-dog nature with which Charles Darwin familiarized the Victorian readership in his *Origin of the Species* (1859). The "poor innocent" of his former encounter makes its uncanny reappearance as the child outside his bedroom window, a child that has been viciously denied existence as a human being and who, with equal viciousness, makes her presence known.

As she and Lockwood struggle to define that space, then, one has to wonder who has made a forced entrance here and who is the victim of the rape. The novel makes it easy to side with the child, who is after all both a "waif" trying to return home after twenty years on the moors and a devoted woman breaching death to reunite with her beloved. Given the sentimentality attached to both these stereotypes, however, it is rather curious that nature in such a form completely overturns the sentimental relationship that Lockwood obviously wants to establish with the landscape. Much like the woman he once rejected, the landscape returns the sentimental observer's look, infiltrates his dreams, and takes possession of the one who sought to possess it through folklore's antiquating words and images. Such violation of Lockwood's expectations could not help but leave readers with the suspicion that the novelist was taking the side of the waif, but for entirely unsentimental reasons. Was Emily Brontë herself committing an act of violence then? Her earliest reviewers evidently thought so.[13]

2. Photography

For twenty years or so before *Wuthering Heights* appeared and caused a minor sensation, a number of individuals in England and France were developing the technology for mechanically reproducing images of the countryside and making them available to urban viewers.[14] This technology brought the more remote regions to the metropolis in much the same way that *Wuthering Heights* did. It made highly

[13]See, for example, the responses by Brontë's contemporaries reprinted in the Norton Critical Edition of *Wuthering Heights,* ed. William M. Sale, Jr., 2nd ed. (New York: Norton, 1972) 277–85.

[14]Although photography was invented in the late 1820s (probably 1827), by the 1840s the daguerreotype and calotype techniques were both already widely available for use by amateurs and professionals throughout England and the Continent. Until around 1850, methods of photography required a very long exposure time during which the subject could not move. This is doubtless one reason why landscapes and set poses were preferred by amateur photographers. I am indebted to Andrew Szegedy-Maszak for his advice on nineteenth-century photography. For an account of the early years of photography, see Beaumont Newhall, *The History of Photography from 1839 to the Present* (New York: Museum of Modern Art, 1982).

textualized images available on a mass basis for consumption in the privacy of respectable homes. These images took their cue from pastoral poetry and picturesque description. They offered the viewer a countryside that was remote, exotic, and utterly passive to view. Although forms of manual labor became a familiar subject of landscape photography, the visibility of work did not overturn the pastoralism. Work was frozen into images that were meant to be received as works of art, images that were supposed to intrigue the viewer. The surface of the native body with its strange, often tattered local costume and primitive implements invited the consumer's gaze to pass over it in wonderment, even pity, but without any sense of a common humanity shared by viewer and photographic subject. Nor did the photograph suggest what might have brought photographers into such remote regions to record the images that came flooding back into the literary marketplace.

Indeed, the new technology left the photographer and his apparatus out of the picture completely. He existed only as an observer, a presence implied by the impressions made on his (camera's) eye and the text that often accompanied them, much like the guidebooks that induced tourists to explore the countryside. Several hundred copies of an album called *The Pencil of Nature* appeared at booksellers in six paper-covered installments between June 1844 and April 1846 and enjoyed immediate success. Along with the crumbling façade of Queen's College, Oxford, shelves of ornamental china and leather-bound books, statues from antiquity, and a fine piece of lace, one finds images of leaves and scenes from what might be called ordinary life, a haystack, a ladder, a cottage door propped open by a broom (Figure 1). It is important, I think, to note the similarity between folklore and the statement made by this selection of objects. The album furthers the dehistoricizing work of the camera. It not only situated snapshots one more step away from the conditions under which they were produced, it also created a kind of equivalence between nature, knowledge, and objects for sale. All are equally things in that they can be translated into and possessed as mechanically reproducible images. Like the leaf or piece of lace, these instruments of common labor operate as synecdoches, broken off and standing in for a whole system of natural, social, or economic relationships.

At the same time, and this is perhaps a more curious feature of such books, the collection presents these images to us as if they are the things in themselves unmediated by human agency. *The Pencil of Nature* included photographer William Henry Fox Talbot's account of his unique process for making calotype images. This is important because his description of the technology of reproduction enhanced the

Figure 1. The Open Door (1844) by William Henry Fox Talbot.
Reproduced by permission of Da Capo Press, a division of Plenum Publishing Corporation, 227 West 17th Street, New York, N.Y. 10011.

ability of his images to disguise the political project they were carrying out. The account calls attention to the photographer's mastery over the scene through the chemistry of image-making, mastery that could not be achieved by hand or with pencil. Talbot's admission that he possesses only the most feeble artistic skills serves to exalt his scientific ingenuity. He strives for an image that completely removes him from the scene. He claims no responsibility for the image because it was nature that put it there for him to reproduce. Thus of his chemically produced negative images he can insist,

> they differ in all respects, and as widely as possible, in their origin, from plates of the ordinary kind, which owe their existence to the united skill of the Artist and the Engraver. They are impressed by Nature's hand, and what they want as yet of delicacy and finish of execution arises chiefly from our want of sufficient knowledge of her laws.[15]

[15]William Henry Fox Talbot, *The Pencil of Nature* (1844; New York: Da Capo, 1969). N. pag.

There are striking similarities between the way Talbot steps outside the photographic frame and the way we receive the wildly Romantic history of Wuthering Heights from Lockwood. For the most part, the story is already over, and he simply reports what he sees and hears from his native informant, Nelly Dean. But who would think of describing the author of such a novel, Emily Brontë herself, in these terms?

Charlotte Brontë did just that in order to make the novel more acceptable to its readership. Of her sister, Charlotte wrote in her "Editor's Preface" to the 1850 edition,

> I am bound to avow that she had scarcely more practical knowledge of the peasantry amongst whom she lived, than a nun has of the country people who sometimes pass her convent gates. My sister's disposition was not naturally gregarious; circumstances favoured and fostered her tendency to seclusion; except to go to church or take a walk on the hills, she rarely crossed the threshold of home. (p. 22)

Emily remained as detached and pristine as the folklorist or the photographer did from the subject whose image, words, or practices he captured in print. "And yet," according to Charlotte, "she knew them; knew their ways, their language, their family histories; she could hear of them with interest, and talk of them with detail, minute, graphic, and accurate; but *with* them, she rarely exchanged a word" (p. 22). Talbot can justify any and all imperfections in *The Pencil of Nature* as signs of his technological immaturity: "At present the Art can hardly be said to have advanced beyond its infancy. . . . Its improvement will be more rapid when more minds are devoted to its improvement." The kind of writing represented by *Wuthering Heights* obviously could not improve. By the time Charlotte Brontë wrote the "Biographical Notice" and "Editor's Preface" to the 1850 edition, Emily Brontë was dead. "Had she but lived," Charlotte admits in the "Preface," "her mind would of itself have grown like a strong tree, loftier, straighter, wider-spreading, and its matured fruits would have attained a mellower ripeness and sunnier bloom; but on that mind time and experience alone could work: to the influence of other intellects, it was not amenable" (p. 23).

Charlotte did the only sensible thing. In order to make the novel more acceptable to a readership shocked at the behavior of Heathcliff and Catherine, she consigned her sister to the rural world caught up in the framework of the novel and packaged for a mass readership. The information appended to the second edition ensured that the author of this particular novel would be received with the same appetite that Victorians brought to accounts of native customs and collections of antiquities. Charlotte as much as placed her sister with the leaf, the delicate pieces of China contained in a curio cabinet, the crumbling façade of Queen's College, or the broom in the doorway. Between them, her "Biographical Notice" and "Editor's Preface" tied the author of *Wuthering Heights* to nature, to a region, and to a regional dialect. Attuned to the rhythms of the place around her, Emily Brontë supposedly perished because she was driven to produce the manuscript according to the dictates of another kind of time that perishes with her: "Never in all her life had she lingered over any task that lay before her, and she did not linger now. She sank rapidly. She made haste to leave us. Yet, while physically she perished, mentally, she grew stronger than we had yet known her" (p. 19).[16] Like the culture indigenous to the north of England, Emily Brontë dropped out of a history that would not have valued her imperfections but only her "improvement." Along with the countryside and way of life in the north of England that her novel memorialized, then, she came to be valued as something extremely rare and perishable that had passed away.

During Emily Brontë's relatively brief lifetime 1818–1848, precisely the years when folklore became enormously popular, an increasing number of amateur photographers went out into the remote areas of Great Britain to document the landscape, customs, and people, in much the same way and presumably for much the same reasons that folklorists had. Especially important was the way they depicted the very forms of labor on which most of the people of Great Britain still depended. A photograph entitled *Gleaners* is but one example of a vast number of images showing how the people of remote regions worked (Figure 2). For the polite readership, the primitive form of labor identifies the two women in the photograph as survivors from an earlier time. Like the landscape itself, the camera transforms their means of livelihood into a curious, if not entirely charming, image.

By looking ahead to the photography of the 1850s, when *Wuthering Heights* had won over the readership, we can observe a change in the style of regional photography. With the popularity of the studio photograph, it no longer seemed so important (as it did when *The*

[16]As the daughter of a minister, Emily had every reason to be aware of the conflict between the older agrarian and more modern concepts of time. Both Thomas Laqueur in *Religion and Respectability* and E. P. Thompson in "Time, Work-Discipline and Industrial Capitalism" point out that John Wesley regularly demanded that his followers practice a rigorous "husbandry of time" implicit in the term "Methodist" itself.

Figure 2. Gleaners (1857). Reproduced by permission of Radio Times Hulton Picture Library.

Pencil of Nature was published) to capture nature in all its imperfections. Many of the same shots that were found and captured during journeys to various regions of Great Britain were restaged in the professional studio. It is instructive, I think, to see how the working women whom photography made into cultural primitives changed again when they were reproduced in this new setting (Figure 3). The artificiality of the painted backdrop seeps into the human subject. Against this background, the clothing of a Scottish fisher girl appears to be a costume, and her baskets, purely ornamental objects. And as nature becomes blatantly artificial, the regional culture loses the aura that depends on its relationship to a specific place in the national landscape and to a particular moment in time. The photograph does not strike us as a relic of a passing way of life so much as a memorial to something that had already passed away by the time the photograph was taken. We might say the same of the Catherine whom Lockwood encounters upon first entering Wuthering Heights. She, too, seems strangely out of place in her

Figure 3. Scottish Fisher Girl (1880), from the Archie Miles Collection. Reproduced by permission of Harper & Row Publishers Inc., 10 East 53rd Street, New York, N.Y. 10022.

setting. On the one hand, she reminds Lockwood of the modern "goddess" whose glances he repelled. At the same time, she is the incarnation of the ghostly Catherine whose mating practices are radically at odds with his. No wonder he has trouble figuring out her name and identity within the local community.

Another photograph entitled *The Colleen Bawm* exhibits the same streak of sensationalism we find in *Wuthering Heights* (Figure 4). It glamorizes a woman otherwise unattractive by Victorian standards. *The Colleen Bawm,* which means either "The White Girl" or "The Golden Girl," was the title given this portrait of a sixteen-year-old Irish girl

Figure 4. The Colleen Bawm (1900), from the Archie Miles Collection. Reproduced by permission of Harper & Row Publishers Inc., 10 East 53rd Street, New York, N.Y. 10022.

named Ellen Harley, who was murdered in 1819 by a local squire and his servant. A story about the fatal beauty of a rural girl was evidently just the sort to inspire several plays and books. It also inspired this sentimentally framed portrait. As Asa Briggs points out, "the photograph could well show an actress playing the part of Ellen, or simply a young country woman dressed as a typical Irish lass for the entertainment of tourists."[17] Thus the image reveals the further effacement of indigenous cultures that occurs when the simulation cannot be distinguished from the authentic object. The culture in question becomes a copy

[17]Asa Briggs, *A Victorian Portrait* (New York: Harper, 1989) 58.

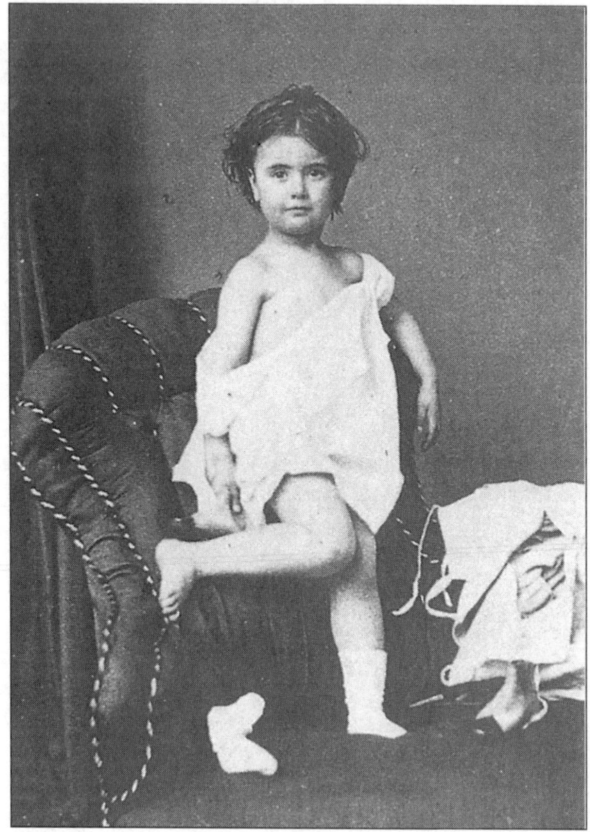

Figure 5. Child Undressing (1865), from the Archie Miles Collection. Reproduced by permission of Harper & Row Publishers Inc., 10 East 53rd Street, New York, N.Y. 10022.

without any original, the photographer's creation rather than an original that photography has copied imperfectly.

Along with *The Colleen Bawm,* I have included one example of an extremely popular genre of Victorian photography, what Asa Briggs calls "slightly *risqué* material" (Figure 5).[18] By charging the image with eroticism, the photograph calls attention to the same constellation of features that come together in Lockwood's dream. In these sexually suggestive portraits, excluded humanity steps forward and presents itself to the public gaze in the form of a nameless, placeless female child. There is something profoundly innocent and vulnerable about the woman's age and child's gender. In contrast with many photographic

[18]Briggs 139.

subjects, this one forces us to ask how she became the object of our gaze. It is definitely wrong for her to have entered our field of vision, although, as in Lockwood's dream, the identity of the perpetrator is not exactly clear. The camera does not simply catch her without her clothes on, any more than the landed gentry happened on Irish peasant girls, or Lockwood accidentally ended up in Catherine's bed. It has all been arranged. Like the prostitute, she appears to have put her body on display. Thus there is something terribly unfeminine about her gender, something primitive about her innocence, something fierce in her vulnerability. Like the women Lockwood encounters, the girls in these photographs look back at the camera. Like the ghostly child in his dream, they seem to disrupt the world of sentimentality and common sense. They intrude into the world dominated by the camera and reveal what such specularity is really all about.

In casting the child's body in its lurid light, the camera has successfully "framed" her — indeed, framed all those who do not appear before it in family portraits, industrial landscapes, and other scenes from modern life. Objectification contains the subject within a framework where almost anything could easily be sentimentalized, as the matting and title of *The Colleen Bawm* proclaim. With the wink of a shutter, entire landscapes and populations within Great Britain were cut down to the size of a single snapshot. Within this framework, various regions tended to appear as similar to one another as they were different from the respectable family that provided the favorite subject of photography. All such images could in turn be placed within a later version of *The Pencil of Nature*, a single album, producing what might be called the Baskin-Robbins effect — just so many flavors of the same thing. To the object so constituted there always sticks a quasi-pornographic aura, generated by its obvious foreignness, its vulnerability, the power of purchasing such an image for private use, and the thrill that comes from just looking. I would suggest that this aura provides the attraction that links such tourists as Lockwood to the collector of photographs as well as to novel-readers like us.

3. Regionalism

Along with folklore and photography, *Wuthering Heights* performs the task of miniaturization. In comparison with present-day reality, the world in miniature appears to be one of nature pure and simple. It places other people in the position of children or of primitive ancestors surviving from an earlier moment in history. In this way, they seem harmless enough to be enjoyed aesthetically.[19] At the same time, we know the miniature is nothing but a copy. It is by thus triumphing over the forces of both time and space that the miniature offers its consumer a fantasy of control, one suggesting that art, knowledge, and/or technology can conquer even death. If we want to move outside the framework of fiction and photography and insert that framing activity in history, however, we need to carry the logic of miniaturization one step farther.

Although we tend to think of British colonialism in terms of the English conquest first of North America and then of parts of Africa and Asia, much the same thing went on inside Great Britain. The pace of internal colonization increased after America won independence and before the 1850s, when Empire took its modern shape. In becoming a modern nation, Great Britain experienced a cultural division of labor that produced an English core and an ethnic periphery.[20] Members of more and less advantaged groups tended to assign each other roles on the basis of visible signs — including dialect, religion, dress, food, and skills, in addition to distinctive physical features — which came to be seen as essential to the very nature of each group. This division was not something that had to be overcome in order for the modern nation state to become coherent as such. To the contrary, a cultural division of labor allowed a certain group of English men and women to establish their particular dialect, religion, clothing, skills, and appearance as those of Great Britain itself. We see this in Lockwood's identification first with Edgar Linton and then with the monogamous couple that monopolizes the frame at the end of the novel (p. 287). They represent the essence of Englishness, an essence from which Lockwood has neurotically excluded himself, rather than a distinction between time frames and ethnic identities.

But once we see the novel as part of the process of internal colonization I call "regionalism," what do we say about the novel and, more specifically, Brontë's place in this process? To work toward a satisfactory

[19]My discussion of miniaturization is indebted to Susan Stewart's *On Longing: Narratives of the Miniature, the Gigantic, the Souvenir, the Collection* (Baltimore: Johns Hopkins UP, 1984).

[20]Michael Hechter has noted that in addition to Scotland, Wales, and Ireland, certain areas within England were made into an ethnic periphery. The English counties and regions that came to be considered ethnic were those that had traditionally been organized for grazing and open wasteland rather than for raising crops in enclosed fields. This use of land followed the "Celtic field system." Although this Celtic model had all but disappeared by the period I am discussing, areas where it had dominated tended to resist the more common English practice of cereal and grass growing and the more typically English distribution of land according to primogeniture. Yorkshire, where Emily Brontë lived and wrote, was one of these peripheral areas. *Internal Colonialism: The Celtic Fringe in British National Development, 1536–1966* (Berkeley: U of California P, 1975) 58–59.

answer to this question, I will draw on the concept of "imperialist nostalgia."[21] Anthropologist Renato Rosaldo formulated this term to describe the tendency among anthropologists to idealize a time before indigenous populations were destroyed, converted, educated, or otherwise transformed by modern Western intellectuals. This state of primitive purity, as he explains, has much in common with miniaturization, and thus with the folklore, photography, and fiction I have been discussing. That is to say, these textualizing practices all exalted another people so as to infuse with longing the very authenticity that they were in fact destroying. The inscription of unfamiliar landscapes and bodies provides not only a record of the passing of regional cultures, then, but also the technology for converting them into an ethnic periphery.[22]

A similar sense of loss accompanies the framing, reduction, and interment of native culture in *Wuthering Heights.* In a well-known photograph of the parsonage at Haworth taken after the death of Emily Brontë, one finds that visitors to the surrounding cemetery are not there simply to pay their respects to the dead (Figure 6). The garden of mingled tombstones and heather surrounding a house reputedly sheltering a family of poets, madmen, and dying women as well as the Reverend Patrick Brontë, was something of a spectacle. Indeed, surviving into the present time, the town and parsonage themselves seem as diminished in size as do the traces of girls apparently afflicted at birth by a mysterious illness that severely reduced their size as well as their span of years. The parsonage exists as a curious spot on the Yorkshire moors to this day, its objects riddled through with captions, signs, and relics pointing to lives that resemble fiction more than history — in short, a text of the very kind I have been describing. Rather than disclosing Emily's true nature, I believe, imperialist nostalgia explains the peculiar way in which Charlotte Brontë presented Emily and her novel to the reading public.

Having described *Wuthering Heights* in relation to the upsurge of interest in local folklore and the development of photography, we can see what binds them all together in a single project. When the reviewers greeted *Wuthering Heights* with suspicion and even outrage, Charlotte

[21]Renato Rosaldo, "Imperialist Nostalgia," *Culture and Truth: The Remaking of Social Analysis* (Boston: Beacon, 1989) 68–87.

[22]John Taylor, "The Alphabetic Universe: Photography and the Picturesque Landscape," in *Reading Landscape,* explains that photographers found it increasingly difficult to find the picturesque in England because of industrialization and the growth of the suburbs: "By 1899 the photographer had to search for the picturesque, but it was still possible to find 'a few villages and hamlets which seem to belong to past centuries — fresh looking plaster and stucco are there unknown; fashion has not quite ousted primitive dress, nor has the din of factories disturbed the sleepy aspect of the surroundings'" (181).

Figure 6. Haworth Parsonage at the Time of the Brontës.
From *Victorian and Edwardian Yorkshire from Old Photographs*, ed. A. B. Craven (1971).

used precisely the textualizing procedures to describe its author that Emily Brontë had used to turn "the outlying hills and hamlets in the West-Riding of Yorkshire" into "things alien and unfamiliar" (p. 21). And thus she eliminated all conflict between the time frames in the novel.[23] To identify the author with the region that she represented, Charlotte infused her with nostalgia. She reframed the novel, much as the studio matting reframed *The Colleen Bawm,* as something "rustic all through. It is moorish, and wild, and knotty as a root of heath" (p. 22). Charlotte's preface arrogated these same qualities to the author as well: "Nor was it natural that it should be otherwise; the author being herself a native and nursling of the moors" (p. 22). Once the preface to the 1850 edition had situated the author of *Wuthering Heights* within the landscape of her own creation, something on the order of a cult began to develop around Emily Brontë, a cult whose presuppositions have determined the way that literary criticism has approached her ever since.

[23]Masao Miyoshi's study of *Wuthering Heights* indicates that Charlotte finished correcting the "errors" in the first edition for the 1850 edition, thus softening the contradictions that produced a gap between time frames in the novel.

Feminist Criticism and *Wuthering Heights*

WHAT IS FEMINIST CRITICISM?

Feminist criticism comes in many forms, and feminist critics have a variety of goals. Some have been interested in rediscovering the works of women writers overlooked by a masculine-dominated culture. Others have revisited books by male authors and reviewed them from a woman's point of view to understand how they both reflect and shape the attitudes that have held women back. A number of contemporary feminists have turned to topics as various as women in postcolonial societies, women's autobiographical writings, lesbians and literature, womanliness as masquerade, and the role of film and other popular media in the construction of the feminine gender.

Until a few years ago, however, feminist thought tended to be classified not according to topic but, rather, according to country of origin. This practice reflected the fact that, during the 1970s and early 1980s, French, American, and British feminists wrote from somewhat different perspectives.

French feminists tended to focus their attention on language, analyzing the ways in which meaning is produced. They concluded that language as we commonly think of it is a decidedly male realm. Drawing on the ideas of the psychoanalytic philosopher Jacques Lacan, they reminded us that language is a realm of public discourse. A child enters the linguistic realm just as it comes to grasp its separateness from its mother, just about the time that boys identify with their father, the family representative of culture. The language learned reflects a binary logic that opposes such terms as active/passive, masculine/feminine, sun/moon, father/mother, head/heart, son/daughter, intelligent/sensitive, brother/sister, form/matter, phallus/vagina, reason/emotion. Because this logic tends to group with masculinity such qualities as light, thought, and activity, French feminists said that the structure of language is phallocentric: it privileges the phallus and, more generally, masculinity by associating them with things and values more appreciated by the (masculine-dominated) culture. Moreover, French feminists suggested, "masculine desire dominates speech and posits woman as an idealized fantasy-fulfillment for the incurable emotional lack caused by separation from the mother" (Jones, "Inscribing" 83).

French feminists associated language with separation from the mother. Its distinctions, they argued, represent the world from the male point of view. Language systematically forces women to choose: either they can imagine and represent themselves as men imagine and represent them (in which case they may speak, but will speak as men) or they can choose "silence," becoming in the process "the invisible and unheard sex" (Jones, "Inscribing" 83).

But some influential French feminists maintained that language only *seems* to give women such a narrow range of choices. There is another possibility, namely, that women can develop a *feminine* language. In various ways, early French feminists such as Annie Leclerc, Xavière Gauthier, and Marguerite Duras suggested that there is something that may be called *l'écriture féminine:* women's writing. More recently, Julia Kristeva has said that feminine language is "semiotic," not "symbolic." Rather than rigidly opposing and ranking elements of reality, rather than symbolizing one thing but not another in terms of a third, feminine language is rhythmic and unifying. If from the male perspective it seems fluid to the point of being chaotic, that is a fault of the male perspective.

According to Kristeva, feminine language is derived from the preoedipal period of fusion between mother and child. Associated with the maternal, feminine language is not only a threat to culture, which is patriarchal, but also a medium through which women may be creative in new ways. But Kristeva paired her central, liberating claim — that truly feminist innovation in all fields requires an understanding of the relation between maternity and feminine creation — with a warning. A feminist language that refuses to participate in "masculine" discourse, that places its future entirely in a feminine, semiotic discourse, risks being politically marginalized by men. That is to say, it risks being relegated to the outskirts (pun intended) of what is considered socially and politically significant.

Kristeva, who associated feminine writing with the female body, was joined in her views by other leading French feminists. Hélène Cixous, for instance, also posited an essential connection between the woman's body, whose sexual pleasure has been repressed and denied expression, and women's writing. "Write your self. Your body must be heard," Cixous urged; once they learn to write their bodies, women will not only realize their sexuality but enter history and move toward a future based on a "feminine" economy of giving rather than the "masculine" economy of hoarding (Cixous 880). For Luce Irigaray, women's sexual pleasure *(jouissance)* cannot be expressed by the dominant, ordered, "logical," masculine language. Irigaray explored the connection between women's sexuality and women's language through the following analogy: as women's *jouissance* is more multiple than men's unitary, phallic pleasure ("woman has sex organs just about everywhere"), so "feminine" language is more diffusive than its "masculine" counterpart. ("That is undoubtedly the reason . . . her language . . . goes off in all directions and . . . he is unable to discern the coherence," Irigaray writes [*This Sex* 101–3].)

Cixous's and Irigaray's emphasis on feminine writing as an expression of the female body drew criticism from other French feminists. Many argued that an emphasis on the body either reduces "the feminine" to a biological essence or elevates it in a way that shifts the valuation of masculine and feminine but retains the binary categories. For Christine Fauré, Irigaray's celebration of women's difference failed to address the issue of masculine dominance, and a Marxist-feminist, Catherine Clément, warned that "poetic" descriptions of what constitutes the feminine will not challenge that dominance in the realm of production. The boys will still make the toys, and decide who gets to use them. In her effort to redefine women as political rather than as sexual beings, Monique Wittig called for the abolition of the sexual categories that Cixous and Irigaray retained and revalued as they celebrated women's writing.

American feminist critics of the 1970s and early 1980s shared with French critics both an interest in and a cautious distrust of the concept of feminine writing. Annette Kolodny, for instance, worried that the "richness and variety of women's writing" will be missed if we see in it only its "feminine mode" or "style" ("Some Notes" 78). And yet Kolodny herself proceeded, in the same essay, to point out that women *have* had their own style, which includes reflexive constructions ("she found herself crying") and particular, recurring themes (clothing and self-fashioning are mentioned by Kolodny; other American feminists have focused on madness, disease, and the demonic).

Interested as they became in the "French" subject of feminine style, American feminist critics began by analyzing literary texts rather than philosophizing abstractly about language. Many reviewed the great works by male writers, embarking on a revisionist rereading of literary tradition. These critics examined the portrayals of women characters, exposing the patriarchal ideology implicit in such works and showing how clearly this tradition of systematic masculine dominance is inscribed in our literary tradition. Kate Millett, Carolyn Heilbrun, and Judith Fetterley, among many others, created this model for American feminist criticism, a model that Elaine Showalter came to call "the feminist critique" of "male-constructed literary history" ("Poetics" 128).

Meanwhile another group of critics including Sandra Gilbert, Susan Gubar, Patricia Meyer Spacks, and Showalter herself created a somewhat different model. Whereas feminists writing "feminist critique" analyzed works by men, practitioners of what Showalter used to refer to as "gynocriticism" studied the writings of those women who, against all odds, produced what she calls "a literature of their own." In *The Female Imagination* (1975), Spacks examined the female literary tradition to find out how great women writers across the ages have felt, perceived themselves, and imagined reality. Gilbert and Gubar, in *The Madwoman in the Attic* (1979), concerned themselves with well-known women writers of the nineteenth century, but they too found that general concerns, images, and themes recur, because the authors that they wrote about lived "in a culture whose fundamental definitions of literary authority" were "both overtly and covertly patriarchal" (45–46).

If one of the purposes of gynocriticism was to (re)study well-known women authors, another was to rediscover women's history and culture, particularly women's communities that nurtured female creativity. Still another related purpose was to discover neglected or forgotten women writers and thus to forge an alternative literary tradition, a canon that better represents the female perspective by better representing the literary works that have been written by women. Showalter, in *A Literature of Their Own* (1977), admirably began to fulfill this purpose, providing a remarkably comprehensive overview of women's writing through three of its phases. She defined these as the "Feminine,

Feminist, and Female" phases, phases during which women first imitated a masculine tradition (1840–80), then protested against its standards and values (1880–1920), and finally advocated their own autonomous, female perspective (1920 to the present).

With the recovery of a body of women's texts, attention returned to a question raised in 1978 by Lillian Robinson: Shouldn't feminist criticism need to formulate a theory of its own practice? Won't reliance on theoretical assumptions, categories, and strategies developed by men and associated with nonfeminist schools of thought prevent feminism from being accepted as equivalent to these other critical discourses? Not all American feminists came to believe that a special or unifying theory of feminist practice was urgently needed; Showalter's historical approach to women's culture allowed a feminist critic to use theories based on nonfeminist disciplines. Kolodny advocated a "playful pluralism" that encompasses a variety of critical schools and methods. But Jane Marcus and others responded that if feminists adopt too wide a range of approaches, they may relax the tensions between feminists and the educational establishment necessary for political activism.

The question of whether feminism weakens or fortifies itself by emphasizing its separateness — and by developing unity through separateness — was one of several areas of debate within American feminism during the 1970s and early 1980s. Another area of disagreement touched on earlier, between feminists who stress universal feminine attributes (the feminine imagination, feminine writing) and those who focus on the political conditions experienced by certain groups of women at certain times in history, paralleled a larger distinction between American feminist critics and their British counterparts.

While it gradually became customary to refer to an Anglo-American tradition of feminist criticism, British feminists tended to distinguish themselves from what they saw as an American overemphasis on texts linking women across boundaries and decades and an underemphasis on popular art and culture. They regarded their own critical practice as more political than that of North American feminists, whom they sometimes faulted for being uninterested in historical detail. They joined such American critics as Myra Jehlen in suggesting that a continuing preoccupation with women writers may bring about the dangerous result of placing women's texts outside the history that conditions them.

British feminists felt that the American opposition to male stereotypes that denigrate women often leads to counterstereotypes of feminine virtue that ignore real differences of race, class, and culture among women. In addition, they argued that American celebrations of individual heroines falsely suggest that powerful individuals may be immune to repressive conditions and may even imply that *any* individual can go through life unconditioned by the culture and ideology in which she or he lives.

Similarly, the American endeavor to recover women's history — for example, by emphasizing that women developed their own strategies to gain power within their sphere — was seen by British feminists like Judith Newton and Deborah Rosenfelt as an endeavor that "mystifies" male oppression, disguising it as something that has created for women a special world of opportunities. More important from the British standpoint, the universalizing and "essentializing" tendencies in both American practice and French theory disguise women's oppression by highlighting sexual difference, suggesting that a dominant system is impervious to political change. By contrast, British feminist theory emphasized an engagement with historical process in order to promote social change.

By now the French, American, and British approaches have so thoroughly critiqued, influenced, and assimilated one another that the work of most Western practitioners is no longer easily identifiable along national boundary lines. Instead, it tends to be characterized according to whether the category of *woman* is the major focus in the exploration of gender and gender oppression or, alternatively, whether the interest in sexual difference encompasses an interest in other differences that also define identity. The latter paradigm encompasses the work of feminists of color, Third World (preferably called postcolonial) feminists, and lesbian feminists, many of whom have asked whether the universal category of woman constructed by certain French and North American predecessors is appropriate to describe women in minority groups or non-Western cultures.

These feminists stress that, while all women are female, they are something else as well (such as African American, lesbian, Muslim Pakistani). This "something else" is precisely what makes them, their problems, and their goals different from those of other women. As Armit Wilson has pointed out, Asian women living in Britain are expected by their families and communities to preserve Asian cultural traditions; thus, the expression of personal identity through clothing involves a much more serious infraction of cultural rules than it does for a Western woman. Gloria Anzaldúa has spoken personally and eloquently about the experience of many women on the margins of Eurocentric North American culture. "I am a border woman," she writes in *Borderlands:*

La Frontera = The New Mestiza (1987). "I grew up between two cultures, the Mexican (with a heavy Indian influence) and the Anglo. . . . Living on the borders and in margins, keeping intact one's shifting and multiple identity and integrity is like trying to swim in a new element, an 'alien' element" (i).

Instead of being divisive and isolating, this evolution of feminism into femin*isms* has fostered a more inclusive, global perspective. The era of recovering women's texts — especially texts by white Western women — has been succeeded by a new era in which the goal is to recover entire cultures of women. Two important figures of this new era are Trinh T. Minh-ha and Gayatri Spivak. Spivak, in works such as *In Other Worlds: Essays in Cultural Politics* (1987) and *Outside in the Teaching Machine* (1993), has shown how political independence (generally looked upon by metropolitan Westerners as a simple and beneficial historical and political reversal) has complex implications for "subaltern" or subproletarian women.

The understanding of woman not as a single, deterministic category but rather as the nexus of diverse experiences has led some white, Western, "majority" feminists like Jane Tompkins and Nancy K. Miller to advocate and practice "personal" or "autobiographical" criticism. Once reluctant to inject themselves into their analyses for fear of being labeled idiosyncratic, impressionistic, and subjective by men, some feminists are now openly skeptical of the claims to reason, logic, and objectivity that have been made in the past by male critics. With the advent of more personal feminist critical styles has come a powerful new interest in women's autobiographical writings.

Shari Benstock, who has written personal criticism in her book *Textualizing the Feminine* (1991), was one of the first feminists to argue that traditional autobiography is a gendered, "masculinist" genre. Its established conventions, feminists have recently pointed out, call for a life-plot that turns on action, triumph through conflict, intellectual self-discovery, and often public renown. The body, reproduction, children, and intimate interpersonal relationships are generally well in the background and often absent. Arguing that the lived experiences of women and men differ — women's lives, for instance, are often characterized by interruption and deferral — Leigh Gilmore has developed a theory of women's self-representation in her book *Autobiographics: A Feminist Theory of Self-Representation* (1994).

Autobiographics and personal criticism are only two of a number of recent developments in contemporary feminist criticism. Others alluded to in the first paragraph of this introduction — lesbian studies, performance or "masquerade" theory, and studies of the role played by film and various other "technologies" in shaping gender today — are prominent in contemporary *gender* criticism. Although there are several differences between the feminist and the newer gender approaches, the fact of this overlap should remind us that categories obscure similarities even as they help us make distinctions. Feminist criticism is, after all, a form of gender criticism, and contemporary gender criticism could never have developed without feminist criticism.

Near the beginning of the essay that follows — "Changing the Names: The Two Catherines" — Lyn Pykett focuses on the three names that Lockwood finds scratched into a ledge. Arguing that the story of *Catherine Earnshaw* hinges on her "socially sanctioned choice" of the name *Catherine Linton* over *Catherine Heathcliff,* Pykett goes on to suggest that the "Catherine–Edgar–Heathcliff plot seems to question" the "social" and "fictional paradigm which structures a woman's life as a choice between two men" (p. 469 in this volume).

The choice Catherine makes is attributable directly to her stay at Thrushcross Grange and the "transformation, described by Nelly as a 'reform,'" that she undergoes there. Mrs. Linton and subsequently Frances Earnshaw seem successfully to reconstruct "an assertive child associated with the realm of nature" into a "genteel young lady" conforming to society's domestic ideal of womanhood (p. 470). But the transformation is incomplete, and "Catherine's ambivalence about her new role and her continued identification with Heathcliff" cause her to adopt what Brontë calls a "double character." In Pykett's words, Catherine's "role" as a "proper lady" is "profoundly at odds . . . with her own nature" (p. 471). Pykett associates that nature with a "female power" that, finding "no channel in the social world," eventually turns destructive and self-destructive (pp. 471–72).

In the second half of her essay, Pykett views Catherine's daughter Cathy as both a "repetition" of and "variation" on her mother (p. 473). But Cathy's *story,* she goes on to argue, "reverses rather than repeats her mother's," taking its heroine from a genteel upbringing to a horribly domestic marriage to eventual rebelliousness fueled by female power (p. 474). And whereas Catherine's power turned destructive and self-destructive, Cathy's "proud resistance" is effective, helping her to "resist mental enslavement" (p. 474). Like Catherine's story, Cathy's is "structured around a choice between two men, but Cathy makes her choice sequentially, and the second choice is informed by her experience . . . of the first" (p. 475). And "whereas Catherine is destroyed by her inability to reconcile conflicting images of her self, and the contradictory definitions of the feminine which confront her, Cathy negotiates them and ultimately constructs a new role for herself" (p. 477).

"Changing the Names" exemplifies feminist criticism in a number of ways. Its early emphasis on women's writing (Lockwood "experiences Catherine as a text" [p. 468]) recalls French and French-influenced feminist criticism, whereas its view of Brontë as a woman novelist writing against societal and novelistic conventions hearkens back to those North American critics who emphasized women writers and their feminist critique of patriarchal structures responsible for holding women back. More British (and contemporary) is Pykett's emphasis on the role played by class in the construction of the feminine (the equation of femininity and domesticity is a feature of *genteel* existence, and certainly not universally applicable). Furthermore, her understanding of femininity *as* a time- and place-bound construct reflects the viewpoint of feminist gender criticism. Finally, Pykett draws upon feminist cultural criticism, persuasively describing Cathy as a "variation on the pattern" of both the "conduct book female" and the "Domestic romance heroine" (pp. 476–77) — cultural constructs that (re)create and (re)enforce the social norms and fictional paradigms so effectively critiqued by Brontë in *Wuthering Heights.*

Ross C Murfin

FEMINIST CRITICISM: A SELECTED BIBLIOGRAPHY

French Feminist Theory

Cixous, Hélène. "The Laugh of the Medusa." Trans. Keith Cohen and Paula Cohen. *Signs* 1 (1976): 875–94.

Cixous, Hélène, and Catherine Clément. *The Newly Born Woman.* Trans. Betsy Wing. Minneapolis: U of Minnesota P, 1986.

Feminist Readings: French Texts/American Contexts. Spec. issue of *Yale French Studies* 62 (1981).

French Feminist Theory. Spec. issue of *Signs* 7.1 (1981).

Irigaray, Luce. *An Ethics of Sexual Difference.* Trans. Carolyn Burke and Gillian C. Gill. Ithaca: Cornell UP, 1993.

———. *This Sex Which Is Not One.* Trans. Catherine Porter. Ithaca: Cornell UP, 1985.

Jardine, Alice A. *Gynesis: Configurations of Woman and Modernity.* Ithaca: Cornell UP, 1985.

Jenson, Deborah, ed. *"Coming to Writing" and Other Essays* (essays by Hélène Cixous). Trans. Sarah Cornell. Cambridge: Harvard UP, 1991.

Jones, Ann Rosalind. "Inscribing Femininity: French Theories of the Feminine." *Making a Difference: Feminist Literary Criticism.* Ed. Gayle Green and Coppélia Kahn. London: Methuen, 1985. 80–112.

———. "Writing the Body: Toward an Understanding of *L'Écriture féminine.*" Showalter, *New Feminist Criticism* 361–77.

Kristeva, Julia. *Desire in Language: A Semiotic Approach to Literature and Art.* Ed. Leon S. Roudiez. Trans. Thomas Gora, Alice Jardine, and Leon S. Roudiez. New York: Columbia UP, 1980.

Marks, Elaine, and Isabelle de Courtivron, eds. *New French Feminisms: An Anthology.* Amherst: U of Massachusetts P, 1980.

Moi, Toril, ed. *French Feminist Thought: A Reader.* Oxford: Basil Blackwell, 1987.

Spivak, Gayatri Chakravorty. "French Feminism in an International Frame." *Yale French Studies* 62 (1981): 154–84.

Stanton, Donna C. "Language and Revolution: The Franco-American Dis-Connection." *The Future of Difference.* Ed. Hester Eisenstein and Alice Jardine. Boston: G. K. Hall, 1980. 73–87.

Wittig, Monique. *Les Guérillères.* 1969. Trans. David Le Vay. New York: Avon, 1973.

Feminist Theory: Classic Texts, General Approaches, Collections

Abel, Elizabeth, and Emily K. Abel, eds. *The "Signs" Reader: Women, Gender, and Scholarship.* Chicago: U of Chicago P, 1983.

Barrett, Michèle, and Anne Phillips. *Destabilizing Theory: Contemporary Feminist Debates.* Stanford: Stanford UP, 1992.

Beauvoir, Simone de. *The Second Sex.* 1949. Trans. and ed. H. M. Parshley. New York: Vintage, 1974.

Benstock, Shari, ed. *Feminist Issues in Literary Scholarship.* Bloomington: Indiana UP, 1987.

de Lauretis, Teresa, ed. *Feminist Studies/Critical Studies.* Bloomington: Indiana UP, 1986.

Fetterley, Judith. *The Resisting Reader: A Feminist Approach to American Fiction.* Bloomington: Indiana UP, 1978.

Fuss, Diana. *Essentially Speaking: Feminism, Nature and Difference.* New York: Routledge, 1989.

Gallop, Jane. *Around 1981: Academic Feminist Critical Theory.* New York: Routledge, 1992.

Greer, Germaine. *The Female Eunuch.* New York: McGraw, 1971.

Herndl, Diana Price, and Robyn Warhol, eds. *Feminisms: An Anthology of Literary Theory and Criticism.* New Brunswick: Rutgers UP, 1991.

hooks, bell. *Feminist Theory: From Margin to Center.* Boston: South End, 1984.

Keohane, Nannerl O., Michelle Z. Rosaldo, and Barbara C. Gelpi, eds. *Feminist Theory: A Critique of Ideology.* Chicago: U of Chicago P, 1982.

Kolodny, Annette. "Dancing Through the Minefield: Some Observations on the Theory, Practice, and Politics of a Feminist Literary Criticism." Showalter, *New Feminist Criticism.* 144–67.

———. "Some Notes on Defining a 'Feminist Literary Criticism.'" *Critical Inquiry* 2 (1975): 75–92.

Lovell, Terry, ed. *British Feminist Thought: A Reader.* Oxford: Basil Blackwell, 1990.

Malson, Micheline, et al., eds. *Feminist Theory in Practice and Process.* Chicago: U of Chicago P, 1986.

Meese, Elizabeth. *Crossing the Double-Cross: The Practice of Feminist Criticism.* Chapel Hill: U of North Carolina P, 1986.

Millett, Kate. *Sexual Politics.* Garden City: Doubleday, 1970.

Rich, Adrienne. *On Lies, Secrets, and Silence: Selected Prose, 1966–1979.* New York: Norton, 1979.

Showalter, Elaine, ed. *The New Feminist Criticism: Essays on Women, Literature, and Theory.* New York: Pantheon, 1985.

———. "Toward a Feminist Poetics." *The New Feminist Criticism* 125–43.

———. "Women's Time, Women's Space: Writing the History of Feminist Criticism." *Tulsa Studies in Women's Literature* 3 (1984): 29–43. Rpt. in Benstock, *Feminist Issues in Literary Scholarship.* 30–44.

Stimpson, Catherine R. "Feminist Criticism." *Redrawing the Boundaries: The Transformation of English and American Literary Studies.* Ed. Stephen Greenblatt and Giles Gunn. New York: MLA, 1992. 251–70.

———. *Where the Meanings Are: Feminism and Cultural Spaces.* New York: Methuen, 1988.

Weed, Elizabeth, ed. *Coming to Terms: Feminism, Theory, Politics.* New York: Routledge, 1989.

Woolf, Virginia. *A Room of One's Own*. New York: Harcourt, 1929.

Women's Writing and Creativity

Abel, Elizabeth, ed. *Writing and Sexual Difference*. Chicago: U of Chicago P, 1982.

Abel, Elizabeth, Marianne Hirsch, and Elizabeth Langland, eds. *The Voyage In: Fictions of Female Development*. Hanover: UP of New England, 1983.

Auerbach, Nina. *Communities of Women: An Idea in Fiction*. Cambridge: Harvard UP, 1978.

Benstock, Shari. "Reading the Signs of Women's Writing." *Tulsa Studies in Women's Literature* 4 (1985): 5–15.

Diehl, Joanne Feit. "Come Slowly Eden: An Exploration of Women Writers and Their Muse." *Signs* 3 (1978): 572–87.

DuPlessis, Rachel Blau. *The Pink Guitar: Writing as Feminist Practice*. New York: Routledge, 1990.

Finke, Laurie. *Feminist Theory, Women's Writing*. Ithaca: Cornell UP, 1992.

Gilbert, Sandra M., and Susan Gubar. *The Madwoman in the Attic: The Woman Writer and the Nineteenth-Century Literary Imagination*. New Haven: Yale UP, 1979.

Homans, Margaret. *Bearing the Word: Language and Female Experience in Nineteenth-Century Women's Writing*. Chicago: U of Chicago P, 1986.

Jacobus, Mary, ed. *Women Writing and Writing about Women*. New York: Barnes, 1979.

Miller, Nancy K., ed. *The Poetics of Gender*. New York: Columbia UP, 1986.

———. *Subject to Change: Reading Feminist Writing*. New York: Columbia UP, 1988.

Montefiore, Janet. "Feminine Identity and the Poetic Tradition." *Feminist Review* 13 (1983): 69–94.

Newton, Judith Lowder. *Women, Power and Subversion: Social Strategies in British Fiction, 1778–1860*. Athens: U of Georgia P, 1981.

Poovey, Mary. *The Proper Lady and the Woman Writer: Ideology as Style in the Works of Mary Wollstonecraft, Mary Shelley, and Jane Austen*. Chicago: U of Chicago P, 1984.

Showalter, Elaine. *Daughters of Decadence: Women Writers of the Fin de Siècle*. New Brunswick: Rutgers UP, 1993.

———. *A Literature of Their Own: British Women Novelists from Brontë to Lessing*. Princeton: Princeton UP, 1977.

———. "Women Who Write Are Women." *New York Times Book Review* I (December 16, 1984): 31–33.

Women's History/Women's Studies

Bridenthal, Renate, et al., ed. *Becoming Visible: Women in European History*. Rev. ed. Boston: Houghton Mifflin, 1998.

Donovan, Josephine. "Feminism and Aesthetics." *Critical Inquiry* 3 (1977): 605–8.

Farnham, Christie, ed. *The Impact of Feminist Research in the Academy*. Bloomington: Indiana UP, 1987.

Kelly, Joan. *Women, History & Theory: The Essays of Joan Kelly*. Chicago: U of Chicago P, 1984.

McConnell-Ginet, Sally, et al., eds. *Woman and Language in Literature and Society*. New York: Praeger, 1980.

Mitchell, Juliet, and Ann Oakley, eds. *The Rights and Wrongs of Women*. London: Penguin, 1976.

Riley, Denise. *"Am I That Name?": Feminism and the Category of "Women" in History*. Minneapolis: U of Minnesota P, 1988.

Rowbotham, Sheila. *Woman's Consciousness, Man's World*. Harmondsworth, UK: Penguin, 1973.

Spacks, Patricia Meyer. *The Female Imagination*. New York: Knopf, 1975.

Feminisms and Sexualities

Snitow, Ann, Christine Stansell, and Sharon Thompson, eds. *Powers of Desire: The Politics of Sexuality*. New York: Monthly Review P, 1983.

Vance, Carole S., ed. *Pleasure and Danger: Exploring Female Sexuality*. Boston: Routledge, 1984.

Feminism, Race, Class, and Nationality

Anzaldúa, Gloria. *Borderlands: La Frontera = The New Mestiza*. San Francisco: Spinsters/Aunt Lute, 1987.

Christian, Barbara. *Black Feminist Criticism: Perspectives on Black Women Writers*. New York: Pergamon, 1985.

Collins, Patricia Hill. *Black Feminist Thought: Knowledge, Consciousness, and the Politics of Empowerment*. Boston: Hyman, 1990.

hooks, bell. *Ain't I a Woman?: Black Women and Feminism*. Boston: South End, 1981.

———. *Black Looks: Race and Representation*. Boston: South End, 1992.

Mitchell, Juliet. *Woman's Estate*. New York: Pantheon, 1971.

Moraga, Cherrie, and Gloria Anzaldúa, eds. *This Bridge Called My Back: Writings by Radical Women of Color.* New York: Kitchen Table, 1981.

Newton, Judith, and Deborah Rosenfelt, eds. *Feminist Criticism and Social Change: Sex, Class, and Race in Literature and Culture*. New York: Methuen, 1985.

Newton, Judith L., et al., eds. *Sex and Class in Women's History.* London: Routledge, 1983.

Pryse, Marjorie, and Hortense Spillers, eds. *Conjuring: Black Women, Fiction, and Literary Tradition*. Bloomington: Indiana UP, 1985.

Robinson, Lillian S. *Sex, Class, and Culture*. 1978. New York: Methuen, 1986.

Smith, Barbara. "Towards a Black Feminist Criticism." Showalter, *New Feminist Criticism* 168–85.

Feminism and Postcoloniality

Emberley, Julia. *Thresholds of Difference: Feminist Critique, Native Women's Writings, Postcolonial Theory.* Toronto: U of Toronto P, 1993.

Minh-ha, Trinh T. *Woman, Native, Other: Writing Postcoloniality and Feminism*. Bloomington: Indiana UP, 1989.

Mohanty, Chandra Talpade, Ann Russo, and Lourdes Torres, eds. *Third World Women and the Politics of Feminism*. Bloomington: Indiana UP, 1991.

Schipper, Mineke, ed. *Unheard Words: Women and Literature in Africa, the Arab World, Asia, the Caribbean, and Latin America*. London: Allison, 1985.

Spivak, Gayatri Chakravorty. *In Other Worlds: Essays in Cultural Politics.* New York: Methuen, 1987.

———. *Outside in the Teaching Machine*. New York: Routledge, 1993.

Wilson, Armit. *Finding a Voice: Asian Women in Britain*. 1979. London: Virago, 1980.

Women's Self-Representation and Personal Criticism

Benstock, Shari, ed. *The Private Self: Theory and Practice of Women's Autobiographical Writings.* Chapel Hill: U of North Carolina P, 1988.

Brodski, Bella, and Celeste Schenck, eds. *Life/Lines: Theorizing Women's Autobiography.* Ithaca: Cornell UP, 1988.

Gilmore, Leigh. *Autobiographics: A Feminist Theory of Self-Representation.* Ithaca: Cornell UP, 1994.

Miller, Nancy K. *Getting Personal: Feminist Occasions and Other Autobiographical Acts.* New York: Routledge, 1991.

Feminism and Other Critical Approaches

Armstrong, Nancy, ed. *Literature as Women's History I.* Spec. issue of *Genre* 19–20 (1986–87).

Barrett, Michèle. *Women's Oppression Today: Problems in Marxist Feminist Analysis.* London: Verso, 1980.

Belsey, Catherine, and Jane Moore, eds. *The Feminist Reader: Essays in Gender and the Politics of Literary Criticism.* New York: Basil Blackwell, 1989.

Benjamin, Jessica. *The Bonds of Love: Psychoanalysis, Feminism, and the Problem of Domination.* New York: Pantheon, 1988.

Benstock, Shari. *Textualizing the Feminine: On the Limits of Genre.* Norman: U of Oklahoma P, 1991.

Butler, Judith, and Joan W. Scott, eds. *Feminists Theorize the Political.* New York: Routledge, 1992.

de Lauretis, Teresa. *Alice Doesn't: Feminism, Semiotics, Cinema.* Bloomington: Indiana UP, 1986.

de Lauretis, Teresa, and Stephen Heath. *The Cinematic Apparatus.* London: Macmillan, 1980.

Delphy, Christine. *Close to Home: A Materialist Analysis of Women's Oppression.* Trans. and ed. Diana Leonard. Amherst: U of Massachusetts P, 1984.

Dimock, Wai-chee. "Feminism, New Historicism, and the Reader." *American Literature* 63 (1991): 601–22.

Doane, Mary Ann. *Re-vision: Essays in Feminist Film Criticism.* Frederick: University Publications of America, 1984.

Felman, Shoshana, ed. *Literature and Psychoanalysis: The Questions of Reading: Otherwise.* Baltimore: Johns Hopkins UP, 1982.

———. "Women and Madness: The Critical Fallacy." *Diacritics* 5 (1975): 2–10.

Feminist Studies. Spec. issue on feminism and deconstruction, 14 (1988).

Gallop, Jane. *The Daughter's Seduction: Feminism and Psychoanalysis.* Ithaca: Cornell UP, 1982.

Gilligan, Carol. *In a Different Voice: Psychological Theory and Women's Development.* Cambridge: Harvard UP, 1982.

Hartsock, Nancy C. M. *Money, Sex, and Power: Toward a Feminist Historical Materialism.* Boston: Northeastern UP, 1985.

Hirsch, Marianne. *The Mother/Daughter Plot: Narrative, Psychoanalysis, Feminism.* Bloomington: Indiana UP, 1989.

Kaplan, Cora. *Sea Changes: Essays on Culture and Feminism.* London: Verso, 1986.

Meese, Elizabeth, and Alice Parker, eds. *The Difference Within: Feminism and Critical Theory.* Philadelphia: John Benjamins, 1989.

Modleski, Tania. *Feminism without Women: Culture and Criticism in a "Postfeminist" Age.* New York: Routledge, 1991.

Mulvey, Laura. *Visual and Other Pleasures.* Bloomington: Indiana UP, 1989.

Newton, Judith Lowder. "History as Usual? Feminism and the New Historicism." *The New Historicism.* Ed. H. Aram Veeser. New York: Routledge, 1989. 152–67.

Nicholson, Linda J., ed. *Feminism/Postmodernism.* New York: Routledge, 1990.

Penley, Constance, ed. *Feminism and Film Theory.* New York: Routledge, 1988.

Riviere, Joan. "Womanliness as a Masquerade." *The International Journal of Psycho-Analysis* 10 (1929): 303–13. Rpt. in *Formations of Fantasy.* Ed. Victor Burgin, James Donald, and Cora Kaplan. New York: Methuen, 1986. 35–44.

Rose, Jacqueline. Introduction II. *Feminine Sexuality: Jacques Lacan and the Ecole Freudienne.* Ed. Juliet Mitchell and Rose. Trans. Rose. New York: Norton, 1983.

Rudnytsky, Peter L., and Andrew M. Gordon, eds. *Psychoanalyses/Feminisms.* Albany and Buffalo: State U of New York P, 2000.

Sargent, Lydia, ed. *Women and Revolution: A Discussion of the Unhappy Marriage of Marxism and Feminism.* Montreal: Black Rose, 1981.

Weedon, Chris. *Feminist Practice and Poststructuralist Theory.* New York: Basil Blackwell, 1987.

Feminist Criticism Relating to *Wuthering Heights*

Boone, Joseph Allen. "*Wuthering Heights:* Uneasy Wedlock and Unquiet Slumbers." *Tradition, Countertradition: Love and the Form of Fiction.* Chicago: U of Chicago P, 1987. 151–72.

Brown, Gillian. "Nuclear Domesticity: Sequence and Survival." *Arms and the Woman: War, Gender, and Literary Representation.* Chapel Hill: U of North Carolina P, 1989. 283–302.

Burns, Bonnie. "Nostalgia, Apostrophe, *Wuthering Heights*: The Queer Destiny of Heterosexuality." *Nineteenth-Century Feminisms* 1 (1999): 81–94.

Davies, Stevie. *Emily Brontë: Heretic.* London: Women's Press, 1994.

———. "The House of Trauma: A Reading of *Wuthering Heights.*" *Emily Brontë.* Plymouth, Eng: Northcote House Publishers, 1998. 77–118.

Gilbert, Sandra M., and Susan Gubar. "Looking Oppositely: Emily Brontë's Bible of Hell." *The Madwoman in the Attic.* New Haven: Yale UP, 1979. 248–308.

Goodman, Charlotte. "The Lost Brother, The Twin: Women Novelists and the Male-Female Double *Bildungsroman.*" *Novel: A Forum on Fiction* 17 (1983): 28–43.

Newman, Beth. "'The Situation of the Looker-on': Gender, Narration, and Gaze in *Wuthering Heights.*" *PMLA* 105 (1990): 1029–41.

Pykett, Lyn. "Gender and Genre in *Wuthering Heights*: Gothic Plot and Domestic Fiction" and "Changing the Names: The Two Catherines." *Emily Brontë.* London: Macmillan, 1989. 71–85, 86–98.

Senf, Carol A. "Emily Brontë's Version of Feminist History: *Wuthering Heights.*" *Essays in Literature* 12 (1985): 201–14.

Stoneman, Patsy. "Feminist Criticism of *Wuthering Heights.*" *Critical Survey* 4 (1992): 147–53.

Yaeger, Patricia. "Violence in the Sitting Room: *Wuthering Heights* and the Woman's Novel." *Genre* 21 (1988): 203–29.

A FEMINIST PERSPECTIVE

LYN PYKETT

Changing the Names: The Two Catherines

> It was a Testament, in lean type, and smelling dreadfully musty: a fly-leaf bore the inscription — "Catherine Earnshaw, her book," and a date some quarter of a century back.
>
> I shut it, and took up another, and another, till I had examined all. Catherine's library was select, and its state of dilapidation proved it to have been well used, though not altogether for a legitimate purpose; scarcely one chapter had escaped a pen and ink commentary — at least, the appearance of one — covering every morsel of blank that the printer had left. Some were detached sentences; other parts took the form of a regular diary. . . . (p. 38 in this volume)

These books discovered by Lockwood are the only self-authored records left by Catherine Earnshaw-Linton. Catherine's diary is a text of discontent and rebellion, recording and speaking out against the domestic tyranny of Hindley and the religious tyranny of Joseph. It is also quite literally a marginal text, scrawled in the margins and on the fly-sheets of her well-used library. The childish scribblings arouse in Lockwood an "immediate interest for the unknown Catherine, and I began, forthwith, to decypher her faded hieroglyphics." The process of deciphering begun by Lockwood is continued in Nelly's narrative and is repeated by the reader who, like Lockwood, experiences Catherine as a text. Indeed much of *Wuthering Heights* is concerned with deciphering the traces of Catherine Earnshaw. The writing Lockwood finds scratched into the paint on the ledge of his sleeping quarters at the Heights foreshadows an important strand of the narrative structure.

> This writing was nothing but a name repeated in all kinds of characters, large and small — *Catherine Earnshaw,* here and there varied to *Catherine Heathcliff,* and then again *Catherine Linton.* (p. 38)

The names Lockwood deciphers circulate through the text, and one of the reader's tasks is to decipher them afresh, to explore the significance of both the names and the roles which attach to them. The first

Catherine begins life as Catherine Earnshaw and ends it as Catherine Linton. Catherine Heathcliff remains an unfulfilled possibility, a route not taken, although some would argue that this unoccupied term in fact names Catherine's true identity, and that she acquires this name-role beyond the narrative when her spirit joins with Heathcliff's to wander the moors eternally. Catherine's daughter, on the other hand, occupies each of the names in turn and traces back the route to her mother's first name. The novel thus begins and ends with Catherine Earnshaw. However, although the names circulate through the text, they create a pattern of asymmetrical repetition rather than of circularity. The stories of the two Catherines, the similarities and differences in their shapes, form a central strand in the elaborately patterned system of repetitions and differences which make this novel's structure.

The story of the first Catherine hinges — as do most novels of the period — on her choice between two men. Choosing the correct husband is the central moral task set for the heroine of most eighteenth- and nineteenth-century novels, particularly those written by women. Catherine's choice of Edgar is socially sanctioned and conforms to the dominant fictional pattern (seen most clearly and familiarly in the novels of Jane Austen) according to which heroines are led to make the rational choice of the sensible, educated man of property and standing in the community. Catherine's self-professed reasons for marrying Edgar are couched in the terms of rationality and prudence:

> "Because he is handsome and pleasant to be with . . . because he loves me . . . And he will be rich, and I shall like to be the greatest woman of the neighbourhood, and I shall be proud of having such a husband." (p. 84)

However, *Wuthering Heights* departs from fictional and social norms by exploring the consequences of the socially sanctioned choice. In Catherine's case, marriage is not the answer to the problem of her life, the resolver of all contradictions, as it usually is in domestic and romantic fiction. On the contrary, marriage compounds the problems of Catherine's life and exposes its contradictions. The return of Heathcliff in the later stages of Catherine's story exposes the inadequacies of an apparently appropriate marriage, and raises questions about both the nature of the choice Catherine had been required to make and the capacity of genteel marriage to comprehend all of a woman's needs. Emily Brontë's particular treatment of the Catherine–Edgar–Heathcliff plot seems to question the fictional paradigm which structures a woman's life as a choice between two men.

Catherine's fundamental inability to choose between Edgar and Heathcliff not only raises the question "what does a woman want?," but more profoundly engages with the "riddle of femininity," "what we men call 'the enigma of woman.'"[1] The novel explores the question "what is a woman?" by charting the process by which Catherine learns to be a woman as defined by the society in which she lives, and by tracing the difficulties which she experiences in living as a woman thus defined. As a motherless, and subsequently fatherless, girl growing up in a geographically isolated and loosely organized working household, Catherine reaches puberty relatively untrammelled by parental notions of suitable feminine conduct. Her childhood is, on the whole, spent with Heathcliff in a private, unsocialized and ungendered moorland world. Her encounters with adult authority, in the form of her brother's petty domestic tyranny and Joseph's rigid Methodism, develop her capacity for rebellion and resistance, and she thus becomes an assertive child associated with the realm of nature, its freedom and power, rather than with the domestic and its constraints.

Emily Brontë's portrayal of Catherine's sudden and dramatic transformation into a genteel young lady during her stay at Thrushcross Grange focuses on the way in which the particular version of femininity involved in the ideal of female gentility is socially produced and reinforced, rather than derived from women's "nature." Catherine's transformation, described by Nelly as a "reform" (p. 63), is shown as, in fact, a process of formation or construction. Frances Earnshaw, acting under Mrs. Linton's guidance and "employing art not force," performs the "maternal" function of subjecting her sister-in-law to a "due restraint" and shaping an acceptably feminine Catherine:

> trying to raise her self-respect with fine clothes and flattery, which she took readily, so that instead of a wild, hatless little savage jumping into the house, and rushing to squeeze us all breathless, there alighted from a handsome black pony a very dignified person with brown ringlets falling from the cover of a feathered beaver. (p. 64)

Nelly's observations on the social climbing of the newly transformed Catherine provide an unwitting comment on the self-division, the "perplexities and untold troubles" (p. 75), that attend the role of the

[1]Sigmund Freud, "Femininity," from "New Introductory Lectures on Psychoanalysis" in *The Standard Edition of the Complete Works of Sigmund Freud,* ed. James Strachey (New York: Norton, 1976), vol. XXII, p. 116.

"proper lady." Catherine's ambition, we are told, "led her to adopt a *double character* without exactly intending to deceive anyone" (p. 75, my emphasis). Catherine's ambivalence about her new role and her continued identification with Heathcliff suggest how profoundly at odds it is with her own nature. Catherine's famous assertion that Heathcliff is "more myself than I am. Whatever our souls are made of, his and mine are the same" (p. 86) is perhaps as much a statement of her identification with an earlier, pre-gendered version of herself, as it is a declaration of elemental passion. The adult Catherine persistently yearns for the self-consistency of the girlhood state that pre-existed the self-divisions induced by her education into the class-gender role of the genteel lady.

> I wish I were a girl again, half savage, and hardy and free; and laughing at injuries, not maddening under them! Why am I so changed? . . . I'm sure I should be myself were I once among the heather on those hills! (p. 123)

Whether in her role as a child of nature, or in her uneasy guise of "proper lady," Catherine Earnshaw is presented as a powerful woman. Even the unsympathetic Nelly concedes that at "fifteen she was the queen of the countryside; she had no peer" (p. 74). The "haughty, headstrong creature" is a kind of Yorkshire Gondal's Queen whose attitude to Edgar and Heathcliff is reminiscent of A.G.A.'s scornful wielding of female power over her lovers. Catherine's power, and the role it plays in shaping her story, may usefully be seen in the context of the issue of female power (what it is and how to use it) which was being debated in the conduct books, designed to inculcate ideas of appropriately feminine behavior, and in periodical articles in the early nineteenth century. Women, as Sarah Ellis argued, must relinquish power and the direct control of their own lives.

> All that has been expected to be enjoyed from the indulgence of selfishness, must then of necessity be left out of our calculations, with all that ministers to the pride of superiority, all that gratifies the love of power, all that converts the woman into the heroine. *(Advice to The Wives of England)*

The love of power, or "heroinism," must be yielded in order that women might be able to exercise feminine influence in the domestic sphere.

> Women in their position in life must consent to be inferior to men, but as their inferiority consists chiefly in their want of power,

> this deficiency is abundantly made up to them by their capability of exercising influence. *(Advice to the Daughters of England)*[2]

Catherine's history demonstrates the difficulties of trying to be the heroine of one's own life in a social and domestic milieu which cannot provide a theater for heroinism. If Catherine is an image of female power, it is a power which is doomed to find no channel in the social world of the novel, and can only turn on itself. It is interesting that Catherine's power over Heathcliff (and arguably over Edgar too) is greater after her death than it was in life, since her power is essentially transcendent rather than material. Catherine's story not only shows the limits of female power but also explores its problematic nature. The novel repeatedly focuses on the realities of gender politics by focusing on the way that Catherine's sense of personal and emotional power is not a means to authority and the resolving of conflict, but is the cause of conflict with others, and uncertainty and ultimately paranoia in herself. Catherine is granted a licensed power which allows her to exercise a whimsical tyranny. As far as her brother is concerned, as long as she advances the family by a favorable marriage, "she might trample on [the servants] like slaves" (p. 93). In addition to exploring the ambivalence of this tyrannical form of female power, the novel also exposes its tendency to become turned against itself, as seen, for example, in Catherine's declaration that "if I cannot keep Heathcliff for my friend, if Edgar will be mean and jealous, I'll try to break their hearts by breaking my own" (p. 116).

Catherine's story also dramatizes the limits of female influence. Her marriage to Edgar, which ironically she sees as a means of empowering herself to assist Heathcliff (p. 87), proves unable to reconcile the two men, and her belief in the power of her influence over Heathcliff is equally illusory. In short, Catherine's story vividly illustrates the fact that no matter how powerful and ruling her personality, a woman, as defined in nineteenth-century ideologies of gender and the family, must always cede definition and control to others and she is always, at least potentially, a victim. The spirited and rebellious Catherine must ultimately submit to the legal control of her father, her brother, and subsequently her husband. As she passes from childhood she becomes the victim of the ideal of feminine gentility. She also becomes the object of a competitive struggle between two men, each of whom wants her to conform to his own version of her.

[2]Sarah Ellis, quoted in Judith Lowder Newton, *Women, Power and Subversion: Social Strategies in British Fiction, 1778–1860* (London: Methuen, 1985), p. 5 and p. 1.

Caught uneasily between these conflicting subject positions, Catherine is ultimately broken by the pressure of the contradictions. She herself blames Edgar and Heathcliff for her predicament.

> You and Edgar have broken my heart, Heathcliff! And you both come to bewail the deed to me as if you were the people to be pitied! I shall not pity you, not I. You have killed me — and thriven on it, I think. How strong you are! How many years do you mean to live after I am gone? (p. 148)

Catherine's final illness is, in effect, a withdrawal from both the world and the self. Her derangement (pp. 118 ff.) enacts her experience of self-alienation. She is unable to recognize the reflection in the mirror as her own, and she regresses to a childhood state, to the Edenic unproblematic period of undivided and undifferentiated selfhood before she became a battleground for conflicting versions of womanhood.

Like so many women in Victorian fiction, Catherine dies in childbirth and is thus not required to negotiate that other profoundly ideological version of womanhood — "the mother." However, although she has been long dead when the novel's action begins, Catherine Earnshaw-Linton persists in the dramatic present of the novel, in the spirit form that haunts Heathcliff and that initiates Lockwood into some of the profundities and mysteries of life at the Heights. Her presence also persists, significantly modified, in the person of her daughter,

> the most winning thing that ever brought sunshine into a desolate house — a real beauty in face — with the Earnshaws' handsome dark eyes, but the Lintons' fair skin, and small features . . . Her spirit was high, though not rough, and qualified by a heart sensitive and lively to excess in its affections. That capacity for intense attachments reminded me of her mother; still she did not resemble her, for she could be soft and mild as a dove, and she had a gentle voice, and pensive expression: her anger was never fierce; it was deep and tender. (pp. 171–72)

If Cathy is a repetition of her mother, she is also a variation. Whereas the older Catherine's childhood prepares her for the role of Gondal's Queen, "half savage, and hardy, and free," her daughter is the spoiled, wilful, and pert fairy tale princess, the empress of her walled domain and mistress of her father and his servants. As the only daughter of a bookish widower she receives a wider education than was perhaps common for girls of the period, but in other respects her life is extremely constricted and protected, and contrasts markedly with her mother's childhood.

> Till she reached the age of thirteen, she had not once been beyond the range of the park by herself . . . Gimmerton was an unsubstantial name in her ears; the chapel, the only building she had approached or entered, except her own home. (p. 172)

In some senses Cathy's story reverses rather than repeats her mother's. For example, whereas the first Catherine's puberty is marked by a rite of passage from the Heights to the Grange, and from rebellious childhood to constrainedly genteel adolescence, her daughter makes the journey in reverse. Cathy's first acquaintance with the Heights, like her mother's with the Grange, is the result of an act of curiosity and rebellion which has misfired. Cathy finds herself at the Heights after illicitly attempting to reach the enchanted and forbidden territory of Penistone Crags, whose "golden rocks" have hitherto marked the physical limits of her horizon and the boundary of her childhood obedience.

While economic dependency, a precarious family position, and the confusions arising from her precipitate education into the role of genteel young lady all combine to propel Catherine into marriage with Edgar, economic security, restricted and over-protected family circumstances, and the steady imbibing of the principles of self-sacrificing feminine gentility render Cathy extremely susceptible to Heathcliff's duplicity and his son's whining vulnerability. Where Catherine apparently made her choice of Edgar freely, Cathy is effectively abducted by Heathcliff and emotionally blackmailed into submission by her cousin Linton, who interestingly employs the supposedly "feminine" strategies previously used by his mother. The marriage between Cathy and Linton thus makes explicit those aspects of genteel marriage which are implicit in the marriage of Catherine and Edgar, and which contribute to Catherine's demise. However, when Cathy is faced with the full horror of domestic imprisonment and the daily experience of Heathcliff's malevolence, the rebellious streak inherited from her mother helps her to resist mental enslavement. In her imprisonment at the Heights Cathy divests herself of the outward signs and mental attitudes of feminine gentility, and salvages an element of imaginative freedom by refusing to conform to certain of the available definitions of the feminine role — housewife, obedient daughter (daughter-in-law), or genteel ornament — opting instead for the role of unsociable slattern with her nose in a book.

Cathy's rebellion, a proud resistance which acknowledges its limitations while asserting its powers, is revealed in an account of an exchange between Heathcliff and Cathy early in Lockwood's narrative.

> "And you, you worthless —" . . . "there you are at your idle tricks again! The rest of them do earn their bread — you live on my charity! Put your trash away, and find something to do."
>
> "I'll put my trash away, because you can make me if I refuse," answered the young lady, closing her book, and throwing it on a chair. "But I'll not do anything, though you should swear your tongue out, except what I please!" (p. 47)

Cathy also empowers herself to resist her circumstances by adopting the guise of witch, a term historically used to describe and contain transgressive female power.

> "I warn you [Joseph] to refrain from provoking me, or I'll ask your abduction as a special favour . . . ," she continued, taking a long, dark book from a shelf. "I'll show you how far I've progressed in the Black Art." (p. 34)

Like her mother's story, Cathy's is structured around a choice between two men, but Cathy makes her choice sequentially, and the second choice is informed by her experience of the consequences of the first. In a sense Cathy's story replays those of both Isabella and Catherine. Like Isabella she is lured, by Heathcliff's scheming, from the petted and suffocating security of the Grange, and like Isabella she experiences directly the force of his brutality. More interestingly, the Cathy–Hareton plot may be seen as a repetition of the Catherine–Heathcliff plot, in which the younger Catherine acts out her mother's unfulfilled relationship with Heathcliff. Indeed, in Lockwood's fantasy (p. 261), Cathy is faced with a similar choice to her mother's: a choice between the genteel man of property, currently inhabiting Thrushcross Grange (Lockwood himself) and the boorish rustic at the Heights (Hareton). However, this is never more than a notional choice for the Cathy produced by the particular history which Emily Brontë has structured for her. Cathy's experience of the discontents of over-civilization in her oppressively restricted genteel life at the Grange and in Linton's peevish and petted gentility, and her experience of domestic incarceration at the Heights all lead to a reassessment of class and gender stereotypes from which her courtship of Hareton proceeds. Indeed, it is perhaps Cathy, rather than Catherine, who gives Emily Brontë the opportunity of writing "the scene of choice," in which the heroine chooses and demands her love, "giving herself freely and, throwing Jane Austen's prudence to the winds, declaring her passion," which Ellen Moers sees as characteristic of "every woman writer who was a feminist in [her depiction of] love."[3] Emily

Brontë's juxtapositioning of the stories of the two Catherines calls into question the view of romantic love implied in Moers' formulation, and also probes the uses as well as the limitations of prudence. Cathy's history (like her mother's) illustrates the problems involved in "throwing . . . prudence to the winds," and is used to explore the dangers involved in women thinking of themselves, or their love, as gifts to be liberally bestowed. In her second marriage Cathy does not *demand* her love, but she chooses freely, after studying Hareton closely, and it is she who initiates their intimacy and nurtures its development.

In the closing stages of the narrative Cathy moves towards occupying spaces and roles previously vacated or refused by her mother. She is to become Catherine Earnshaw, and in doing so will redeem Heathcliff's protégé and other self, Hareton. In the process Cathy relinquishes her role as the victim of a gothic plot for that of the heroine of a domestic romance. In this latter role Cathy comes to represent both female power and feminine influence. Although she is trapped and imprisoned by Heathcliff and a patriarchal legal system, Cathy exercises one of the few forms of power available to the powerless — resistance. This initial strategy of resistance frees her to choose a version of the role of feminine influence advocated by the conduct books. In conduct book fashion Catherine reclaims the noble savage Hareton, offering him culture which is — as Terry Eagleton rather nervously puts it — "unemasculating."[4]

However, Emily Brontë's presentation of the relationship between Cathy and Hareton offers variations on the pattern of the nurturing female. Unlike the conduct book females, Cathy is not all sweet virtue. Although she is (as is so often the case in the Victorian novel) the stimulus for Hareton's cultural ambition, she also mocks and frustrates his efforts to teach himself to read, causing him to burn the small library he has acquired (p. 259). When Cathy regrets her former actions, she adopts "feminine" strategies of stealth and indirection to rekindle Hareton's interest in books. *Wuthering Heights* is perhaps franker than are the conduct books about the manipulations and particularly the sexual exploitation involved in the exercise of feminine influence. Cathy's cultivation of Hareton is portrayed fairly openly as a form of sexual control. Her gift of the book illustrates the point. Having wrapped a handsome book, she sends it to Hareton via Nelly who is instructed to "tell

[3]Ellen Moers, *Literary Women: The Great Writers* (New York: Oxford UP, 1963), p. 157.

[4]Terry Eagleton, *Myths of Power: A Marxist Study of the Brontës* (London: Macmillan, 1975), p. 118.

him, if he'll take it I'll come and teach him to read it right . . . and if he refuse it, I'll go upstairs and never trouble him again" (p. 269).

In another interesting variation on the pattern of the conduct book female, and the domestic romance heroine, Cathy is not made to pay the usual price for her feminine influence, which, according to Judith Lowder Newton, "was made contingent upon the renunciation of such self-advancing forms of power as control or self-definition."[5] In exercising influence over Hareton, Cathy is also resuming control of her own life and defining herself anew. Her early history has demonstrated (to the character and the reader) the limitations of feminine gentility, and her later history shows how just as this cultural construct is learned it can be unlearned. Having learned to divest herself of many of the forms of feminine gentility, Cathy reconstructs both herself and Hareton. Whereas Catherine is destroyed by her inability to reconcile conflicting images of herself and the contradictory definitions of the feminine which confront her, Cathy negotiates them and ultimately constructs a new role for herself.

[5]Lowder Newton, p. 4.

Combining Perspectives on *Wuthering Heights*

So far, this volume's emphasis has been on mapping the boundaries of particular contemporary critical approaches and traditions. In presenting this final essay, by Susan Meyer, the emphasis is reversed, for the intention is to demonstrate the permeability of such approaches, traditions, and boundaries. The goal is to show how supposedly diverse critical assumptions and traditions can mix, merge, and metamorphose. To put it more plainly, Meyer's essay allows us to see how a critic can draw on the insights of *several* approaches (in effect, combining perspectives) to present a view of a work unavailable from any one window, any single critical perspective.

Meyer initially focuses on the scene in *Wuthering Heights* in which Edgar Linton's father, after a cursory inspection of the young Heathcliff's features, supposes the child to be the castoff son either of an Indian "Lascar" pressed into service on a British ship or of a black slave headed for a British or Spanish American colony. In either case, Meyer points out, old Mr. Linton "speculates that the boy is of a race subject to European imperialism" (p. 481 in this volume). Furthermore, Linton's (and his family's) arrogant assumption that someone of Heathcliff's color and features is bound to prove wicked and, ultimately, turn criminal reflects "the British desire to contain and control the 'dark races' through a reductive and predictive reading of physiognomy" (pp. 482–83).

In arguing that Brontë "makes an extended critique of British imperialism" (p. 483), Meyer references the association that Marxist critics (including Terry Eagleton, whose work is represented in this volume) have long made between Heathcliff and the alienated working class. (See "What is Marxist Criticism?" pp. 379–94). While arguing that the novel is undisputably "concerned with class inequality," Meyer maintains that the servant classes most potently represented by Heathcliff are the nonwhite people from "India, China, Africa, and the West Indes" with whom he "accru[es] associations" and (odd as it may at first seem) with certain white British women — "ladies" whose economic subservience and "constraining social role" are metaphorically signified by racial otherness (pp. 484–85).

"And yet," Meyer goes on to argue, "the novel does not simply, or primarily, represent the discontents of gender . . . through racial metaphor," thus approvingly using but moving beyond feminist and gender analysis much as she did a mere Marxist reading of the text. (See "What Is Feminist Criticism?" pp. 451–67.) As the novel progresses, Heathcliff's growing rage less and less implies concern metaphorically with gender or class oppression and, instead, "becomes an increasingly literal response to the oppression of the 'dark races' themselves" (p. 488). And as race becomes less figurative, plot — not metaphor — more and more becomes the means by which *Wuthering Heights* critiques not only "British social structures" but also the "traditional moves of fictional closure," which in Meyer's view typically "act to suppress the energies of social resistance" (p. 485).

In analyzing the novel's ending that is not an ending (it involves a marriage but not a traditional marriage and a death that brings no closure), Meyer shows certain affinities with practitioners of deconstruction, who unsettle the distinctions, oppositions, and hierarchies taken for granted by Western culture and much of its literature. (See the Glossary definition of *deconstruction*.) In her subsequent analysis of Heathcliff's relationship to the English language (even more "marginal" than that of women like Catherine, it is the relationship of colonized speakers to the "language of power"), Meyer shows even closer affinities to those cultural critics more specifically identified with postcolonial criticism. (See "What Is Cultural Criticism," p. 411, and the Glossary definition of *postcolonial criticism*.) Indeed, in the concluding pages of "Reverse Imperialism in *Wuthering Heights*," Meyer fully adopts the stance of a postcolonial critic, grounding Heathcliff's three-year disappearance from England in a "historical moment" associated "precisely" with "colonial insurrection" and defining the ruthless, acquisitive activities he undertakes following his return from the colonies as manifestations of "reverse colonization" (pp. 495–96).

COMBINING PERSPECTIVES

SUSAN MEYER

From "Your Father Was Emperor of China, and Your Mother an Indian Queen": Reverse Imperialism in *Wuthering Heights*

I

When Catherine and Heathcliff are captured by the Lintons in *Wuthering Heights,* after gazing in at their opulent splendor through the "great glass panes" of Thrushcross Grange, Heathcliff is subjected to a visual scrutiny that relegates him to what is to be his place in the social order. "Oh, my dear Mary, look here!" exclaims Mr. Linton:

> "'Don't be afraid, it is but a boy — yet, the villain scowls so plainly in his face, would it not be a kindness to the country to hang him at once, before he shows his nature in acts, as well as features?'
>
> "He pulled me under the chandelier, and Mrs. Linton placed her spectacles on her nose and raised her hands in horror. The cowardly children crept nearer also, Isabella lisping —
>
> "'Frightful thing! Put him in the cellar, papa. He's exactly like the son of the fortune-teller, that stole my tame pheasant.'" (pp. 61–62 in this volume)

Pulled under the chandelier, scrutinized through spectacles and pronounced upon as if he were a specimen of some strange animal species, Heathcliff is subjected to the potent gaze of a racial arrogance deriving from British imperialism. In Heathcliff's dark face, the Lintons read his nature and his destiny, and they find in it a license to punish him for crimes of property putatively committed by others of similar appearance. Isabella first describes Heathcliff as a gypsy, giving him the generic designation for a dark-complexioned alien in England which is attributed to him throughout the novel. But in a moment Mr. Linton's gaze becomes more historically specific, as he recognizes in Heathcliff "that strange acquisition my late neighbour made in his journey to Liverpool — a little Lascar, or an American or Spanish castaway." He speculates that the boy is of a race subject to European imperialism: Heathcliff may be the child of one of the Indian seamen, termed lascars, recruited by the East India Company to replace members of the British crews who died on exposure to disease in India or in military encounters with the Indians. Discharged at the end of the voyage, the lascars remained unemployed and starving in England's port cities for several months before their return journey home.[1]

Or perhaps, Mr. Linton hints with his second, ambiguous designation, the dark-skinned child arrived in Liverpool as a result of the trade for which the city was most famous in the late eighteenth century. In 1769, the year in which Mr. Earnshaw found Heathcliff in the Liverpool streets, the city was England's largest slave-trading port, conducting seventy to eighty-five percent of the English slave trade along the Liverpool Triangle, exchanging manufactured goods from the Mersey region for West African slaves, who were exchanged for plantation crops in the American and the Spanish American colonies.[2] Perhaps the young Heathcliff, Linton suggests, is the cast-off offspring of one of those slaves, or "an American or Spanish castaway." Thousands of black slaves were living in England itself in the late eighteenth century, concentrated particularly in the port cities of London, Liverpool, and Bristol, to which they had been brought by captains of slaving vessels and planters, government officials, and military officers returning from the West Indies.[3] Black slavery within England did not come to an end until 1834, when the English slaves were emancipated by the same legislative act of Parliament that (gradually) put an end to slavery in the English colonies.[4] In

[1]See Peter Stallybrass, "Marx and Heterogeneity: Thinking the Lumpenproletariat," *Representations* 31 (1990): 76–77.

[2]Suzanne Miers, *Britain and the Ending of the Slave Trade* (New York: Africana Publishing, 1975), 4. For accounts of the Liverpool slave trade, see C. Northcote Parkinson, *The Rise of the Port of Liverpool* (Liverpool: University Press of Liverpool, 1952), especially 86–101; Gomer Williams, *History of the Liverpool Privateers and Letters of Marque with an Account of the Liverpool Slave Trade* (London: William Heinemann, 1897). I calculate the date to be 1769 based on the following information. Nelly says (p. 72) that in the summer of 1778 Catherine is fifteen and Heathcliff about sixteen. We are told (p. 51) that Catherine is "hardly six" when Heathcliff is brought home, which makes him about seven and the date nine years earlier, or 1769.

[3]F. O. Shyllon, *Black Slaves in Britain* (New York: Oxford University Press, 1974), 3–4.

[4]Shyllon points out that there has been considerable misunderstanding about the results of Lord Mansfield's decision of 1772 that a slave, upon setting foot in England, is legally free. This decision did not bring slavery in England to an end. An 1827 ruling in the case of Grace Jones declared that a slave brought into England did not become free unless she had proof of having been manumitted by her master. Not until 1834, with the legislative act of Parliament, were all English slaves emancipated. Shyllon, ix–xi, 230–31.

1764, the *Gentlemen's Magazine* estimated that there were more than 20,000 black slaves in London alone. A street in eighteenth-century Liverpool was nicknamed "Negro Row," and slaves were sold in the city at public auctions held in warehouses, coffee houses, and shops, and outside the custom house.[5] Newspapers ran advertisements announcing the sale of slaves, giving notice of their escape, and offering rewards for recapture. In 1768, for example, the *Liverpool Chronicle* advertised the sale of "A fine Negroe Boy, of about 4 Feet 5 Inches high. Of a sober, tractable, humane Disposition, Eleven or Twelve Years of Age, talks English very well, and can Dress Hair in a tolerable way."[6] When Mr. Earnshaw finds the dark Heathcliff in the streets of Liverpool in 1769 and inquires for "its owner" (p. 52), he is simply following the dictates of contemporary English property law. By taking Heathcliff into his home and giving him the name (although not the surname or the property) of a son, Mr. Earnshaw attempts to give him a more favorable social status. But as the Lintons inspect the adolescent Heathcliff and describe him as "an American or Spanish castaway," they return him, with the power of the gaze of empire, to the status of racial property — he is the late Mr. Earnshaw's "acquisition" — and fix him into the role of inferior racial outsider, a thoroughgoing outsider, as the servant's derogatory phrase, "an out-and-outer," suggests, or, in Mrs. Linton's terms, "a wicked boy . . . unfit for a decent house" (p. 62).

Catherine's laughter on hearing the Lintons' horrified commentary alerts us to Emily Brontë's satirical attitude toward the Lintons' literal and moral myopia, as they peer through spectacles at Heathcliff, and toward their exploitative racial arrogance. In this passage Brontë only slightly exaggerates the sublime irrationality of nineteenth-century British racism, a typical, and similar, example of which could be found in an essay in the Brontës' favorite periodical, *Blackwood's,* in which the writer, meditating upon the scenes of his boyhood in Scotland, chances upon a gang of gypsies, and comments: "I should not be surprised to read some day in the newspapers, that the villain who leads the van had been executed for burglary, arson, and murder. That is the misfortune of having a bad physiognomy, a side-long look, a scarred cheek, and a cruel grin about the muscles of the mouth. . . ."[7] In describing the Lintons' simultaneously frightened and arrogant inspection of Heathcliff's dark face, Emily Brontë satirizes the British desire to contain and con-

[5]Gomer Williams, 474.

[6]Quoted in Shyllon, 6.

[7]"May-Day," *Blackwood's Edinburgh Magazine* 21, no. 125 (May 1827): 517.

trol the "dark races" through a reductive and predictive reading of physiognomy.

Yet at the same time, in this passage Emily Brontë reveals the force of the imperialist gaze wielded against Heathcliff. In the moment of inspection itself, the various participants in the scene behave in a manner that would seem to bear out the Lintons' assumptions about the brute-like, dumb character of people with dark skin. But Brontë reveals the way in which the power dynamics of the imperialist encounter artificially distribute the agency of language by having Heathcliff himself tell the story of his own capture and silencing to Nelly, fully revealing his capacity to form judgments about his captors and to give an account of the imperialist encounter from his own perspective. In the moment of inspection, however, he is, as when first brought home and examined by the Earnshaws, "as good as dumb" (p. 51). In that first appearance in the novel Heathcliff is incapable of communication because he speaks a foreign language — "some gibberish that nobody could understand," as Nelly puts it (p. 51) — but here he is silenced by the relentless gaze and commentary of the Lintons. They react to him as if he is a visual object only, or an animal, incapable of speech. First termed "foul-mouthed" and told to hold his tongue by the servant, and then heard only in the style rather than the substance of his speech — "Did you notice his language, Linton?" asks his wife, "I'm shocked that my children should have heard it" — Heathcliff might say, with Caliban, "You taught me language, and my profit on't / Is, I know how to curse."[8]

In *Wuthering Heights,* Emily Brontë makes an extended critique of British imperialism. She does so in part by exploring what would happen if the suppressed power of the "savage" outsiders were unleashed. Brontë relentlessly explores the nature of forces external to, subordinated to, marginalized by, or excluded from the British social order. And like her sister Charlotte, Emily Brontë invokes the metaphorical link between white women and people of nonwhite races as she explores energies of resistance to the existing social structure. In *Wuthering Heights* these energies have a universal resonance — they suggest the external, untamable energies that forever threaten the cozy domestic internal. But the novel also gives them a local specificity, associating them with nineteenth-century social issues of topical significance.

Critics such as David Wilson, Arnold Kettle, and Terry Eagleton have accounted for the threatening power of *Wuthering Heights* by

[8]Shakespeare, *The Tempest,* 1.2.363–64.

reading Heathcliff as a representative of the discontented working class of the "hungry forties," rising in rebellion against an oppressive society and learning himself to wield the oppressive tools of capitalism.[9] As Eagleton puts it, Heathcliff's "rise to power symbolizes at once the triumph of the oppressed over capitalism, and the triumph of capitalism over the oppressed" (p. 403). The issue of economic injustice is certainly central to *Wuthering Heights.* But the novel is most powerfully concerned, I would argue, not with economic injustice within the domestic class system, but with the economic injustice imposed by British imperialism on the "dark races" of the world. To read Heathcliff simply as a working man within a domestic context does not sufficiently account for the novel's threatening power. Read as a discontented worker, Heathcliff does not behave in a particularly dangerous manner. He does not form alliances with other workers (Nelly, Joseph, or Michael, for example), as the middle class most feared discontented laborers would. Instead, Heathcliff simply makes an individual rise, enacting, although in a vengeful form, the individualistic rags-to-riches plot, a plot that in fact reinforces the values of capitalism. Such a reading thus fails to explain what remains menacingly resonant in the novel. Considered in the interpretive context of imperialist history, however, Heathcliff suddenly looks, as it were, collective — accruing associations with India, China, Africa, and the West Indies. Reading the novel in this context, one also linked with the discontents of gender, helps to explain its potently disruptive and threatening energy. This is not to say that the novel is not concerned with class inequality — it obviously is — but that it locates the energies of resistance to social inequality not so much in the English working class as in the "dark races" beyond the margins of England.

Heathcliff, with his dark skin and indeterminate, widely suggestive colonial origins, is at once the novel's "ghoul" or "vampire" — its "incarnate demon" (p. 281) — and its incarnation of the resistant ener-

[9]David Wilson, "Emily Brontë: First of the Moderns," *Modern Quarterly Miscellany* 1 (1947): 94–115; Arnold Kettle, "Emily Brontë: *Wuthering Heights,*" in *An Introduction to the English Novel* (1951; reprint New York: Harper, 1968), 130–45; Terry Eagleton, *Myths of Power: A Marxist Study of the Brontës* (London: Macmillan, 1975). Raymond Williams, *The English Novel from Dickens to Lawrence* (London: Chatto, 1970), 50–61, contends that the historical problems of the 1840s are not so much directly represented as displaced into psychological events in the novel; Nancy Armstrong similarly suggests that although Heathcliff comes from Liverpool and appears "around the time of the provincial hunger riots (1766)," by the end of the novel "he has become a phantasm of unfulfilled sexual desire." Nancy Armstrong, *Desire and Domestic Fiction: A Political History of the Novel* (New York: Oxford University Press, 1987), 187.

gies of those subjected to British imperialism, those made, as entire peoples, into a servant class for England. The other, most potent asocial energies in the novel are located in Catherine, in the "savage" free child trapped within her adult ladyhood. Again in this novel these resistant energies are linked, here through the passionate sense of identity that Catherine feels with Heathcliff. And yet the novel does not simply, or primarily, represent the discontents of gender and class through the racial metaphor. In *Wuthering Heights* the energies embodied in the dark-skinned Heathcliff have a potency that exceeds the role of metaphor. . . . *Wuthering Heights* makes no attempt to represent a reformed social order: this novel instead persists through its ending in affirming transgression against British social structures. In so doing, *Wuthering Heights* also suggests the ways in which traditional moves of fictional closure act to suppress energies of social resistance.

II

The yoking of the rebellious Catherine with Heathcliff, the novel's representative of the "dark races," is central to *Wuthering Heights* and is established early in the novel. *Wuthering Heights* tells the story of a pre-adolescent girl, "half savage and hardy, and free" (p. 122), whose desire to resist a constraining female social role is figured through her identity with the "dark races" — "I *am* Heathcliff," Catherine proclaims (p. 88). The young Catherine Earnshaw's wildness and rejection of the female role are represented in *Wuthering Heights:* before she is tamed and whitened by her confinement at the Lintons, Catherine is, according to Nelly, a "wild, hatless little savage" (p. 63).

Catherine Earnshaw's resistance to female acculturation, her "half savage" nature (p. 122), is metaphorically represented not on her own body but associatively, in the companion from whom in her childhood she is inseparable: the dark-skinned gypsy Heathcliff. . . . Brontë explores the way in which the constraining life of adult womanhood splits her off from what for Brontë are her most vital energies, energies that remain fully present in the novel, yet painfully divided from Catherine, in the character of Heathcliff.

It is possible that Emily Brontë's Heathcliff owes something to the African Quashia Quamina of the Glass Town stories. The Brontë children collaborated on these juvenile tales in the beginning, and later, even after Emily and Anne separated from their older sister and brother to create an imaginary world of their own, all four children may well have discussed their imaginative creations or read them to each other.

Brontë biographer Winifred Gérin believes that Quashia finds an echo "not only in the enigmatic figure of the dark-haired orphan boy, of 'the iron man,' the 'accursèd man' of the Gondal poems, but preeminently in the conception of Heathcliff, the louring 'gypsy brat' whose origins . . . Emily deliberately left undefined."[10] Some of the imagery surrounding Heathcliff in *Wuthering Heights* does seem strikingly similar to that in the early tales, particularly the imagery of glass structures of privilege and racially alien outsiders. Particularly reminiscent of the juvenilia is the episode in which the two children are discovered peering in through the enormous windows of Thrushcross Grange: Catherine is seized and entrapped by the world inside the glass structure of British civilization — much like the "diamond House with golden windows" through which the African Quashia sees the image of his own exclusion in the Glass Town stories.[11] Meanwhile Heathcliff, left outside because of his dark features, remains excluded from the world within what he calls those "great glass panes" (p. 62), and thus uncivilized and unacculturated.

At Thrushcross Grange, Catherine is inserted into a social role internal to the domestic civilization of Britain. While Heathcliff, at this determining moment in their adolescence, becomes fixed into the external role of "out-and-outer," Catherine becomes civilized in the British fashion — she becomes, as Hindley exclaims in delight, "a lady" (p. 63). In the scene of her return, Brontë concisely demonstrates the way in which Catherine's enclosure in this role is accompanied by a painful splitting of herself, a division of herself, from her earlier "savage" energies. As an adult woman, Catherine is separated from her former physical vitality and emotional immediacy: instead of "jumping into the house, and rushing to squeeze us all breathless" (p. 63) as Nelly expects, she arrives attired in cumbersome clothes, which hamper her movement and her emotions. She is obliged to hold up her new riding habit "with both hands" in order to walk (p. 63). Her new social role also breaks her bond with the natural world: Nelly reports that "while her eyes sparkled joyfully when the dogs came bounding up to welcome her, she dare hardly touch them lest they should fawn upon her splendid garments" (p. 64). Catherine's attire creates a new division between her and the servants — "I was all flour making the Christmas cake," Nelly reports, "and it would not have done to give me a hug"

[10]Winifred Gérin, *Emily Brontë: A Biography* (Oxford: Clarendon Press, 1971), 23.

[11]Charlotte Brontë, *Caroline Vernon*, in *Five Novelettes*, ed. Winifred Gérin (London: The Folio Press, 1971), 283.

(p. 64) — and causes her to require waiting on for things she could once do by herself. "Ellen, help Miss Catherine off with her things," commands Hindley's wife (p. 64). This new need for service both renders Catherine physically helpless and enforces social distinctions: "little Cathy" (p. 51) becomes "Miss Catherine."

Most painfully, of course, Catherine's insertion into the social structure, her restrictive, isolating attire of "ladyhood," splits her off from Heathcliff, who is now divided from her by "great glass panes" at once as transparent and as deadly as the jagged window glass into which Lockwood forces the flesh of the ghostly Catherine's bare wrist. Catherine for the first time sees Heathcliff from the perspective of the inside: he looks "dirty" and startlingly "black and cross," now that she is divided from her own "savage" anger and resistance (p. 64). Heathcliff's fingers, as she sees when she takes them in her own, are "dusky" (p. 65), while her own are "wonderfully whitened with doing nothing and staying indoors" (p. 64). Brontë's phrase at once marks the new racial divide between Catherine and Heathcliff and mocks the association of dark skin with dirt by associating white skin with a "civilized" indoor idleness and physical frailty.

Catherine is at first able to connect with the split-off part of herself. When Hindley locks Heathcliff in the garret, much as Bertha is imprisoned in *Jane Eyre,* instead of existing separately from this angry, revengeful aspect of herself, as Jane does, Catherine climbs in through the skylight to join him and later takes him out with her the same way. But the two are soon at odds: Heathcliff complains of the "silly frock" that divides Catherine from him (p. 76), while Catherine objects to the absence of speech that marks Heathcliff's mutilation by the social order: "You might be dumb . . . for anything you say to amuse me" (p. 77). Catherine's lamenting protestations of her bond with Heathcliff are eulogistic, as if she needs to assert the connection verbally only when it is being broken. Yet Catherine's protestations are at the same time accurate: struggling to resist the loss of her unacculturated, free self as she discusses her engagement to Linton with Nelly, she says of Heathcliff: "He's more myself than I am" (p. 86). As Catherine conforms to the constraining role of womanhood, and as Heathcliff remains energized by resistance, this statement rings increasingly true.

When Catherine makes her famous assertion in the same exchange — "Nelly, I *am* Heathcliff — he's always, always in my mind — not as a pleasure, any more than I am always a pleasure to myself — but as my own being" (p. 88) — Brontë clearly establishes the metaphorical bond between these two characters. But Emily Brontë's use of the metaphor in this novel is in several respects unusual. The construction of the metaphor in *Wuthering Heights* gives Heathcliff, and through him the "dark races," an exceptionally fully realized status. After Catherine dies, sickening from being split off from the most vital part of herself, Heathcliff lives on, embodying energies of resistance that persist after his original figurative role seems over. The novel is indeed not so much the story of Catherine as it is the story of Heathcliff: the need for the narration of a story is evoked by his arrival and ends with his death. The anger Heathcliff expresses in the course of the novel does imply some resistance to the social constraints imposed on women, since he is linked early on with Catherine's "half savage" energies, and since he passionately wants, when she is an adult, to enable her to escape from the constricting social role she has assumed. But as the novel goes on, Heathcliff increasingly escapes the bounds of metaphor. *Wuthering Heights* becomes so interested in the dark character's position in and of itself, rather than in its figurative capacity, that in the latter part of the novel Heathcliff himself becomes, in an apparent paradox, one of the novel's most horrific oppressors of women. The dark character's role in *Wuthering Heights* so much exceeds the metaphorical that as the novel proceeds, it virtually loses the concern with women's oppression so important in its earlier chapters, while Heathcliff's rage becomes an increasingly literal response to the oppression of the "dark races" themselves.

III

In the early chapters of *Wuthering Heights,* Emily Brontë explores the rationale for the association of white women with colonized races by suggesting that white women and races subject to imperialism both experience an oppressive disempowerment. Brontë even subtly suggests that the situation is harsher for colonized peoples. As Heathcliff says, on being thrust out of Thrushcross Grange, "She was a young lady and they made a distinction between her treatment and mine" (p. 62). One of the forms of mutual disempowerment with which the novel is most concerned is economic. Catherine's only access to money is through marriage, for apparently her father, following patriarchal tradition, has bequeathed all his property to his oldest son. "Did it never strike you that, if Heathcliff and I married, we should be beggars?" (p. 57) Catherine asks Nelly. Hindley forces Heathcliff into the role of servant — probably an unpaid one, to judge from Heathcliff's later re-creation of his own situation in Hareton, whom he "deprive[s] of the advantage of wages" (p. 171). Forced to labor in the fields, deprived of literacy, and beaten by his "master" (one who certainly, despite their upbringing, never treats him as "a man and a brother"), Heathcliff is little better off than if he had remained on a Liverpool slave ship. The novel reveals the constraining economic situation of women, while demonstrating that the economic situation of the colonized peoples who are made into a servant class for England is even worse.

Wuthering Heights also emphatically demonstrates the mutual exclusion of women and of colonized races from the language of power, from the "good books," like the ones Catherine and Heathcliff cast into the dog kennel, that embody law and authority in British society. Catherine and Heathcliff's mutual exclusion from the central texts of the culture is made evident in Heathcliff's complaint to Nelly that, as a punishment for incorrectly answering questions about Joseph's sermons, he and Catherine are "set to learn a column of scripture names" (p. 59). The two children are forced to learn a text explicitly constructed so as to exclude them: neither has any part in such self-authorizing genealogies, lists of ancestral names that establish a current generation's claim to sanctity and to the land. Heathcliff's missing surname marks his unknown ancestry: deprived of his history by British imperialism, he is simultaneously deprived of the authority and the claim to ancestral ownership of the land that such a list of names establishes. Catherine also has no place in the genealogy: as a woman she would exist in such a list usually as an unmentioned link. Like Heathcliff, she is also essentially without a stable name and a solid identity and place in the succession of generations, as her scratching of multiple surnames for herself on the window sill of Wuthering Heights makes clear.

More critical attention has been paid to Catherine's relation to language and writing than to Heathcliff's, but the novel is equally concerned with Heathcliff's marginal position in relation to the dominant stories the culture tells itself, with the way in which he too, indeed, more extremely than Catherine, is silenced and suppressed by them.[12] Although Lockwood piles up books against the broken window in his dream to keep Catherine out, she has already demonstrated, through

[12]See, for example, Margaret Homans, *Bearing the Word: Language and Female Experience in Nineteenth-Century Women's Writing* (Chicago: University of Chicago Press, 1986), 68–83; Patricia Yaeger, "Violence in the Sitting Room: *Wuthering Heights* and the Woman's Novel," *Genre* 21 (1988): 203–29. Yaeger notes that Catherine's marginal writing "is the prototype of the novel as the site where violence surfaces, where the 'aphoristic energy' of women's writing begins to usurp the encyclopedic grasp of the tradition itself" (211; see also 220–21).

her marginal writing, that she can use those books to create a defiant and destructive telling of her own story. The terrified Lockwood, screaming in his sleep, realizes that the books will not serve as an impenetrable barrier to her. Her marginal writing in the religious texts simultaneously mocks the patriarchs (as in her caricature of Joseph), asserts her own, contrary experience, and, in so doing, damages the dominating text. In his childhood, Heathcliff has been able to follow Catherine's lead in aggressively fighting with that text. As Catherine reports in the destructive diary itself, when the children rebel against the "good books" he forces on them, Joseph cries out in despair that Catherine has "riven th' back off 'Th' Helmet uh Salvation,'" and that Heathcliff, kicking his book after Catherine's, has "pawsed his fit intuh t' first part uh 'T' Broad Way to Destruction!'" (p. 39). His outraged wording suggests that Catherine has damaged more than simply the material book: one might say that the whole armor of the Lord emerges from its confrontation with her a bit the worse for wear. But Heathcliff's relation to the text, Joseph's words suggest, is quite different: even in violently rejecting the text, he seems to be drawn into the deleterious plot within which it would insert him. Heathcliff's foot is already on the broad way to destruction.

On his own, Heathcliff has yet more difficulty with the language of power. When he is first brought home to Wuthering Heights, he is about seven years old — his face looks older than that of the six-year old Catherine — and he can of course already speak his native language. But nothing that he has experienced in that language, which Nelly dismissively terms "gibberish" (p. 51), ever makes its way into the cognitive space of the novel. Oddly, no one ever even seems to ask Heathcliff, once he can speak English, where he is from or who his parents are, and he does not seem himself to remember. It is as if everything he has experienced in his native language is somehow untranslatable into the language of the colonizer. Already as a child, when he learns that language, Heathcliff is subdued by it: he speaks "precious little," Nelly reports, ("and that generally the truth," she comments [pp. 52–53]). As an adolescent, Heathcliff is deprived of instruction in literacy: he is forced into what Nelly terms "savage sullenness" and ignorance by Hindley's attempts to make him into his idea of a savage (p. 74). Told that "the first word he spoke to Miss Catherine should ensure a dismissal" (p. 63), he becomes "dumb" with her, thus earning her annoyance and exacerbating the separation between them. Even when Heathcliff returns to Wuthering Heights after his absence, newly in control of economic power, his marginal relation to the English language is immediately indicated in the text:

his newly deep voice, Nelly notes, is "foreign in tone" (p. 96). Gilbert and Gubar note that "the power of the patriarch, Edgar's power, begins with words. . . . Edgar does not need a strong, conventionally masculine body, because his mastery is contained in books, wills, testaments, leases . . . languages, all the paraphernalia by which patriarchal culture is transmitted from one generation to the next."[13] It is telling then that the feeble Edgar Linton lands his one blow on Heathcliff in his point of greatest vulnerability, the same place that his culture has been striking Heathcliff— "full on the throat" (p. 115). When Heathcliff mourns for Catherine, later, his voice is again "strangled in his throat" (p. 160).

Heathcliff does achieve some control over authoritative language at the apex of his power: he is able to prevent Edgar Linton from altering his will by paying off the lawyer. But his linguistic power in this case is, interestingly, only negative: he is able to prevent Edgar Linton from exercising the power of language, but never fully wields it himself. The second Catherine, obviously without comprehension of his reasons, complains that Heathcliff has taken it into his head to burn all the books in the house. Even when Heathcliff owns Wuthering Heights, that structure itself marks the tenuousness of his occupation: the name of Hareton Earnshaw is the one written over its door. Catherine may self-assertively (and with mild destructiveness) scratch her name on the window sill of the house, but Heathcliff's name is never written, except as part of Catherine's exploration of her own identity, anywhere on Wuthering Heights. The name of Earnshaw engraved over the door marks the genealogy, the tradition, the culture, and the class, as well as the race, from which Heathcliff is permanently excluded.

Heathcliff's namelessness is emphasized at the beginning of the novel, and again, as the novel draws to a close, Brontë reminds the reader of Heathcliff's anonymity and his status as racial and linguistic outsider.[14] Nelly has a dream, in the novel's final pages, which exposes Heathcliff's problematic relation to the language of the colonizer; it is parallel to Lockwood's dream about Catherine's relation to language in the novel's opening. "Where did he come from, the little dark thing, harboured by a good man to his bane?" muses Nelly. Half-asleep, she wearies herself "imaging some parentage for him," and recalling the course of his existence (p. 281). In the ensuing dream, she has the

[13]Sandra M. Gilbert and Susan Gubar, *The Madwoman in the Attic: The Woman Writer and the Nineteenth-Century Literary Imagination* (New Haven: Yale University Press, 1979), 281.

[14]For a provocative discussion of names and social class in *Wuthering Heights,* see Miles, 56–61.

vexing task of dictating the inscription on his gravestone. She cannot, of course, tell his surname or his age, and in the end dictates only "the single word, 'Heathcliff.'" ("That came true," she adds [p. 281]). Even Heathcliff's final mark in the world, the writing his existence inscribes on the blank page of his tombstone, is suffused more with absence than with presence. Even the one word written on the stone denotes his tangential relationship to the colonizing language into which he has been inserted. It is the name of a son already dead, a used name, empty and waiting for an occupant, and a name to which he has only a fragile and secondary claim. His claim is more secondary, than, for example, the claim of the second Catherine to the name of her mother, because this is a name already used *within* his generation: this Heathcliff, who was given some other, untranslatable name at birth, will, always remain, in relation to his belated English name, only a shadow Heathcliff. His relation to even the one word with which his gravestone is marked is as tenuous as his temporary claim to the building of Wuthering Heights. The gravestone of Heathcliff denotes his exile from history, genealogy, and property through his exile from the language of the colonizing race, and reveals the effect of that exile in erasing his identity.

IV

Both Catherine and Heathcliff are excluded from the dominant language, from the central stories of the culture, and both Catherine and Heathcliff are economically disempowered. But Catherine, whose exclusion is less extreme, assimilates to the oppressive society, assuming her designated social role and essentially, although with outbursts of now self-destructive fury, accepting her limited position. This one "wild, hatless little savage" is successfully colonized. Now "more [her]self than [she]," however, Heathcliff, remains an angry outsider who continues to express all the energies of resistance to subjugation that he once shared with Catherine. Indeed as the novel proceeds and the character of Heathcliff gathers energy, the novel seems largely to lose its interest in women's social subjugation. Emily Brontë gleefully unleashes Heathcliff's energies of social resistance, and that resistance takes the form of the worst nightmare of the imperialist power: reverse colonization. As Heathcliff takes this revenge on an oppressive British society, however, he himself becomes a subjugator of women.

That Heathcliff will enact the drama of resistance in this form is already predicted in his childhood. Nelly, helping Heathcliff to wash and comb, and encouraging him to join Catherine and the Linton children, offers a reading of the colonial dynamics written in his face quite different from that given by the Linton family. "'You're fit for a prince in disguise," she tells him:[15]

> "Who knows, but your father was Emperor of China, and your mother an Indian queen, each of them able to buy up, with one week's income, Wuthering Heights and Thrushcross Grange together? And you were kidnapped by wicked sailors, and brought to England. Were I in your place, I would frame high notions of my birth; and the thoughts of what I was should give me courage and dignity to support the oppressions of a little farmer!" (pp. 67–68)

Nelly's reconstruction of Heathcliff's history turns from the speculative to the definite, as indicated by the punctuation, at a telling place: Heathcliff may have an impressive parentage, but he was more certainly brought unwillingly to England by "wicked sailors." But Nelly's speculations about Heathcliff's parentage offer him a fantasy of retribution for his unwilling colonization. In this predictive moment, Nelly associates Heathcliff with the appropriation of English land and property by countries subject to British imperialism, that is, with the reverse colonization of England.

Brontë has Nelly imagine for Heathcliff a particularly telling royal colonial lineage, one that would have evoked specific forms of political anxiety in a British audience in 1847. When Emily Brontë published *Wuthering Heights,* the British were on their way to establishing solid political control in India, governing directly and through subordinate princes. But a reference to the Chinese emperor would have been fraught with more political uncertainty in Britain in 1847. China was by no means under such strong British control as India, although it had recently had an encounter with the might of British imperialism during the first Opium War of 1840–42. As the nineteenth century began, Britain had been purchasing increasingly large quantities of tea from China, yet was unable to develop much Chinese interest in the products it had to offer in exchange. The resulting drain of British silver into China made the British uneasy, and, to prevent it, British merchants began a triangular trade, using India's exports of opium and cotton to

[15]To a twentieth-century reader, Nelly's suggestion that Heathcliff might be the son of the Emperor of China would seem to be visually at odds with the description of him as looking like a gypsy. But that to English eyes in this era these two groups looked far more similar than different is suggested in the account an Oxford country parson, James Woodforde, gave in 1775 of the appearance of the Chinese: they were like "the runabout gypsies," he noted, and "uncommonly ugly." Quoted in Jerome Ch'en, *China and the West: Society and Culture 1815–1937* (London: Hutchinson & Co., 1979), 43.

pay for the tea Britain bought from China. As this resulted in a drain of Chinese silver from the economy and increasing Chinese addiction to opium, the Peking court banned the opium trade. The British continued to smuggle opium into China, but in the late 1830s, Chinese authorities began to enforce the ban more successfully. In June 1840, British warships arrived in Hong Kong, claiming the principle of free trade, and began the first Opium War. In 1842, China yielded and was forced to sign a treaty opening five ports to the British, limiting import and export duties, and ceding Hong Kong to Britain. For a few years, the British were able to congratulate themselves on their relatively easy dissolution of the mighty, ancient Chinese empire by their own.[16]

Yet despite Britain's military triumph, China was still able to resist its forcible opening with some success. The British were disappointed to find their trade with China dropping off after 1846. The Chinese also succeeded in keeping the British out of the important walled city of Guangzhou (Canton), and the economically self-sufficient communities in China proved more resistant than those in India to British control. When Emily Brontë published *Wuthering Heights* in 1847, the British were feeling less confident about their success in dissolving the Chinese empire. When Nelly asks Heathcliff to consider that his father may be the Emperor of China, able to buy up the two English houses with " 'one week's income," she hints at a possible relationship between the Chinese and the British empire in which the British might not find themselves so easily triumphant. While Indian exports had been used by the British as a way of wielding their economic power over China, Nelly's imaginative recreation of Heathcliff's ancestry suggests, in fantasy, the prospect of an alliance between the two countries — a marriage between an Emperor of China and an Indian queen — and the possibility of their joint economic occupation of Britain. Together they might readily buy up, as trifles, pieces of England — the Heights and the Grange. In restoring to Heathcliff a history, Nelly suggests to the nineteenth-century British reader a way in which dark-skinned people

[16]For an example of this triumphant British attitude, see "War with China, and the Opium Question," *Blackwood's Edinburgh Magazine* 47 (1840): 368. "The day may come when the empire boasting its thousands of years shall reach the term of its immortality. . . . A formidable and outraged power shall press and inflict the first wound. . . . The cackling of geese once saved an empire; the incident, almost as trivial, or opium-smoking or eating, instead of tobacco — a mere matter of taste — may chance to ruin one." For an overview of the events of the first Opium War, see Sheng Hu, *Imperialism and Chinese Politics* (1955, rpt. Beijing: Foreign Languages Press, 1981), 1–19; Shouyi Bai, ed., *An Outline History of China* (Beijing: Foreign Languages Press, 1982), 431–36.

like Heathcliff might be able to take revenge for the subjugation they have suffered at British hands.

In addition, Brontë situates the three years of Heathcliff's absence from Wuthering Heights, from which he returns with a new bearing, money, and a sense of his own power, at a historical moment that associates him with precisely such colonial insurrection. The novel is set in a historical period, the late eighteenth century, which enables the expression of mid-nineteenth-century political anxieties about loss of empire. Lockwood speculates that Heathcliff has "escape[d] to America, and earn[ed] honours by drawing blood, from his foster country" (p. 95), and his theory seems to be borne out by Nelly's comments that Heathcliff seems to have "been for a soldier" (p. 97) and that his "upright carriage suggested the idea of his having been in the army" (p. 99). Heathcliff's absence, as a calculation of dates in the novel reveals, takes place between 1780 and 1783, the last three years of the American Revolutionary War.[17] By suggesting that Heathcliff has been in the American army in the years he was away, Brontë associates him with the archetypal war of successful colonial rebellion, one in which England was even at one point in fear of invasion. The revolution of the American colonies, accompanied by Canadian discontent and disturbances in the West Indies, demonstrated to the British the possibility of the loss of their colonies and the dissolution of their empire. Because the West Indies were dependent on the American colonies for food, at some points during the Revolutionary War it seemed likely that they would join the American colonies in the revolt against Britain.[18] An 1833 article in *Blackwood's* commented on the remarkable growth and progress of the East India Company and its ability to win "the native affections" at this very time, the time "when the Colonies of England, under the direct control of the mother country, were brought into such a state of discontent, as led to the dismemberment of a large portion of the empire, and threatens soon to sever from the parent state its colonial possessions."[19] Heathcliff, gaining a new sense of power by "drawing blood from his foster country," is the disconcerting representative of all the British colonies that, however subtly, may threaten to turn

[17]Heathcliff returns to Wuthering Heights when Catherine and Edgar have been married six months (p. 96). As Hareton is nearly five when they marry (p. 94), and as he was born in the summer of 1778 (p. 72), Catherine and Edgar marry in the spring of 1783. Heathcliff arrives in September of that year (p. 96) and has been absent three years (p. 99).

[18]Parkinson, 124.

[19]"The East India Question," *Blackwood's Edinburgh Magazine* 33 (May 1833): 783.

against the "parent state" — a parent state that, like Mr. Earnshaw, may turn out to have "harboured" them "to [its] bane."

The American Revolutionary War had other detrimental effects on the British empire as well. The war brought the trade with Africa to a standstill, and, with America and the West Indies ruled out as markets, completely cut off the slave trade, threatening to put a permanent end to it. As Liverpool's shipping industry was hit even harder than London's by the destruction of these two forms of trade, Brontë's association of Heathcliff with the Revolutionary War hints at the beginnings of his revenge on the "'wicked sailors" of Liverpool who brought him to England.[20] If Heathcliff has indeed "been for a soldier" during these three years, "drawing blood from his foster country," he has begun his retribution by impeding and threatening the business of the British empire.

And on his return from those three years away, Heathcliff immediately proceeds with the revenge Nelly had hinted at, as he begins to appropriate English land and wealth. He takes possession of Hindley's land, piece by piece, and soon installs himself as the master of Wuthering Heights, easily acquiring the estates Nelly had once suggested his father and mother, as Emperor of China and Indian queen, could readily buy up. He simultaneously drains Hindley's silver and encourages his self-destructive addictions (to drink and gambling), in a way reminiscent of the demoralizing effects of the British opium trade on the Chinese — but in reverse.[21] He sexually appropriates, imprisons, and beats British women, and subjects them to sexual and economic coercion. He creates a world in which physical force and economic power — coming from a mysterious external source — take the place of law or local standards of morality. His actions hideously mimic the ugly brutality of British imperialism.

Heathcliff's first indication of his intent to engage in reverse colonization takes place in a scene that recalls his subjection to the imperialist gaze on his capture by the Lintons. In a reversal of that earlier scene, Catherine and Heathcliff now wield the imperialist gaze, bringing it to bear on the captive Isabella Linton and treating her, as she and her family had once treated Heathcliff, as an object to be scrutinized and com-

[20]See Parkinson, 125, for an account of the effect of the war on Liverpool.

[21]It is perhaps worth noting here that one of Brontë's nineteenth-century biographers, A. Mary F. Robinson, claimed that Hindley's drunken debauchery was modeled on Branwell Brontë's demeanor when, dismissed from his tutoring job for making romantic advances to the (married) mother of his students, he returned home in despair to the parsonage where he drank to excess and smoked opium. A. Mary F. Robinson, *Emily Brontë* (Boston: Roberts, 1883), 217.

mented on, rather than spoken to, as an exotic, subhuman creature. When Catherine, after her marriage and Heathcliff's return, torments Isabella by telling Heathcliff, in her presence, that Isabella has been pining for him, she holds the young woman fast, just as Heathcliff was once held by the Lintons, so that Heathcliff can fix his eyes upon her in her humiliation and confusion. Heathcliff gazes at Isabella, as she had once at him, in a way that deprives her of human status, and he comments on her as if she now were incapable of speech:

> "I think you belie her," said Heathcliff, twisting his chair to face them. "She wishes to be out of my society now, at any rate!"
>
> And he stared hard at the object of discourse, as one might do at a strange repulsive animal, a centipede from the Indies, for instance, which curiosity leads one to examine in spite of the aversion it raises.
>
> The poor thing couldn't bear that; she grew white and red in rapid succession, and, while tears beaded her lashes, bent the strength of her small fingers to loosen the firm clutch of Catherine. (p. 107)

Heathcliff, who had once been denigrated as colonial detritus, as "an American or Spanish castaway," looks at Isabella as one might at a centipede crawling out of a hogshead of West Indian sugar. And Catherine, holding Isabella captive as she and Heathcliff were once held, participates in the reversal of the imperialist gaze, by describing the young woman, who is using her fingernails to free herself, as another exotic, colonial animal: she shakes Isabella off, exclaiming, "There's a tigress!" (p. 107).[22] Isabella, unable to speak under such tormenting scrutiny and commentary, is silenced, like Heathcliff before her, and becomes the object, rather than the subject, of imperialist discourse.

In Heathcliff's childhood, Nelly had coaxed him, rather inanely, in ways of making his face look more white: he must smooth his forehead and learn to change his "black fiends" of eyes into "confident, innocent angles" (p. 67). Heathcliff, decoding the impossible agenda of racial transformation in her beauty advice, comments wryly that in other words he must "wish for Edgar Linton's great blue eyes, and even forehead." "I do," he says, "and that won't help me to them." Nelly insists, however, that "A good heart will help you to a bonny face, my lad . . . if

[22]Compare Harriet Ritvo, *The Animal Estate: The English and Other Creatures in the Victorian Age* (Cambridge: Harvard University Press, 1987), 205–42. Ritvo argues that the creation of menageries and zoos in nineteenth-century Britain, filled with exotic animals from the colonies safely held captive, figured for the British the power of empire.

you were a regular black" (p. 67). Nelly evidently believes that washing will turn the gypsy white, and that such a transformation is to be desired. When Heathcliff acquires power, in his years away from Wuthering Heights, however, he threatens to make the attempted racial metamorphosis work in the opposite direction, as he proposes to take his revenge on the white skin and blue eyes that have tyrannized over him. He tells Catherine: "You'd hear of odd things, if I lived alone with that mawkish, waxen face; the most ordinary would be painting on its white the colours of the rainbow, and turning the blue black, every day or two; they detestably resemble Linton's" (p. 108). When Heathcliff, now "master" at the Heights, describes Isabella as an animal — "a mean-minded brach" — and terms her "slavish" (p. 143), the reversal is accomplished and his imperialist power over her is complete.

As Heathcliff was once himself locked up in Wuthering Heights, he locks up Isabella, the younger Catherine, and Nelly. And as Heathcliff was once kept from education and language, he deprives Hareton of literacy to the point where, in the ultimate metaphor of disinheritance, he cannot read his own name over the door of Wuthering Heights. Hareton himself, with his animal-like appearance — "his whiskers encroached bearishly over his cheeks" — and his "embrowned" skin, is Heathcliff's reverse enactment of his own colonization (p. 143).

The "vivid and fearful" scenes in *Wuthering Heights,* of which Charlotte Brontë complained, are primarily scenes in which the ugliness of starkly wielded colonial power, usually exercised in areas remote from the reach of British law or putative moral standards, is enacted through Heathcliff's fearful reversals. Here too British law seems strangely powerless, and Heathcliff's actions, as he reverses the colonizing process, take on the quality of nightmare. The shifting white shape espied by Nelly outside Thrushcross Grange "mov[ing] irregularly, evidently by another agent than the wind" (p. 125), gasping for breath in the last throes of hanging, is a sinister reminder and reversal of Mr. Linton's suggestion that Heathcliff should be hanged simply on account of his dark complexion. The gasping, dangling white shape turns out to be only a dog, but Heathcliff's implicit threat is clear.

In *Wuthering Heights,* Emily Brontë gives imaginative life to the colonial "other" who is kept outside the "great glass panes" surrounding the prosperity of the colonizing power, and empowers him to shatter those barriers surrounding and protecting the secure domestic prosperity of Britain. Isabella and Hindley attempt to prevent Heathcliff from entering Wuthering Heights after his vigils over Catherine's body, repeating the scene in which he looked in the windows of

Thrushcross Grange as a child. Isabella describes their attempt to lock Heathcliff out: "The casement behind me was banged on to the floor by a blow from the latter individual; and his black countenance looked blightingly through. The stanchions stood too close to suffer his shoulders to follow; and I smiled, exulting in my fancied security. His hair and clothes were whitened with snow, and his sharp cannibal teeth, revealed by cold and wrath, gleamed through the dark" (p. 162). Much like the African Quashia of the Brontë children's juvenilia, lurking outside the fragile imperial palaces of Glass Town, Heathcliff represents the return of the colonial repressed. In Emily Brontë's novel, he enacts the worst nightmare of empire: he gets in. Isabella is "unnerved by terror for the consequences of [her] taunting speech" when Heathcliff, with his "black countenance" and "sharp cannibal teeth" easily takes a stone, "[strikes] down the division between two windows" (p. 163), and, with preternatural energy, forcibly enters, the "decent house."

The repeated motif of Heathcliff's cannibalism is yet another image of the imperialist's nightmare of being subjected to reverse colonization. A cannibal treats other men — in the nightmare of empire, the colonizers — as if they were animals, and then takes this metaphor literally. Cannibalism is also the ultimate manifestation of the violation of boundaries, and represents the fear, on the most immediately horrifying personal and bodily level, of being invaded and used by another for his own purposes. Heathcliff, who Catherine suspects will "devour" Isabella (p. 104), whose mouth waters, according to Isabella, to tear Hindley "with his teeth" (p. 165), who claims that had he been born "where laws are less strict, and tastes less dainty" he would have treated himself to the "slow vivisection" of the younger Catherine and Isabella's son Linton (p. 234), is the imperialist's horrific image of retribution for having treated colonized peoples like animals. This treatment of the "dark races" as animals rarely reached the extreme it did on a nineteenth-century hunting expedition in Southern Africa, where a group of Dutch settlers shot and killed a Bushman and then cooked and ate him, thinking him an orangutan, but this incident suggests why being eaten by cannibals was one of the deepest fears of empire.[23] This horror is evoked in *Jane Eyre* through Bertha Rochester, who has bitten, and to the physician's horror, *chewed* the shoulder of Richard Mason: "She worried me like a tigress," he murmurs. "She sucked the

[23]Martin Guenther, "The Changing Western Image of the Bushmen," *Paideuma* 26 (1980): 123–40, cited in Stephen Jay Gould, "The Hottentot Venus," in *The Flamingo's Smile: Reflections in Natural History* (New York: Norton, 1985), 295.

blood: she said she'd drain my heart."[24] But while the resolution of *Jane Eyre* controls these fearful energies of resistance to empire, the impulse of *Wuthering Heights,* even in its ending, is to let these energies loose. Even at the novel's end, when Heathcliff dies, Nelly is horrified by the "sarcastic, savage face" of the corpse, horrified that she cannot compose the face and get the lips to close over the threatening "sharp, white teeth" (p. 286).

V

By the time *Wuthering Heights* comes to its own ending, the novel has already satirized some common moves of narrative closure in nineteenth-century fiction. In doing so Brontë mocks the sensibilities of novelists like her sister Charlotte, who would use just such moves to come to a resolution to the complicated metaphorical maneuvers of *Jane Eyre. Wuthering Heights* points out that marriage need not lead to permanent domestic happiness, as nineteenth-century novel closures commonly suggest, and as Charlotte Brontë, for example, will indicate that it does for Jane and Rochester. Instead Emily Brontë shows in Isabella's story what happens *after* an innocent girl marries a surly, difficult hero. The tradition of the blissful deathbed of the saintly man is also ferociously mocked in *Wuthering Heights.* The novel unmasks the horrible truths that may lurk beneath the surface of such scenes when, in order that Edgar Linton may die in tranquility, Nelly instructs young Cathy to tell her father that she will be very happy with her whining, malicious husband, Linton Heathcliff, whom she has been forced to marry. Nelly knows how the good are supposed to die. But storytellers with Nelly's narrative conventionality, Emily Brontë demonstrates, must suppress a great deal in order to force a plot into traditional shape. It is the evil man, not the good one, who dies joyfully in *Wuthering Heights.* The artificiality of Edgar's happy passing is all the more evident when Heathcliff dies, taking a wild, ferocious joy in the event and so disconcerting Nelly with the "frightful, life-like gaze of exultation" on his corpse that she tries earnestly, like a good nineteenth-century narrator, to extinguish it (pp. 285–86).

The inevitable gestures of nineteenth-century fictional closure, marriage and death, both of which will be crucial to the resolution of *Jane Eyre,* are unsettled in *Wuthering Heights:* they begin to look like artificial fictional impositions, intended to quiet troubling yet uncon-

[24]Charlotte Brontë, *Jane Eyre,* ed. Ian Jack and Margaret Smith (Oxford: Clarendon Press, 1969), 266–67.

tainable passions and energies. The duality in the ending of *Wuthering Heights* itself works similarly to reveal that such closures suppress the energies of social resistance. The passion of Heathcliff and the first Catherine ends in Heathcliff's sneering death, but *Wuthering Heights* provides an alternate, more socially acceptable ending, as the second Cathy and Hareton reenact Catherine and Heathcliff's passionate bonding as a love story with a happy, traditional consummation. With this alternate ending, the resolution to the second Cathy/Hareton plot, rather than to the first Catherine/Heathcliff plot, Brontë writes a double ending to mock the expectations of her readers and to satirize the conventional conclusion of the domestic novel. Charlotte Brontë's *Jane Eyre* (like her earlier *The Professor*) ends in happy, slightly uneasy, self-enclosed domesticity; Emily Brontë mockingly provides her novel with a *faux* version of this kind of fictional conclusion with a courtship at Easter, time of rebirth, a marriage and a new start on New Year's Day, plans for domesticated gardens, and a removal to the "civilized" domestic sanctuary of Thrushcross Grange.

The marriage of Hareton and the second Cathy may indeed at first seem like an adequate resolution to the problems of social marginality and oppression experienced by Heathcliff and Catherine. Their marriage brings an end to class inequality, as Hareton, the former servant, marries the once pampered and wealthy young Cathy. The image of the second Cathy's "light, shining ringlets blending, at intervals, with [Hareton's] brown locks" (p. 263) reminds the reader of a crossing of racial barriers, Hareton's reading lessons suggest the process of decolonization, and the two heads bent avidly over the book they are jointly reading suggest a mutual access to the language of power.

But closer attention reveals the inadequacy of this resolution. The marriage between Hareton and Cathy is an instance neither of true class mobility nor of racial rapprochement. Hareton, although transformed for a while into a "boor," is not truly of another class or race from the second Cathy, and therefore can be incorporated into the British middle class in a way that Heathcliff never can. Hareton is readily civilized: when he washes, *his* dusky skin lightens, although washing will never turn Heathcliff white. The second Cathy, too, has little of the socially resistant energy of the first Catherine. When Cathy and Hareton read the book together, although they pause on the word "contrary," they are at quite a remove from the first Catherine's carelessly blasphemous marginal commentary (p. 263).

Brontë's dual ending mockingly draws attention to the type of conclusion she is not giving her novel. It reveals who is excluded from such endings, what energies they tame and dilute, what they cannot imagine. The last images in the novel ironize the exclusive, walled-in domestic bliss of the Cathy/Hareton ending, which assumes a position only slightly "contrary" to the dominant culture. After showing us, through Lockwood's eyes, the young couple entering the house, the novel moves on to an image of a badly decayed building, the kirk, with its broken windows and collapsing roof. Outside forces have invaded and destroyed this central structure of British society, leaving only "black gaps" where windows, "glass panes," once successfully kept the outside — and the outsiders — out (p. 287). Last, the novel shows us the three headstones above the graves, where, even as Lockwood watches unseeingly, a radical merging is taking place. Catherine and Heathcliff, divided since adolescence by the "great glass panes" of British civilization, return in their deaths to a unity in social transgression: Heathcliff has arranged to have his coffin constructed with a removable panel, and has already knocked the side of Catherine's loose, so that their bodies, no longer artificially divided, will dissolve together, finally consummating their passionate sense of identity. In the context of nineteenth-century British culture, Emily Brontë's image of the two bodies uniting in dissolution, the barrier lifted between the white woman and the dark colonial outsider, has a dramatically defiant power.[25] Lockwood, a civilized narrator and a violent defender of British social boundaries against transgression, can see only what is above the ground and denies the possibility of "unquiet slumbers, for the sleepers in that quiet earth" (p. 288). But by returning us to the novel's first plot, in that final image of a radical unity in marginality, Emily Brontë points out what is suppressed by the type of literary imagination that curbs troubling energies with quiescent endings. At the same time she intimates that the invisible barriers separating those within the glass house of British imperialist civilization from the wrathful dark faces outside are hardly as impenetrable as they might at first seem.

[25]Thackeray, for example, evokes shudders at a much less startling image of the dissolution of barriers between races, when he expresses disgust at the thought of "Desdemona's golden curls on swart Othello's shoulder." Charles Lamb, like others in this century, felt that *Othello* should not be performed on stage; he found "something extremely revolting in the courtship and wedded caresses of Othello and Desdemona." William Makepeace Thackeray, *The Adventures of Philip,* vol. 11 of *The Works of William Makepeace Thackeray* (New York: Harper & Brothers, 1899), 185; Charles Lamb, "On the Tragedies of Shakespeare, Considered with Reference to Their Fitness for Stage Representation," in *The Works of Charles Lamb,* ed. William MacDonald (London: J. M. Dent, 1903), 3:34. For an account of nineteenth-century reactions to performances of *Othello,* see Ruth Cowhig, "Blacks in English Renaissance Drama," in *The Black Presence in English Literature,* ed. David Dabydeen (Manchester: Manchester University Press, 1985), 1–25.

Glossary of Critical and Theoretical Terms

ABSENCE The idea, advanced by French theorist Jacques Derrida, that authors are not present in texts and that meaning arises in the absence of any authority guaranteeing the correctness of any one interpretation.

See **Presence and Absence** for a more complete discussion.

AFFECTIVE FALLACY *See* **New Criticism; Reader-Response Criticism.**

BASE *See* **Marxist Criticism.**

CANON A term used since the fourth century to refer to those books of the Bible that the Christian church accepts as being Holy Scripture — that is, divinely inspired. Books outside the canon (noncanonical books) are referred to as *apocryphal. Canon* has also been used to refer to the Saints Canon, the group of people officially recognized by the Catholic Church as saints. More recently, it has been employed to refer to the body of works generally attributed by scholars to a particular author (for example, the Shakespearean canon is currently believed to consist of thirty-seven plays that scholars feel can be definitively attributed to him). Works sometimes attributed to an

Note: The following definitions are adapted and/or abridged verisons of ones found in *The Bedford Glossary of Critical and Literary Terms,* by Ross C Murfin and Supryia M. Ray.

author, but whose authorship is disputed or otherwise uncertain, are called apocryphal. *Canon* may also refer more generally to those literary works that are "privileged," or given special status, by a culture. Works we tend to think of as classics or as "Great Books"— texts that are repeatedly reprinted in anthologies of literature — may be said to constitute the canon.

Contemporary **Marxist, feminist,** minority, and **postcolonial** critics have argued that, for political reasons, many excellent works never enter the canon. Canonized works, they claim, are those that reflect — and respect — the culture's dominant ideology or perform some socially acceptable or even necessary form of "cultural work." Attempts have been made to broaden or redefine the canon by discovering valuable texts, or versions of texts, that were repressed or ignored for political reasons. These have been published both in traditional and in nontraditional anthologies. The most outspoken critics of the canon, especially certain critics practicing **cultural criticism,** have called into question the whole concept of canon or "canonicity." Privileging no form of artistic expression, these critics treat cartoons, comics, and soap operas with the same cogency and respect they accord novels, poems, and plays.

CHICAGO SCHOOL Originally a group of literary critics associated with the University of Chicago; other critics who have followed in their footsteps have also been referred to as Chicago School critics or, more simply, as Chicago Critics. In 1952, the original group of Chicago Critics collectively published a landmark book entitled *Critics and Criticism,* which outlined their thinking about both practical criticism (a type of literary criticism) and the general history of criticism.

Chicago School critics typically examine works on an individual basis (as do practical critics and objective critics). They view the text in terms of its form, or shaping principle, and the way in which that form is articulated in the work's structure. They also, however, consider the relationship between individual works and broadly defined categories of works, or **genres.** Because they combine a historical interest in schools of criticism and literary genres with a practical or objective focus on the internal structure and relations of elements within individual works, the Chicago School critics are sometimes said to be **Neo-Aristotelian** critics. The approach of the Chicago critics has also been called formalist insofar as it involves analyzing works on an individual basis; it is important to note, however, that the Chicago critics' interest in historical matters is decidedly not formalist. Influential Chicago critics include such figures as R. S. Crane, Elder Olson, and Wayne Booth.

CULTURAL CRITICISM, CULTURAL STUDIES *See* "What Is Cultural Criticism?" pp. 411–24.

DECONSTRUCTION Deconstruction involves the close reading of **texts** in order to demonstrate that any given text has irreconcilably contradictory meanings, rather than being a unified, logical whole. As J. Hillis Miller, the preeminent American deconstructor, has explained in an essay entitled "Stevens' Rock and Criticism as Cure" (1976), "Deconstruction is not a dismantling of the structure of a text, but a demonstration that it has already dismantled itself. Its apparently solid ground is no rock but thin air."

Deconstruction was both created and has been profoundly influenced by the French philosopher of language Jacques Derrida. Derrida, who coined the term *deconstruction,* argues that in Western culture, people tend to think and express their thoughts in terms of *binary oppositions.* Something is white but not black, masculine and therefore not feminine, a cause rather than an effect. Other common and mutually exclusive pairs include beginning/end, conscious/unconscious, **presence/absence,** and speech/writing. Derrida suggests these oppositions are hierarchies in miniature, containing one term that Western culture views as positive or superior and another considered negative or inferior, even if only slightly so. Through deconstruction, Derrida aims to erase the boundary between binary oppositions — and to do so in such a way that the hierarchy implied by the oppositions is thrown into question.

Although its ultimate aim may be to criticize Western logic, deconstruction arose as a response to **structuralism** and to **formalism.** Structuralists believed that all elements of human culture, including literature, may be understood as parts of a system of signs. Derrida did not believe that structuralists could explain the laws governing human signification and thus provide the key to understanding the form and meaning of everything from an African village to Greek myth to a literary text. He also rejected the structuralist belief that texts have identifiable "centers" of meaning, a belief structuralists shared with formalists.

Formalist critics, such as the **New Critics,** assume that a work of literature is a freestanding, self-contained object whose meaning can be found in the complex network of relations between its parts (allusions, images, rhythms, sounds, etc.). Deconstructors, by contrast, see works in terms of their *undecidability.* They reject the formalist view that a work of literary art is demonstrably unified from beginning to end, in one certain way, or that it is organized around a single center that ultimately can be identified. As a result, deconstructors see texts as more radically heterogeneous than do formalists. Formalists ultimately make sense of the ambiguities they find in a given text, arguing that every ambiguity serves a definite, meaningful — and demonstrable — literary function. Undecidability, by contrast, is never reduced, let alone mastered. Though a deconstructive reading can reveal the incompatible possibilities generated by the text, it is impossible for the reader to decide among them.

DIALECTIC Originally developed by Greek philosophers, mainly Socrates and Plato (in *The Republic* and *Phaedrus* [c. 360 B.C.]), a form and method of logical argumentation that typically addresses conflicting ideas or positions. When used in the plural, dialectics refer to any mode of argumentation that attempts to resolve the contradictions between opposing ideas.

The German philosopher G. W. F. Hegel described dialectic as a process whereby a *thesis,* when countered by an *antithesis,* leads to the *synthesis* of a new idea. Karl Marx and Friedrich Engels, adapting Hegel's idealist theory, used the phrase *dialectical materialism* to discuss the way in which a revolutionary class war might lead to the synthesis of a new socioeconomic order.

In literary criticism, *dialectic* typically refers to the oppositional ideas and/or mediatory reasoning that pervade and unify a given work or group of works. Critics may thus speak of the dialectic of head and heart (reason and passion) in William Shakespeare's plays. The American **Marxist critic** Fredric Jameson has coined the phrase "dialectical criticism" to refer to a Marxist critical approach that synthesizes **structuralist** and **poststructuralist** methodologies.

DIALOGIC *See* **Discourse.**

DISCOURSE Used specifically, (1) the thoughts, statements, or dialogue of individuals, especially of characters in a literary work; (2) the words in, or text of, a **narrative** as opposed to its story line; or (3) a "strand" within a given narrative that argues a certain point or defends a given value system. Discourse of the first type is sometimes categorized as *direct* or *indirect.* Direct discourse relates the thoughts and utterances of individuals and literary characters to the reader unfiltered by a third-person narrator. ("Take me home this instant!" she insisted.) Indirect discourse (also referred to as free indirect discourse) is more impersonal, involving the reportage of thoughts, statements, or dialogue by a third-person narrator. (She told him to take her home immediately.)

More generally, *discourse* refers to the language in which a subject or area of knowledge is discussed or a certain kind of business is transacted. Human knowledge is collected and structured in discourses. Theology and medicine are defined by their discourses, as are politics, sexuality, and literary criticism.

Contemporary literary critics have maintained that society is generally made up of a number of different discourses or *discourse communities,* one or more of which may be dominant or serve the dominant ideology. Each discourse has its own vocabulary, concepts, and rules — knowledge of which constitutes power. The psychoanalyst and **psychoanalytic critic** Jacques Lacan has treated the unconscious as a form of discourse, the patterns of which are repeated in literature. **Cultural critics,** following Soviet critic Mikhail Bakhtin, use the word *dialogic* to discuss the dialogue between discourses that takes place within language or, more specifically, a literary text. Some **poststructuralists** have used *discourse* in lieu of **text** to refer to any verbal structure whether literary or not.

FEMINIST CRITICISM *See* "What Is Feminist Criticism?" pp. 451–59.

FIGURE, FIGURE OF SPEECH *See* **Trope.**

FORMALISM A general term covering several similar types of literary criticism that arose in the 1920s and 1930s, flourished during the 1940s and 1950s, and are still in evidence today. Formalists see the literary work as an object in its own right. Thus, they tend to devote their attention to its intrinsic nature, concentrating their analyses on the interplay and relationships between the text's essential verbal elements. They study the form of the work (as opposed to its content), although form to a formalist can connote anything from **genre** (for example, one may speak of "the sonnet form") to grammatical or rhetorical structure to the "emotional imperative" that engenders the work's (more mechanical) structure. No matter which connotation of form pertains, however, formalists seek to be objective in their analysis, focusing on the work itself and eschewing external considerations. They pay particular attention to literary devices used in the work and to the patterns these devices establish.

Formalism developed largely in reaction to the practice of interpreting literary **texts** by relating them to "extrinsic" issues, such as the historical circumstances and politics of the era in which the work was written, its philosophical or theological milieu, or the experiences and frame of mind of its author. Although the term *formalism* was coined by critics to disparage the movement, it is now used simply as a descriptive term.

Formalists have generally suggested that everyday language, which serves simply to communicate information, is stale and unimaginative. They argue that "literariness" has the capacity to overturn common and expected patterns (of grammar, of storyline), thereby rejuvenating language. Such novel uses of language supposedly enable readers to experience not only language but also the world in an entirely new way.

A number of schools of criticism have adopted a formalist orientation, or at least make use of formalist concepts. The **New Criticism,** an American approach to literature that reached its height in the 1940s and 1950s, is perhaps the most famous type of formalism. But Russian formalism was the first major formalist movement; after the Stalinist regime suppressed it in the early 1930s, the Prague Linguistic Circle adopted its analytical methods. The **Chicago School** has also been classified as formalist insofar as the Chicago critics examined and analyzed works on an individual basis; their interest in historical material, on the other hand, was clearly not formalist.

Another sort of formalism, namely **Neo-Aristotelian criticism**, coexisted (but often quarreled) with the New Criticism. Centered at the University of Chicago, and practiced by such critics as R. S. Crane, Wayne Booth, and Sheldon Sacks, Neo-Aristotelian criticism derived from Aristotle's *Poetics* an appreciation for plot and the belief that, in a successful novel, plot and such other elements of fiction as characters, themes, and language would cohere to form an integrated work. The "structural" analysis of the Chicago School came into conflict, first, with the "textural" analysis of the New Critics and, later, with the theories of **reader-response** and **deconstructive** critics, who, in variously insisting on the indeterminacy of the literary text, opposed what they saw as authoritarian in the Neo-Aristotelian method.

GAPS When used by **reader-response critics** familiar with the theories of Wolfgang Iser, the term refers to "blanks" in **texts** that must be filled in by readers. A gap may be said to exist whenever and wherever a reader perceives something to be missing between words, sentences, paragraphs, stanzas, or chapters. Readers respond to gaps actively and creatively, explaining apparent inconsistencies in point of view, accounting for jumps in chronology, speculatively supplying information missing from plots, and resolving problems or issues left ambiguous or "indeterminate" in the text.

Reader-response critics sometimes speak as if a gap actually exists in a text; a gap, of course, is to some extent a product of readers' perceptions. One reader may find a given text to be riddled with gaps while another reader may view that text as comparatively consistent and complete; different readers may find different gaps in the same text. Furthermore, they may fill in the gaps they find in different ways, which is why, a reader-response critic might argue, works are interpreted in different ways.

Although the concept of the gap has been used mainly by reader-response critics, it has also been used by critics taking other theoretical approaches. Practitioners of **deconstruction** might use *gap* when explaining that every text contains opposing and even contradictory discourses that cannot be reconciled. **Marxist critics** have used the term gap to speak of everything from the gap that opens up between economic **base** and cultural **superstructure** to two kinds of conflicts or contradictions found in literary texts. The first of these conflicts or contradictions, they would argue, results from the fact that even realistic texts reflect an **ideology**, within which there are inevitably subjects and attitudes that cannot be represented or even recognized. As a result, readers at the edge or outside of that ideology perceive that something is missing. The second kind of conflict or contradiction within a text results from the fact that works do more than reflect ideology; they are also fictions that, consciously or unconsciously, distance themselves from that ideology.

GAY AND LESBIAN CRITICISM Sometimes referred to as *queer theory,* an approach to literature currently viewed as a form of **gender criticism**.

See **Gender Criticism.**

GENDER CRITICISM A type of literary criticism that focuses on — and critiques — gender as it is commonly conceived, seeking to expose its insufficiency as a categorizing device. Gender critics reject the view that gender is something natural or innate, arguing instead that gender is a social construct, a learned behavior, a product of culture and its institutions. **Gay and lesbian criticism** is generally viewed as a major emphasis within gender criticism, although not all gay and lesbian critics would so categorize their work.

Many commentators have argued that feminist criticism is also a type of gender criticism, despite the fact that feminist criticism arose as an approach to literary criticism in the 1970s, whereas gender criticism appeared on the critical scene a decade later. Gender critics have drawn heavily upon feminist theory and practice even as they have attacked many feminist concepts and claims.

Many gender critics hold "constructionist" views and take issue with those feminists who urge an "essentialist" approach. Stated simply, the word *essentialist* refers to the view that women are essentially — that is, naturally — different from men. The most essentialist feminists write as if no amount of enculturation could alter female nature, female difference. *Constructionist,* by conrast, refers to the view that most of the differences between men and women are characteristics not of the male and female sex (nature) but, rather, of the masculine and feminine genders (nurture). Constructionist gender critics vehemently disagree with those feminists who emphasize the female body, its sexual difference, and the manifold implications of that difference, especially those French feminist critics who argue that the female body gives rise to a special feminine language, writing, and style. Unlike these essentialist feminists, constructionist gender critics would attribute differences in language, writing, and style to cultural influences, not to sexual differences between female and male bodies.

Following the lead of French philosophical historian Michel Foucault, gay and lesbian cultural critics associated with so-called *queer theory* have argued that the heterosexual/homosexual distinction is as much a cultural construct as is the masculine/feminine dichotomy. These critics have been especially critical of heterosexuality as a norm, arguing that it is an enforced corollary and consequence of a "sex/gender system" which presupposes that men are masculine, that masculinity carries with it an attraction to women, and that it is therefore unnatural for men to be attracted to other men. Gay and lesbian writings have produced compelling, if controversial, reinterpretations of works by authors as diverse as Herman Melville, Emily Dickinson, Henry James, Virginia Woolf, and Toni Morrison.

Gay and lesbian critics are not the only gender critics who have critiqued masculinity. An unprecedented number of gender theorists have analyzed masculinity as a complex construct which produces and reproduces a constellation of behaviors and goals such as performance and conquest, many of them destructive and injurious to women. The construct of masculinity has been studied in works by Stephen Crane, T. S. Eliot, F. Scott Fitzgerald, and Nathaniel Hawthorne.

GENRE From the French *genre* for "kind" or "type," the classification of literary works on the basis of their content, form, or technique. The term also refers to individual classifications. For centuries works have been grouped and associated according to a number of classificatory schemes and distinctions, such as prose/poem/fiction/drama/lyric, and the traditional classical divisions: comedy/tragedy/lyric/pastoral/epic/satire. More recently, Northrop Frye has suggested that all literary works may be grouped with one of four sets of archetypal myths that are in turn associated with the four seasons; for Frye, the four main genre classifications are comedy (spring), romance (summer), tragedy (fall), and satire (winter). Many more specific genre categories exist as well, such as autobiography, the essay, the Gothic novel, the picaresque novel, the sentimental novel. Current usage is thus broad enough to permit varieties of a given genre (such as the novel) as well as the novel in general to be legitimately denoted by the term *genre*.

Traditional thinking about genre has been revised and even roundly criticized by contemporary critics. For example, the prose/poem dichotomy has been largely discarded in favor of a lyric/drama/fiction (or narrative) scheme. The more general idea that works of imaginative literature can be solidly and satisfactorily classified according to set, specific categories has also come under attack in recent times.

HEGEMONY Most commonly, one nation's dominance or dominant influence over another. The term was adopted (and adapted) by the Italian **Marxist critic** Antonio Gramsci to refer to the process of consensus formation and to the pervasive system of assumptions, meanings, and values — the web of **ideologies**, in other words — that shape the way things look, what they mean, and therefore what reality is for the majority of people within a given culture. Although Gramsci viewed hegemony as being powerful and persuasive, he did not believe that extant systems were immune to change; rather, he encouraged people to resist prevailing ideologies, to form a new consensus, and thereby to alter hegemony.

Hegemony is a term commonly used by **cultural critics** as well as by Marxist critics.

IDEOLOGY A set of beliefs underlying the customs, habits, and practices common to a given social group. To members of that group, the beliefs seem obviously true, natural, and even universally applicable. They may seem just as obviously arbitrary, idiosyncratic, and even false to those who adhere to another ideology. Within a society, several ideologies may coexist; one or more of these may be dominant.

Ideologies may be forcefully imposed or willingly subscribed to. Their component beliefs may be held consciously or unconsciously. In either case, they come to form what Johanna M. Smith has called "the unexamined ground of our experience." Ideology governs our perceptions, judgments, and prejudices — our sense of what is acceptable, normal, and deviant. Ideology may cause a revolution; it may also allow discrimination and even exploitation.

Ideologies are of special interest to politically oriented critics of literature because of the way in which authors reflect or resist prevailing views in their texts. Some **Marxist critics** have argued that literary texts reflect and reproduce the ideologies that produced them; most, however, have shown how ideologies are riven with contradictions that works of literature manage to expose and widen. Other Marxist critics have focused on the way in which texts themselves are characterized by gaps, conflicts, and contradictions between their ideological and anti-ideological functions.

Fredric Jameson, an American Marxist critic, argues that all thought is ideological, but that ideological thought that knows itself as such stands the chance of seeing through and transcending ideology.

Not all of the politically oriented critics interested in ideology have been Marxists. Certain non-Marxist **feminist critics** have addressed the question of ideology by seeking to expose (and thereby call into question) the patriarchal ideology mirrored or inscribed in works written by men — even men who have sought to counter sexism and break down sexual stereotypes. **New historicists** have been interested in demonstrating the ideological underpinnings not only of literary representations but also of our interpretations of them.

IMAGINARY ORDER *See* **Psychological Criticism and Psychoanalytic Criticism**.

IMPLIED READER *See* **Reader-Response Criticism**.

INTENTIONAL FALLACY *See* **New Criticism**.

INTERTEXTUALITY The condition of interconnectedness among texts, or the concept that any text is an amalgam of others, either because it exhibits signs of influence or because its language inevitably contains common points of reference with other texts through such things as allusion, quotation, genre, stylistic features, and even revisions. The critic Julia Kristeva, who popularized and is often credited with coining this term, views any given work as part of a larger fabric of literary **discourse**, part of a continuum including the future as well as the past. Other critics have argued for an even broader use and understanding of the term *intertextuality,* maintaining that literary history per se is too narrow a context within which to read and understand a literary text. When understood this way, *intertextuality* could be used by a **new historicist** or **cultural critic** to refer to the significant interconnectedness between a literary text and contemporary, nonliterary discussions of the issues represented in the literary text. Or it could be used by a **poststructuralist** to suggest that a work of literature can only be recognized and read within a vast field of signs and **tropes** that is like a text and that makes any single text self-contradictory and **undecidable.**

MARXIST CRITICISM *See* "What Is Marxist Criticism?" pp. 379–91.

METAPHOR A **figure of speech** (more specifically a **trope**) that associates two unlike things; the representation of one thing by another. The image (or activity or concept) used to represent or "figure" something else is known as the **vehicle** of the metaphor; the thing represented is called the **tenor**. For instance, in the sentence "That child is a mouse," the child is the tenor, whereas the mouse is the vehicle. The image of a mouse is being used to represent the child, perhaps to emphasize his or her timidity.

Metaphor should be distinguished from **simile**, another figure of speech with which it is sometimes confused. Similes compare two unlike things by using a connective word such as *like* or *as.* Metaphors use no connective word to make their comparison. Furthermore, critics ranging from Aristotle to I. A. Richards have argued that metaphors equate the vehicle with the tenor instead of simply comparing the two.

This identification of vehicle and tenor can provide much additional meaning. For instance, instead of saying, "Last night I read a book," we might say, "Last night I plowed through a book." "Plowed through" (or the activity of plowing) is the vehicle of our metaphor; "read" (or the act of reading) is the tenor, the thing being figured. (As this example shows, neither vehicle nor tenor need be a noun; metaphors may employ other parts of speech.) The increment in meaning through metaphor is fairly obvious. Our audience knows not only *that* we read but also *how* we read, because to read a book in the way that a plow rips through earth is surely to read in a relentless, unreflective way. Note that in the sentence above, a new metaphor —"rips through"— has been used to explain an old one. This serves (which is a metaphor) as an example of just how thick (another metaphor) language is with metaphors!

Metaphors may be classified as *direct* or *implied.* A direct metaphor, such as "That child is a mouse" (or "He is such a doormat!"), specifies both tenor and vehicle. An implied metaphor, by contrast, mentions only the vehicle; the tenor is implied by the context of the sentence or passage. For instance, in the sentence "Last night I plowed through a book" (or "She sliced through traffic"), the tenor — the act of reading (or driving) — can be inferred.

Traditionally, metaphor has been viewed as the principal trope. Other figures of speech include simile, **symbol**, personification, allegory, **metonymy**, synecdoche, and conceit. **Deconstructors** have questioned the distinction between metaphor and metonymy.

METONYMY **A figure of speech** (more specifically a **trope**), in which one thing is represented by another that is commonly and often physically associated with it. To refer to a writer's handwriting as his or her "hand" is to use a metonymic figure.

Like other figures of speech (such as **metaphor**), metonymy involves the replacement of one word or phrase by another; thus, a monarch might be referred to as "the crown." As narrowly defined by certain contemporary critics, particularly those associated with **deconstruction**, the **vehicle** of a metonym is arbitrarily, not intrinsically, associated with the **tenor**. (There is no special, intrinsic likeness between a crown and a monarch; it's just that crowns traditionally sit on monarchs' heads and not on the heads of university professors.)

More broadly, metonym and metonymy have been used by recent critics to refer to a wide range of figures. **Structuralists** such as Roman Jakobson, who emphasized the difference between metonymy and metaphor, have recently been challenged by deconstructors, who have further argued that *all* figuration is arbitrary. Deconstructors such as Paul de Man and J. Hillis Miller have questioned the "privilege" granted to metaphor and the metaphor/metonymy distinction or "opposition," suggesting instead that all metaphors are really metonyms.

MODERNISM *See* **Postmodernism**.

NARRATIVE A story or a telling of a story, or an account of a situation or events. Narratives may be fictional or true; they may be written in prose or verse. Some critics use the term even more generally; Brook Thomas, a **new historicist**, has critiqued "narratives of human history that neglect the role human labor has played."

NARRATOLOGY The analysis of the **structural** components of a **narrative**, the way in which those components interrelate, and the relationship between this complex of elements and the narrative's basic story line. Narratology incorporates techniques developed by other critics, most notably Russian **formalists** and French **structuralists**, applying in addition numerous traditional methods of analyzing narrative fiction (for instance, those methods outlined in the "Showing as Telling" chapter of Wayne Booth's *The Rhetoric of Fiction* [1961]). Narratologists treat narratives as explicitly, intentionally, and meticulously constructed systems rather than as simple or natural vehicles for an author's representation of life. They seek to analyze and explain how authors transform a chronologically organized story line into a literary plot. (Story is the raw material from which plot is selectively arranged and constructed.)

Narratologists pay particular attention to such elements as point of view; the relations among story, teller, and audience; and the levels and types of **discourse** used in narratives. Certain narratologists concentrate on the question of whether any narrative can actually be neutral (like a clear pane of glass through which some subject is objectively seen) and on how the practices of a given culture influence the shape, content, and impact of "historical" narratives. Mieke Bal's *Narratology: Introduction to the Theory of Narrative* (1980) is a standard introduction to the narratological approach.

NEO-ARISTOTELIAN CRITICISM *See* **Chicago School, Formalism**.

NEW CRITICISM, THE A type of **formalist** literary criticism that reached its height during the 1940s and 1950s, and that received its name from John Crowe Ransom's 1941 book *The New Criticism*. New Critics treat a work of literary art as if it were a self-contained, self-referential object. Rather than basing their interpretations of a **text** on the reader's response, the author's stated intentions, or parallels between the text and historical contexts (such as the author's life), New Critics perform a close reading of the text, concentrating on the internal relationships that give it its own distinctive character or form. New Critics emphasize that the structure of a work should not be divorced from meaning, viewing the two as constituting a quasi-organic unity. Special attention is paid to repetition, particularly of images or symbols, but also of sound effects and rhythms in poetry. New critics especially appreciate the use of literary devices, such as irony and paradox, to achieve a balance or reconciliation between dissimilar, even conflicting, elements in a text.

Because of the importance placed on close textual analysis and the stress on the text as a carefully crafted, orderly object containing observable formal patterns, the New Criticism has sometimes been called an "objective" approach to literature. New Critics are more likely than certain other critics to believe and say that the meaning of a text can be known objectively. For instance, **reader-response critics** see meaning as a function either of each reader's experience or of the norms that govern a particular interpretive community, and **deconstructors** argue that texts mean opposite things at the same time.

The foundations of the New Criticism were laid in books and essays written during the 1920s and 1930s by I. A. Richards (*Practical Criticism* [1929]), William Empson (*Seven Types of Ambiguity* [1930]), and T. S. Eliot ("The Function of Criticism" [1933]). The approach was significantly developed later, however, by a group of American poets and critics, including R. P. Blackmur, Cleanth Brooks, John Crowe Ransom, Allen Tate, Robert Penn Warren, and William K. Wimsatt. Although we associate the New Criticism with certain principles and terms (such as the *affective fallacy* — the notion that the reader's response is relevant to the meaning of a work — and the *intentional fallacy* — the notion that the author's intention determines the work's meaning), the New Critics were trying to make a cultural statement rather than to establish a critical dogma. Generally Southern, religious, and culturally conservative, they advocated the inherent value of literary works (particularly of literary works regarded as beautiful art objects) because they were sick of the growing ugliness of modern life and contemporary events. Some recent theorists even link the rising popularity after World War II of the New Criticism (and other types of formalist literary criticism such as the **Chicago School**) to American isolationism. These critics tend to view the formalist tendency to isolate literature from biography and history as symptomatic of American fatigue with wider involvements. Whatever the source of the New Criticism's popularity (or the reason for its eventual decline), its practitioners and the textbooks they wrote were so influential in American academia that the approach became standard in college and even high school curricula through the 1960s and well into the 1970s.

NEW HISTORICISM, THE A type of literary criticism that developed during the 1980s, largely in reaction to the text-only approach pursued by **formalist New Critics** and the critics who challenged the New Criticism in the 1970s. New historicists, like formalists and their critics, acknowledge the importance of the literary **text**, but they also analyze the text with an eye to history. In this respect, the new historicism is not "new"; the majority of critics between 1920 and 1950 focused on a work's historical content and based their interpretations on the interplay between the text and historical contexts (such as the author's life or intentions in writing the work).

In other respects, however, the new historicism differs from the historical criticism of the 1930s and 1940s. It is informed by the **poststructuralist** and **reader-response theory** of the 1970s, as well as by the thinking of **feminist**, **cultural**, and **Marxist** critics whose work was also "new" in the 1980s. They are less fact- and event-oriented than historical critics used to be, perhaps because they have come to wonder whether the truth about what really happened can ever be purely and objectively known. They are less likely to see history as linear and progressive, as something developing toward the present, and they are also less likely to think of it in terms of specific eras, each with a definite, persistent, and consistent zeitgeist (spirit of the times). Hence, they are unlikely to suggest that a literary text has a single or easily identifiable historical context.

New historicist critics also tend to define the discipline of history more broadly than did their predecessors. They view history as a social science like anthropology and sociology, whereas older historicists tended to view history as literature's "background" and the social sciences as being properly historical. They have erased the line dividing historical and literary materials, showing not only that the production of one of William Shakespeare's historical plays was both a political act and a historical event, but also that the coronation of Elizabeth I was carried out with the same care for staging and symbol lavished on works of dramatic art.

New historicists remind us that it is treacherous to reconstruct the past as it really was — rather than as we have been conditioned by our own place and time to believe that it was. And they know that the job is impossible for those who are unaware of that difficulty, insensitive to the bent or bias of their own historical vantage point. Hence, when new historicist critics describe a historical change, they are highly conscious of (and even likely to discuss) the theory of historical change that informs their account.

Many new historicists have acknowledged a profound indebtedness to the writings of Michel Foucault. A French philosophical historian, Foucault brought together incidents and phenomena from areas normally seen as unconnected, encouraging new historicists and new cultural historicists to redefine the boundaries of historical inquiry. Like the philosopher Friedrich Nietzsche, Foucault refused to see history as an evolutionary process, a continuous development from cause to effect, from past to present toward *the end*, a moment of definite closure, a day of judgment. No historical event, according to Foucault, has a single cause; rather, each event is tied into a vast web of economic, social, and political factors. Like Karl Marx, Foucault saw history in terms of power, but, unlike Marx, he viewed power not simply as a repressive force or a tool of conspiracy but rather as a complex of forces that produces what happens. Not even a tyrannical aristocrat simply wields power, for the aristocrat is himself empowered by discourses and practices that constitute power.

Not all new historicist critics owe their greatest debt to Foucault. Some, like Stephen Greenblatt, have been most nearly influenced by the British cultural critic Raymond Williams, and others, like Brook Thomas, have been more influenced by German Marxist Walter Benjamin. Still others — Jerome McGann, for example — have followed the lead of Soviet critic Mikhail Bakhtin, who viewed literary works in terms of polyphonic **discourses** and dialogues between the official, legitimate voices of a society and other, more challenging or critical voices echoing popular culture.

POSTCOLONIAL CRITICISM, POSTCOLONIAL STUDIES A type of **cultural criticism,** *postcolonial criticism* usually involves the analysis of literary texts produced in countries and cultures that have come under the control of European colonial powers at some point in their history. Alternatively, it can refer to the analysis of texts written about colonized places by writers hailing from the colonizing culture. In *Orientalism* (1978), Edward Said, a pioneer of postcolonial criticism and studies, has focused on the way in which the colonizing First World has invented false images and myths of the Third (postcolonial) World, stereotypical images and myths that have conveniently justified Western exploitation and domination of Eastern and Middle Eastern cultures and peoples. In an essay entitled "Postcolonial Criticism" (1992), Homi K. Bhabha has shown how certain cultures (mis)represent other cultures, thereby extending their political and social domination in the modern world order.

Postcolonial studies, a type of **cultural studies**, refers more broadly to the study of cultural groups, practices, and **discourses** — including but not limited to literary discourses — in the colonized world. The term *postcolonial* is usually used broadly to refer to the study of works written at any point after colonization first occurred in a given country, although it is sometimes used more specifically to refer to the analysis of texts and other cultural discourses that emerged after the end of the colonial period (after the success of liberation and independence movements). Among **feminist critics**, the postcolonial perspective has inspired an attempt to recover whole cultures of women heretofore ignored or marginalized, women who speak not only from colonized places but also from the colonizing places to which many of them fled.

Postcolonial criticism has been influenced by **Marxist** thought, by the work of Michel Foucault — whose theories about the power of discourses have influenced **the new historicism** — and by **deconstruction**, which has challenged not only hierarchical, binary oppositions such as West/East and North/South but also the notions of superiority associated with the first term of each opposition.

POSTMODERNISM A term referring to certain radically experimental works of literature and art produced after World War II. *Postmodernism* is distinguished from *modernism,* which generally refers to the revolution in art and literature that occurred during the period 1910–1930, particularly following the disillusioning experience of World War I. The postmodern era, with its potential for mass destruction and its shocking history of genocide, has evoked a continuing disillusionment similar to that widely experienced during the modern period. Much of postmodernist writing reveals and highlights the alienation of individuals and the meaninglessness of human existence. Postmodernists frequently stress that humans desperately (and ultimately unsuccessfully) cling to illusions of security to conceal and forget the void on which their lives are perched.

Not surprisingly, postmodernists have shared with their modernist precursors the goal of breaking away from traditions (including certain modernist traditions, which, over time, had become institutionalized and conventional to some degree) through experimentation with new literary devices, forms, and styles. While preserving the spirit and even some of the themes of modernist literature (such as the alienation of humanity and historical discontinuity), postmodernists have rejected the order that a number of modernists attempted to instill in their work through patterns of allusion, symbol, and myth. They have also taken some of the meanings and methods found in modernist works to extremes that most modernists would have deplored. For instance, whereas modernists such as T. S. Eliot perceived the world as fragmented and represented that fragmentation through poetic language, many also viewed art as a potentially integrating, restorative force, a hedge against the cacophony and chaos that postmodernist works often imitate (or even celebrate) but do not attempt to counter or correct.

Because postmodernist works frequently combine aspects of diverse **genres**, they can be difficult to classify — at least according to traditional schemes of classification. Postmodernists, revolting against a certain modernist tendency toward elitist "high art," have also generally made a concerted effort to appeal to popular culture. Cartoons, music, "pop art," and television have thus become acceptable and even common media for postmodernist artistic expression. Postmodernist literary developments include such genres as the Absurd, the antinovel, concrete poetry, and other forms of avant-garde poetry written in free verse and challenging the **ideological** assumptions of contemporary society. What postmodernist theater, fiction, and poetry have in common is the view (explicit or implicit) that literary language is its own reality, not a means of representing reality.

Postmodernist critical schools include **deconstruction**, whose practitioners explore the **undecidability** of texts, and **cultural criticism**, which erases the boundary between "high" and "low" culture. The foremost theorist of postmodernism is Jean-François Lyotard, best known for his book *La Condition Postmoderne* (*The Postmodern Condition*) (1979).

POSTSTRUCTURALISM The general attempt to contest and subvert **structuralism** and to formulate new theories regarding interpretation and meaning, initiated particularly by **deconstructors** but also associated with certain aspects and practitioners of **psychoanalytic, Marxist, cultural, feminist,** and **gender criticism**. Poststructuralism, which arose in the late 1960s, includes such a wide variety of perspectives that no unified poststructuralist theory can be identified. Rather, poststructuralists are distinguished from other contemporary critics by their opposition to structuralism and by certain concepts they embrace.

Structuralists typically believe that meaning(s) in a text, as well as the meaning of a text, can be determined with reference to the system of signification — the "codes" and conventions that governed the text's production and that operate in its reception. Poststructuralists reject the possibility of such "determinate" knowledge. They believe that signification is an interminable and intricate web of associations that continually defers a determinate assessment of meaning. The numerous possible meanings of any word lead to contradictions and ultimately to the dissemination of meaning itself. Thus, poststructuralists contend that texts contradict not only structuralist accounts of them but also themselves.

To elaborate, poststructuralists have suggested that structuralism rests on a number of distinctions — between signifier and signified, self and language (or **text**), texts and other texts, and text and world — that are overly simplistic, if not patently inaccurate, and they have made a concerted effort to discredit these oppositions. For instance, poststructuralists have viewed the self as the subject, as well as the user, of language, claiming that although we may speak through and shape language, it also shapes and speaks through us. In addition, poststructuralists have demonstrated that in the grand scheme of signification, all "signifieds" are also signifiers, for each word exists in a complex web of language and has such a variety of denotations and connotations that no one meaning can be said to be final, stable, and invulnerable to reconsideration and substitution. Signification is unstable and indeterminate, and thus so is meaning. Poststructuralists, who have generally followed their structuralist predecessors in rejecting the traditional concept of the literary "work" (as the work of an individual and purposeful author) in favor of the impersonal "text," have gone structuralists one better by treating texts as "intertexts": crisscrossed strands within the infinitely larger text called language, that weblike system of denotation, connotation, and signification in which the individual text is inscribed and read and through which its myriad possible meanings are ascribed and assigned. (Poststructuralist **psychoanalytic critic** Julia Kristeva coined the term **intertextuality** to refer to the fact that a text is a "mosaic" of preexisting texts whose meanings it reworks and transforms.)

Although poststructuralism has drawn from numerous critical perspectives developed in Europe and in North America, it relies most heavily on the work of French theorists, especially Jacques Derrida, Kristeva, Jacques Lacan, Michel Foucault, and Roland Barthes. Derrida's 1966 paper "Structure, Sign and Play in the Discourse of the Human Sciences" inaugurated poststructuralism as a coherent challenge to structuralism. Derrida rejected the structuralist presupposition that texts (or other structures) have self-referential centers that govern their language (or signifying system) without being in any way determined, governed, co-opted, or problematized by that language (or signifying system). Having rejected the structuralist concept of a self-referential center, Derrida also rejected its corollary: that a text's meaning is thereby rendered determinable (capable of being determined) as well as determinate (fixed and reliably correct). Lacan, Kristeva, Foucault, and Barthes have all, in diverse ways, arrived at similarly "antifoundational" conclusions, positing that no foundation or "center" exists that can ensure correct interpretation.

Poststructuralism continues to flourish today. In fact, one might reasonably say that poststructuralism serves as the overall paradigm for many of the most prominent contemporary critical perspectives. Approaches ranging from **reader-response criticism** to **the new historicism** assume the "antifoundationalist" bias of poststructuralism. Many approaches also incorporate the poststructuralist position that texts do not have clear and definite meanings, an argument pushed to the extreme by those poststructuralists identified with deconstruction. But unlike deconstructors, who argue that the process of signification itself produces irreconcilable contradictions, contemporary critics oriented toward other poststructuralist approaches (**discourse** analysis or Lacanian psychoanalytic theory, for instance) maintain that texts do have real meanings underlying their apparent or "manifest" meanings (which often contradict or cancel out one another). These underlying meanings have been distorted, disguised, or repressed for psychological or **ideological** reasons but can be discovered through poststructuralist ways of reading.

PRESENCE AND ABSENCE Words given a special literary application by French theorist of **deconstruction** Jacques Derrida when he used them to make a distinction between speech and writing. An individual speaking words must actually be present at the time they are heard, Derrida pointed out, whereas an individual writing words is absent at the time they are read. Derrida, who associates presence with *logos* (the creating spoken Word of a present God who "In the beginning" said, "Let there be light"), argued that the Western concept of language is **logocentric**. That is, it is grounded in "the metaphysics of presence," the belief that any linguistic system has a basic foundation (what Derrida terms an "ultimate referent"), making possible an identifiable and correct meaning or meanings for any potential statement that can be made within that system. Far from supporting this common Western view of language as logocentric, however, Derrida argues that presence is not an "ultimate referent" and that it does not guarantee determinable (capable of being determined) — much less determinate (fixed and reliably correct) — meaning. Derrida in fact calls into question the "privileging" of speech and presence over writing and absence in Western thought.

PSYCHOLOGICAL CRITICISM AND PSYCHOANALYTIC CRITICISM *See* "What Is Psychoanalytic Criticism?" pp. 348–59.

QUEER THEORY *See* **Gay and Lesbian Criticism, Gender Criticism.**

READER-RESPONSE CRITICISM A critical approach encompassing various approaches to literature that explore and seek to explain the diversity (and often divergence) of readers' responses to literary works.

Louise Rosenblatt is often credited with pioneering the approaches in *Literature as Exploration* (1938). In a 1969 essay entitled "Towards a Transactional Theory of Reading," she summed up her position as follows: "a poem is what the reader lives through under the guidance of the text and experiences as relevant to the text." Recognizing that many critics would reject this definition, Rosenblatt wrote: "The idea that a *poem* presupposes a *reader* actively involved with a *text* is particularly shocking to those seeking to emphasize the objectivity of their interpretations." Rosenblatt implicitly and generally refers to formalists (the most influential of whom are the **New Critics**) when she speaks of supposedly objective interpreters shocked by the notion that a *"poem"* is cooperatively produced by a *"reader"* and a *"text."* Formalists spoke of "the poem itself," the "concrete work of art," the "real poem." They had no interest in what a work of literature makes a reader "live through." In fact, in *The Verbal Icon* (1954), William K. Wimsatt and Monroe C. Beardsley used the term **affective fallacy** to define as erroneous the very idea that a reader's response is relevant to the meaning of a literary work.

Stanley Fish, whose early work is seen by some as marking the true beginning of contemporary reader-response criticism, also took issue with the tenets of formalism. In "Literature in the Reader: Affective Stylistics" (1970), he argued that any school of criticism that sees a literary work as an object, claiming to describe what it is and never what it does, misconstrues the very essence of literature and reading. Literature exists and signifies when it is read, Fish suggests, and its force is an affective force. Furthermore, reading is a temporal process, not a spatial one as formalists assume when they step back and survey the literary work as if it were an object spread out before them. The German critic Wolfgang Iser has described that process in his books *The Implied Reader: Patterns of Communication in Prose Fiction from Bunyan to Beckett* (1974) and *The Act of Reading: A Theory of Aesthetic Response* (1976). Iser argues that texts contain **gaps** (or blanks) that powerfully affect the reader, who must explain them, connect what they separate, and create in his or her mind aspects of a work that aren't *in* the text but that the text incites.

With the redefinition of literature as something that only exists meaningfully in the mind of the reader, with the redefinition of the literary work as a catalyst of mental events, comes a redefinition of the reader. No longer is the reader the passive recipient of those ideas that an author has planted in a text. "The reader is *active*," Rosenblatt had insisted. Fish makes the same point in "Literature in the Reader": "reading is . . . something you *do*." Iser, in focusing critical interest on the gaps in texts, on the blanks that readers have to fill in, similarly redefines the reader as an active maker of meaning. Other reader-response critics define the reader differently. Wayne Booth uses the phrase *the implied reader* to mean the reader "created by the work." Like Booth, Iser employs the term *the implied reader,* but he also uses *the educated reader* when he refers to what Fish calls the "intended reader."

Since the mid-1970s, reader-response criticism has evolved into a variety of new forms. Subjectivists like David Bleich, Norman Holland, and Robert Crosman have viewed the reader's response not as one "guided" by the text but rather as one motivated by deep-seated, personal, psychological needs. Holland has suggested that, when we read, we find our own "identity theme" in the text using "the literary work to symbolize and finally to replicate ourselves. We work out through the text our own characteristic patterns of desire." Even Fish has moved away from reader-response criticism as he had initially helped define it, focusing on "interpretive strategies" held in common by "interpretive communities" — such as the one comprised by American college students reading a novel as a class assignment.

Fish's shift in focus is in many ways typical of changes that have taken place within the field of reader-response criticism — a field that, because of those changes, is increasingly being referred to as *reader-oriented criticism.* Recent reader-oriented critics, responding to Fish's emphasis on interpretive communities and also to the historically oriented perception theory of Hans Robert Jauss, have studied the way a given reading public's "horizons of expectations" change over time. Many of these contemporary critics view themselves as reader-oriented critics and as practitioners of some other critical approach as well. Certain **feminist** and **gender critics** with an interest in reader response have asked whether there is such a thing as "reading like a woman." Reading-oriented **new historicists** have looked at the way in which racism affects and is affected by reading and, more generally, the way in which politics can affect reading practices and outcomes. **Gay and lesbian critics,** such as Wayne Koestenbaum, have argued that sexualities have been similarly constructed within and by social **discourses** and that there may even be a homosexual way of reading.

REAL, THE *See* **Psychological Criticism and Psychoanalytic Criticism**.

SEMIOLOGY Another word for **semiotics**, created by Swiss linguist Ferdinand de Saussure in his 1915 book *Course in General Linguistics.*

SEMIOTICS A term coined by Charles Sanders Peirce to refer to the study of signs, sign systems, and the way meaning is derived from them. **Structuralist** anthropologists, psychoanalysts, and literary critics developed semiotics during the decades following 1950, but much of the pioneering work had been done at the turn of the century by Peirce and by the founder of modern linguistics, Ferdinand de Saussure.

To a semiotician, a sign is not simply a direct means of communication, such as a stop sign or a restaurant sign or language itself. Rather, signs encompass body language (crossed arms, slouching), ways of greeting and parting (handshakes, hugs, waves), artifacts, and even articles of clothing. A sign is anything that conveys information to others who understand it based upon a system of codes and conventions that they have consciously learned or unconsciously internalized as members of a certain culture. Semioticians have often used concepts derived specifically from linguistics, which focuses on language, to analyze all types of signs.

Although Saussure viewed linguistics as a division of semiotics (semiotics, after all, involves the study of all signs, not just linguistic ones), much semiotic theory rests on Saussure's linguistic terms, concepts, and distinctions. Semioticians subscribe to Saussure's basic concept of the linguistic sign as containing a *signifier* (a linguistic "sound image" used to represent some more abstract concept) and *signified* (the abstract concept being represented). They have also found generally useful his notion that the relationship between signifiers and signified is arbitrary; that is, no intrinsic or natural relationship exists between them, and meanings we derive from signifiers are grounded in the differences among signifiers themselves. Particularly useful are Saussure's concept of the *phoneme* (the smallest basic speech sound or unit of pronunciation) and his idea that phonemes exist in two kinds of relationships: diachronic and synchronic.

A phoneme has a diachronic, or "horizontal," relationship with those other phonemes that precede and follow it (as the words appear, left to right, on this page) in a particular usage, utterance, or **narrative** — what Saussure called *parole* (French for "word"). A phoneme has a synchronic, or "vertical," relationship with the entire system of language within which individual usages, utterances, or narratives have meaning — what Saussure called *langue* (French for "tongue," as in "native tongue," meaning language). *An* means what it means in English because those of us who speak the language are plugged in to the same system (think of it as a computer network where different individuals access the same information in the same way at a given time). A principal tenet of semiotics is that signs, like words, are not significant in themselves, but instead have meaning only in relation to other signs and the entire system of signs, or *langue*. Meaning is not inherent in the signs themselves, but is derived from the differences among signs.

Given that semiotic theory underlies structuralism, it is not surprising that many semioticians have taken a broad, structuralist approach to signs, studying a variety of phenomena ranging from rites of passage to methods of preparing and consuming food to understand the cultural codes and conventions they reveal. Because of the broad-based applicability of semiotics, furthermore, structuralist anthropologists such as Claude Lévi-Strauss, literary critics such as Roland Barthes, and **psychoanalytic theorists** such as Jacques Lacan and Julia Kristeva have made use of semiotic theories and practices. Kristeva, who is generally considered a pioneer of feminism (although she eschews the feminist label), has argued that there is such a thing as *feminine language* and that it is semiotic, not **symbolic** in nature. She thus employs both terms in an unusual way, using *semiotic* to refer to language that is rhythmic, unifying, and fluid, and *symbolic* to refer to the more rigid associations redefined in the Western canon. The affinity between semiotics and structuralist literary criticism derives from the emphasis placed on *langue,* or system. Structuralist critics were reacting against formalists and their method of focusing on individual words as if meanings did not depend on anything external to the text.

See also **Symbolic Order; Structuralism.**

SIMILE *See* **Metaphor; Trope.**

STRUCTURALISM A theory of humankind whose proponents attempted to show systematically, even scientifically, that all elements of human culture, including literature, may be understood as parts of a system of **signs**. Critic Robert Scholes has described structuralism as a reaction to " 'modernist' alienation and despair."

European structuralists such as Roman Jakobson, Claude Lévi-Strauss, and Roland Barthes (before his shift toward poststructuralism) attempted to develop a **semiology**, or **semiotics** (science of signs). Barthes, among others, sought to recover literature and even language from the isolation in which they had been studied and to show that the laws that govern them govern all signs, from road signs to articles of clothing.

Structuralism was heavily influenced by linguistics, especially by the pioneering work of linguist Ferdinand de Saussure. Particularly useful to structuralists were Saussure's concept of the *phoneme* (the smallest basic speech sound or unit of pronunciation) and his idea that phonemes exist in two kinds of relationships: diachronic and synchronic. A phoneme has a diachronic, or "horizontal," relationship with those other phonemes that precede and follow it (as the words appear, left to right, on this page) in a particular usage, utterance, or narrative — what Saussure called *parole* (French for "word"). A phoneme has a synchronic, or "vertical," relationship with the entire system of language within which individual usages, utterances, or narratives have meaning — what Saussure called *langue* (French for "tongue," as in "native tongue," meaning language). *An* means what it means in English because those of us who speak the language are plugged in to the same system (think of it as a computer network where different individuals can access the same information in the same way at a given time).

Following Saussure, Lévi-Strauss, an anthropologist, studied hundreds of myths, breaking them into their smallest meaningful units, which he called "mythemes." Removing each from its diachronic relations with other mythemes in a single myth (such as the myth of Oedipus and his mother), he vertically aligned those mythemes that he found to be homologous (structurally correspondent). He then studied the relationships within as well as between vertically aligned columns, in an attempt to understand scientifically, through ratios and proportions, those thoughts and processes that humankind has shared, both at one particular time and across time. Whether Lévi-Strauss was studying the structure of myths or the structure of villages, he looked for recurring, common elements that transcended the differences within and among cultures.

Structuralists followed Saussure in preferring to think about the overriding *langue* or language of myth, in which each mytheme and mytheme-constituted myth fits meaningfully, rather than about isolated individual *paroles,* or narratives. Structuralists also followed Saussure's lead in believing that sign systems must be understood in terms of binary oppositions (a proposition later disputed by poststructuralist Jacques Derrida). In analyzing myths and texts to find basic structures, structuralists found that opposite terms modulate until they are finally resolved or reconciled by some intermediary third term. Thus a structuralist reading of Milton's *Paradise Lost* (1667) might show that the war between God and the rebellious angels becomes a rift between God and sinful, fallen man, a rift that is healed by the Son of God, the mediating third term.

Although structuralism was largely a European phenomenon in its origin and development, it was influenced by American thinkers as well. Noam Chomsky, for instance, who powerfully influenced structuralism through works such as *Reflections on Language* (1975), identified and distinguished between "surface structures" and "deep structures" in language and linguistic literatures, including texts.

SYMBOL Something that, although it is of interest in its own right, stands for or suggests something larger and more complex — often an idea or a range of interrelated ideas, attitudes, and practices.

Within a given culture, some things are understood to be symbols: the flag of the United States is an obvious example, as are the five intertwined Olympic rings. More subtle cultural symbols might be the river as a symbol of time and the journey as a symbol of life and its manifold experiences. Instead of appropriating symbols generally used and understood within their culture, writers often create their own symbols by setting up a complex but identifiable web of associations in their works. As a result, one object, image, person, place, or action suggests others, and may ultimately suggest a range of ideas.

A symbol may thus be defined as a **metaphor** in which the **vehicle** — the image, activity, or concept used to represent something else — represents many related things (or **tenors**), or is broadly suggestive. The urn in Keats's "Ode on a Grecian Urn" (1820) suggests many interrelated concepts, including art, truth, beauty, and timelessness.

Symbols have been of particular interest to **formalists**, who study how meanings emerge from the complex, patterned relationships among images in a work, and **psychoanalytic critics**, who are interested in how individual authors and the larger culture both disguise and reveal unconscious fears and desires through symbols. Recently, French **feminist critics** have also focused on the symbolic. They have suggested that, as wide-ranging as it seems, symbolic language is ultimately rigid and restrictive. They favor **semiotic** language and writing — writing that neither opposes nor hierarchically ranks qualities or elements of reality nor symbolizes one thing but not another in terms of a third — contending that semiotic language is at once more fluid, rhythmic, unifying, and feminine.

SYMBOLIC ORDER *See* **Psychological Criticism and Psychoanalytic Criticism; Symbol.**

TENOR *See* **Metaphor; Metonymy; Symbol.**

TEXT From the Latin *texere,* meaning "to weave," a term that may be defined in a number of ways. Some critics restrict its use to the written word, although they may apply the term to objects ranging from a poem to the words in a book to a book itself to a biblical passage used in a sermon to a written transcript of an oral statement or interview. Other critics include nonwritten material in the designation text, as long as that material has been isolated for analysis.

French **structuralist** critics took issue with the traditional view of literary compositions as "works" with a form intentionally imposed by the author and a meaning identifiable through analysis of the author's use of language. These critics argued that literary compositions are texts rather than works, texts being the product of a social institution they called *écriture* (writing). By identifying compositions as texts rather than works, structuralists denied them the personalized character attributed to works wrought by a particular, unique author. Structuralists believed not only that a text was essentially impersonal, the confluence of certain preexisting attributes of the social institution of writing, but that any interpretation of the text should result from an impersonal *lecture* (reading). This *lecture* included reading with an active awareness of how the linguistic system functions.

The French writer and theorist Roland Barthes, a structuralist who later turned toward **poststructuralism**, distinguished text from *work* in a different way, characterizing a text as open and a work as closed. According to Barthes, works are bounded entities, conventionally classified in the canon, whereas texts engage readers in an ongoing relationship of interpretation and reinterpretation. Barthes further divided texts into two categories: *lisible* (readerly) and *scriptible* (writerly). Texts that are *lisible* depend more heavily on convention, making their interpretation easier and more predictable. Texts that are *scriptible* are generally experimental, flouting or seriously modifying traditional rules. Such texts cannot be interpreted according to standard conventions.

TROPE One of the two major divisions of **figures of speech** (the other being *rhetorical figures*). Trope comes from a word that literally means "turning"; to trope (with figures of speech) is, figuratively speaking, to turn or twist some word or phrase to make it mean something else. **Metaphor, metonymy, simile**, personification, and synecdoche are sometimes referred to as the principal tropes.

UNDECIDABILITY *See* **Deconstruction**.

VEHICLE *See* **Metaphor, Metonymy, Symbol**.

About the Contributors

THE VOLUME EDITOR

Linda H. Peterson is the Niel Gray Jr. Professor of English and codirector of the Bass Writing Program at Yale University, where she teaches Victorian poetry and prose. She is the coauthor of *Victorian Women Artists and Authors* (1994) and author of *Victorian Autobiography: The Tradition of Self-Interpretation* (1986) and *Traditions of Women's Autobiography: The Poetics and Politics of Life Writing* (1999).

THE CRITICS

Nancy Armstrong, the Nancy Duke Lewis Professor of English at Brown University, has published numerous articles on eighteenth- and nineteenth-century fiction and culture, feminism, and cultural theory. She is coauthor of *The Imaginary Puritan: Literature, Intellectual Labor, and the Origins of Personal Life* (1992) and author of *Desire and Domestic Fiction: A Political History of the Novel* (1987) and *Fiction in the Age of Photography: The Legacy of British Realism* (1999). She has also served as managing editor of the journal *NOVEL.*

Terry Eagleton is a professor of English at St. Catherine's College, Oxford University. His many books include *Criticism and Ideology* (1976), *Literary Theory: An Introduction* (1983), *The Ideology of the*

Aesthetic (1990), *Heathcliff and the Great Hunger* (1995), *The Illusions of Postmodernism* (1996), *The Function of Criticism: From the Spectator to Post-Structuralism* (1997), and *The Idea of Culture* (2000). He is also the editor of *Ideology* (1994) and *Critical Perspectives* (1997).

Susan Meyer, professor of English at Wellesley College, is a scholar of the nineteenth-century British novel, literature and imperialism, and twentieth-century American literature. She is author of *Imperialism at Home: Race in Victorian Women's Fiction* (1996) and coeditor of *The New Nineteenth Century* (1996), an anthology of feminist readings of Victorian fiction. She has also published work on the contemporary Jewish writer Lynne Sharon Schwartz and American photographer Lewis Hine.

Lyn Pykett, professor of English at the University of Wales, Aberystwyth, is the author of several books and articles on nineteenth-century writing, including *Emily Brontë* (1989), *The Improper Feminine* (1992), *The Sensation Novel from "The Woman in White" to "The Moonstone"* (1994), and *Engendering Fictions* (1995). She has also edited two collections of essays: *Reading Fin de Siècle Fictions* (1996) and a volume on Wilkie Collins in the *New Casebooks* series (1998).

Philip K. Wion is an associate professor of English at the University of Pittsburgh, where he teaches Renaissance literature and psychoanalytic criticism. His publications include psychoanalytically oriented articles on Marlowe's *Doctor Faustus* and Brontë's *Wuthering Heights.*

THE SERIES EDITOR

Ross C Murfin, general editor of the series, is provost of Southern Methodist University. He has taught literature at Yale University and the University of Virginia and has published scholarly studies on Joseph Conrad, Thomas Hardy, and D. H. Lawrence. With Supryia M. Ray, he is the author of *The Bedford Glossary of Critical and Literary Terms.*

(continued from p. iv)

"Myths of Power: A Marxist Study on *Wuthering Heights*" by Terry Eagleton. Reprinted from Terry Eagleton: *Myths of Power* Second Edition, 1988, Macmillan Publishing Company, reproduced with permission of Palgrave Macmillan.

"Changing Names: The Two Catherines" by Lyn Pykett. Reprinted from Lyn Pykett: *Emily Bronte,* 1989, Rowman & Littlefield Publishers, reproduced with permission of Palgrave Macmillan.

"The Absent Mother in Emily Bronte's *Wuthering Heights*" by Philip K. Wion, from *American Imago* 42:2 (1985), 143–164. © The Johns Hopkins Press. Reprinted by permission of the Johns Hopkins University Press.

" 'Your Father Was Emperor of China, and Your Mother an Indian Queen': Reverse Imperialism in *Wuthering Heights*" by Susan Meyer. Reprinted from Susan Meyer: *Imperialism at Home: Race and Victorian Women's Fiction.* Copyright © 1996 by Cornell University. Used by permission of the publisher, Cornell University Press.